D

SECOND EDITION

The Legal Foundations of Public Administration

SECOND EDITION

The Legal Foundations of Public Administration

DONALD D. BARRY
HOWARD R. WHITCOMB
Professors of Government
Lehigh University

WEST PUBLISHING COMPANY
ST. PAUL   NEW YORK   LOS ANGELES   SAN FRANCISCO

Copyediting: William N. Olson
Design: Lucy Lesiak Design

COPYRIGHT © 1981 By WEST PUBLISHING COMPANY
COPYRIGHT © 1987 By WEST PUBLISHING COMPANY
                    50 W. Kellogg Boulevard
                    P.O. Box 64526
                    St. Paul, MN 55164–1003

Library of Congress Cataloging-in-Publication Data
Barry, Donald D.
   The legal foundations of public administration.

   Includes index.
   1. Administrative law—United States.
2. Administrative procedure—United States.
3. Public administration—United States. I. Whitcomb,
Howard R., 1939–   . II. Title.

KF5402.B37 1987   342.73'06   86–22447
ISBN 0–314–30387–1   347.3026

THIS BOOK IS DEDICATED TO

Emily, Brian, Amy, Colleen, Dan, and Gerry, the younger adults, and to
Myrt and Dianne, the older adults

Summary of Contents

Table of Contents

Table of Cases

Principal cases are in italic type.   Cases cited or discussed in roman type. References are to pages.

Preface

The major objective of this book is to introduce students of public administration to a selection of important issues in administrative law. While the book may be used with profit by others, including law school students, it is intended primarily for those who have had little or no prior experience with legal analysis or the use of the case method. The treatment here is briefer by a considerable margin than that found in the typical administrative law casebook-textbook. As indicated, only a *selection* of important issues in administrative law is included, although we consider these to be the issues of most importance to the present or future administrator. And these issues may not be treated as exhaustively as in the typical law school casebook: while a large number of recent cases and other up-to-date information will be found in the book, we do not consider it our primary function to set out for the reader "the law" as it has evolved in all of its particulars and in the most recent court opinions; rather, we are much more interested in making the administrator aware of the kinds of legal problems with which or she is likely to be confronted. In a number of instances, therefore, we use one or two cases to illustrate the problem rather than discussing numerous cases in order to sketch the broad contours of the present law. Moreover, the analysis that follows largely excludes questions involving the technicalities of legal procedure. These are matters which would be better left to the attention of agency attorneys, on whom a public official with competence in other areas of administration will necessarily rely heavily when it comes to legal problems.

During the six years that have elapsed since the first edition of this book, numerous developments have taken place in administrative law. In this revision we have tried to give attention to these developments and to integrate them into the framework of the book as originally written.

The most important development, as we see it, has been the emphasis on administrative deregulation in the past several years. This is reflected most prominently in two new sections in the book, "Deregulation and Rulemaking" in chapter 6, and "The Political Component of Administrative Law" in chapter 1.

In addition, there have been numerous important changes in statutory and case law during this period, and these, too, have been prominently featured in the revision. In the statutory realm changes discussed have ranged from minor amendments in the Freedom of Information Act to the massive Gramm-Rudman "Balanced Budget and Emergency Deficit Control Act of 1985." In addition, it is clear that further statutory changes are likely, and some of these are also discussed: for instance, the package of proposed revisions of tort law put forward by the Reagan administration in 1986.

In terms of court cases, one could not discuss contemporary administrative law without commenting on the Supreme Court's 1983 ruling that the legislative veto is unconstitutional. And the case in which the Supreme Court made that declaration, *Immigration and Naturalization Service* v. *Chadha*, is discussed in detail in two chapters in the book. There have been numerous other important cases decided in recent years as well, which explains why about one-third of the 44 cases in the book are new to this edition.

The first edition received considerable attention from students and teachers of public administration. We appreciate the numerous helpful comments received from them, which we have taken into consideration in preparing this revision. Among the major changes that have been made at their suggestion are the inclusion of the text of the U.S. Constitution as appendix B and the shortening and simplifying of some of the court case excerpts. As an aid to the student reading court cases for the first time, we have provided short summaries of the facts for most of the cases. In our editing of primary and secondary sources we have selectively omitted statute and case citations, as well as footnotes. Where footnotes have been retained we have renumbered them to run consecutively through the chapter.

A number of people have provided important help to the authors in the writing of this book. The staff of the Lehigh University Libraries helped in the location and acquisition of many of the sources we used. The secretaries in Lehigh's Department of Government, Dorothy Windish and Chris Baran, handled the word processing skillfully and cheerfully. The book is dedicated to several people who are very close to us.

Donald D. Barry
Howard R. Whitcomb

Bethlehem, Pennsylvania
July, 1986

Acknowledgments

We acknowledge the courtesy of the following publishers, publications, and authors who have permitted us to reprint excerpts from publications:

Cambridge University Press: James O. Freedman, *Crisis and Legitimacy: The Administrative Process and American Government,* 1978, excerpts from pages 4–6. Copyrighted by and reprinted with the permission of Cambridge University Press.

Administrative Law Review: Alfred E. Kahn and Michael Roach, "Commentary: A Paean to Legal Creativity," 31 Ad.Law Rev. 97 (1979), excerpts from pp. 101–102; Jerre S. Williams, "Chairman's Message," 28 Ad.Law Rev. v (1976), excerpts from pages v-xii. *Administrative Law Review* is a publication of the Administrative Law Section of the American Bar Association.

Praeger Publishers: Marshall E. Dimock, *Law and Dynamic Administration,* excerpts from pages 68–80. Copyright © 1980 Praeger Publishers. Reprinted and abridged by permission of Praeger Publishers.

Public Administration Review: Phillip J. Cooper, "Conflict or Constructive Tension: The Changing Relationship of Judges and Administrators," *Public Administration Review* (Nov. 1985). Reprinted with permission from *Public Administration Review* © 1985 by the American Society for Public Administration, 1120 G Street, N.W., Suite 500, Washington, D.C. All rights reserved.

The *New York Times:* Alan Richman, "Radiation Overdose: All in a Day's Work," April 4, 1979, page 1. © 1979 by The New York Times Company. Reprinted by permission.

American University Law Review: Warner W. Gardner, "The Informal Actions of the Federal Government," 26 *American University Law Review* 799 (1979). Reprinted by permission.

The Legal Foundations of Public Administraton

Chapter 1

Administrative Authority and Law

The legal rules regarding the administrator's exercise of governmental authority on the one hand, and the private party's rights in relation to governmental authority on the other, constitute the basic subject matter of administrative law. As a separate area of study, administrative law is rather new in the United States, dating only from the late nineteenth century. It is also one of the broadest of general legal subjects, since it embraces the activities of any and all governmental agencies other than courts and legislatures, at all levels of government. A study of the Environmental Protection Agency could be considered an environmental law topic, but it might also fall within the broader field of administrative law. Many of the activities of the National Labor Relations Board are appropriate for analysis in both administrative law and labor law. An examination of the executive functions of departments in city or county government might be narrowly called municipal law, but it fits within the broader context of administrative law as well.

ADMINISTRATIVE LAW AS AN AMALGAM OF CENTRIFUGAL FORCES

Considered from this perspective, administrative law should not be seen as a unified body of law but rather as a variety of administrative procedures and regulations whose content depends, to some extent, on the agencies and departments involved. As one student of the subject commented over twenty-five years ago:

> I am not sure that there is *an* administrative process. There are a series of . . . processes which, perhaps, bear more resemblance to one another than to anything else, but still not too much to one another. Those processes vary, and they

should vary, in accordance with the social problems and the practical needs which particular agencies were established to handle.[1]

Since this statement was made, the range and volume of administrative activity has grown significantly, and commentators continue to raise the question of whether "centrifugal forces" (separate bodies of labor law, tax law, public utility law, etc.) have made it unrealistic to maintain a disciplinary entity known as administrative law. This has led Robert L. Rabin to ask "whether there is in fact an administrative process about which useful generalizations can be made, or whether one should be content with more modest—and, one might argue, more practical—efforts to contribute to our understanding of particular agencies." His answer articulates an underlying premise of this book: "While it is indisputable that there is no single administrative process, it seems equally clear . . . that there are a sufficient number of important characteristics shared by *some* agencies to create a fertile field for teaching and scholarship on administrative processes."[2]

It should be noted that in spite of the centrifugal forces mentioned above, some commentators would expand the scope of administrative law even more. Kenneth Culp Davis, for instance, acknowledges that some of the subject matter in his recent writing is "outside of what is traditionally administrative law."[3] He argues persuasively, nevertheless, that certain aspects of criminal law, namely the activities of police and prosecutors, should be brought into the mainstream of the subject.[4] While not disagreeing with the logic of Davis' proposal (police and prosecutors do, after all, perform a variety of administrative functions), the analysis in this book will be limited largely to activities of administrative agencies and officers traditionally covered in administrative law analyses.

Independent Regulatory Commissions

Some of the earlier treatments of the subject tended to equate administrative law with the law of the independent regulatory commissions.[5] These commis-

---

[1] Paul M. Herzog, "Comment," in Monrad G. Paulsen, ed., *Legal Institutions Today and Tomorrow* 169 (1959).

[2] Robert L. Rabin, "Administrative Law in Transition: A Discipline in Search of an Organizing Principle," 72 *Northwestern University Law Review* 120, 136 (1977). The term "centrifugal forces" is from Rabin at 127. See also the criticism of the "conception of administrative law as a unified body of doctrine with general applicability" in Richard B. Stewart, "The Reformation of American Administrative Law," 88 *Harvard Law Review* 1667, 1670 (1975).

[3] Kenneth Culp Davis, *Administrative Law of the Seventies* 40 (1976).

[4] Kenneth Culp Davis, 1 *Administrative Law Treatise* 2–3 (2d ed., 1978).

[5] Regulatory commissions, typically multi-headed agencies rather than being under a single administrator, possess several characteristics that give them a degree of independence. Commission members, although appointed by the president, serve terms longer than that of the president. The terms are staggered, and bipartisanship is assured by the provision that no more than a bare majority·of the membership may be from one political party. Unlike appointees in the regular executive departments, commission members may not be removed at the pleasure of the president, but only for grounds specified in the appropriate act of Congress. But the independence of such agencies is by no means complete. One of the important areas of executive control is in budgetary matters. For further information see, for example, Bernard Schwartz, *Administrative Law* 13–16 (1976).

sions played an important role in the development of the subject, and in many of the early landmark decisions, the Federal Communications Commission (FCC), Federal Trade Commission (FTC), Securities and Exchange Commission (SEC), or some other independent commission was one of the parties involved. As important as they continue to be, however, the independent commissions no longer play so dominant a role in the overall administrative process. Several of the older independent agencies have been abolished (the Civil Aeronautics Board and the Federal Power Commission, for instance), their remaining functions absorbed by various executive branch bodies. Those that remain (the FCC, FTC, SEC, Interstate Commerce Commission (ICC), and National Labor Relations Board (NLRB) are the most well known) employ only a fraction of the personnel who work in the Veterans Administration alone. Numerous other independent agencies have been created in more recent times, and the total number of such bodies is large. But if one excludes the three biggest of these (the U.S. Postal Service with seven hundred fifty thousand employees, the Veterans Administration with two hundred fifty thousand employees, and the Tennessee Valley Authority with thirty-two thousand employees), then the total number of employees in the seventy-six other independent agencies listed by the Office of Personnel Management for late 1985 is about the same as that of the Department of Health and Human Services alone.[6]

Administrative Functions

Nor is the major thrust of administrative activity so strongly regulatory as it once was. A large part of administrative activity involves other kinds of functions, such as awarding benefits to qualifying private parties. As a result, some students have sought to break down the broad subject of administrative law into logical subcategories, within which a higher degree of uniformity of procedure might be expected. Rabin, in the work cited above, suggests that there are three "major fields of administrative activity": regulation, public management, and benefit distribution.[7] Others simplify the classification to that of a dichotomy: Paul R. Verkuil sees the distinction as between "regulatory (or economic)" and "non-regulatory (or social benefit)" spheres,[8] and Judge Henry J. Friendly, in an important article that will be referred to frequently in succeeding chapters, writes in a similar vein of "mass justice" as opposed to economic regulation.[9]

Within these broad categories, a number of different kinds of administrative functions are performed. Verkuil has isolated six types of activity which "seem to encompass most administrative decision making." These are "imposition of sanctions," "ratemaking, licensing and other regulatory decisions," "environmental and safety decisions," "awards of benefits, loans, grants and

---

[6] *Federal Civilian Workforce Statistics*, (Monthly Release) Table 2, 10–13 (August, 1985).

[7] Rabin, above, note 2, 143.

[8] Paul R. Verkuil, "The Emerging Concept of Administrative Procedure," 78 *Columbia Law Review* 258, 283 (1978).

[9] Henry J. Friendly, "Some Kind of Hearing," 123 *University of Pennsylvania Law Review* 1267, 1316 (1975).

subsidies," "inspections, audits, and approvals," and "planning and poli-cymaking." Verkuil explains the relationship of these categories to each other:

> These six categories of administrative decisions reflect a variety of formal and informal procedural solutions. In terms of ordering the procedural values one might organize these categories on a scale of maximum to minimum procedures. At the top of the scale, the hearing procedures employed may come close to the full adjudicative model, since the issues at stake resemble those decided in the civil or criminal process. Toward the bottom of the scale, there may be a few, if any, procedural requirements. The issues may not be resolved in a hearing context at all, as is the case with planning and policy making; or as with inspections and tests, there may be alternatives for resolving disputes that are superior to hearing procedures. Even in these categories, however, certain procedural ingredients appear; in effect, notice and reasons requirements approximate a minimum procedural model. While it is possible to avoid giving notice or reasons, arguments for going below this floor should be very strong.[10]

This attempt at classification of types of administrative procedures, while among the more recent, is certainly not the only one that might be mentioned.[11] The important thing to emphasize here is the general recognition that: (1) the multiplicity of functions now performed in this country by administrative agencies has necessitated the creation of a variety of arrangements for administrative decision making, which may differ from each other considerably in their procedural requirements; and (2) the basic concept of administrative law as fundamentally involving regulatory activity has yielded to an understanding that, in addition to regulation, a great deal of attention is now also given to benefit distribution.

---

[10] Verkuil, above, note 8, at 303–304. Verkuil then goes on to list twelve ingredients which "constitute the maximum procedures found in adjudicatory hearings" and appear to be applicable to proceedings at the top of his scale. These twelve include ten from the landmark case of *Goldberg* v. *Kelly*, 397 U.S. 254, 90 S.Ct. 1011, 25 L.Ed.2d 287 (1970) and two from the Administrative Procedure Act. The twelve are stated by Verkuil as follows: "The ten *Goldberg* ingredients are: 1. timely and adequate notice; 2. confronting adverse witnesses; 3. oral presentation of arguments; 4. oral presentation of evidence; 5. cross-examination of adverse witnesses; 6. disclosure to the claimant of opposing evidence; 7. the right to retain an attorney; 8. a determination on the record of the hearing; 9. a statement of reasons for the determination and an indication of the evidence relied on; and 10. an impartial decisionmaker . . . The APA formal adjudication provisions add two ingredients not required by *Goldberg*: an ALJ [Administrative Law Judge] decisionmaker and the requirement of findings of fact and conclusions of law."

Friendly, in the article cited (above, note 9), also categorizes "the nature of governmental action" on the basis of "its seriousness to the individual" (at 1295) and comes up with a list of eleven "elements of a fair hearing," noting that the "required degree of procedural safeguards varies directly with the importance of the private interest protected and the need for and usefulness of the particular safeguard in the given circumstances and inversely with the burden and any other adverse consequences of affording it" (at 1278). Although somewhat different in phraseology, Verkuil's list of twelve and Friendly's list of eleven are quite similar in content.

[11] See above, note 9, on Judge Friendly's similar classification, and see, for instance, the discussion of seven "characteristic forms of administrative action," followed by an analysis of the procedures for administrative policy making in Louis L. Jaffe and Nathaniel L. Nathanson, *Administrative Law: Cases and Materials* 15–28 (3d ed., 1968).

ADMINISTRATIVE LAW AS A UNIFIED SUBJECT

Neither of these points should be taken to suggest that no uniformity in administrative law and procedure has been achieved, however. On the federal level there is the Administrative Procedure Act (APA), adopted in 1946 and applicable to most federal executive agencies, including the independent regulatory commissions. Developments leading up to the adoption of the APA will be reviewed in the next chapter. Many states have their own administrative procedure acts, administrative codes, or statutes contained in the general laws that cover administrative procedure, and a number of municipalities have ordinances covering the activities of numerous agencies. The National Conference of Commissioners on Uniform State Laws has drafted a Model State Administrative Procedure Act. The current act, approved in 1981, supersedes an earlier version adopted in 1961, which in turn replaced the original Model Act adopted in 1946. As of 1985 over half of the states had an administrative procedure act based, at least in part, on one of the model acts.[12]

In addition to these legislative acts, the courts also contribute to the development of administrative law. The due process and equal protection clauses of the Constitution, as well as other sections of that document, have served as the basis for significant litigation concerning the rights and powers of administrators and agencies. State constitutions also have provisions which courts apply in determining the propriety of administrative acts. And, of course, courts may also interpret the language of statutes covering administrative procedure when no constitutional issue is involved. When the United States Supreme Court makes a ruling on the constitutionality of a particular administrative action, especially if it is an action of a state or local body, it is contributing not just to the uniformity of administrative law but to the "nationalization" of that law as well. A significant amount of the material in succeeding chapters is given over to selections from court opinions which are either landmark decisions or cases which illustrate important aspects of administrative law. For students without previous experience in studying judicial decisions, the final section of this chapter, "A Note on Analyzing Court Cases," should prove helpful.

THE ADMINISTRATIVE PROCESS [13]

Consonant with the major objectives of this book and the primary audience for whom it is intended, little attention will be devoted to technical matters of legal procedure. We will concentrate, rather, on the major aspects of the administrative process and the important legal issues that arise under each of them. The following is both a brief description of the major aspects of the administrative process and a rationale for the organization of the book.

---

[12] *14 Uniform Laws Annotated*, "1985 Cumulative Annual Pocket Part," 73.

[13] Parts of this section are based on Donald D. Barry, Thomas E. Baynes, Jr., W. Donald Heisel, and John M. Urie, *Resource Mobilizer* (1977).

Delegation of Power

After a chapter devoted to the historical development of administrative law, the first subject examined deals with the basis for the exercise of administrative power, namely, the granting by the legislature to administrative agencies of the authority to act. The conditions under which this authority is granted, and the extent and nature of the grant, are crucial issues of administrative law that remain alive to this day. The basic questions in this chapter concern the appropriate level of legislative control over administrative action, and the best means of achieving that control.

Judicial Review

Chapters 3 through 10 all concern judicial review, in the sense that all discuss cases in which courts have reviewed the propriety of administrative acts. Just as the chapter on delegation of power deals with the proper role of the legislature regarding administrative action, this chapter examines the proper role of the courts in attempting to keep administrative power within appropriate bounds. The basic questions have to do with the kinds of administrative actions the courts can review, when review can take place, who can seek review, and the degree of scrutiny the courts will give to the administrative actions in question.

Investigatory Power

An important element in the performance of administrative duties is information: the administrator must have facts and data to carry out the functions assigned to his agency by the legislative body. But this need sometimes runs counter to the rights or interests of private parties. Legal rules which strike an appropriate balance in this area between governmental needs and private rights are still evolving.

Rules and the Rule-making Process

The two major formal processes of administrative agencies are rule making and adjudication. Rules can be characterized as normally having general application and future effect. They are "quasi-legislative" in nature. The major issues connected with the subject involve the question of whether an agency has the authority to adopt "legislative-type" rules, and the appropriate procedures to be used in the rule-making process.

The Right to Be Heard and Adjudicatory Policy Making

The right to a hearing implies an adjudicatory hearing, a "quasi-judicial" as opposed to "quasi-legislative" proceeding. Such hearings might involve the granting or revoking of a license, the suspension of a pupil from school or termination of welfare benefits to an individual, or a myriad of other matters in which important legal interests are at stake. The most important questions with regard to hearings of this kind are. Who has the right to a hearing? If a hearing is required, at what stage in the process must it come? and What procedural rules should apply in the hearing itself?

Can agency policy be developed through proceedings involving this kind of a hearing, that is, through adjudicatory proceedings? The answer to this question is yes, but a conditional yes. The policy of an agency can be developed through orders adopted in quasi-judicial proceedings and through rules adopted via the rule-making process. Most observers hold that, where possible, rule making is superior to adjudication for the articulation of agency policy, but some agencies have not been granted clear rule-making power, and others, in spite of having such authority, prefer to develop policy on a case-by-case basis.

Informal Activity and the Exercise of Discretion

The informal administrative process refers to a wide range of administrative action that takes place outside of such formal proceedings as rule making and adjudication. Such action might involve advice from an administrator to a private party on the latter's problem with the government (concerning a pension, for instance), bank supervision by governmental authorities, administration of drivers' tests, or accepting and processing applications. The range of possible examples is endless. Such activity may have legal consequences, but it is not so commonly reviewed by courts as are formal administrative actions.

The exercise of discretion may take place in the context of the informal administrative process, but administrative discretion may also be treated as a somewhat distinct subject. Recent years have seen a revival of interest in studying administrative discretion, inspired in large part by Kenneth Culp Davis' important 1969 book *Discretionary Justice*. All commentators acknowledge that administrators need some discretion in order to carry out their functions in a reasonable and efficient manner. But excessive discretion can lead to violation of the rights of private parties. Again, the problem is one of finding the proper balance. Recent efforts have been directed at devising mechanisms (both within the courts and in more informal complaint-handling systems) which will provide appropriate means for reviewing informal administrative activity and the exercise of discretion.

Remedies Against Improper Administrative Acts

A private party who thinks that he has been the victim of an illegal administrative act has several options. If it is an act that is subject to judicial review, he or she may seek an injunction and/or a declaration by the court that the act is illegal. If a governmental action has caused harm to an individual that cannot be corrected by a court's voiding of the administrative act, a suit for damages might be instituted. A threshold question will involve the concept of "sovereign immunity," that is, whether the governmental unit in question has consented to be sued. The history of the waiver of sovereign immunity in the United States is interesting and complex. A separate question is whether a plaintiff may sue a culpable official for damages. While sovereign immunity does not apply in these cases, a fairly high level of protection is available to many governmental officials who have acted in a reasonable manner and within the sphere of their duties, even if their acts have harmed private parties.

There are instances where neither the governmental unit nor the individual official will be held liable by a court, and yet it seems unjust for the private party to have to bear a loss incurred through no fault of his own. Remedies that go beyond the bounds of the traditional law of damages are increasingly being proposed to cover such cases.

Opening Up the Government

No other area of administrative law has experienced such impressive development over the past ten to fifteen years as this one. The direction of development has been strongly toward citizen access and participation in the administrative process. If information or participation is denied under the law in some concrete circumstances—and there are good reasons why government operations should not be open in certain cases—the presumption has definitely shifted in recent years in favor of public access wherever possible. As is the case with regard to most controversial questions of administrative law, the basic issue involves the search for an appropriate balance between citizen interests and governmental needs.

THE POLITICAL COMPONENT OF ADMINISTRATIVE LAW

Perhaps more than other branches of law, administrative law contains within it a large political element. Given the fact that one side of an administrative law relationship is the government, this is understandable. Many aspects of administrative activity, from the appointment and dismissal of administrative personnel through the budgetary process which funds administrative programs to the policy framework within which administrators are expected to perform their functions. In the broadest sense, the problem of the political aspect of administrative law reduces itself to the following: How to maintain a reasonable check on the administration, by nonelected officials, of broad and often vague policies adopted by popularly elected officials, without unduly restricting the administrator's discretion or improperly influencing his or her decisions. This issue, which some commentators treat as a central problem of administrative law,[14] will receive considerable attention in this book.

President's Power to Remove Administrators

An example of potential political influence on the administrative process involves the president's power to remove administrative officials. While many officials in the executive branch serve at the president's pleasure, a great number of others are protected by civil service status and can only be dis-

---

[14] See, for instance, *Administrative Law and Process* by Richard J. Pierce, Jr., Sidney A. Shapiro, and Paul R. Verkuil (1985). The first chapter of this recent treatise is called ''The Political Nature of the Administrative Process.''

missed for specifically defined reasons and after certain procedural requirements have been met. Others, while appointed by the president and not under civil service status, serve in agencies that contain some degree of insulation from presidential control. The rise of such "independent" agencies, created in part to protect the administrators in question from partisan political influences, will be described in the next chapter. The power of the president to remove such officials has been the subject of continuing controversy over a number of decades. The following case is one example of this controversy. The excerpt reproduced below, from a Supreme Court opinion, summarizes legal developments in this area prior to the case at hand.

Wiener v. United States

SUPREME COURT OF THE UNITED STATES, 1958.
357 U.S. 349, 78 S.CT. 1275, 2 L.ED.2D 1377.

[This case is based on a suit for back pay by a former member of the War Claims Commission, who asserted that he had been removed illegally. Wiener was appointed to the commission in 1950 by President Truman, and was removed by President Eisenhower in 1953. Eisenhower stated in removing Wiener that he wanted "personnel of my own selection" for the commission. Because of the commission's temporary nature (it went out of existence in 1954), Congress made no provision for removal of a commissioner. The Court of Claims dismissed the suit, and it came to the U.S. Supreme Court. In his opinion for the Court, Justice Frankfurter discusses two earlier Supreme Court cases involving the president's removal power: *Myers* v. *United States*, 272 U.S. 52, 47 S.Ct. 21, 71 L.Ed. 160 (1926) (opinion by a former president, Chief Justice Taft); and *Humphrey's Executor* v. *United States*, 295 U.S. 602, 55 S.Ct. 869, 79 L.Ed. 1611 (1935).]

Mr. Justice FRANKFURTER delivered the opinion of the Court . . .

We brought the case here . . . because it presents a variant of the constitutional issue decided in *Humphrey's Executor* v. *United States*, 295 U.S. 602, 55 S.Ct. 869, 79 L.Ed. 1611.

Controversy pertaining to the scope and limits of the President's power of re-moval fills a thick chapter of our political and judicial history. The long stretches of its history, beginning with the very first Congress, with early echoes in the Reports of this Court, were laboriously traversed in *Myers* v. *United States*, 272 U.S. 52, 47 S.Ct. 21, 71 L.Ed. 160, and need not be retraced. President Roosevelt's reliance upon the pronouncements of the Court in that case in removing a member of the Federal Trade Commission on the ground that "the aims and purposes of the Administration with respect to the work of the Commission can be carried out most effectively with personnel of my own selection" reflected contemporaneous professional opinion regarding the significance of the *Myers* decision. Speaking through a Chief Justice who himself had been President, the Court did not restrict itself to the immediate issue before it, the President's inherent power to remove a postmaster, obviously an executive official. As of set purpose and not by way of parenthetic casualness, the Court announced that the President had inherent constitutional power of removal also of officials who have "duties of a quasi-judicial character . . . whose decisions after hearing affect interests of individuals, the discharge of which the President cannot in a particular case properly influence or control." *Myers* v.

United States, supra, 272 U.S. at page 135, 47 S.Ct. at page 31. This view of presidential power was deemed to flow from his "constitutional duty of seeing that the laws be faithfully executed." Ibid.

The assumption was short-lived that the *Myers* case recognized the President's inherent constitutional power to remove officials, no matter what the relation of the executive to the discharge of their duties and no matter what restrictions Congress may have imposed regarding the nature of their tenure. The versatility of circumstances often mocks a natural desire for definitiveness. Within less than ten years a unanimous Court, in *Humphrey's Executor* v. *United States,* 295 U.S. 602, 55 S.Ct. 869, 79 L.Ed. 1611, narrowly confined the scope of the *Myers* decision to include only "all purely executive officers." 295 U.S. at page 628, 55 S.Ct. at page 874. The Court explicitly "disapproved" the expressions in *Myers* supporting the President's inherent constitutional power to remove members of quasi-judicial bodies. 295 U.S. at pages 626–627, 55 S.Ct. at pages 873–874. Congress had given members of the Federal Trade Commission a seven-year term and also provided for the removal of a Commissioner by the President for inefficiency, neglect of duty or malfeasance in office. In the present case, Congress provided for a tenure defined by the relatively short period of time during which the War Claims Commission was to operate—that is, it was to wind up not later than three years after the expiration of the time for filing of claims. But nothing was said in the Act about removal.

This is another instance in which the most appropriate legal significance must be drawn from congressional failure of explicitness. Necessarily this is a problem in probabilities. We start with one certainty. The problem of the President's power to remove members of agencies entrusted with duties of the kind with which the War Claims Commission was charged was within the lively knowledge of Congress.

Few contests between Congress and the President have so recurringly had the attention of Congress as that pertaining to the power of removal. Not the least significant aspect of the *Myers* case is that on the Court's special invitation Senator George Wharton Pepper, of Pennsylvania, presented the position of Congress at the bar of this Court.

Humphrey's case was a *cause célèbre*—and not least in the halls of Congress. And what is the essence of the decision in *Humphrey's* case? It drew a sharp line of cleavage between officials who were part of the Executive establishment and were thus removable by virtue of the President's constitutional powers, and those who are members of a body "to exercise its judgment without the leave or hindrance of any other official or any department of the government," 295 U.S. at pages 625–626, 55 S.Ct. at page 873, as to whom a power of removal exists only if Congress may fairly be said to have conferred it. This sharp differentiation derives from the difference in functions between those who are part of the Executive establishment and those whose tasks require absolute freedom from Executive interference. "For it is quite evident," again to quote *Humphrey's Executor,* "that one who holds his office only during the pleasure of another, cannot be depended upon to maintain an attitude of independence against the latter's will." 295 U.S. at page 629, 55 S.Ct. at page 874.

Thus, the most reliable factor for drawing an inference regarding the President's power of removal in our case is the nature of the function that Congress vested in the War Claims Commission. What were the duties that Congress confided to this Commission? And can the inference fairly be drawn from the failure of Congress to provide for removal that these Commissioners were to remain in office at the will of the President? For such is the assertion of power on which petitioner's removal must rest. The ground of President Eisenhower's removal of petitioner was precisely the same as President Roosevelt's removal of *Humphrey*. Both Presidents desired to have Commissioners, one on the Federal Trade Commission, the other on the War Claims Commission, "of my own selection." They wanted these Commissioners to be their men. The terms of removal in the two cases are identic and express the assumption that the agencies of which the two Commissioners were members were subject in the discharge of their duties to the control of the Executive. An analysis of the Federal Trade Commission Act, 15 U.S. C.A. § 41 et seq., left this Court in no doubt that such was not the conception of Congress in creating the Federal Trade Commission. The terms of the War Claims Act of 1948 leave no doubt that such was not the conception of Congress regarding the War Claims Commission.

The history of this legislation emphatically underlines this fact. The short of it is that the origin of the Act was a bill, H.R. 4044, 80th Cong., 1st Sess., passed by the House that placed the administration of a very limited class of claims by Americans against Japan in the hands of the Federal Security Administrator and provided for a Commission to inquire into and report upon other types of claims. See H.R.Rep. No. 976, 80th Cong., 1st Sess. The Federal Security Administrator was indubitably an arm of the President. When the House bill reached the Senate, it struck out all but the enacting clause, rewrote the bill, and established a Commission with "jurisdiction to receive and adjudicate according to law" three classes of claims, as defined by §§ 5, 6 and 7. The Commission was established as an adjudicating body with all the paraphernalia by which legal claims are put to the test of proof, with finality of determination "not subject to review by any other official of the United States or by any court by mandamus or otherwise," § 11. Awards were to be paid out of a War Claims Fund in the hands of the Secretary of the Treasury, whereby such claims were given even more assured collectability than adheres to judgments rendered in the Court of Claims. . . .

Congress could, of course, have given jurisdiction over these claims to the District Courts or to the Court of Claims. The fact that it chose to establish a Commission to "adjudicate according to law" the classes of claims defined in the statute did not alter the intrinsic judicial character of the task with which the Commission was charged. The claims were to be "adjudicated according to law," that is, on the merits of each claim, supported by evidence and governing legal considerations, by a body that was "entirely free from the control or coercive influence, direct or indirect," *Humphrey's Executor* v. *United States*, supra, 295 U.S. at page 629, 55 S.Ct. at page 874 of either the Executive or the Congress. If, as one must take for granted, the War Claims Act precluded the President from influencing the Commission in passing on a particular claim, *a fortiori* must it be inferred that Congress did not wish to have hang over the Commission the Damocles' sword of removal by the President for no reason other than that he preferred to have on that Commission men of his own choosing.

For such is this case. We have not a removal for cause involving the rectitude of a member of an adjudicatory body, nor even a suspensory removal until the Senate could act upon it by confirming the appointment of a new Commissioner or otherwise dealing with the matter. Judging the matter in all the nakedness in which it is presented, namely, the claim that the President could remove a member of an adjudicatory body like the War Claims Commission merely because he wanted his own appointees on such a Commission, we are compelled to conclude that no such power is given to the President directly by the Constitution, and none is impliedly conferred upon him by statute simply because Congress said nothing about it. The philosophy of *Humphrey's Executor,* in its

explicit language as well as its implications, precludes such a claim.

The judgment is reversed.
Reversed.

How Independent Are "Independent" Agencies?

In 1983 President Reagan sought to remove several members of the Civil
Rights Commission and replace them with persons whose views were closer
to his own on matters such as affirmative action. These members refused to
resign, and the president was unable to get his new appointees confirmed by
the Senate. The commission, which was established in 1957, was composed of
six members appointed by the president on a bipartisan basis (no more than
three members from the same party) for terms not prescribed in the statute.
Unlike the FTC or the War Claims Commission (independent agencies discussed in the *Wiener* case), the Civil Rights Commission did not perform
adjudicatory functions. Its major tasks were to carry out investigations in the
area of civil rights and to report its findings to the president and Congress.

The Civil Rights Commission, then, was not a prototype independent
agency. Still, the attempted dismissals produced strong, largely partisan, concern that the president was trying improperly to influence the commission.
The impasse was broken later in 1983 when a compromise was reached under
which the old commission was abolished and a new eight-member panel was
created. Four members of the new bipartisan Civil Rights Commission are
appointed by the president and two each are named by the Senate and the
House of Representatives. Members serve six-year terms and may be removed
by the president "only for neglect of duty or malfeasance in office," terms
typically used in legislation covering independent agencies.[15] The 1957 act
described the Civil Rights Commission as an agency "in the executive
branch." No such designation is found in the 1983 act.

A potentially more fundamental challenge to the "independent" agencies
surfaced in a 1985 speech by the attorney general of the United States.[16] Edwin
Meese's remarks, which were largely overlooked at the time of delivery,[17]
amounted to a direct challenge to the constitutionality of agencies that were
not politically accountable to the president, that is, not subject to executive
removal power as outlined in the aforementioned case of *Myers* v. *United
States* (1926). Meese stated, in part, that "federal agencies performing executive functions are properly agents of the executive. They are not 'quasi' this, or
'independent' that."[18] Meese's assertion that a body that exercises enforcement powers is a part of the executive branch appeared to be a challenge to
the Supreme Court's decision in *Humphrey's Executor* v. *United States* (1935),
which was discussed in the *Wiener* case excerpt earlier in this chapter. This

---

[15] P.L. 98–183, 97 *Stat.* 1301.

[16] Address by The Honorable Edwin Meese III to the Federal Bar Association, Detroit, Michigan, September 13, 1985. A copy of the speech is in the authors' possession.

[17] The *New York Times,* for instance, did not report on the content of the speech until Stuart
Taylor, Jr., did so in the issue of November 6, 1985.

[18] Meese, above, 10.

interpretation was confirmed in a subsequent speech in 1986 [19] in which he explicitly challenged the foundations of the *Humphrey's* precedent. In referring to that case he said the Court "spawned a radically new view of separation of powers" and, furthermore, Meese seemingly accepted the characterization of it having created "a sanctuary for bureaucratic domination." [20]

It remains to be seen whether the attorney general's views, which are already being incorporated into Justice Department briefs, will prevail; however, it has led one prominent Member of Congress, John D. Dingell (D., Michigan), to characterize the Meese stance as "being the culmination of a long-planned raid on independent agencies." [21]

A NOTE ON ANALYZING COURT CASES

A good bit of the reading that follows involves court cases—either discussions of rules courts have made on certain issues or selections from actual court opinions. The person encountering court opinions for the first time may have difficulty in understanding precisely what the court has decided, let alone seeing how the decision fits into the overall context of the subject being discussed. The facts of some cases are quite complex, and it is important to the understanding of any case to extract from the opinion the issues on which the court is being asked to rule. Even the most experienced analysts of court cases, therefore, often find it helpful to prepare an outline of the salient points of the case—usually called a "brief"—as an aid to understanding and discussion.

Briefing a Case

It is recommended that each of the forty-four cases set forth in the following chapters be briefed by the student. As suggested, the brief typically uses an outline form and covers the following points:

1. Name and citation [22] of case
2. Brief statement of the facts

---

[19] Address by The Honorable Edwin Meese III at the University of Dallas, Irving, Texas, February 27, 1986. A copy of the speech is in the authors' possession.

[20] Ibid., at 9 and 11, respectively.

[21] As reported by Stuart Taylor, Jr., in the *New York Times*, November 6, 1985.

[22] A uniform system of citation is used for case law reports (and many other legal citations) throughout the United States. It consists of three parts: volume number, name of publication, and page number. Thus, for instance, 100 So.2d 53 (1957) means volume 100 of the *Southern Reporter, Second Series*, page 53. This is a citation of a case included in chapter 8 which was decided by the Supreme Court of Florida in 1957. The date is included in parentheses in the citation. Since Florida has discontinued its official state reports, this unofficial regional reporter published by West Publishing Company becomes the main source where one can find opinions of that state's highest court along with comparable opinions for the states of Alabama, Mississippi, and Louisiana. Three versions of U.S. Supreme Court cases are usually cited. The official *U.S. Reports* ("U.S."), the *Supreme Court Reporter*, published by West Publishing Company ("S.Ct.") and the *Lawyers' Edition of the U.S. Supreme Court Reports* ("L.Ed."), published by the Lawyers Cooperative Publishing Company and the Bancroft-Whitney Company. Thus, a full citation for the first case set forth in this book, *Wiener v. United States*, is 357 U.S. 349, 78 S.Ct. 1275, 2 L.Ed.2d

3. Issue(s) the court must decide
4. Holding(s) of the court on these issues
5. Order of the court
6. Reasoning employed by the court to support the holding(s)
7. Major points of the concurring and/or dissenting opinions, if any

Since many of the cases presented below were decided by courts with more than one judge participating, it is also useful to indicate the voting lineup of the judges.

A brief need not be long. Most cases can be briefed on one side of an 8½-by-11-inch sheet of paper. Many students err in the direction of writing briefs that are too long, often by becoming bogged down in the facts. Remember that the brief is not a crutch but an aid to facilitate one's ability to understand and explain the case. And keep in mind above all that mastering a case means little in itself unless it serves to enhance understanding of the larger picture. The most important task in analyzing a case is to determine what it illustrates about the question of law being examined.

At this point the student will be asked to prepare a brief. Turn to page 11, where *Wiener* v. *United States*, the first case set forth in this book, will be found. Brief this case, and then compare your brief with the one prepared by the authors, which is printed below.

Wiener v. United States, 357 U.S. 349, 78 S.Ct. 1275, 2 L.Ed.2d 1377 (1958)

Facts:

Wiener, who was appointed to the War Claims Commission by President Truman, was dismissed by President Eisenhower because the president wanted "personnel of his own selection" on the commission. Wiener sued for back pay, claiming that his dismissal was illegal. The Court of Claims dismissed the petition and the Supreme Court took the case for review.

1377 (1958). A few cases reproduced in this book are U.S. Court of Appeals or U.S. District Court opinions. These cases, published in unofficial editions by the West Publishing Company, appeared originally in the *Federal Reporter* ("F."—for Court of Appeals cases) and the *Federal Supplement* ("F.Supp."—for District Court cases). In many of the cases below there will also be citations to legislative and administrative materials. The most common are: (1) for statutes, the U.S. *Statutes at Large* (abbreviated as Stat.), a chronological publication arranged by sessions of Congress, and the *U.S. Code* (U.S.C.), in which the statutes in force are arranged by subject. There are also privately published, annotated versions of the *U.S. Code*, for instance, *U.S. Code Annotated* (U.S.C.A.), published by West Publishing Company; (2) for administrative regulations, the *Federal Register* (F.R.), a daily publication, and the *Code of Federal Regulations* (C.F.R.), a compilation of federal regulations arranged by subject. Citations of statutes and regulations follow the same uniform format mentioned above, i.e., volume number (or "title" in the case of U.S.C. and C.F.R.), name of publication, and page number (or section number). Most of the states have equivalent publications for their statutes and administrative regulations. For more information on citation style and legal research, see Morris L. Cohen, *Legal Research in a Nutshell* (4th ed., 1985).

Issue:

Does the president have authority to remove Wiener for political reasons, namely, because he wanted his own appointee on the commission?

Holding:

No.

Order:

The judgment of the Court of Claims is reversed.

Reasoning:

(Opinion by Mr. Justice Frankfurter for a unanimous Court)

The most important factor in determining whether the president has removal power on the grounds stated is "the nature of the function" of the War Claims Commission. The commission's basic function is to adjudicate claims brought before it. Its task is of an "intrinsic judicial character." Such functions should be protected from outside interference both as to particular cases and as to the removal of a commissioner for the reasons stated: "no such power is given to the president directly by the Constitution, and none is impliedly conferred upon him by the statute simply because Congress said nothing about it." The Court suggested that it might be another matter if removal were based on reasons related to improper performance of official duties.

The Court relied heavily on the authority of *Humphrey's Executor* v. *United States* (1935), where the Supreme Court rejected the president's assertion of authority to remove a member of the Federal Trade Commission, a body with an essentially adjudicatory function, for basically the same reasons. It distinguished the present case from *Myers* v. *United States* (1926), which upheld the president's power to remove an official from the purely executive position of postmaster.

Separate Concurring or Dissenting Opinions:

Frankfurter wrote for a unanimous Court. There were no concurring or dissenting opinions.

Chapter 2

Origin and Development of the Administrative Process

Many studies of the origin and development of the administrative process have focused upon the creation of the Interstate Commerce Commission in 1887 as the point at which the United States embarked on a new pattern of unified, national regulation by independent administrative agencies.[1] This event admittedly was the classic example of Congress creating an administrative agency to provide continuous expert supervision over matters of regulatory policy that were alien to the basic functions of either the courts or legislatures. The history of the post–Civil War period had amply demonstrated that neither the individual states nor the federal courts were in a position to fashion remedies for the general public, which was suffering from a variety of unfair practices and the exorbitant rate structure of the railroad industry.[2] Congressional acknowledgment that national regulatory policy was needed to cope with problems such as unfair methods of competition and unfair labor practices led to the establishment of additional independent regulatory commissions in the twentieth century.[3]

---

[1] For more information on the origins of the independent regulatory commissions see Robert E. Cushman, *The Independent Regulatory Commissions* (1941), and Marver Bernstein, *Regulating Business by Independent Commission* (1955).

[2] For a discussion of the catalytic role of the Supreme Court's decision in *Wabash, St. Louis and Pacific R.R. Co.* v. *Illinois*, 118 U.S. 557, 7 S.Ct. 4, 30 L.Ed. 244 (1886) in the congressional decision to pass the Interstate Commerce Act, see Cushman, above, note 1, at 44.

[3] For an exhaustive compilation of articles and documents associated with twentieth century development of the administrative process, see Legislative Reference Service of the Library of Congress, *Separation of Powers and the Independent Agencies: Cases and Selected Readings*, S.Doc. No. 49, 91st Cong., 1st sess. (1969).

HISTORICAL DEVELOPMENT OF AMERICAN ADMINISTRATIVE PROCESS

However, if we are to take a comprehensive look at the origin and development of the administrative process in the United States we must go much further back than 1887 and the creation of the first independent regulatory commission. One logical point would be the creation of the Republic for, in fact, the forerunners of several of our administrative agencies date back to the 1790s. More appropriately, however, we need to go back still further to the Anglo-American origins.

Professor R. John Tresolini [4] traced the origins of Anglo-American administrative law from the latter part of the twelfth century in England, when the first book on the common law was published. In the process he examined the role of the sheriff in the centralization of royal authority, the judicial and administrative activities of itinerant justices, and, most importantly, the justices of the peace, who by the eighteenth and early nineteenth centuries had become chief administrators. Only with the advent of the Industrial Revolution did a more centralized system of administration evolve in Britain, which gradually resulted in the diminution of the powers of the justices of the peace.

Tresolini also described the justices of peace and magistrates as being the most important officers in the colonial period in America. The administration of many local laws and ordinances was entrusted to them. The agrarian nature of American society, coupled with the fear of centralized authority, obviated the need for complex administrative systems. Eventually, however, administrative power began to shift from local governmental units to those at the state or federal level. As in England, this gradual centralization of administrative power was accentuated by the onset of the Industrial Revolution, which required intervention by the national government in a variety of previously unregulated areas. As federal regulatory jurisdiction expanded, Congress increasingly delegated responsibility over technical matters to newly created administrative agencies. The enabling legislation creating these agencies authorized wide grants of discretionary authority to administrative officers. These grants of legislative and judicial authority were the forerunners of the rule-making and adjudicatory powers commonly exercised by independent regulatory bodies during the past half century.

Tresolini also recounted the process whereby administrative law eventually received recognition as a legitimate component of public law. With the exception of several enlightened scholars who perceived the need for the exploration of the workings of administrative law, the major thrust of the nineteenth and early twentieth century writings on the subject in both Great Britain and the United States either sought to condemn its growth or deny its existence as a body of law. It was A. V. Dicey, the foremost scholar of English constitutional law, who was to exert the greatest influence in retarding the recognition of administrative law. He was eventually forced to capitulate in the face of court decisions upholding the exercise of administrative powers

---

[4] R. John Tresolini, "The Development of Administrative Law," 12 *University of Pittsburgh Law Review* 362 (1951).

and, ultimately, the findings of the Committee on Ministers' Powers. Likewise, in the United States, administrative law was to receive belated recognition. The scholarly contributions of Frank J. Goodnow and Ernst Freund were to prove instrumental in that regard, as was the *Final Report of the Attorney General's Committee on Administrative Procedure*.[5]

The edited selections reproduced in this chapter constitute an overview of the historical development of the American administrative process. Collectively, they provide the student of the administrative process with a basis from which contemporary developments may be analyzed. They also demonstrate, to use Felix Frankfurter's words, that "administrative law has not come like a thief in the night." [6]

As noted earlier, the precursors of the Interstate Commerce Commission date back to the founding of the Republic. The following brief excerpt from James O. Freedman's book, *Crisis and Legitimacy: The Administrative Process and American Government*, traces the development of our modern regulatory system from these modest beginnings.

Crisis and Legitimacy: The Administrative Process and American Government

James O. Freedman
Cambridge University Press, 1978, pages 4–6.[a]

Roots of the Modern Administrative Process

The growth of the administrative process in the United States occurred gradually, as the original thirteen states matured into a continental nation, increasingly industrialized and urbanized, facing economic and social problems that required responses more technologically expert, more institutionally flexible, and more procedurally expeditious than either the Congress or the federal courts could provide. The creation of administrative agencies was designed to supply these institutional deficiencies in the formulation and administration of public policy.

Although the rise of the administrative process is often identified with the presidency of Franklin D. Roosevelt, in fact reliance upon administrative agencies to meet emerging national problems long antedates the New Deal. It is as old as the Republic itself. The First Congress of the United States, meeting in 1789, enacted legislation authorizing administrative officers to "estimate the duties payable" on imports and to adjudicate claims to military pensions for "invalids who were wounded and disabled during the late war." The forerunner of the Patent Office was created in 1790, of the Office of Indian

---

[5] Attorney General's Committee on Administrative Procedure, *Final Report of the Attorney General's Committee on Administrative Procedure*, S.Doc. No. 8, 77th Cong., 1st sess. (1941).

[6] Felix Frankfurter, "Foreword," 47 *Yale Law Journal* 515 (1938).

[a] Reprinted by permission of the publisher.

Affairs in 1796. The General Land Office was established in 1812. The administrative process thus has deep historical roots.

Approximately one-third of the federal administrative agencies were created before 1900, notably the Civil Service Commission in 1883 and the Interstate Commerce Commission in 1887. By 1891, the Pension Office of the Department of the Interior, with six thousand employees and more than a half-million cases pending for adjudication, was, according to its commissioner, the "largest executive bureau in the world." [7] Still another third of the federal agencies were created between 1900 and 1930, notably the Federal Reserve Board in 1913, the Federal Trade Commission in 1914, and the United States Tariff Commission in 1916. During these same decades, many state governments, responding to the influence of the Granger and Progressive movements, created administrative agencies to regulate banking, bridges, canals, ferries, grain elevators, insurance, railroad freight rates, and warehouses.

Reliance upon the administrative process was thus an established practice by the time that Roosevelt became president in 1933. But it nevertheless seems natural to associate the dominant position of the administrative process in modern government with President Roosevelt because the New Deal radiated a faith in the capacity of the administrative process perhaps exceeding that of any previous administration.

Faced with the devastating consequences of a major depression, the New Deal created a large number of administrative agencies to attack the nation's economic and social problems. These agencies, almost all of which eventually wrought major changes in American life, included the Federal Deposit Insurance Corporation (1933), the Tennessee Valley Authority (1933), the Federal Communications Commission (1934), the Securities and Exchange Commission (1934), the National Labor Relations Board (1935), and the Civil Aeronautics Board (1938).

In 1937, the President's Committee on Administrative Management reported critically to President Roosevelt that Congress had created more than a dozen major independent regulatory agencies since 1887, and went on to complain that "Congress is always tempted to turn each new responsibility over to a new independent commission. This is not only following the line of least resistance. It is also following a fifty-year-old tradition." [8]

The tradition persists to this day. The demonstrated utility of the administrative process in meeting serious national problems during the New Deal years undoubtedly influenced the decision to create additional administrative agencies to meet the problems of controlling materials, manpower, prices, and production presented by World War II. In the decades since the war, the creation of new administrative agencies to deal with emerging national problems has continued apace. Under Democratic and Republican presidents alike, Congress has regularly chosen to rely upon administrative regulation—rather than upon civil remedies, criminal penalties, subsidies to the private sector, or the free market, for example—to implement public policies in new

---

[7] See L. White, *The Republican Era, 1869–1901*, at 211–14 (1958).

[8] *Report of the President's Comm. on Administrative Management* 41 (1937).

and complex areas of federal concern. These areas have included atomic energy (the Atomic Energy Commission, 1946), military conscription (the Selective Service Commission, 1948), space exploration (the National Aeronautics and Space Administration, 1958), shipping (the Federal Maritime Commission, 1961), employment discrimination (the Equal Employment Opportunity Commission, 1965), environmental protection (the Environmental Protection Agency, 1970), occupational safety (the Occupational Safety and Health Review Commission, 1970), and consumer product safety (the Consumer Product Safety Commission, 1972).

The continuing growth in the administrative process has led to a corresponding increase in the prominence of administrative law in the decisions of the Supreme Court. The role of the Supreme Court in the shaping of American administrative law dates at least from the decision in *The Brig Aurora* in 1813.[9] (At one time, in 1957, decisions involving review of administrative action constituted the largest single category of cases decided by the Court on the merits, about one-third of the total.[10]) In the decades of the 1960s and 1970s, however, the Court considered proportionally fewer administrative law cases as other classes of litigation, particularly those involving criminal procedure and civil rights, assumed a heightened national importance and claimed a greater share of the Court's attention.

By the time of the nation's bicentennial in 1976, the federal administrative process had achieved a considerable status. It embraced more than sixty independent regulatory agencies as well as perhaps several hundred administrative agencies located in the executive departments. Administrative agencies exercised regulatory responsibilities in scores of important and sensitive areas. The decisions rendered by the federal administrative agencies were many times the number rendered by the federal courts and probably affected the lives of more ordinary citizens more pervasively and more intimately than the decisions of the federal courts. In virtually every relevant respect, the administrative process has become a fourth branch of government, comparable in the scope of its authority and the impact of its decision making to the three more familiar constitutional branches.

The United States thus has increasingly become an administrative state. Americans have sought to understand the implications of this fact for the character of American democracy, the nature of American justice, and the quality of American life. These implications have often been troubling—even though the administrative process had deep historical roots, even though its growth has been gradual and evolutionary, and even though that growth has occurred only by deliberative acts of democratic choice. If the United States is to realize the promise and respect the limitations of the administrative process, the quest for understanding its implications must be regularly renewed. . . .

---

[9] 11 U.S. (7 Cranch) 382 (1813).

[10] Frankfurter, *The Supreme Court in the Mirror of Justices*, 105 U.Pa.L.Rev. 781, 793 (1957).

The APA

A major event in the evolution of administrative law was the adoption of the Administrative Procedure Act (APA) in 1946. But the APA was not conceived and brought into being overnight. It can be traced back at least as far as the early 1930s.

Concurrent with the *de facto* growth of federal regulatory agencies, described above by Freedman, a major debate raged in both governmental and nongovernmental circles over the structural relationships between these administrative agencies and the courts. However, while the debate continued over the degree of judicial accountability of the administrative process, that process itself became more and more deeply entrenched in the everyday operations of American government. The interaction of agencies and courts continued, giving rise to both an ever expanding caselaw and an increasingly more mature administrative process. During the 1930s proposals for the creation of a separate administrative court system were made by the American Bar Association's Special Committee on Administrative Law [11] and the President's Committee on Administrative Management; [12] however, the *de facto* growth and acceptance of the administrative process destined them to failure from the outset.

Acknowledging the failure of the administrative court proposals, the American Bar Association's Special Committee later shifted its focus to advocating greater judicialization of the then-existing administrative process. Its efforts culminated in the passage of the Walter-Logan bill; however, President Roosevelt vetoed the bill, and efforts to override the veto were unsuccessful. [13] The Walter-Logan bill emphasized structural reforms designed primarily to enlarge judicial controls, specifically involving the scope and subject matter of judicial review, over the agencies affected. James N. Landis described the impact the bill would have had on the administrative process:

> Only one thing can be certain and that is, that to apply the Procrustean formula suggested by the Association's [ABA] pending proposals is to cut off here a foot and there a head, leaving broken and bleeding the process of administrative law. [14]

With the failure to override the president's veto, the high point of the movement for basic judicialization of the administrative process had been reached. Roughly simultaneously, there was a growing conviction that judicial review itself would not solve the structural problems between agencies and courts. Virtually everyone agreed that some clarification of judicial review was necessary; however, it was no longer to be considered an end in itself. Carl McFarland captured the mood of the times quite accurately:

[11] 59 *American Bar Association Report* 539–564 (1934) and 61 *American Bar Association Report* 720–793 (1936).

[12] President's Committee on Administrative Management, *Report of the President's Committee on Administrative Management*, V, Part D., 39–42 (1937).

[13] Message of December 18, 1940, H. Doc. 986, 76th Cong., 3d sess. (1940); sustained by House of Representatives, 86 *Congressional Record*, Part 12, 76th Cong., 3d sess., 13953 (1940).

[14] James Landis, "Crucial Areas in Administrative Law," 53 *Harvard Law Review* 1077, 1102 (1940).

Partly out of recognition of the real substance of the problem, partly to avoid undue expansion of judicial review through legislative action, and partly because of recent and rapid expansion in the realm of federal administration which has driven home bluntly the methods and operation of administrative agencies, attention has turned to the principles and details, the needs and inefficiencies, the virtues and injustices of the actual operation of the administrative system in the federal government.[15]

Although the legislative history of the Administrative Procedure Act has been traced back to the Seventy-third Congress (1933–34),[16] its more direct source was two bills introduced during the Second Session of the Seventy-eighth Congress (1944), which were revised and simplified during the early days of the First Session of the Seventy-ninth Congress in 1945. The act itself was finally adopted in 1946 [17] by unanimous vote in both houses. According to Davis, "[t]he battle over fundamentals had ceased . . . [and] the federal administrative process seemed secure." [18]

Evaluations of the newly enacted legislation ran the full gamut, from claims that the Administrative Procedure Act was the "Magna Carta of Administrative Law" to the statement that the act constituted a "sabotage of the administrative process." [19] The intervening years have moderated the assessments and Bernard Schwartz's views are probably not unrepresentative today. Although Schwartz noted that the APA was not a comprehensive code of administrative procedure, he felt that it was a general framework of fundamental importance. In particular, he saw in the Administrative Procedure Act the initial "legislative attempt in the common-law world to state the essential principles of fair administrative procedure," [20] a step which imposed on all federal agencies the best procedures developed up to that time.[21]

Another assessment was offered by Marver Bernstein in his classic, *Regulating Business by Independent Commission:*

> Its significance seems . . . to be not so much in specific changes it has brought about in the procedure of adjudication as in the extent to which the Act represents an important stage in the unfolding of ideas and attitudes concerning the role of administrative discretion in modern government and the possibilities of achieving a fair measure of equity in the dispensing of administrative justice. It is more important for its political implications than for its specific procedural requirements and definitions.[22]

---

[15] Carl McFarland, "The False Standard in Administrative Procedures," 27 *Cornell Law Quarterly* 433, 439 (1942).

[16] See *Legislative History of the Administrative Procedure Act*, S.Doc. No. 248, 79th Cong., 2d sess., 187–191 (1946), for a chronological chart of main bills introduced dating back to the 73rd Congress.

[17] Administrative Procedure Act, 60 *Stat.* 237 (1946).

[18] Kenneth C. Davis, 1 *Administrative Law Treatise* 30 (1958).

[19] Frederick F. Blachly and Miriam E. Oatman, "Sabotage of the Administrative Process," 6 *Public Administration Review* 213 (1946).

[20] Bernard Schwartz, *Introduction to American Administrative Law* 134 (2d ed., 1962).

[21] Ibid., 135.

[22] Bernstein, above, note 1, at 194.

Thus, the enactment of the Administrative Procedure Act marked the maturation of the administrative process. In Nathaniel Nathanson's words "the turbulent administrative issues of the thirties have developed into a more or less peaceful maturity." [23]

Although related to administrative procedure, regulatory reform is a subject in its own right. As the following excerpt from a six-volume Senate study on federal regulation suggests, regulatory reform has also been the subject of repeated examinations through the years.

Regulatory Organization

Report by the Committee on Governmental Affairs
Senate, Ninety-fifth Congress, First Session, Washington, 1977, Volume V, pages 14–22.

Previous Efforts to Improve Regulatory Organization

Brownlow Report (the department as regulator)

President Franklin Roosevelt made executive-branch reorganization a major item in his agenda for a second term. As part of the president's more general strategy to increase his influence over administrative operations and policy, he submitted to Congress the report of his Committee on Administrative Management (Brownlow Committee) in January 1937. The committee proposed to integrate all the programs and agencies of the executive branch into twelve departments. This consolidation was to include all the independent regulatory commissions.

The attack on the commissions in the report was uncompromising, characterizing the commissions as a "headless fourth branch of the Government, a haphazard deposit of irresponsible agencies and uncoordinated powers. They do violence to the basic theory of the American Constitution that there should be three major branches of the Government and only three. The Congress has found no effective way of supervising them, they cannot be controlled by the President, and they are answerable to the courts only in respect to the legality of their activities."

The report further stated:

> Power without responsibility has no place in a government based on the theory of democratic control, for responsibility is the people's only weapon, their only insurance against abuse of power.
>
> But though the commissions enjoy power without responsibility, they also leave the President with responsibility without power. Placed by the Constitution at the head of a unified and centralized Executive Branch, and charged with the duty to see that the laws are faithfully executed, he must detour around powerful administrative agencies which are in no way subject to his authority and which are, therefore, both actual and potential obstructions to his effective overall management of national administration. The commissions practice confusion, conflict,

---

[23] Nathaniel Nathanson, "Central Issues in American Administrative Law," 45 *American Political Science Review* 348 (1951).

and incoherence in the formulation and in the execution of the President's policies. Not only by constitutional theory, but by a steady and mounting insistence of public opinion, the President is held responsible for the wise and efficient management of the Executive Branch of the Government. The people look to him for leadership. And yet we whittle away the effective control essential to that leadership by parceling out to a dozen or more irresponsible agencies important powers of policy and administration.

The committee recommended that the commissions become agencies within the executive departments. These regulatory agencies would then each be divided into an administrative section and a judicial section. The administrative section would be a regular bureau or division within the department, headed by a chief with career tenure and staffed under Civil Service regulations. It would be directly responsible to the secretary and through him to the president. The judicial section, on the other hand, would be "in" the department only for purposes of "administrative house-keeping", such as the budget, general personnel administration, and material. It would be wholly independent of the department and the president with respect to its work and its decisions. Its members would be appointed by the president with the approval of the Senate for long, staggered terms and would be removable only for specific causes as stated in the statute.

> This proposed plan meets squarely the problems presented by the independent commissions. It creates effective responsibility for the administrative and policy-determining aspects of the regulatory job and, at the same time, guarantees the complete independence and neutrality for that part of the work which must be performed after the manner of a court. It facilitates and strengthens administrative management without lessening judicial independence.

The committee continued by arguing that there was nothing novel or dangerous about their proposal. Important regulatory functions had long been carried out by executive departments. Cited in particular was the Agriculture Department, which in 1937 had numerous regulatory functions not unlike those performed by the regulatory commissions.

Under this arrangement, the judicial phases of the regulatory process, involving important rights of property, are handled by politically responsive, policy-determining officials. This is a system far more open to attack than the proposed plan which carefully places the adjudication of private rights in an independent judicial section.

The point the Brownlow Committee was attempting to make was that policy and administration could only be coordinated in the several regulatory fields if the units were responsible to a secretary and ultimately to the president. To the committee, it was both undemocratic and unwise to add responsibility for the making and administration of public policy to the duties of officials charged with the adjudication of private rights and the public interest.

The Executive Reorganization bill of 1938, which contained many of the recommendations of the Brownlow Committee, was defeated in Congress, in part over concern that it would give too much power to the president and abet what many saw that year as a trend towards "presidential dictatorship." In 1939, another Executive Reorganization bill was introduced and passed which simply provided the president with authority to initiate reorganization plans, subject to Congressional veto, and statutorily provided that the president could appoint six assistants.

However, one of the key changes that was made as a result of the Brownlow study concerned regulatory agency budgets. Prior to 1939, the budgets of the independent agencies were submitted to Congress directly. In 1939, however, the Budget and Accounting Act was amended at the president's urging, and thereafter the president's budget office was given the power to review and modify the budgets of all executive branch agencies, including the independent regulatory agencies.

The concept of including a regulatory agency with adjudicating powers within an executive department, first suggested by the Brownlow Committee in 1937, was revived in the creation of the Department of Energy in 1977. The Department of Energy Organization Act (P.L. 95–91) created the Federal Energy Regulatory Commission (FERC) to administer the principle pricing and related regulatory activities transferred to DOE from the Federal Power Commission, the Federal Energy Administration, and the Interstate Commerce Commission. The Congress recognized the need for assuring that important regulatory decisions would be consistent with the nation's overall energy policies. At the same time, Congress was concerned that full, impartial and independent consideration be given these important regulatory decisions.

It consequently created FERC as a collegial regulatory body within DOE, but gave the Secretary of Energy certain initiatory powers to assure the secretary an opportunity to participate actively in the commission's decision-making process and to assure expeditious commission consideration of important regulatory matters. The details of this merger are discussed in chapter 8 dealing with energy regulation. Suffice it to say here that certain aspects of this reorganization may represent a model worthy of consideration in other areas where regulatory agency activities may impact on national policy and planning goals.

Ash Council Study (commission consolidation)

Soon after taking office in 1969, President Nixon announced the appointment of a President's Advisory Council on Executive Organization to be chaired by Roy L. Ash, President of Litton Industries. The council would eventually submit some thirteen memorandums to the president, three of which would be made public. One of the memorandums later made public (1971) was a report on selected independent regulatory agencies.

The Ash Council report on regulatory agencies contended that the independent regulatory commissions are not sufficiently adaptable to changing economic conditions. This inability to adapt to changing circumstances is attributable to several causes, such as their "independence and remoteness in practice" from the president and the Congress. The council appeared to accept the notion that the problems of regulating the economy through independent commissions was not necessarily endemic to the nature of the regulation itself, but was largely a structural problem and subject to resolution. The council's principal solution was to alter the structure of the commissions.

To assure coordination of regulatory matters with policy goals, to improve the management efficiency of regulatory functions, to improve accountability to the Congress and the executive branch, and to increase the probability of superior leadership for regulatory activities, the transportation, power, securities and consumer protection regulatory functions should be administered by single administrators, appointed by the President. These functions should be performed by agencies respectively designated Transportation Regulatory Agency, Federal Power Agency, Securities and Exchange Agency, and the Federal Trade Practices Agency.

For reasons not entirely clear either then or now, the council excluded one regulatory commission and one function from their generalization about the wisdom of a single administrator agency.

The communications regulatory functions and the antitrust enforcement function should, as now, be carried out by multimember bodies for reasons supervening the advantages of a single administrator. The FCC should be reduced in size from seven to five members, to serve 5 year terms.

The council recommended that the following functional responsibilities among the independent regulatory commissions be realigned:

To reflect the increasing interdependence of the structure, economics, and technology of the transportation modes, regulatory responsibilities of the ICC, CAB, and the FMC should be combined within a new Transportation Regulatory Agency.

To correct the conflict inherent in performing regulatory and promotional functions in the same agency, the promotional subsidy-granting activities of the CAB should be transferred to the Department of Transportation.

To assure that each of its missions is more effectively performed, the FTC's consumer protection responsibilities should be vested in a new Federal Trade Practices Agency and its antitrust enforcement responsibilities should be vested in a new Federal Antitrust Board. The Board should consist of a chairman and two economist members, each appointed by the President with the consent of the Senate.

To provide an organization placement which better reflects current realities, the regulatory responsibilities of the SEC under the Public Utilities Holding Company Act should be transferred to the Federal Power Agency.

The improved coordination sought by the Ash Council was to be achieved, in their view, largely by the substitution of single administrators for plural commissions. The agencies would, presumably, become independent agencies within the executive branch with a status similar to that of the Environmental Protection Agency.

We believe single administrators will enhance leadership, improve the management of operations, and insure accountability in the regulatory agencies, where these vital requirements for program effectiveness are now often weak. This form of organization would also strengthen program coordination where two or more agencies need to work together to achieve a common goal.

The Ash Council considered the commissions to be ineffective for three reasons: "collegial organization, the judicial caste of agency activities, and the misalignment of certain functional responsibilities."

It was thought that if the multi-member commissions became agencies headed by a single administrator, they would attract more capable executives. Such an organization would also tend to enhance administrative policy making rather than relying on case-by-case adjudication for the development of policy. Coordination between these agencies and other regulatory agencies within the executive branch would be improved.

Criticism of the Ash Council's report tended to center on two points: that whatever merits there might be to any of the specific proposals, the overall study suffered from a lack of empirical evidence and too great a reliance "... on the intrinsic persuasiveness of its intuition;" and second, that the council did not relate its organizational proposals to any policy objectives. The Ash Council's report also failed to discuss regulatory agencies within the executive branch.

Landis Report (the executive office as coordinator)

In 1960, President-elect John Kennedy asked James M. Landis to prepare a study on regulatory commissions with the intent to recommend improvements in the operations of these commissions. Landis was concerned with several problems: delay in the disposition of adjudicatory proceedings, costs, personnel, ethical conduct, administrative procedures, formulation of policy within and between agencies, and the relationship of the commissions to the president and Congress. Landis placed special emphasis on the inadequacy of institutional efforts to coordinate regulatory policies.

The report recites examples of the absence or breakdown of policy coordination both within agencies and between agencies in a particular regulatory field. It states:

> A prime criticism of the regulatory agencies is their failure to develop broad policies in the areas subject to their jurisdiction ...
>
> A series of ... hiatuses in various regulatory fields can be mentioned, arising out of the inability to fashion viable patterns through the process of adjudication.
>
> If there is a lack of policy formulation within agencies, there is an almost complete barenness of such formulation for those matters with which groups of agencies are concerned. The few interagency committees that have been set up have accomplished too little in conducting their separate approaches to a common problem....
>
> The inability to effect inter-agency coordination has been responsible for the lack of any policy as to the nature of the competition that should exist as between forms of transportation and also between the carriers themselves. Military transportation, as presently conducted, competes heavily with commercial transportation, and there are patent abuses that attach to the government as a mass shipper, but it still insists on going its own way regardless of the effects its policies may have upon other carriers.

Various alternative means to improve coordination were suggested by Landis, but he concluded that the type of coordination he desired would have to be hierarchically imposed and ultimately involve the president. The Bureau of the Budget (now OMB) was specifically ruled out as coordinative unit. Consolidation of these agencies into executive departments, as recommended by the Brownlow Committee, might "eventually be the right answer," but the problem was "too pressing to await the initation of what would be a mammoth project of consolidation in the fields of transportation, communications, and energy . . . . "

The solution, according to Landis, was to develop and coordinate policy at a high staff level, in this case within the Executive Office of the President. The report was published at a time when much academic and media support could be found for increasing the size, functions, and power of the Executive Office as an institution. The report specifically proposed, among other things, that four new offices be established within the Executive Office of the President, as follows:

(1) An Office for the Coordination and Development of Transportation Policy to develop and implement a national transportation policy. This should be accomplished by Reorganization Plan transferring to this Office all the responsibilities now vested in the Undersecretary of Commerce for Transportation.

(2) An Office for the Coordination and Development of Communications Policy and simultaneously by executive order transfer to this Office all powers relating to telecommunications now vested in the Office of Civil and Defense Mobilization.

(3) An Office for the Coordination and Development of Energy Policy with authority to propose to the President plans for the development of energy resources of this nation.

(4) An Office for the Oversight of Regulatory Agencies which will assist the President in discharging his responsibility of assuring the efficient execution of those laws that these agencies administer.

The Landis Report, while innovative in terms of its proposals for new units within the Executive Office, was similar to earlier studies in its avoidance of the subject of regulatory policy administered by executive-branch agencies and concentrated, instead, on the independent regulatory commissions and their alleged structural deficiencies. Marver Bernstein observed: "Perhaps because of his desire or instructions to avoid any proposal requiring legislation, Landis did not relate problems of regulatory agencies to the character of the legislative mandates, and the lack of effective sanctions for securing compliance with regulations."

The president subsequently submitted to Congress seven proposals on reorganizing the regulatory commissions. All of the reorganization plans had the same basic aim of speeding up and streamlining agency procedures. The first four plans—those for the Securities and Exchange Commission, the Federal Communications Commission, the Civil Aeronautics Board, the Federal Trade Commission—contained three basically identical steps to accomplish this. They authorized the board or commission to delegate some of its functions to certain members or employees; they empowered the chairman to assign the delegated functions; and they made review of certain lower-level decisions discretionary.

The plan for the National Labor Relations Board was the same as the first four but omitted the chairman's power of assignment; the plan for the Federal Home Loan Bank Board only restored some hiring and firing powers formerly held by the chairman; in the seventh plan, the Federal Maritime Board, was abolished and its functions delegated to other agencies. Congress rejected four of the seven reorganization plans submitted. The rejections were essentially the result of particular congressional committees coming to the defense of "their" commissions. The rejections were construed, however, as a rebuff to the president. This defeat apparently cooled whatever ardor the president might have felt for reorganizing the regulatory agencies.

A common thread running through the Brownlow, Landis, and Ash studies of regulatory organization discussed above is the need to impose some degree of political (i.e., congressional and presidential) influence on at least the policy-related activities of the regulatory bodies. It is commonly agreed that many of the tasks assigned by Congress to regulatory agencies are political in nature, involving critical choices of selecting among conflicting interests. Agencies must often decide which economic and social goals to pursue and at what economic and social costs. These are unquestionably political decisions. At the same time, of course, agencies make decisions such as in rate making and in choosing between applicants for a particular license which should be insulated from political influence. But even some of these decisions are fringed with political overtones. For example, should the CAB authorize a route between cities exceeding a certain population size is a political choice; the choice of which particular route, or which carrier should operate that route, is closer to adjudication. However, instead of having a broad perspective on the political aspect of issues they decide, most agencies are concerned solely with their particular industry and with a narrower perspective. Their decisions are inevitably based on the facts and issues presented to them rather than on any concern for national goals or policy. Coordination mechanisms such as interagency committees are designed to settle jurisdictional conflicts and avoid obvious overlaps or duplication, but they are not intended to nor do they deal with the problem of relating the work of a particular agency to overall national policy.

The Brownlow Committee, Dean Landis, and the Ash Council all recognized these problems and recommended various proposals to give the executive greater influence in regulatory agency decision making. In our view, none of these reports sufficiently recognized the importance of maintaining independence for regulatory decision making. However, they did point to the single deficiency which continues to persist—the inability of the political arms of government to influence policy-related activities of the regulatory bodies. We deal with these issues in this volume's chapter on independence and in our recommendations. One of our recommendations attempts to resolve the dilemma of maintaining independence at the same time that some measure of political initiative is provided to the executive to institute proceedings before regulatory bodies.

It is our view that the appropriate way to gain political control of regulatory agencies is certainly not to impose a provision of doubtful constitutionality such as the legislative veto. If agencies are acting in ways believed by Congress to deviate from congressional intent, then Congress should either amend the laws under which agencies operate to ensure that they understand congressional intent or Congress should narrow delegations of authority and engage in more thorough oversight. One of our recommendations is that Congress review and consolidate the disparate laws under which some agencies operate. We also recommend that in order to improve congressional oversight that Congress should draft its statutes for regulatory agencies as narrowly as possible. Since one problem encountered in certain substantive areas is the absence of clear legislative policy goals, we also recommend that statutes incorporating national goals or policy be enacted for areas such as transportation, energy, and banking.

Whether or not a given organizational structure for regulatory administration should be favored over all others will depend, in large part, on what political values are to be promoted. Regulation is not an end in itself. It is a means toward some other end, and the test of any regulatory structure is whether it is attaining the goals and purposes which gave rise to its creation. When it can no longer meet this test, the structure, and possibly even the underlying regulation, is in need of change. . . .

Recent Efforts at Reform of Administrative Processes

Efforts at reform of the regulatory and administrative processes have continued in recent years. During the Carter administration, for example, the Airline Deregulation Act of 1978 [24] constituted the first major legislative effort to deregulate an entire industry. The act not only provided for the gradual phaseout of price and market-entry controls, but it also called for the abolition of the Civil Aeronautics Board (CAB) as of January 1, 1985.[25] Additional industries affected by deregulation initiatives during the Carter presidency were natural gas, trucking, and railroads. President Carter also was intent upon improving the quality of governmental regulations. His March 1978 Executive Order #12044, for example, specified that regulations were to be written in plain English and that new methods were to be adopted to facilitate public comment in the rule-making process.

President Reagan has not only expanded the single-industry deregulation initiatives of the Carter administration, for example, decontrol of the price of crude oil and gasoline and of the banking industry, but he has also, and more importantly, called for the reduction of social, environmental, and health regulations so as to minimize costs of industrial compliance.[26] An integral component of these deregulation initiatives is the requirement that all existing and proposed regulations be subjected to cost-benefit and/or cost-effectiveness analysis. Final review authority over the adequacy and accuracy of these analyses has been vested in the Office of Management and Budget. The regulatory missions of prominent federal agencies, such as the Environmental Protection Agency (EPA) and the Occupational Safety and Health Administration (OSHA), are likely to be significantly affected by these deregulatory initiatives. Some of these recent changes and proposals will be discussed more fully elsewhere in this book.

---

[24] P.L. 95–504, 92 *Stat.* 1705 (1978).

[25] See, in particular, the chapter on airline deregulation in Stephen Breyer, *Regulation and Its Reform*, 317–340 (1982).

[26] See Florence Heffron (with Neil McFeeley), *The Administrative Regulatory Process*, 372–387 (1983) for tripartite categorization of deregulation initiatives of the Carter and Reagan presidencies.

Where, then, does the administrative process stand today? The following excerpt will suggest some answers to that question. It is by the former chairman of the American Bar Association's section on administrative law and was prepared for a special issue of the *Administrative Law Review* commemorating the Bicentennial of the Declaration of Independence. On the eve of the bicentennial of the drafting of the U.S. Constitution it still is an insightful and succinct overview of the development of American administrative law.

Cornerstones of American Administrative Law [a]

Jerre S. Williams
28 Administrative Law Review v–xii (1976).

[Williams begins by saying that in the course of studying the subject he came to the conclusion that there were "four cornerstones of the development of traditional administrative law up to the present time."]

... After I had isolated these four cornerstones, it came home to me that all four of them are American inventions. Certainly we have relied upon our English heritage in developing these fundamental principles of American administrative law, but the creative spark of advance in each of them is our own. These four traditional cornerstones are:

1. The independent regulatory agency
2. A uniform administrative procedure law—the APA
3. Substantial evidence judicial review
4. Notice and comment rulemaking

Let met state a few critical observations with respect to each of these cornerstones.

Reference to the first cornerstone, the "independent regulatory agency," should be in quotation marks. Rather than being independent, as we all know, these agencies are in a unique and peculiar way highly dependent upon both the executive and legislative branches of the government, and indirectly upon the judicial branch as well. But independence is gained out of their trifurcated dependency.

These agencies grow out of the American constitutional separation of powers concept—not characteristic of British law and governmental organization. Their status and posture give them strength but also weaknesses at the same time. The independent agency in attempting to give flesh to the broad, general, and usually disputed delegations of power from the Congress must at the same time satisfy the executive branch of the government on its budgetary and legislative proposals and satisfy the courts as to the scope of its activities and the fidelity with which they are carried out. All of these restraints lead to a peculiar and frequently a difficult life for an administrative agency. Yet at

---

[a] Jerre S. Williams wrote this "Chairman's Message" during his tenure as chairman of the Administrative Law Section of the American Bar Association. The author is now a Circuit Judge, Fifth Circuit Court of Appeals. It is reprinted from 28 *Administrative Law Review* v–xii (1976), a publication of the Administrative Law Section of the American Bar Association.

the same time, this constant pull from three directions at once constitutes an innate strength to the agency's existence and its particular kind of effectiveness.

The effectiveness of our administrative agencies is not demonstrated in sweeping programs of reform in government as much as it is demonstrated in a buffer relationship which enables the executive and legislative branches to accomplish something in delicate areas where accomplishment would be exceedingly difficult without the usually genteel, but often not gentle, tug of war between those governmental branches.

It is my view that the independent regulatory agency has also set the pattern for much of the bridging of the separate postures of the executive and legislative branches by the governmental agencies within the executive branch itself. We have the independent agencies within the executive branch; we have other bureaus, boards, and programs within the executive branch— all of which are successfully able to maintain a measure of independence from a monolithic control by the president probably because we learn through the independent agencies how such a measure of independence can be maintained.

All this does not lead to crisp, efficient decision making. But it does lead ultimately to decision making which is responsive to the demands of the two political branches of the government and ultimately to the demands of the judicial branch as well.

It is axiomatic that regulatory agencies have their lean years and their effective years. We perhaps could wish that all years would be effective. But a lack of effectiveness in the agencies almost certainly telegraphs notice that the legislative and executive branches of the government do not wish effective activity by that agency at that time.

An example of the point that I here make is readily seen in the rapid development of environmental concerns in the last few years. When our nation quite suddenly became environmentally conscious, there was a substantial amount of criticism of the regulatory agencies for not having taken the leadership in environmental matters. Except in a minor and rather interstitial way, the regulatory agencies could not have taken leadership in environmental matters at an earlier time because their activities in doing so would immediately have been undermined and barred through congressional hearings and executive supervisory action. The reason for this, of course, is that the Congress and the executive were not at that time concerned about environmental matters, and they would not have wanted agencies running off on new trails which they themselves at that time did not perceive.

The independent regulatory agency is not the spearhead of government. In a democratic government, it should not be. The agency should be the working administrator that carries out the spearhead actions of the legislative and executive bodies. Whatever leadership given by a regulatory agency is only the mirror reflecting the leadership given by the Congress and the executive. Frequent impatience with regulatory bodies should more properly be directed toward those that set them up and oversee their activities.

The second traditional cornerstone is the development and enactment of a uniform administrative procedure law—the Administrative Procedure Act. I am not stating that this law by any means creates complete uniformity. But the Administrative Procedure Act has played a remarkable role in bringing a measure of standardization to administrative practices and procedures and enabling access to those procedures by citizens.

Chaos in administrative procedure was much the order of the day before the APA. The only regularity was found in court decisions based upon constitutional grounds. And the warning was that we were moving down the road of deciding all manner of administrative practice and procedure questions on a constitutional basis. This would have been a tragic outcome, blocking creative activity to develop effective administrative processes.

The remarkable enactment by unanimous vote of both Houses of Congress of the Administrative Procedure Act at once regularized and recognized a corpus of administrative law, but at the same time created it. The two most critical aspects of the statute form the other two cornerstones. But the over-all idea that agencies must follow the fundamental outlines of this broad and general statute, unless they can find justifiable exception, was an advance of immeasurable proportions in administrative law and in the protection of the rights of citizens.

In contrast, the British are just now moving to the adoption of an overall Administrative Procedure Act. Our general statute of 1946 was a particular American advance and invention.

The third cornerstone is the principle of substantial evidence judicial review. Until the enactment of this standard in the Administrative Procedure Act, the courts and the legislative bodies were floundering. Judicial review of formal administrative action was mercurial and carried strong constitutional overtones. In some areas those overtones threatened to be obstructive, as in the "constitutional fact" analysis.

Of course, the Administrative Procedure Act did not invent substantial evidence review. Congress developed this scope of review in various statutes. But insertion of the substantial evidence review standard in the Administrative Procedure Act regularized it and justified the use of judicial review precedents under one statute to define the breadth of judicial review under the substantial evidence test in other statutes. The substantial evidence review test might well have developed different nuances under different statutes if it had not been for the Administrative Procedure Act.

Substantial evidence review has been a dominant aspect of administrative practice and procedure. It has been the means by which the courts can intrude in the merits of an agency action when it has badly gone wrong. At the same time, however, this standard of review has not in the overview been too broad an invitation for the courts to move constantly and deeply into the administrative process. It enables a delicate, yet effective, balance in the role the courts play in ensuring that the administrative process is fair yet unstifled.

Again, we have a noteworthy contrast. The British in their new Administrative Procedure Act proposals are for the first time undertaking to develop a regularized process of judicial review. In the past, the British have had to rely upon the common-law extraordinary writs, particularly the writ of certiorari, as the framework for judicial review of administrative action. While the British have subtly achieved a measure of judicial review of the merits through this device, it is not a well-defined and accepted means of judicial oversight of the merits of administrative action.

The substantial evidence test recognizes and accepts court intrusion into the merits of administrative action to a restricted, yet effective, level. Every indication we get is that the Congress and the executive, and indeed the American people, want this to be so. If the administrative body goes too badly wrong on the merits, they want the courts to reverse by finding an inadequacy in the record.

The final traditional cornerstone in the development of administrative law in the United States is the rule making procedure. Kenneth Culp Davis has called notice and comment rule making one of the most creative and important jurisprudential developments of this century. In the rule-making procedure we gave birth to a means by which we can get public participation in the development of administrative policy decisions.

Perhaps the most important aspect of the rule making procedure as it relates to the overall body of administrative law is that notice and comment rule making demonstrates there are means by which the public can be enabled to participate effectively in their governmental processes which are short of full participation as parties in an adjudicatory-type hearing with a transcript and complete record.

The Administrative Procedure Act is polarized into two procedures, the informal rule-making procedure and the formal adjudicatory procedure. But as we know, and as a number of other statutes separately provide, there are many means by which informal public participation such as in rule making under Section 4 of the APA can be broadened without becoming a full adjudicatory procedure under Sections 5, 6, and 7. Certain aspects of rule making can be subjected to more intensive public participation than others. In some situations, the comments under the informal procedure need not be limited to written comments mailed into the agency but can include oral hearings at various locations around the country, and especially at locations where the license granted by the agency or the regulation of the agency will have particular impact.

So not only has the rule-making procedure in its own right been a significant contribution to administrative process, but it also serves as the catalyst and guide to force us into consideration of other possible procedures for public participation short of the full formal requirements of adjudication.

Lest the reader be left hanging with the thought that in the preparation of the paper for the American Bar Association I considered only the traditional development of administrative law, I go on to mention briefly the three additional cornerstones which I see as becoming critical in the future development of administrative law. I do not dwell upon them here. Contemporary and future administrative law are best left to the outstanding articles in this special Bicentennial Issue of the *Review.* I mention them only to round out my own brief observations. And, in mentioning these new cornerstones, I stress that in the last ten to fifteen years new developments in administrative process have burgeoned. There have been radical changes manifested in new procedures and in the application of procedures to new areas of citizen-government relationships.

The three contemporary cornerstones are:

1. Public participation in the administrative process
2. Administrative process in informal and discretionary governmental activity
3. Continuing definition of the mission of administrative agencies and development of effective oversight of their activities

The first contemporary cornerstone is public participation in the administrative process. Only ten to fifteen years ago, the prevailing view was that the agency itself was the representative of the public interest. All this has now drastically changed. Through court decisions insisting that the public has the right to participate in the administrative process, and through recognition by Congress and within the agencies themselves that public participation in new and effective ways must be accepted, citizen participation in government has become a significant contemporary theme.

A current manifestation of this drive for public participation is the noteworthy development of proposals for the government to pay attorneys' fees to those who participate in the administrative process as representatives of the public and make a significant contribution to that process. A number of government programs to pay such fees are already in effect, and broader proposals are under consideration.

Yet, public participation creates problems in expense and delay and raises serious questions about the effective functioning of the democratic process. Self-selected groups appearing before agencies may or may not be adequately representing the public and yet may be viewed by the agency as the voice of the people. But accepting these concerns, the increased public participation is an exciting and challenging development which cannot and should not be stayed.

The second contemporary and future cornerstone is the new awareness of the need for and application of the administrative process in informal and discretionary governmental activity. We are increasingly beginning to realize that the administrative process in some regularized form must be applied to areas which have hitherto been treated as purely discretionary.

The treatment of persons in public institutions, the treatment of aliens, and the entire area of governance in educational institutions are manifestations of the kind of governmental activity demanding this new awareness. Here we are beginning to develop a great deal of procedural law where, it is fair to say, a few years ago no procedural law at all existed. It would be difficult to overemphasize the importance of this broadening development to the protection of the rights of citizens.

Again, problems surface. Delay continues its never ending irritation. So also it may well be urged that formalizing procedures is not worth the expense and effort in many minor situations. But government is for the benefit of citizens, and we had better be willing to take on the burden of developing fair and effective procedures in these erstwhile neglected areas.

The third and final contemporary cornerstone is the continuing definition of the mission of administrative agencies and the development of oversight of their activities. This final cornerstone is not so much new as it represents a new awakening.

This is one place where the old is ever new. Each new administration decides there must be regulatory reform. But each new administration falls short of the sweeping regulatory reform promised. Much of the reason for failure to achieve announced goals is the reason mentioned earlier. The administrative bodies fulfill a buffer function which militates against their spearheading creative and sweeping programs.

The reformers seek new ways of control of the administrative process. Legislative oversight is now to be enhanced, perhaps, by proposals for legislative veto of proposed administrative regulations. Certainly, the last few years has seen an increased scope of judicial review with the courts demanding hearing processes more complete than statutory requirements and with the courts playing the major administrative role in statutes such as the National Environmental Policy Act.

And we must not overlook the ombudsman. Although we have not yet figured out how to introduce the ombudsman broadly in the federal government, the institution is alive and healthy in a number of state and local governmental entities.

With the perennial problem of delay and the demonstrable instances where administrative bodies act unacceptably by overregulation or underregulation, affirmative efforts to improve and enhance the process must continue. A holding operation is not only unseemly but a denial of citizen rights. The challenges of the days ahead must be met and they can be met only by innovative change and growth in process, as well as in substantive standards.

So the final cornerstone must be continuing development of mission and fulfillment of mission, and continuing improvement in oversight. The issue is what is the best way among the alternatives presented, rather than whether improvements are needed. . . .

The Literature of Administrative Law

This chapter's review of the origin and development of the administrative process would be incomplete without some reference to the rich literature of administrative law. The final excerpt is a highly personalized literature review by an individual who has devoted his career, both as an academic and a practitioner, to the integration of the fields of law and public administration. According to Marshall E. Dimock, future lawyers and administrators would be well served if they familiarized themselves with the classic literature of the other's field.

Law and Dynamic Administration

Marshall E. Dimock

Praeger Publishers, 1980, pages 68–80.[a]

Up to this point, the focus of this book has been almost entirely on the governmental, or institutional, application of public administration and administrative law. However, attention now will be turned to the academic setting where the teaching, research, and book and article writing take place, and where both lawyers and administrators get their mental set. Before one can hope to reform the application, one needs to go back to the origin of manpower supply and improve scholarly understanding and cooperation.

In the United States, the divorcement of the public administration offering in arts and sciences faculties and the teaching of administrative law in law schools was apparent by 1940, but the trend started in the 1920s. Fortunately, the divorcement has never been complete, because there are still scholars in both faculties who have tried valiantly to hold the two strands together, realizing that their complete separation represents not merely a tilt but a distortion, with serious social consequences.

In historical perspective, three main periods may be distinguished in the United States. Between 1880 and 1923, both subjects were unified because they grew out of the same source, the administrative law of the Continent and the early political science of England. Between 1923 and 1940, the two subjects tended to differentiate more clearly but were still effectively collaborating within political science and law school faculties. The stimulus to the eventual separation occurred when, in a series of lectures on *The Growth of American Administrative Law* sponsored by the American Bar Association, administrative law was defined as "a convenient term to indicate that branch of modern law relating to the executive department *when acting in a quasi-legislative or quasi-judicial capacity.*" In the final period from 1940 to the present, the two fields have grown steadily apart, as political science and public administration neglected law, and as law school courses on administrative law stopped teaching administration and concentrated on private rights, or regulation. It was in the 1940s, therefore, that the two subjects finally got off the track.

The significance of these developments may be assessed more clearly when it is realized that in continental countries and wherever the Roman law tradition prevails today, the two subjects have been continuously taught in the same faculty since the early part of the nineteenth century. Only recently, as in France and Germany, has the operational or functional approach to public administration (which is characterized as "American") begun to receive separate treatment in separate courses or training programs for future officials. In England, due largely to the influence of the London School of Economics and Political Science, administrative law and public administration, as distinct courses, arrived much later on the scene in the 1930s, and with wider emphasis only since the end of World War II.

It is not too much to say, therefore, that both administrative law and public administration, as academic subjects in the United States, received

---

[a] Reprinted by permission of the publisher.

their original impetus from the Continent, where the attempt was to teach the whole of administration in a single course, and where treatises on administrative law sometimes run to seven or more volumes by the same author. . . .

Since there is some disagreement about the history of administrative law in the United States, with some occasionally claiming that it is a twentieth-century invention, and since a knowledge of authors is desirable, what follows is a general sequence of scholarly effort in the United States to date.

Some Steps in the Evolution of Administrative Law and Public Administration

In 1886 Frank J. Goodnow wrote an article on "Judicial Remedies against Administrative Actions" in volume one of Columbia's *Political Science Quarterly*. He noted that there were already certain books in existence that form a part of administrative law. Dillon's *Law of Municipal Corporations* (1872), and Cooley's *Law of Taxation* (1876). In 1890 Mechem's *Law of Officers* appeared. In 1887, a year after Goodnow's article was published, Woodrow Wilson's famous essay, "A Study of Administration," was published in volume two of the *Political Science Quarterly*. This article of Wilson's in which he describes public administration by analogy to business, marked the real beginning of public administration in the United States, and gave it its orientation.

The acknowledged father of administrative law, Goodnow published *Comparative Administrative Law* in 1893, *Politics and Administration*, which represented an initial attempt to combine the two fields, in 1900, and *The Principles of the Administrative Law of the United States* in 1905. Goodnow also was interested in municipal government and social legislation and wrote *Municipal Home Rule, Municipal Problems, Municipal Government*, and *Social Reform and the Constitution*.

Another pioneer, W. F. Willoughby, was both public lawyer and the earliest sustained writer in the field of public administration. He was for many years director of governmental studies at the Brookings Institution in Washington, D.C. As early as 1891 he coauthored with his brother, W. W. Willoughby, *Government and Administration in the United States*. However, his main distinction is his trilogy, *Principles of Public Administration* (1927), *Principles of Judicial Administration* (1929), and *Principles of Legislative Organization and Administration* (1934). Not only is Willoughby the only author who has written definitive books on the administration of all three branches in the United States, but he also is justly famous for inventing the idea that there is a legitimate fourth branch of government, the administrative, which is properly distinguished from the executive and reports to both Congress, as board of directors, and to the president, as chief executive.

In 1926 Leonard D. White of the University of Chicago published *An Introduction to Public Administration*, which became the first textbook in this field. His primary emphasis was upon personnel management, but being both a student and colleague of Ernst Freund, he was interested in administrative law and shared Freund's orientation. He later distinguished himself by writing several good books on government career service and was a member of the United States Civil Service Commission during the Roosevelt administration.

In addition to the other books of Ernst Freund that already have been noted, prominent consideration should be given to his scholarship in the field of legislation, where he was a pioneer. *Legislative Drafting* (1916), *Standards of Legislation* (1917), and *Legislative Regulation: A Study of the Ways and Means of Written Law* (1932). He also is justly famous for his interest in aliens and the Chicago School of Social Work, plus several monographs dealing with labor law. Freund also was a prime mover in the uniform state law movement. In addition, he was a pioneer in the study of police power, as exemplified by his book, *The Police Power: Public Policy and Constitutional Rights* (1904). This early book doubtless had something to do with his espousal of private rights in his 1928 book, *Administrative Powers over Persons and Property*.

Felix Frankfurter not only wrote one of the earliest casebooks on administrative law, but he also had a lifelong interest in practical administration, having served in Washington around the time of World War I. This practical experience is reflected in books such as *The Business of the Supreme Court* (with James M. Landis, 1928), *The Labor Injunction* (with Nathan Greene, 1930), *The Public and Its Government* (1930), *Mr. Justice Holmes* (1931), *Cases on Federal Jurisdiction* (with Wilber G. Katz, 1931), and *Mr. Justice Brandeis* (1932). It is possible that Frankfurter early had a better understanding of practical administration than any other law school writer of books on administrative law.

Another pioneer, Roscoe Pound, also was close to the interests of political scientists and public administrators all his life. He was essentially a philosopher and statesman of the law, but his interest in administration was intense. Among his many books the following are especially relevant: *Outlines of Lectures on Jurisprudence* (1914), *The Spirit of the Common Law* (1921), *An Introduction to the Philosophy of Law* (1922), *Law and Morals* (1924), *Criminal Justice in America* (1930), and *Administrative Law: Its Growth, Procedure and Significance* (1942).

During the 1920s and 1930s a number of political scientists exercised a considerable influence in the field of administrative law: James Hart, *Ordinance Making Power of the President* (1925); J. P. Comer, *Legislative Functions of National Administrative Authorities* (1927); John Dickinson, *Administrative Justice and the Supremacy of Law* (1927); W. C. Van Vleck, *The Administrative Control of Aliens* (1932); Frederick E. Blachly and Miriam E. Oatman, *Administrative Legislation and Adjudication* (1934); and J. P. Chamberlain et al., *The Judicial Function in Federal Administrative Agencies* (1942).

Because of their impact on U.S. thinking, a number of books by English authors also should be mentioned: Robert Carr, *Delegated Legislation* (1921); William A. Robson, *Justice and Administrative Law* (1928); F. J. Port, *Administrative Law* (1929); and Lord Hewart's polemic, *The New Despotism* (1929).

Another U.S. political scientist who has distinguished himself equally in law and administration is J. Roland Pennock. His earliest book, *Administration and the Rule of Law* (1941), is something of a classic. Because of his deep insights into legal philosophy, two more recent books of Pennock are equally rewarding (both with John W. Chapman): *The Limits of Law* (1974) and *Due Process* (1977). Pennock is one of those rare spirits who throughout a long professional life has helped to keep law and administration congenially intertwined.

The present author is another U.S. political scientist who always has kept one foot in administrative law and the other in public administration. Following the appearance of his *Congressional Investigating Committees* (1929), he edited (with C. G. Haines) *The Law and Practice of Administration* (1935); published *The Frontiers of Public Administration* (with Gaus and White, 1936), *Modern Politics and Administration* (1937), *The Immigration and Naturalization Service* (with Henry M. Hart, Jr. and John McIntire, 1940), four editions of *Public Administration* (with Gladys Ogden Dimock), the first in 1953, *A Philosophy of Administration* (1958), and *Casebook in Public Administration* (joint author, 1969). His early articles on administrative law, reflecting Goodnow's influence, whose student he was, are found in *Public Administration* (London, 1931), *American Political Science Review* (1932), and various other publications.

Among those law school professors who have been mentioned earlier, Walter Gellhorn has continued his interest in discovering alternative ways to formal courts of law for dispensing justice. This is reflected in two of his recent books, *Ombudsmen and Other Citizens' Protectors in Nine Countries* (1966), and *When Americans Complain: Governmental Grievance Procedures* (1966). Of all the law school professors active today, Gellhorn probably has a better appreciation of the virtue of interdisciplinary solidarity than anyone else.

Bernard Schwartz of New York University is, like Kenneth Davis, another prolific author. In addition to his 1976 *Administrative Law*, which has been cited often, his book entitled *The Professor and the Commissions* (1959), will be found interesting, and his book written with H.W.R. Wade, *Legal Control of Government: Administrative Law in Britain and the United States* (1972), presents some interesting contrasts.

I realize that in this brief review I have neglected significant authors such as Louis Jaffe, Ralph Fuchs, Nathaniel Nathanson, and many others, some of whom are close friends. Yet I beg forgiveness because my object has been quite limited: to convey some impression of the stages through which joint scholarship has gone and the degree to which authors from the two fields have either interlaced or gone their separate ways. I hope even this brief historical résumé has contributed something to an understanding of the historical integration of the two fields.

What is one to conclude from this chapter's survey of one-hundred years of courtship and alienation? The first thing is that administrative law is by no means a twentieth-century invention. It had a long history on the Continent before it was transplanted over here. At the outset the partners enjoyed connubial bliss because both came out of the legal-juristic tradition: political science was law and law was political science. Both were subdivisions under their patron saint, philosophy. There was no special merit in being called a lawyer or a political scientist. Political science was a point of view: comparative, analytical, believing in first principles, willing to experiment, not averse to turning its attention to municipal corruption, the exploitation of aliens, labor relations, or Sacco and Vanzetti, as Felix Frankfurter did in his first book.

Even as late as 1938, as I can recall from personal experience, lawyers and political scientists seemed unaware of any hereditary differences. Roscoe Pound courted Charles Grove Haines to go to Harvard Law School and give his lectures on the revival of natural law concepts; Edward S. Corwin of Princeton was, in both fields, the acknowledged expert on the presidency; lawyers pored over W. W. Willoughby's four volumes on constitutional law and marveled at the breadth of his scholarship and the accuracy of his interpretations; when I went to Chicago in 1932, one of the inducements held out to me was that Freund and I both were students of Frank J. Goodnow and Freund was about to retire (he died the same year).

Unlike now, neither side hesitated to quote the other profession as readily as its own. All this is now changed. One may read an entire book on administrative law and never find a reference to any of those works dealt with in the above historical summary. But this, unfortunately, is true today of most professional fields, with the possible exceptions of sociology and philosophy, which are considered mavericks.

But as has been seen, there have been throughout some who refused to budge from their fealty to a common citizenship. Frankfurter and Gellhorn are good examples in law, Haines and Pennock in political science. Another like this was Oliver P. Field of the University of Minnesota. The impression is that there were giants abroad in former times, men in both law and political science who were big enough to rise above any petty personal, professional, or scholastic rivalries.

One naturally wonders whether the accelerated drawing apart that began to occur in 1940 was due to differences in conservative or liberal philosophy. Perhaps in a few cases, but not in many. Most of those mentioned, such as Frankfurter, Goodnow, and Freund, were conservative in some things, liberal in others. Pound was that way, too. Some have suspected that as he got older he became more conservative, some would say ultraconservative; but if one reads his Claremont lectures, which is one of the last things he did, that impression is rapidly dispelled. His theme still was change and adjusting to change, but he continued to seek values in law and political philosophy that were congruent.

In terms of understanding the history of ideas, it was the New Deal, not so much the individual philosophies of scholars, that tended to create polarities. New agencies were being established at a rapid rate, as I learned from the vantage point of assistant secretary of labor in charge of legislation and administration. Lawyers understandably felt that administrative justice might, if the trend was not checked, overwhelm the traditional common law. Perhaps, in their concern, some individuals and the legal profession as a whole overreacted. In hindsight, it seems to this observer that they did. But as Aristotle pointed out long ago, this excessive zeal still can be righted, because the pendulum always has swung from one extreme to another, in short time cycles, and seldom, if ever, stands still.

The problem now is that of correctly appraising the requirements of the period that appears to lie ahead. In this period, as Mr. Justice Scarman said in his lectures, *English Law—The New Dimension* (1975), problems such as the European Community, the rival claims of organized labor and management, and the whole complex of social welfare cannot help but challenge the best thought of both professional disciplines, working together on solutions. The central problem is still, as it was in 1890 when Mechem wrote, a matter of political philosophy in its deepest sense. Society is an interconnected organism and hardly any problem can be dealt with adequately in splendid isolation. Pound and Goodnow were both clear about this in their heyday. Philosophers still believe that this is true, as seen in such seminal works as Summers' *Essays in Legal Philosophy* (1976) and Ronald Dworkin's *Taking Rights Seriously* (1977), which are attempting to revitalize this idea.

The field of law and administration needs big men with wide and deep insights and a charitable attitude toward cousins and second cousins. Future lawyers and administrators can develop this intimate knowledge of each other's fields simply by reading a few well-selected books. The case method should continue to be utilized in the preparation of both sets of experts, but it should not be used exclusively. Public lawyers and public administrators both can combine private and public interest without neglecting either. Perhaps the necessary first step in accomplishing this adjustment is to take a hard look at the preconceptions of one's academic field, as Dwight Waldo did in *The Administrative State* (1948), and more recently in *The Study of Public Administration* (1955).

One need not reject the past to build the future. The past is needed, with appropriate innovations, to assure the kind of future that measures up to the attainments of the past.

PART TWO

Legislative and Judicial Controls over the Administrative Process

Chapter 3

Delegation of Power

The starting point for the analysis of administrative activity is the authority provided to the administrator by the legislature. "All legislative powers herein granted shall be vested in a Congress of the United States," reads Article I of the U.S. Constitution. Article I also provides Congress with the power to "collect taxes," "borrow money," "coin money," and many other specific functions, but it was clearly not contemplated that members of Congress would personally and directly take part in these activities. Article II states that the president "shall take care that the laws be faithfully executed" and mentions "executive departments" and "officers" under the president whose functions would involve administration of the legislation adopted by Congress.

DELEGATION BY CONGRESS

From the start, then, there was an expectation that participation by governmental departments and officials outside of Congress would be required to realize the objectives of legislation promulgated by Congress. Whether such activity involves "delegation" by Congress to the executive is open to question. The term "delegation" does not appear in the Constitution, and there is some disagreement as to its precise meaning. "That Congress cannot delegate legislative power ... is a principle universally recognized as vital to the integrity and maintenance of the system of government ordained by the Constitution" is an often repeated quotation from an 1892 Supreme Court case. *Field* v. *Clark*, 143 U.S. 649, 692, 12 S.Ct. 495, 504, 36 L.Ed. 294, 310. It is also a statement with which most people would agree if "legislative power" is used in a very narrow sense. But the concept of delegation is often employed more loosely. A writer has recently called it the "power to 'fill in the details' of legislative enactments." [1] In this sense, delegation is an activity that has been

---

[1] Sotirios A. Barber, *The Constitution and the Delegation of Congressional Power* 7 (1975).

practiced at least since the time of the adoption of the Constitution.[2] The inspiration for this definition is the well-known statement by Chief Justice Marshall in 1825: "The line has not been exactly drawn which separates those important subjects, which must be entirely regulated by the legislature itself, from those of less interest, in which a general provision may be made, and power given to those who are to act under such general provision, to fill up the details." *Wayman* v. *Southard*, 23 U.S. (10 Wheat.) 1, 43, 6 L.Ed. 253, 263. Marshall's statement is an acknowledgement, at an early point in American history, that some aspects of governmental policy, the details of broader frameworks set out by Congress, would have to be left to administrative officials. And the fact that "the line has not been exactly drawn" between what only Congress can do and what may be left to other governmental officials is the nub of the problem.

The Panama Case

It wasn't until the end of the nineteenth century that the so-called nondelegation doctrine began to be asserted. The statement quoted above from *Field* v. *Clark* (1892), to the effect that "Congress cannot delegate legislative power," was an important expression of the doctrine. In spite of such statements, however, the Supreme Court uniformly sustained delegations by Congress until the 1930s. The year 1935 saw the only two Supreme Court decisions invalidating congressional delegations to governmental authorities. In *Panama Refining Co.* v. *Ryan*, 293 U.S. 388, 55 S.Ct. 241, 79 L.Ed. 446 (1935), the Supreme Court declared section 9(c) of the National Industrial Recovery Act of 1933 to be an improper delegation of power because of the absence in the statute of a standard under which the president was to act. Section 9(c) gave the president the power to prohibit the transportation in interstate commerce of "hot oil" (oil produced in violation of state laws), but provided no guidelines for the exercise of presidential power. As Mr. Justice Cardozo pointed out in the sole dissent, policy objectives stated elsewhere in the act asserted that the legislation was designed "to eliminate unfair competitive practices," and "to conserve natural resources," but these were not considered adequate by the majority of the Court.

The Schechter Case

The second delegation held invalid, in *Schechter Poultry Corp.* v. *United States*, 295 U.S. 495, 55 S.Ct. 837, 79 L.Ed. 1570 (1935), was much broader. Under section 3 of the National Industrial Recovery Act, the president was empowered to approve "codes of fair competition" for various branches of industry and commerce to regulate such matters as maximum hours, minimum wages, and collective bargaining. When petitioners were convicted for violation of the "Live Poultry Code" adopted under section 3, they contended that the code had been adopted pursuant to an unconstitutional delegation of

---

[2] For examples see Mr. Justice Cardozo's dissenting opinion in *Panama Refining Co.* v. *Ryan*, 293 U.S. 388, 442, 55 S.Ct. 241, 257–8, 79 L.Ed. 446, 470 (1935).

power. The Supreme Court unanimously supported this view. Said Chief Justice Hughes for the Court:

> Section 3 of the Recovery Act is without precedent. It supplies no standards for any trade, industry or activity. It does not undertake to prescribe rules of conduct to be applied to particular states of fact determined by appropriate administrative procedure.... [T]he discretion of the President, in approving or prescribing codes, and thus enacting laws for the government of trade and industry throughout the country, is virtually unfettered. We think that the code-making authority thus conferred is an unconstitutional delegation of legislative power.

Mr. Justice Cardozo, who had dissented in the *Panama Refining* case, wrote a concurring opinion in *Schechter* in which he stated the following: "The delegated power ... which has found expression in this code is not canalized within banks that keep it from overflowing. It is unconfined and vagrant.... This is delegation running riot. No such plenitude of power is susceptible of transfer."

Since *Panama* and *Schechter*, delegations by Congress have been uniformly upheld. Commentators appear to agree that "no delegation since has equalled the scope of the Recovery Act,"[3] but there have been numerous broad grants of power from Congress based on quite vague legislative standards, all of which have been sustained in constitutional challenges.[4] Writers are divided on the propriety and wisdom of this uncritical approach to delegation. Kenneth Culp Davis, in his important *Administrative Law Treatise* (1958), took the view that "the test of the validity of delegation ought to have more to do with [procedural] safeguards than with standards.... [T]he standards test is on the way out and the safeguards test in the ascendancy."[5] Davis has argued elsewhere that the objective of requiring every delegation to be accompanied by meaningful standards "had to fail, should have failed, and did fail."[6] But others regret the reluctance of the courts to demand more of Congress. The political scientist Theodore Lowi states that this "offers a jurisprudential carte blanche for poor legislative drafting and at the same time sweeps away all concern for the consequences." He favors a "revival of the still valid but universally disregarded rule in the *Schechter* case," adding that "[u]nder present conditions, when Congress delegates without a shred of guidance, the courts usually end up rewriting many of the statutes in the course of construction." Rather than such judicial activism, "a blanket invalidation under the *Schechter* rule is tantamount to a court order for Congress to do its own

---

[3] Barber, above, note 1, 95.

[4] Representative examples are *Yakus* v. *United States*, 321 U.S. 414, 64 S.Ct. 660, 88 L.Ed. 834 (1941); *Lichter* v. *United States*, 334 U.S. 742, 68 S.Ct. 1294, 92 L.Ed. 1694 (1948); *Arizona* v. *California*, 373 U.S. 546, 83 S.Ct. 1468, 10 L.Ed.2d 542 (1963). As Bernard Schwartz has put it in discussing delegation, "*Schechter* stands apart in any discussion of delegation. It involves the broadest delegation Congress has ever made.... But the federal courts now sustain standards at least as broad as that condemned in *Panama*." *Administrative Law* 38 and 41 (1976).

[5] 1965 Pocket Part to Volume 1 §§ 2.17, 55.

[6] "A New Approach to Delegation," 36 *University of Chicago Law Review* 713, 719 (1969). Davis' later writings contain a more elaborate discussion of these matters, in which he tries to "alter the nondelegation doctrine to make it effective and useful." But he still rejects the standards test as workable. See the second edition of his 1 *Administrative Law Treatise* 206 (2d ed., 1978).

work. Therefore, the rule of law is a restraint upon rather than an expansion of judicial function."[7]

It is said that Congress is sometimes unable to provide clearer standards because the questions that it is dealing with are too complex or new,[8] and that it is sometimes unwilling to do so because the issues in question are too controversial.[9] Whatever its motivation, it seems clear that Congress is disinclined to do much more than it had been doing in recent years to lay down precise standards for delegation.

RECENT JUDICIAL VIEWS ON NONDELEGATION

Recently, however, the voices of two Supreme Court justices—William Rehnquist and Warren Burger—were added to those supporting a return to the nondelegation doctrine. Their views were expressed in two nonprincipal opinions (the first a concurrence and the second a dissent) in cases decided by the Supreme Court in the early 1980s. Rehnquist wrote both opinions and Burger joined in the second. In both cases, *Industrial Union Department, AFL–CIO* v. *American Petroleum Institute*, 448 U.S. 607, 100 S.Ct. 2844, 65 L.Ed.2d 1010 (1980) and *American Textile Manufacturers Institute* v. *Donovan*, 452 U.S. 490, 101 S.Ct. 2478, 69 L.Ed.2d 185 (1981), the nondelegation issue centered on the same statutory provision: the statement in section 6(b)(5) of the Occupational Health and Safety Act of 1970, 29 U.S.C. 655(b)(5) that in establishing standards dealing with toxic materials or harmful physical agents, the Secretary of Labor "shall set the standard which most adequately assures, to the extent feasible, on the basis of the best available evidence, that no employee will suffer material impairment of health or functional capacity" from exposure to such substances. In the first case producers of benzene objected to the standard set by the Occupational Health and Safety Administration (OSHA, an agency within the Department of Labor) for exposure to benzene, and in the second, representatives of the cotton industry challenged OSHA's cotton dust standard. These cases have relevance to other aspects of administrative law and will be discussed later in this book. Suffice it to say here that in the first case, the Supreme Court affirmed a lower court decision which held the benzene standard invalid, and in the second it agreed with a lower court that a cost-benefit analysis by OSHA was not required in establishing the cotton

---

[7] Theodore J. Lowi, *The End of Liberalism* 125, 300 (2d ed., 1979). Other writings advocating a revival of the nondelegation doctrine include Judge J. Skelly Wright, "Beyond Discretionary Justice," 81 *Yale Law Journal* 575, 582 (1972) and John Hart Ely, *Democracy and District: A Theory of Judicial Review* 131–134 (1980).

[8] Concerning the National Environmental Policy Act of 1969, Kenneth Culp Davis has written: "The reason Congress refrained from stating meaningful guides as to whether or when environmental values should prevail is simply that no one knew how to write meaningful guides." 1 *Administrative Law Treatise* 153 (2d ed., 1978).

[9] See, e.g., Ely, above, note 7, 131–2: "How much more comfortable it must be simply to vote in favor of a bill calling for safe cars, clean air, or nondiscrimination, and to leave to others the chore of fleshing out what such a mandate might mean. How much safer, too—and here we get to the nub. For the fact seems to be that on most hard issues our representatives quite shrewdly prefer not to have to stand up and be counted but rather to let some executive-branch bureaucrat, or perhaps some independent regulatory commission, 'take the inevitable political heat.' "

dust standard. What does concern us here is Justice Rehnquist's attack, on delegation grounds, on the statutory language just quoted. The excerpt printed below contains the gist of Rehnquist's argument.

Industrial Union Department, AFL–CIO v. American Petroleum Institute

SUPREME COURT OF THE UNITED STATES, 1980.
448 U.S. 607, 100 S.CT. 2844, 65 L.ED.2D 1010.

Mr. Justice REHNQUIST, concurring in the judgment.

The statutory provision at the center of the present controversy, § 6(b)(5) of the Occupational Safety and Health Act of 1970, states, in relevant part, that the Secretary of Labor

... in promulgating standards dealing with toxic materials or harmful physical agents ... shall set the standard which most adequately assures, *to the extent feasible*, on the basis of the best available evidence, that no employee will suffer material impairment of health or functional capacity even if such employee has regular exposure to the hazard dealt with by such standard for the period of his working life. 84 Stat. 1594, 29 U.S.C. § 655(b)(5) (emphasis added).

According to the Secretary, who is one of the petitioners herein, § 6(b)(5) imposes upon him an absolute duty, in regulating harmful substances like benzene for which no safe level is known, to set the standard for permissible exposure at the lowest level that "can be achieved at bearable cost with available technology." Brief for Federal Parties 57. While the Secretary does not attempt to refine the concept of "bearable cost," he apparently believes that a proposed standard is economically feasible so long as its impact "will not be such as to threaten the financial welfare of the affected firms or the general economy." 43 Fed. Reg. 5939 (1978).

Respondents reply, and the lower court agreed, that § 6(b)(5) must be read in light of another provision in the same Act, § 3(8), which defines an "occupational health and safety standard" as

... a standard which requires conditions, or the adoption or use of one or more practices, means, methods, operations, or processes, reasonably necessary or appropriate to provide safe or healthful employment and places of employment. 84 Stat. 1591, 29 U.S.C. § 652(8).

According to respondents, § 6(b)(5), as tempered by § 3(8), requires the Secretary to demonstrate that any particular health standard is justifiable on the basis of a rough balancing of costs and benefits.

In considering these alternative interpretations, my colleagues manifest a good deal of uncertainty, and ultimately divide over whether the Secretary produced sufficient evidence that the proposed standard for benzene will result in any appreciable benefits at all. This uncertainty, I would suggest, is eminently justified, since I believe that this litigation presents the Court with what has to be one of the most difficult issues that could confront a decisionmaker: whether the statistical possibility of future deaths should ever be disregarded in light of the economic costs of preventing those deaths. I would also suggest that the widely varying positions advanced in the briefs of the parties and in the opinions of Mr. Justice STEVENS, THE CHIEF JUSTICE, Mr. Justice POWELL, and Mr. Justice MARSHALL demonstrate, perhaps better than any other fact, that Congress, the governmental body best suited and most obligated to make the choice confronting us in this litigation, has improperly delegated that choice to the Secretary of Labor and, derivatively, to this Court. . . .

[Rehnquist then engages in a wide-ranging analysis of legislative power and its delegation, starting with John Locke's *Second Treatise on Civil Government* (1690). In discussing the legislative history of the Occupational Safety and Health Act, he points out that during its passage through Congress, the bill originally did not contain the phrase "to the extent feasible," this being added only after concern was expressed that the standard might be interpreted to require "absolute health and safety in all cases, regardless of feasibility" and he concludes, on the basis of his reading of the legislative history, that the addition of the feasibility limitation to the statute added little, if anything, of practical importance.* Rehnquist then returns to the nondelegation doctrine and its relevance to this case.]

As formulated and enforced by this Court, the nondelegation doctrine serves three important functions. First, and most abstractly, it ensures to the extent consistent with orderly governmental administration that important choices of social policy are made by Congress, the branch of our Government most responsive to the popular will. See *Arizona* v. *California*, 373 U.S. 546, 626, 83 S.Ct. 1468, 1511, 10 L.Ed.2d 542 (1963) (Harlan, J., dissenting in part); *United States* v. *Robel*, 389 U.S. 258, 276, 88 S.Ct. 419, 430, 19 L.Ed.2d 508 (1967) (BRENNAN, J., concurring in result). Second, the doctrine guarantees that, to the extent Congress finds it necessary to delegate authority, it provides the recipient of that authority with an "intelligible principle" to guide the exercise of the delegated discretion. See *J. W. Hampton & Co.* v. *United States*, 276 U.S., at 409, 48 S.Ct., at 352, 72 L.Ed. 624 (1928); *Panama Refining Co.* v. *Ry-*

an, 293 U.S., at 430, 55 S.Ct., at 252. Third, and derivative of the second, the doctrine ensures that courts charged with reviewing the exercise of delegated legislative discretion will be able to test that exercise against ascertainable standards. See *Arizona* v. *California, supra*, 373 U.S., at 626, 83 S.Ct., at 1511 (Harlan, J., dissenting in part); *American Power & Light Co.* v. *SEC, supra*, at 106, 67 S.Ct., at 142.

I believe the legislation at issue here fails on all three counts. The decision whether the law of diminishing returns should have any place in the regulation of toxic substances is quintessentially one of legislative policy. For Congress to pass that decision on to the Secretary in the manner it did violates, in my mind, John Locke's caveat—reflected in the cases cited earlier in this opinion—that legislatures are to make laws, not legislators. Nor, as I think the prior discussion amply demonstrates, do the provisions at issue or their legislative history provide the Secretary with any guidance that might lead him to his somewhat tentative conclusion that he must eliminate exposure to benzene as far as technologically and economically possible. Finally, I would suggest that the standard of "feasibility" renders meaningful judicial review impossible. . . .

If we are ever to reshoulder the burden of ensuring that Congress itself make the critical policy decisions, these are surely the cases in which to do it. It is difficult to imagine a more obvious example of Congress simply avoiding a choice which was both fundamental for purposes of the statute and yet politically so divisive that the necessary decision or compromise was difficult, if not impossible, to hammer out in the legislative forge. Far from detracting from the substantive authority of Congress, a declaration that the first sentence of § 6(b)(5) of the Occupational Safety and

---

* "In sum, the legislative history contains nothing to indicate that the language 'to the extent feasible' does anything other than render what had been a clear, if somewhat unrealistic, standard largely, if not entirely, precatory."

Health Act constitutes an invalid delegation to the Secretary of Labor would preserve the authority of Congress. If Congress wishes to legislate in an area which it has not previously sought to enter, it will in today's political world undoubtedly run into opposition no matter how the legislation is formulated. But that is the very essence of legislative authority under our system. It is the hard choices, and not the filling in of the blanks, which must be made by the elected representatives of the people. When fundamental policy decisions underlying important legislation about to be enacted are to be made, the buck stops with Congress and the President insofar as he exercises his constitutional role in the legislative process. . . .

Admonitions to Congress

In the "cotton dust" case Justice Rehnquist, now joined by Chief Justice Burger, continued his attempt to revive the nondelegation doctrine. He stated that Congress could have been more precise in addressing the issue of exposure levels (for instance, by requiring the Secretary to engage in cost-benefit analysis), but it did not:

> Rather than make that choice and resolve the difficult policy issue, however, Congress passed. . . . The words "to the extent feasible" were used to mask a fundamental policy disagreement in Congress. I have no doubt that if Congress had been required to choose whether to mandate, permit, or prohibit the Secretary from engaging in cost-benefit analysis, there would have been no bill for the President to sign. . . . Congress simply left the crucial policy choices in the hands of the Secretary of Labor. As I stated at greater length last term, I believe that in so doing Congress unconstitutionally delegated its legislative responsibility to the Executive Branch.[10]

The addition of the voices of two Supreme Court justices to those calling for a return to the nondelegation doctrine undoubtedly adds authority to this development. It might be interpreted by members of Congress as an admonition to delegate more carefully. It is doubtful, however, that support for the nondelegation doctrine will command a majority of the Supreme Court in the near future. More likely is a court response of attempting to "manage" unwieldy delegations on a case-by-case basis.

A practical problem with legislation lacking clear standards is that courts are deprived of a reasonable basis for reviewing agency action. As Justice Rehnquist put it in the excerpt from the *Benzene* case quoted above, in his view "the standard of 'feasibility' renders meaningful judicial review impossible." Some observers, therefore, have looked to the courts, not for invalidation of delegations *a la Schechter*, but for other means of control of standardless delegations. Two measures, employed by the courts on occasion, are (1) interpreting broad delegations narrowly in order to avoid constitutional issues and (2) requiring that agencies develop their own standards when legislative standards are lacking.

---

[10] 452 U.S. 490, at 545–48, 101 S.Ct. 2478, at 2509–10, 69 L.Ed. 2d 195, at 224–25.

JUDICIAL NARROWING OF CONGRESSIONAL DELEGATION

In the next case excerpt, *Kent* v. *Dulles*, Kent and Briehl were denied passports under a regulation promulgated by the secretary of state providing that no passport would be issued for travel by Communists or others for purposes of furthering the Communist movement. The regulation was adopted under a statute which provided: "The Secretary of State may grant and issue passports . . . under such rules as the President shall designate and prescribe for and on behalf of the United States, and no other person shall grant, issue or verify such passports." (22 U.S.C.A. § 211a). Another statute made it unlawful to depart from or enter into the United States without a valid passport. (8 U.S. C.A. § 1185). Both plaintiffs sued in U.S. District Court for declaratory relief, but on that level and at the Court of Appeals their pleas were rejected. The case came to the U.S. Supreme Court on certiorari. This case is a good example of judicial narrowing of congressional delegation.

Kent v. Dulles

SUPREME COURT OF THE UNITED STATES, 1958.
357 U.S. 116, 78 S.CT. 1113, 2 L.ED.2D 1204.

Mr. Justice DOUGLAS delivered the opinion of the Court. . . .

The right to travel is a part of the "liberty" of which the citizen cannot be deprived without the due process of law under the Fifth Amendment. So much is conceded by the Solicitor General. . . . We need not decide the extent to which it can be curtailed. We are first concerned with the extent, if any, to which Congress has authorized its curtailment.

The difficulty is that while the power of the Secretary of State over the issuance of passports is expressed in broad terms, it was apparently long exercised quite narrowly. So far as material here, the cases of refusal of passports generally fell into two categories. First, questions pertinent to the citizenship of the applicant and his allegiance to the United States had to be resolved by the Secretary, for the command of Congress was that "No passport shall be granted or issued to or verified for any other persons than those owing allegiance, whether citizens or not, to the United States." 32 Stat. 386, 22 U.S.C. § 212, 22 U.S. C.A. § 212. Second, was the question whether the applicant was participating in illegal conduct, trying to escape the toils of the law, promoting passport frauds, or otherwise engaging in conduct which would violate the laws of the United States.

The grounds for refusal asserted here do not relate to citizenship or allegiance on the one hand or to criminal or unlawful conduct on the other. Yet, so far as relevant here, those two are the only ones which it could fairly be argued were adopted by Congress in light of prior administrative practice. One can find in the records of the State Department rulings of subordinates covering a wider range of activities than the two indicated. But as respects Communists these are scattered rulings and not consistently of one pattern. We can say with assurance that whatever may have been the practice after 1926, at the time the Act of July 3, 1926, was adopted, the administrative practice, so far as relevant here, had jelled only around the two categories mentioned. We, therefore, hesitate to impute to Congress, when in 1952 it made a passport necessary for foreign travel and left its issuance to the discretion of the Secretary of State, a purpose to give him unbridled discretion to grant or withhold a passport from a citizen for any substantive reason he may choose. . . .

Since we start with an exercise by an American citizen of an activity included in constitutional protection, we will not readily infer that Congress gave the Secretary of State unbridled discretion to grant or withhold it. If we were dealing with political questions entrusted to the Chief Executive by the Constitution we would have a different case. But there is more involved here. In part, of course, the issuance of the passport carries some implication of intention to extend the bearer diplomatic protection, though it does no more than "request all whom it may concern to permit safely and freely to pass, and in case of need to give all lawful aid and protection" to this citizen of the United States. But that function of the passport is subordinate. Its crucial function today is control over exit. And, as we have seen, the right of exit is a personal right included within the word "liberty" as used in the Fifth Amendment. If that "liberty" is to be regulated, it must, be pursuant to the law-making functions of the Congress. And if that power is delegated, the standards must be adequate to pass scrutiny by the accepted tests. Where

activities or enjoyment, natural and often necessary to the well-being of an American citizen, such as travel, are involved, we will construe narrowly all delegated powers that curtail or dilute them. We hesitate to find in this broad generalized power an authority to trench so heavily on the rights of the citizen.

Thus we do not reach the question of constitutionality. We only conclude that § 1185 and § 211a do not delegate to the Secretary the kind of authority exercised here. . . .

To repeat, we deal here with a constitutional right of the citizen, a right which we must assume Congress will be faithful to respect. We would be faced with important constitutional questions were we to hold that Congress by § 1185 and § 211a had given the Secretary authority to withhold passports to citizens because of their beliefs or associations. Congress has made no such provision in explicit terms; and absent one, the Secretary may not employ that standard to restrict the citizens' right of free movement.

Reversed.

[The dissenting opinion of Mr. Justice Clark, with whom Mr. Justice Burton, Mr. Justice Harlan, and Mr. Justice Whittaker concur, is omitted.]

Professor Richard Stewart believes that a policy of judicial narrowing of broad statutory delegations might encourage Congress to write clear statements of legislative purpose to accompany their delegations.[11] But judicial narrowing is a device that the courts do not always choose to employ. For example, in the 1980 case *United States* v. *Euge*, which is discussed in chapter 5 (see below, p. 135), Justice Rehnquist specifically rejected "a narrower interpretation of the duty imposed . . . by the actual language of the statute." *Kent* v. *Dulles* thus stands as a illustration of the judicial narrowing technique, but it is not necessarily the last word on passport policy or freedom of travel.

Philip Agee was a former employee of the CIA who embarked on a campaign to expose CIA agents operating secretly in foreign countries. His passport was revoked by the secretary of state under a regulation authorizing

---

[11] Richard B. Stewart, "The Reformation of American Administrative Law," 88 *Harvard Law Review* 1667, 1697 (1975).

revocation where an American citizen's activities "are causing or likely to cause serious damage to the national security or the foreign policy of the United States." Two lower courts ruled, on the basis of *Kent* v. *Dulles* and other precedents, that the secretary had exceeded his statutory powers in revoking Agee's passport. But the Supreme Court by a vote of 7 to 2 reversed, distinguishing *Kent* v. *Dulles* from the present case. It upheld the broad rule-making authority granted the secretary under the Passport Act of 1926, and ruled that the regulation in question, and its application to Agee, were proper. The dissenters, justices Brennan and Marshall, thought that the decision in *Kent* v. *Dulles* should be controlling. And Justice Blackmun, who voted with the majority, wrote a separate concurring opinion stating that the decision "cannot be fully reconciled with all the reasoning of *Zemel* v. *Rusk* [another relevant freedom-of-travel case] ... and particularly *Kent* v. *Dulles....*" Blackmun would have preferred directly overruling *Zemel* and *Kent* in upholding the revocation of Agee's passport. *Haig* v. *Agee*, 453 U.S. 280, 101 S.Ct. 2766, 69 L.Ed. 2d 640 (1981).

REQUIRING AGENCY-DEVELOPED STANDARDS

The idea of court-required agency standards has been developed most fully in the work of Kenneth Culp Davis. A succinct statement of the proposal is "that the courts should continue their requirement of meaningful standards, except that when the legislative body fails to prescribe the required standards the administrator should be allowed to satisfy the requirement by prescribing them with a reasonable time." [12] A case often cited as representing a concrete application of the idea is the following.

Environmental Defense Fund, Inc. v. Ruckelshaus

United States Court of Appeals, District of Columbia Circuit, 1971.
439 F.2d 584.

[The Federal Insecticide, Fungicide and Rodenticide Act (FIFRA) provides that certain pesticides must be registered with the secretary of agriculture. When a registered substance appears to fail to conform to statutory standards relating to safety, administrative procedures are available to terminate that registration. The ordinary process, cancellation of registration, is commenced by a notice of cancellation to the registrant followed by certain prescribed procedures, including a public hearing, before the secretary issues an order cancelling or continuing the registra-

---

[12] Kenneth Culp Davis, *Discretionary Justice: A Preliminary Inquiry* 59 (1969). A more detailed treatment of the concept, linking it directly to the delegation problem, is Davis' "A New Approach to Delegation," above, note 8, at 725f. A recent discussion is Davis' *Administrative Law Treatise* above, note 8, at 207–208. Among numerous writings advocating the requirement of agency-developed standards see "Comment: Judicially Required Rulemaking as Fourth Amendment Policy: An Applied Analysis of the Supervisory Power of Federal Courts," 72 *Northwestern University Law Review* 595 (1978). Professor Stewart, above, note 11, at 1699, states that the proposal of "structuring agency discretion as an alternative to legislative specification was apparently first advocated" in a 1937 report by the President's Committee on Administrative Management.

tion. Alternatively, the secretary may summarily suspend such a registration when "necessary to prevent imminent hazard to the public." The process of suspension thus provides an expeditious, if temporary, alternative to what could be lengthy administrative proceedings under cancellation.

The Environmental Defense Fund submitted petitions to the secretary of agriculture requesting both cancellation and suspension of all registrations of pesticides containing DDT. The secretary issued cancellation notices with regard to some uses of DDT, but was silent on the request for suspension. The case reached the court of appeals two times in connection with petitioners' interests in both cancellation and suspension. The excerpt below deals with the court's view on the suspension issue, followed by Judge Bazelon's more general discussion of the judiciary's role in monitoring the work of administrative agencies in carrying out their mandated functions. It is an important example of the advocacy of agency-developed standards.]

Before BAZELON, Chief Judge, and ROBINSON and ROBB, Circuit Judges.

BAZELON, Chief Judge:

... While the Secretary recognized a substantial question concerning the safety of DDT, he concluded that the evidence did not warrant summary suspension of its registration for any purpose. That conclusion reflects both a factual determination and the application of a legal standard. Suspension is designed to protect the public from an "imminent hazard" during the course of further administrative proceedings. In order to decide whether it is warranted in a particular case, the Secretary must first determine what harm, if any, is likely to flow from the use of the product in question during the course of administrative proceedings. He must consider both the magnitude of the anticipated harm, and the likelihood that it will occur. Then, on the basis of that factual determination, he must decide whether the anticipated

harm amounts to an "imminent hazard to the public."

Petitioners do not challenge the Secretary's determination of the kinds of harm that may be associated with DDT. They argue that his estimate of the probability that harm will occur is too low, in light of the available reports of scientific studies. They also argue that he has set the standard of proof too high, in light of the clear legislative purpose. On the first point, we think it appropriate in the circumstances of this case to defer to the administrative judgment. We have neither an evidentiary record, nor the scientific expertise, that would permit us to review the Secretary's findings with respect to the probability of harm. We have found no error of law that infects the Secretary's inferences from the scientific data. And we have recognized that it is particularly appropriate to defer to administrative findings of fact in reviewing a decision on a question of interim relief.

The second part of the petitioners' challenge, however, is entirely appropriate for judicial consideration at this time. The formulation of standards for suspension is entrusted to the Secretary in the first instance, but the court has an obligation to ensure that the administrative standards conform to the legislative purpose, and that they are uniformly applied in individual cases.

The statute provides for suspension in order "to prevent an imminent hazard to the pulic." Congress clearly intended to protect the public from some risks by summary administrative action pending further proceedings. The administrator's problem is to determine which risks fall in that class. The Secretary has made no attempt to deal with that problem, either by issuing regulations relating to suspension, or by explaining his decision in this case. If regulations of general applicability were formulated, it would of course be possible to explain individual decisions by reference to the appropriate regulation. It may well be, however, that standards for suspension can best be developed piecemeal, as the Secretary evaluates the hazards presented by particular products. Even so, he has an obligation to articulate the criteria that he develops in making each individual decision. We cannot assume, in the absence of adequate explanation, that proper standards are implicit in every exercise of administrative discretion.

Since the Secretary has not yet provided an adequate explanation for his decision to deny interim relief in this case, it will be necessary to remand the case once more, for a fresh determination on that issue. On remand, the Secretary should consider whether the information presently available to him calls for suspension of any registrations of products containing DDT, identifying the factors relevant to that determination, and relating the evidence to those factors in a statement of the reasons for his decision.

In the course of this and subsequent litigation, the Secretary has identified some of the factors he deems relevant to the question of suspension, and resolved some questions of statutory interpretation. He has concluded that the most important element of an "imminent hazard to the public" is a serious threat to public health, that a hazard may be "imminent" even if its impact will not be apparent for many years, and that the "public" protected by the suspension provision includes fish and wildlife. These interpretations all seem consistent with the statutory language and purpose. An important beginning has been made, and the task of formulating standards must not be abandoned now.

We stand on the threshold of a new era in the history of the long and fruitful collaboration of administrative agencies and reviewing courts. For many years, courts have treated administrative policy decisions with great deference, confining judicial attention primarily to matters of procedure. On matters of substance, the courts regularly upheld agency action, with a nod in the direction of the "substantial evidence" test, and a bow to the mysteries of administrative expertise. Courts occasionally asserted, but less often exercised, the power to set aside agency action on the ground that an impermissible factor had entered into the decision, or a crucial factor had not been considered. Gradually, however, that power has come into more frequent use, and with it, the requirement that administrators articulate the factors on which they base their decisions.

Strict adherence to that requirement is especially important now that the character of administrative litigation is changing. As a result of expanding doctrines of standing and reviewability, and new statutory causes of action, courts are increasingly asked to review administrative action that touches on fundamental personal interests in life, health, and liberty. These interests have always had a special claim to judicial protection, in comparison with the economic interests at stake in a ratemaking or licensing proceeding.

To protect these interests from administrative arbitrariness, it is necessary, but not sufficient, to insist on strict judicial scrutiny of administrative action. For judicial review alone can correct only the most egregious abuses. Judicial review must operate to ensure that the administrative process itself will confine and control the exercise of discretion. Courts should require administrative officers to articulate the standards and principles that govern their discretionary decisions in as much detail as possible. Rules and regulations should be freely formulated by administrators, and revised when necessary. Discretionary decisions should more often be supported with findings of fact and reasoned opinions. When administrators provide a framework for principled decision-making, the result will be to diminish the importance of judicial review by enhancing the integrity of the administrative process, and to improve the quality of judicial review in those cases where judicial review is sought.

Remanded for further proceedings consistent with this opinion.

ROBB, Circuit Judge (dissenting):

In my view the majority opinion substitutes the judgment of this court for the judgment of the Secretary in a matter committed to his discretion by law. This action is taken without the benefit of any administrative hearing in which the validity of the petitioner's forebodings and the soundness of the Secretary's discretionary action might be tested. In effect, the court is undertaking to manage the Department of Agriculture. Finding nothing in the statutes that gives us such authority I respectfully dissent.

In one of the most frequently-cited passages in the above case, Judge Bazelon predicted: "We stand on the threshold of a new era in the history of the long and fruitful collaboration of administrative agencies and reviewing courts." This new era, he added, would be one in which the courts would do more to require "that administrators articulate the factors on which they base their decisions." The almost two decades since this prediction have seen a number of decisions where courts have cast themselves in this role,[13] but the idea seems not to have taken hold in the nation's highest court. Indeed, the Supreme Court, in more than one recent decision, has indicated that the Court of Appeals for the D.C. Circuit, the source of *E.D.F.* v. *Ruckelshaus*, has sometimes gone too far in what it requires from administrative agencies. An example is the Supreme Court's unanimous decision in the important 1978 case of *Vermont Yankee Nuclear Power Corp.* v. *Natural Resources Defense Council, Inc.*, 435 U.S. 519, 98 S.Ct. 1197, 55 L.Ed.2d 460, which is discussed in chapter 6.

THE LEGISLATIVE VETO

In the previous two sections of this chapter, devices for judicial "correction" of broad legislative delegations have been discussed. A different approach, intended to provide a legislative check on the administrative implementation of a statute, has been referred to as "congressional reassertion of control via post-delegation review,"[14] or the legislative veto.

The utility of this mechanism, which had been written into a significant number of statutes since the 1930s, was obviated in 1983 when the U.S. Supreme Court declared the legislative veto unconstitutional. The case was *Immigration and Naturalization Service* v. *Chadha*, 462 U.S. 919, 103 S.Ct. 2764, 77 L.Ed.2d 317. Several considerations have made the *Chadha* decision particularly notable: its elimination of a potentially important device for controlling administration; the significant constitutional questions addressed by the case; and the broad sweep of Chief Justice Burger's majority opinion, which brought forth expressions of concern both from other members of the Su-

---

[13] See the discussion in Davis, above, note 8, at 212–13 and Davis' *1982 Supplement to Administrative Law Treatise* 23 (1982).

[14] This phrase is from Judge Carl McGowan, "Congress, Court and Control of Delegated Power," 77 *Columbia Law Review* 1119, 1133 (1977).

preme Court and from a number of commentators. As a consequence, *Chadha* has been one of the most-discussed Supreme Court cases in recent years. The aspects of the decision relevant to the issue of delegation are examined below. Because the case also has significance with regard to the rule-making powers of administrative agencies, it will be discussed again in chapter 6.

In its generic form, the legislative veto involved a statutory stipulation by Congress that it reserves the right to disapprove of an action taken by an executive agency under the statute. Often the executive action in question is the adoption of an administrative regulation. But the executive act vetoed by Congress could also be an administrative decision of narrow application, which is the case in *Chadha*. Some of the statutes which contained legislative vetoes required that both houses of Congress participate in disapproving an administrative act, while others allowed a one-house veto. The one-house veto was authorized in the statute the Supreme Court reviewed in *Chadha*, which is the reason for the discussion of "bicameralism" in Chief Justice Burger's majority opinion. Although bicameralism is a significant issue in the case, for our purposes the more important consideration is the relationship of the legislative veto to delegation. The question may be stated as follows: once Congress has delegated authority to an administrator or an agency, can it then, on its own and without resort to the full legislative process (in which the president has a role through signing or vetoing a bill), disapprove of action taken under that delegated power? This consideration is embraced in the discussion in *Chadha* involving separation of powers and the presentment clauses of the Constitution.

Immigration and Naturalization Service v. Chadha

SUPREME COURT OF THE UNITED STATES, 1983.
462 U.S. 919, 103 S.CT. 2764, 77 L.ED.2D 317.

[The Immigration and Nationality Act, § 244(a)(1), codified as 8 U.S.C. 1254(a)(1), granted the attorney general the discretion to suspend deportation proceedings and grant permanent resident status to certain aliens "whose deportation would in the opinion of the Attorney General, result in extreme hardship to the alien or to his spouse, parent, or child, who is a citizen of the United States or an alien lawfully admitted for permanent residence." The Immigration and Naturalization Service, a division of the Department of Justice, discharges these responsibilities for the attorney general.

The act also provided, in § 244(c)(2), codified as 8 U.S.C. § 1254(c)(2), that one house of Congress, by resolution, could invalidate the attorney general's decision to allow a particular alien to remain in the United States.

Jagdish Rai Chadha was an East Indian born in Kenya and holding a British passport who spent a number of years in the United States on a student visa. After the student visa expired the Immigration Service began deportation proceedings against him. He petitioned for suspension of deportation, and, after a hearing, an immigration judge ordered that the deportation be suspended. But in late 1975 a resolution was introduced in the House of Representatives opposing the granting of permanent residence to Chadha and five other aliens, on the grounds that they did not meet the statutory requirements, particularly that relating to extreme hardship. The resolution passed without debate or recorded vote, and, as a resolution, it was not submitted to the Senate or presented to the president. The immigration judge then reopened the proceedings to implement the House resolution, and Chadha was ordered deported. Chadha appealed and, after exhausting his administrative remedies, filed for a review of the deportation order in the U.S. Court of Appeals. That court declared the legislative veto provision of the Immigration and Nationality Act unconstitutional, and the case came to the Supreme Court.

The Supreme Court was presented with numerous issues to resolve, several connected with whether the Supreme Court had the authority to decide the case at hand, as well as whether the legislative veto was "severable" from the rest of the statute. The severability issue involved the question of whether, if the legislative veto provision were struck down as unconstitutional, the rest of the Immigration and Naturalization Act could still stand as valid law. These are interesting issues, but they are of only tangential importance to the subject matter of this chapter. The excerpt below, therefore, from Chief Justice Burger's opinion for six members of the Court, will concentrate only on the part of the decision concerning separation of powers and bicameralism.]

Chief Justice BURGER delivered the opinion of the court . . .

We turn now to the question whether action of one House of Congress under § 244(c)(2) violates strictures of the Constitution. We begin, of course, with the presumption that the challenged statute is valid. Its wisdom is not the concern of the courts; . . .

By the same token, the fact that a given law or procedure is efficient, convenient, and useful in facilitating functions of government, standing alone, will not save it if it is contrary to the Constitution. Convenience and efficiency are not the primary objectives—or the hallmarks—of democratic government and our inquiry is sharpened rather than blunted by the fact that Congressional veto provisions are appearing with increasing frequency in statutes which delegate authority to executive and independent agencies:

> Since 1932, when the first veto provision was enacted into law, 295 congressional veto-type procedures have been inserted in 196 different statutes as follows: from 1932 to 1939, five statutes were affected; from 1940–49, nineteen statutes; between 1950–59, thirty-four statutes; and from 1960–69, forty-nine. From the year 1970 through 1975, at least one hundred sixty-three such provisions were included in eighty-nine laws. Abourezk, The Congressional Veto: A Contemporary Response to Executive Encroachment on Legislative Prerogatives, 52 Ind.L. Rev. 323, 324 (1977). . . .

But policy arguments supporting even useful "political inventions" are subject to the demands of the Constitution which defines powers and, with respect to this subject, sets out just how those powers are to be exercised.

Explicit and unambiguous provisions of the Constitution prescribe and define the respective functions of the Congress and of the Executive in the legislative process. Since the precise terms of those familiar provisions are critical to the resolution of this case, we set them out verbatim. Art. I provides:

> All legislative Powers herein granted shall be vested in a Congress of the United States, which shall consist of a Senate *and* a House of Representatives. Art. I, § 1. (Emphasis added).
> Every Bill which shall have passed the House of Representatives *and* the Senate, *shall*, before it becomes a Law, be presented to the President of the United States; . . . Art. I, § 7, cl. 2. (Emphasis added).

Every Order, Resolution, or Vote to which the Concurrence of the Senate and House of Representatives may be necessary (except on a question of Adjournment) *shall* be presented to the President of the United States; and before the Same shall take Effect, *shall* be approved by him, or being disapproved by him, *shall* be repassed by two thirds of the Senate and House of Representatives, according to the Rules and Limitations prescribed in the Case of a Bill. Art. I, § 7, cl. 3. (Emphasis added).

These provisions of Art. I are integral parts of the constitutional design for the separation of power.... The very structure of the articles delegating and separating powers under Arts. I, II, and III exemplify the concept of separation of powers and we now turn to Art. I.

The Presentment Clauses

The records of the Constitutional Convention reveal that the requirement that all legislation be presented to the President before becoming law was uniformly accepted by the Framers. Presentment to the President and the Presidential veto were considered so imperative that the draftsmen took special pains to assure that these requirements could not be circumvented. During the final debate on Art. I, § 7, cl. 2, James Madison expressed concern that it might easily be evaded by the simple expedient of calling a proposed law a "resolution" or "vote" rather than a "bill." 2 M. Farrand, The Records of the Federal Convention of 1787 301–302. As a consequence, Art. I, § 7, cl. 3, . . . was added. *Id.*, at 304–305.

The decision to provide the President with a limited and qualified power to nullify proposed legislation by veto was based on the profound conviction of the Framers that the powers conferred on Congress were the powers to be most carefully circumscribed. It is beyond doubt that lawmaking was a power to be shared by both Houses and the President. In The Federal-

ist No. 73 (H. Lodge ed. 1888), Hamilton focused on the President's role in making laws:

> If even no propensity had ever discovered itself in the legislative body to invade the rights of the Executive, the rules of just reasoning and theoretic propriety would of themselves teach us that the one ought not to be left to the mercy of the other, but ought to possess a constitutional and effectual power of self-defense. Id., at 457–458.

See also The Federalist No. 51. In his Commentaries on the Constitution, Joseph Story makes the same point. 1 J. Story, Commentaries on the Constitution of the United States 614–615 (1858).

The President's role in the lawmaking process also reflects the Framers' careful efforts to check whatever propensity a particular Congress might have to enact oppressive, improvident, or ill-considered measures. The President's veto role in the legislative process was described later during public debate on ratification:

> It establishes a salutary check upon the legislative body, calculated to guard the community against the effects of faction, precipitancy, or of any impulse unfriendly to the public good which may happen to influence a majority of that body.... The primary inducement to conferring the power in question upon the Executive is to enable him to defend himself; the secondary one is to increase the chances in favor of the community against the passing of bad laws through haste, inadvertence, or design. The Federalist No. 73, *supra*, at 458 (A. Hamilton)....

Bicameralism

The bicameral requirement of Art. I, §§ 1, 7 was of scarcely less concern to the Framers than was the Presidential veto and indeed the two concepts are interdependent. By providing that no law could take effect without the concurrence of the prescribed majority of the Members of both Houses, the Framers reemphasized their belief, already remarked upon in connection with the Presentment Clauses, that legislation should not be enacted unless it has been carefully and fully considered by the Nation's elected officials.... [The chief justice then quotes from several authorities to support this view.]

We see therefore that the Framers were acutely conscious that the bicameral requirement and the Presentment Clauses would serve essential constitutional functions. The President's participation in the legislative process was to protect the Executive Branch from Congress and to protect the whole people from improvident laws. The division of the Congress into two distinctive bodies assures that the legislative power would be exercised only after opportunity for full study and debate in separate settings. The President's unilateral veto power, in turn, was limited by the power of two thirds of both Houses of Congress to overrule a veto thereby precluding final arbitrary action of one person.... It emerges clearly that the prescription for legislative action in Art. I, §§ 1, 7 represents the Framers' decision that the legislative power of the Federal government be exercised in accord with a single, finely wrought and exhaustively considered, procedure.

The Constitution sought to divide the delegated powers of the new federal government into three defined categories, legislative, executive and judicial, to assure, as nearly as possible, that each Branch of government would confine itself to its assigned responsibility. The hydraulic pressure inherent within each of the separate Branches to exceed the outer limits of its power, even to accomplish desirable objectives, must be resisted.

Although not "hermetically" sealed from one another, ... the powers delegated to the three Branches are functionally identifiable. When any Branch acts, it is presumptively exercising the power the Constitution has delegated to it. See *Hampton & Co.* v. *United States*, 276 U.S. 394, 406, 48 S.Ct. 348, 351, 72 L.Ed. 624 (1928). When

the Executive acts, it presumptively acts in an executive or administrative capacity as defined in Art. II. And when, as here, one House of Congress purports to act, it is presumptively acting within its assigned sphere.

Beginning with this presumption, we must nevertheless establish that the challenged action under § 244(c)(2) is of the kind to which the procedural requirements of Art. I, § 7 apply. Not every action taken by either House is subject to the bicameralism and presentment requirements of Art. I.... Whether actions taken by either House are, in law and fact, an exercise of legislative power depends not on their form but upon "whether they contain matter which is properly to be regarded as legislative in its character and effect." S.Rep. No. 1335, 54th Cong., 2d Sess., 8 (1897).

Examination of the action taken here by one House pursuant to § 244(c)(2) reveals that it was essentially legislative in purpose and effect. In purporting to exercise power defined in Art. I, § 8, cl. 4 to "establish an uniform Rule of Naturalization," the House took action that had the purpose and effect of altering the legal rights, duties and relations of persons, including the Attorney General, Executive Branch officials and Chadha, all outside the legislative branch. Section 244(c)(2) purports to authorize one House of Congress to require the Attorney General to deport an individual alien whose deportation otherwise would be cancelled under § 244. The one-House veto operated in this case to overrule the Attorney General and mandate Chadha's deportation; absent the House action, Chadha would remain in the United States. Congress has *acted* and its action has altered Chadha's status.

The legislative character of the one-House veto in this case is confirmed by the character of the Congressional action it supplants. Neither the House of Representatives nor the Senate contends that, absent the veto provision in § 244(c)(2), either of them, or both of them acting together, could effectively require the Attorney General to deport an alien once the Attorney General, in the exercise of legislatively delegated authority, had determined the alien should remain in the United States. Without the challenged provision in § 244(c)(2), this could have been achieved, if at all, only by legislation requiring deportation. Similarly, a veto by one House of Congress under § 244(c)(2) cannot be justified as an attempt at amending the standards set out in § 244(a)(1), or as a repeal of § 244 as applied to Chadha. Amendment and repeal of statutes, no less than enactment, must conform with Art. I.

The nature of the decision implemented by the one-House veto in this case further manifests its legislative character. After long experience with the clumsy, time consuming private bill procedure, Congress made a deliberate choice to delegate to the Executive Branch, and specifically to the Attorney General, the authority to allow deportable aliens to remain in this country in certain specified circumstances. It is not disputed that this choice to delegate authority is precisely the kind of decision that can be implemented only in accordance with the procedures set out in Art. I. Disagreement with the Attorney General's decision on Chadha's deportation—that is, Congress' decision to deport

Chadha—no less than Congress' original choice to delegate to the Attorney General the authority to make that decision, involves determinations of policy that Congress can implement in only one way; bicameral passage followed by presentment to the President. Congress must abide by its delegation of authority until that delegation is legislatively altered or revoked. . . .

The bicameral requirement, the Presentment Clauses, the President's veto, and Congress' power to override a veto were intended to erect enduring checks on each Branch and to protect the people from the improvident exercise of power by mandating certain prescribed steps. To preserve those checks, and maintain the separation of powers, the carefully defined limits on the power of each Branch must not be eroded. To accomplish what has been attempted by one House of Congress in this case requires action in conformity with the express procedures of the Constitution's prescription for legislative action: passage by a majority of both Houses and presentment to the President. . . .

We hold that the Congressional veto provision in § 244(c)(2) is severable from the Act and that it is unconstitutional. Accordingly, the judgment of the Court of Appeals is

Affirmed.

As the above excerpt indicates, Chief Justice Burger was intent on showing that the House of Representatives' action regarding Chadha was a legislative act. Having determined that, he asserted that, because it was not accomplished through the regular legislative process, it was unconstitutional. Justice Powell concurred in the result, but justified his decision on narrower grounds. He felt that the use of the legislative veto in the *Chadha* case was not an exercise of legislative power, but "clearly adjudicatory," "a function ordinarily entrusted to the federal courts." He would have invalidated the legislative veto used in the *Chadha* case on that basis, not reaching "the broader question whether legislative vetoes are invalid under the Presentment Clauses."

A question for students to ponder is whether the House's action regarding Chadha was basically legislative or judicial. As decided by the majority, all legislative vetoes were declared invalid. This result was questioned not only by Justice Powell in his concurring opinion, but also by Justice White in his comprehensive dissenting opinion. Because White's dissent and other statements that take a similar position have important relevance for administrative rule making, they will be examined in chapter 6.

POST-CHADHA *DELEGATION (GRAMM-RUDMAN-HOLLINGS)*

The adoption of Gramm-Rudman-Hollings, formally known as the Balanced Budget and Emergency Deficit Control Act of 1985,[15] provided yet another opportunity for the federal courts to rule on a major delegation of congressional power. Gramm-Rudman-Hollings mandated annual reductions in the federal deficit so as to produce a balanced budget by 1991. The key provision of that act was a determination to be made by the comptroller general of the United States that the automatic deficit reduction provisions of the act were to be implemented. The comptroller general, the head of the General Accounting Office (GAO), was to make this determination on the basis of data provided by the Office of Management and Budget (OMB) and the Congressional Budget Office (CBO). The president, in turn, would prepare the sequestration order which would result in the budget cuts necessary to achieve the deficit reduction specified in the comptroller general's report.[16]

Both proponents and detractors of Gramm-Rudman-Hollings foresaw the likelihood of constitutional challenges to the bill and, consequently, provisions were incorporated in it so as to ensure expedited judicial review. The legislature also provided a fallback procedure in the event that the OMB/CBO/GAO reporting procedures were declared unconstitutional. If that were the case the OMB/CBO report would be transmitted to a temporary joint House and Senate committee on deficit reduction which would be empowered to report a joint resolution which could trigger sequestration if it were passed by both houses and signed by the president. This fallback procedure was obviously sensitive to the principle of "bicameralism" and to "the presentment clause," which had recently been the focus of the Supreme Court's deliberation in *Chadha*, the "legislative veto" case.

Constitutional Objections to Gramm-Rudman-Hollings

Quite predictably, constitutional objections surfaced early and often during congressional consideration of Gramm-Rudman-Hollings. Chairman Peter Rodino of the House Judiciary Committee, for instance, argued that the bill's provisions deviated from established lawmaking procedures which placed taxing and spending decisions in the hands of Congress. In Rodino's words, "Congress *can* delegate the authority to implement laws, it *cannot* delegate

---

[15] See summary of conference agreement in the *Congressional Record*, vol. 131, no. 172, pp. H 11876–77 (Proceedings of December 11, 1985).

[16] Ibid.

authority to repeal laws.'' [17] Even President Reagan, in his statement of December 12, 1985, when he signed the bill into law, acknowledged potential constitutional flaws, although they were different from those noted by Rodino. Specifically, President Reagan objected to the conferring of an executive function on the comptroller general, who is an agent of Congress, not an officer in the executive branch. Reagan stated, in part, that "[u]nder our constitutional system, an agent of Congress may not exercise supervisory authority over the President.'' [18]

The principal suit challenging the law's delegation of power to unelected officials (i.e., in the Office of Management and Budget, the Congressional Budget Office, and the General Accounting Office), was brought by Representative Synar on behalf of fellow members of Congress. The Justice Department's brief on the merits of the case echoed those of the president, namely that the comptroller general's role violated the principle of separation of powers. As an officer of the legislative branch he was encroaching upon executive branch prerogatives. The three-judge federal court panel ruled on February 7, 1986, that Gramm-Rudman-Hollings was unconstitutional for the reasons articulated earlier by President Reagan and the Justice Department. More specifically, the panel concluded that while Congress could delegate its authority to make spending decisions, it could not delegate those responsibilities to the comptroller general, who is removable by a joint resolution of both the House and the Senate. The three-judge court stayed the effect of its decision pending an appeal to the Supreme Court.

On July 7, 1986, the Supreme Court by a seven-to-two margin affirmed the lower court ruling that the comptroller general's role in the deficit reduction process violated the doctrine of separation of powers.[19] More specifically, by virtue of the congressional retention of the removal authority of the official responsible for the execution of the Deficit Control Act, Congress had in effect intruded into the executive function. Chief Justice Burger's majority opinion included an explicit refusal to consider Congressman Synar's principal challenge to the act, i.e., that the assignment of automatic budget cutting powers to the Comptroller General violated the delegation of powers [20]. In contrast, the two dissenting jurists, White and Blackmun, accepted the District Court's finding that the statute did not violate the nondelegation doctrine. The only jurist to write an opinion focusing on the delegation issue was Justice Stevens, who did so in a concurrence which Justice Marshall joined. According to Stevens, "the critical inquiry in this case concerns not the manner in which Executive officials or agencies may act, but the manner in which Congress and its agents may act.'' [21] Stevens viewed the comptroller general as an agent of Congress and, consequently, the duties delegated to him contravened the

---

[17] Letter from Peter W. Rodino, Jr., Chairman of the Committee on the Judiciary, to Dan Rostenkowski dated October 16, 1985, reprinted in the *Congressional Record*, vol. 131, no. 172, pp. H 11893–94 (Proceedings of December 11, 1985).

[18] *Weekly Compilation of Presidential Documents*, December 16, 1986, vol. 21, no. 50, pp. 1471–99, at 1490–91.

[19] *Bowsher* v. *Synar*, 54 *U.S.L.W.* 5064.

[20] Ibid., at 5070.

[21] Ibid., at 5076.

Constitution's prescription for legislative action as outlined in the *Chadha* decision, i.e., the bicameralism and presentation requirements. In this particular instance, Stevens stated, it was unlawful to "authorize a lesser representative of the Legislative Branch to act on its behalf." [22]

The Supreme Court's ruling left intact the aforementioned fallback provision, which calls for using the ordinary legislative process to enact the mandated cuts; however, it left unresolved the question as to whether the Deficit Control Act might be modified so as to avoid the constitutional infirmity. For example, the budgetary cutting power might be assigned to an officer of the executive branch such as the director of the Office of Management and Budget. This solution, if enacted, may raise anew the delegation of powers question that the Court has chosen so far to avoid.

DELEGATION AT THE STATE LEVEL

As noted earlier, the Supreme Court has found congressional delegations to governmental bodies constitutionally deficient only two times in history. The situation is somewhat different at the state level, where courts have shown more readiness to overturn standardless delegation. Numerous explanations are advanced for this difference in judicial practice, such as a lower assessment of the impartiality and competency of state administrators and legislators by state judges than is the case on the federal level.[23] Whatever the reasons, however, it certainly is the case that invalidation of delegation is still a part of state-court practice, as numerous analyses of the subject have pointed out.[24]

---

[22] Ibid.

[23] On this and other explanations for the federal-state differences on this matter, see Richard J. Pierce, Jr., Sidney A. Shapiro, and Paul R. Verkuil, *Administrative Law and Process* 63–64 (1985), and Kenneth Culp Davis, *Administrative Law: Cases—Text—Problems* 45 (6th ed., 1977).

[24] In addition to the discussions cited in the previous note, see Bernard Schwartz, above, note 4, at 48–50 and Bernard Schwartz, "Administrative Law Cases During 1978," 31 *Administrative Law Review* 123, 126 (1979).

Chapter 4

Judicial Review of Administrative Determinations

As indicated in chapter 1, since the judicial check is one of the foremost mechanisms for control of improper administrative activity, much of this book deals with scrutiny by courts of administrative action. In this chapter attention is given to the ground rules of judicial review. Considered are such basic questions as what administrative actions are reviewable, who can seek review, at what point in the process is judicial review permitted, and what is the scope of the court's reviewing power.

THE COMMON LAW OF JUDICIAL REVIEW

The authority for judicial review to scrutinize allegedly illegal administrative action is derived from both statutory and nonstatutory sources.[1] In the former case one looks to the statute books and in the latter case to the continuously evolving common law. The statutory authority for judicial review can be either of a "general" variety, such as section 701 et seq. of the Administrative Procedure Act, or a more "specific" variety, where regulatory statutes explicitly authorize review of certain agency actions. The principle bases of nonstatutory judicial review of administrative actions are the prerogative writs, such as certiorari and mandamus, and their simplified contemporary counterparts, "injunctions" and "declaratory relief."[2]

---

[1] For a discussion of the constitutional bases of judicial review in both federal and state jurisdictions see Louis L. Jaffe, *Judicial Control of Administrative Action* 376 et seq. (1965).

[2] See Walter Gellhorn, Clark Byse, and Peter L. Strauss, *Administrative Law: Cases and Comments*, (7th ed., 1979) for an excellent discussion of injunctive and declaratory relief (919 et seq.) and the prerogative writs (923 et seq.).

The Reviewability Question

A leading authority, Louis L. Jaffe, has argued that "[i]n most cases statutes or common-law decisions make clear the reviewability of an administrative action at the suit of at least one or more classes of potential plaintiffs." [3] However, the more difficult question, and one that needs to be explored here, is whether, in cases of statutory silence or ambiguity, there is a common-law reviewability.

The mixed interpretations of the complex case law on the reviewability/unreviewability question [4] can be illustrated by juxtaposing [5] the views of Mr. Justice Frankfurter with those of the Attorney General's Committee. Mr. Justice Frankfurter stated, in dissent, in *Stark* v. *Wickard* (1944) that "[a]part from the text and texture of a particular law in relation to which judicial review is sought, 'judicial review' is a mischievous abstraction. There is no such thing as a common law of judicial review in the federal courts." [6] However, the Attorney General's Committee expressed a divergent view: "Legislation has played little part in defining the area of reviewable administrative action. Such limits as there are to that area have been marked out largely by the gradual judicial process of inclusion and exclusion, aided at times by the courts' judgment as to the probable legislative intent derived from the spirit of the statutory scheme." [7]

One can further complicate the situation by citing Louis L. Jaffe, who asserts that "in our system of remedies, an individual whose interest is acutely and immediately affected by an administrative action presumptively has a right to secure at some point a judicial determination of its validity." [8] Although analysis of these mixes of prescription and description is not possible here, a brief recounting of the historical development of the presumption of reviewability is in order. As this survey will make clear, the evolution toward a presumption of judicial review has not been a straight line development. Nor should such a presumption be taken to mean that judicial review of administrative acts will be available to all persons at all times.

Case Law Concerning Reviewability

An examination of the nineteenth-century case law on the question of presumption of reviewability/unreviewability reveals a clear disposition against reviewability. The classic precedent of this period is *Decatur* v. *Paulding* (1840),[9] which involved a mandamus action brought by Mrs. Stephen Decatur, the naval hero's widow, against the Secretary of the Navy to pay her two pensions, one a general naval pension and the other granted her by private

---

[3] Jaffe, above, note 1, at 336.

[4] See Kenneth C. Davis, 4 *Administrative Law Treatise* 5–8 (1958).

[5] Ibid., 9 (note 1).

[6] *Stark* v. *Wickard*, 321 U.S. 228, 312, 64 S.Ct. 559, 572, 88 L.Ed. 733, 749 (1944).

[7] Attorney General's Committee on Administrative Procedure, *Final Report of the Attorney General Committee on Administrative Procedure*, S.Doc. No. 8, 77th Cong., 1st sess. (1941).

[8] Jaffe, above, note 1, at 336.

[9] 39 U.S. (14 Pet.) 497, 10 L.Ed. 559 (1840).

legislation. The Secretary of the Navy had ruled that she might have either one, but not both. The Supreme Court, in denying mandamus, held that "[t]he interference of the Courts with the performance of the ordinary duties of the executive departments of the government, would be productive of nothing but mischief; and we are quite satisfied that such a power was never intended to be given to them." [10]

In the latter part of the nineteenth century, the question of the propriety of judicial control of executive action arose again in cases involving public land grants [11] and the exclusion or deportation of aliens,[12] and not surprisingly, the reasoning and dispositions in these cases were similar to that in *Decatur* v. *Paulding*.[13] Davis gives the following explanation for the judicial preference for unreviewability:

> The probable explanation for the early judicial attitude is that the judges had not yet developed a clear vision of the possibility of a limited review. If the choice was between something approaching a judicial assumption of administrative tasks and a refusal of all review, a preference for unreviewability was easy. But the courts gradually developed systems of limited review. As soon as the judges clearly perceived that they could restrict their review to questions of jurisdiction, statutory interpretation, fair procedure, and substantial evidence, it is hardly surprising that the presumption gradually shifted to the side of reviewability.[14]

Although this common-law attitude of unreviewability persisted into the twentieth century, unless Congress had made an affirmative effort to make administrative determinations reviewable, a 1902 decision signaled the shift toward the presumption of reviewability. *American School of Magnetic Healing* v. *McAnnulty* [15] involved review of the postmaster general's fraud order barring use of the mails for conducting plaintiff's business. The question brought before the court in this bill of equity was "as to the power of the court to grant relief where the Postmaster has assumed and exercised jurisdiction in a case not covered by the statutes, and where he has ordered the detention of mail matter when the statutes have not granted him power so to order." [16] The Court answered:

> That the conduct of the Post Office is a part of the administrative department of the government is entirely true, but that does not necessarily and always oust the courts of jurisdiction to grant relief to a party aggrieved in any action by the head or one of the subordinate officials of the department which is unauthorized by the statute under which he assumes to act. . . . Otherwise, the individual is left to the absolutely uncontrolled and arbitrary action of a public and administrative officer, whose action is unauthorized by any law and is in violation of the rights of the individual.[17]

---

[10] Ibid., at 516 and 568, respectively.

[11] *Lem Moon Sing* v. *United States*, 158 U.S. 538, 15 S.Ct. 967, 39 L.Ed. 1082 (1895).

[12] *Gaines* v. *Thompson*, 74 U.S. (7 Wall.) 347, 19 L.Ed. 62 (1868).

[13] Jaffe, above, note 1, at 337–38.

[14] Davis, above, note 4, at 31.

[15] 187 U.S. 94, 23 S.Ct. 33, 47 L.Ed. 90 (1902).

[16] Ibid., at 107–8, 38, and 96, respectively.

[17] Ibid., at 108–10, 39, and 96, respectively.

The Court in the next decade moved on to reverse the presumption in immigration [18] and land grant [19] cases, which had been bastions of the nineteenth-century presumption against reviewability. Although the presumption of reviewability was temporarily sidetracked in *Switchmen's Union* v. *National Mediation Board* (1943),[20] which has been described as "an expression of the mood of judicial self-deprecation and abdication," [21] the Supreme Court quickly reverted back to the presumption in *Stark* v. *Wickard* (1944).[22] In that case, Mr. Justice Reed, in spite of Mr. Justice Frankfurter's protestations in dissent, held that:

> The responsibility of determining the limits of statutory grants of authority ... is a judicial function entrusted to the courts by Congress by the statutes establishing courts and marking their jurisdiction..... [U]nder Article 3, Congress established courts to adjudicate cases and controversies as to claims of infringement of individual rights whether by unlawful action of private persons or by the exertions of unauthorized administrative power.[23]

Summing up the situation in 1965, on the basis of *Stark* v. *Wickard*, Professor Jaffe wrote, "it can safely be said that the prevailing and the correct view is that of Mr. Justice Reed.... Congress, barring constitutional impediments, may indeed exclude judicial review. But judicial review is the rule. It rests on the congressional grant of general jurisdiction to the article III courts. It is a basic right; it is a traditional power and the intention to exclude it must be made specifically manifest." [24]

Professor Jaffe's view has been confirmed by more recent case law. In the important case of *Abbott Laboratories* v. *Gardner*, 387 U.S. 136, 87 S.Ct. 1507, 18 L.Ed.2d 681 (1967), the Supreme Court stated that "only upon a showing of 'clear and convincing evidence' of a contrary legislative intent should the courts restrict access to judicial review." 387 U.S. 141, 87 S.Ct. 1511, 18 L.Ed.2d 687. Elsewhere in the same opinion the Court described the general legislative intent at the federal level (as manifested in the APA): "the Administrative Procedure Act ... embodies the basic presumption of judicial review ... so long as no statute precludes such relief or the action is not one committed by law to agency discretion.... " 387 U.S. 140, 87 S.Ct. 1511, 18 L.Ed.2d 686–7.

The pertinent provisions of the APA are § 704 and § 701. Section 704 provides: "Agency action made reviewable by statute and final agency action for which there is no adequate remedy in a court are subject to judicial review." This general provision is conditioned, however, by § 701: "This chapter applies, according to the provisions thereof, except to the extent

---

[18] *Gegiow* v. *Uhl*, 239 U.S. 3, 36 S.Ct. 2, 60 L.Ed. 114 (1915).

[19] *Lane* v. *Hoglund*, 244 U.S. 174, 37 S.Ct. 558, 61 L.Ed. 1066 (1917).

[20] *Switchmen's Union* v. *National Mediation Bd.*, 320 U.S. 297, 64 S.Ct. 95, 88 L.Ed. 61 (1943).

[21] Jaffe, above, note 1, at 344.

[22] *Stark* v. *Wickard*, 321 U.S. 288, 64 S.Ct. 559, 88 L.Ed. 733 (1944).

[23] Ibid., at 310, 571, and 748, respectively. Although *American School of Magnetic Healing* v. *McAnnulty, Gegiow* v. *Uhl, Lane* v. *Hoglund*, and *Stark* v. *Wickard*, cited previously, support the conclusion that generally there is a right to judicial review, one must be aware of the exceptions. In this regard, see either Davis, above, note 4, at 25–30 or Jaffe, above, note 1, at 348–353.

[24] Jaffe, above, note 1, at 346.

that—(1) statutes preclude judicial review; or (2) agency action is committed to agency discretion by law."

PRECLUSION OF JUDICIAL REVIEW

Under the APA, then, the two bases for denying review are statutory preclusion and cases involving agency discretion. The quotation from Professor Jaffe given above stated that preclusion of judicial review "must be made specifically manifest." Earlier there was some basis for saying, however (and this is confirmed by Jaffe later in his analysis), that preclusion could be either implied or express. But with the strengthening of the presumption in favor of review, the willingness of courts to find an implied preclusion has become rare.[25]

Express preclusion is a different matter. While statutory provisions specifically barring judicial review are not common, a few congressional enactments do contain such statements. A current example is § 211(a) of Title 38 of the U.S.Code, on the authority of the Veterans' Administration in the area of veteran's benefits: "the decisions of the Administrator of any question of law or fact under any law administered by the Veterans' Administration providing benefits for veterans . . . shall be final and conclusive and no . . . court of the United States shall have the power or jurisdiction to review such decision . . . . "

The following case involves an attempt by a private individual to gain judicial review of his grievance, in spite of the apparently clear intent of Congress as spelled out in the statute.

Johnson v. Robison

SUPREME COURT OF THE UNITED STATES, 1974.
415 U.S. 361, 94 S.CT. 1160, 39 L.ED.2D 389.

[Robison, a conscientious objector who had satisfactorily completed two years of alternate service, was denied educational assistance benefits by the Veterans' Administration on the ground that he did not qualify as an "eligible veteran" under 38 U.S.C.A. § 1661(a). Robison filed a class-action suit in a U.S. district court seeking a declaratory judgment that this and related provisions violated the First Amendment's guarantee of religious freedom and the Fifth Amendment's guarantee of equal protection of the laws. Johnson, the Administrator of Veterans' Affairs, moved to dismiss the action on the ground that on the basis of 38 U.S.C.A. § 211(a) (quoted above), judicial review of decisions of the administrator is prohibited. The district court

---

[25] See the discussion and citation of cases in Gellhorn, Byse and Strauss, above, note 2, at 938–942; also Bernard Schwartz, *Administrative Law* 441–444 (1976). But courts have shown some reluctance to permit judicial review of functions that fall within the area of foreign affairs and international diplomacy, even where the statute appears to confer review. See *Chicago and Southern Air Lines* v. *Waterman Steamship Corp.*, 333 U.S. 103, 68 S.Ct. 431, 92 L.Ed. 568 (1948). The Court of Appeals for the District of Columbia recently reaffirmed the principle of this decision in *Braniff Airways, Inc.* v. *C.A.B.*, 581 F.2d 846 (D.C.Cir., 1978).

ruled that judicial review was available, rejected Robison's First-Amendment claim, but upheld his equal-protection claim. The Supreme Court, one justice dissenting, rejected both Robison's First-Amendment and equal-protection claims. The only part of the Supreme Court opinion set forth below deals with the issue of judicial review of Veterans' Administration decisions.]

Mr. Justice Brennan delivered the opinion of the Court. . . .

We consider first appellants' contention that § 211(a) bars federal courts from deciding the constitutionality of veterans' benefits legislation. Such a construction would, of course, raise serious questions concerning the constitutionality of § 211(a), and in such case "it is a cardinal principle that this Court will first ascertain whether a construction of the statute is fairly possible by which the [constitutional] question[s] may be avoided." United States v. Thirty-seven Photographs, 402 U.S. 363, 369, 91 S.Ct. 1400, 1404, 28 L.Ed.2d 822 (1971).

Plainly, no explicit provision of § 211(a) bars judicial consideration of appellee's constitutional claims. That section provides that "the *decisions* of the Administrator on any question of law or fact *under* any law administered by the Veterans' Administration providing benefits for veterans . . . shall be final and conclusive and no . . . court of the United States shall have power or jurisdiction to review any such decision. . . . " (Emphasis added.) The prohibitions would appear to be aimed at review only of those decisions of law or fact that arise in the *administration* by the Veterans' Administration of a *statute* providing benefits for veterans. A decision of law or fact "under" a statute is made by the Administrator in the interpretation or application of a particular provision of the statute to a particular set of facts, Appellee's constitutional challenge is not to any such decision of the *Administrator*, but rather to a decision of *Congress* to create a statutory class entitled to benefits that does

not include I–O conscientious objectors who performed alternative civilian service. Thus, as the District Court stated: "The questions of law presented in these proceedings arise under the Constitution, not under the statute whose validity is challenged." 352 F.Supp., at 853.

This construction is also supported by the administrative practice of the Veterans' Administration. "When faced with a problem of statutory construction, this Court shows great deference to the interpretation given the statute by the officers or agency charged with its administration." Udall v. Tallman, 380 U.S. 1, 16, 85 S.Ct. 792, 801, 13 L.Ed.2d 61 (1965). The Board of Veterans' Appeals expressly disclaimed authority to decide constitutional questions in Appeal of Sly, C–27 593 725 (May 10, 1972). There the Board, denying a claim for educational assistance by a I–O conscientious objector, held that "[t]his decision does not reach the issue of the constitutionality of the pertinent laws as this matter is not within the jurisdiction of this Board." *Sly* thus accepts and follows the principle that "[a]djudication of the constitutionality of congressional enactments has generally been thought beyond the jurisdiction of administrative agencies. . . . "

Nor does the legislative history accompanying the 1970 amendment of § 211(a) demonstrate a congressional intention to bar judicial review even of constitutional questions. No-review clauses similar to § 211(a) have been a part of veterans' benefits legislation since 1933. While the legislative history accompanying these precursor no-review clauses is almost nonexistent, the Administrator, in a letter written in 1952 in connection with a revision of the clause under consideration by the Subcommittee of the House Committee on Veterans' Affairs, comprehensively explained the policies necessitating the no-review clause and identified two primary purposes: (1) to insure that veterans' benefits claims will not burden the courts and the Veterans' Administration with expensive and time-consuming litigation, and (2) to insure that the technical and complex determinations and applications of Veterans' Administration policy connected with veterans' benefits decisions will be adequately and uniformly made.

The legislative history of the 1970 amendment indicates nothing more than a congressional intent to preserve these two primary purposes. Before amendment, the no-review clause made final "the decisions of the Administrator on any question of law or fact *concerning a claim for benefits or payments* under [certain] law[s] administered by the Veterans' Administration" (emphasis added), 38 U.S.C. § 211(a) (1964 ed.), 71 Stat. 92. In a series of decisions, e.g., Wellman v. Whittier, 104 U.S.App.D.C. 6, 259 F.2d 163 (1958); Thompson v. Gleason, 115 U.S.App.D.C. 201, 317 F.2d 901 (1962); and Tracy v. Gleason, 126 U.S.App. D.C. 415, 379 F.2d 469 (1967), the Court of Appeals for the District of Columbia Circuit interpreted the term "claim" as a limitation upon the reach of § 211(a), and as a consequence held that judicial review of actions by the Administrator *subsequent* to an original grant of benefits was not barred.

Congress perceived this judicial interpretation as a threat to the dual purposes of the no-review clause. First, the interpretation would lead to an inevitable increase in litigation with consequent burdens upon the courts and the Veterans' Administration. In its House Report, the Committee on Veterans' Affairs stated that "[s]ince the decision in the *Tracy* case—and as the result of that decision and the *Wellman* and *Thompson* decisions—suits in constantly increasing numbers have been filed in the U.S. District Court for the District of Columbia by plaintiffs seeking a resumption of terminated benefits." H.R.Rep. No. 91–1166, p. 10 (1970), U.S.Code Cong. & Admin. News 1970, p. 3730. This same concern over the rising number of court cases was expressed by the Administrator in a letter to the Committee:

The *Wellman, Thompson*, and *Tracy* decisions have not been followed in any of the other 10 Federal judicial circuits throughout the country. Nevertheless, soon after the *Tracy* decision, suits in the nature of mandamus or for declaratory judgment commenced to be filed in the U.S. District Court for the District of Columbia in constantly increasing numbers by plaintiffs seeking resumption of terminated benefits. As of March 8, 1970, 353 suits of this type had been filed in the District of Columbia circuit....

The scope of the *Tracy* decision and the decisions upon which it is based is so broad that it could well afford a basis for judicial review of millions of decisions terminating or reducing many types of benefits provided under laws administered by the Veterans' Administration. Such review might even extend to the decisions of predecessor agencies made many years ago. Id., at 21, 24, U.S.Code Cong. & Admin. News 1970, p. 3740.

Second, Congress was concerned that the judicial interpretation of § 211(a) would involve the courts in day-to-day determination and interpretation of Veterans' Administration policy. The House Report states that the cases already filed in the courts in response to *Wellman, Thompson*, and *Tracy*

involve a large variety of matters—a 1930's termination of a widow's pension payments under a statute then extant, because of her open and notorious adulterous cohabitation; invalid marriage to a veteran; severance of a veteran's service connection for disability compensation; reduction of such compensation because of lessened disability ... [and] suits ... brought by [Filipino] widows of World War II servicemen seeking restoration of death compensation or pension benefits terminated after the Administrator raised a presumption of their remarriage on the basis of evidence gathered through field examination. Notwithstanding the 1962 endorsement by the Congress of the Veterans' Administration's [sic] administrative presumption of remarriage rule, most of [the suits brought by Filipino widows] have resulted in judgments adverse to the Government. Id., at 10, U.S. Code Cong. & Admin.News 1970, p. 3730.

The Administrator voiced similar concerns, stating that "it seems obvious that suits similar to the several hundred already filed can—and undoubtedly will—subject nearly every aspect of our benefit determinations to judicial review, including rating decisions, related Veterans' Administration regulations, Administrator's decisions, and various adjudication procedures." Letter to the Committee on Veterans' Affairs 23–24, U.S.Code Cong. & Admin.News 1970, p. 3742.

Thus, the 1970 amendment was enacted to overrule the interpretation of the Court of Appeals for the District of Columbia Circuit, and thereby restore vitality to the two primary purposes to be served by the no-review clause. Nothing whatever in the legislative history of the 1970 amendment, or predecessor no-review clauses, suggests any congressional intent to preclude judicial cognizance of constitutional challenges to veterans' benefits legislation.

Such challenges obviously do not contravene the purposes of the no-review clause, for they cannot be expected to burden the courts by their volume, nor do they involve technical considerations of Veterans' Administration policy. We therefore conclude, in agreement with the District Court, that a construction of § 211(a) that does not extend the prohibitions of that section to actions challenging the constitutionality of laws providing benefits for veterans is not only "fairly possible" but is the most reasonable construction, for neither the text nor the scant legislative history of § 211(a) provides the "clear and convincing" evidence of congressional intent required by this Court before a statute will be construed to restrict access to judicial review. See Abbott Laboratories v. Gardner, 387 U.S. 136, 141, 87 S.Ct. 1507, 1511, 18 L.Ed.2d 681 (1967). . . .

[The dissenting opinion of Mr. Justice Douglas is omitted.]

What this case suggests is that when constitutional questions involving important personal interests are raised, courts will sometimes choose not to interpret finality provisions literally. The effect is to strengthen the presumption in favor of judicial review, as the principles articulated in cases such as these are applied to other governmental agencies.[26] But this is not to imply that courts permit all constitutional challenges to overcome statutory preclusion provisions, or that cases like *Johnson* v. *Robison* have made all claims against the Veterans' Administration subject to judicial review. In fact, the vast majority of veterans' claims remain beyond judicial review, a situation that several commentators believe invites agency abuse of the system.[27]

---

[26] See, for instance, *Eskra* v. *Morton*, 380 F.Supp. 205 (D.C.Wis., 1974), applying the principle of *Johnson* v. *Robison* to a similar statutory provision relevant to the authority of the Board of Indian Appeals of the Department of the Interior.

On appeal, the U.S. Court of Appeals for the Seventh Circuit affirmed the holding of the district court concerning that court's authority to review the administrative determination, but reversed the district court on the merits. 524 F.2d 9 (1975).

[27] See, e.g., Kim Lacy Morris, "Judicial Review of Non-Reviewable Administrative Action: Veterans Administration Benefits Claims," 29 *Administrative Law Review* 65 (1977); Robert L. Rabin, "Preclusion of Judicial Review in Processing of Claims for Veterans' Benefits: A Preliminary Analysis," 27 *Stanford Law Review* 905 (1975). As Rabin puts it at 923: "On the existing information about the system, the case for access to court seems strong—sufficiently strong to cast a long shadow over the preclusion statute." Bills introduced in Congress to broaden judicial review of veterans' claims have so far not been adopted.

ADMINISTRATIVE ACTIONS COMMITTED BY LAW TO AGENCY DISCRETION

Most commentators agree that this is "a tricky problem." [28] Section 706 of the APA provides that the court shall vacate agency action found to be "arbitrary, capricious, an abuse of discretion, or otherwise not in accordance with the law." But § 701 states: "This chapter applies ... except to the extent that ... agency action is committed to agency discretion by law." Numerous analysts have wrestled with these seemingly contradictory provisions and have reached varying conclusions. Most, however, appear to minimize the importance of the "committed to agency discretion by law" provision of § 706. Davis states: "When legislative intent is unexpressed or unclear, the best generalization may be that courts limit themselves to issues appropriate for judicial determination." [29] Schwartz concludes that "the exception for agency discretion [is limited] to situations where the statute shows some positive intention to eliminate review.... The exception ... accordingly adds little or nothing to that of cases where 'statutes preclude judicial review.' " [30] Jaffe states: "Presumptively, an exercise of discretion is reviewable for legal error, procedural defect, or 'abuse.' " [31] *Overton Park* is an important Supreme Court case that deals with the issue. It is followed, however, by the more recent *Heckler* case in which the Court expresses its reservations about judicial oversight of agencies by establishing a presumption of unreviewability of an agency's decision not to take an enforcement action.

Citizens to Preserve Overton Park, Inc. v. Volpe

SUPREME COURT OF THE UNITED STATES, 1971.
401 U.S. 402, 91 S.CT. 814, 28 L.ED.2D 136.

Opinion of the Court by Mr. Justice MARSHALL, announced by Mr. Justice STEWART.

The growing public concern about the quality of our natural environment has prompted Congress in recent years to enact legislation designed to curb the accelerating destruction of our country's natural beauty. We are concerned in this case with § 4(f) of the Department of Transportation Act of 1966, as amended, and § 18(a) of the Federal-Aid Highway Act of 1968, 82 Stat. 823, 23 U.S.C.A. § 138 (hereafter § 138).

These statutes prohibit the Secretary of Transportation from authorizing the use of federal funds to finance the construction of highways through public parks if a "feasible and prudent" alternative route exists. If no such route is available, the statutes allow him to approve construction through parks only if there has been "all possible planning to minimize harm" to the park.

Petitioners, private citizens as well as local and national conservation organizations, contend that the Secretary has violat-

---

[28] Jaffe, above, note 1, at 359. See also Kenneth Culp Davis, *Administrative Law: Cases—Text—Problems* 63 (6th ed., 1977).

[29] Davis, above, note 28, at 64.

[30] Schwartz, above, note 25, at 454.

[31] Jaffe, above, note 1, at 363.

ed these statutes by authorizing the expenditure of federal funds for the construction of a six-lane interstate highway through a public park in Memphis, Tennessee. Their claim was rejected by the District Court, which granted the Secretary's motion for summary judgment, and the Court of Appeals for the Sixth Circuit affirmed. After oral argument, this Court granted a stay that halted construction and, treating the application for the stay as a petition for certiorari, granted review. 400 U.S. 939, 91 S.Ct. 246, 27 L.Ed.2d 262. We now reverse the judgment below and remand for further proceedings in the District Court.

Overton Park is a 342-acre city park located near the center of Memphis. The park contains a zoo, a nine-hole municipal golf course, an outdoor theater, nature trails, a bridle path, an art academy, picnic areas, and 170 acres of forest. The proposed highway, which is to be a six-lane, high-speed, expressway, will sever the zoo from the rest of the park. Although the roadway will be depressed below ground level except where it crosses a small creek, 26 acres of the park will be destroyed. The highway is to be a segment of Interstate Highway I–40, part of the National System of Interstate and Defense Highways. I–40 will provide Memphis with a major east-west expressway which will allow easier access to downtown Memphis from the residential areas on the eastern edge of the city.

Although the route through the park was approved by the Bureau of Public Roads in 1956 and by the Federal Highway Administrator in 1966, the enactment of § 4(f) of the Department of Transportation Act prevented distribution of federal funds for the section of the highway designated to go through Overton Park until the Secretary of Transportation determined whether the requirements of § 4(f) had been met. Federal funding for the rest of the project was, however, available; and the state acquired a right-of-way on both sides of the park. In April 1968, the Secretary an-

nounced that he concurred in the judgment of local officials that I–40 should be built through the park. And in September 1969 the State acquired the right-of-way inside Overton Park from the city. Final approval for the project—the route as well as the design—was not announced until November 1969, after Congress had reiterated in § 138 of the Federal-Aid Highway Act that highway construction through public parks was to be restricted. Neither announcement approving the route and design of I–40 was accompanied by a statement of the Secretary's factual findings. He did not indicate why he believed there were no feasible and prudent alternative routes or why design changes could not be made to reduce the harm to the park.

Petitioners contend that the Secretary's action is invalid without such formal findings and that the Secretary did not make an independent determination but merely relied on the judgment of the Memphis City Council. They also contend that it would be "feasible and prudent" to route I–40 around Overton Park either to the north or to the south. And they argue that if these alternative routes are not "feasible and prudent," the present plan does not include "all possible" methods for reducing harm to the park. Petitioners claim that I–40 could be built under the park by using either of two possible tunneling methods, and they claim that, at a minimum, by using advanced drainage techniques the expressway could be depressed below ground level along the entire route through the park including the section that crosses the small creek.

Respondents argue that it was unnecessary for the Secretary to make formal findings, and that he did, in fact, exercise his own independent judgment which was supported by the facts. In the District Court, respondents introduced affidavits, prepared specifically for this litigation, which indicated that the Secretary had made the decision and that the decision was supportable. These affidavits were contradicted by affidavits introduced by petitioners, who also sought to take the deposition of a former Federal Highway Administrator who had participated in the decision to route I–40 through Overton Park.

The District Court and the Court of Appeals found that formal findings by the Secretary were not necessary and refused to order the deposition of the former Federal Highway Administrator because those courts believed that probing of the mental processes of an administrative decisionmaker was prohibited. And, believing that the Secretary's authority was wide and reviewing courts' authority narrow in the approval of highway routes, the lower courts held that the affidavits contained no basis for a determination that the Secretary had exceeded his authority.

We agree that formal findings were not required. But we do not believe that in this case judicial review based solely on litigation affidavits was adequate.

A threshold question—whether petitioners are entitled to any judicial review—is easily answered. Section 701 of the Administrative Procedure Act, 5 U.S.C.A. § 701, provides that the action of "each authority of the Government of the United States," which includes the Department of Transportation, is subject to judicial review except where there is a statutory prohibition on review or where "agency action is committed to agency discretion by law." In this case, there is no indication that Congress sought to prohibit judicial review and there is most certainly no "showing of 'clear and convincing evidence' of a . . . legislative intent" to restrict access to judicial review. Abbott Laboratories v. Gardner, 387 U.S. 136, 141, 87 S.Ct. 1507, 1511, 18 L.Ed.2d 681 (1967).

Similarly, the Secretary's decision here does not fall within the exception for action "committed to agency discretion." This is a very narrow exception. Berger, Administrative Arbitrariness and Judicial Review, 65 Col.L.Rev. 55 (1965). The legisla-

tive history of the Administrative Procedure Act indicates that it is applicable in those rare instances where "statutes are drawn in such broad terms that in a given case there is no law to apply." S.Rep. No. 752, 79th Cong., 1st Sess., 26 (1945).

Section 4(f) of the Department of Transportation Act and § 138 of the Federal Aid Highway Act are clear and specific directives. Both the Department of Transportation Act and the Federal-Aid to Highway Act provide that the Secretary "shall not approve any program or project" that requires the use of any public parkland "unless (1) there is no feasible and prudent alternative to the use of such land, and (2) such program includes all possible planning to minimize harm to such park. . . . " 23 U.S.C.A. § 138; 49 U.S.C.A. § 1653(f). This language is a plain and explicit bar to the use of federal funds for construction of highways through parks—only the most unusual situations are exempted.

Despite the clarity of the statutory language, respondents argue that the Secretary has wide discretion. They recognize that the requirement that there be no "feasible" alternative route admits of little administrative discretion. For this exemption to apply the Secretary must find that as a matter of sound engineering it would not be feasible to build the highway along any other route. Respondents argue, however, that the requirement that there be no other "prudent" route requires the Secretary to engage in a wide-ranging balancing of competing interests. They contend that the Secretary should weigh the detriment resulting from the destruction of parkland against the cost of other routes, safety considerations, and other factors, and determine on the basis of the importance that he attaches to these other factors whether, on balance, alternative feasible routes would be "prudent."

But no such wide-ranging endeavor was intended. It is obvious that in most cases considerations of cost, directness of route, and community disruption will indicate that parkland should be used for high-way construction whenever possible. Although it may be necessary to transfer funds from one jurisdiction to another, there will always be a smaller outlay required from the public purse when parkland is used since the public already owns the land and there will be no need to pay for right-of-way . . . .

Congress clearly did not intend that cost and disruption of the community were to be ignored by the Secretary. But the very existence of the statutes indicates that protection of parkland was to be given paramount importance. The few green havens that are public parks were not to be lost unless there were truly unusual factors present in a particular case or the cost or community disruption resulting from alternative routes reached extraordinary magnitudes. If the statutes are to have any meaning, the Secretary cannot approve the destruction of parkland unless he finds that alternative routes present unique problems.

Plainly, there is "law to apply" and thus the exemption for action "committed to agency discretion" is inapplicable. But the existence of judicial review is only the start: the standard for review must also be determined . . . .

[There follows a discussion of the scope of judicial review to be applied in the case, in which the petitioners' alternative pleas for review under the substantial evidence test and *de novo* review of whether the secretary's decision was "unwarranted by the facts" are rejected by the Court.]

. . . The lower courts based their review on the litigation affidavits that were presented. These affidavits were merely "*post hoc*" rationalizations, Burlington Truck Lines v. United States, 371 U.S. 156, 168–169, 83 S.Ct. 239, 245–246, 9 L.Ed.2d 207 (1962), which have traditionally been found to be an inadequate basis for review. And they clearly do not constitute the "whole record" compiled by the agency:

the basis for review required by § 706 of the Administrative Procedure Act.

Thus it is necessary to remand this case to the District Court for plenary review of the Secretary's decision. That review is to be based on the full administrative record that was before the Secretary at the time he made his decision. But since the bare record may not disclose the factors that were considered or the Secretary's construction of the evidence it may be necessary for the District Court to require some explanation in order to determine if the Secretary acted within the scope of his authority and if the Secretary's action was justifiable under the applicable standard.

The court may require the administrative officials who participated in the decision to give testimony explaining their action. Of course, such inquiry into the mental processes of administrative decisionmakers is usually to be avoided. United States v. Morgan, 313 U.S. 409, 422, 61 S.Ct. 999, 1004–1005, 85 L.Ed. 1429 (1941). And where there are administrative findings that were made at the same time as the decision, as was the case in *Morgan*, there must be a strong showing of bad faith or improper behavior before such inquiry may be made. But here there are no such formal findings and it may be that the only way there can be effective judicial review is by examining the decisionmakers themselves.

The District Court is not, however, required to make such an inquiry. It may be that the Secretary can prepare formal findings including the information required by DOT Order 5610.1 that will provide an adequate explanation for his action. Such an explanation will, to some extent, be a "*post hoc* rationalization" and thus must be viewed critically. If the District Court decides that additional explanation is necessary, that court should consider which method will prove the most expeditious so that full review may be had as soon as possible.

Reversed and remanded.

Mr. Justice DOUGLAS took no part in the consideration or decision of this case.

[The separate opinion of Mr. Justice Black, with whom Mr. Justice Brennan joins, is omitted.]

Heckler, Secretary of Health and Human Services v. Chaney

SUPREME COURT OF THE UNITED STATES, 1985.
470 U.S. 821, 105 S.CT. 1649, 84 L.ED. 714.

[After being convicted of capital offenses and sentenced to death by lethal injection of drugs, prison inmates requested that the Federal Drug Administration (FDA) take enforcement action to prevent violations of the Federal Food, Drug, and Cosmetic Act (FDCA). The inmates alleged that the use of certain drugs in human executions was a violation of the FDCA. They argued, for instance, that the FDA was required to approve drugs as "safe and effective" for human executions before they were distributed in interstate commerce. When the FDA commissioner refused to take the requested investigatory and enforcement actions, the inmates filed suit in U.S. district court seeking review of the agency action under the judicial review provisions of the Administrative Procedure Act, 5 U.S.C. §§ 701–706. The district court granted summary judgment for the FDA, but the U.S. court of appeals reversed on the grounds that the FDA's refusal to act was reviewable and an abuse of discretion. Following the court of appeal's denial of a petition for a rehearing, the Supreme Court granted certiorari. In Justice Rehnquist's words, the Court "granted certiorari to review the implausible result that the FDA is required to exercise its enforcement power to ensure that States only use drugs that are 'safe and effective' for human execution."]

Justice REHNQUIST delivered the opinion of the Court . . .

The Court of Appeals' decision addressed three questions: (1) whether the FDA had jurisdiction to undertake the enforcement actions requested, (2) whether if it did have jurisdiction its refusal to take those actions was subject to judicial review, and (3) whether if reviewable its refusal was arbitrary, capricious, or an abuse of discretion. In reaching our conclusion that the Court of Appeals was wrong, however, we need not and do not address the thorny question of the FDA's jurisdiction. For us, this case turns on the important question of the extent to which determinations by the FDA *not to exercise* its enforcement authority over the use of drugs in interstate commerce may be judicially reviewed. That decision in turn involves the construction of two separate but necessarily interrelated statutes, the APA and the FDCA.

The APA's comprehensive provisions for judicial review of "agency actions" are contained in 5 U.S.C. §§ 701–706. Any person "adversely affected or aggrieved" by agency action, see § 702, including a "failure to act," is entitled to "judicial review thereof," as long as the action is a "final agency action for which there is no other adequate remedy in a court," see § 704. The standards to be applied on review are governed by the provisions of § 706. But before any review at all may be had, a party must first clear the hurdle of § 701(a). That section provides that the chapter on judicial review "applies, according to the provisions thereof, except to the extent that—(1) statutes preclude judicial review; or (2) agency action is committed to agency discretion by law." Petitioner urges that the decision of the FDA to refuse enforcement is an action "committed to agency discretion by law" under § 701(a)(2).

This Court has not had occasion to interpret this second exception in § 701(a) in any great detail. On its face, the section does not obviously lend itself to any particular construction; indeed, one might wonder what difference exists between § (a)(1) and § (a)(2). The former section seems easy in application; it requires construction of the substantive statute involved to determine whether Congress intended to preclude judicial review of certain decisions. . . .

This Court first discussed § (a)(2) in *Citizens to Preserve Overton Park* v. *Volpe*. That case dealt with the Secretary of Transportation's approval of the building of an interstate highway through a park in Memphis, Tennessee. The relevant federal statute provided that the Secretary "shall not approve" any program or project using public parkland unless the Secretary first determined that no feasible alternatives were available. *Overton Park*, 401 U.S., at 411, 91 S.Ct., at 821. Interested citizens challenged the Secretary's approval under the APA, arguing that he had not satisfied the substantive statute's requirements. This Court first addressed the "threshold question" of whether the agency's action was at all reviewable. After setting out the language of § 701(a), the Court stated:

> In this case, there is no indication that Congress sought to prohibit judicial review and there is most certainly no "showing of 'clear and convincing evidence' of a . . . legislative intent" to restrict access to judicial review. *Abbott Laboratories* v. *Gardner*, 387 U.S. 136, 141 [87 S.Ct. 1507, 1511, 18 L.Ed.2d 681] (1967).
>
> Similarly, the Secretary's decision here does not fall within the exception for action "committed to agency discretion." This is a very narrow exception. . . . The legislative history of the Administrative Procedure Act indicates that it is applicable in those rare instances where "statutes are drawn in such broad terms that in a given case there is no law to apply." S.Rep. No. 752, 79th Cong., 1st Sess., 26 (1945). *Overton Park*, supra, 401 U.S., at 410, 91 S.Ct., at 820–821 (footnote omitted).

The above quote answers several of the questions raised by the language of § 701(a), although it raises others. First, it clearly separates the exception provided by § (a)(1) from the § (a)(2) exception. The former applies when Congress has expressed an intent to preclude judicial review. The latter applies in different circumstances; even where Congress has not affirmatively precluded review, review is not to be had if the statute is drawn so that a court would have no meaningful standard against which to judge the agency's exercise of discretion. In such a case, the statute ("law") can be taken to have "committed" the decisionmaking to the agency's judgment absolutely. . . .

To this point our analysis does not differ significantly from that of the Court of Appeals. That court purported to apply the "no law to apply" standard of *Overton Park*. We disagree, however, with that court's insistence that the "narrow construction" of § (a)(2) required application of a presumption of reviewability even to an agency's decision not to undertake certain enforcement actions. Here we think the Court of Appeals broke with tradition, case law, and sound reasoning.

Overton Park did not involve an agency's refusal to take requested enforcement action. It involved an affirmative act of approval under a statute that set clear guidelines for determining when such approval should be given. Refusals to take enforcement steps generally involve precisely the opposite situation, and in that situation we think the presumption is that judicial review is not available. This Court has recognized on several occasions over many years that an agency's decision not to prosecute or enforce, whether through civil or criminal process, is a decision generally committed to an agency's absolute discretion. See *United States* v. *Batchelder*, 442 U.S. 114, 123–124, 99 S.Ct. 2198, 2203–2204, 60 L.Ed.2d 755 (1979); *United States* v. *Nixon*, 418 U.S. 683, 693, 94 S.Ct. 3090, 3100, 41 L.Ed.2d 1039 (1974); *Vaca* v. *Sipes*, 386 U.S.

171, 182, 87 S.Ct. 903, 912, 17 L.Ed.2d 842 (1967); *Confiscation Cases*, 7 Wall. 454, 19 L.Ed. 196 (1869). This recognition of the existence of discretion is attributable in no small part to the general unsuitability for judicial review of agency decisions to refuse enforcement.

The reasons for this general unsuitability are many. First, an agency decision not to enforce often involves a complicated balancing of a number of factors which are peculiarly within its expertise. Thus, the agency must not only assess whether a violation has occurred, but whether agency resources are best spent on this violation or another, whether the agency is likely to succeed if it acts, whether the particular enforcement action requested best fits the agency's overall policies, and indeed, whether the agency has enough resources to undertake the action at all. An agency generally cannot act against each technical violation of the statute it is charged with enforcing. The agency is far better equipped than the courts to deal with the many variables involved in the proper ordering of its priorities. Similar concerns animate the principles of administrative law that courts generally will defer to an agency's construction of the statute it is charged with implementing, and to the procedures it adopts for implementing that statute. . . .

In addition to these administrative concerns, we note that when an agency refuses to act it generally does not exercise its *coercive* power over an individual's liberty or property rights, and thus does not infringe upon areas that courts often are called upon to protect. Similarly, when an agency *does* act to enforce, that action itself provides a focus for judicial review, inasmuch as the agency must have exercised its power in some manner. The action at least can be reviewed to determine whether the agency exceeded its statutory powers. . . . Finally, we recognize that an agency's refusal to institute proceedings shares to some extent the characteristics of

the decision of a prosecutor in the Executive Branch not to indict—a decision which has long been regarded as the special province of the Executive Branch, inasmuch as it is the executive who is charged by the Constitution to "take Care that the Laws be faithfully executed." U.S. Const., Art. II, § 3.

We of course only list the above concerns to facilitate understanding of our conclusion that an agency's decision not to take enforcement action should be presumed immune from judicial review under § 701(a)(2). For good reasons, such a decision has traditionally been "committed to agency discretion," and we believe that the Congress enacting the APA did not intend to alter that tradition. . . . In so stating, we emphasize that the decision is only presumptively unreviewable; the presumption may be rebutted where the substantive statute has provided guidelines for the agency to follow in exercising its enforcement powers. Thus, in establishing this presumption in the APA, Congress did not set agencies free to disregard legislative direction in the statutory scheme that the agency administers. Congress may limit an agency's exercise of enforcement power if it wishes, either by setting substantive priorities, or by otherwise circumscribing an agency's power to discriminate among issues or cases it will pursue. How to determine when Congress has done so is the question left open by *Overton Park*.

Dunlop v. *Bachowski*, 421 U.S. 560, 95 S.Ct. 1851, 44 L.Ed.2d 377 (1975) relied upon heavily by respondents and the majority in the Court of Appeals, presents an example of statutory language which supplied sufficient standards to rebut the presumption of unreviewability. *Dunlop* involved a suit by a union employee, under the Labor-Management Reporting and Disclosure Act, . . . asking the National Labor Relations Board to investigate and file suit to set aside a union election. Section 482 provided that, upon filing of a complaint by a union member, "[t]he Secretary shall investigate such complaint and, if he finds probable cause to believe that a violation ... has occurred ... he shall ... bring a civil action.... " After investigating the plaintiff's claims the Secretary of Labor declined to file suit, and the plaintiff sought judicial review under the APA. This Court held that review was available. It rejected the Secretary's argument that the statute precluded judicial review, and in a footnote it stated its agreement with the conclusion of the Court of Appeals that the decision was not "an unreviewable exercise of prosecutorial discretion." 421 U.S., at 567, n. 7, 95 S.Ct., at 1858, n. 7. Our textual references to the "strong presumption" of reviewability in *Dunlop* were addressed only to the § (a)(1) exception; we were content to rely on the Court of Appeals' opinion to hold that the § (a)(2) exception did not apply. The Court of Appeals, in turn, had found the "principle of absolute prosecutorial discretion" inapplicable, because the language of the LMRDA indicated that the Secretary was required to file suit if certain "clearly defined" factors were present. The decision therefore was not " 'beyond the judicial capacity to supervise.' " ...

Dunlop is thus consistent with a general presumption of unreviewability of decisions not to enforce. The statute being administered quite clearly withdrew discretion from the agency and provided guidelines for exercise of its enforcement power. Our decision that review was available was not based on "pragmatic considerations," such as those cited by the Court of Appeals, see 231 U.S.App.D.C., at 147, 718 F.2d, at 1185, that amount to an assessment of whether the interests at stake are important enough to justify intervention in the agencies' decisionmaking. The danger that agencies may not carry out their delegated powers with sufficient vigor does not necessarily lead to the conclusion that courts are the most appropriate body to police this aspect of their performance. That decision is in the first instance for

Congress, and we therefore turn to the FDCA to determine whether in this case Congress has provided us with "law to apply." If it has indicated an intent to circumscribe agency enforcement discretion, and has provided meaningful standards for defining the limits of that discretion, there is "law to apply" under § 701(a)(2), and courts may require that the agency follow that law; if it has not, then an agency refusal to institute proceedings is a decision "committed to agency discretion by law" within the meaning of that section.

To enforce the various substantive prohibitions contained in the FDCA, the Act provides for injunctions, 21 U.S.C. § 332, criminal sanctions, §§ 333 and 335, and seizure of any offending food, drug, or cosmetic article, § 334. The Act's general provision for enforcement, § 372, provides only that "[t]he Secretary is *authorized* to conduct examinations and investigations.... " Unlike the statute at issue in *Dunlop*, § 332 gives no indication of when an injunction should be sought, and § 334, providing for seizures, is framed in the permissive—the offending food, drug or cosmetic "shall be liable to be proceeded against." The section on criminal sanctions states baldly that any person who violates the Act's substantive prohibitions "shall be imprisoned ... or fined." Respondents argue that this statement mandates criminal prosecution of every violator of the Act but they adduce no indication in case law or legislative history that such was Congress' intention in using this language, which is commonly found in the criminal provisions of Title 18 of the United States Code.... We are unwilling to attribute such a sweeping meaning to this language, particularly since the Act charges the Secretary only with recommending prosecution; any criminal prosecutions must be instituted by the Attorney General. The Act's enforcement provisions thus commit complete discretion to the Secretary to decide how and when they should be exercised....

We therefore conclude that the presumption that agency decisions not to institute proceedings are unreviewable under § 701(a)(2) of the APA is not overcome by the enforcement provisions of the FDCA. The FDA's decision not to take the enforcement actions requested by respondents is therefore not subject to judicial review under the APA. The general exception to reviewability provided by § 701(a)(2) for action "committed to agency discretion" remains a narrow one, see *Overton Park*, 401 U.S. 402, 91 S.Ct. 814, 28 L.Ed.2d 136 (1971), but within that exception are included agency refusals to institute investigative or enforcement proceedings, unless Congress has indicated otherwise. In so holding, we essentially leave to Congress, and not to the courts, the decision as to whether an agency's refusal to institute proceedings should be judicially reviewable. No colorable claim is made in this case that the agency's refusal to institute proceedings violated any constitutional rights of respondents, and we do not address the issue that would be raised in such a case. Cf. *Johnson* v. *Robison*, 415 U.S. 361, 366, 94 S.Ct. 1160, 1165, 39 L.Ed.2d 389 (1974); *Yick Wo* v. *Hopkins*, 118 U.S. 356, 372–374, 6 S.Ct. 1064, 1072–1073, 30 L.Ed. 220 (1886). The fact that the drugs involved in this case are ultimately to be used in imposing the death penalty must not lead this Court or other courts to import profound differences of opinion over the meaning of the Eighth Amendment to the United States Constitution into the domain of administrative law.

The judgment of the Court of Appeals is

Reversed.

[The concurring opinion of Justice Brennan is omitted.]

Justice MARSHALL, concurring in the judgment.

Easy cases at times produce bad law, for in the rush to reach a clearly ordained result, courts may offer up principles, doctrines, and statements that calmer reflec-

tion, and a fuller understanding of their implications in concrete settings, would eschew. In my view, the "presumption of unreviewability" announced today is a product of that lack of discipline that easy cases make all too easy. The majority, eager to reverse what it goes out of its way to label as an "implausible result," *ante*, at 1654, not only does reverse, as I agree it should, but along the way creates out of whole cloth the notion that agency decisions not to take "enforcement action" are unreviewable unless Congress has rather specifically indicated otherwise. Because this "presumption of unreviewability" is fundamentally at odds with rule-of-law principles firmly embedded in our jurisprudence, because it seeks to truncate an emerging line of judicial authority subjecting enforcement discretion to rational and principled constraint, and because, in the end, the presumption may well be indecipherable, one can only hope that it will come to be understood as a relic of a particular factual setting in which the full implications of such a presumption were neither confronted nor understood.

I write separately to argue for a different basis of decision: that refusals to enforce, like other agency actions, are reviewable in the absence of a "clear and convincing" congressional intent to the contrary, but that such refusals warrant deferrence when, as in this case, there is nothing to suggest that an agency with enforcement discretion has abused that discretion.

In response to respondents' petition, the FDA Commissioner stated that it would not pursue the complaint

> under our inherent discretion to decline to pursue certain enforcement matters. The unapproved use of approved drugs is an area in which the case law is far from uniform. Generally, enforcement proceedings in this area are initiated only when there is a serious danger to the public health or a blatant scheme to defraud. We cannot conclude that those dangers are present under State lethal

injection laws.... [W]e decline, as a matter of enforcement discretion, to pursue supplies of drugs under State control that will be used for execution by lethal injection.

The FDA may well have been legally required to provide this statement of basis and purpose for its decision not to take the action requested. Under the Administrative Procedure Act, such a statement is required when an agency denies a "written application, petition, or other request of an interested person made in connection with any agency proceedings." 5 U.S.C. § 555(e). Whether this written explanation was legally required or not, however, it does provide a sufficient basis for holding, *on the merits*, that the FDA's refusal to grant the relief requested was within its discretion....

The Court, however, is not content to rest on this ground. Instead, the Court transforms the arguments for deferential review on the merits into the wholly different notion that "enforcement" decisions are presumptively unreviewable altogether—unreviewable whether the resource-allocation rationale is a sham, unreviewable whether enforcement is declined out of vindictive or personal motives, and unreviewable whether the agency has simply ignored the request for enforcement.... But surely it is a far cry from asserting that agencies must be given substantial leeway in allocating enforcement resources among valid alternatives to suggesting that agency enforcement decisions are presumptively unreviewable *no matter what factor caused the agency to stay its hand*.

This "presumption of unreviewability" is also a far cry from prior understandings of the Administrative Procedure Act. As the Court acknowledges, the APA presumptively entitles any person "adversely affected or aggrieved by agency action," 5 U.S.C. § 702—which is defined to include the "failure to act," 5 U.S.C. § 551(13)—to judicial review of that action. That presumption can be defeated if the substantive stat-

ute precludes review, § 701(a)(1), or if the action is committed to agency discretion *by law*, § 701(a)(2), but as Justice Harlan's opinion in *Abbott Laboratories* v. *Gardner*, 387 U.S. 136, 87 S.Ct. 1507, 18 L.Ed.2d 681 (1967), made clear in interpreting the APA's judicial review provisions,

> The legislative material elucidating [the APA] manifests a congressional intention that it cover a broad spectrum of administrative actions, and this Court has echoed that theme by noting that the Administrative Procedure Act's "generous review provisions" must be given a "hospitable" interpretation.... [O]nly upon a showing of "clear and convincing evidence" of a contrary legislative intent should the courts restrict access to judicial review. Id., at 140–141, 87 S.Ct., at 1511 (citations omitted; footnote omitted).... Rather than confront *Abbott Labs*, perhaps the seminal case on judicial review under the APA, the Court chooses simply to ignore it. Instead, to support its newfound "presumption of unreviewability," the Court resorts to completely undefined and unsubstantiated references to "tradition," see *ante*, at 1656, and to citation of four cases. See *United States* v. *Batchelder*, 442 U.S. 114, 99 S.Ct. 2198, 60 L.Ed.2d 755 (1979); *United States* v. *Nixon*, 418 U.S. 683, 94 S.Ct. 3090, 41 L.Ed.2d 1039 (1974); *Vaca* v. *Sipes*, 386 U.S. 171, 87 S.Ct. 903, 17 L.Ed.2d 842 (1967); *Confiscation Cases*, 7 Wall. 454, 19 L.Ed. 196 (1869). Because the Court's "tradition" rationale, which flies in the face of *Abbott Labs*, stands as a flat, unsupported *ipse dixit*, these four cases form the only doctrinal foundation for the majority's presumption of unreviewability.

Yet these cases hardly support such a broad presumption with respect to agency refusal to take enforcement action. The only one of these cases to involve administrative action, *Vaca* v. *Sipes*, suggests, in dictum, that the General Counsel of the National Labor Relations Board has unreviewable discretion to refuse to initiate an unfair labor practice complaint. To the extent this dictum is sound, later cases indicate that unreviewability results from the particular structure of the National Labor Relations Act and the explicit statutory intent to withdraw review found in 29 U.S.C. § 153(d), rather than from some general "presumption of unreviewability" of enforcement decisions. See *NLRB* v. *Sears, Roebuck & Co.*, 421 U.S. 132, 138, 95 S.Ct. 1504, 1510, 44 L.Ed.2d 29 (1975). Neither *Vaca* nor *Sears, Roebuck* discuss the APA. The other three cases—*Batchelder, Nixon*, and the *Confiscation Cases*—all involve prosecutorial discretion to enforce the criminal law. . . .

Perhaps most important, the *sine qua non* of the APA was to alter inherited judicial reluctance to constrain the exercise of discretionary administrative power—to rationalize and make fairer the exercise of such discretion. Since passage of the APA, the sustained effort of administrative law has been to "continuously narro[w] the category of actions considered to be so discretionary as to be exempted from review." Shapiro, Administrative Discretion: The Next Stage, 92 Yale L.J. 1487, 1489, n. 11 (1983). Discretion may well be necessary to carry out a variety of important administrative functions, but discretion can be a veil for laziness, corruption, incompetency, lack of will, or other motives, and for that reason *"the presence of discretion should not bar a court from considering a claim of illegal or arbitrary use of discretion."* L. Jaffe, Judicial Control of Administrative Action 375 (1965). Judicial review is available under the APA in the absence of a clear and convincing demonstration that Congress intended to preclude it precisely so that agencies, whether in rulemaking, adjudicating, acting or failing to act, do not become stagnant backwaters of caprice and lawlessness. "Law has reached its finest moments when it has freed man from the unlimited discretion of some ruler, some civil or military official, some bureaucrat." *United States* v. *Wunderlich*, 342 U.S. 98, 101, 72 S.Ct. 154, 156, 96 L.Ed. 113 (1951).

For these and other reasons, reliance on prosecutorial discretion, itself a fading talisman, to justify the unreviewability of agency inaction is inappropriate. See generally Stewart & Sunstein, Public Programs and Private Rights, 95 Harv.L.Rev. 1195, 1285–1286, n. 386 (1982) (discussing differences between agency inaction and prosecutorial discretion); Note, Judicial Review of Administrative Inaction, 83 Colum.L. Rev. 627, 658–661 (1983) (same). To the extent arguments about traditional notions of prosecutorial discretion have any force at all in this context, they ought to apply only to an agency's decision to decline to seek penalties against an individual for past conduct, not to a decision to refuse to investigate or take action on a public health, safety, or welfare problem. . . .

The problem of agency refusal to act is one of the pressing problems of the modern administrative state, given the enormous powers, for both good and ill, that agency inaction, like agency action, holds over citizens. As *Dunlop* v. *Bachowski*, 421 U.S. 560, 95 S.Ct. 1851, 44 L.Ed.2d 377 (1975), recognized, the problems and dangers of agency inaction are too important, too prevalent, and too multifaceted to admit of a single facile solution under which "enforcement" decisions are "presumptively unreviewable." Over time, I believe the approach announced today will come to be understood, not as mandating that courts cover their eyes and their reasoning power when asked to review an agency's failure to act, but as recognizing that courts must approach the substantive task of reviewing such failures with appropriate deference to an agency's legitimate need to set policy through the allocation of scarce budgetary and enforcement resources. Because the Court's approach, if taken literally, would take the courts out of the role of reviewing agency inaction in far too many cases, I join only the judgment today.

A SAMPLING OF THRESHOLD QUESTIONS: STANDING AND PRIMARY JURISDICTION

Assuming that judicial review is not precluded, the person petitioning a court for review of administrative action may face other barriers, including such "threshold questions" as standing, ripeness, exhaustion, and primary jurisdiction. These are rather technical matters that are of more significance to the legal practitioner than the public administrator, and all are treated extensively in the standard law school texts. The discussion that follows will only sketch the broad outlines of these four issues, giving greater attention to the first and the last of them.

To state these issues in their most brief form, *standing* involves the question of whether a party has a sufficient interest in a controversy to bring an action in court; *ripeness* concerns the issue of whether a problem has matured to the point where it is real and imminent, as opposed to abstract and remote, and thus is appropriate for court review; *exhaustion* (exhaustion of administrative remedies) raises the question of whether a party should be required to pursue further administrative appeal *before* bringing the matter to court; and *primary jurisdiction* involves the somewhat similar but distinct question of whether a court or an administrative body is the appropriate organ to decide the issue in question. On all of these matters the relevant statutory law may provide some answers, but the present law on each of these issues is based on a substantial body of case law as well.

Standing

Standing, a recent analysis suggests, "is part of the law of judicial jurisdiction, that law which defines the role of the courts in society and is, of all law, the most judge-made. Standing in particular determines whom a court may hear make arguments about the legality of an official decision." [32] Barriers to gaining standing were relaxed substantially during the 1960s and 1970s. As an important 1962 Supreme Court case put it, one must demonstrate a "personal stake in the outcome" in order to have standing in a controversy,[33] and many of the more recent standing decisions have amounted to assessments of the presence or absence of such a personal stake. The Supreme Court, for example, accorded standing in one important case when it was able to answer affirmatively "the question whether the interest to be protected by the complainant is arguably within the zone of interests to be protected by the statute or constitutional guarantee in question." *Association of Data Processing Service Organizations, Inc.* v. *Camp*, 397 U.S. 150, 153, 90 S.Ct. 827, 830, 25 L.Ed.2d 184, 188 (1970). However, it denied standing in another significant case where it found "a mere interest in a problem" rather than "injury in fact." *Sierra Club* v. *Morton*, 405 U.S. 727, 92 S.Ct. 1361, 31 L.Ed.2d 636 (1972).

---

[32] Joseph Vining, *Legal Identity* 1 (1978). The author also notes that in this area of judge-made law it is difficult to find a common thread in recent judicial decisions. Judicial behavior, he says, is "erratic, even bizarre." Ibid.

[33] *Baker* v. *Carr*, 369 U.S. 186, 204, 82 S.Ct. 691, 703, 7 L.Ed.2d 663, 678 (1962).

In 1983 Kenneth C. Davis characterized the law of standing in the following manner:

> The main failure of the law of standing is neither that the judicial doors are in general opened too much nor that they are opened too little; the main failure is the inconsistency, unreliability and inordinate complexity.[34]

The 1983 case set forth below at the very minimum illustrates the inordinate complexities of present standing law. Furthermore, it reveals the Court's predisposition to make it more difficult for civil rights litigants to obtain injunctive relief.

City of Los Angeles v. Lyons

SUPREME COURT OF THE UNITED STATES, 1983.
461 U.S. 95, 103 S.CT. 1660, 75 L.ED. 675.

[The respondent, Adolph Lyons, was stopped during the early morning hours by officers of the Los Angeles Police Department for a vehicle code violation, namely, one of his taillights was burned out according to Lyons' undisputed testimony. Even though Lyons offered no resistance, the officers seized him and applied a "chokehold" which rendered him unconscious and damaged his larynx. Lyons subsequently filed a complaint in the U.S. District Court against the City of Los Angeles and the police officers for damages and for both injunctive and declaratory relief. The excerpts below deal primarily with the fifth count of the complaint, which sought a preliminary and permanent injunction barring the use of control holds "except in situations where the proposed victim of said control reasonably appears to be threatening the immediate use of deadly force." In the final count of the complaint, Lyons sought a declaratory judgment against the city, namely, a ruling that the use of chokeholds in the absence of a deadly force threat would constitute a per se violation of various constitutional rights.

In the injunctive relief count Lyons alleged that the police officers, "pursuant to the authorization, instruction and encouragement of defendant City of Los Angeles, regularly and routinely apply these chokeholds in innumerable situations where they are not threatened by the use of any deadly force whatsoever," that a number of individuals have been injured as a result of the application of the chokeholds, that Lyons and others in similar situations face irreparable injury or even loss of life, and that Lyons "justifiably fears that any contact he has with Los Angeles police officers may result in his being choked and strangled to death without provocation, justification or other legal excuse."

The U.S. district court, on remand, entered a preliminary injunction prohibiting "the use of both the carotid-artery and bar arm holds under circumstances which do not threaten death or serious bodily injury." The Court of Appeals for the Ninth Circuit affirmed, stating that the district court had not abused its discretion in the issuance of the preliminary injunction. The Supreme Court granted certiorari.]

Justice WHITE delivered the opinion of the Court.

The issue here is whether respondent Lyons satisfied the prerequisites for seek-

---

[34] 4 *Administrative Law Treatise*, 208 (2d ed., 1983).

ing injunctive relief in the federal district court. . . .

It goes without saying that those who seek to invoke the jurisdiction of the federal courts must satisfy the threshold requirement imposed by Article III of the Constitution by alleging an actual case or controversy. . . . Plaintiffs must demonstrate a "personal stake in the outcome" in order to "assure that concrete adverseness which sharpens the presentation of issues" necessary for the proper resolution of constitutional questions. *Baker* v. *Carr*, 369 U.S. 186, 204, 82 S.Ct. 691, 703, 7 L.Ed.2d 663 (1962). Abstract injury is not enough. The plaintiff must show that he "has sustained or is immediately in danger of sustaining some direct injury" as the result of the challenged official conduct and the injury or threat of injury must be both "real and immediate," not "conjectural" or "hypothetical." . . .

In *O'Shea* v. *Littleton*, 414 U.S. 488, 94 S.Ct. 669, 38 L.Ed.2d 674 (1974), we dealt with a case brought by a class of plaintiffs claiming that they had been subjected to discriminatory enforcement of the criminal law. Among other things, a county magistrate and judge were accused of discriminatory conduct in various respects, such as sentencing members of plaintiff's class more harshly than other defendants. The Court of Appeals reversed the dismissal of the suit by the District Court, ruling that if the allegations were proved, an appropriate injunction could be entered.

We reversed for failure of the complaint to allege a case or controversy. . . . Although it was claimed in that case that particular members of the plaintiff class had actually suffered from the alleged unconstitutional practices, we observed that "[p]ast exposure to illegal conduct does not in itself show a present case or controversy regarding injunctive relief . . . if unaccompanied by any continuing, present adverse effects." . . . Past wrongs were evidence bearing on "whether there is a real and immediate threat of repeated injury."

. . . But the prospect of future injury rested "on the likelihood that [plaintiffs] will again be arrested for and charged with violations of the criminal law and will again be subjected to bond proceedings, trial, or sentencing before petitioners." . . . The most that could be said for plaintiffs' standing was "that *if* [plaintiffs] proceed to violate an unchallenged law and *if* they are charged, held to answer, and tried in any proceedings before petitioners, they will be subjected to the discriminatory practices that petitioners are alleged to have followed." . . . We could not find a case or controversy in those circumstances: the threat to the plaintiffs was not "sufficiently real and immediate to show an existing controversy simply because they anticipate violating lawful criminal statutes and being tried for their offenses. . . . " . . . Id., at 496, 94 S.Ct., at 676. It was to be assumed "that [plaintiffs] will conduct their activities within the law and so avoid prosecution and conviction as well as exposure to the challenged course of conduct said to be followed by petitioners." . . .

We further observed that case or controversy considerations "obviously shade into those determining whether the complaint states a sound basis for equitable relief," . . . and went on to hold that even if the complaint presented an existing case or controversy, an adequate basis for equitable relief against petitioners had not been demonstrated:

> [Plaintiffs] have failed, moreover, to establish the basic requisites of the issuance of equitable relief in these circumstances—the likelihood of substantial and immediate irreparable injury, and the inadequacy of remedies at law. We have already canvassed the necessarily conjectural nature of the threatened injury to which [plaintiffs] are allegedly subjected. And if any of the [plaintiffs] are ever prosecuted and face trial, or if they are illegally sentenced, there are available state and federal procedures which could provide relief from the wrongful conduct alleged. . . .

Another relevant decision for present purposes is *Rizzo* v. *Goode*, 423 U.S. 362, 96 S.Ct. 598, 46 L.Ed.2d 561 (1976), a case in which plaintiffs alleged widespread illegal and unconstitutional police conduct aimed at minority citizens and against City residents in general. The Court reiterated the holding in *O'Shea* that past wrongs do not in themselves amount to that real and immediate threat of injury necessary to make out a case or controversy. The claim of injury rested upon "what one or a small, unnamed minority of policemen might do to them in the future because of that unknown policeman's perception" of departmental procedures.... This hypothesis was "even more attenuated than those allegations of future injury found insufficient in *O'Shea* to warrant [the] invocation of federal jurisdiction." ... The Court also held that plaintiffs' showing at trial of a relatively few instances of violations by individual police officers, without any showing of a deliberate policy on behalf of the named defendants, did not provide a basis for equitable relief....

No extension of *O'Shea* and *Rizzo* is necessary to hold that respondent Lyons has failed to demonstrate a case or controversy with the City that would justify the equitable relief sought. Lyons' standing to seek the injunction requested depended on whether he was likely to suffer future injury from the use of the chokeholds by police officers. Count V of the complaint alleged the traffic stop and choking incident five months before. That Lyons may have been illegally choked by the police on October 6, 1976, while presumably affording Lyons standing to claim damages against the individual officers and perhaps against the City, does nothing to establish a real and immediate threat that he would again be stopped for a traffic violation, or for any other offense, by an officer or officers who would illegally choke him into unconsciousness without any provocation or resistance on his part. The additional allegation in the complaint that the police in Los Angeles routinely apply chokeholds in situations where they are not threatened by the use of deadly force falls far short of the allegations that would be necessary to establish a case or controversy between these parties.

In order to establish an actual controversy in this case, Lyons would have had not only to allege that he would have another encounter with the police but also to make the incredible assertion either, (1) that *all* police officers in Los Angeles *always* choke any citizen with whom they happen to have an encounter, whether for the purpose of arrest, issuing a citation or for questioning or, (2) that the City ordered or authorized police officers to act in such manner. Although Count V alleged that the City authorized the use of the control holds in situations where deadly force was not threatened, it did not indicate why Lyons might be realistically threatened by police officers who acted within the strictures of the City's policy. If, for example, chokeholds were authorized to be used only to counter resistance to an arrest by a suspect, or to thwart an effort to escape, any future threat to Lyons from the City's policy or from the conduct of police officers would be no more real than the possibility that he would again have an encounter with the police and that either he would illegally resist arrest or detention or the officers would disobey their instructions and again render him unconscious without any provocation.

Under *O'Shea* and *Rizzo*, these allegations were an insufficient basis to provide a federal court with jurisdiction to entertain Count V of the complaint. This was apparently the conclusion of the District Court in dismissing Lyons' claim for injunctive relief. Although the District Court acted without opinion or findings, the Court of Appeals interpreted its action as based on lack of standing, i.e., that under *O'Shea* and *Rizzo*, Lyons must be held to have made an "insufficient showing that the police were likely to do this to the plaintiff again." . . . For several reasons—each of them infirm, in our view—the Court of Appeals thought reliance on *O'Shea* and *Rizzo* was misplaced and reversed the District Court.

First, the Court of Appeals thought that Lyons was more immediately threatened than the plaintiffs in those cases since, according to the Court of Appeals, Lyons need only be stopped for a minor traffic violation to be subject to the strangleholds. But even assuming that Lyons would again be stopped for a traffic or other violation in the reasonably near future, it is untenable to assert, and the complaint made no such allegation, that strangleholds are applied by the Los Angeles police to every citizen who is stopped or arrested regardless of the conduct of the person stopped. We cannot agree that the "odds" . . . that Lyons would not only again be stopped for a traffic violation but would also be subjected to a chokehold without any provocation whatsoever are sufficient to make out a federal case for equitable relief. We note that five months elapsed between October 6, 1976, and the filing of the complaint, yet there was no allegation of further unfortunate encounters between Lyons and the police.

Of course, it may be that among the countless encounters between the police and the citizens of a great city such as Los Angeles, there will be certain instances in which strangleholds will be illegally applied and injury and death unconstitutionally inflicted on the victim. As we have said, however, it is no more than conjecture to suggest that in every instance of a traffic stop, arrest, or other encounter between the police and a citizen, the police will act unconstitutionally and inflict injury without provocation or legal excuse. And it is surely no more than speculation to assert either that Lyons himself will again be involved in one of those unfortunate instances, or that he will be arrested in the future and provoke the use of a chokehold by resisting arrest, attempting to escape, or threatening deadly force or serious bodily injury.

Second, the Court of Appeals viewed *O'Shea* and *Rizzo* as cases in which the plaintiffs sought "massive structural" relief against the local law enforcement systems and therefore that the holdings in those cases were inapposite to cases such as this where the plaintiff, according to the Court of Appeals, seeks to enjoin only an "established," "sanctioned" police practice assertedly violative of constitutional rights. *O'Shea* and *Rizzo*, however, cannot be so easily confined to their facts. If Lyons has made no showing that he is realistically threatened by a repetition of his experience of October, 1976, then he has not met the requirements for seeking an injunction in a federal court, whether the injunction contemplates intrusive structural relief or the cessation of a discrete practice. . . .

Our conclusion is that the Court of Appeals failed to heed *O'Shea*, *Rizzo*, and other relevant authority, and that the District Court was quite right in dismissing Count V.

Lyons fares no better if it be assumed that his pending damages suit affords him Article III standing to seek an injunction as a remedy for the claim arising out of the October 1976 events. The equitable remedy is unavailable absent a showing of irreparable injury, a requirement that cannot be met where there is no showing of any real or immediate threat that the plaintiff will be wronged again—a "likelihood of substantial and immediate irreparable injury." . . . The speculative nature of Lyons' claim of future injury requires a finding that this prerequisite of equitable relief has not been fulfilled.

Nor will the injury that Lyons allegedly suffered in 1976 go unrecompensed; for that injury, he has an adequate remedy at law. Contrary to the view of the Court of Appeals, it is not at all "difficult" under our holding "to see how anyone can ever challenge police or similar administrative practices." . . . The legality of the violence to which Lyons claims he was once subjected is at issue in his suit for damages and can be determined there.

Absent a sufficient likelihood that he will again be wronged in a similar way, Lyons is no more entitled to an injunction than any other citizen of Los Angeles; and a federal court may not entertain a claim by any or all citizens who no more than assert that certain practices of law enforcement officers are unconstitutional.... This is not to suggest that such undifferentiated claims should not be taken seriously by local authorities. Indeed, the interest of an alert and interested citizen is an essential element of an effective and fair government, whether on the local, state or national level. A federal court, however, is not the proper forum to press such claims unless the requirements for entry and the prerequisites for injunctive relief are satisfied.

We decline the invitation to slight the preconditions for equitable relief, for as we have held, recognition of the need for a proper balance between state and federal authority counsels restraint in the issuance of injunctions against state officers engaged in the administration of the states' criminal laws in the absence of irreparable injury which is both great and immediate.... But this holding did not displace the normal principles of equity, comity and federalism that should inform the judgment of federal courts when asked to oversee state law enforcement authorities. In exercising their equitable powers federal courts must recognize "[t]he special delicacy of the adjustment to be preserved between federal equitable power and State administration of its own law." ... The Court of Appeals failed to apply these factors properly and therefore erred in finding that the District Court had not abused its discretion in entering an injunction in this case.

As we noted in *O'Shea*, 414 U.S., at 503, 94 S.Ct., at 679, withholding injunctive relief does not mean that the "federal law

will exercise no deterrent effect in these circumstances." If Lyons has suffered an injury barred by the Federal Constitution, he has a remedy for damages under § 1983. Furthermore, those who deliberately deprive a citizen of his constitutional rights risk conviction under the federal criminal laws....

Beyond these considerations the state courts need not impose the same standing or remedial requirements that govern federal-court proceedings. The individual States may permit their courts to use injunctions to oversee the conduct of law enforcement authorities on a continuing basis. But this is not the role of a federal court, absent far more justification than Lyons has proffered in this case.

The judgment of the Court of Appeals is accordingly

Reversed.

Justice MARSHALL, with whom Justice BRENNAN, Justice BLACKMUN, and Justice STEVENS join, dissenting.

The District Court found that the city of Los Angeles authorizes its police officers to apply life-threatening chokeholds to citizens who pose no threat of violence, and that respondent, Adolph Lyons, was subjected to such a chokehold. The Court today holds that a federal court is without power to enjoin the enforcement of the city's policy, no matter how flagrantly unconstitutional it may be. Since no one can show that he will be choked in the future, no one—not even a person who, like Lyons, has almost been choked to death—has standing to challenge the continuation of the policy. The city is free to continue the policy indefinitely as long as it is willing to pay damages for the injuries and deaths that result. I dissent from this unprecedented and unwarranted approach to standing.

There is plainly a "case or controversy" concerning the constitutionality of the city's chokehold policy. The constitutionality of that policy is directly implicated by Lyons' claim for damages against the city.

The complaint clearly alleges that the officer who choked Lyons was carrying out an official policy, and a municipality is liable under 42 U.S.C. § 1983 for the conduct of its employees only if they acted pursuant to such a policy. . . . Lyons therefore has standing to challenge the city's chokehold policy and to obtain whatever relief a court may ultimately deem appropriate. None of our prior decisions suggests that his requests for particular forms of relief raise any additional issues concerning his standing. Standing has always depended on whether a plaintiff has a "personal stake in the outcome of the controversy," . . . not on the "precise nature of the relief sought." . . .

Respondent Adolph Lyons is a 24-year-old Negro male who resides in Los Angeles. According to the uncontradicted evidence in the record, at about 2 a.m. on October 6, 1976, Lyons was pulled over to the curb by two officers of the Los Angeles Police Department (LAPD) for a traffic infraction because one of his taillights was burned out. The officers greeted him with drawn revolvers as he exited from his car. Lyons was told to face his car and spread his legs. He did so. He was then ordered to clasp his hands and put them on top of his head. He again complied. After one of the officers completed a pat-down search, Lyons dropped his hands, but was ordered to place them back above his head, and one of the officers grabbed Lyons' hands and slammed them onto his head. Lyons complained about the pain caused by the ring of keys he was holding in his hand. Within five to ten seconds, the officer began to choke Lyons by applying a forearm against his throat. As Lyons struggled for air, the officer handcuffed him, but continued to apply the chokehold until he blacked out. When Lyons regained consciousness, he was lying face down on the ground, choking, gasping for air, and spitting up blood and dirt. He had urinated and defecated. He was issued a traffic citation and released.

On February 7, 1977, Lyons commenced this action under 42 U.S.C. § 1983 against the individual officers and the City, alleging violations of his rights under the Fourth, Eighth, and Fourteenth Amendments to the Constitution and seeking damages and declaratory and injunctive relief. . . .

Although the City instructs its officers that use of a chokehold does not constitute deadly force, since 1975 no less than 16 persons have died following the use of a chokehold by an LAPD police officer. Twelve have been Negro males. The evidence submitted to the District Court established that for many years it has been the official policy of the City to permit police officers to employ chokeholds in a variety of situations where they face no threat of violence. In reported "altercations" between LAPD officers and citizens the chokeholds are used more frequently than any other means of physical restraint. Between February 1975 and July 1980, LAPD officers applied chokeholds on at least 975 occasions, which represented more than three-quarters of the reported altercations.

It is undisputed that chokeholds pose a high and unpredictable risk of serious injury or death. Chokeholds are intended to bring a subject under control by causing pain and rendering him unconscious. Depending on the position of the officer's arm and the force applied, the victim's voluntary or involuntary reaction, and his state of health, an officer may inadvertently crush the victim's larynx, trachea, or thyroid. The result may be death caused by either cardiac arrest or asphyxiation. An LAPD officer described the reaction of a person to being choked as "do[ing] the chicken," . . . in reference apparently to the reactions of a chicken when its neck is wrung. The victim experiences extreme pain. His face turns blue as he is deprived of oxygen, he goes into spasmodic convulsions, his eyes roll back, his body wriggles, his feet kick up and down, and his arms move about wildly. . . .

At the outset it is important to emphasize that Lyons' entitlement to injunctive relief and his entitlement to an award of damages both depend upon whether he can show that the City's chokehold policy violates the Constitution. An indispensable prerequisite of municipal liability under 42 U.S.C. § 1983 is proof that the conduct complained of is attributable to an unconstitutional official policy or custom. . . . It is not enough for a § 1983 plaintiff to show that the employees or agents of a municipality have violated or will violate the Constitution, for a municipality will not be held liable solely on a theory of *respondeat superior* . . . .

In sum, it's absolutely clear that Lyons' requests for damages and for injunctive relief call into question the constitutionality of the City's policy concerning the use of chokeholds. If he does not show that that policy is unconstitutional, he will be no more entitled to damages than to an injunction.

Since Lyons' claim for damages plainly gives him standing, and since the success of that claim depends upon a demonstration that the City's chokehold policy is unconstitutional, it is beyond dispute that Lyons has properly invoked the District Court's authority to adjudicate the constitutionality of the City's chokehold policy. The dispute concerning the constitutionality of that policy plainly presents a "case or controversy" under Article III. The Court nevertheless holds that a federal court has no power under Article III to adjudicate Lyons' request, in the same lawsuit, for injunctive relief with respect to that very policy. This anomalous result is not supported either by precedent or by the fundamental concern underlying the standing requirement. Moreover, by fragmenting a single claim into multiple claims for particular types of relief and requiring a separate showing of standing for each form of relief, the decision today departs

from this Court's traditional conception of standing and of the remedial powers of the federal courts. . . .

The Court's decision likewise finds no support in the fundamental policy underlying the Article III standing requirement—the concern that a federal court not decide a legal issue if the plaintiff lacks a sufficient "personal stake in the outcome of the controversy as to assure that concrete adverseness which sharpens the presentation of issues upon which the court so largely depends for illumination of difficult . . . questions." . . . As this Court stated in *Flast* v. *Cohen*, 392 U.S. 83, 101, 88 S.Ct. 1942, 1953, 20 L.Ed.2d 947 (1968), "the question of standing is related only to whether the dispute sought to be adjudicated will be presented in an adversary context and in a form historically viewed as capable of judicial resolution."

Because Lyons has a claim for damages against the City, and because he cannot prevail on that claim unless he demonstrates that the City's chokehold policy violates the Constitution, his personal stake in the outcome of the controversy adequately assures an adversary presentation of his challenge to the constitutionality of the policy. Moreover, the resolution of this challenge will be largely dispositive of his requests for declaratory and injunctive relief. No doubt the requests for injunctive relief may raise additional questions. But these questions involve familiar issues relating to the appropriateness of particular forms of relief, and have never been thought to implicate a litigant's standing to sue. The denial of standing separately to seek injunctive relief therefore cannot be justified by the basic concern underlying the Article III standing requirement.

By fragmenting the standing inquiry and imposing a separate standing hurdle with respect to each form of relief sought, the decision today departs significantly from this Court's traditional conception of the standing requirement and of the remedial powers of the federal courts. We have never required more than that a plaintiff have standing to litigate a claim. Whether he will be entitled to obtain particular forms of relief should he prevail has never been understood to be an issue of standing. In determining whether a plaintiff has standing, we have always focused on his personal stake in the outcome of the controversy, not on the issues sought to be litigated, . . . or the "precise nature of the relief sought." . . .

Our cases uniformly state that the touchstone of the Article III standing requirement is the plaintiff's personal stake in the underlying dispute, not in the particular types of relief sought. Once a plaintiff establishes a personal stake in a dispute, he has done all that is necessary to "invok[e] the court's authority . . . to challenge the action sought to be adjudicated." . . .

The personal stake of a litigant depends, in turn, on whether he has alleged a legally redressable injury. In determining whether a plaintiff has a sufficient personal stake in the outcome of a controversy, this Court has asked whether he "personally has suffered some actual *or* threatened injury," . . . whether the injury "fairly can be traced to the challenged action." . . . and whether plaintiff's injury "is likely to be redressed by a favorable decision." . . . These well-accepted criteria for determining whether a plaintiff has established the requisite personal stake do not fragment the standing inquiry into a series of discrete questions about the plaintiff's stake in each of the particular types of relief sought. Quite the contrary, they ask simply whether the plaintiff has a sufficient stake in seeking a judicial resolution of the controversy.

Lyons has alleged past injury and a risk of future injury and has linked both to the City's chokehold policy. Under established principles, the only additional question in determining standing under Article III is whether the injuries he has alleged can be remedied or prevented by *some* form of judicial relief. Satisfaction of this requirement ensures that the lawsuit does not entail the issuance of an advisory opinion without the possibility of any judicial relief, and that the exercise of a court's remedial powers will actually redress the alleged injury. Therefore Lyons needs to demonstrate only that, should he prevail on the merits, "the exercise of the Court's remedial powers would redress the claimed injuries." . . . Lyons has easily made this showing here, for monetary relief would plainly provide redress for his past injury, and prospective relief would reduce the likelihood of any future injury. Nothing more has ever been required to establish standing.

The Court's decision turns these well accepted principles on their heads by requiring a separate standing inquiry with respect to each request for relief. Until now, questions concerning remedy were relevant to the threshold issue of standing only in the limited sense that some relief must be possible. The approach adopted today drastically alters the inquiry into remedy that must be made to determine standing. . . .

Apparently because it is unwilling to rely solely on its unprecedented rule of standing, the Court goes on to conclude that, even if Lyons has standing, "[t]he equitable remedy is unavailable." *Ante*, at 1670. The Court's reliance on this alternative ground is puzzling for two reasons.

If, as the Court says, Lyons lacks standing under Article III, the federal courts have no power to decide his entitlement to equitable relief on the merits. . . . Under the Court's own view of Article III, the Court's discussion in Part V is purely an advisory opinion.

In addition, the question whether injunctive relief is available under equitable principles is simply not before us. We granted certiorari only to determine whether Lyons has standing and whether, if so, the preliminary injunction must be set aside because it constitutes an impermissible interference in the operation of a municipal police department. We did not grant certiorari to consider whether Lyons satisfies the traditional prerequisites for equitable relief. . . .

Even if the issue had been properly raised, I could not agree with the Court's disposition of it. . . .

The Court's decision removes an entire class of constitutional violations from the equitable powers of a federal court. It immunizes from prospective equitable relief any policy that authorizes persistent deprivations of constitutional rights as long as no individual can establish with substantial certainty that he will be injured, or injured again, in the future. THE CHIEF JUSTICE asked in *Bivens* v. *Six Unknown Fed. Narcotics Agents*, 403 U.S. 388, 419, 91 S.Ct. 1999, 2016, 29 L.Ed.2d 619 (1971) (dis-

senting opinion), "what would be the judicial response to a police order authorizing 'shoot to kill' with respect to every fugitive?" His answer was that it would be "easy to predict our collective wrath and outrage." Ibid. We now learn that wrath and outrage cannot be translated into an order to cease the unconstitutional practice, but only an award of damages to those who are victimized by the practice and live to sue and to the survivors of those who are not so fortunate. Under the view expressed by the majority today, if the police adopt a policy of "shoot to kill," or a policy of shooting one out of ten suspects, the federal courts will be powerless to enjoin its continuation. . . . The federal judicial power is now limited to levying a toll for such a systematic constitutional violation.

Primary Jurisdiction

A court may decline to review an agency's act because further recourse to the administrative process is still available. This is what is involved in exhaustion of administrative remedies. There are some circumstances, however, in which both a court and an agency arguably have the authority to consider the same issue. The question then arises as to which body should have *primary* jurisdiction. The difference between exhaustion and primary jurisdiction was stated as follows in a 1956 Supreme Court case:

> Exhaustion applies where a claim is cognizable in the first instance by an administrative agency alone; judicial interference is withheld until the administrative process has run its course. "Primary jurisdiction," on the other hand, applies where a claim is originally cognizable in the courts, and comes into play whenever enforcement of the claim requires the resolution of issues which, under a regulatory scheme, have been placed within the special competence of an administrative body; in such a case the judicial process is suspended pending referral of such issues to the administrative body for its views. United States v. Western Pacific Railroad Co., 352 U.S. 59, 63–64, 77 S.Ct. 161, 165, 1 L.Ed.2d 126, 132 (1956).

There may be good reasons why a party would want a court rather than an agency to rule on an issue, but this may be contested by the other party to the controversy. This is the issue in the following case, a recent primary jurisdiction ruling.

Nader v. Allegheny Airlines, Inc.

SUPREME COURT OF THE UNITED STATES, 1976.
426 U.S. 290, 96 S.CT. 1978, 48 L.ED.2D 643.

[Ralph Nader held a confirmed reservation on a scheduled Allegheny Airlines flight from Washington, D.C., to Hartford, Connecticut, where he was to make two speeches. When he arrived for the flight he was informed that all seats were occupied and that he, like several other passengers, could not be accommodated. It was acknowledged by Allegheny that Nader's reservation was not honored because more reservations had been accepted for the flight than there were available seats. Such overbooking was a common airlines industry practice aimed at coping with the problem of "no-shows"—reservation-holding passengers who did not appear. Such overbooking sometimes resulted in more passengers appearing than could be accommodated, and when this occurred, some passengers would be denied boarding ("bumped"). As a result of being bumped, Nader filed suit in U.S. District Court for compensatory and punitive damages based on, among other grounds, fraudulent misrepresentation for failure to inform Nader in advance of the deliberate overbooking practices. The District Court ruled for Nader and awarded him $10 in compensatory damages and $25,000 in punitive damages. The Court of Appeals reversed. The case came to the Supreme Court on certiorari. The excerpt below deals basically with the issue of primary jurisdiction. Despite the Supreme Court's ruling on the primary jurisdiction question, Ralph Nader eventually lost his suit

against Allegheny Airlines—he received neither compensatory nor punitive damages as a result of the "bumping" episode. 626 F.2d 1031.]

Mr. Justice POWELL delivered the opinion of the Court.

In this case we address the question whether a common-law tort action based on alleged fraudulent misrepresentation by an air carrier subject to regulation by the Civil Aeronautics Board (Board) must be stayed pending reference to the Board for determination whether the practice is "deceptive" within the meaning of § 411 of the Federal Aviation Act of 1958, 72 Stat. 769, 49 U.S.C.A. § 1381. We hold that under the circumstances of this case a stay pending reference is inappropriate. . . .

The only issue before us concerns the Court of Appeals' disposition on the merits of petitioner's claim of fraudulent misrepresentation. Although the court rejected respondent's argument that the existence of the Board's cease-and-desist power under § 411 of the Act eliminates all private remedies for common-law torts arising from unfair or deceptive practices by regulated carriers, it held that a determination by the Board that a practice is not deceptive within the meaning of § 411 would, as a matter of law, preclude a common-law tort action seeking damages for injuries caused by that practice.[35] Therefore, the court held that the Board must be allowed to determine in the first instance whether the challenged practice (in this case, the al-

---

[35] Section 411 provides in full:

"The Board may, upon its own initiative or upon complaint by any air carrier, foreign air carrier, or ticket agent, if it considers that such action by it would be in the interest of the public, investigate and determine whether any air carrier, foreign air carrier, or ticket agent has been or is engaged in unfair or deceptive practices or unfair methods of competition in air transportation or the sale thereof. If the Board shall find, after notice and hearing, that such air carrier, foreign air carrier, or ticket agent is engaged in such unfair or deceptive practices or unfair methods of competition, it shall order such air carrier, foreign air carrier, or ticket agent to cease and desist from such practices or methods of competition."

leged failure to disclose the practice of overbooking) falls within the ambit of § 411. The court took judicial notice that a rulemaking proceeding concerning possible changes in reservation practices in response to the 1973–1974 fuel crisis was already underway and that a challenge to the carriers' overbooking practices had been raised by an intervenor in that proceeding. The District Court was instructed to stay further action on petitioner's misrepresentation claim pending the outcome of the rulemaking proceeding. The Court of Appeals characterized its holding as "but another application of the principles of primary jurisdiction, a doctrine whose purpose is the coordination of the workings of agency and court." 167 U.S.App. D.C., at 367, 512 F.2d, at 544.

II

The question before us, then, is whether the Board must be given an opportunity to determine whether respondent's alleged failure to disclose its practice of deliberate overbooking is a deceptive practice under § 411 before petitioner's common-law action is allowed to proceed. The decision of the Court of Appeals requires the District Court to stay the action brought by petitioner in order to give the Board an opportunity to resolve the question. If the Board were to find that there had been no violation of § 411, respondent would be immunized from common-law liability.

A

Section 1106 of the Act, 49 U.S.C.A. § 1506, provides that "[n]othing contained in this chapter shall in any way abridge or alter the remedies now existing at common law or by statute, but the provisions of this chapter are in addition to such remedies." The Court of Appeals found that "although the saving clause of section 1106 purports to speak in absolute terms it cannot be read so literally." 167 U.S.App.D.C., at 367,

512 F.2d, at 544. In reaching this conclusion, it relied on Texas & Pacific R. Co. v. Abilene Cotton Oil Co., 204 U.S. 426, 27 S.Ct. 350, 51 L.Ed. 553 (1907). In that case, the Court, despite the existence of a saving clause virtually identical to § 1106, refused to permit a state-court common-law action challenging a published carrier rate as "unjust and unreasonable." The Court conceded that a common-law right, even absent a saving clause, is not to be abrogated "unless it be found that the preexisting right is so repugnant to the statute that the survival of such right would in effect deprive the subsequent statute of its efficacy; in other words, render its provisions nugatory." 204 U.S., at 437, 27 S.Ct., at 354, 51 L.Ed., at 557. But the Court found that the continuance of private damages actions attacking the reasonableness of rates subject to the regulation of the Interstate Commerce Commission would destroy the purpose of the Interstate Commerce Act, which was to eliminate discrimination by requiring uniform rates. The saving clause, the Court found, "cannot in reason be construed as continuing in shippers a common law right, the continued existence of which would be absolutely inconsistent with the provisions of the act. In other words, the act cannot be held to destroy itself." Id., at 446, 27 S.Ct., at 358, 51 L.Ed., at 561.

In this case, unlike *Abilene*, we are not faced with an irreconcilable conflict between the statutory scheme and the persistence of common-law remedies. In *Abilene* the carrier, if subject to both agency and court sanctions, would be put in an untenable position when the agency and a court disagreed on the reasonableness of a rate. The carrier could not abide by the rate filed with the Commission, as required by statute, and also comply with a court's determination that the rate was excessive. The conflict between the court's common-law authority and the agency's rate-making power was direct and unambiguous. The court in the present case, in contrast, is not called upon to substitute its judgment for the agency's on the reasonableness of a rate—or, indeed, on the reasonableness of any carrier practice. There is no Board requirement that air carriers engage in overbooking or that they fail to disclose that they do so. And any impact on rates that may result from the imposition of tort liability or from practices adopted by a carrier to avoid such liability would be merely incidental. Under the circumstances, the common-law action and the statute are not "absolutely inconsistent" and may coexist, as contemplated by § 1106.

B

Section 411 of the Act allows the Board, where "it considers that such action . . . would be in the interest of the public," "upon its own initiative or upon complaint by any air carrier, foreign air carrier, or ticket agent," to "investigate and determine whether any air carrier . . . has been or is engaged in unfair or deceptive practices or unfair methods of competition. . . . " Practices determined to be in violation of this section "shall" be the subject of a cease-and-desist order. The Court of Appeals concluded—and respondent does not challenge the conclusion here—that this section does not totally preclude petitioner's common-law tort action. But the Court of Appeals also held, relying on the nature of the airline industry as "a regulated system of limited competition," *American Airlines, Inc. v. North American Airlines, Inc.,* 351 U.S. 79, 84, 76 S.Ct. 600, 604, 100 L.Ed. 953, 961 (1956), and the Board's duty to promote "adequate, economical, and efficient service," § 102(c) of the Act, 49 U.S.C.A. § 1302(c), "at the lowest cost consistent with the furnishing of such service," § 1002(e)(2) of the Act, 49 U.S.C.A. § 1482(e)(2), that the Board has the power in a § 411 proceeding to approve practices that might otherwise be considered deceptive and thus to immunize carriers from common-law liability. 167 U.S. App.D.C., at 366, 512 F.2d, at 543.

We cannot agree. No power to immunize can be derived from the language of § 411. . . . Section 411 . . . is purely restrictive. It contemplates the elimination of "unfair or deceptive practices" that impair the public interest. . . . As such, § 411 provides an injunctive remedy for vindication of the public interest to supplement the compensatory common-law remedies for private parties preserved by § 1106.

Thus, a violation of § 411, contrary to the Court of Appeals' conclusion, is not coextensive with a breach of duty under the common law. . . .

In sum, § 411 confers upon the Board a new and powerful weapon against unfair and deceptive practices that injure the public. But it does not represent the only, or best, response to all challenged carrier actions that result in private wrongs.

C

The doctrine of primary jurisdiction "is concerned with promoting proper relationships between the courts and administrative agencies charged with particular regulatory duties." *United States v. Western Pacific R. Co.,* 352 U.S. 59, 63, 77 S.Ct. 161, 165, 1 L.Ed.2d 126, 132 (1956). Even when common-law rights and remedies survive and the agency in question lacks the power to confer immunity from common-law liability, it may be appropriate to refer specific issues to an agency for initial determination where that procedure would secure "[u]niformity and consistency in the regulation of business entrusted to a particular agency" or where

the limited functions of review by the judiciary [would be] more rationally exercised, by preliminary resort for ascertaining and interpreting the circumstances underlying legal issues to agencies that are better equipped than courts by specialization, by insight gained through experience, and by more flexible procedure. *Far East Conference v.*

United States, 342 U.S., at 574–575, 72 S.Ct., at 494, 96 L.Ed., at 582.

The doctrine has been applied, for example, when an action otherwise within the jurisdiction of the court raises a question of the validity of a rate or practice included in a tariff filed with an agency, e.g., Danna v. Air France, 463 F.2d 407 (C.A.2 1972); Southwestern Sugar & Molasses Co. v. River Terminals Corp., 360 U.S. 411, 417–418, 79 S.Ct. 1210, 1214–1215, 3 L.Ed.2d 1334, 1340–1341 (1959), particularly when the issue involves technical questions of fact uniquely within the expertise and experience of an agency—such as matters turning on an assessment of industry conditions, e.g., United States v. Western Pacific R. Co., supra, 352 U.S., at 66–67, 77 S.Ct., at 166, 1 L.Ed.2d, at 133–134. In this case, however, considerations of uniformity in regulation and of technical expertise do not call for prior reference to the Board.

Petitioner seeks damages for respondent's failure to disclose its overbooking practices. He makes no challenge to any provision in the tariff, and indeed there is no tariff provision or Board regulation applicable to disclosure practices. Petitioner also makes no challenge, comparable to those made in Southwestern Sugar & Molasses Co. v. River Terminals Corp., supra, and Lichten v. Eastern Airlines, Inc., 189 F.2d 939 (C.A.2 1951), to limitations on common-law damages imposed through exculpatory clauses included in a tariff.

Referral of the misrepresentation issue to the Board cannot be justified by the interest in informing the court's ultimate decision with "the expert and specialized knowledge," United States v. Western Pacific R. Co., supra, at 64, 77 S.Ct., at 165, 1 L.Ed.2d, at 132, of the Board. The action brought by petitioner does not turn on a determination of the reasonableness of a challenged practice—a determination that could be facilitated by an informed evaluation of the economics or technology of the regulated industry. The standards to be applied in an action for fraudulent misrepresentation are within the conventional competence of the courts, and the judgment of a technically expert body is not likely to be helpful in the application of these standards to the facts of this case.

We are particularly aware that, even where the wrong sought to be redressed is not misrepresentation but bumping itself, which has been the subject of Board consideration and for which compensation is provided in carrier tariffs, the Board has contemplated that there may be individual adjudications by courts in common-law suits brought at the option of the passenger. The present regulations dealing with the problems of overbooking and oversales were promulgated by the Board in 1967. They provide for denied boarding compensation to bumped passengers and require each carrier to establish priority rules for seating passengers and to file reports of passengers who could not be accommodated. The order instituting these regulations contemplates that the bumped passenger will have a choice between accepting denied boarding compensation as "liquidated damages for all damages incurred ... as a result of the carrier's failure to provide the passenger with confirmed reserved space," or pursuing his or her common-law remedies. The Board specifically provided for a 30-day period before the specified compensation need be accepted so that the passenger will not be forced to make a decision before "the consequences of denied boarding have occurred and are known." After evaluating the consequences, passengers may choose as an alternative "to pursue their remedy under the common law."

III

We conclude that petitioner's tort action should not be stayed pending reference to the Board and accordingly the decision of

the Court of Appeals on this issue is reversed. . . .

[The concurring opinion of Mr. Justice
White is omitted.]

SCOPE OF JUDICIAL REVIEW

Assuming that none of the barriers to judicial review discussed above exists,
the next relevant matter is the scope of review. Scope of review has to do with
the degree or extent of judicial scrutiny of agency action. The extent of review
achieved should strike an appropriate balance: a judicial posture which treats
agency action with too much deference, or too cursorily, tends toward making review meaningless; review that probes too deeply can result in decisions
being made, in effect, by the courts, rather than by the agencies charged with
such functions.

It is generally said that administrators are charged with making findings
of fact while courts decide questions of law. The distinction is stated more
fully by Professor Jaffe as follows:

> The distinction between fact and law is vital to a correct appreciation of the
> respective roles of the administrative and the judiciary. The administrative is the
> sole fact finder. The judiciary may set aside a finding of fact not adequately
> supported by the record, but, with certain exceptions its function is at that point
> exhausted. It has, as it were, a veto but no positive power of determination. On the
> other hand, the administrative and the judiciary share the role of law pronounc-
> ing and law making. They are in partnership. The court may supersede the
> administrative and itself determine the question of law; it is the senior partner.[36]

On review, therefore, the general function of the court is to assure that the
law has been applied correctly and that the administrative decision has a
basis in fact. While these principles have evolved over time through court
articulation, they have to some extent been codified in the statutory law as
well. A good example is the Administrative Procedure Act. As noted earlier in
the chapter, § 701 provides for judicial review except to the extent that it is
precluded by statute or committed to agency discretion. Section 706, on scope
of review, reads as follows:

> To the extent necessary to decision and when presented, the reviewing court shall
> decide all relevant questions of law, interpret constitutional and statutory provi-
> sions, and determine the meaning or applicability of the terms of an agency
> action. The reviewing court shall—

> (1) compel agency action unlawfully withheld or unreasonably delayed; and

> (2) hold unlawful and set aside agency action, findings, and conclusions found to
> be—

>   (A) arbitrary, capricious, an abuse of discretion, or otherwise not in accordance
>   with law;
>   (B) contrary to constitutional right, power, privilege, or immunity;

---

[36] Jaffe, above, note 1, p. 546.

(C) in excess of statutory jurisdiction, authority, or limitations, or short of statutory right;

(D) without observance of procedure required by law;

(E) unsupported by substantial evidence in a case subject to sections 556 and 557 of this title or otherwise reviewed on the record of an agency hearing provided by statute; or

(F) unwarranted by the facts to the extent that the facts are subject to trial de novo by the reviewing court.

In making the foregoing determinations, the court shall review the whole record or those parts of it cited by a party, and due account shall be taken of the rule of prejudicial error.

As the numerous provisions of § 706 suggest, a variety of issues might be treated in this part of the chapter. We will concentrate on a broad examination of just two: the substantial evidence rule and the law-fact distinction.

Substantial Evidence

Section 706(2)(E) of the APA, just quoted, indicates that agency action must be based on substantial evidence. But the substantial evidence test far predates the APA.[37] The precise meaning of the term is not readily apparent. An oft-quoted statement by Chief Justice Hughes is that substantial evidence "is more than a mere scintilla. It means such relevant evidence as a reasonable mind might accept as adequate to support a conclusion." [38] And others have suggested that it represents a compromise between the "clearly erroneous" test, which allows broad judicial review, and a narrower standard that requires agency findings to be upheld when supported by any evidence on the record.[39] Still, there is "often greater difficulty in applying the test than in formulating it." [40] A leading case on the meaning of substantial evidence, decided just a few years after the adoption of the APA, is the *Universal Camera* case.

Universal Camera Corp. v. NLRB

SUPREME COURT OF THE UNITED STATES, 1951.
340 U.S. 474, 71 S.CT. 456, 95 L.ED. 456.

Mr. Justice FRANKFURTER delivered the opinion of the Court.

The essential issue raised by this case and its companion, National Labor Relations Board v. Pittsburgh Steamship Co., 340 U.S. 498, 71 S.Ct. 453, infra, is the effect of the Administrative Procedure Act and the legislation colloquially known as the

---

[37] Schwartz (above, note 25, at 592) writes that the principle of substantial evidence "was first developed in connection with review of the Interstate Commerce Commission." He cites a 1912 ICC case in which the term was used.

[38] *Consolidated Edison Co.* v. *NLRB*, 305 U.S. 197, 229, 59 S.Ct. 206, 217, 83 L.Ed. 126, 140 (1938).

[39] Ernest Gellhorn, *Administrative Law and Process* 265 (1972).

[40] *Stork Restaurant, Inc.* v. *Boland*, 282 N.Y. 256, 274, 26 N.E.2d 247, 255 (1940), as quoted in Schwartz, above, note 25, at 592.

Taft-Hartley Act, 5 U.S.C.A. § 1001 et seq.; 29 U.S.C.A. § 141 et seq., on the duty of Courts of Appeals when called upon to review orders of the National Labor Relations Board.

The Court of Appeals for the Second Circuit granted enforcement of an order directing, in the main, that petitioner reinstate with back pay an employee found to have been discharged because he gave testimony under the Wagner Act, 29 U.S.C.A. § 151 et seq., and cease and desist from discriminating against any employee who files charges or gives testimony under that Act. The court below, Judge Swan dissenting, decreed full enforcement of the order. 2 Cir., 179 F.2d 749. Because the views of that court regarding the effect of the new legislation on the relation between the Board and the courts of appeals in the enforcement of the Board's orders conflicted with those of the Court of Appeals for the Sixth Circuit we brought both cases here. 339 U.S. 951, 70 S.Ct. 842 and 339 U.S. 962, 70 S.Ct. 998. The clash of opinion obviously required settlement by this Court.

I

Want of certainty in judicial review of Labor Board decisions partly reflects the intractability of any formula to furnish definiteness of content for all the impalpable factors involved in judicial review. But in part doubts as to the nature of the reviewing power and uncertainties in its application derive from history, and to that extent an elucidation of this history may clear them away.

The Wagner Act provided: "The findings of the Board as to the facts, if supported by evidence, shall be conclusive." Act of July 5, 1935, § 10(e), 49 Stat. 449, 454, 29 U.S.C. § 160(e), 29 U.S.C.A. § 160(e). This Court read "evidence" to mean "substantial evidence," Washington, V. & M. Coach Co. v. Labor Board, 301 U.S. 142, 57 S.Ct. 648, 81 L.Ed. 965, and we said that "[s]ubstantial evidence is more than a mere scintilla. It means such relevant evidence as a reasonable mind might accept as adequate to support a conclusion." Consolidated Edison Co. v. National Labor Relations Board, 305 U.S. 197, 229, 59 S.Ct. 206, 217, 83 L.Ed. 126. Accordingly, it "must do more than create a suspicion of the existence of the fact to be established. . . . [I]t must be enough to justify, if the trial were to a jury, a refusal to direct a verdict when the conclusion sought to be drawn from it is one of fact for the jury." National Labor Relations Board v. Columbian Enameling & Stamping Co., 306 U.S. 292, 300, 59 S.Ct. 501, 505, 83 L.Ed. 660.

The very smoothness of the "substantial evidence" formula as the standard for reviewing the evidentiary validity of the Board's findings established its currency. But the inevitably variant applications of the standard to conflicting evidence soon brought contrariety of views and in due course bred criticism. Even though the whole record may have been canvassed in order to determine whether the evidentiary foundation of a determination by the Board was "substantial," the phrasing of this Court's process of review readily lent itself to the notion that it was enough that the evidence supporting the Board's result was "substantial" when considered by itself. It is fair to say that by imperceptible steps regard for the fact-finding function of the Board led to the assumption that the requirements of the Wagner Act were met when the reviewing court could find in the record evidence which, when viewed in isolation, substantiated the Board's findings. This is not to say that every member of this Court was consciously guided by this view or that the Court ever explicitly avowed this practice as doctrine. What matters is that the belief justifiably arose that the Court had so construed the obligation to review. . . .

The final report of the Attorney General's Committee was submitted in January, 1941. The majority concluded that "[d]issatisfaction with the existing standards as to the scope of judicial review derives largely from dissatisfaction with the fact-finding procedures now employed by the administrative bodies." Departure from the "substantial evidence" test, it thought, would either create unnecessary uncertainty or transfer to courts the responsibility for ascertaining and assaying matters the significance of which lies outside judicial competence. Accordingly, it recommended against legislation embodying a general scheme of judicial review.

Three members of the Committee registered a dissent. Their view was that the "present system or lack of system of judicial review" led to inconsistency and uncertainty. They reported that under a "prevalent" interpretation of the "substantial evidence" rule "if what is called 'substantial evidence' is found anywhere in the record to support conclusions of fact, the courts are said to be obliged to sustain the decision without reference to how heavily the countervailing evidence may preponderate—unless indeed the stage of arbitrary decision is reached. Under this interpretation, the courts need to read only one side of the case and, if they find any evidence there, the administrative action is to be sustained and the record to the contrary is to be ignored." Their view led them to recommend that Congress enact principles of review applicable to all agencies not excepted by unique characteristics. One of these principles was expressed by the formula that judicial review could extend to "findings, inferences, or conclusions of fact unsupported, upon the whole record, by substantial evidence." So far as the history of this movement for enlarged review reveals, the phrase "upon the whole record" makes its first appearance in this recommendation of the minority of the Attorney General's Committee. This evidence of the close relationship between the phrase and the criticism out of which it arose is important, for the substance of this formula for judicial review found its way into the statute books when Congress with unques-

tioning—we might even say uncritical—unanimity enacted the Administrative Procedure Act. . . .

Similar dissatisfaction with too restricted application of the "substantial evidence" test is reflected in the legislative history of the Taft-Hartley Act. The bill as reported to the House provided that the "findings of the Board as to the facts shall be conclusive unless it is made to appear to the satisfaction of the court either (1) that the findings of fact are against the manifest weight of the evidence, or (2) that the findings of fact are not supported by substantial evidence." The bill left the House with this provision. Early committee prints in the Senate provided for review by "weight of the evidence" or "clearly erroneous" standards. But, as the Senate Committee Report relates, "it was finally decided to conform the statute to the corresponding section of the Administrative Procedure Act where the substantial evidence test prevails. In order to clarify any ambiguity in that statute, however, the committee inserted the words 'questions of fact, if supported by substantial evidence *on the record considered as a whole*. . . . ' "

This phraseology was adopted by the Senate. The House conferees agreed. They reported to the House: "It is believed that the provisions of the conference agreement relating to the courts' reviewing power will be adequate to preclude such decisions as those in N.L.R.B. v. Nevada Consol. Copper Corp., 316 U.S. 105, 62 S.Ct. 960, 86 L.Ed. 1305 and in the Wilson, Columbia Products, Union Pacific Stages, Hearst, Republic Aviation, and Le Tourneau, etc. cases, supra, without unduly burdening the courts." The Senate version became the law.

It is fair to say that in all this Congress expressed a mood. And it expressed its mood not merely by oratory but by legislation. As legislation that mood must be respected, even though it can only serve as a standard for judgment and not as a body of rigid rules assuring sameness of application. Enforcement of such broad standards implies subtlety of mind and solidity of judgment. But it is not for us to question that Congress may assume such qualities in the federal judiciary.

From the legislative story we have summarized, two concrete conclusions do emerge. One is the identity of aim of the Administrative Procedure Act and the Taft-Hartley Act regarding the proof with which the Labor Board must support a decision. The other is that now Congress has left no room for doubt as to the kind of scrutiny which a court of appeals must give the record before the Board to satisfy itself that the Board's order rests on adequate proof.

It would be mischievous word-playing to find that the scope of review under the Taft-Hartley Act is any different from that under the Administrative Procedure Act. The Senate Committee which reported the review clause of the Taft-Hartley Act expressly indicated that the two standards were to conform in this regard, and the wording of the two Acts is for purposes of judicial administration identical. And so we hold that the standard of proof specifically required of the Labor Board by the Taft-Hartley Act is the same as that to be exacted by courts reviewing every administrative action subject to the Administrative Procedure Act.

Whether or not it was ever permissible for courts to determine the substantiality of evidence supporting a Labor Board decision merely on the basis of evidence which in and of itself justified it, without taking into account contradictory evidence or evidence from which conflicting inferences could be drawn, the new legislation definitively precludes such a theory of review and bars its practice. The substantiality of evidence must take into account whatever in the record fairly detracts from its weight. This is clearly the significance of the requirement in both statutes that courts consider the whole record. Commit-

tee reports and the adoption in the Administrative Procedure Act of the minority views of the Attorney General's Committee demonstrate that to enjoin such a duty on the reviewing court was one of the important purposes of the movement which eventuated in that enactment. . . .

We conclude, therefore, that the Administrative Procedure Act and the Taft-Hartley Act direct that courts must now assume more responsibility for the reasonableness and fairness of Labor Board decisions than some courts have shown in the past. Reviewing courts must be influenced by a feeling that they are not to abdicate the conventional judicial function. Congress has imposed on them responsibility for assuring that the Board keeps within reasonable grounds. That responsibility is not less real because it is limited to enforcing the requirement that evidence appear substantial when viewed, on the record as a whole, by courts invested with the authority and enjoying the prestige of the Courts of Appeals. The Board's findings are entitled to respect; but they must nonetheless be set aside when the record before a Court of Appeals clearly precludes the Board's decision from being justified by a fair estimate of the worth of the testimony of witnesses or its informed judgment on matters within its special competence or both. . . .

The decision of the Court of Appeals is assailed on two grounds. It is said (1) that the court erred in holding that it was barred from taking into account the report of the examiner on questions of fact insofar as that report was rejected by the Board, and (2) that the Board's order was not supported by substantial evidence on the record considered as a whole, even apart from the validity of the court's refusal to consider the rejected portions of the examiner's report.

The latter contention is easily met. . . . [I]t is clear from the court's opinion in this case that it in fact did consider the "record as a whole," and did not deem itself merely the judicial echo of the Board's conclusion. . . . On such a record we could not say that it would be error to grant enforcement.

The first contention, however, raises serious questions to which we now turn. . . .

We do not require that the examiner's findings be given more weight than in reason and in the light of judicial experience they deserve. The "substantial evidence" standard is not modified in any way when the Board and its examiner disagree. We intend only to recognize that evidence supporting a conclusion may be less substantial when an impartial, experienced examiner who has observed the witnesses and lived with the case has drawn conclusions different from the Board's than when he has reached the same conclusion. The findings of the examiner are to be considered along with the consistency and inherent probability of testimony. The significance of his report, of course, depends largely on the importance of credibility in the particular case. To give it this significance does not seem to us materially more difficult than to heed the other factors which in sum determine whether evidence is "substantial."

The direction in which the law moves is often a guide for decision of particular cases, and here it serves to confirm our conclusion. However halting its progress, the trend in litigation is toward a rational inquiry into truth, in which the tribunal considers everything "logically probative of some matter requiring to be proved." Thayer, A Preliminary Treatise on Evidence, 530. This Court has refused to accept assumptions of fact which are demonstrably false, even when agreed to by the parties. Machinery for discovery of evidence has been strengthened; the boundaries of judicial notice have been slowly but perceptibly enlarged. It would reverse this process for courts to deny examiners' findings the probative force they would have in the conduct of affairs outside a courtroom.

We therefore remand the cause to the Court of Appeals. On reconsideration of the record it should accord the findings of the trial examiner the relevance that they reasonably command in answering the comprehensive question whether the evidence supporting the Board's order is substantial. But the court need not limit its reexamination of the case to the effect of that report on its decision. We leave it free to grant or deny enforcement as it thinks the principles expressed in this opinion dictate.

Judgment vacated and cause remanded.

The Law-Fact Distinction

As suggested above, the general rule is that the agency is charged with making findings of fact while courts, on review, decide questions of law. Thus, "a court is theoretically free to determine for itself the correctness of the agency's legal judgments. However, even then the agency's interpretations are often entitled to great weight."[41] In addition to such judicial deference to agency interpretation, another factor which sometimes favors the agency position is that there is "surprisingly little agreement on how questions of fact

---

[41] Gellhorn, above, note 39, at 263.

and law can be distinguished." [42] A leading case on this question is the following.

National Labor Relations Board v. Hearst Publications, Inc.

SUPREME COURT OF THE UNITED STATES, 1944.
322 U.S. 111, 64 S.CT. 851, 88 L.ED. 1170.

[The respondents refused to bargain collectively with a union representing newsboys, contending that the latter were not "employees" within the meaning of that term under the National Labor Relations Act, 49 Stat. 450, 29 U.S.C.A. § 152. Proceedings were instituted before the NLRB, which found that the respondents had violated sections of the Act, and ordered them to cease and desist from such violations and to bargain collectively with the union upon request.

The Court of Appeals, on review, set aside the NLRB order. It concluded that the Act imported common law standards for determining the employee question and held that the newsboys were not employees. The case came to the Supreme Court on certiorari.]

Mr. Justice RUTLEDGE delivered the opinion of the Court.

... The papers are distributed to the ultimate consumer through a variety of channels, including independent dealers and newsstands often attached to drug, grocery or confectionery stores, carriers who make home deliveries, and newsboys who sell on the streets of the city and its suburbs. Only the last of these are involved in this case.

The newsboys work under varying terms and conditions. They may be "bootjackers," selling to the general public at places other than established corners, or they may sell at fixed "spots." They may sell only casually or part-time, or full-time; and they may be employed regularly and continuously or only temporarily. The units which the Board determined to be appropriate are composed of those who sell full-time at established spots. Those vendors, misnamed boys, are generally mature men, dependent upon the proceeds of their sales for their sustenance, and frequently supporters of families. Working thus as news vendors on a regular basis, often for a number of years, they form a stable group with relatively little turnover, in contrast to schoolboys and others who sell as bootjackers, temporary and casual distributors.

Over-all circulation and distribution of the papers are under the general supervision of circulation managers. But for purposes of street distribution each paper has divided metropolitan Los Angeles into geographic districts. Each district is under the direct and close supervision of a district manager. His function in the mechanics of distribution is to supply the newsboys in his district with papers which he obtains from the publisher and to turn over to the publisher the receipts which he collects from their sales, either directly or with the assistance of "checkmen" or "main spot" boys. The latter, stationed at the important corners or "spots" in the district, are newsboys who, among other things, receive delivery of the papers, redistribute them to other newsboys stationed at less important corners, and collect receipts from their sales. For that service, which occupies a minor portion of their working day, the checkmen receive a small salary from the publisher. The bulk of their day, however, they spend in hawking papers at their

---

[42] Ibid., at 264.

"spots" like other full-time newsboys. A large part of the appropriate units selected by the Board for the News and the Herald are checkmen who, in that capacity, clearly are employees of those papers.

The newsboys' compensation consists in the difference between the prices at which they sell the papers and the prices they pay for them. The former are fixed by the publishers and the latter are fixed either by the publishers or, in the case of the News, by the district manager. In practice the newsboys receive their papers on credit. They pay for those sold either sometime during or after the close of their selling day, returning for credit all unsold papers. Lost or otherwise unreturned papers, however, must be paid for as though sold. Not only is the "profit" per paper thus effectively fixed by the publisher, but substantial control of the newsboys' total "take home" can be effected through the ability to designate their sales areas and the power to determine the number of papers allocated to each. While as a practical matter this power is not exercised fully, the newsboys' "right" to decide how many papers they will take is also not absolute. In practice, the Board found, they cannot determine the size of their established order without the cooperation of the district manager. And often the number of papers they must take is determined unilaterally by the district managers.

In addition to effectively fixing the compensation, respondents in a variety of ways prescribe, if not the minutiae of daily activities, at least the broad terms and conditions of work. This is accomplished largely through the supervisory efforts of the district managers, who serve as the nexus between the publishers and the newsboys. The district managers assign "spots" or corners to which the newsboys are expected to confine their selling activities. Transfers from one "spot" to another may be ordered by the district manager for reasons of discipline or efficiency or other cause. Transportation to the spots from the newspaper building is offered by each of respondents. Hours of work on the spots are determined not simply by the impersonal pressures of the market, but to a real extent by explicit instructions from the district managers. Adherence to the prescribed hours is observed closely by the district managers or other supervisory agents of the publishers. Sanctions, varying in severity from reprimand to dismissal, are visited on the tardy and the delinquent. By similar supervisory controls minimum standards of diligence and good conduct while at work are sought to be enforced. However wide may be the latitude for individual initiative beyond those standards, district managers' instructions in what the publishers apparently regard as helpful sales technique are expected to be followed. Such varied items as the manner of displaying the paper, of emphasizing current features and headlines, and of placing advertising placards, or the advantages of soliciting customers at specific stores or in the traffic lanes are among the subjects of this instruction. Moreover, newsboys are furnished with sales equipment, such as racks, boxes and change aprons, and advertising placards by the publishers. In this pattern of employment the Board found that the newsboys are an integral part of the publishers' distribution system and circulation organization. And the record discloses that the newsboys and checkmen feel they are employees of the papers and respondents' supervisory employees, if not respondents themselves, regard them as such.

In addition to questioning the sufficiency of the evidence to sustain these findings, respondents point to a number of other attributes characterizing their relationship with the newsboys and urge that on the entire record the latter cannot be considered their employees. They base this conclusion on the argument that by common-law standards the extent of their control and direction of the newsboys' working activities creates no more than an "independent contractor" relationship and that common-law standards determine the "employee" relationship under the Act....

I

The principal question is whether the newsboys are "employees." Because Congress did not explicitly define the term, respondents say its meaning must be determined by reference to common-law standards. In their view "common-law standards" are those the courts have applied in distinguishing between "employees" and "independent contractors" when working out various problems unrelated to the Wagner Act's purposes and provisions.

The argument assumes that there is some simple, uniform and easily applicable test which the courts have used, in dealing with such problems, to determine whether persons doing work for others fall in one class or the other. Unfortunately this is not true.... Few problems in the law have given greater variety of application and conflict in results than the cases arising in the borderland between what is clearly an employer-employee relationship and what is clearly one of independent entrepreneurial dealing....

Two possible consequences could follow. One would be to refer the decision of who are employees to local state law. The alternative would be to make it turn on a sort of pervading general essence distilled from state law. Congress obviously did not intend the former result. It would introduce variations into the statute's operation as wide as the differences the forty-eight states and other local jurisdictions make in applying the distinction for wholly different purposes. Persons who might be "employees" in one state would be "independent contractors" in another. They would be within or without the statute's protection depending not on whether their situation falls factually within the ambit Congress had in mind, but upon the accidents

of the location of their work and the attitude of the particular local jurisdiction in casting doubtful cases one way or the other. Persons working across state lines might fall in one class or the other, possibly both, depending on whether the Board and the courts would be required to give effect to the law of one state or of the adjoining one, or to that of each in relation to the portion of the work done within its borders.

Both the terms and the purposes of the statute, as well as the legislative history, show that Congress had in mind no such patchwork plan for securing freedom of employees' organization and of collective bargaining. The Wagner Act is federal legislation, administered by a national agency, intended to solve a national problem on a national scale. It is an Act, therefore, in reference to which it is not only proper, but necessary for us to assume, "in the absence of a plain indication to the contrary, that Congress ... is not making the application of the federal act dependent on state law." ...

II

Whether, given the intended national uniformity, the term "employee" includes such workers as these newsboys must be answered primarily from the history, terms and purposes of the legislation ... It will not do, for deciding this question as one of uniform national application, to import wholesale the traditional common-law conceptions or some distilled essence of their local variations as exclusively controlling limitations upon the scope of the statute's effectiveness. To do this would be merely to select some of the local, hairline variations for nation-wide application and thus to reject others for coverage under the Act. That result hardly would be consistent with the statute's broad terms and purposes....

The mischief at which the Act is aimed and the remedies it offers are not confined exclusively to "employees" within the traditional legal distinctions separating them from "independent contractors." Myriad forms of service relationship, with infinite and subtle variations in the terms of employment, blanket the nation's economy. Some are within this Act, others beyond its coverage. Large numbers will fall clearly on one side or on the other, by whatever test may be applied. But intermediate there will be many, the incidents of whose employment partake in part of the one group, in part of the other, in varying proportions of weight. And consequently the legal pendulum, for purposes of applying the statute, may swing one way or the other, depending upon the weight of this balance and its relation to the special purpose at hand.

Unless the common-law tests are to be imported and made exclusively controlling, without regard to the statute's purposes, it cannot be irrelevant that the particular workers in these cases are subject, as a matter of economic fact, to the evils the statute was designed to eradicate and that the remedies it affords are appropriate for preventing them or curing their harmful effects in the special situation. . . .

It is not necessary in this case to make a completely definitive limitation around the term "employee." That task has been assigned primarily to the agency created by Congress to administer the Act. Determination of "where all the conditions of the relation require protection" involves inquiries for the Board charged with this duty. Everyday experience in the administration of the statute gives it familiarity with the circumstances and backgrounds of employment relationships in various industries, with the abilities and needs of the workers for self organization and collective action, and with the adaptability of collective bargaining for the peaceful settlement of their disputes with their employers. The experience thus acquired must be brought frequently to bear on the question who is an employee under the Act. Resolving that

question, like determining whether unfair labor practices have been committed, "belongs to the usual administrative routine" of the Board. Gray v. Powell, 314 U.S. 402, 411, 62 S.Ct. 326, 332, 86 L.Ed. 301.

In making that body's determinations as to the facts in these matters conclusive, if supported by evidence, Congress entrusted to it primarily the decision whether the evidence establishes the material facts. Hence in reviewing the Board's ultimate conclusions, it is not the court's function to substitute its own inferences of fact for the Board's, when the latter have support in the record. Undoubtedly questions of statutory interpretation, especially when arising in the first instance in judicial proceedings, are for the courts to resolve, giving appropriate weight to the judgment of those whose special duty is to administer the questioned statute. But where the question is one of specific application of a broad statutory term in a proceeding in which the agency administering the statute must determine it initially, the reviewing court's function is limited. Like the commissioner's determination under the Longshoremen's & Harbor Workers' Act, that a man is not a "member of a crew" (South Chicago Coal & Dock Co. v. Bassett, 309 U.S. 251, 60 S.Ct. 544, 547, 84 L.Ed. 732) or that he was injured "in the course of his employment" (Parker v. Motor Boat Sales, Inc., 314 U.S. 244, 62 S.Ct. 221, 222, 86 L.Ed. 184) and the Federal Communications Commission's determination that one company is under the "control" of another (Rochester Telephone Corp. v. United States, 307 U.S. 125, 59 S.Ct. 754, 83 L.Ed. 1147), the Board's determination that specified persons are "employees" under this Act is to be accepted if it has "warrant in the record" and a reasonable basis in law.

In this case the Board found that the designated newsboys work continuously and regularly, rely upon their earnings for the support of themselves and their families, and have their total wages influenced in large measure by the publishers who dictate their buying and selling prices, fix their markets and control their supply of papers. Their hours of work and their efforts on the job are supervised and to some extent prescribed by the publishers or their agents. Much of their sales equipment and advertising materials is furnished by the publishers with the intention that it be used for the publisher's benefit. Stating that "the primary consideration in the determination of the applicability of the statutory definition is whether effectuation of the declared policy and purposes of the Act comprehend securing to the individual the rights guaranteed and protection afforded by the Act," the Board concluded that the newsboys are employees. The record sustains the Board's findings and there is ample basis in the law for its conclusion. . . .

Mr. Justice REED concurs in the result . . . .

Reversed and remanded.

Mr. Justice ROBERTS.

I think the judgment of the Circuit Court of Appeals should be affirmed. . . .

I think it plain that newsboys are not "employees" of the respondents within the meaning and intent of the National Labor Relations Act. When Congress, in § 2(3), 29 U.S.C.A. § 152(3), said: "The term 'employee' shall include any employee, . . . " it stated as clearly as language could do it that the provisions of the Act were to extend to those who, as a result of decades of tradition which had become part of the common understanding of our people, bear the named relationship. Clearly also Congress did not delegate to the National Labor Relations Board the function of defining the relationship of employment so as to promote what the Board understood to be the underlying purpose of the statute. The question who is an employee, so as to make the statute applicable to him, is a question of the meaning of the Act and, therefore, is a judicial and not an administrative question.

THE JUDICIAL–ADMINISTRATIVE RELATIONSHIP: EVIDENCE OF GREATER DEFERENCE?

The final selection of this chapter has been excerpted from the lead article in a November 1985 "Law and Public Affairs" symposium issue of the *Public Administration Review*. In it the author, Phillip J. Cooper, examines the relationship between judges and administrators and concludes that the federal courts, including the Supreme Court, have in recent years been much less intrusive in administrative matters than the conventional wisdom would lead us to believe. Several of the illustrative cases cited by Cooper, such as *Mathews* v. *Eldridge* and *Harlow* v. *Fitzgerald*, will be examined in more detail in subsequent chapters of this text.

Conflict or Constructive Tension: The Changing Relationship of Judges and Administrators [a]

Phillip J. Cooper

Administrators these days often express frustration, resentment, and anxiety over judicial intervention into administrative operations. The indictment is familiar. Beginning in the late 1960s and early 1970s, the story goes, federal courts began a movement toward greater interference in administrative matters that has become progressively more intrusive. The trend, the argument runs, continues to this day.

It should not be at all surprising that administrators resent judicial rulings limiting their discretion and mandating procedural or substantive policy changes in agency operations. After all, one of the administrator's primary tasks is to anticipate and eliminate contingencies in the organizational environment.[43] Judicial rulings would seem to be just one more troublesome factor constraining administrative flexibility.

However, the courts perform a variety of essential functions required of them by the Constitution and statutes. They must ensure that administrators do not exceed their statutory authority, ignore basic procedural requisites, conduct themselves in a manner that is arbitrary and capricious or an abuse of discretion, make important policy determinations without some kind of reasoned decision based upon a record, or violate the provisions of the Constitution.[44] Neither these functions nor the courts designated to perform them are going to be eliminated.

The problem then is to develop an effective working relationship between judges and administrators. But before such an accommodation can be reached it will be necessary to assess the current relationship between these legal and administrative institutions. The starting point for such a reassessment must be a realization that the federal courts, led by the Supreme Court, have changed the law governing administrative agencies in ways more charitable to administrators. It is not true that there is a continuing trend toward greater interference in administration. Recent cases indicate an increasing judicial sensitivity to management problems and priorities.

This article examines the premises underlying current tensions between judges and administrators. It then turns to a consideration of the various counts in the indictment brought by administrators against the courts indicating the importance of recent federal court rulings.... Finally, the article suggests that law is a discretion-reinforcing agent, a fact that argues for improved judicial-administrative relations and against continued hostility.

[a] 45 *Public Administration Review* 643 (1985), a publication of the American Society for Public Administration. Reprinted by permission.

[43] Victor Thompson, *Bureaucracy and the Modern World* (Morristown, N.J.: General Learning Press, 1976), p. 10.

[44] 5 U.S.C. § 706.

Law and Administration: Natural Animosity or Constructive Tension

Two premises are essential to any discussion about law and administration. First, discretion is an essential commodity in modern public administration. Problems are simply too diverse and specialized and the environment too dynamic for legislators to provide more than a moderate amount of guidance to those who must administer public programs. Beyond that, managers must have sufficient flexibility to adapt their organizations and practices to changing conditions in order to perform effectively and efficiently. A lack of discretion would stifle creativity and confine administrators to rigid behavior patterns producing a panoply of bureaucratic dysfunctions long feared by scholars of organizational theory.[45]

The second premise is that law is intended to, and does in fact, limit discretion. Internal checks acquired by careful recruitment and training of promising public servants and the external checks provided by executive supervision and legislative oversight have never been thought adequate substitutes for the opportunity to call an official into court to demonstrate the validity of his or her actions. "No man in this country," the Supreme Court has admonished us, "is so high that he is above the law. No officer of the law may set that law at defiance with impunity. All of the officers of government, from the highest to the lowest, are creatures of the law, and are bound to obey it." [46]

From these two premises it follows that there will inevitably be tension between judges and administrators. Adding to that conflict are the differing perspectives of legally trained professionals and management-educated professional administrators.[47] The former tend to treat as core values the utility of law as a defense against government intervention in personal and business affairs, the commitment to due process of law, an insistence upon equal protection of the law, and a concern for substantial justice. The latter, on the other hand, are by degrees more concerned with the latitude necessary to apply expertise to complex problems, the need for flexibility in meeting new challenges, and the goal of efficiency—what Gulick referred to as "the basic good." [48]

However, the fact that some tension exists between judges and administrators is not necessarily destructive nor should it transform natural tension into animosity. Such a polarized view of the judicial-administrative relationship would be understandable only if managers could successfully argue that absolute discretion is absolutely good and necessary or if legalists could contend that all discretion is bad. Neither argument has merit. Discretion does

[45] See Robert K. Merton, "Bureaucratic Structure and Personality," in Merton et al. (eds.), *Reader in Bureaucracy* (New York: Free Press, 1952).

[46] *United States* v. *Lee*, 106 U.S. 196, 220 (1882).

[47] It is, of course, understood that many are administrators as a second profession and that a substantial proportion of those managers have not received advanced training in public administration. See Frederick Mosher, *Democracy and the Public Service* (New York: Oxford University Press, 1984).

[48] Luther Gulick and L. Urwick (eds.), *Papers on the Science of Administration* (Fairfield, N.J.: A. M. Kelley, 1977), p. 192.

not necessarily have a straight-line correlation with efficiency.[49] The relationship is more curvilinear. No discretion would paralyze management. On the other hand, complete discretion may undermine efficiency. Sofaer, for example, found in his study of an agency with extremely wide discretion that broad flexibility can lead to "inconsistency, arbitrariness, and inefficiency."[50] He concluded that "the evidence seemed to refute the hypothesis that discretion results in less costly, speedier administration.... The presence of discretionary power seemed throughout the administrative process, disproportionately to attract political intervention."[51] Legalists have the same problem. The relationship between just decisions and discretion is again nothing so simple as a straight-line negative correlation. Absolute discretion would mean a high probability of arbitrary and inconsistent administrative judgments. On the other hand, no discretion would mean rule-bound administration without accommodation for equity or any other consideration of individualized justice.

The challenge, then, is to find useful mixes of discretion and checks on abuses of discretion not only to achieve just decisions and bolster accountability but also to protect necessary administrative flexibility so that managers can administer their organizations efficiently. The most useful approach to thinking about law and administration is not a juxtaposition of law against administration, but development of an understanding of the interaction of courts and agencies as a necessarily ongoing relationship.

Before progress can be made in improving the judicial-administrative relationship, administrators must be made aware of some of the important changes in the law. There are indications in a variety of recent rulings of increased judicial sensitivity to administrative concerns.

Judges Neither Understand nor Care About Administrative Problems: Mythology and Reality in Recent Legal Developments

A common misconception is that a straight-line progression of judicial assumption of authority has occurred, substituting legal judgment for administrative discretion. Examination of administrative law cases over the past decade, however, indicates that part of this management perception is based upon a number of myths or misunderstandings, which are not generally supported by the case law. True, there are important controversies, but the relationship is not as adversarial as it may seem.

The last decade or so has witnessed significant changes in direction within the Supreme Court and some lower courts on issues of importance to administrators. In several areas, judges have openly recognized the importance of administrative discretion and have moved to protect it. One way to understand the importance of these rulings is to consider the charges issued

---

[49] Phillip J. Cooper, *Public Law and Public Administration* (Palo Alto, Calif.: Mayfield, 1983), pp. 217–219.

[50] Abraham Sofaer, "Judicial Control of Informal Discretionary Adjudication and Enforcement," *Columbia Law Review*, vol. 72 (December 1972), p. 1374.

[51] Ibid., pp. 1301–1302.

by administrators against the judiciary and the manner in which a federal judge might respond to them.

1. *Courts do not care about costs.* There is substantial evidence to the contrary. Consider the development of standards for administrative due process, judicial acknowledgment of the need to avoid supplanting legislative budgeting, and the recognition of fiscal problems faced by administrators in institutional reform litigation.

Even before the important recent changes in the requirements of administrative due process, the Supreme Court acknowledged the need to permit a flexible approach to due process to accommodate administrative circumstances. In a 1976 ruling, *Mathews* v. *Eldridge*, the court went even further.[52] In *Eldridge*, the court found that Social Security disability recipients were not entitled to a hearing before the termination of their benefits, though they would have an opportunity to be heard at some point later in the process. The significance of this decision lies not in permitting administrators to deny claimants any due process, but in granting flexibility in assessing what process is due under varying administrative conditions. In *Eldridge*, the Supreme Court developed a balancing test for determining how much process is due someone before an administrative agency which specifically recognizes fiscal and administrative burden as a major element of the balance. In order to decide what process is due, the court said, one must consider:

> first, the private interest that will be affected by the official action; second, the risk of an erroneous deprivation of such interest through the procedure used, and the probable value, if any, of additional or substitute safeguards; and finally, *the Government's interest, including the function involved and the fiscal and administrative burdens that the additional or substitute procedural requirements would entail.*[53] (Emphasis added.)

The *Eldridge* balancing test has been the controlling due process standard since 1976.[54] The court has consistently rejected calls for expanded administrative due process since that time and has, in fact, relaxed some of the requirements imposed in earlier cases.[55] . . .

Some question exists, however, as to whether administrators have tried in complex litigation to assist judges to understand relevant fiscal dimensions and to work out accommodations where necessary to minimize judicial-administrative tension. For example, in one northern school desegregation case, the state, when called upon by the judge to produce a proposed remedy, sent six plans, recommended none of them, and provided only one witness for the remedy hearing whose only role was to explain what was in the

---

[52] *Mathews* v. *Eldridge*, 424 U.S. 319 (1976).

[53] Ibid., p. 335.

[54] Evidence for this is provided in my study on administrative due process since *Goldberg* v. *Kelly* which was reported in "Due Process, the Burger Court, and Public Administration," *Southern Review of Public Administration*, vol. 6 (Spring 1982), pp. 65–98.

[55] See, e.g., *Parham* v. *J.R.*, 422 U.S. 584 (1979); *Bishop* v. *Wood*, 426 U.S. 341 (1976); *Paul* v. *Davis*, 424 U.S. 693 (1976); *Board of Curators* v. *Horowitz*, 435 U.S. 78 (1978); and *Ingraham* v. *Wright*, 430 U.S. 651 (1977). The court has spoken of the *Eldridge* balancing formula as "the familiar test prescribed in Mathews v. Eldridge." *Schweiker* v. *McClure*, 72 L.Ed.2d 1, 9–10 (1982).

plans.[56] The state provided the judge no help whatsoever in understanding the administrative and fiscal problems involved in implementing any of the proposed remedies. In an Alabama case, state mental health officials were given six months to take action to remedy unconstitutional conditions at state mental health facilities, but they took no action at all. Moreover, the state refused offers of assistance from federal agencies. After indicating his understanding that state administrators may have lacked funds to implement reforms, the judge asked just how that prevented the administrators from producing a plan that could be implemented when funds did become available.[57]

Administrators can improve their relationship with judges in such cases by making careful decisions about when to fight and when to negotiate. They can present detailed and understandable explanations of their concerns about financial and administrative feasibility. They can resist the temptation simply to ignore likely judicial action until it is forced upon them.

2. *Courts are increasingly unwilling to defer to the expertise of administrators.* Again, there have been a number of opinions, particularly Supreme Court rulings, demanding deference to administrative expertise. The court has issued these admonitions in two types of cases, rule-making review and institutional reform litigation.

The court's leading ruling on judicial review of administrative rule making was the unanimous opinion issued in *Vermont Yankee Nuclear Power Corp.* v. *United States Nuclear Regulatory Commission*.[58] *Vermont Yankee* warned lower courts against fashioning procedural requirements beyond those contained in the statutes administered by the agency involved. Lower courts are to examine the record prepared by the agency during rule making, and, if it is adequately supported and within the statutory authority of the agency, the action is to be affirmed.[59] While there has been disagreement among members of the court as to precisely how much deference is due,[60] the prime forces expanding rule-making procedural requirements in recent years have been legislation and executive orders, not judicial mandates.

The court subsequently issued a number of rulings demanding lower court respect for and deference to administrative expertise at the state as well as the federal level. Two of the more forceful decisions concerned administration of programs for handicapped children and mental health treatment.

Amy Rowley's parents objected to the individual education plan (IEP) developed for their daughter by the Hendrick Hudson School District under the requirements of the Education for All Handicapped Children Act. While school officials had provided an FM microphone, training for teachers, tutorial assistance, and speech therapy for the hearing-impaired child, they refused the Rowley's request for a sign language interpreter in the classroom. Amy

---

[56] See, generally, *Bradley* v. *Milliken*, 345 F.Supp. 914 (E.D.Mich.1972).

[57] *Wyatt* v. *Stickney*, 334 F.Supp. 1341, 1344 (M.D.Ala.1971).

[58] *Vermont Yankee Nuclear Power Corp.* v. *U.S. Nuclear Regulatory Commission*, 435 U.S. 519 (1978).

[59] See, e.g., *Federal Communications Commission* v. *WNCN Listeners Guild*, 450 U.S. 582 (1981) and *Office of Communications of the United Church of Christ* v. *FCC*, 707 F.2d 1413 (D.C.Cir.1983).

[60] See, e.g., *Industrial Union Dept, AFL–CIO* v. *American Petroleum Institute*, 448 U.S. 607 (1980) and *American Textile Manufacturers Institute* v. *Donovan*, 452 U.S. 490 (1981).

was acknowledged by all to be a bright child who read lips well enough to earn passing marks at least in her elementary grades in a regular classroom. But she did this in spite of the fact that she could only understand about half of the information conveyed. In sum, she was not able to perform up to anything like her potential without the additional assistance of a sign language interpreter. For that reason, they argued, Amy was denied the "free appropriate public education" required by the EHCA. The lower courts agreed, but the Supreme Court reversed.

The court concluded that the act did not require the state to do more than ensure that "personalized instruction is being provided with sufficient support services to permit the child to benefit from instruction" plus meet the procedural requirements for parental participation in development of plans. If that was done, the child was by definition receiving a "free appropriate public education." [61] Perhaps of equal importance, however, was the court's discussion of how judges are to decide whether the child is in fact receiving benefit from the plan. The court insisted upon increased deference to administrative expertise.

> In assuring that the requirements of the Act have been met, courts must be careful to avoid imposing their view of preferable educational methods upon the States. The primary responsibility for formulating the education to be accorded a handicapped child, and for choosing the educational method most suitable to the child's needs was left by the Act to state and local educational agencies in cooperation with the parents or guardian of the child....
>
> We previously have cautioned that courts lack the "specialized knowledge and experience" necessary to resolve "persistent and difficult questions of educational policy." [62]

But the court's admonition to judges on the need for deference was not limited to this particular program. In the same term, the court issued a decision in *Youngberg* v. *Romeo* which, though it recognized a constitutional claim for protection against abuse and a requirement for some mental health care for institutionalized retarded persons, carried a strong warning against judicial second-guesses of expert administrative judgment.[63] Justice Powell insisted that "courts must show deference to the judgment exercised by a qualified professional." He concluded:

> By so limiting judicial review of challenges to conditions in state institutions, interferences by the federal judiciary with the internal operations of these institutions should be minimized. Moreover, there certainly is no reason to think judges or juries are better qualified than appropriate professionals in making such decisions [about the kind of care and treatment needed by a patient].... (Courts should not "second-guess the expert administrator on matters on which they are better informed.") [64]

---

[61] *Hendrick Hudson Bd. of Ed.* v. *Rowley*, 458 U.S. 176, 189 (1982).

[62] Ibid., p. 208.

[63] *Youngberg* v. *Romeo*, 457 U.S. 307 (1982).

[64] Ibid., pp. 322–323.

This was a suit which asked, among other things, for damages against hospital and state officials for the lack of treatment. Pressing the need to protect administrative discretion and recognize fiscal difficulties, the court wrote:

> [L]iability may be imposed only when the decision by the professional is such a substantial departure from accepted professional judgment, practice, or standards as to demonstrate that the person responsible actually did not base the decision on such a judgment. In an action for damages against a professional in his individual capacity, however, *the professional will not be liable if he was unable to satisfy his normal professional standards because of budgetary constraints. . . .* [65] (Emphasis added.) . . .

3. *The Supreme Court is continually expanding the authority of federal district courts to issue complex remedial orders obstructing administrative operations.* There are two important factors to be considered in assessing the remedial decree cases. First, administrators have often welcomed suits against prisons and mental hospitals as means to pressure legislators for increased appropriations.[66] Thus, it is not always clear that the relationship of court to agency in these cases is primarily adversarial.

In fact, for a decade now the Supreme Court has been moving to make it harder for trial judges to justify issuance of a remedial order,[67] narrowing the scope of such orders [68] and limiting the duration for which district judges may retain supervisory jurisdiction over administrative institutions.[69] In cases involving school desegregation, mental health, and prison conditions, the court has admonished lower courts to avoid unnecessary orders, to carefully tailor those which are necessary to remedy constitutional violations without undue interference in agency operations, and to terminate control over those institutions as soon as possible.

4. *The Supreme Court keeps expanding legal protections available to employees at the expense of managers' discretion.* An expansion of employee rights did occur in the late 1960s and early 1970s. Once again, however, care must be exercised in judgments about judicial interference with administration. In the first place, many employee rights were created by statute or executive order and not judicial rulings.[70] It is, of course, true that federal

---

[65] Ibid.

[66] Stephen L. Wasby, "Arrogation of Power or Accountability: 'Judicial Imperialism Revisited,'" *Judicature*, vol. 65 (October 1981), p. 213. See also, Stonewall B. Stickney, "Problems in Implementing the Right to Treatment in Alabama: The Wyatt v. Stickney Case," *Hospital & Community Psychiatry*, vol. 25 (July 1974), pp. 454–455.

[67] See, e.g., *San Antonio Independent School District* v. *Rodriquez*, 411 U.S. 1 (1973); *Washington* v. *Davis*, 426 U.S. 229 (1976); *Personnel Administrator* v. *Feeney*, 442 U.S. 256 (1979); *Rizzo* v. *Goode*, 423 U.S. 362 (1976); and *Rhodes* v. *Chapman, op. cit.*

[68] See, e.g., *Milliken* v. *Bradley*, 418 U.S. 717 (1974); *Dayton Bd. of Ed.* v. *Brinkman*, 433 U.S. 406 (1977); *Columbus Bd. of Ed.* v. *Penick*, 443 U.S. 449 (1979); *Dayton Bd. of Ed.* v. *Brinkman*, 443 U.S. 526 (1979); and *Firefighters Local Union No. 1784* v. *Stotts*, 81 L.Ed.2d 483 (1984).

[69] *Pasadena Bd. of Education* v. *Spangler*, 427 U.S. 424 (1976).

[70] Indeed one purpose of the Civil Service Reform Act of 1978 was to assemble and clarify the various statutory protections for civil servants provided by, among others, the Civil Rights Act of 1964 as amended, the Age Discrimination in Employment Act of 1967, the Fair Labor Standards Act, and the Rehabilitation Act of 1973. 5 U.S.C. § 2302(b) (1978).

courts added protections, particularly in the area of First Amendment free speech and association as well as due process requirements in adverse personnel actions. However, important changes have been made in recent Supreme Court decisions that define employee rights, particularly in the First Amendment and due process fields.

Using the *Eldridge* balancing formula, the court has drawn back from what were some years ago expanding administrative due process requirements in employee terminations concerning which employees are entitled to a hearing [71] and the type and timing of any hearing that is required.[72] These cases have indicated that the court will be reticent to require more elements of due process than are specified in statutes and regulations. Moreover, they have rejected claims by employees that civil servants are entitled to a hearing before they are removed from their jobs rather than some time later in the administrative process.

In the First Amendment field, the court has shifted the burden and increased the level of proof required for the employee to prevail on complaints of unlawful termination in violation of First Amendment free speech protections.[73] The most direct statement of the court's intention to leave managers free of unnecessary judicial involvement in personnel decisions came recently in *Connick* v. *Myers*.[74]

The *Connick* case arose when Myers, a deputy district attorney in Orleans Parish, Louisiana, got into a disagreement with her supervisor regarding a job transfer. She had been offered a transfer and promotion based upon her performance, but she resisted the step up because it would have required her to prosecute cases in the court of a judge with whom she had been working for some time on an offender diversion program. She saw the move as a conflict of interest. When her supervisor disagreed and insisted upon the move she charged that this was another example of his poor administration of the office. Her criticism alleged a range of administrative problems including attempts to coerce employees into participating in partisan political activities. The supervisor indicated her views were not widely shared within the office. At that, Myers went home and prepared a questionnaire which she circulated to other employees. Her supervisor summoned Myers who was summarily dismissed. The district court awarded damages on grounds that there was no question that she had been fired because of her First Amendment protected speech and there was no showing of significant impairment of organizational operations as defined by previous case law that justified the termination.[75]

The Supreme Court reversed, finding that Myers had not adequately demonstrated the public significance of her speech. In so doing, the court added a new requirement to the existing burden an employee must carry in defending his or her speech against reprisal. It was not, however, merely the

---

[71] *Bishop*, 426 U.S. 341, and *Paul*, 424 U.S. 693.

[72] *Arnett* v. *Kennedy*, 416 U.S. 134 (1974).

[73] Consider the shift from *Pickering* v. *Bd. of Education*, 391 U.S. 563 (1968), to *Mt. Healthy Bd. of Ed.* v. *Doyle*, 429 U.S. 274 (1977), to *Givhan* v. *Western Line Consolidated School Dist.*, 439 U.S. 410 (1979).

[74] *Connick* v. *Myers*, 75 L.Ed 2d 708 (1983).

[75] *Myers* v. *Connick*, 507 F.Supp. 752 (E.D.La.1981), aff'd 654 F.2d 719 (5th Cir. 1981).

court's change of this test regarding when an employee can be disciplined that made the case so important, but it was also Justice White's insistence upon deference to management discretion in such matters.

> When employee expression cannot fairly be considered as relating to any matter of political, social, or other concern of the community, government officials should enjoy wide latitude in managing their officers, without intrusive oversight by the judiciary in the name of the First Amendment. Perhaps the government employer's dismissal of the worker may not be fair, but ordinary dismissals from government service which violate no fixed tenure or applicable statute or regulation are not subject to judicial review even if the reasons for the dismissal are alleged to be mistaken or unreasonable.[76]
>
> We hold that where a public employee speaks not as a citizen upon matters of public concern, but instead as an employee upon matters only of personal interest, absent the most unusual circumstances, a federal court is not the appropriate forum in which to review the wisdom of a personnel decision taken by a public agency allegedly in reaction to the employee's behavior. . . .
>
> When close working relationships are essential to fulfilling public responsibilities, a wide degree of deference to employers' judgment is appropriate. Furthermore, we do not see the necessity for an employer to allow events to unfold to the extent that the disruption of the office and the destruction of working relationships is manifest before taking action.[77]

The court's language in *Connick* coupled with its cautions against extensive judicially imposed due process requirements indicates a significant shift toward deference to administrative interests.

5. *The Supreme Court has consistently issued rulings that make it easier to bring suit in federal court.* It is true that in the late 1960s and early 1970s the Warren court relaxed the rules governing who could bring a suit in federal court, permitting a wider range of litigation. However, the Burger court has issued a string of decisions placing significant limits on standing to sue and other procedural standards governing access to federal courts.[78] In fact, it is in the area of court access rules that the Burger court has made some of the most dramatic changes from the Warren-court precedents.

The Burger court has sent other signals indicating that groups interested in changing policy should look to arenas other than the federal courts. For example, it rejected the claim that public interest groups acting as private attorneys general could collect attorneys' fees when they sued successfully.[79] (Congress later reversed that ruling by statute.) The court has also restricted the ability of private groups to claim a right to sue under statutes that do not specifically authorize private litigation, the so-called implied right of action.[80]

---

[76] *Connick*, 75 L.Ed.2d at 719–720.

[77] Ibid.

[78] See *Allen* v. *Wright*, 82 L.Ed.2d 556 (1984); *Valley Forge Christian College* v. *Americans United for Separation of Church and State*, 454 U.S. 464 (1982); *Duke Power Co.* v. *Carolina Environmental Study Group*, 438 U.S. 59 (1978); *Simon* v. *Eastern Kentucky Welfare Rights Organization*, 426 U.S. 26 (1976); and *Warth* v. *Seldin*, 422 U.S. 490 (1975).

[79] *Alyeska Pipeline* v. *Wilderness Society*, 421 U.S. 240 (1975).

[80] *Middlesex County Sewerage Authority* v. *National Sea Clammers Assn.*, 453 U.S. 1 (1981); *California* v. *Sierra Club*, 451 U.S. 287 (1981); *Touche Ross & Co.* v. *Redington*, 442 U.S. 560 (1979); and *Cannon* v. *University of Chicago*, 441 U.S. 677 (1979).

Just because there may be a violation of law that government is unable or unwilling to prosecute, does not mean that a group of private individuals may step into the breach and demand court action. For several reasons, then, it simply is not true that the trend of the Warren-court years to open the doors of the federal courthouse to more lawsuits has been continued by the current court.

6. *Federal courts are constantly expanding the threat to administrators from tort liability judgments.* The controversy surrounding the vulnerability of officials and units of government to damage claims is considered elsewhere in this symposium. But since administrators' frustration and anxiety about tort lawsuits is an important part of the conflict between judges and managers, some caveats are worthy of brief mention here.

First, while the Supreme Court has permitted more types of suits for damages over the past decade, it has brought about a kind of trade-off for administrators. At the same time that it has been allowing a wider range of damage suits, it has been limiting broad remedial orders that interfere with ongoing administration.[81] The message to lower courts is to limit interference with current administrative operations, but to let claimants come into court after the fact and collect damages if they can make their case.

Second, recent liability rulings are not unrestricted invitations to sue public officials. Even in the decisions expanding the range of possible damage claims, the Supreme Court has created a series of immunities making it relatively difficult for a plaintiff to win a case.[82] More recently, the court has recognized that its official liability decisions have placed added burdens upon public administrators discouraging initiative and producing time-consuming and costly litigation.[83] In *Harlow* v. *Fitzgerald*, the court expanded the standard immunity afforded public officials in federal tort suits and instructed judges to guard against unnecessary pretrial discovery and other burdensome procedures.[84]

In sum, the rules and judicial trends affecting the judicial-administrative relationship are not part of a continuing judicial assault on public administration. In a variety of areas the federal courts have demonstrated a sensitivity to the problems administrators must face. That does not mean that they have been willing to serve as rubber stamps for administrative action, but it does give lie to some of the more extreme charges that the courts are about the business of undermining administrators. . . .

Law as a Discretion-Reinforcing Agent

There are and always will be natural tensions between administrators and judges over the nature and boundaries of administrative authority. Yet there is a simultaneous positive aspect to this law-administration relationship. It is

---

[81] See, *Rizzo*, 423 U.S. 362. See also, David Rosenbloom, "Public Administrators' Official Immunity: Developments During the Seventies," *Public Administration Review*, vol. 40 (March–April 1980), pp. 166–173.

[82] See, e.g., *Butz* v. *Economou*, 438 U.S. 478 (1978).

[83] 457 U.S. 800 (1982).

[84] Ibid., pp. 817–818.

worthwhile to assess the reasons administrators ought to attempt to foster better working relations with judges, notwithstanding the difficulties such a prescription entails.

Knowledge of the legal elements of administration is an enabling force. Formal authority of administrators is derived from a statute or executive order. Care in using such authority supports effective administration. There is an admittedly rough but useful analogy to the budget process. An agency without adequate fiscal resources is in serious trouble. The amount of funds available is a significant factor in the agency's ability to perform. It is both an enabling force and, in a sense, a constraint. The fact that budgetary politics are complex and often disappointing does not indicate that a good manager ought to abandon concern for the subject or cease efforts to improve relationships with appropriations committees. The same is true of law and administration.

An understanding of legal developments is also important as a defensive matter. It can help to avoid liability judgments, prevent the loss of invested time and effort when agency decisions are reversed, avoid loss of control over one's agency to a complex remedial court order, and lead to savings of money as well as time from having to replicate and improve work rejected in judicial review.

Two other key functions are served by enhancing the relationship between administrators and judges. Understanding the relationship provides increased predictability which is critical to any manager. The first task is to understand judicial trends sufficiently to anticipate likely judicial responses to agency actions. An awareness of legal limits on administration provides an ability to predict not only what courts will do with respect to one's own but also to other agencies. Administrators thus informed can manage their operations with some expectation of how other agencies will be able to respond. Administration without attention to law would not mean more efficiency, it would mean chaos.

Finally, administrators need legal support for their claim to legitimacy within government and, perhaps more importantly, within the larger society. There is a certain irony in the fact that administrators busy challenging the legitimacy of judicial involvement in policy making are in danger of being convicted by their own arguments. Many of the charges made against judges can be made in only slightly modified form against administrators. They are not elected. Many cannot be removed from office except for cause. It is extremely difficult to keep them responsive and responsible. They frequently do precisely what the majority of the people do not wish them to do. The list goes on. Beyond that particular threat to legitimacy, however, is the need for assistance in establishing a legitimate place for administrators in the constitutional framework. Our constitutional authority is derivative. We obtain our authority by inference and indirectly.[85] We must always be able to trace our authority back through the chain of statutes and judicial rulings that support us. . . .

---

[85] I am indebted for this idea, if not these precise words, to John Rohr.

PART THREE

The Internal Administrative Process

Chapter 5

Investigatory Power

Part III of the book concerns the activities of administrators in carrying out the functions they are charged with by law. We have divided the subject into four categories. In discharging their duties, administrators often need to make factual determinations: whether a party is entitled to a governmental benefit, or is covered by a regulatory statute, or is engaging in an allegedly illegal activity, or a myriad of other matters of this kind. This chapter deals with the legal issues associated with efforts by administrators to gather information in situations such as these.

One of the ways in which governmental agencies attempt to spell out in more detail the sometimes vague statements of legislative intent found in statutes is through the adoption of substatutory pronouncements of their own. These statements are usually called "rules" or "regulations" (the terms are normally considered equivalents) and the process of adoption is called "rule making." This is the subject of chapter 6.

Rule making normally affects a whole group of private parties, such as all taxpayers or property owners in a city or all airlines or television licensees. But administrators also interact with individuals and smaller groups. They may have to make individual decisions, such as whether an advertiser is engaged in deceptive advertising, whether a welfare recipient is entitled to continue to receive benefits, whether a petitioner is entitled to a zoning variance. If sufficiently important interests are at stake, a proceeding with some degree of formality, sometimes approaching that of a court proceeding, must be held. This kind of procedure goes under a number of names, including "adjudication" and "quasi-judicial proceedings." The most formal of these are called "trial-type" hearings. A recurring question which is continually being addressed by courts, legislatures, and commentators on administrative procedure is whether the interests at stake in a particular administrative proceeding are sufficiently important to require "some kind of hearing." [1] It

---

[1] Henry J. Friendly, "Some Kind of Hearing," 123 *University of Pennsylvania Law Review* 1267 (1975).

takes little reflection to realize that rule making often amounts to "administrative policy making" or at least supplementation of legislative policy. What may not be so immediately apparent is that an administrative agency can also create policy by adjudication as well. In chapter 7 we will address these aspects of administrative adjudication.

Finally, a great deal of the activity of administrative agencies in their dealings with private parties involves neither rule making nor adjudication. Advice given to a citizen by a governmental employee; the refusal by immigration authorities to allow an alien to enter the country; a telephone call from a regulatory commission lawyer to a company official indicating that, in the lawyer's opinion, the company may be doing something illegal—these and many other administrative activities can be placed in the categories "informal activity and the exercise of discretion"—categories which, until fairly recently, were rather neglected areas of administrative law. Chapter 8 examines this emerging and extremely important area.

Administrative investigations generally take one of two broad forms: (1) the examination of papers, records or other documents (as well as testimony by individuals), and (2) the inspection of premises and other objects. Administrators derive their investigatory authority from legislation describing the functions and duties of their agencies.[2] Legal controversies typically arise over the alleged clash between statutory investigatory authority and constitutional guarantees protecting private parties, most often the Fourth Amendment's protection against unreasonable search and seizure and the Fifth Amendment's guarantee against self-incrimination. Although both amendments are brief and rather directly stated,[3] a great number of disputes over the years have involved the precise meaning of their terms. Moreover, it is clear that there has been some evolution over time in the judicial interpretation of these provisions.

As indicated in the introduction to this volume, administrative law and criminal law are separate subjects with some degree of overlap, in the sense that those engaged in criminal law enforcement often perform functions analogous to those performed by other administrators. Investigatory activity is an area where this overlapping is particularly evident. The enormous body of law concerning criminal investigatory authority is of tangential importance to the present discussion, which will concentrate on more traditional examples of administrative investigations.

----

[2] Such authority may also be provided in general legislation such as the Administrative Procedure Act. In the case of the APA, the relevant provisions are derivative. Section 555(c) provides: "Process, requirement of a report, inspection, or other investigative act or demand may not be issued, made, or enforced except as authorized by law.... " Section 555(d) provides: "Agency subpoenas authorized by law shall be issued to a party on request and, when required by rules of procedure, on a statement or showing of general relevance and reasonable scope of the evidence sought. On contest, the court shall sustain the subpoena or similar process or demand to the extent that it is found to be in accordance with law."

[3] The Fourth Amendment reads: "The right of the people to be secure in their persons, houses, papers, and effects, against unreasonable searches and seizures, shall not be violated, and no warrants shall issue, but upon probable cause, supported by oath or affirmation, and particularly describing the place to be searched, and the persons or things to be seized."

The Fifth Amendment reads in part: "No person ... shall be compelled in any criminal case to be a witness against himself.... "

THE SUBPOENA POWER AND RELATED PROCESSES

Records and other data may be required to be kept by private parties and filed with governmental agencies. Thus, for instance, taxpayers are required to submit income tax statements by April 15 of each year, and governmental contractors are required to provide various kinds of information to government agencies, such as data on their affirmative action programs. Records and other documents not required to be routinely filed with government agencies may also be within the reach of the government, through what is broadly referred to as compulsory process. This is one of the areas where the interpretation of the law has evolved considerably over the years.

A case often cited as indicative of the early position of the courts on the matter is FTC v. American Tobacco Company.

FTC v. American Tobacco Co.

SUPREME COURT OF THE UNITED STATES, 1924.
264 U.S. 298, 44 S.CT. 336, 68 L.ED. 696.

[The FTC under a broad statutory subpoena power, undertook an investigation of charges that two tobacco companies had engaged in unfair competition by controlling prices. It ordered the companies to produce "all letters and telegrams received by the Company from, or sent by it to, all of its jobber customers between January 1, 1921, to December 31, 1921, inclusive." The companies refused, on constitutional grounds, to provide the information. The District Court upheld the position of the companies, and the Supreme Court affirmed in a unanimous opinion by Mr. Justice Holmes.]

Mr. Justice HOLMES delivered the opinion of the Court. . . .

The mere facts of carrying on a commerce not confined within State lines and of being organized as a corporation do not make men's affairs public. . . . Anyone who respects the spirit as well as the letter of the Fourth Amendment would be loath to believe that Congress intended to authorize one of its subordinate agencies to sweep all our traditions into the fire (Interstate Commerce Commission v. Brimson, 154 U.S. 447, 479, 14 Sup.Ct. 1125, 38 L.Ed. 1047), and to direct fishing expeditions into private papers on the possibility that they may disclose evidence of crime. We do not discuss the question whether it could do so if it tried, as nothing short of the most explicit language would induce us to attribute to Congress that intent. The interruption of business, the possible revelation of trade secrets, and the expense that compliance with the Commission's wholesale demand would cause are the least considerations. It is contrary to the first principles of justice to allow a search through all the respondents' records, relevant or irrelevant, in the hope that something will turn up. . . .

The right of access given by the statute is to documentary evidence—not to all documents, but to such documents as are evidence. The analogies of the law do not allow the party wanting evidence to call for all documents in order to see if they do not contain it. Some ground must be shown for supposing that the documents called for do contain it. . . . A general subpoena in the form of these petitions would be bad. Some evidence of the materiality of the papers demanded must be produced. . . .

We have considered this case on the general claim of authority put forward by the Commission. The argument for the

Government attaches some force to the investigations and proceedings upon which the Commission had entered. The investigations and complaints seem to have been only on hearsay or suspicion—but even if they were induced by substantial evidence under oath the rudimentary principles of justice that we have laid down would apply. We cannot attribute to Congress an intent to defy the Fourth Amendment or even to come so near to doing so as to raise a serious question of constitutional law.

Judgments affirmed.

But the hand of the government was strengthened by later interpretations of the Supreme Court. A particularly significant case in this evolution was the 1946 *Oklahoma Press* decision.

Oklahoma Press Pub. Co. v. Walling

Supreme Court of the United States, 1946.
327 U.S. 186, 66 S.Ct. 494, 90 L.Ed. 614.

[A grant of subpoena power similar to that in the FTC case was the basis for a request by the administrator of the Fair Labor Standards Act for records from certain employers. Appellants objected that it had not even been shown that they were covered by the act, and therefore resisted complying with the subpoena, a position that was rejected at the court of appeals level.]

Mr. Justice RUTLEDGE delivered the opinion of the Court.

These cases bring for decision important questions concerning the Administrator's right to judicial enforcement of subpoenas duces tecum issued by him in the course of investigations conducted pursuant to § 11(a) of the Fair Labor Standards Act, 52 Stat. 1060, 29 U.S.C.A. § 211(a)....
The subpoenas sought the production of specified records to determine whether petitioners were violating the Fair Labor Standards Act, including records relating to coverage. Petitioners, newspaper publishing corporations, maintain that the Act is not applicable to them, for constitutional and other reasons, and insist that the question of coverage must be adjudicated before the subpoenas may be enforced....

Other questions pertain to whether enforcement of the subpoenas as directed by the Circuit Courts of Appeals will violate any of petitioners' rights secured by the Fourth Amendment and related issues concerning Congress' intent. It is claimed that enforcement would permit the Administrator to conduct general fishing expeditions into petitioners' books, records and papers, in order to secure evidence that they have violated the Act, without a prior charge or complaint and simply to secure information upon which to base one, all allegedly in violation of the Amendment's search and seizure provisions....

The short answer to the Fourth Amendment objections is that the records in these cases present no question of actual search and seizure, but raise only the question whether orders of court for the production of specified records have been validly made; and no sufficient showing appears to justify setting them aside. No officer or other person has sought to enter petitioners' premises against their will, to search them, or to seize or examine their books, records or papers without their assent, otherwise than pursuant to orders of court authorized by law and made after adequate opportunity to present objections, which in fact were made. Nor has any objection been taken to the breadth of the subpoenas or to any other specific defect which would invalidate them.... The very purpose of the subpoena and of the order, as of the authorized investigation, is to discover and procure evidence, not to prove a pending charge or complaint, but upon which to make one if, in the Administrator's judgment, the facts thus discovered should justify doing so. . . .

The primary source of misconception concerning the Fourth Amendment's function lies perhaps in the identification of cases involving so-called "figurative" or "constructive" search with cases of actual search and seizure. . . .

The confusion, obscuring the basic distinction between actual and so-called "constructive" search has been accentuated where the records and papers sought are of corporate character, as in these cases. Historically private corporations have been subject to broad visitorial power, both in England and in this country. And it long has been established that Congress may exercise wide investigative power over them, analogous to the visitorial power of the incorporating state, when their activities take place within or affect interstate commerce. Correspondingly it has been settled that corporations are not entitled to all of the constitutional protections which private individuals have in these and related matters. As has been noted, they are not at all within the privilege against self-incrimination. . . .

Without attempt to summarize or accurately distinguish all of the cases, the fair distillation, in so far as they apply merely to the production of corporate records and papers in response to a subpoena or order authorized by law and safeguarded by judicial sanction, seems to be that the Fifth Amendment affords no protection by virtue of the self-incrimination provision, whether for the corporation or for its officers; and the Fourth, if applicable, at the most guards against abuse only by way of too much indefiniteness or breadth in the things required to be "particularly described," if also the inquiry is one the demanding agency is authorized by law to make and the materials specified are relevant. The gist of the protection is in the requirement, expressed in terms, that the disclosure sought shall not be unreasonable. . . .

[I]t is impossible to conceive how a violation of petitioners' rights could have been involved. Both were corporations. The only records or documents sought were corporate ones. No possible element of self-incrimination was therefore presented or in fact claimed. All the records sought were relevant to the authorized inquiry, the purpose of which was to determine two issues, whether petitioners were subject to the Act and, if so, whether they were violating it. These were subjects of investigation authorized by § 11(a), the latter expressly, the former by necessary implication. It is not to be doubted that Congress could authorize investigation of these matters. In all these respects, the specifications more than meet the requirements long established by many precedents. . . .

What has been said disposes of petitioners' principal contention upon the sufficiency of the showing. Other assignments, however, present the further questions whether any showing is required beyond the Administrator's allegations of coverage and relevance of the required materials to that question; and, if so, of what character. Stated otherwise they are whether the court may order enforcement only upon a finding of "probable cause," that is, probability in fact, of coverage. . . .

Congress has made no requirements in terms of any showing of "probable cause"; and, in view of what has already been said, any possible constitutional requirement of that sort was satisfied by the Administrator's showing in this case, including not only the allegations concerning coverage, but also that he was proceeding with his investigation in accordance with the mandate of Congress and that the records sought were relevant to that purpose. . . .

Accordingly the judgments in both causes, . . . are affirmed.

Affirmed.

[The dissenting opinion of Mr. Justice Murphy is omitted.]

Legality of Investigative Devices

Four years after *Oklahoma Press* the Supreme Court suggested how outmoded the thrust of the *American Tobacco* case was by referring to "the colorful and nostalgic slogan 'no fishing expeditions.' " In the same opinion the Court brought out an important distinction between the judicial and administrative processes, which, impliedly at least, had not received recognition at the time of *American Tobacco*:

> Because judicial power is reluctant if not unable to summon evidence until it is shown to be relevant to issues in litigation, it does not follow that an administrative agency charged with seeing that the laws are enforced may not have and exercise powers of original inquiry. It has a power of inquisition, if one chooses to call it that, which is not derived from the judicial function. It is more analogous to the Grand Jury, which does not depend on a case or controversy for power to get evidence but can investigate merely on suspicion that the law is being violated, or even just because it wants assurance that it is not. United States v. Morton Salt Co., 338 U.S. 632, 642–3, 70 S.Ct. 357, 364, 94 L.Ed. 401, 411 (1950).

In addition to the holding in the *Oklahoma Press* case, which sanctioned the use of wide-ranging subpoena power by administrators, two other important points in the opinion should be noted. The first is the distinction between "constructive" search of papers and documents and actual search and seizure. As Justice Rutledge pointed out, the latter is based on "probable cause," an element not required in constructive search. This will be an important consideration in the cases on inspection of premises covered below. Second, *Oklahoma Press* makes it clear that corporations and their officers have long been excluded from the protection of the Fifth Amendment's self-incrimination provisions. By a series of judicial decisions, this exclusion has been extended to other organizations such as trade unions and even small partnerships. The self-incrimination clause may also be bypassed in several other ways as well. For instance, a grant of immunity from prosecution may be used to require a person to testify. And the courts have ruled that if one person's records are in the custody of another person, the Fifth Amendment provides no protection for such papers.[4]

The following case is an illustration of the broad reach of government investigatory power in more recent times. Justice Rehnquist's majority opinion clearly states the facts and issues. Although his opinion, as well as Justice Marshall's dissent, mentions the constitutional implications of the case, the reasoning of all of the opinions (including the dissent by Justice Brennan) largely turns on *statutory construction*, namely, the determination as to whether the statute permitted the investigative device used in this case.

---

[4] On these and other ways around the self-incrimination provision, see Kenneth Culp Davis, 1 *Administrative Law Treatise* 274–298 (2d ed., 1978).

United States v. Euge

SUPREME COURT OF THE UNITED STATES, 1980.
444 U.S. 707, 100 S.CT. 874, 63 L.ED.2D 141.

Mr. Justice REHNQUIST delivered the opinion of the Court.

The United States sued in the District Court seeking enforcement of an Internal Revenue Service summons requiring respondent to appear and provide handwriting exemplars. Enforcement was denied by the Court of Appeals for the Eighth Circuit, United States v. Euge, 587 F.2d 25 (CA8 1978) (en banc), and we granted certiorari. We now hold that Congress has empowered the IRS to compel handwriting exemplars under its summons authority conferred by 26 U.S.C.A. § 7602.

I

The facts are not in dispute. In October 1977, an agent in the Intelligence Division of the Internal Revenue Service was assigned to investigate respondent's income tax liability for the years 1973 through 1976. Respondent had not filed any tax returns for those years. The Service sought to employ the "bank deposits method" of reconstructing respondent's income for those years, as a means of calculating his tax liability. Under this method of proof, the sums deposited in the taxpayer's bank accounts are scrutinized to determine whether they represent taxable income.

During the course of the investigation, the agent found only two bank accounts registered in respondent's name. Twenty other bank accounts were discovered, however, which the agent had reason to believe were being maintained by respondent under aliases to conceal taxable income. The statements for these accounts were sent to post office boxes held in respondent's name; the signature cards for the accounts listed addresses of properties owned by respondent; and the agent had documented frequent transfers of funds between the accounts.

In an effort to determine whether the sums deposited in these accounts represented income attributable to respondent, the agent issued a summons on October 7, 1977, requiring respondent to appear and execute handwriting exemplars of the various signatures appearing on the bank signature cards. Respondent declined to comply with the summons.

The United States commenced this action under 26 U.S.C.A. § 7604(a). The District Court held that the summons should be enforced, ordering respondent to provide 10 handwriting exemplars of eight different signatures. The Court of Appeals reversed, ruling that the summons authority vested in the Internal Revenue Service under 26 U.S.C.A. § 7602 does not authorize the IRS to compel the execution of handwriting exemplars.

II

The structure and history of the statutory authority of the Internal Revenue Service to summon witnesses to produce evidence necessary for tax investigations has been repeatedly reviewed by this Court in recent years. Under § 7602, the Secretary of the Treasury, and therefore the IRS as his designate, is authorized to summon individuals to "appear before the Secretary . . . and to produce such books, papers, records, or other data, and to give testimony, under oath, as may be relevant or material to such inquiry. . . . " The question presented here is whether this power to compel a witness to "appear," to produce "other data," and to "give testimony," includes the power to compel the execution of handwriting exemplars. We conclude that it does, for several reasons. While the language may not be explicit in its authorization of handwriting exemplars, the duty to appear and give testimony, a duty imposed by § 7602, has traditionally encompassed a duty to provide some forms of nontestimonial, physical evidence, including handwriting exemplars. Further this Court has consistently construed congressional intent to require that if the summons authority claimed is necessary for the effective performance of congressionally imposed responsibilities to enforce the tax code, that authority should be upheld absent express statutory prohibition or substantial countervailing policies. The authority claimed here is necessary for the effective exercise of the Service's enforcement responsibilities; it is entirely consistent with the statutory language; and it is not in derogation of any constitutional rights or countervailing policies enunciated by Congress.

A

Through § 7602, Congress has imposed a duty on persons possessing information "relevant or material" to an investigation of federal tax liability to produce that information at the request of the Secretary or his delegate. That duty to provide relevant information expressly obligates the person summoned to produce documentary evidence and to "appear" and "give testimony." Imposition of such an evidentiary obligation is, of course, not a novel innovation attributable to § 7602. The common law has been the source of a comparable evidentiary obligation for centuries. In determining the scope of the obligation Congress intended to impose by use of this language, we have previously analogized, as an interpretive guide, to the common-law duties attaching to the issuance of a testimonial summons. Congress, through legislation, may expand or contract the duty imposed, but absent some contrary expression, there is a wealth of

history helpful in defining the duties imposed by the issuance of a summons.

The scope of the "testimonial" or evidentiary duty imposed by common law or statute has traditionally been interpreted as an expansive duty limited principally by relevance and privilege. . . .

This broad duty to provide most relevant, nonprivileged evidence has not been considered to exist only in the common law. The Court has recognized that by statute "Congress may provide for the performance of this duty." Blackmer v. United States, 284 U.S. 421, 438, 52 S.Ct. 252, 255, 76 L.Ed. 375 (1932). By imposing an obligation to produce documents as well as to appear and give testimony, we believe the language of § 7602 suggests an intention to codify a broad testimonial obligation, including an obligation to provide some physical evidence relevant and material to a tax investigation, subject to the traditional privileges and limitations. This conclusion seems inherent in the imposition of an obligation to "appear," since an obligation to appear necessarily entails an obligation to display physical features to the summoning authority. Congress thereby authorized the Service to compel the production of some physical evidence and it is certainly possible to conclude that this authorization extended to the execution of handwriting exemplars, one variety of relevant physical evidence. This construction of the language conforms with the historical notions of the testimonial duty attaching to the issuance of a summons. . . . Section 7602 does not, by its terms, compel the production of handwriting exemplars, and therefore, a narrower interpretation of the duty imposed is not precluded by the actual language of the statute. A narrower interpretation *is* precluded, however, by the precedents of this Court construing that statute. As early as 1911, this Court established the benchmarks for interpreting the authority of the Internal Revenue Service to enforce tax obligations in holding that, "the administration of this statute may well be taken to embrace all appropriate measures for its enforcement, [unless] there is ... substantial reason for assigning to the phrase[s] ... a narrower interpretation." United States v. Chamberlin, 219 U.S. 250, 269, 31 S.Ct. 155, 162, 55 L.Ed. 204 (1911). This precise mode of construction has consistently been applied by this Court in construing the breadth of the summons authority Congress intended to confer in § 7602.... There is thus a formidable line of precedent construing congressional intent to uphold the claimed enforcement authority of the Service if such authority is necessary for the effective enforcement of the revenue laws and is not undercut by contrary legislative purposes.

Applying these principles, we conclude that Congress empowered the Service to seek, and obliged the witness to provide handwriting exemplars relevant to the investigation....

There is certainly nothing in the statutory language, or in the legislative history, precluding the interpretation asserted by the Service. Nor is there any constitutional privilege of the taxpayer or other parties that is violated by this construction. Compulsion of handwriting exemplars is neither a search or seizure subject to Fourth Amendment protections, nor testimonial evidence protected by the Fifth Amendment privilege against self-incrimination. Gilbert v. California, 388 U.S. 263, 87 S.Ct. 1951, 18 L.Ed.2d 1178 (1967). The compulsion of handwriting exemplars has been the subject of far less protection than the compulsion of testimony and documents. Since Congress has explicitly established an obligation to provide the more protected forms of evidence, it would seem curious had it chosen not to impose an obligation to produce a form of evidence tradition has found it less important to protect.

As we have emphasized in other cases dealing with § 7602 proceedings, the summoned party is entitled to challenge the issuance of the summons in an adversary proceeding in federal court prior to enforcement, and may assert appropriate defenses. The Service must also establish compliance with the good-faith requirements recognized by this Court, United States v. LaSalle National Bank, 437 U.S. 298, 318, 98 S.Ct. 2357, 2368, 57 L.Ed.2d 221 (1978), and with the requirement of § 7605(b) that "No taxpayer shall be subjected to unnecessary examination or investigations...." These protections are quite sufficient to lead us to refuse to strain to imply additional ones from the neutral language Congress has used in § 7602.

We accordingly reverse the judgment of the Court of Appeals refusing enforcement of the summons.

Reversed.

Mr. Justice BRENNAN, with whom Mr. Justice MARSHALL and Mr. Justice STEVENS join, dissenting.

The Internal Revenue Service, unlike common-law courts, has only such authority as Congress gives it. Congress has granted the Service authority to summon individuals "to appear before the Secretary ... at a time and place named in the summons and to produce such books, papers, records, or other data, and to give such testimony, under oath, as may be relevant or material to such inquiry...." 26 U.S. C.A. § 7602. The Court holds today that this authority to compel "testimony" includes authority to compel the creation of handwriting exemplars. The Court, however, is unable to point to anything in the statutory language or legislative history that even suggests that the obligation to "give testimony" includes an obligation to *create* a handwriting exemplar. Indeed, the Court concedes, as it must, that a handwriting exemplar is a kind of *nontestimonial* physical evidence. Certainly, Congress has the power to authorize the Service to compel the creation of exemplars, but it has not chosen to do so in § 7602. Accordingly, I dissent.

Mr. Justice MARSHALL, dissenting.

In my view, the Fifth Amendment's privilege against compulsory self-incrimination prohibits the Government from requiring a person to provide handwriting exemplars. As I stated in my dissenting opinion in United States v. Mara, 410 U.S. 19, 33, 93 S.Ct. 774, 782, 35 L.Ed.2d 99 (1973), "I cannot accept the notion that the Government can compel a man to cooperate affirmatively in securing incriminating evidence when that evidence could not be obtained without the cooperation of the suspect." The Fifth Amendment privilege is rooted in "the basic stream of religious and political principle[,] . . . reflects the limits of the individual's attornment to the state," In re Gault, 387 U.S. 1, 47, 87 S.Ct. 1428, 1454, 18 L.Ed.2d 527 (1967), and embodies the "respect a government—state or federal—must accord to the dignity and integrity of its citizens," Miranda v. Arizona, 384 U.S. 436, 460, 86 S.Ct. 1602, 1620, 16 L.Ed.2d 694 (1966). I continue to believe, then, that "[i]t is only by prohibiting the Government from compelling an individual to cooperate affirmatively in securing incriminating evidence which could not be obtained without his active assistance, that 'the inviolability of the human personality' is assured." United States v. Mara, supra, 410 U.S., at 34–35, 93 S.Ct., at 782–83 (dissenting opinion) (quoting Miranda v. Arizona, supra, 384 U.S., at 460, 86 S.Ct., at 1620).

In order to avoid this constitutional problem, I agree with my Brother BRENNAN . . . that 26 U.S.C.A. § 7602 should be construed not to permit Internal Revenue Service personnel to compel the production of handwriting exemplars. Accordingly, I dissent.

THE INSPECTION OF PREMISES

The line of development traced through the preceding cases is strongly in the direction of increasing governmental investigatory power. At first glance, the direction with regard to administrative inspection of premises appears to be otherwise. Let us look at the relevant cases.

The Supreme Court did not take up constitutional questions of administrative inspection of premises until 1959. Then, in *Frank* v. *Maryland*, 359 U.S. 360, 79 S.Ct. 804, 3 L.Ed.2d 877, the Court upheld by a five-to-four vote a provision of the Baltimore City Code allowing warrantless inspections of private dwellings by a health inspector based on suspicion that a nuisance existed. The *Frank* decision remained controlling until the *Camara* case of 1967.

Camara v. Municipal Court of the City and County of San Francisco

Supreme Court of the United States, 1967.
387 U.S. 523, 87 S.Ct. 1727, 18 L.Ed.2d 930.

Mr. Justice WHITE delivered the opinion of the Court.

In Frank v. State of Maryland, 359 U.S. 360, 79 S.Ct. 804, 3 L.Ed.2d 877, this Court upheld, by a five-to-four vote, a state court conviction of a homeowner who refused to permit a municipal health inspector to enter and inspect his premises without a search warrant. In Ohio ex rel. Eaton v. Price, 364 U.S. 263, 80 S.Ct. 1463, 4 L.Ed.2d 1708, a similar conviction was affirmed by an equally divided Court. Since those closely divided decisions, more intensive efforts at all levels of government to contain and eliminate urban blight have led to increasing use of such inspection techniques, while numerous decisions of this Court have more fully defined the Fourth Amendment's effect on state and municipal action. . . .

Appellant brought this action in a California Superior Court alleging that he was awaiting trial on a criminal charge of violating the San Francisco Housing Code by refusing to permit a warrantless inspection of his residence, and that a writ of prohibition should issue to the criminal court because the ordinance authorizing such inspections is unconstitutional on its face. The Superior Court denied the writ, the District Court of Appeal affirmed, and the Supreme Court of California denied a petition for hearing. Appellant properly raised and had considered by the California courts the federal constitutional questions he now presents to this Court.

Though there were no judicial findings of fact in this prohibition proceeding, we shall set forth the parties' factual allegations. On November 6, 1963, an inspector of the Division of Housing Inspection of the San Francisco Department of Public Health entered an apartment building to make a routine annual inspection for possible violations of the city's Housing Code. The building's manager informed the inspector that appellant, lessee of the ground floor, was using the rear of his leasehold as a personal residence. Claiming that the building's occupancy permit did not allow residential use of the ground floor, the inspector confronted appellant and demanded that he permit an inspection of the premises. Appellant refused to allow the inspection because the inspector lacked a search warrant.

The inspector returned on November 8, again without a warrant, and appellant again refused to allow an inspection. A citation was then mailed ordering appellant to appear at the district attorney's office.

When appellant failed to appear, two inspectors returned to his apartment on November 22. They informed appellant that he was required by law to permit an inspection under § 503 of the Housing Code:

> Sec. 503 RIGHT TO ENTER BUILDING. Authorized employees of the City departments or City agencies, so far as may be necessary for the performance of their duties, shall, upon presentation of proper credentials, have the right to enter, at reasonable times, any building, structure, or premises in the City to perform any duty imposed upon them by the Municipal Code.

Appellant nevertheless refused the inspectors access to his apartment without a search warrant. Thereafter, a complaint was filed charging him with refusing to permit a lawful inspection in violation of § 507 of the Code. Appellant was arrested on December 2 and released on bail. When his demurrer to the criminal complaint was denied, appellant filed this petition for a writ of prohibition.

Appellant has argued throughout this litigation that § 503 is contrary to the Fourth and Fourteenth Amendments in that it authorizes municipal officials to enter a private dwelling without a search warrant and without probable cause to believe that a violation of the Housing Code exists therein. Consequently, appellant contends, he may not be prosecuted under § 507 for refusing to permit an inspection unconstitutionally authorized by § 503. Relying on Frank v. State of Maryland, Eaton v. Price, and decisions in other States, the District Court of Appeal held that § 503 does not violate Fourth Amendment rights because it "is part of a regulatory scheme which is essentially civil rather than criminal in nature, inasmuch as that section creates a right of inspection which is limited in scope and may not be exercised under unreasonable conditions." Having concluded that Frank v. State of Maryland, to the extent that it sanctioned such warrantless inspections, must be overruled, we reverse.... [W]e hold that administrative searches of the kind at issue here are significant intrusions upon the interests protected by the Fourth Amendment, that such searches when authorized and conducted without a warrant procedure lack the traditional safeguards which the Fourth Amendment guarantees to the individual, and that the reasons put forth in Frank v. State of Maryland and in other cases for upholding these warrantless searches are insufficient to justify so substantial a weakening of the Fourth Amendment's protections. Because of the nature of the municipal programs under consideration, however, these conclusions must be the beginning, not the end, of our inquiry. The *Frank* majority gave recognition to the unique character of these inspection programs by refusing to require search warrants; to reject that disposition does not justify ignoring the question whether some other accommodation between public need and individual rights is essential.

II

The Fourth Amendment provides that, "no Warrants shall issue, but upon probable cause." Borrowing from more typical Fourth Amendment cases, appellant argues not only that code enforcement inspection programs must be circumscribed by a warrant procedure, but also that warrants should issue only when the inspector possesses probable cause to believe that a particular dwelling contains violations of the minimum standards prescribed by the code being enforced. We disagree.

In cases in which the Fourth Amendment requires that a warrant to search be obtained, "probable cause" is the standard by which a particular decision to search is tested against the constitutional mandate of reasonableness. To apply this standard, it is obviously necessary first to focus upon the governmental interest which allegedly justifies official intrusion upon the constitutionally protected interests of the private

citizen. For example, in a criminal investigation, the police may undertake to recover specific stolen or contraband goods. But that public interest would hardly justify a sweeping search of an entire city conducted in the hope that these goods might be found. Consequently, a search for these goods, even with a warrant, is "reasonable" only when there is "probable cause" to believe that they will be uncovered in a particular dwelling.

Unlike the search pursuant to a criminal investigation, the inspection programs at issue here are aimed at securing citywide compliance with minimum physical standards for private property. The primary governmental interest at stake is to prevent even the unintentional development of conditions which are hazardous to public health and safety....

There is unanimous agreement among those most familiar with this field that the only effective way to seek universal compliance with the minimum standards required by municipal codes is through routine periodic inspections of all structures. It is here that the probable cause debate is focused, for the agency's decision to conduct an area inspection is unavoidably based on its appraisal of conditions in the area as a whole, not on its knowledge of conditions in each particular building.... [W]e think that a number of persuasive factors combine to support the reasonableness of area code-enforcement inspections. First, such programs have a long history of judicial and public acceptance. See Frank v. State of Maryland, 359 U.S., at 367–371, 79 S.Ct. at 809–811. Second, the public interest demands that all dangerous conditions be prevented or abated, yet it is doubtful that any other canvassing technique would achieve acceptable results. Many such conditions—faulty wiring is an obvious example—are not observable from outside the building and indeed may not be apparent to the inexpert occupant himself. Finally, because the inspections are neither personal in nature nor aimed at the discovery of evidence of crime, they involve a relatively limited invasion of the urban citizen's privacy. . . .

Having concluded that the area inspection is a "reasonable" search of private property within the meaning of the Fourth Amendment, it is obvious that "probable cause" to issue a warrant to inspect must exist if reasonable legislative or administrative standards for conducting an area inspection are satisfied with respect to a particular dwelling. Such standards, which will vary with the municipal program being enforced, may be based upon the passage of time, the nature of the building (e.g., a multi-family apartment house), or the condition of the entire area, but they will not necessarily depend upon specific knowledge of the condition of the particular dwelling. It has been suggested that to so vary the probable cause test from the standard applied in criminal cases would be to authorize a "synthetic search warrant" and thereby to lessen the overall protections of the Fourth Amendment. Frank v. State of Maryland, 359 U.S., at 373, 79 S.Ct. at 812. But we do not agree. The warrant procedure is designed to guarantee that a decision to search private property is justified by a reasonable governmental interest. But reasonableness is still the ultimate standard. If a valid public interest justifies the intrusion contemplated, then there is probable cause to issue a suitably restricted search warrant. Cf. Oklahoma Press Pub. Co. v. Walling, 327 U.S. 186, 66 S.Ct. 494, 90 L.Ed. 614. . . .

Since our holding emphasizes the controlling standard of reasonableness, nothing we say today is intended to foreclose prompt inspections, even without a warrant, that the law has traditionally upheld in emergency situations. See North American Cold Storage Co. v. City of Chicago, 211 U.S. 306, 29 S.Ct. 101, 53 L.Ed. 195 (seizure of unwholesome food); Jacobson v. Commonwealth of Massachusetts, 197 U.S. 11, 25 S.Ct. 358, 49 L.Ed. 643 (compulsory smallpox vaccination); Compagnie Francaise de Navigation à Vapeur v. Louisiana State Board of Health, 186 U.S. 380, 22 S.Ct. 811, 46 L.Ed. 1209 (health quarantine); Kroplin v. Truax, 119 Ohio St. 610, 165 N.E. 498 (summary destruction of tubercular cattle). On the other hand, in the case of most routine area inspections, there is no compelling urgency to inspect at a particular time or on a particular day. Moreover, most citizens allow inspections of their property without a warrant. Thus, as a practical matter and in light of the Fourth Amendment's requirement that a warrant specify the property to be searched, it seems likely that warrants should normally be sought only after entry is refused unless there has been a citizen complaint or there is other satisfactory reason for securing immediate entry. Similarly, the requirement of a warrant procedure does not suggest any change in what seems to be the prevailing local policy, in most situations, of authorizing entry, but not entry by force, to inspect. . . .

The judgment is vacated and the case is remanded for further proceedings not inconsistent with this opinion. It is so ordered.

Judgment vacated and case remanded.

[Mr. Justice Clark, Mr. Justice Harlan and Mr. Justice Stewart dissented.]

Warrants in Administrative Investigations

Looking back at the *Camara* holding from a perspective of twenty years, it is clear that the decision was just the first in a series of cases questioning the need for a warrant in a wide range of administrative investigations. In *Wyman* v. *James*, 400 U.S. 309, 91 S.Ct. 381, 27 L.Ed.2d 408 (1971), a welfare recipient sought to prevent a periodic home visit by a welfare caseworker on the grounds that such a visit constituted a search and thus a warrant was required. But the Supreme Court ruled that the home visit was a reasonable administrative tool and need not be based on a warrant. It contrasted the home visit to the situation in *Camara* in these terms: "Mrs. James is not being prosecuted for her refusal to permit a home visit and is not about to be so prosecuted. . . . If a statute made her refusal a criminal offense, and if this case were one concerning her prosecution under the statute, *Camara* . . . would have conceivable pertinency."

A companion to the *Camara* case, decided on the same day, was *See* v. *City of Seattle*, 387 U.S. 541, 87 S.Ct. 1737, 8 L.Ed.2d 943 (1967). The case was based on an action by the city against a warehouse owner who refused to submit to fire inspection. The lower courts ruled for the city but the Supreme Court, with the same voting lineup as in *Camara*, reversed, holding that "warrants are a necessary and a tolerable limitation on the right to enter upon and inspect commercial premises" and that there is "no justification for so relaxing Fourth Amendment safeguards where the official inspection is intended to aid enforcement of laws prescribing minimum physical standards for commercial enterprises." (387 U.S. 543–544). Some commentators wondered whether *See* implied a warrant requirement for all administrative entries into business establishments, although the majority in *See* did note that they were not questioning "such accepted regulatory techniques as licensing programs." (387 U.S. 546). The Supreme Court soon had occasion to consider cases falling into this category.

In *Colonnade Catering Corp.* v. *United States*, 397 U.S. 72, 90 S.Ct. 774, 25 L.Ed.2d 60 (1970) IRS agents, suspecting a violation of federal excise tax laws, visited petitioner's establishment, which was licensed to serve alcoholic beverages. They requested to inspect the locked liquor storeroom, and when refused entry they broke in and removed bottles of liquor that they suspected of being refilled, which would have been a violation of a federal statute. Pertinent articles of the U.S. Code gave the secretary of the treasury or his agents broad power to enter and inspect the premises of retail dealers in liquor. In case of refusal to permit entry, the code provided for forfeiture of a five-hundred-dollar fine. In a proceeding on the question of suppression of the seized liquor as evidence, the Supreme Court found that while "Congress has broad power to design such powers of inspection under the liquor laws as it deems necessary to meet the evils at hand," the statutory scheme did not provide for using force when entry was refused, but only for the assessing of a fine. In other words, while the government lost the case, the principle of warrantless inspection in this case was left undisturbed.

United States v. *Biswell*, 406 U.S. 311, 92 S.Ct. 1593, 32 L.Ed.2d 87 (1972) involved the inspection by a treasury agent of a locked gun storeroom of a pawn shop operator who was federally licensed to deal in sporting weapons. Such warrantless inspections were authorized under the Gun Control Act of 1968. The operator asked the agent if he had a warrant, and when told that warrantless inspections were authorized under the statute he permitted entry. When the pawn shop operator was convicted of possessing illegal weapons found in the search, he moved to overturn the conviction by charging that the search violated the Fourth Amendment.

The Supreme Court, with only one justice dissenting, ruled that a warrantless inspection in this case was justified:

> When a dealer chooses to engage in this pervasively regulated business and to accept a federal license, he does so with the knowledge that his business records, firearms and ammunition will be subject to effective inspection.... [W]e have little difficulty in concluding that where, as here, regulatory inspections further urgent federal interest and the possibility of abuse and the threat of privacy are not of impressive dimensions, the inspection may proceed without a warrant where specifically authorized by statute.

A capstone case in the area of inspection of commercial establishments is *Marshall* v. *Barlow's*, decided in 1978. It amounted to a showdown of sorts between the line of cases requiring warrants and those condoning warrantless inspections.[5]

Marshall v. Barlow's, Inc.

SUPREME COURT OF THE UNITED STATES, 1978.
436 U.S. 307, 98 S.CT. 1816, 56 L.ED.2D 305.

[The Occupational Safety and Health Act of 1970 (OSHA) empowered the Secretary of Labor to search the work area of facilities covered by the act for purposes of uncovering safety hazards and violations of OSHA regulations. The act provided no requirement of a search warrant. An OSHA inspector was denied admission to the employee area of Barlow's Inc., an electrical and plumbing installation business in Pocatello, Idaho. The secretary of labor obtained a court order compelling Mr. Barlow to admit the inspector, and Barlow again refused. Barlow then sought injunctive relief against the warrantless search OSHA claimed it had the authority to conduct, asserting that such searches violated the Fourth Amendment. A federal district court ruled in Barlow's favor, holding that *Camara* and *See* controlled this case. The secretary appealed, and the case came to the Supreme Court.]

Mr. Justice WHITE delivered the opinion of the Court....

I

The Secretary urges that warrantless inspections to enforce OSHA are reasonable within the meaning of the Fourth Amendment. Among other things, he relies on § 8(a) of the Act, 29 U.S.C.A. § 657(a), which authorizes inspection of business premises without a warrant and which the Secretary urges represents a congressional construction of the Fourth Amendment that the courts should not reject. Regretfully, we are unable to agree....

This Court has already held that warrantless searches are generally unreasonable, and that this rule applies to commercial premises as well as homes. In Camara v. Municipal Court, 387 U.S. 523, 528–529, 87 S.Ct. 1727, 1731, 18 L.Ed.2d 930 (1967), we held:

[E]xcept in certain carefully defined classes of cases, a search of private property without proper consent is 'unreasonable' unless

[5] As Mr. Justice Rehnquist made clear in granting a stay pending Supreme Court consideration of a district court order based on this case, which had enjoined further government searches, the district court relied on *Camara* and *See* while the government relied on *Colonnade* and *Biswell* in urging a contrary result. *Marshall* v. *Barlow's, Inc.*, 429 U.S. 1347, 97 S.Ct. 776, 50 L.Ed.2d 739 (1977).

it has been authorized by a valid search warrant.

On the same day, we also ruled:

As we explained in *Camara*, a search of private houses is presumptively unreasonable if conducted without a warrant. The businessman, like the occupant of a residence, has a constitutional right to go about his business free from unreasonable official entries upon his private commercial property. The businessman, too, has that right placed in jeopardy if the decision to enter and inspect for violation of regulatory laws can be made and enforced by the inspector in the field without official authority evidenced by a warrant. See v. City of Seattle, 387 U.S. 541, 543, 87 S.Ct. 1737, 1739, 18 L.Ed.2d 943 (1967).

These same cases also held that the Fourth Amendment prohibition against unreasonable searches protects against warrantless intrusions during civil as well as criminal investigations. See v. City of Seattle, supra, at 543, 87 S.Ct. at 1739. The reason is found in the "basic purpose of this Amendment ... [which] is to safeguard the privacy and security of individuals against arbitrary invasions by governmental officials." *Camara*, supra, 387 U.S., at 528, 87 S.Ct. at 1730. If the government intrudes on a person's property, the privacy interest suffers whether the government's motivation is to investigate violations of criminal laws or breaches of other statutory or regulatory standards. It therefore appears that unless some recognized exception to the warrant requirement applies, See v. City of Seattle, supra, would require a warrant to conduct the inspection sought in this case.

The Secretary urges that an exception from the search warrant requirement has been recognized for "pervasively regulated business[es]," United States v. Biswell, 406 U.S. 311, 316, 92 S.Ct. 1593, 1596, 32 L.Ed.2d 87 (1972), and for "closely regulated" industries "long subject to close supervision and inspection." Colonnade Catering Corp. v. United States, 397 U.S. 72, 74, 77, 90 S.Ct.

774, 777, 25 L.Ed.2d 60 (1970). These cases are indeed exceptions, but they represent responses to relatively unique circumstances. Certain industries have such a history of government oversight that no reasonable expectation of privacy, see Katz v. United States, 389 U.S. 347, 351–352, 88 S.Ct. 507, 511, 19 L.Ed.2d 576 (1967), could exist for a proprietor over the stock of such an enterprise. Liquor (*Colonnade*) and firearms (*Biswell*) are industries of this type; when an entrepreneur embarks upon such a business, he has voluntarily chosen to subject himself to a full arsenal of governmental regulation....

The clear import of our cases is that the closely regulated industry of the type involved in *Colonnade* and *Biswell* is the exception. The Secretary would make it the rule....

The Secretary submits that warrantless inspections are essential to the proper enforcement of OSHA because they afford the opportunity to inspect without prior notice and hence to preserve the advantages of surprise. While the dangerous conditions outlawed by the Act include structural defects that cannot be quickly hidden or remedied, the Act also regulates a myriad of safety details that may be amenable to speedy alteration or disguise. The risk is that during the interval between an inspector's initial request to search a plant and his procuring a warrant following the owner's refusal of permission, violations of this latter type could be corrected and thus escape the inspector's notice. To the suggestion that warrants may be issued *ex parte* and executed without delay and without prior notice, thereby preserving the element of surprise, the Secretary expresses concern for the administrative strain that would be experienced by the inspection system, and by the courts, should *ex parte* warrants issued in advance become standard practice.

We are unconvinced, however, that requiring warrants to inspect will impose serious burdens on the inspection system or the courts, will prevent inspections necessary to enforce the statute, or will make them less effective. . . . [T]he great majority of businessmen can be expected in normal course to consent to inspection without warrant; the Secretary has not brought to this Court's attention any widespread pattern of refusal. . . .

Whether the Secretary proceeds to secure a warrant or other process, with or without prior notice, his entitlement to inspect will not depend on his demonstrating probable cause to believe that conditions in violation of OSHA exist on the premises. Probable cause in the criminal law sense is not required. For purposes of an administrative search such as this, probable cause justifying the issuance of a warrant may be based not only on specific evidence of an existing violation but also on a showing that "reasonable legislative or administrative standards for conducting an . . . inspection are satisfied with respect to a particular [establishment]." Camara v. Municipal Court, supra, at 538, 87 S.Ct., at 1736. A warrant showing that a specific business has been chosen for an OSHA search on the basis of a general administrative plan for the enforcement of the Act derived from neutral sources such as, for example, dispersion of employees in various types of industries across a given area, and the desired frequency of searches in any of the lesser divisions of the area, would protect an employer's Fourth Amendment rights. We doubt that the consumption of enforcement energies in the obtaining of such warrants will exceed manageable proportions.

Finally, the Secretary urges that requiring a warrant for OSHA inspectors will mean that, as a practical matter, warrantless search provisions in other regulatory statutes are also constitutionally infirm. The reasonableness of a warrantless search, however, will depend upon the specific enforcement needs and privacy guarantees of each statute. Some of the statutes cited apply only to a single indus-

try, where regulations might already be so pervasive that a *Colonnade-Biswell* exception to the warrant requirement could apply. Some statutes already envision resort to federal court enforcement when entry is refused, employing specific language in some cases and general language in others. In short, we base today's opinion on the facts and law concerned with OSHA and do not retreat from a holding appropriate to that statute because of its real or imagined effect on other, different administrative schemes. . . .

III

We hold that Barlow was entitled to a declaratory judgment that the Act is unconstitutional insofar as it purports to authorize inspections without warrant or its equivalent and to an injunction enjoining the Act's enforcement to that extent. The judgment of the District Court is therefore affirmed.

So ordered.

Mr. Justice BRENNAN took no part in the consideration or decision of this case.

Mr. Justice STEVENS, with whom Mr. Justice BLACKMUN and Mr. Justice REHNQUIST join, dissenting.

Congress enacted the Occupational Safety and Health Act to safeguard employees against hazards in the work areas of businesses subject to the Act. To ensure compliance, Congress authorized the Secretary of Labor to conduct routine, nonconsensual inspections. Today the Court holds that the Fourth Amendment prohibits such inspections without a warrant. The Court also holds that the constitutionally required warrant may be issued without any showing of probable cause. I disagree with both of these holdings.

The Fourth Amendment contains two separate clauses, each flatly prohibiting a category of governmental conduct. The first clause states that the right to be free from unreasonable searches "shall not be violated"; the second unequivocally prohibits the issuance of warrants except "upon probable cause." In this case the ultimate question is whether the category of warrantless searches authorized by the statute is "unreasonable" within the meaning of the first clause.

In cases involving the investigation of criminal activity, the Court has held that the reasonableness of a search generally depends upon whether it was conducted pursuant to a valid warrant. There is, however, also a category of searches which are reasonable within the meaning of the first clause even though the probable cause requirement of the Warrant Clause cannot be satisfied. The regulatory inspection program challenged in this case, in my judgment, falls within this category.

I

The warrant requirement is linked "textually . . . to the probable-cause concept" in the Warrant Clause. South Dakota v. Opperman, supra, 428 U.S., at 370 n.5, 96 S.Ct. at 3097. The routine OSHA inspections are, by definition, not based on cause to believe there is a violation on the premises to be inspected. Hence, if the inspections were measured against the requirements of the Warrant Clause, they would be automatically and unequivocally unreasonable.

Because of the acknowledged importance and reasonableness of routine inspections in the enforcement of federal regulatory statutes such as OSHA, the Court recognizes that requiring full compliance with the Warrant Clause would invalidate all such inspection programs. Yet, rather than simply analyzing such programs under the "reasonableness" clause of the Fourth Amendment, the Court holds the OSHA program invalid under the Warrant Clause and then avoids a blanket prohibition on all routine, regulatory inspections by relying on the notion that the "probable cause" requirement in the Warrant Clause may be relaxed whenever the Court believes that the governmental need to conduct a category of "searches" outweighs the intrusion on interests protected by the Fourth Amendment. . . .

Fidelity to the original understanding of the Fourth Amendment, therefore, leads to the conclusion that the Warrant Clause has no application to routine, regulatory inspections of commercial premises. If such inspections are valid, it is because they comport with the ultimate reasonableness standard of the Fourth Amendment. If the Court were correct in its view that such inspections, if undertaken without a warrant, are unreasonable in the constitutional sense, the issuance of a "new-fangled warrant"—to use Mr. Justice Clark's characteristically expressive term— without any true showing of particularized probable cause would not be sufficient to validate them. . . .

SUBPOENAS AND INSPECTIONS: DIVERGING TRENDS?

As suggested earlier, the trend of the inspection cases, at least as represented in *Camara, See,* and *Barlow's,* which required warrants prior to entry onto premises, seems to diverge from that of the constructive search cases covered at the beginning of the chapter, which have allowed an ever wider use of the subpoena power by government agencies. For two reasons, however, the differences between these two categories of cases may not be as great as it initially appears. First is the court-developed relaxation of the warrant requirement in inspection cases, and second is the number of exceptions to the warrant requirement that have surfaced over the years.

Regarding the relaxation of the warrant requirement, in *Camara* the Court said that probable cause could be satisfied on an area basis, without reference to "the condition of the particular building," while in *Barlow's* the Court indicated approval of a "warrant showing that a specific business has been chosen for an OSHA search on the basis of a general administrative plan for the enforcement of the Act...." In other words, a warrant in such cases would appear to be quite easy to obtain. To quote the *Barlow's* majority again, a warrant "with or without prior notice ... will not depend on [the Secretary's] demonstrating probable cause...." The relaxation of the warrant requirement in *Camara* and *Barlow's* has led one commentator to conclude that "[t]he practical difference between what the Court requires and what could be done through warrantless inspections may be so slight as to be almost nonexistent." [6]

Regarding the second point mentioned above, exceptions to the warrant requirement in inspection cases, *Wyman* (1971), *Colonnade* (1970), and *Biswell* (1972), have already been mentioned. In the first of these it was concluded that the home visit to a welfare recipient was not subject to the warrant requirement. The other two cases established the principle that warrantless inspections would be permitted in pervasively regulated businesses such as selling liquor and firearms. More recently, the Supreme Court has condoned warrantless administrative inspections in another line of cases. In 1981 the right of inspectors to conduct a warrantless inspection of a stone quarry under provisions of the Federal Mine Safety and Health Act of 1977 was upheld. Writing for the majority, Justice Marshall distinguished the situation from that in *Marshall* v. *Barlow's* and justified the warrantless search on the ground that "the Mine Safety and Health Act applies to industrial activity with a notorious history of serious accidents and unhealthful working conditions." *Donovan* v. *Dewey*, 452 U.S. 594, 603, 101 S.Ct. 2534, 2540, 69 L.Ed.2d 262, 272 (1981).

Justice Rehnquist concurred in the judgment in *Donovan* v. *Dewey* because he concluded that the stone quarry being inspected "was largely visible to the naked eye" and there was no need to enter the buildings or enclosed property of the defendant. Justice Rehnquist went on to invoke the "open fields exception" in support of his view. When public officials enter outdoor premises belonging to a firm or individual for investigative purposes, a somewhat different situation obtains. The Supreme Court held in 1974 that a health inspector did not violate the Fourth Amendment when he went onto the land of a corporation without its knowledge or consent to make observations of smoke being emitted from the plant's chimneys. These observations were "well within the 'open fields' exception to the Fourth Amendment" and were not controlled by the rulings in *Camara* or *See*. *Air Pollution Variance Board of the State of Colorado* v. *Western Alfalfa Corp.*, 416 U.S. 861, 94 S.Ct. 2114, 40 L.Ed.2d 607 (1974). In 1984 the Supreme Court indicated (in two cases covered in a single decision) that the open fields exception could apply to warrantless inspections of farmlands and woodlands where marijuana was being grown. *Oliver* v. *United States*, 466 U.S. 170, 104 S.Ct. 1735, 80 L.Ed.2d 214 (1984). And,

---

[6] Davis, above, note 4, at 258.

in a pair of five-to-four decisions rendered on the same day in 1986, the Court ruled that the open fields exception covered aerial surveillance where the evidence in question, although not within buildings, was behind walls or fences. One case involved monitoring pollution from an industrial plant, and the other concerned aerial surveillance of a marijuana garden in the fenced-in yard of a private home.[7]

A case which combines some of the features of the two major subjects of this chapter, the use of the subpoena power and the administrative entry on to private premises, was decided by the Supreme Court in 1984. Justice Rehnquist's short opinion for a unanimous Court cites and discusses several of the important precedents covered previously in this chapter.

Donovan v. Lone Steer, Inc.

SUPREME COURT OF THE UNITED STATES, 1984.
464 U.S. 408, 104 S.CT. 769, 78 L.ED.2D 567.

Justice REHNQUIST delivered the opinion of the Court.

Section 11(a) of the Fair Labor Standards Act of 1938 (FLSA or Act), 29 U.S.C. § 211(a), authorizes the Secretary of Labor to investigate and gather data regarding wages, hours, and other conditions of employment to determine whether an employer is violating the Act. § 9 of the FLSA, 29 U.S.C. § 209, empowers the Secretary of Labor to subpoena witnesses and documentary evidence relating to any matter under investigation. Pursuant to those provisions, an official of the Department of Labor served an administrative subpoena *duces tecum* on an employee of appellee Lone Steer, Inc., a motel and restaurant located in Steele, North Dakota. The subpoena directed an officer or agent of appellee with personal knowledge of appellee's records to appear at the Wage and Hour Division of the United States Department of Labor in Bismarck, North Dakota, and to produce certain payroll and sales records. In an action filed by appellee to challenge the validity of the subpoena, the District Court for the District of North Dakota, 565 F.Supp. 229, held that, although the Secretary of Labor had complied with the appli-

cable provisions of the FLSA in issuing the subpoena, enforcement of the subpoena would violate the Fourth Amendment of the United States Constitution because the Secretary had not previously obtained a judicial warrant. We noted probable jurisdiction of the Secretary's appeal, 462 U.S. 1105, 103 S.Ct. 2451, 77 L.Ed.2d 1331 (1983), and we now reverse the judgment of the District Court.

On January 6, 1982, Al Godes, a Compliance Officer with the Wage and Hour Division of the Department of Labor, telephoned Susann White, appellee's manager, to inform her that he intended to begin an investigation of appellee the following morning and to request that she have available for inspection payroll records for all employees for the past two years. White telephoned Godes later that day to inform him that it would not be convenient to conduct the inspection on the following morning. After some preliminary skirmishing between the parties, during which appellee inquired about the scope and reason for the proposed investigation and appellants declined to provide specific information, Godes and Gerald Hill, Assistant Area Director from the Wage and Hour Division

---

[7] The first case was *Dow Chemical* v. *U.S.*, ___ U.S. ___, 106 S.Ct. 1019, 90 L.Ed.2d 226. The second case was *California* v. *Ciraola*, ___ U.S. ___, 106 S.Ct. 1809, 90 L.Ed.2d 210.

in Denver, arrived at appellee's premises on February 2, 1982, for the purpose of conducting the investigation. After waiting for White, Godes served the administrative subpoena at issue here on one of appellee's other employees. The subpoena was directed to any employee of appellee having custody and personal knowledge of the records specifically described therein, records which appellee was required by law to maintain. See 29 CFR §§ 516.2(a), 516.5(c) (1983). The subpoena directed the employee to appear with those records at the Wage and Hour Office of the Department of Labor in Bismarck, North Dakota.

Appellee refused to comply with the subpoena and sought declaratory and injunctive relief in the District Court, claiming that the subpoena constituted an unlawful search and seizure in violation of the Fourth Amendment. Appellants counterclaimed for enforcement of the subpoena. The District Court concluded that the actions of appellants in issuing the administrative subpoena "unquestionably comport with the provisions of the Fair Labor Standards Act, as amended, 29 U.S.C. § 201, et seq." Juris. Statement 6a. Relying on our decision in *Marshall* v. *Barlow's, Inc.*, 436 U.S. 307, 98 S.Ct. 1816, 56 L.Ed.2d 305 (1978), however, the District Court held that the applicable provisions of the FLSA violate the Fourth Amendment insofar as they authorize the Secretary of Labor to issue an administrative subpoena without previously having obtained a judicial warrant. In *Barlow's* this Court declared unconstitutional the provisions of the Occupational Safety and Health Act of 1970 (OSHA) which authorized inspectors to enter an employer's premises without a warrant to conduct inspections of work areas. The District Court rejected appellants' arguments that *Barlow's* is not dispositive of the issue here by stating:

> It is reasonable to conclude that the exigencies of an entry upon commercial premises for the purpose of conducting a safety and health inspection designed to protect the

personal well-being of employees supply more compelling bases for proceeding without a warrant than the circumstances presented here, where the entry is sought for the purpose of determining compliance with wage and hour regulations. The reasoning of the Supreme Court in *Barlow's* applies with equal—if not greater—force in the instant situation.

In sum, I hold that the Secretary of Labor may *not* proceed to enter upon the premises of Lone Steer, Inc., for the purpose of inspecting its records under § 11 of the Fair Labor Standards Act without first having obtained a valid warrant.

Juris. Statement 8a.

We think that the District Court undertook to decide a case not before it when it held that appellants may not "enter upon the premises" of appellee to inspect its records without first having obtained a warrant. The only "entry" upon appellee's premises by appellants, so far as the record discloses, is that of Godes on February 2, 1982, when he and Gerald Hill entered the motel and restaurant to attempt to conduct an investigation. The stipulation of facts entered into by the parties, app. 11–17, and incorporated into the opinion of the District Court, juris. statement 2a–8a, describe what happened next:

> They asked for Ms. White and were told she was not available but expected shortly. They were offered some coffee, and waited in the lobby area. After 20–30 minutes, when Ms. White had not appeared, Mr. Godes served an Administrative Subpoena Duces Tecum on employee Karen Arnold.

App. 15.

An entry into the public lobby of a motel and restaurant for the purpose of serving an administrative subpoena is scarcely the sort of governmental act which is forbidden by the Fourth Amendment. The administrative subpoena itself did not authorize either entry or inspection of appellee's premises; it merely directed appellee to produce relevant wage and hour records at appellants' regional office some 25 miles away.

The governmental actions which required antecedent administrative warrants in *Marshall* v. *Barlow's, Inc.*, supra, and *Camara* v. *Municipal Court*, 387 U.S. 523, 87 S.Ct. 1727, 18 L.Ed.2d 930 (1967), are quite different from the governmental action in this case. In *Barlow's* an OSHA inspector sought to conduct a search of non-public working areas of an electrical and plumbing installation business. In *Camara* a San Francisco housing inspector sought to inspect the premises of an apartment building in that city. See also *See* v. *City of Seattle*, 387 U.S. 541, 87 S.Ct. 1737, 18 L.Ed.2d 943 (1967) (involving a similar search by a fire inspector of commercial premises). In each case, this Court held that an administrative warrant was required before such a search could be conducted without the consent of the owner of the premises.

It is plain to us that those cases turned upon the effort of the government inspectors to make non-consensual entries into areas not open to the public. As we have indicated, no such entry was made by appellants in this case. Thus the enforceability of the administrative subpoena *duces tecum* at issue here is governed, not by our decision in *Barlow's* as the District Court concluded, but rather by our decision in *Oklahoma Press Publishing Co.* v. *Walling*, 327 U.S. 186, 66 S.Ct. 494, 90 L.Ed. 614 (1946). In *Oklahoma Press* the Court rejected an employer's claim that the subpoena power conferred upon the Secretary of Labor by the FLSA violates the Fourth Amendment.

> The short answer to the Fourth Amendment objections is that the records in these cases present no question of actual search and seizure, but raise only the question whether orders of court for the production of specified records have been validly made; and no sufficient showing appears to justify setting them aside. No officer or other person has sought to enter petitioners' premises against their will, to search them, or to seize or examine their books, records or papers without their assent, otherwise than pursuant to orders of court authorized by law and made after adequate opportunity to present objections. . . .

327 U.S., at 195, 66 S.Ct., at 498 (footnotes omitted). We cited *Oklahoma Press* with approval in *See* v. *City of Seattle*, supra, a companion case to *Camara*, and described the constitutional requirements for administrative subpoenas as follows:

> It is now settled that, when an administrative agency subpoenas corporate books or records, the Fourth Amendment requires that the subpoena be sufficiently limited in scope, relevant in purpose, and specific in directive so that compliance will not be unreasonably burdensome.

See v. *City of Seattle*, supra, 387 U.S., at 544, 87 S.Ct., at 1740 (footnote omitted). See also *United States* v. *Morton Salt Co.*, 338 U.S. 632, 652–653, 70 S.Ct. 357, 368–369, 94 L.Ed. 401 (1950).

Thus although our cases make it clear that the Secretary of Labor may issue an administrative subpoena without a warrant, they nonetheless provide protection for a subpoenaed employer by allowing him to question the reasonableness of the subpoena, before suffering any penalties for refusing to comply with it, by raising objections in an action in district court. *See* v. *City of Seattle*, supra, 387 U.S., at 544–545, 87 S.Ct., at 1739–1740; *Oklahoma Press*, supra, 327 U.S., at 208–209, 66 S.Ct., at 505. Our holding here, which simply reaffirms our holding in *Oklahoma Press*, in no way leaves an employer defenseless against an unreasonably burdensome administrative subpoena requiring the production of documents. We hold only that the defenses available to an employer do not include the right to insist upon a judicial warrant as a condition precedent to a valid administrative subpoena.

Appellee insists that "[t]he official inspection procedure used by the appellants reveal[s] that the use of the administrative subpoena is inextricably intertwined with the entry process," Brief for Appellee 11, and states that it is appellants' established policy to seek entry inspections by expressly relying on its inspection authority under § 11 of the FLSA. Id., at 12. We need only observe that no non-consensual entry into protected premises was involved in this case.

The judgment of the District Court is accordingly.

Reversed.

Chapter 6

Rules and Rule Making

Radiation Overdose: All in a Day's Work [a]

Alan Richman

Special to the New York Times

Harrisburg, Pa., April 3—Last Wednesday afternoon Edward Houser dressed more carefully than usual for work.

He put on a pair of coveralls, something like a jumpsuit. On top of the coveralls, he put two more pairs. He put on three pairs of gloves, one pair of rubber boots and a full-face respirator. Then he walked into more nuclear radiation than a human body can endure for very long.

"I never felt a thing," he said.

Mr. Houser is a chemistry foreman at the Three Mile Island nuclear power plant, one of four men who received overdoses of gamma radiation on the day that unit No. 2 went out of control. Of the four, he received the most, exceeding the limit mandated by federal regulations by an amount equivalent to 35 chest X rays. . . . [Six days later] Mr. Houser is back on the job at Three Mile Island, although he is not working in the vicinity of high radiation. He was cleared to return to work so soon after overexposure because federal guidelines are based on the calendar, not on the body.

Each calendar quarter a nuclear industry employee is permitted to absorb no more than three rem. Each year he is allowed no more than five. The yearly figure is flexible.

Any unused portion of the yearly total of five rem may be carried forward, just as an investor on Wall Street carries forward a long-term capital loss. Mr. Houser, for example, is 32 years old. Since the rem savings system begins

---

[a] The *New York Times*, April 4, 1979, 1. © 1979 by the New York Times Company. Reprinted by permission.

when an individual is 18 years old, his nuclear bank contains seventy rem minus whatever radiation he has absorbed in his career.

Last Wednesday, he received a dose of approximately four rem. That exceeded his quarterly quota, but the quarter ended three days later. The four rem did not exceed his yearly quota of five. Officials did not even have to consider how much he had in his bank.

"It's a fact of life," said Mr. Elsasser [state liaison officer for the Nuclear Regulatory Commission] "that everything is based on quarterly exposure. Its a matter of how you set up your bookkeeping. Once the quarter is over, the accumulation is considered removed, and it so happened April 1 began the next quarter. It's a matter of coincidence that this accident occurred so close to the end of the quarter. (When April 1 came, he was assigned back to work in the radiation field.) . . .

The calendar-related radiation exposure limits discussed in this dispatch from the Three Mile Island plant are *rules*, duly adopted by the Nuclear Regulatory Commission and to be found in Volume 10 of the Code of Federal Regulations for 1979, Part 20, "Standards for Protection Against Radiation," pages 185 to 191. It's all there, in somewhat more complex and technical language than in the newspaper dispatch, but there nevertheless.

That these radiation standards are *rules* suggests several things of importance for the reader of this book. One is the tremendous reach of administrative rules, and therefore of administrative authority, into the lives of all Americans. Another is that rules can be quite complex in themselves and can deal with extremely complex aspects of the scientific-technological level achieved in this country at the end of the twentieth century. A third is that rules may be less than perfect when it comes to their application in practice. That the Three Mile Island accident happened at the end of a calendar quarter made it possible for Mr. Houser to receive a higher level of radiation than may have been desirable, but the rules were not violated.

This chapter will deal with the characteristics of administrative rules and the modes of their promulgation.

RULES

For most purposes an administrative rule can be distinguished from an administrative adjudicatory decision in two ways. First, a rule generally has future effect while a decision applies to a present fact situation. And, second, a rule is a statement of general applicability while a decision applies to an individual or a small number of parties. These distinctions operate satisfactorily in most cases and reflect the general understanding of the differences between the two terms. Some administrative activities confound this basic classification, however. For instance, a licensing proceeding or the issuing of an injunction typically apply to individual parties but can be said to have future effect. Yet they clearly fall into the category of adjudicatory proceedings.

The most well-known statutory definitions of rules only partially embrace the two characteristics mentioned above. The Model State Administrative Procedure Act emphasizes the general nature of a rule by stating that the term "means the whole or part of an agency statement of *general* applicability that implements, interprets, or prescribes (i) law or policy, or (ii) the organization, procedure, or practice requirements of an agency." [1] The federal Administrative Procedure Act stresses the prospective nature of a rule by defining it as "the whole or a part of an agency statement of *general or particular applicability and future effect* designed to implement, interpret or prescribe policy. . . ." [2] In spite of these definitional inconsistencies, however, it is clear that most administrative rules are designed to have both prospective effect and general applicability.

The distinction between rules and decisions is not unimportant. Significant procedural differences have traditionally been associated with the processes by which these two kinds of acts are adopted. We will take up that matter in the discussion of rule making.

Three Kinds of Rules

It is generally said that there are three kinds of rules: procedural, interpretive and legislative (or substantive). Procedural rules have caused little difficulty for analysts. They are internal "housekeeping" types of rules adopted by the agency to guide it in the procedures it will follow in carrying out its duties. If an agency fails to follow one of its procedural rules (even if it was not required to adopt such rules), its decision based on that faulty procedure may be reversed by a court. Thus, for instance, when the secretary of state discharged a foreign service officer without following the State Department's regulation that such decisions "shall be reached after consideration of the complete file, arguments, briefs, and testimony presented," a unanimous Supreme Court reversed the secretary's action. *Service* v. *Dulles*, 354 U.S. 363, 77 S.Ct. 1152, 1 L.Ed.2d 1403 (1957).

More difficult to deal with are legislative and interpretive rules. Distinguishing these two kinds of rules is not always easy, but important legal consequences depend upon which category rules are seen to fall into. The recognition of a difference between the two types of rules has been traced back to the 1920s. At first it was said that legislative rules were only "those promulgated pursuant to a *specific* delegation of rule-making power." [3] But later discussions have said that such rules can be based on a legislative grant "whether specific or not." [4] In any case, legislative rules are akin to statutes in

---

[1] 14 *Uniform Laws Annotated* § 1–102(10). 1985 Cumulative Annual Pocket Part.

[2] Section 551(4), emphasis added. See appendix A of this book. The original draft of the APA limited the definition of rules to "statements of general applicability." The change of language was made to assure that rule making could, when necessary, be addressed to named persons. See Bernard Schwartz, *Administrative Law* 147–8 (2d ed., 1984).

[3] Michael Asimow, "Public Participation in the Adoption of Interpretive Rules and Policy Statements," 75 *Michigan Law Review* 520, 561 (1977), emphasis in the original.

[4] Kenneth Culp Davis, 1 *Administrative Law Treatise* 358 (1958). Essentially the same conclusion is reached by Davis in the second edition of his treatise. See Vol. 2, 54 (1979).

their legal effect; they "receive statutory force upon going into effect," as the Attorney General's Committee's *Final Report* put it.[5] They are said to have the force of law, and courts are not supposed to substitute their judgment on the wisdom of such rules.

Interpretive rules, on the other hand, are considered to be merely the agency's interpretation of the statute.[6] They do not supplement the statute or prescribe conduct under a grant from the legislature. While such rules will not bind a court, they are entitled to some weight. As the important case of *Skidmore* v. *Swift Co.* put it, they "do constitute a body of experience and informed judgment to which courts and litigants may properly resort for guidance." 323 U.S. 134, 65 S.Ct. 161, 89 L.Ed. 124 (1944).

Aside from the difference in degree of deference, courts must show the two types of rules, another important difference between them involves procedures for adoption. The notice and comment provisions of section 553 of the APA do not apply to *interpretative rules* (most commentators now use the term "interpretive rules"), although both substantive rules and interpretive rules of general applicability must be published in the Federal Register.

One of the problems with the legislative-interpretive dichotomy has been the difficulty, in concrete cases, of distinguishing the two, a problem that is heightened by the great increase in rule making at the federal level in recent years. Rules are not always labelled legislative or interpretive by the issuing agency, and even when they are, some courts have found that the labels given are not reliable.

In connection with this point, the recent case law has gone in two directions on the matter of categorizing rules. The so-called "legal effect" standard either accepts the agency's label for its rules or attempts otherwise to determine whether the agency has a clear legislative mandate to adopt such rules. It accepts, in effect, the legislative rule-interpretive rule distinction. The "substantial impact" test pays less attention to the labels attached to rules, including those provided by the agency. Rather, it raises the question as to whether the regulation in question will have a substantial impact on the persons who will be affected by it. If this is the case, then section 553 of the APA, allowing notice and comment, must be applied. Those courts using the substantial impact test are saying, in effect, "if the regulations will have substantial impact, they are substantive rules no matter what they are called by the agency." It should be said however, that neither of these tests has proved fully satisfactory in practice. They both present problems in their application to specific fact situations, and their merit continues to be debated by scholars.[7]

---

[5] As quoted in Manning Gilbert Warren III, "The Notice Requirement in Administrative Rulemaking: An Analysis of Legislative and Interpretive Rules," 29 *Administrative Law Review* 367, 372 (1977).

[6] As Asimow, above, note 3, at 541, has pointed out, agency interpretation can also occur in less formal agency statements such as "press releases, internal memoranda, or advice letters to members of the public" as well as adjudication, both formal and informal, "negotiations, speechmaking, dispensing of grants, and even the lifting of the administrative eyebrow."

[7] See Michael Asimow, "Nonlegislative Rulemaking and Regulatory Reform," 1985 *Duke Law Journal* 381 (1985); William T. Mayton, "A Concept of a Rule and the 'Substantial Impact Test' in Rulemaking," 33 *Emory Law Journal* 889 (1984); "The Substantial Impact Test: Victim of the

The following two cases contain recent discussions of many of the points mentioned in this section. The first case is notable in that both tests are discussed in both the majority and dissenting opinions, while the *Chrysler* case is particularly interesting as one of the most thorough Supreme Court discussions of legislative and interpretive rules.

Energy Reserves Group, Inc. v. Department of Energy

TEMPORARY EMERGENCY COURT OF APPEALS, 1978.
589 F.2D 1082.

[The Emergency Petroleum Allocation Act (EPAA), as amended, exempts from price and allocation regulation the first sale of crude oil from any lease "whose average daily production of crude oil for the preceding calendar year does not exceed 10 barrels per well." Duly adopted legislative regulations of the Cost of Living Council and the Federal Energy Administration (FEA) expressly provided with regard to this "stripper well" exemption that only wells "which produce crude petroleum" could be counted in the calculation of the average daily production. While these provisions were in force appellees and others proposed that "injection wells" (nonproducing wells) should be included in the well count for purposes of determining average daily production. The FEA thereupon adopted what it called an interpretive ruling, "ruling 1974–29," the relevant part of which reads: "Thus, the F.E.A. regulations by their specific language provide that only wells 'which produce crude petroleum' are to be counted in calculating average daily production for the purpose of determining whether the stripper well lease exemption applies. While injection techniques help to 'produce' crude petroleum, they are not wells which themselves, 'produce' crude petroleum. Therefore, wells which did not actually yield or produce crude petroleum during the preceding calendar year are not production wells

for this purpose. Whether the non-producing well was an 'injection' well, a disposal well, a dry well, a spent well or a shut-in well will not change this result."]

Before CHRISTENSEN, BECKER and ZIRPOLI, Judges.

BECKER, Judge:

Introduction

In these cases the appellees question the validity of Ruling 1974–29 of the Federal Energy Administration (FEA), designated as an "interpretative" rule by FEA. If Ruling 1974–29 was interpretative, the ruling was exempt from the rule making requirements of § 553(b) and (c) Title 5 U.S.C.A., a part of the Administrative Procedure Act (APA). Section 553(b) of the APA permits all administrative agencies to issue interpretative rules without prior notice and opportunity for submission of written views, data and argument. The district court held that Ruling 1974–29 was not interpretative, but was legislative, and therefore invalid under § 553(b) and (c) of the APA, requiring notice and opportunity to comment prior to its adoption.

Appellants, Department of Energy (DOE) and the Secretary of Energy, contend that Ruling 1974–29 was properly designated as interpretative of a regulation, 10 C.F.R. § 210.32(b), and of the underlying statutory provisions exempting crude pe-

Fallout from *Vermont Yankee?*" 53 George Washington Law Review 118 (1984). See also Administrative Conference of the United States, *A Guide to Federal Agency Rulemaking* 33–39 (1983).

troleum produced by "stripper wells" from allocation and price regulation.

Statement of the Issue

Appellants, DOE and the Secretary of Energy, properly state that the issue in these consolidated appeals is as follows:

> Whether the District Court erred in holding that Federal Energy Administration ("FEA") Ruling 1974–29 (39 F.R. 44414, December 24, 1974), which interpreted the stripper well exemption as excluding injection wells from the "well count" for purposes of applying the exemption, is null and void and without effect because it was published without utilizing the notice and comment provisions of the Administrative Procedure Act ("APA"), 5 U.S.C.A. § 553(b). . . .

As stated above, FEA had previously dealt with this question by carefully setting forth in the mandatory regulations that only "wells which produced crude petroleum and petroleum condensates" were a factor in the formula for determining "average daily production." FEA consistently disallowed the count of injection wells in the formula. Despite the apparently clear statutory and regulatory provisions, FEA, confronted with claims such as those advanced in these cases, determined to put firmly at rest its official position concerning its interpretation of the term "average daily production" as used in the regulations (and statutes) by issuing in December 1974, its Ruling 1974–29, quoted above, interpreting the statutory stripper well exemption defined in the existing mandatory legislative regulation 10 C.F.R. § 210.32.

It is submitted that Ruling 1974–29 is interpretative because (1) FEA deemed it to be interpretative; (2) in its nature and effect the ruling was in fact and law an interpretation of the mandatory stripper well exemptions provided by EPAA and earlier by TAPAA, and defined by 10 C.F.R. § 210.32; (3) the ruling has no "impact," if its impact

is a consideration in determining its nature. These reasons will be developed in detail hereinafter.

(1) Ruling 1974–29 was deemed by FEA to be interpretative. While this characterization by FEA is not controlling, its interpretation of its statutory mandate is entitled to judicial deference, under persuasive authorities and the prior rulings of this Court. . . .

(2) By its nature and effect, Ruling 1974–29 was an interpretation of the stripper well exemption provided by EPAA and TAPAA, and defined in 10 C.F.R. § 210.32. An examination of the statute and Ruling 1974–29 makes this evident. The ruling does not purport to expand or constrict the meaning of the term "average daily production" as used in EPAA, TAPAA, and 10 C.F.R. § 210.32. It is in its nature a clarifying interpretation of the underlying statutes EPAA and TAPAA, and of the mandatory regulation 10 C.F.R. § 210.32, caused by the ingenious attempt to include injection wells in the statutory and regulatory formula. Further, Ruling 1974–29 was not only a reasonable construction (interpretation) of the statute and the regulation (the validity of which was accepted by the district court), but in addition may be the construction ultimately preferred by the courts. . . .

It is argued in support of the contention that Ruling 1974–29 is legislative rather than interpretative, that the ruling, though classified as interpretative, must be found to be legislative if it had a "substantial impact." This contention is unsound in law and experience. The words "substantial impact" do not appear in § 553 of the APA. They constitute an unwarranted judicial gloss on the statute misapplied in the context of these cases.

Even when a rule is legislative in form it will be treated as interpretative unless the administrative agency possesses and exercises delegated legislative authority in issuing it. The weight of persuasive and controlling legal authorities does not support application of this substantial impact test....

If Ruling 1974–29 was a reasonable interpretation of the stripper well statutory exception of EPAA and TAPAA, or of 10 C.F.R. § 210.32, or both, it had no impact. In that event the impact came from the statute and valid legislative regulation being interpreted, not from the interpretative ruling.

It is submitted that Ruling 1974–29 is a reasonable interpretation of the term "average daily production" as used in § 406 of TAPAA, § 4(e)(2)(A) of EPAA, and in 10 C.F.R. § 210.32(b). As such it had no "impact" if such be a test. The "impact," if any, resulted earlier from the statute and from the regulation 10 C.F.R. § 210.32(b) found to be valid by the district court. The interpretation of § 406 of TAPAA and § 4(e)(2)(A) of EPAA to exclude injection wells in computing "average daily production" was a reasonable contemporaneous construction of the statute and created no new law or legislative rule....

In each of these actions the judgment is reversed and the action remanded for further proceedings consistent with this opinion....

[The concurring opinion of Judge Christensen is omitted.]

ZIRPOLI, Judge, dissenting:

For the reasons stated below, I must respectfully dissent....

Rulemaking under the APA

A. Legislative and Interpretative Rules

The APA requires notice and an opportunity for interested persons to comment prior to the promulgation of a new rule. An exception to such formal rulemaking requirements, however, is provided in 5 U.S.C.A. § 553(b) for interpretative rules, and the FEA contends that Ruling 1974–29 is the epitome of an interpretative rule, since it merely seeks to define a term contained in an underlying regulation. The mere fact that a rule appears to be defini-

tional in form, however, does not preclude a finding that it is legislative rather than interpretative and thus subject to the formal rulemaking procedures of the APA. If Congress has delegated lawmaking power to the agency, then rules issued pursuant to that grant are legislative, whether such rules are cast in the form of definitions or in more traditional statutory form. The existence of such a delegation of power does not limit an agency to the issuance of legislative rules, but if such a grant has been made, a reviewing court must determine into which category the rule falls, and that determination is constrained neither by the form of the rule nor by the label attached to it by the agency. The FEA's contention that Ruling 1974–29 defines a term contained in an underlying regulation and is therefore interpretative rather than legislative is particularly difficult to sustain in view of the fact that the agency itself chose to define the other central terms of the stripper well exemption through the issuance of a legislative regulation.

Rather than be bound by the agency's own classification, many courts have attempted to discern the impact of the rule on regulated parties and have held those rules with substantial impact to be legislative and thus subject to formal rulemaking procedures. The FEA asserts that the substantial impact test has been discredited and abandoned as a means for distinguishing legislative from interpretative rules, but the agency's interment of the test appears to be premature....

While I believe that the FEA's obligation to employ formal rulemaking procedures in its promulgation of Ruling 1974–29 can be discerned in the APA itself, without regard to the agency's specific statutory framework, it is clear that Congress intended the FEA to proceed with an extra measure of caution, a caution deemed advisable in the case of a new agency whose actions would necessarily have widespread impact on the economy. In view of the clear and substantial impact of Ruling

1974–29, on consumers as well as producers of crude oil, the agency was required to observe formal rulemaking procedures....

I would affirm the judgment of the district court.

Chrysler Corp. v. Brown

SUPREME COURT OF THE UNITED STATES, 1979.
441 U.S. 281, 99 S.CT. 1705, 60 L.ED.2D 208.

[The Chrysler Corporation sued to enjoin the release, under the Freedom of Information Act, of documents it had submitted to the Defense Logistics Agency (DLA) in compliance with an executive order which applied to government contractors. This aspect of the case, a "reverse-Freedom-of-Information-Act" suit, is discussed elsewhere in this book. Chrysler contended that, in addition to the Freedom of Information Act, its suit could also be premised on the Trade Secrets Act, 18 U.S.C.A. § 1905, which provides that any officer or employee of the United States who divulges in a manner "not authorized by law" any information concerning trade secrets or other confidential data of a private organization may be subject to fine, imprisonment, and removal from office or employment. Chrysler argued that § 1905 was applicable to the type of disclosure at issue in this case, Affirmation Action Programs and related documents for two Chrysler plants, which were required under regulations promulgated by the Department of Labor's Office of Federal Contract Compliance Programs (OFCCP), and that the act also provided Chrysler a right to obtain injunctive relief. The court of appeals ruled that § 1905 was not applicable because the regulations in question provided authorization by law. Justice Rehnquist for a unanimous Court ruled that the Trade Secrets Act provided no direct private right of action to seek an injunction. But an injunction could be sought under § 706(2)(A) of the APA, which provides in part that a reviewing Court shall "hold unlawful and set aside agency action ... not in accordance with law." Thus, if disclosure violated the Trade Secrets Act, it would also be "not in accordance with law" under the APA. The Court's job, therefore, was to determine if the regulations in question satisfied the "authorized by law" language of the Trade Secrets Act. The passages excerpted below from Justice Rehnquist's opinion amount to an essay on the nature of administrative rules.]

Mr. Justice REHNQUIST delivered the opinion of the Court....

In order for a regulation to have the "force and effect of law," it must have certain substantive characteristics and be the product of certain procedural requisites. The central distinction among agency regulations found in the Administrative Procedure Act (APA) is that between "substantive rules" on the one hand and "interpretive rules, general statements of policy, or rules of agency organization, procedure, or practice" on the other. A "substantive rule" is not defined in the APA, and other authoritative sources essentially offer definitions by negative inference. But in Morton v. Ruiz, 415 U.S. 199, 94 S.Ct. 1055, 39 L.Ed.2d 270 (1974), we noted a characteristic inherent in the concept of a "substantive rule." We described a substantive rule—or a "legislative-type rule," id., at 236, 94 S.Ct., at 1074—as one "affecting individual rights and obligations." Id., at 232, 94 S.Ct., at 1073. This characteristic is an important touchstone for distinguishing those rules that may be "binding" or have the "force of law."

That an agency regulation is "substantive," however, does not by itself give it the "force and effect of law." The legislative power of the United States is vested in the Congress, and the exercise of quasi-legislative authority by governmental departments and agencies must be rooted in a grant of such power by the Congress and subject to limitations which that body imposes. As this Court noted in Batterton v. Francis, 432 U.S. 416, 425 n. 9, 97 S.Ct. 2399, 2405 n. 9, 53 L.Ed.2d 448 (1977):

> Legislative, or substantive, regulations are "issued by an agency pursuant to statutory authority and . . . implement the statute, as, for example, the proxy rules issued by the Securities and Exchange Commission. . . . Such rules have the force and effect of law."

Likewise the promulgation of these regulations must conform with any procedural requirements imposed by Congress. For agency discretion is not only limited by substantive, statutory grants of authority, but also by the procedural requirements which "assure fairness and mature consideration of rules of general application." NLRB v. Wyman-Gordon Co., 394 U.S. 759, 764, 89 S.Ct. 1426, 1429, 22 L.Ed.2d 709 (1969). The pertinent procedural limitations in this case are those found in the APA.

The regulations relied on by the Government in this case as providing "authoriz[ation] by law" within the meaning of § 1905 certainly affect individual rights and obligations; they govern the public's right to information in records obtained under Executive Order 11246 and the confidentiality rights of those who submit information to OFCCP and its compliance agencies. It is a much closer question, however, whether they are the product of a congressional grant of legislative authority.

In his published memorandum setting forth the disclosure regulations at issue in this case, the Secretary of Labor states that the authority upon which he relies in promulgating the regulations are § 201 of Executive Order 11246, as amended, and 29 CFR § 70.71, which permits units in the Department of Labor to promulgate supplemental disclosure regulations consistent with 29 CFR pt. 70 and the FOIA. 38 Fed.Reg. 3192–3194 (1973). . . .

Section 201 of Executive Order 11246 directs the Secretary of Labor to "adopt such rules and regulations and issue such orders as he deems necessary and appropriate to achieve the purposes thereof." But in order for such regulations to have the "force and effect of law," it is necessary to establish a nexus between the regulations and some delegation of the requisite legislative authority by Congress. . . . The pertinent inquiry is whether under any of the arguable *statutory* grants of authority, the OFCCP disclosure regulations relied on by the Government are reasonably within the contemplation of that grant of authority. We think that it is clear that when it enacted these statutes, Congress was not concerned with public disclosure of trade secrets or confidential business information, and, unless we were to hold that any federal statute that implies some authority to collect information must grant *legislative* authority to disclose that information to the public, it is simply not possible to find in these statutes a delegation of the disclosure authority asserted by the Government here.

The relationship between any grant of legislative authority and the disclosure regulations becomes more remote when one examines § 201 of the Executive order. It speaks in terms of rules and regulations "necessary and appropriate" to achieve the purposes of the Executive order. Those purposes are an end to discrimination in employment by the Federal Government and those who deal with the Federal Government. One cannot readily pull from the logic and purposes of the Executive order any concern with the public's access to information in Government files or the importance of protecting trade secrets or confidential business statistics.

The "purpose and scope" section of the disclosure regulations indicates two underlying rationales: OFCCP's general policy "to disclose information to the public," and its policy "to cooperate with other public agencies as well as private parties seeking to eliminate discrimination in employment." 41 CFR § 60–40.1 (1977). The government argues that "[t]he purpose of the Executive Order is to combat discrimination in employment, and a disclosure policy designed to further this purpose is consistent with the Executive Order and an appropriate subject for regulation under its aegis." Were a grant of legislative authority as a basis for Executive Order 11246 more clearly identifiable, we might agree with the Government that this "compatibility" gives the disclosure regulations the necessary legislative force. But the thread between these regulations and any grant of authority by the Congress is so strained that it would do violence to established principles of separations of powers to denominate these particular regulations "legislative" and credit them with the "binding effect of law."

This is not to say that any grant of legislative authority to a federal agency by Congress must be specific before regulations promulgated pursuant to them can be binding on courts in a manner akin to statutes. What is important is that the reviewing court reasonably be able to conclude that the grant of authority contemplates the regulations issued. . . .

There is also a procedural defect in the OFCCP disclosure regulations which precludes courts from affording them the force and effect of law. That defect is a lack of strict compliance with the APA. . . .

Section 4 of the APA, 5 U.S.C.A. § 553, specifies that an agency shall afford interested persons general notice of proposed rulemaking and an opportunity to comment before a substantive rule is promulgated. "Interpretative rules, general statements of policy or rules of agency organization, procedure or practice" are exempt from these requirements. When the Secretary of Labor published the regulations pertinent in this case, he stated:

> As the changes made by this document relate solely to interpretive rules, general statements of policy, and to rules of agency procedure and practice, neither notice of proposed rule making nor public participation therein is required by 5 U.S.C. 553. Since the changes made by this document either relieve restrictions or are interpretative rules, no delay in effective date is required by 5 U.S.C. 553(d). These rules shall therefore be effective immediately.
>
> In accordance with the spirit of the public policy set forth in 5 U.S.C. 553, interested persons may submit written comments, suggestions, data, or arguments to the Director, Office of Federal Contract Compliance. . . . 38 Fed.Reg. 3192, 3193 (1973).

Thus the regulations were essentially treated as interpretative rules and interested parties were not afforded the notice of proposed rulemaking required for substantive rules under 5 U.S.C.A. § 553(b). As we observed in Batterton v. Francis, 432 U.S. 416, 425 n. 9, 97 S.Ct. 2399, 2405, 53 L.Ed.2d 448 (1977), "a court is not required to give effect to an interpretative regulation. Varying degrees of deference are accorded to administrative interpretations, based on such factors as the timing and consistency of the agency's position, and the nature of its expertise." We need not decide whether these regulations are properly characterized "interpretative rules." It is enough that such regulations are not properly promulgated as substantive rules, and therefore not the product of procedures which Congress prescribed as necessary prerequisites to giving a regulation the binding effect of law. An interpretative regulation or general statement of agency policy cannot be the "authoriz[ation] by law" required by § 1905.

RULE MAKING

As suggested above, different procedural requirements are associated with the adoption of rules on the one hand and adjudicatory decisions on the other. These differences have their roots in interpretations of the constitutional provisions guaranteeing due process of law made in the early part of this century, specifically, the two Supreme Court cases of *Londoner* v. *Denver*, 210 U.S. 373, 28 S.Ct. 708, 52 L.Ed. 1103 (1908) and *Bi-Metallic Investment Co.* v. *State Bd. of Equalization*, 239 U.S. 441, 36 S.Ct. 141, 60 L.Ed. 372 (1915). The important recent case of *United States* v. *Florida East Coast Ry. Co.*, 410 U.S. 224, 93 S.Ct. 810, 35 L.Ed.2d 223 (1973), which will be discussed below, explains the significance of these two cases well. As Mr. Justice Rehnquist said for the majority:

> The basic distinction between rulemaking and adjudication is illustrated by this Court's treatment of two related cases under the Due Process Clause of the Fourteenth Amendment. In Londoner v. Denver, . . . 210 U.S. 373, 28 S.Ct. 708, 52 L.Ed. 1103 (1908), the Court held that due process had not been accorded a landowner who objected to the amount assessed against his land as its share of the benefit resulting from the paving of a street. Local procedure had accorded him the right to file a written complaint and objection, but not to be heard orally. This Court held that due process of law required that he "have the right to support his allegations by argument, however brief; and, if need be, by proof, however informal." But in the later case of Bi-Metallic Investment Co. v. State Board of Equalization, 239 U.S. 441, 36 S.Ct. 141, 60 L.Ed. 372 (1915), the Court held that no hearing at all was constitutionally required prior to a decision by state tax officers in Colorado to increase the valuation of all taxable property in Denver by a substantial percentage. The Court distinguished *Londoner* by stating that there a small number of persons "were exceptionally affected, in each case upon individual grounds."
>
> Later decisions have continued to observe the distinction adverted to in *Bi-Metallic Investment Co.* . . .

The importance of these two old cases can hardly be exaggerated. They are said to have "introduced the modern era of administrative law." [8] And their basic thrust, that a hearing with oral participation will be required in adjudication but not in rule making, is the orthodox view on the matter to this day. Thus, for instance, the U.S. Administrative Procedure Act (§ 553(c)) provides that rules may be adopted without oral participation by interested parties.

Particularly in recent years, however, this simple distinction between rule making and adjudication has been increasingly challenged. A number of statutes applying to particular agencies provide for oral participation in rule making, and some court decisions have required agencies to provide more than the minimum requirements of § 553. Moreover, some commentators believe that the distinction is no longer a satisfactory one in contemporary administrative law. We will return to this matter below.

---

[8] Paul R. Verkuil, "The Emerging Concept of Administrative Procedure," 78 *Columbia Law Review* 258, 264 (1978).

Notice and Public Procedure

Section 553 of the APA provides the following:

(a) This section applies, according to the provisions thereof, except to the extent that there is involved—

(1) a military or foreign affairs function of the United States; or

(2) a matter relating to agency management or personnel or to public property, loans, grants, benefits, or contracts.

(b) General notice of proposed rule making shall be published in the Federal Register, unless persons subject thereto are named and either personally served or otherwise have actual notice thereof in accordance with law. The notice shall include—

(1) a statement of the time, place, and nature of public rule making proceedings;

(2) reference to the legal authority under which the rule is proposed; and

(3) either the terms or substance of the proposed rule or a description of the subjects and issues involved.

After notice, the agency is required to "give interested persons an opportunity to participate in the rule making through submission of written data, views or arguments with or without opportunity for oral participation." This is followed by adoption of the rule, with publication no less than thirty days before its effective date.

Official notice is provided through publication in the *Federal Register*. This daily publication has been in existence since 1936. Regulations of "current general and permanent" [9] importance are codified by subject in the *Code of Federal Regulations*, a publication containing 50 Titles which is updated yearly. The Federal Register system was created by act of Congress in 1935 when problems arose as a result of the absence of an official notice publication for administrative rules.

Publications analogous to the *Federal Register* and the *Code of Federal Regulations* do not exist in all states. But a recognition of the advantages of providing a unified source of official notice with easy access for the public appear to be growing. By 1983 over three-fourths of the states were either publishing or preparing to publish state administrative codes containing all important administrative rules and regulations.[10]

Interpretive rules of general application are required to be published in the *Federal Register* but are not subject to the procedures of § 553. Because of the importance of many interpretive rules, the Administrative Conference of the United States in 1976 recommended that an interpretive rule or policy statement "which is likely to have a substantial impact on the public" be adopted, amended, or repealed according to the provisions of § 553.[11]

---

[9] See *The Federal Register: What It Is and How to Use It* 1 (1977).

[10] Henry P. Tseng and Donald B. Pederson, "Acquisition of State Administrative Rules and Regulations—Update 1983," 35 *Administrative Law Review* 349–389 (1983).

[11] Asimow, above, note 3, at 578; Warren, above, note 5, at 367.

The "Good Cause" Exemption

Sections 553(b)(B) and 553(d)(3) of the APA allow agencies to dispense with the notice and public-procedure provisions regarding rule making for "good cause." To invoke these provisions the agency must make a finding that regular procedures are "impracticable, unnecessary, or contrary to the public interest." Because the good-cause exemption might be subject to potential abuse, courts have taken the position that it is to be construed narrowly. The Administrative Conference of the United States adopted a resolution in 1983 proposing that agencies that invoke the good-cause exemption should provide interested persons an opportunity for postpromulgation comment when it is determined that prior notice and comment was "impracticable" or "contrary to the public interest." Such postpromulgation notice and comment would not be required when an agency determined that public procedures were "unnecessary." [12]

Since publication in the *Federal Register* constitutes official notice, failure to so publish may cause problems. An unpublished regulation may be ruled by a court to have no legal effect. An important recent case is *Morton* v. *Ruiz*, 415 U.S. 199, 94 S.Ct. 1055, 39 L.Ed.2d 270 (1974). The appellees, husband and wife, were members of an Indian tribe who lived off, but near, a reservation. The Bureau of Indian Affairs had denied them relief benefits, basing its decision on a BIA manual in effect since 1952 which limited such assistance to Indians living on reservations. But the manual had never been published in the *Federal Register*, and the BIA in congressional appropriation hearings had made numerous representations to the effect that Indians living near reservations were eligible for BIA services. The unanimous decision of the Supreme Court was based on a number of considerations, but one of their reasons for ruling against the BIA was that a rule of this importance, affecting "substantial individual rights and obligations," should have been published in the *Federal Register*.

Informal and Formal Rule Making

The section 553 procedure is often called "notice-and-comment" rule making because of the provision which allows exclusion of opportunity for oral participation. Lately this procedure has also been referred to as "informal rule making," to distinguish it from more formal rule-making procedures. "When rules are required by statute to be made on the record after opportunity for agency hearing," it says elsewhere in section 553, sections 556 and 557 of the APA will apply. These sections, which cover what are normally called adjudicatory hearings, provide for a good deal of formality in proceedings, including oral arguments, the right to submit rebuttal evidence, and the right to cross-examination. Such proceedings are based on the "common-law judicial

---

[12] *1983 Annual Report, Administrative Conference of the United States*, 29; see also *A Guide to Federal Agency Rulemaking*, above, note 7, 39; James T. O'Reilly, *Administrative Rulemaking: Structuring, Opposing and Defending Federal Agency Regulations*, 36–42 (1983); Ellen R. Jordan, "The Administrative Procedure Act's 'Good Cause' Exemption," 36 *Administrative Law Review* 113 (1984).

model." They generally involve "adverse parties litigating a relatively particularized factual issue." [13]

A small number of federal statutes provide for "on-the-record" proceedings in rule making. These are very much the exception rather than the rule. While it might be argued that these more formal proceedings provide interested parties a greater opportunity to present their views, the costs, both in terms of person-hours of agency time and in slowness of policy making, can be considerable. Professor Robert W. Hamilton succinctly summarizes the results of sixteen on-the-record hearings held by the FDA in the 1960s, which he says varied from "unnecessarily drawn out proceedings to virtual disasters":

> In not one instance did the agency complete a rulemaking proceeding involving a hearings in less than two years, and in two instances more than ten years elapsed between the first proposal and the final order. The *average* time lapse was roughly four years. The hearings themselves tended to be drawn out, repetitious and unproductive. The *Foods for Special Dietary Uses* hearing consumed over 200 days of testimony and amassed a transcript of more than 32,000 pages. Most of the hearing was devoted to cross examination of expert government witnesses. Another proceeding involving the standard of identity for peanut butter developed a transcript of over 7,700 pages, largely directed to the question of whether the product peanut butter should consist of 90 percent peanuts or 87½ percent peanuts.[14]

As might be expected, formal rule making of this kind is widely condemned by commentators.[15] There has emerged, however, some support for a middle ground between the basic notice and comment provisions of section 553 of the APA (informal rule making) and the trial-type procedures just discussed (formal rule making). What has been referred to as "hybrid" or "553-plus" rule making, in which "an oral stage of rulemaking is mixed with the notice and comment process of § 553," [16] has been imposed upon some agencies by both the courts and Congress. Occasionally agencies themselves will voluntarily provide further procedural steps, such as limited cross-examination. As will be shown below, judicial imposition of procedures beyond those required by section 553 has been specifically rejected by the Supreme Court in the *Vermont Yankee* case. But Congress may authorize additional rule-making procedures for individual agencies, and this was done on a number of occasions during the 1960s and 1970s.[17] Assessments of the utility of such hybrid

---

[13] Antonin Scalia, "Two Wrongs Make a Right: The Judicializing of Standardless Rulemaking," *Regulation* 38 (July/August, 1977).

[14] Robert W. Hamilton, "Procedures for the Adoption of Rules of General Applicability: The Need for Procedural Innovations in Administrative Rule-making," 60 *California Law Review* 1278, 1287–88 (1972).

[15] See, e.g., O'Reilly, above, note 12, 158–9, and sources cited therein.

[16] Id., 97.

[17] *A Guide to Federal Agency Rulemaking*, above, note 7, 131. An example is the Federal Trade Commission Improvement Act (Magnuson-Moss Act) of 1975, 15 U.S.C.A. § 45 et seq. This act goes beyond § 553 (but stops short of a full trial-type hearing) by allowing an "informal hearing" at which an interested person may "present his position orally or by documentary submissions (or both)" and, if the commission determines that there are "disputed issues of material fact," a person may "present such rebuttal submissions" and conduct such cross-examinations as the

procedures have not so far been very positive.[18]

The Supreme Court's attitude with regard to rule making has been clarified to a considerable extent in recent years. The Court has made several important decisions supporting the adequacy of notice and comment rule making under section 553, and it has rejected efforts by lower courts to require, in the absence of specific statutory provisions, more formal rule-making proceedings. The following two cases illustrate these points.

United States v. Florida East Coast Ry. Co.

SUPREME COURT OF THE UNITED STATES, 1973.
410 U.S. 224, 93 S.CT. 810, 35 L.ED.2D 223.

[The Interstate Commerce Act empowers the ICC "after hearing" to establish "rules, regulations and practices" with regard to freight car service. Section 1(14)(a). Traditionally the commission had accorded full trial-type hearings under this provision, but recently it had begun to use the less formal notice-and-comment proceedings. Acting under specific authority provided by a 1966 amendment to the ICC Act to cope with the shortage of rail cars, the commission had adopted "incentive per diem rates" for use by one railroad of freight cars owned by another. Two railroad companies moved to set aside the rates on the ground that the APA and the "hearing" provision of the Interstate Commerce Act required opportunity for greater participation than they had been accorded. The district court sustained the railroads' position and the case came to the Supreme Court.]

Mr. Justice REHNQUIST delivered the opinion of the Court. . . .

Following our decision last Term in United States v. Allegheny-Ludlum Steel Corp., 406 U.S. 742, 92 S.Ct. 1941, 32 L.Ed.2d 453 (1972), we noted probable jurisdiction, 407 U.S. 908, 92 S.Ct. 2431, 32 L.Ed.2d 682

(1972), and requested the parties to brief the question of whether the Commission's proceeding was governed by 5 U.S.C.A. § 553, or by 556 and 557, of the Administrative Procedure Act. We here decide that the Commission's proceeding was governed only by § 553 of that Act, and that appellees received the "hearing" required by § 1(14)(a) of the Interstate Commerce Act. . . .

In United States v. Allegheny-Ludlum Steel Corp., supra, we held that the language of § 1(14)(a) of the Interstate Commerce Act authorizing the Commission to act "after hearing" was not the equivalent of a requirement that a rule be made "on the record after opportunity for an agency hearing" as the latter term is used in § 553(c) of the Administrative Procedure Act. Since the 1966 amendment to § 1(14)(a), under which the Commission was here proceeding, does not by its terms add to the hearing requirement contained in the earlier language, the same result should obtain here unless that amendment contains language that is tantamount to such a requirement. Appellees contend that such language is found in the provisions of that Act requiring that:

---

commission considers appropriate. The commission retains considerable flexibility in conducting such hearings, including having the discretion to impose "reasonable time limits on each interested person's oral presentations."

[18] See, e.g., id 131–137; O'Reilly, above, note 12, 97–8; Richard J. Pierce, Jr., Sidney A. Shapiro, and Paul R. Verkuil, *Administrative Law and Process*, 333–335 (1985).

[T]he Commission shall give consideration to the national level of ownership of such type of freight car and to other factors affecting the adequacy of the national freight car supply, and shall, on the basis of such consideration, determine whether compensation should be computed....

While this language is undoubtedly a mandate to the Commission to consider the factors there set forth in reaching any conclusion as to imposition of per diem incentive charges, it adds to the hearing requirements of the section neither expressly nor by implication. We know of no reason to think that an administrative agency in reaching a decision cannot accord consideration to factors such as those set forth in the 1966 amendment by means other than a trial-type hearing or the presentation of oral argument by the affected parties. Congress by that amendment specified necessary components of the ultimate decision, but it did not specify the method by which the Commission should acquire information about those components....

The term "hearing" in its legal context undoubtedly has a host of meanings. Its meaning undoubtedly will vary, depending on whether it is used in the context of a rulemaking-type proceeding or in the context of a proceeding devoted to the adjudication of particular disputed facts. It is by no means apparent what the drafters of the Esch Car Service Act of 1917, 40 Stat. 101, which became the first part of § 1(14)(a) of the Interstate Commerce Act, meant by the term. Such an intent would surely be an ephemeral one if, indeed, Congress in 1917 had in mind anything more specific than the language it actually used, for none of the parties refer to any legislative history that would shed light on the intended meaning of the words "after hearing." What is apparent, though, is that the term was used in granting authority to the Commission to make rules and regulations of a prospective nature....

[C]onfronted with a grant of substantive authority made after the Administrative Procedure Act was enacted, we think that reference to that Act, in which Congress devoted itself exclusively to questions such as the nature and scope of hearings, is a satisfactory basis for determining what is meant by the term "hearing" used in another statute. Turning to that Act, we are convinced that the term "hearing" as used therein does not necessarily embrace either the right to present evidence orally and to cross-examine opposing witnesses, or the right to present oral argument to the agency's decisionmaker.

Section 553 excepts from its requirements rulemaking devoted to "interpretative rules, general statements of policy, or rules of agency organization, procedure, or practice," and rulemaking "when the agency for good cause finds ... that notice and public procedure thereon are impracticable, unnecessary, or contrary to the public interest." This exception does not apply, however, "when notice or hearing is required by statute"; in those cases, even though interpretative rulemaking be involved, the requirements of § 553 apply. But since these requirements themselves do not mandate any oral presentation, see *Allegheny-Ludlum*, supra, it cannot be doubted that a statute that requires a "hearing" prior to rulemaking may in some circumstances be satisfied by procedures that meet only the standards of § 553. The Court's opinion in FPC v. Texaco Inc., 377 U.S. 33, 84 S.Ct. 1105, 12 L.Ed.2d 112 (1964), supports such a broad definition of the term "hearing."

Similarly, even where the statute requires that the rulemaking procedure take place "on the record after opportunity for an agency hearing," thus triggering the applicability of § 556, subsection (d) provides that the agency may proceed by the submission of all or part of the evidence in written form if a party will not be "prejudiced thereby." Again, the Act makes it plain that a specific statutory mandate that the proceedings take place on the record after hearing may be satisfied in some circumstances by evidentiary submission in written form only.

We think this treatment of the term "hearing" in the Administrative Procedure Act affords a sufficient basis for concluding that the requirement of a "hearing" contained in § 1(14)(a); in a situation where the Commission was acting under the 1966 statutory rulemaking authority that Congress had conferred upon it, did not by its own force require the Commission either to hear oral testimony, to permit cross-examination of Commission witnesses, or to hear oral argument. Here, the Commission promulgated a tentative draft of an order, and accorded all interested parties 60 days in which to file statements of position, submissions of evidence, and other relevant observations. The parties had fair notice of exactly what the Commission proposed to do, and were given an opportunity to comment, to object, or to make some other form of written submission. The final order of the Commission indicates that it gave consideration to the statements of the two appellees here. Given the "open-ended" nature of the proceedings, and the Commission's announced willingness to consider proposals

for modification after operating experience had been acquired, we think the hearing requirement of § 1(14)(a) of the Act was met....

[The opinion then turns to the basic distinction between rule making and adjudication, as illustrated in the Supreme Court cases of *Londoner* v. *Denver* and *Bi-Metallic Investment Co.* v. *State Board of Equalization*. This passage is quoted above, p. 163.]

The Commission's procedure satisfied both the provisions of § 1(14)(a) of the Interstate Commerce Act and of the Administrative Procedure Act, and were [*sic*] not inconsistent with prior decisions of this Court. We, therefore, reverse the judgment of the District Court, and remand the case so that it may consider those contentions of the parties that are not disposed of by this opinion.

It is so ordered.

Reversed and remanded.

Mr. Justice POWELL took no part in the consideration or decision of this case.

[The *dissenting* opinion of Mr. Justice Douglas, with whom Mr. Justice Stewart concurs, is omitted.]

The change effected by the *Florida East Coast* decision was quite significant. Justice Douglas, in his dissent, called it "a sharp break with traditional concepts of procedural due process." 410 U.S. 246, 93 S.Ct. 821, 35 L.Ed.2d 240. One commentator said that the Court redefined "the procedural ingredients that traditionally defined the term 'hearing.' " [19] Judge Friendly said the decision "signals a large expansion of what can be done by notice and comment rule making and a corresponding retraction of the area where a trial type hearing is required in the regulatory field." [20]

The *Florida East Coast* decision was a stimulus to an already-developing trend toward greater use of rule making at the federal level. This development, in turn, began giving rise to attempts to place checks on agency rule making. We will discuss below the efforts of Congress, the president, and private interests in this area.

[19] Verkuil, above, note 8, at 284.

[20] Henry J. Friendly, "Some Kind of Hearing," 123 *University of Pennsylvania Law Review* 1267, 1308 (1975).

Even before the *Florida East Coast* decision some lower courts, led by the Court of Appeals for the D.C. Circuit, had sometimes imposed additional procedural requirements for informal rule making even when not mandated by statute. After *Florida East Coast* this practice continued, to the point where, as one commentator put it, "the D.C. Circuit was in the process of replacing the rudimentary procedural mandates" of the APA.[21] This development set the stage for the landmark *Vermont Yankee* decision of 1978.

Vermont Yankee Nuclear Power Corp. v. Natural Resources Defense Council, Inc.

SUPREME COURT OF THE UNITED STATES, 1978.
435 U.S. 519, 98 S.CT. 1197, 55 L.ED.2D 460.

[This long and complex case concerns a number of issues growing out of the licensing of two nuclear power plants. The most important issue for our purposes is the procedure used in the Atomic Energy Commission in promulgating a "spent-fuel-cycle rule." The licensing proceedings employed full adjudicatory hearings, but the rule making, although it included oral comment, did not allow for discovery or cross-examination, and thus did not utilize full adjudicatory procedures. The Court of Appeals for the D.C. Circuit overturned the rule because of shortcomings in the procedures, and the Supreme Court reviewed on certiorari. Mr. Justice Rehnquist's opinion represents the unanimous view of seven participating members of the Court.]

Mr. Justice REHNQUIST delivered the opinion of the Court.

In 1946, Congress enacted the Administrative Procedure Act, which as we have noted elsewhere was not only "a new, basic and comprehensive regulation of procedures in many agencies," Wong Yang Sun v. McGrath, 339 U.S. 33, 70 S.Ct. 445, 94 L.Ed. 616 (1950), but was also a legislative enactment which settled "long-continued and hard-fought contentions, and enacts a formula upon which opposing social and political forces have come to rest." Id., at

40, 70 S.Ct., at 448. Section 553 of the Act, dealing with rulemaking, requires that ". . . notice of proposed rulemaking shall be published in the Federal Register . . . ," describes the contents of that notice, and goes on to require in subsection (c) that after the notice the agency "shall give interested persons an opportunity to participate in the rulemaking through submission of written data, views, or arguments with or without opportunity for oral presentation. After consideration of the relevant matter presented, the agency shall incorporate in the rules adopted a concise general statement of their basis and purpose." 5 U.S.C.A. § 553. Interpreting this provision of the Act in United States v. Allegheny-Ludlum Steel Corp., 406 U.S. 742, 92 S.Ct. 1941, 32 L.Ed.2d 453 (1972), and United States v. Florida East Coast Railroad Co., 410 U.S. 224, 93 S.Ct. 810, 35 L.Ed.2d 223 (1973), we held that generally speaking this section of the Act established the maximum procedural requirements which Congress was willing to have the courts impose upon agencies in conducting rulemaking procedures. Agencies are free to grant additional procedural rights in the exercise of their discretion, but reviewing courts are generally not free to impose them if the agencies have not chosen to

---

[21] Antonin Scalia, "Vermont Yankee: The A.P.A., The D.C. Circuit, and The Supreme Court," in Philip B. Kurland and Gerhard Casper (eds.), *The Supreme Court Review, 1978* 359 (1979).

grant them. This is not to say necessarily that there are no circumstances which would ever justify a court in overturning agency action because of a failure to employ procedures beyond those required by the statute. But such circumstances, if they exist, are extremely rare.

Even apart from the Administrative Procedure Act this Court has for more than four decades emphasized that the formulation of procedures was basically to be left within the discretion of the agencies to which Congress had confided the responsibility for substantive judgments....

It is in the light of this background of statutory and decisional law that we granted certiorari to review two judgments of the Court of Appeals for the District of Columbia Circuit because of our concern that they had seriously misread or misapplied this statutory and decisional law cautioning reviewing courts against engrafting their own notions of proper procedures upon agencies entrusted with substantive functions by Congress. We conclude that the Court of Appeals has done just that in these cases, and we therefore remand them to it for further proceedings....

[After disposing of other issues, the Court turned to the rule-making issue.]

We next turn to the invalidation of the spent fuel cycle rule. But before determining whether the Court of Appeals reached a permissible result, we must determine exactly what result it did reach, and in this case that is no mean feat. Vermont Yankee argues that the court invalidated the rule because of the inadequacy of the procedures employed in the proceedings. Petitioner Vermont Yankee Nuclear Power Corp. Brief 30–38. Respondent NRDC, on the other hand, labeling petitioner's view of the decision a "straw man," argues to this Court that the court merely held that the record was inadequate to enable the reviewing court to determine whether the agency had fulfilled its statutory obligation. Respondent NRDC Brief 28–30, 40. But we unfortunately have not found the par-

ties' characterization of the opinion to be entirely reliable; it appears here, as in Orloff v. Willoughby, 345 U.S. 83, 87, 73 S.Ct. 534, 537, 97 L.Ed. 842 (1953), that "in this Court the parties changed positions as nimbly as if dancing a quadrille."

After a thorough examination of the opinion itself, we conclude that while the matter is not entirely free from doubt, the majority of the Court of Appeals struck down the rule because of the perceived inadequacies of the procedures employed in the rulemaking proceedings. The court first determined the intervenors' primary argument to be "that the decision to preclude 'discovery or cross-examination' denied them a meaningful opportunity to participate in the proceedings as guaranteed by due process." 178 U.S.App.D.C., at 346, 547 F.2d, at 643. The court then went on to frame the issue for decision thusly:

> Thus, we are called upon to decide whether the procedures provided by the agency were sufficient to ventilate the issues. 178 U.S.App. D.C., at 346, 547 F.2d, at 643 (footnotes omitted).

The court conceded that absent extraordinary circumstances it is improper for a reviewing court to prescribe the procedural format an agency must follow, but it likewise clearly thought it entirely appropriate to "scrutinize the record as a whole to insure that genuine opportunities to participate in a meaningful way were provided....." 178 U.S.App.D.C., at 347, 547 F.2d, at 644. The court also refrained from actually ordering the agency to follow any specific procedures, 178 U.S.App.D.C., at 356–357, 547 F.2d, at 653–654, but there is little doubt in our minds that the ineluctable mandate of the court's decision is that the procedures afforded during the hearings were inadequate....

In prior opinions we have intimated that even in a rulemaking proceeding when an agency is making a "quasi-judicial" determination by which a very small number of persons are " 'exceptionally affected, in each case upon individual grounds,' " in some circumstances additional procedures may be required in order to afford the aggrieved individuals due process. United States v. Florida East Coast R. Co., 410 U.S. 224, 242–245, 93 S.Ct. 810, 819–821, 35 L.Ed.2d 223, quoting from Bi-Metallic Investment Co. v. State Board of Equalization, 239 U.S. 441, 446, 36 S.Ct. 141, 142, 60 L.Ed. 372 (1915). It might also be true, although we do not think the issue is presented in this case and accordingly do not decide it, that a totally unjustified departure from well settled agency procedures of long standing might require judicial correction.

But this much is absolutely clear. Absent constitutional constraints or extremely compelling circumstances "the administrative agencies 'should be free to fashion their own rules of procedure and to pursue method of inquiry capable of permitting them to discharge their multitudinous duties.' " . . .

Respondent NRDC argues that § 553 of the Administrative Procedure Act merely establishes lower procedural bounds and that a court may routinely require more than the minimum when an agency's proposed rule addresses complex or technical factual issues or "issues of great public import." NRDC Brief, p. 49. We have, however, previously shown that our decisions reject this view. . . .

There are compelling reasons for construing § 553 in this manner. In the first place, if courts continually review agency proceedings to determine whether the agency employed procedures which were, in the Court's opinion, perfectly tailored to reach what the court perceives to be the "best" or "correct" result, judicial review would be totally unpredictable. And the agencies, operating under this vague injunction to employ the "best" procedures and facing the threat of reversal if they did not, would undoubtedly adopt full adjudicatory procedures in every instance. Not only would this totally disrupt the statuto-

ry scheme, through which Congress enacted "a formula upon which opposing social and political forces have come to rest," Wong Yang Sun v. McGrath, supra, at 40, 70 S.Ct., at 450, but all the inherent advantages of informal rulemaking would be totally lost.

Secondly, it is obvious that the court in this case reviewed the agency's choice of procedures on the basis of the record actually produced at the hearing, 178 U.S.App. D.C., at 347, 547 F.2d, at 645, and not on the basis of the information available to the agency when it made the decision to structure the proceedings in a certain way. This sort of Monday morning quarterbacking not only encourages but almost compels the agency to conduct all rulemaking proceedings with the full panoply of procedural devices normally associated only with adjudicatory hearings.

Finally, and perhaps most importantly, this sort of review fundamentally misconceives the nature of the standard for judicial review of an agency rule. The court below uncritically assumed that additional procedures will automatically result in a more adequate record because it will give interested parties more of an opportunity to participate and contribute to the proceedings. But informal rulemaking need not be based solely on the transcript of a hearing held before an agency. Indeed, the agency need not even hold a formal hearing. See 5 U.S.C.A. § 553(c). Thus, the adequacy of the "record" in this type of proceeding is not correlated directly to the type of procedural devices employed, but rather turns on whether the agency has followed the statutory mandate of the Administrative Procedure Act or other relevant statutes. If the agency is compelled to support the rule which it ultimately adopts with the type of record produced only after a full adjudicatory hearing, it simply will have no choice but to conduct a full adjudicatory prior to promulgating every rule. In sum, this sort of unwarranted judicial examination of perceived procedural shortcomings of a rulemaking proceeding can do nothing but seriously interfere with that process prescribed by Congress. . . .

In short, nothing in the APA, NEPA, the circumstances of this case, the nature of the issues being considered, past agency practice, or the statutory mandate under which the Commission operates permitted the court to review and overturn the rulemaking proceeding on the basis of the procedural devices employed (or not employed) by the Commission so long as the Commission employed at least the statutory *minima*, a matter about which there is no doubt in this case. . . .

All this leads us to make one further observation of some relevance to this case. To say that the Court of Appeals' final reason for remanding is insubstantial at best is a gross understatement. Consumers Power first applied in 1969 for a construction permit—not even an operating license, just a construction permit. The proposed plant underwent an incredibly extensive review. The reports filed and reviewed literally fill books. The proceedings took years. The actual hearings themselves over two weeks. To then nullify that effort seven years later because one report refers to other problems, which problems admittedly have been discussed at length in other reports available to the public, borders on the Kafkaesque. Nuclear energy may some day be a cheap, safe source of power

or it may not. But Congress has made a choice to at least try nuclear energy, establishing a reasonable review process in which courts are to play only a limited role. The fundamental policy questions appropriately resolved in Congress and in the state legislatures are *not* subject to reexamination in the federal courts under the guise of judicial review of agency action. Time may prove wrong the decision to develop nuclear energy, but it is Congress or the States within their appropriate agencies which must eventually make that judgment. In the meantime courts should perform their appointed function. NEPA does set forth significant substantive goals for the Nation, but its mandate to the agencies is essentially procedural. It is to insure a fully informed and well-considered decision, not necessarily a decision the judges of the Court of Appeals or of this Court would have reached had they been members of the decisionmaking unit of the agency. Administrative decisions should be set aside in this context, as in every other, only for substantial procedural or substantive reasons as mandated by statute, Consolo v. Fed. Maritime Comm'n, 383 U.S. 607, 620, 86 S.Ct. 1018, 1026, 16 L.Ed.2d 131 (1966), not simply because the court is unhappy with the result reached. . . .

Reversed and remanded.

Mr. Justice BLACKMUN and Mr. Justice POWELL took no part in the consideration or decision of these cases.

DEREGULATION AND RULE MAKING

Before the Reagan administration took office in 1981, only limited attention had been devoted by administrative law specialists to practical problems associated with *deregulation*. As shown in chapter 2, the strong political impulses to reduce the role of government in American life were translated in a number of ways into concrete results in the area of administrative law (as, for instance, in the significant drop in the number of pages in the *Federal Register*, suggesting a reduction in the number of regulations adopted by agencies [22]). This was bound to produce a variety of legal problems, many of which would be referred to the courts for resolution. Several of these problems will be discussed in this section.

Perhaps the most obvious and certainly one of the most important issues involves the decision of an agency to rescind a rule that had been adopted earlier. The following case is an important Supreme Court decision on that subject. For purposes of this chapter, the most important consideration is the process the agency is required to follow in rescinding a rule. In addition to this, the Supreme Court, in the case excerpted below, speaks to the issue of the appropriate judicial role in reviewing administrative action.

Motor Vehicle Manufacturers Association v. State Farm Mutual Automobile Insurance Company

SUPREME COURT OF THE UNITED STATES, 1983.
463 U.S. 29, 103 S.CT. 2856, 77 L.ED.2D 443.

[Congress in 1966 enacted the National Traffic and Motor Vehicle Safety Act, 15 U.S.C. §§ 1381 et seq., for the purpose of reducing "traffic accidents and deaths and injuries to persons resulting from traffic accidents." The act directs the secretary of transportation or his delegate to issue motor vehicle safety standards that "shall be practicable, shall meet the need for motor vehicle safety, and shall be stated in objective terms."

The regulation at issue in this case, according to Justice White in his majority opinion, "bears a complex and convoluted history." A standard requiring that passive restraints (air bags or automatic seat belts) be installed in automobiles was first proposed in 1969. But is was not until 1977 that Modified Standard 208 was adopted. It mandated the installation of passive restraints in large cars in model year 1982 and the phasing in of the requirement to cover all cars by model year 1984.

In February 1981, however, the new secretary of transportation reopened the rule-making process. Acting for the secretary, the National Highway Traffic Safety

Administration (NHTSA) first ordered a one-year delay in the application of the standard and later rescinded the passive restraint requirement altogether.

The respondent brought suit for review of the rescission, and the U.S. Court of Appeals for the District of Columbia ruled in 1982 that the rescission was arbitrary and capricious. The Supreme Court granted certiorari to review the court of appeals' decision. As indicated above, the two main issues the Supreme Court considered were the scope of the Court's reviewing power and the basis upon which NHTSA rescinded the regulation.]

Justice WHITE delivered the opinion of the Court. . . .

Both the Motor Vehicle Safety Act and the 1974 Amendments concerning occupant crash protection standards indicate that motor vehicle safety standards are to be promulgated under the informal rulemaking procedures of § 553 of the Administrative Procedure Act. 5 U.S.C. § 553 (1976). The agency's action in promulgating such standards therefore may be set aside if found to be "arbitrary, capricious,

---

[22] The Alliance for Justice, in a 1983 report, suggested that Reagan administration efforts went beyond reducing the number of regulations adopted to a systematic practice of discouraging or reducing public participation in the rule-making process. See *Contempt for Law: Excluding the Public from the Rulemaking Process* (1983).

an abuse of discretion, or otherwise not in accordance with law." 5 U.S.C. § 706(2)(A). *Citizens to Preserve Overton Park* v. *Volpe*, 401 U.S. 402, 414, 91 S.Ct. 814, 822, 28 L.Ed. 2d 136 (1971); *Bowman Transportation, Inc.* v. *Arkansas-Best Freight System, Inc.*, 419 U.S. 281, 95 S.Ct. 438, 42 L.Ed.2d 447 (1974). We believe that the rescission or modification of an occupant protection standard is subject to the same test. Section 103(b) of the Motor Vehicle Safety Act, 15 U.S.C. § 1392(b), states that the procedural and judicial review provisions of the Administrative Procedure Act "shall apply to all orders establishing, amending, or revoking a Federal motor vehicle safety standard," and suggests no difference in the scope of judicial review depending upon the nature of the agency's action.

Petitioner Motor Vehicle Manufacturers Association (MVMA) disagrees, contending that the rescission of an agency rule should be judged by the same standard a court would use to judge an agency's refusal to promulgate a rule in the first place—a standard Petitioner believes considerably narrower than the traditional arbitrary and capricious test and "close to the borderline of nonreviewability." Brief of Petitioner MVMA, at 35. We reject this view. The Motor Vehicle Safety Act expressly equates orders "revoking" and "establishing" safety standards; neither that Act nor the APA suggests that revocations are to be treated as refusals to promulgate standards. Petitioner's view would render meaningless Congress' authorization for judicial review of orders revoking safety rules. Moreover, the revocation of an extant regulation is substantially different than a failure to act. Revocation constitutes a reversal of the agency's former views as to the proper course. . . .

Accordingly, an agency changing its course by rescinding a rule is obligated to supply a reasoned analysis for the change beyond that which may be required when an agency does not act in the first instance. . . .

The ultimate question before us is whether NHTSA's rescission of the passive restraint requirement of Standard 208 was arbitrary and capricious. We conclude, as did the Court of Appeals, that it was. We also conclude, but for somewhat different reasons, that further consideration of the issue by the agency is therefore required. We deal separately with the rescission as it applies to airbags and as it applies to seatbelts.

A

The first and most obvious reason for finding the rescission arbitrary and capricious is that NHTSA apparently gave no consideration whatever to modifying the Standard to require that airbag technology be utilized. Standard 208 sought to achieve automatic crash protection by requiring automobile manufacturers to install either of two passive restraint devices: airbags or automatic seatbelts. There was no suggestion in the long rulemaking process that led to Standard 208 that if only one of these options were feasible, no passive restraint standard should be promulgated. Indeed, the agency's original proposed standard contemplated the installation of inflatable restraints in all cars. Automatic belts were added as a means of complying with the standard because they were believed to be as effective as airbags in achieving the goal of occupant crash protection. 36 Fed.Reg. 12,858, 12,859 (July 8, 1971). At that time, the passive belt approved by the agency could not be detached. Only later, at a manufacturer's behest, did the agency approve of the detachability feature—and only after assurances that the feature would not compromise the safety benefits of the restraint. Although it was then foreseen that 60% of the new cars would contain airbags and 40% would have automatic seatbelts, the ratio between the two was not significant as long as the passive belt would also assure greater passenger safety.

The agency has now determined that the detachable automatic belts will not attain anticipated safety benefits because so many individuals will detach the mechanism. Even if this conclusion were acceptable in its entirety, ... standing alone it would not justify any more than an amendment of Standard 208 to disallow compliance by means of the one technology which will not provide effective passenger protection. It does not cast doubt on the need for a passive restraint standard or upon the efficacy of airbag technology. In its most recent rule-making, the agency again acknowledged the lifesaving potential of the airbag:

> The agency has no basis at this time for changing its earlier conclusions in 1976 and 1977 that basic airbag technology is sound and has been sufficiently demonstrated to be effective in those vehicles in current use.... NHTSA Final Regulatory Impact Analysis (RIA) at XI–4 (App. 264).

Given the effectiveness ascribed to airbag technology by the agency, the mandate of the Safety Act to achieve traffic safety would suggest that the logical response to the faults of detachable seatbelts would be to require the installation of airbags. At the very least this alternative way of achieving the objectives of the Act should have been addressed and adequate reasons given for its abandonment. But the agency not only did not require compliance through airbags, it did not even consider the possibility in its 1981 rulemaking. Not one sentence of its rulemaking statement discusses the airbags-only option.... We have frequently reiterated that an agency must cogently explain why it has exercised its discretion in a given manner, ... and we reaffirm this principle again today....

Although the agency did not address the mandatory airbags option and the Court of Appeals noted that "airbags seem to have none of the problems that NHTSA identified in passive seatbelts," petitioners recite a number of difficulties that they believe would be posed by a mandatory airbag standard. These range from ques-

tions concerning the installation of airbags in small cars to that of adverse public reaction. But these are not the agency's reasons for rejecting a mandatory airbag standard. Not having discussed the possibility, the agency submitted no reasons at all. The short—and sufficient—answer to petitioners' submission is that the courts may not accept appellate counsel's *post hoc* rationalizations for agency action....

B

Although the issue is closer, we also find that the agency was too quick to dismiss the safety benefits of automatic seatbelts. NHTSA's critical finding was that, in light of the industry's plans to install readily detachable passive belts, it could not reliably predict "even a 5 percentage point increase as the minimum level of expected usage increase." 46 Fed.Reg., at 53,423. The Court of Appeals rejected this finding because there is "not one iota" of evidence that Modified Standard 208 will fail to increase nationwide seatbelt use by at least 13 percentage points, the level of increased usage necessary for the standard to justify its cost. Given the lack of probative evidence, the court held that "only a well-justified refusal to seek more evidence could render rescission non-arbitrary." 680 F.2d, at 232.

Petitioners object to this conclusion. In their view, "substantial uncertainty" that a regulation will accomplish its intended purpose is sufficient reason, without more, to rescind a regulation. We agree with petitioners that just as an agency reasonably may decline to issue a safety standard if it is uncertain about its efficacy, an agency may also revoke a standard on the basis of serious uncertainties if supported by the record and reasonably explained. Rescission of the passive restraint requirement would not be arbitrary and capricious simply because there was no evidence in direct support of the agency's conclusion. It is not infrequent that the available data does not settle a regulatory issue and the agency must then exercise its judgment in moving from the facts and probabilities on the record to a policy conclusion. Recognizing that policymaking in a complex society must account for uncertainty, however, does not imply that it is sufficient for an agency to merely recite the terms "substantial uncertainty" as a justification for its actions. The agency must explain the evidence which is available, and must offer a "rational connection between the facts found and the choice made." *Burlington Truck Lines, Inc.* v. *United States*, supra, 371 U.S., at 168, 83 S.Ct., at 246. Generally, one aspect of that explanation would be a justification for rescinding the regulation before engaging in a search for further evidence.

In this case, the agency's explanation for rescission of the passive restraint requirement is *not* sufficient to enable us to conclude that the rescission was the product of reasoned decisionmaking. . . .

VI

"An agency's view of what is in the public interest may change, either with or without a change in circumstances. But an agency changing its course must supply a reasoned analysis. . . ." *Greater Boston Television Corp.* v. *FCC*, 444 F.2d 841, 852 (CADC), cert. denied, 403 U.S. 923, 91 S.Ct.

2233, 29 L.Ed.2d 701 (1971). We do not accept all of the reasoning of the Court of Appeals but we do conclude that the agency has failed to supply the requisite "reasoned analysis" in this case. Accordingly, we vacate the judgment of the Court of Appeals and remand the case to that court with directions to remand the matter to the NHTSA for further consideration consistent with this opinion.

So ordered.

Justice REHNQUIST, with whom THE CHIEF JUSTICE, Justice POWELL, and Justice O'CONNOR join, concurring in part and dissenting in part. . . .

The agency's changed view of the standard seems to be related to the election of a new President of a different political party. It is readily apparent that the responsible members of one administration may consider public resistance and uncertainties to be more important than do their counterparts in a previous administration. A change in administration brought about by the people casting their votes is a perfectly reasonable basis for an executive agency's reappraisal of the costs and benefits of its programs and regulations. As long as the agency remains within the bounds established by Congress, it is entitled to assess administrative records and evaluate priorities in light of the philosophy of the administration.

After the *Motor Vehicle Manufacturers Association* decision was handed down, the secretary of transportation promulgated another rule requiring the installation of airbags or automatic seat belts in all automobiles after 1989. The regulation provided that this requirement would be rescinded if at least two-thirds of the country's population were covered by state laws requiring mandatory seat belt use by 1989.[23]

---

[23] 49 Fed.Reg. 28,962 (1984).

POLITICS AND ADMINISTRATIVE POLICY

In the *Motor Vehicle Manufacturers* case, from the separate opinion of Justice Rehnquist, the point is made that the change in policy regarding passive restraints in automobiles seems traceable to a new president of a different party taking over the White House. Rehnquist goes on to say that a reappraisal of policy that grows out of a popularly-mandated change in governmental personnel is reasonable, as long as it doesn't involve a violation of existing law. This assertion emphasizes the point, discussed in chapter 1, concerning the political aspects of administrative law: substantive problems addressed by administrative agencies often involve controversial policy considerations. Policy choices may be expressed through formally-adopted regulations, and sometimes, as in the passive restraint case just discussed, political considerations impinge upon the legal aspects of the administrative process. Nor is the passive restraint case an isolated example.

The Bubble Concept

Chevron U.S.A., Inc. v. *Natural Resources Defense Council, Inc.*, 467 U.S. 837, 104 S.Ct. 2778, 81 L.Ed.2d 694 (1984) is another important Supreme Court case involving political aspects of agency rule making. The 1977 amendments to the Clean Air Act required states that have not achieved national air-quality standards established by the Environmental Protection Agency (EPA) to create a permit program regulating "new or modified major stationary sources" of air pollution. Of considerable significance is the meaning of "stationary source," which is not explicitly defined in the 1977 amendments. The so-called "bubble concept" involves adopting a plantwide definition of a stationary source. Under this definition, a plant containing pollution devices could install or modify one piece of pollution equipment as long as this alternation would not increase total emissions from the plant. Thus, to quote from the Supreme Court opinion in the case, "all of the pollution-emitting devices within the same industrial grouping" would be treated "as though they were encased within a single bubble." In 1980 the EPA adopted a regulation that precluded using the "bubble concept" in the particular circumstances that became the issue in this case. But, as the Supreme Court noted in its opinion, the EPA view changed after the 1980 election: "[I]n 1981 a new administration took office and initiated a 'government-wide reexamination of regulatory burdens and complexities.' 46 Fed.Reg. 16281. In the context of that review, the EPA reevaluated the various arguments that had been advanced in connection with the proper definition of the term 'source.' . . . " It concluded that the plantwide definition of source was appropriate, and thus embraced the bubble concept as a general standard.

The Natural Resources Defense Council brought suit in the court of appeals, which ruled the regulation invalid on the ground that the bubble concept as applied to the pollution-control areas in question was contrary to law. In reviewing this decision, the Supreme Court addressed two basic issues: (1) whether the regulation allowing the use of the bubble concept was a reasonable construction by the EPA of legislative intent, and (2) the degree of judicial deference that should be given to the agency's ruling. The Supreme

Court reversed the decision of the court of appeals. In a unanimous decision for the six members of the Court who participated, Justice Stevens stated that the use of the bubble concept "is a reasonable policy choice for the agency to make." It "is a permissible construction of the statute which seeks to accommodate progress in reducing air pollution with economic growth." Regarding the fact that the agency had changed its definition of the term source:

> [this] does not, as respondents argue, lead us to conclude that no defense should be accorded to the agency's interpretation of the statute. An initial agency interpretation is not instantly carved in stone. On the contrary, the agency, to engage in informed rulemaking, must consider varying interpretations and the wisdom of its policy on a continuing basis.

Stevens added that policy arguments of this sort should not be waged in court. They "are more properly addressed to legislators or administrators, not to judges." Among the "well-settled principles" that the court of appeals ignored in its decision was the following: "Sometimes the legislative delegation to an agency on a particular question is implicit rather than explicit. In such a case, a court may not substitute its own construction of a statutory provision for a reasonable interpretation made by the administrator of an agency."

The two cases discussed in this part of the chapter involve what one commentator (in analyzing the passive restraint case) has called "the political nature of much of administrative decisionmaking." [24] They also bring to the forefront one of the principal problems that this political component creates: uncertainty as to the appropriate role for the courts in reviewing these kinds of cases. While the Supreme Court appears to accord considerable deference to administrative action in the bubble concept case, its more intrusive posture in the passive restraint case is seen by one analyst as an example of the so-called "hard-look" doctrine: a more searching examination of the reasonableness of the exercise of agency discretion.[25]

RULE MAKING AND ITS CONTROL

Kenneth Culp Davis has called rule-making procedure "one of the greatest inventions of modern government," [26] and many others have noted the increase in its use recently. It is what Antonin Scalia has described as "perhaps the most notable development in federal government administration during

---

[24] Merrick B. Garland, "Deregulation and Judicial Review," 98 *Harvard Law Review* 591 (1984).

[25] Cass R. Sunstein, "Deregulation and the Hard-Look Doctrine." *1983 Supreme Court Review*, eds. Philip B. Kurkland, Gerhard Casper, and Dennis J. Hutchinson (1984), 177–215. Sunstein says about the hard-look doctrine at 181: "The purpose of the hard-look doctrine is primarily to facilitate review of the reasonableness of the exercise of discretion, not to ascertain whether agency action has been authorized by the governing substantive law." Sunstein sees *Motor Vehicles Manufacturers Association* as casting doubt on the long-term importance of the Supreme Court's more deferential stance in the *Vermont Yankee* case.

[26] Kenneth Culp Davis, *Administrative Law: Cases—Text—Problems* 241 (6th ed., 1977). In Volume 1 second edition of his *Administrative Law Treatise* (1978), Davis notes at 448 that that statement, made originally in 1970, preceded a "virtual revolution" in that procedures since then. As a result, "[w]hat was one of the greatest inventions of modern government in 1970 has been vastly improved."

the past two decades: 'the contrivance of more expeditious administrative methods'—that is, the constant and accelerating flight away from individualized, adjudicatory proceedings to generalized disposition through rulemaking." [27] Rule making has grown of necessity, in the sense that the many new responsibilities charged to federal administrators under sweeping mandates from Congress "could not possibly" be discharged, according to one governmental official, "through case-by-case adjudication in formal hearings." [28]

This tremendous increase in rule making has not been without problems and critics, however. The economic impact of regulations on private parties, particularly business organizations, can be considerable, and many representatives of this area of the public are calling for restraints on the regulators. At the same time, other areas of public opinion increasingly want to make sure that their views, on matters such as pollution control and nuclear power, for instance, are not ignored in administrative rule making. Whether in direct response to these appeals or not, a view which appears to be expressed increasingly of late states, in effect, "let's try to keep a closer check on what the agencies are doing by means of rules and regulations." The developments and recommendations relevant to this point involve Congress, the president, and the courts.

THE ROLE OF CONGRESS

In addition to general bills pending before Congress that would effect more comprehensive administrative reform, Congress has made use of or considered the following measures which affect rule making directly or indirectly.

Increased Formality for Rule Making in Certain Agencies

Congress, in some cases, has required that agencies go beyond the requirements of § 553 of the APA in rule making. But the attractiveness of either formal or hybrid rule making, both discussed earlier in this chapter, seems to have waned in recent years.[29]

Legislative Veto

The term *legislative veto* refers to congressional authority to annul executive or administrative action—often administrative rules—by resolution of one or both houses or by a congressional committee. As discussed in chapter 3, however, the Supreme Court declared the legislative veto to be unconstitutional in 1983 in *Immigration and Naturalization Service* v. *Chadha*, 462 U.S. 919, 103 S.Ct. 2764, 88 L.Ed.2d 317. As pointed out there, Chief Justice Burger's majority opinion in *Chadha* had the effect of invalidating all legislative ve-

---

[27] Scalia, above, note 21, at 376.

[28] William F. Pederson, Jr., "Formal Records and Informal Rulemaking," 85 *Yale Law Journal* 38 (1975).

[29] O'Reilly, above, note 12, 97 and 158.

toes.[30] Justice Powell, in a concurring opinion, said that only the adjudicatory-type vetoes, such as that exercised in *Chadha*, should be struck down in the case, leaving open the question of the validity of other types of vetoes, including those involving administrative regulations. Justice White, dissenting in *Chadha*, expressed concern about the broad implications of the decision for a large amount of federal legislation. The gist of this part of Justice White's long dissenting opinion is set forth below:

Today the Court not only invalidates § 244(c)(2) of the Immigration and Nationality Act, but also sounds the death knell for nearly 200 other statutory provisions in which Congress has reserved a "legislative veto." For this reason, the Court's decision is of surpassing importance. And it is for this reason that the Court would have been well-advised to decide the case, if possible, on the narrower grounds of separation of powers, leaving for full consideration the constitutionality of other congressional review statutes operating on such varied matters as war powers and agency rulemaking, some of which concern the independent regulatory agencies. . . .

[O]ver the past five decades, the legislative veto has been placed in nearly 200 statutes. The device is known in every field of governmental concern: reorganization, budgets, foreign affairs, war powers, and regulation of trade, safety, energy, the environment and the economy. . . .

[T]his brief review suffices to demonstrate that the legislative veto is more than "efficient, convenient, and useful." Ante, at 2780–2781. It is an important if not indispensable political invention that allows the President and Congress to resolve major constitutional and policy differences, assures the accountability of independent regulatory agencies, and preserves Congress' control over lawmaking. Perhaps there are other means of accommodation and accountability, but the increasing reliance of Congress upon the legislative veto suggests that the alternatives to which Congress must now turn are not entirely satisfactory.

For all these reasons, the apparent sweep of the Court's decision today is regrettable. The Court's Article I analysis appears to invalidate all legislative vetoes irrespective of form or subject. Because the legislative veto is commonly found as a check upon rulemaking by administrative agencies and upon broad-based policy decisions of the Executive Branch, it is particularly unfortunate that the Court reaches its decision in a case involving the exercise of a veto over deportation decisions regarding particular individuals. Courts should always be wary of striking statutes as unconstitutional; to strike an entire class of statutes based on consideration of a somewhat atypical and more-readily indictable exemplar of the class is irresponsible. . . .

I regret that I am in disagreement with my colleagues on the fundamental questions that this case presents. But even more I regret the destructive scope of the Court's holding. It reflects a profoundly different conception of the Constitution than that held by the Courts which sanctioned the modern administrative state. Today's decision strikes down in one fell swoop provisions in more laws enacted by Congress than the Court has cumulatively invalidated in its history. . . .

---

[30] Two weeks after *Chadha*, the Supreme Court in memorandum decisions affirmed lower court opinions invalidating legislative vetoes in several other cases. *Process Gas Consumers Group* v. *Consumer Energy Council*, 463 U.S. 1216, 103 S.Ct. 3556, 77 L.Ed.2d 1402, *reh den* 463 U.S. 1250, 104 S.Ct. 40, 77 L.Ed.2d 1457.

The above-quoted excerpts from Justice White's dissent concentrate mostly on the unnecessary breadth of the majority opinion. Elsewhere in the dissent White argues that the legislative veto is not just a useful device, but that it comports with the Constitution and should be declared valid. He concludes his opinion with an appendix containing brief descriptions of many statutes affected by the *Chadha* decision.

Chadha is one of the most-discussed Supreme Court decisions in years. Many commentators have expressed concern about the broad sweep of the majority opinion. But some have doubted that its practical impact will be of great significance.[31] And in spite of *Chadha*, Congress continues to write legislative-veto provisions into some statutes.[32] Thus, the end of this issue is apparently not yet in sight. And this is understandable: Congress seeks to assert its authority in various ways, and it naturally resists losing a tool intended to enhance its exercise of power. Some support has been expressed for a constitutional amendment to provide for a legislative veto.[33] And other avenues have been proposed or have already been utilized.

The Joint Resolution of Approval

Under the joint-resolution arrangement, Congress might stipulate by statute that an executive action (say, an arms sale), would need to be approved by Congress within a certain period of time. This could make the situation for the executive more difficult than under a legislative veto. As one commentator put it: "Prior to *Chadha*, it took a two-house legislative veto to disapprove a major arms sale. If Congress now insists on a joint resolution of approval for major sales, they would be 'vetoed' if either house refused its support. The administration would face not a two-house but a one-house veto." [34]

Congressional Voiding of Regulations by Statute

The congressional-voiding device is rarely used, but it is a legitimate exercise of congressional power. An example of its use is a 1975 statute which suspended a food-stamp-coupon cost increase which had been promulgated under Department of Agriculture regulations.[35] Since this involves the exercise

---

[31] See, e.g., Pierce, Shapiro, and Verkuil, above note 18, 68.

[32] Louis Fisher of the Library of Congress reported in 1985: "In the 16 months between *Chadha* and the end of the 98th Congress, 53 Legislative vetoes (generally the committee veto variety) have been enacted into law in 18 different statutes." Fisher added that "the Court's prestige has been damaged by a decision that was broader than necessary and unpersuasive in reasoning." Fisher argues that in addition to the legislative veto, Congress possesses a variety of devices for exercising control over agency action, and that these several tools will be used to achieve "comity and cooperation among the branches." Fisher, "Legislative Vetoes, Phoenix Style," in *Courts, Judges and Politics: An Introduction to the Judicial Process*, eds. Walter F. Murphy and C. Herman Pritchett (1986), 347–349. The quotations are from 349.

[33] See, e.g., Senator Dennis DeConcini and Robert Faucher, "The Legislative Veto: A Constitutional Amendment," 21 *Harvard Journal of Legislation* 29 (1984).

[34] Fisher, above, note 32, 348.

[35] P.L. 94–4, 89 Stat. 6, February 22, 1975. See also 33 *Congressional Quarterly Weekly Report* 305 (February 8, 1975).

of statutory power by Congress, the president performs his regular role of either assenting to or vetoing the legislation.

Sunset Legislation

Several proposals recently considered by Congress would require periodic congressional review of agency programs, with spending authority to terminate unless Congress acted to renew or revise the program. While sunset measures are not specifically aimed at agency rule making, certain regulations would clearly make some agencies likely targets.

Environmental Impact Statements

The National Environmental Policy Act of 1969 (NEPA), 83 Stat. 852, 42 U.S.C.A. §§ 4321, 4331–4347, requires environmental impact statements (EIS) on every recommendation for legislation or "other major Federal actions significantly affecting the quality of the human environment." Thousands of such statements have been prepared since the act was adopted, some of them running to thousands of pages and costing millions of dollars to compile. The Council on Environmental Quality has interpreted NEPA to require that procedures for the adoption of EIS are not significantly different from APA rule-making provisions.[36]

Benefit/Cost Analysis

Congress in recent years has passed some forty statutes in areas such as health, education, transportation, housing and the environment that require an assessment of the economic impact of regulations adopted under them. These laws are at least in part in response to charges from critics that over-regulation hurts business and that it is reasonable to ask for some relative balancing by administrators between benefits to be gained and costs incurred from the regulations they adopt.[37] Benefit/cost analysis is part of a broader impulse toward regulatory reform which has lately taken the name "regulatory analysis." Attempts to adopt broad legislation requiring regulatory analysis by all administrative agencies has so far failed in Congress, and initiative in this area has passed to the president.[38] Relevant presidential executive orders will be discussed below.

Congress has adopted two pieces of general legislation which bear on this subject, however. The Regulatory Flexibility Act, adopted in 1980, requires agencies to consider the impact of proposed rules on "small entities," including businesses and other organizations. The agencies, in the course of rule making, must look into alternatives that are less burdensome to small entities

---

[36] J. Skelly Wright, "New Judicial Requisites for Informal Rulemaking: Implications for the Environmental Impact Statement Process," 29 *Administrative Law Review* 59 (1977). See also O'Reilly, above, note 12, 199–215.

[37] Robert B. Reich, "Warring Critiques of Regulation," *Regulation* 37 (January/February, 1979).

[38] On regulatory analysis and a congressional attempt to adopt legislation mandating it, see O'Reilly, above, note 12, 173–215; Pierce, Shapiro, and Verkuil, above, note 18, 512–523.

and, if not adopted, explain why such alternatives were rejected.[39] The Paperwork Reduction Act has among its objectives the reduction of the paperwork burden on the public. To achieve this end, agencies are required to gain the approval of the Office of Management and Budget (OMB) before engaging in the collection of information from the public.[40] Because of the relationship between information collected by agencies and agency rule making, this act could be of considerable importance to the regulatory process.

Increased Citizen Participation

Several statutes from the 1970s provided for funding for interested parties to participate in agency proceedings. The federal Trade Commission Improvement Act of 1975 provides that the commission may compensate a necessary party for attorneys' fees and costs of rule-making participation if that party could not otherwise be represented. Bills have been introduced in Congress to make such aid available for participation in agency proceedings generally.[41]

THE ROLE OF THE PRESIDENT

Recent years have seen increased efforts on the part of the chief executive to influence the regulatory activities of administrative agencies. Since much agency policy is spelled out in rules, a prime target of presidential attention is agency rule making. While presidential influence has taken various forms, including appeals to public opinion (President Reagan's pledge to "get government off our backs" [42] is an obvious example), the most straightforward approach has been the issuance of executive orders.

Regulatory Analysis

Presidents Ford, Carter, and Reagan have issued executive orders affecting rule making, and while these documents have appeared to impose increasingly stringent requirements on agency rule making, their objectives and approach, as one commentator has put it, "amount essentially to the same thing" [43]: requiring agencies to engage in some systematic process of analysis, overseen by a coordinating agency close to the president, before regulations are promulgated. As mentioned above, this process has now come to be referred to as "regulatory analysis." President Ford's Executive Order No. 11821 of 1974 required agencies to examine the inflationary impact of all proposed rules and charged the director of OMB with monitoring agency

---

[39] P.L. 96–354, 94 Stat. 1156 (1980), 5 U.S.C. §§ 601–612. For further discussion of this act, see *A Guide to Federal Agency Rulemaking*, above, note 7, 47–51.

[40] P.L. 96–511, 94 Stat. 2812 (1980), 44 U.S.C. §§ 3501–3520.

[41] See O'Reilly, above, note 12, chapter 11, "Public Participation," 216–229, and sources cited therein. O'Reilly believes that the prevailing mood in Congress in the early 1980s was opposed to funding participation.

[42] "[I]t is not my intention to do away with government. It is rather to make it work . . . not ride on our back." President Reagan's Inaugural Address, January 20, 1981, 39 *Congressional Quarterly Weekly Report* 187 (1981).

[43] Pierce, Shapiro, and Verkuil, above, note 18, 514.

activity in this area.[44] President Carter's 1978 Executive Order No. 12044, "Improving Government Regulations," required, among other things, a "regulatory analysis" for significant regulations which "may have major economic consequences." Agencies were to attempt to avoid placing unnecessary burdens on those affected by regulations and to explore alternative ways of dealing with problems. Again, the OMB was assigned a coordinating role, and an interagency Regulatory Advisory Review Group undertook the actual review of regulations.[45]

Recent Efforts to Control Rule Making

President Reagan's 1981 Executive Order No. 12291 is the most ambitious effort to control rule making yet attempted. It applies to all regulations, major and minor, of all agencies except independent regulatory bodies (to which Carter's and Ford's executive orders also did not apply), which are requested to comply voluntarily with the order. A key provision is that all proposed or final rules must be submitted to OMB for review (a Task Force on Regulatory Relief, headed by the vice-president, also plays a review role). Rules designated as "major" (those estimated to have an annual effect on the economy of $100 million or a major impact on a particular area of the economy) must be accompanied by a "regulatory impact analysis." And no regulatory action, whether a major rule or not, "shall be undertaken unless the potential benefits to society outweigh the potential costs to society." [46]

For the first years of the Reagan administration, only a small percentage of proposed or final rules submitted to OMB for review were considered "major," and thus requiring the preparation of regulatory impact analyses.[47] But this should not be taken to mean that the impact of the Reagan administration on regulatory activity has been insignificant. The total number of pages in the *Federal Register*, where rules and proposed rules are published, reached a high point of 87,012 in 1980, the last year of the Carter administration. It dropped steadily under Reagan, to 50,998 in 1984.[48] In January 1985 President Reagan adopted another executive order with further potential effect on rule making. Executive Order No. 12498, "Regulatory Planning Process," requires, among other things, that agencies annually provide OMB with their agendas for the coming year, including any activities such as studies, which might eventually lead to regulations.[49]

These executive orders have undoubtedly placed rule making under closer scrutiny of the president and his advisors. In theory, at least, this should facilitate achieving consistency in the aims of regulatory programs

---

[44] Executive Order No. 11821, 3 C.F.R. Pt. 926 (1975).

[45] Executive Order No. 12044, 3 C.F.R. Pt. 152 (1979).

[46] Executive Order No. 12291, 3 C.F.R. Pt. 127 (1982).

[47] *A Guide to Federal Agency Rulemaking*, above, note 7, 108.

[48] Communication from the Office of the Federal Register, National Archives, January 24, 1986. In 1985 the number of pages rose slightly to 53,480. These figures should be treated only a general indicator of changes in agency rule making, since the *Federal Register* publishes other material besides regulations, such as presidential proclamations, and announcements.

[49] Executive Order No. 12498, "Regulatory Planning Process," January 4, 1985, 21 *Weekly Compilation of Presidential Documents* 1 (1985).

across a wide range of agencies. But this intervention by or on behalf of the president is not without its critics. It is argued, for instance, that Congress has delegated rule-making power to particular agencies, and when representatives of the president outside of these agencies effect changes in rules, this violates the spirit of the legislation. It is further suggested that off-the-record intervention from OMB, perhaps after the notice-and-comment period has ended, violates the spirit and intent of the Administrative Procedure Act. It seems likely that judicial resolution of issues of this kind will be sought.[50]

THE ROLE OF THE COURTS

The problem just referred to, that of off-the-record input in rule making, brings the discussion back to one of the central problems of recent rule making under the APA.

The "original understanding"[51] with regard to rule making under the APA was that in rule making "on the record," the record established at the hearing, was "exclusive." No *ex parte* contacts with decision makers were to be allowed, and no material not in the record should be considered in developing a rule. By contrast, the "record" of a notice-and-comment proceeding accompanying informal rule making was not considered "exclusive," but could be supplemented by discussions among staff members, outside contacts, and the like. Under these kinds of assumptions, RARG review of rules, at least to the extent that they were promulgated under § 553 of the APA, would not be objectionable.

The problem with this original understanding is that it assumed that the absence of a complete record in a § 553 rule-making proceeding could be overcome by having a U.S. district court proceeding to build an adequate record, to be followed by a court of appeals review of legal questions. However, statutory and judicial developments have led to a situation where it is common for courts of appeal to accept review of § 553 rule making directly, with the result that the record, for review purposes, is exclusive and may be

---

[50] The problems of presidential intervention in rule making have been widely discussed. See, for instance, "Symposium: Cost-Benefit Analysis and Agency Decision-Making: An Analysis of Executive Order No. 12,291," 23 *Arizona Law Review* 1195–1298 (1981); "Symposium: Presidential Intervention in Administrative Rulemaking," 56 *Tulane Law Review* 811–902 (1982); Kenneth Culp Davis, *1982 Supplement to Administrative Law Treatise* 147–159 (1982). Alan B. Morrison, "OMB Interference with Agency Rulemaking: The Wrong way to Write a Regulation," 99 *Harvard Law Review* 1059 (1986); Christopher C. DeMuth and Douglas H. Ginsburg, "White House Review of Agency Rulemaking," 99 *Harvard Law Review* 1075 (1986). These issues have not yet been addressed by the Supreme Court. Two relevant lower court opinions are *Sierra Club* v. *Costle,* 657 F.2d 298 (C.A.D.C., 1981), holding that meetings during the post-comment period of an EPA rule making proceeding with presidential advisors did not violate due process or the Clean Air Act; and *Wolfe* v. *Department of Health and Human Services,* 54 U.S.L.W. 2309 (U.S.CD.C., D.C., 1985), holding that agency records concerning transmission of proposed rule from Health and Human Services to OMB is not exempt from disclosure under Freedom of Information Act.

[51] The term is that of Carl A. Auerbach. The analysis in this passage is based largely on his "Informal Rulemaking: A Proposed Relationship Between Administrative Procedures and Judicial Review," 72 *Northwestern University Law Review* 15, 16–30 (1977).

inadequate as well. The inadequacy of the record of § 553 rule-making proceedings for review purposes has been one of the stimuli for requiring more
formal procedures than § 553 calls for. A senior court of appeals judge, in an
off-the-bench comment, put it this way: [52]

> But if courts are going to make a searching and careful review of the facts in an
> informal rulemaking proceeding, they will need a proper record. Today's informal
> rulemaking proceedings do not provide a proper record. The government agen-
> cies and departments seem to be operating under the old assumption that agency
> expertise is a proper blanket with which to insulate themselves from searching
> judicial review. But the insulation is occurring at a time when lower courts are
> being required by the Supreme Court to pierce the blanket and get to the facts—
> not to weigh them but to consider them to determine whether the agency action
> under review is rational. The result is that courts spend an inordinate amount of
> time in review of informal rule-making cases attempting to find documents that
> presumably are in the record but which are somehow unavailable. Often there is
> not even a list of the documents that make up the record. Perhaps the most
> distressing aspect of such reviews is that documents seem to surface one at a time,
> first from one party, then from another. And one understandably gets the uneasy
> feeling that the whole record is not really before the court.

And once it is determined that a more complete administrative record is
necessary for judicial review of informal rule making, it is only a short step
from there to determining that this record should be "exclusive" and that no
ex parte contacts should be allowed. Lower court rulings on this part have not
been consistent.[53] It is an issue appropriate for consideration by the Supreme
Court.

The Partnership Metaphor

In addition to the problem of the adequacy of the record, another major
stimulus for court imposition of hybrid rule-making procedures has been the
perception among some federal judges that the great significance of administrative policy making requires a closer judicial check on administrative action.
This attitude has been referred to as the "partnership metaphor," [54] and it is
best expressed in an oft-quoted statement of Judge David Bazelon of the Court
of Appeals for the District of Columbia in the case of *Environmental Defense
Fund, Inc.* v. *Ruckelshaus*, 439 F.2d 584, 598 (D.C.Cir., 1971):

> We stand on the threshold of a new era in the history of the long and fruitful
> collaboration of administrative agencies and reviewing courts. For many years,
> courts have treated administrative policy decisions with great deference, confin-
> ing judicial attention primarily to matters of procedure. On matters of substance,
> the courts regularly upheld agency action, with a nod in the direction of the

---

[52] Wright, above, note 36, at 61.

[53] See the general discussion, including a review of lower court cases, of "The Problems of Ex
Parte Contacts" in Pierce, Shapiro, and Verkuil, above, note 18, 492–505.

[54] The term is Daniel D. Polsby's and is used in "*FCC* v. *National Citizens Committee for
Broadcasting and the Judicious Use of Administrative Discretion,*" in Philip B. Kurland and
Gerhard Casper (eds)., *The Supreme Court Review, 1978,* 34 (1979).

"substantial evidence" test, and a bow to the mysteries of administrative expertise. Courts occasionally asserted, but less often exercised, the power to set aside agency action on the ground that an impermissible factor had entered into the decision, or a crucial factor had not been considered. Gradually, however, that power has come into more frequent use and with it, the requirement that administrators articulate the factors on which they base their decisions.

In giving closer scrutiny to administrative actions in this collaborative relationship, reviewing courts came to require more procedural guarantees than the informal rule-making provisions the APA provided. And this, of course, is where the Supreme Court came into the picture, particularly with its *Vermont Yankee* opinion.

That opinion did not solve the problems with which the lower courts were grappling, however. The inadequacy of informal rule-making records and the need for scrutiny of administrative action still remain. As a result, doubts have been expressed as to the decision's long-term significance,[55] and writers have speculated about ways to get around the decision. Courts may still find ways to distinguish cases from *Vermont Yankee* and require hybrid procedures. Or Congress may consider any of several recommendations for dealing with these problems. We will mention just three of these recommendations briefly:

1. Extending of the provision in the FTC Improvement Act of 1975 which allows hearings with cross examination and rebuttal submissions on "disputed issues of material fact." This proposal is based on the distinction between legislative fact and adjudicative fact long favored by several analysts.[56]
2. Restoring fully the distinction between rule making and adjudication by leaving section 553 as it is, but not having proceedings based thereon serve as the basis for judicial review. Instead, "any person seeking review of a section-553 rule" would be required "to file a protest against the rule with the agency." This would be followed by an on-the-record proceeding before the agency, which would be subject to direct judicial review. Under this arrangement, no rules would be adopted under any other provision of the APA than section 553.[57]
3. Dispensing with the rule-making and adjudication categories, in fact if not in name, and designing "unitary procedural solutions" which provide a range of procedural guarantees. The particular procedure would depend on the category of administrative action, ranging from

---

[55] Professor Davis calls it "largely one of those rare opinions in which a unanimous Supreme Court speaks with little or no authority." 1 *Administrative Law Treatise* 616 (2nd ed., 1978). See also Scalia, above, note 21, at 375–409.

[56] See Davis, above, note 26, at 261–263; Friendly, above, note 10, at 1268; Lionel Kestenbaum, "Rulemaking Beyond A.P.A.: Criteria for Trial-Type Procedures and the F.T.C. Improvement Act," 44 *George Washington Law Review* 679, 691 (1976).

[57] Auerbach, above, note 51, at 61f.

the most informal (for planning and policy-making functions) to the most formal (for the imposition of sanctions).[58]

As Judge Friendly said in his celebrated article, "Some Kind of Hearing," "the problem is always the same—to devise procedures that are both fair and feasible." [59] The range of recommendations just discussed indicates that that elusive goal is still being sought.

---

[58] Verkuil, above, note 8, at 293.

[59] Friendly, above, note 20, at 1315.

Chapter 7

The Right to Be Heard and Adjudicatory Policy Making

THE RIGHT TO BE HEARD

As noted in the last chapter, rule making may at times resemble adjudication in the procedural requirements that are built into the process. But in general, discussions of "the right to a hearing" imply adjudication, a quasi-judicial as opposed to quasi-legislative process. The types of such hearings that one could mention are nearly endless: proceedings to receive a license of some kind or to be awarded a television channel by the FCC, or renewal or revocation of such licenses; a hearing on a charge of improper dealing in securities before the SEC; proceedings involving the firing, supervision, or disciplining of a governmental employee; a conference or interview involving one's pension or tax problems; a discussion with school authorities about the suspension or expulsion of one's child from school; an appeal of a zoning ruling concerning one's property; and many more such examples. Whatever the matter at issue, the right to be heard involves some form of oral participation by the party affected by the administrative action. The degree of required formality of the hearing may vary from situation to situation. If a hearing is required, there may be a question as to when it must be held. And there are some situations when no hearing of any kind is necessary. These are the matters that will be examined in this part of the chapter.

The question of who has a right to a hearing has been a controversial one in administrative law for decades. While there has been considerable judicial attention to this matter in recent years, controversies still arise frequently, and it is impossible to state with precision the conditions when a hearing will or will not be required. One should start by looking at the applicable legislation, both general statutes and those applying specifically to the administrative agency in question. Typically, the general statute will reference particular statutes. For instance, section 554 of the APA, on adjudication, applies to "every case of adjudication required by statute to be determined on the record after opportunity for agency hearing."

The absence in a particular statute of a provision for a hearing may not be conclusive, however. Much litigation has involved allegations that the denial of a hearing, even when no hearing is mandated by the legislature, contravenes the constitutional rights of the plaintiff. The constitutional basis for most such litigation are the provisions of the Fifth and Fourteenth Amendments stating that a person may not be deprived of "life, liberty, or property, without due process of law."

The Right-Privilege Distinction

In applying these provisions in concrete cases, how do courts determine if a deprivation of life, liberty, or property actually is involved? A test frequently applied over the years has been the so-called "right-privilege distinction," which essentially holds that if a privilege rather than a right is at stake, then due process does not require a hearing. The distinction has a long history and is usually traced to Judge Oliver Wendell Holmes, Jr.[1] It has been stated many times by the courts, but perhaps nowhere was it put so succinctly as in a 1950 Supreme Court opinion upholding the exclusion from the country without a hearing of the alien wife of a U.S. citizen, "solely upon a finding by the Attorney General that her admission would be prejudicial to the interests of the United States"; "... we are dealing here with a matter of *privilege*. Petitioner had no vested *right* of entry...." *United States of America ex rel. Knauff* v. *Shaughnessy*, 338 U.S. 537, 539, 544, 70 S.Ct. 309, 310–311, 313, 94 L.Ed. 317, 322, 325 (1950) (emphasis in the original).

By the 1970s, however, the impact of the right-privilege distinction had been eroded to a considerable extent. Commentators wrote of a "due process explosion"[2] which, among other things, discredited the right-privilege distinction and extended the requirement of a hearing into areas where it would not have been deemed necessary some years earlier. This "revolution" did not proceed as far as most analysts, either proponents or critics, had prophesied, however. By the end of the decade, a drawing back from the expectations of the early and mid 1970s regarding the development of due process was clear. The dominant theme of those assessing the Supreme Court's role in this development has been the inconsistency and lack of clarity in the Court's

---

[1] The kernel of the Holmes position is contained in his statement that a "petitioner may have a constitutional right to talk politics, but he has no constitutional right to be a policeman," made in *McAuliffe* v. *Mayor of New Bedford*, 155 Mass. 216, 220, 29 N.E. 517 (Supreme Judicial Court of Massachusetts, 1892). This quotation, as well as a general discussion of the case, provide the introduction to Professor William W. Van Alstyne's comprehensive article on the right-privilege distinction. "The Demise of the Right-Privilege Distinction in Constitutional Law," 81 *Harvard Law Review* 1439 (1968).

[2] The term was used by Judge Henry J. Friendly in "Some Kind of Hearing," 123 University of *Pennsylvania Law Review* 1267, 1268 (1975). In this article Judge Friendly stated (at 1273) that "we have witnessed a greater expansion of procedural due process in the last five years than in the entire period since ratification of the Constitution."

pronouncements. These assessments will be discussed further below. But first the outlines of the abbreviated "revolution" should be sketched.

The first key case is *Goldberg* v. *Kelly*, a 1970 decision that spoke to the right-privilege distinction in the course of spelling out the due process [3] status of a welfare recipient.

Goldberg v. Kelly

SUPREME COURT OF THE UNITED STATES, 1970.
397 U.S. 254, 90 S.CT. 1011, 25 L.ED.2D 287.

Mr. Justice BRENNAN delivered the opinion of the Court.

The question for decision is whether a State that terminates public assistance payments to a particular recipient without affording him the opportunity for an evidentiary hearing prior to termination denies the recipient procedural due process in violation of the Due Process Clause of the Fourteenth Amendment. . . .

Pursuant to [a relevant regulation] the New York City Department of Social Services promulgated Procedure No. 68–18. A caseworker who has doubts about the recipient's continued eligibility must first discuss them with the recipient. If the caseworker concludes that the recipient is no longer eligible, he recommends termination of aid to a unit supervisor. If the latter concurs, he sends the recipient a letter stating the reasons for proposing to terminate aid and notifying him that within seven days he may request that a higher official review the record, and may support the request with a written statement prepared personally or with the aid of an attorney or other person. If the reviewing official affirms the determination of ineligibility, aid is stopped immediately and the recipient is informed by letter of the reasons for the action. Appellees' challenge to this procedure emphasizes the absence of any provisions for the personal appearance of the recipient before the reviewing official, for oral presentation of evidence, and for confrontation and cross-examination of adverse witnesses. However, the letter does inform the recipient that he may request a post-termination "fair hearing." . . .

The constitutional issue to be decided, therefore, is the narrow one whether the Due Process Clause requires that the recipient be afforded an evidentiary hearing *before* the termination of benefits. The District Court held that only a pre-termination evidentiary hearing would satisfy the constitutional command, and rejected the argument of the state and city officials that the combination of the post-termination "fair hearing" with the informal pre-termination review disposed of all due process claims. The court said: "While post-termination review is relevant, there is one overpowering fact which controls here. By hypothesis, a welfare recipient is destitute, without funds or assets. . . . Suffice it to say that to cut off a welfare recipient in the face of . . . 'brutal need' without a prior hearing of some sort is unconscionable, unless overwhelming considerations justify it." *Kelly* v. *Wyman*, 294 F.Supp. 893, 899, 900 (1968). The court rejected the argument that the need to protect the public's tax revenues supplied the requisite "overwhelming consideration." "Against the jus-

---

[3] So important is this case that one writer referred to the "Goldberg v. Kelly revolution." Bernard Schwartz, "Administrative Law: The Third Century," 29 *Administrative Law Review* 291, 300 (1977).

tified desire to protect public funds must be weighed the individual's overpowering need in this unique situation not to be wrongfully deprived of assistance. . . . While the problem of additional expense must be kept in mind, it does not justify denying a hearing meeting the ordinary standards of due process. Under all the circumstances, we hold that due process requires an adequate hearing before termination of welfare benefits, and the fact that there is a later constitutionally fair proceeding does not alter the result." . . .

Appellant does not contend that procedural due process is not applicable to the termination of welfare benefits. Such benefits are a matter of statutory entitlement for persons qualified to receive them. Their termination involves state action that adjudicates important rights. The constitutional challenge cannot be answered by an argument that public assistance benefits are "a 'privilege' and not a 'right.'" *Shapiro* v. *Thompson*, 394 U.S. 618, 627 n. 6, 89 S.Ct. 1322, 1327 (1969). . . .

It is true, of course, that some governmental benefits may be administratively terminated without affording the recipient a pre-termination evidentiary hearing. But we agree with the District Court that when welfare is discontinued, only a pre-termination evidentiary hearing provides the recipient with procedural due process. . . . Welfare recipients must . . . be given an opportunity to confront and cross-examine the witnesses relied on by the department. . . . We do not say that counsel must be provided at the pre-termination hearing, but only that the recipient must be allowed to retain an attorney if he so desires. Counsel can help delineate the issues, present the factual contentions in an orderly manner, conduct cross-examination, and generally safeguard the interests of the recipient. . . . We agree with the District Court that prior involvement in some aspects of a case will not necessarily bar a welfare official from acting as a decision maker. He should not, however, have participated in making the determination under review.

Affirmed.

[The dissenting opinion of Mr. Justice Black is omitted.]

Liberty and Due Process

Two years after *Goldberg* came *Morrissey* v. *Brewer*, a case involving the liberty rather than the property aspects of due process. 408 U.S. 471, 92 S.Ct. 2593, 33 L.Ed.2d 484 (1972). The Supreme Court in *Morrissey* ruled that the Due Process Clause of the Fourteenth Amendment afforded an individual the right to be heard prior to the revocation of his parole. The Court stated: "it is hardly useful any longer to try to deal with this problem in terms of whether the parolee's liberty is a 'right' or a 'privilege.' By whatever name the liberty is valuable and must be seen as within the protection of the Fourteenth Amendment." The Court called for a two-stage parole revocation process, with a preliminary hearing at the time of arrest and a more formal revocation hearing later. While the Court said that it "cannot write a code of procedure," it did lay down "minimum requirements of due process" for the second hearing, including written notice, disclosure of evidence against the parolee, opportunity to be heard in person and to present witnesses and documentary evidence, the right to confront and cross-examine adverse witnesses ("unless the hearing officer specifically finds good cause for not allowing confrontation"), a neutral and detached hearing body, and a written statement as to the evidence relied on and the reasons for revoking parole. The Court did not decide the question of the parolee's entitlement to retain counsel, however, as it had in *Goldberg*.

In another opinion issued on the same day as *Morrissey*, the Supreme Court appeared to dispense completely with the right-privilege distinction when it stated that "the Court has fully and finally rejected the wooden distinction between 'rights' and 'privileges' that once seemed to govern the applicability of procedural due process rights." *Board of Regents* v. *Roth*, 408 U.S. 564, 571, 92 S.Ct. 2701, 2706, 33 L.Ed.2d 548, 557 (1972). But in this case the majority of the Supreme Court held that Roth, an assistant professor at a state university hired on a one-year contract, was not entitled under the Fourteenth Amendment to either a statement of reasons or a hearing on the decision not to rehire him. As Mr. Justice Stewart stated for the majority, "the range of interests protected by procedural due process is not infinite."[4]

Roth, then, is a decision that cuts both ways: it continues the condemnation of the right-privilege distinction, but it rules that Roth's due process interest is sufficiently minor that a hearing was not required. Some commentators trace to the *Roth* case a change in direction in the Supreme Court's treatment of right to be heard cases. Thereafter, "the lack of a coherent methodology in dealing with this area of the law" is discerned.[5] The new orientation was particularly manifested in the 1976 case of *Mathews* v. *Eldridge*, which is close to *Goldberg* in that both involved the right to a pretermination hearing over the continued receipt of benefit payments.

Mathews v. Eldridge

SUPREME COURT OF THE UNITED STATES, 1976.
424 U.S. 319, 96 S.CT. 893, 47 L.ED.2D 18.

Mr. Justice POWELL delivered the opinion of the Court.

The issue in this case is whether the Due Process Clause of the Fifth Amendment requires that prior to the termination of Social Security disability benefit payments the recipient be afforded an opportunity for an evidentiary hearing.

I

Cash benefits are provided to workers during periods in which they are completely disabled under the disability insurance benefits program created by the 1956 amendments to Title II of the Social Security Act. 70 Stat. 815, 42 U.S.C.A. § 423. Respondent Eldridge was first awarded bene-

---

[4] In the companion case of *Perry* v. *Sinderman*, the Court ruled that a professor who had been employed for a number of years at the same institution was entitled to attempt to show that a de facto tenure system existed at his institution and that proof of such a system would entitle him to a hearing on the matter of his dismissal. 408 U.S. 593, 92 S.Ct. 2694, 33 L.Ed.2d 570 (1972).

[5] Victor G. Rosenblum, "Schoolchildren: Yes, Policemen: No—Some Thoughts About the Supreme Court's Priorities Concerning the Right to a Hearing in Suspension and Removal Cases," 72 *Northwestern University Law Review* 146 (1977), at 155. See also "Democratic Due Process: Administrative Procedure After *Bishop* v. *Wood*," 77 *Duke Law Journal* 453 (1977), at 456, and Rolf Dolzer, "Welfare Benefits as Property Interests: A Constitutional Right to a Hearing and Judicial Review," 29 *Administrative Law Review* 525 (1977).

fits in June 1968. In March 1972, he received a questionnaire from the state agency charged with monitoring his medical condition. Eldridge completed the questionnaire, indicating that his condition had not improved and identifying the medical sources, including physicians, from whom he had received treatment recently. The state agency then obtained reports from his physician and a psychiatric consultant. After considering these reports and other information in his file the agency informed Eldridge by letter that it had made a tentative determination that his disability had ceased in May 1972. The letter included a statement of reasons for the proposed termination of benefits, and advised Eldridge that he might request reasonable time in which to obtain and submit additional information pertaining to his condition.

In his written response, Eldridge disputed one characterization of his medical condition and indicated that the agency already had enough evidence to establish his disability. The state agency then made its final determination that he had ceased to be disabled in May 1972. This determination was accepted by the Social Security Administration (SSA), which notified Eldridge in July that his benefits would terminate after that month. The notification also advised him of his right to seek reconsideration by the state agency of this initial determination within six months.

Instead of requesting reconsideration, Eldridge commenced this action challenging the constitutional validity of the administrative procedures established by the Secretary of Health, Education, and Welfare for assessing whether there exists a continuing disability. He sought an immediate reinstatement of benefits pending a hearing on the issue of his disability. . . .

The District Court concluded that the administrative procedures pursuant to which the Secretary had terminated Eldridge's benefits abridged his right to procedural due process. The court viewed the interest of the disability recipient in uninterrupted benefits as indistinguishable from that of the welfare recipient in *Goldberg*. . . . Relying entirely upon the District Court's opinion, the Court of Appeals for the Fourth Circuit affirmed the injunction barring termination of Eldridge's benefits prior to an evidentiary hearing. 493 F.2d 1230 (1974). We reverse. . . .

Procedural due process imposes constraints on governmental decisions which deprive individuals of "liberty" or "property" interests within the meaning of the Due Process Clause of the Fifth or Fourteenth Amendment. The Secretary does not contend that procedural due process is inapplicable to terminations of Social Security disability benefits. . . .

This Court consistently has held that some form of hearing is required before an individual is finally deprived of a property interest. . . .

Eldridge agrees that the review procedures available to a claimant before the initial determination of ineligibility becomes final would be adequate if disability benefits were not terminated until after the evidentiary hearing stage of the administrative process. The dispute centers upon what process is due prior to the initial termination of benefits, pending review.

In recent years this Court increasingly has had occasion to consider the extent to which due process requires an evidentiary hearing prior to the deprivation of some type of property interest even if such a hearing is provided thereafter. In only one case, Goldberg v. Kelly, 397 U.S., at 266–271, 90 S.Ct., at 1019–1022, 25 L.Ed.2d 287, has the Court held that a hearing closely approximating a judicial trial is necessary. In other cases requiring some type of pre-termination hearing as a matter of constitutional right the Court has spoken sparingly about the requisite procedures. . . .

[The Court then described the legally-mandated procedures for determining disability and monitoring continuing eligibility for disability payments. This monitoring is carried out by mail or telephone, supplemented by information from the recipient's source of medical treatment. If a recipient's benefits are to be terminated, he is notified, provided with a summary of the evidence on which the proposed termination is based, and given an opportunity "to respond in writing and submit additional evidence." No pre-termination hearing is provided, although the procedures do allow for a post-termination evidentiary hearing.]

Despite the elaborate character of the administrative procedures provided by the Secretary, the courts below held them to be constitutionally inadequate, concluding that due process requires an evidentiary hearing prior to termination. In light of the private and governmental interests at stake here and the nature of the existing procedures, we think this was error.

Since a recipient whose benefits are terminated is awarded full retroactive relief if he ultimately prevails, his sole interest is in the uninterrupted receipt of this source of income pending final administrative decision on his claim. His potential injury is thus similar in nature to that of the welfare recipient in *Goldberg*, see 397 U.S., at 263–264, 90 S.Ct., at 1018–1019, the nonprobationary federal employee in *Arnett*, see 416 U.S., at 146, 94 S.Ct., at 1640, 1641, and the wage earner in *Sniadach*.

Only in *Goldberg* has the Court held that due process requires an evidentiary hearing prior to a temporary deprivation. It was emphasized there that welfare assistance is given to persons on the very margin of subsistence:

> The crucial factor in this context—a factor not present in the case of . . . virtually anyone else whose governmental entitlements are ended—is that termination of aid pending resolution of a controversy over eligibility may deprive an *eligible* recipient of the very means by which to live while he waits. 397 U.S., at 264, 90 S.Ct., at 1018 (emphasis in original).

Eligibility for disability benefits, in contrast, is not based upon financial need. Indeed, it is wholly unrelated to the worker's income or support from many other sources, such as earnings of other family members, workmen's compensation awards, tort claims awards, savings, private insurance, public or private pensions, veterans' benefits, food stamps, public assistance, or the "many other important programs, both public and private, which contain provisions for disability payments affecting a substantial portion of the work force. . . ."

As *Goldberg* illustrates, the degree of potential deprivation that may be created by a particular decision is a factor to be considered in assessing the validity of any administrative decisionmaking process. Cf. Morrissey v. Brewer, 408 U.S. 471, 92 S.Ct. 2593, 33 L.Ed.2d 484 (1972). The potential deprivation here is generally likely to be less than in *Goldberg*, although the degree of difference can be overstated. As the District Court emphasized, to remain eligible for benefits a recipient must be "unable to engage in substantial gainful activity." 42 U.S.C.A. § 423; 361 F.Supp., at 523. Thus, in contrast to the discharged federal employee in *Arnett*, there is little possibility that the terminated recipient will be able to find even temporary employment to ameliorate the interim loss. . . . The Secretary concedes that the delay between a request for a hearing before an administrative law judge and a decision on the claim is currently between 10 and 11 months. Since a terminated recipient must first obtain a reconsideration decision as a prerequisite to invoking his right to an evidentiary hearing, the delay between the actual cutoff of benefits and final decision after a hearing exceeds one year.

In view of the torpidity of this administrative review process, cf. id., at 383–384, 386, 95 S.Ct., at 536–537, 538, and the typically modest resources of the family unit of the physically disabled worker, the hardship imposed upon the erroneously terminated disability recipient may be significant. Still, the disabled worker's need is likely to be less than that of a welfare recipient. In addition to the possibility of access to private resources, other forms of government assistance will become available where the termination of disability benefits places a worker or his family below the subsistence level. In view of these potential sources of temporary income, there is less reason here than in *Goldberg* to depart from the ordinary principle, established by our decisions, that something less than an evidentiary hearing is sufficient prior to adverse administrative action.

D

An additional factor to be considered here is the fairness and reliability of the existing pretermination procedures, and the probable value, if any, of additional procedural safeguards. Central to the evaluation of any administrative process is the nature of the relevant inquiry. In order to remain eligible for benefits the disabled worker must demonstrate by means of "medically acceptable clinical and laboratory diagnostic techniques," 42 U.S.C.A. § 423(d)(3), that he is unable "to engage in any substantial gainful activity by reason of any *medically determinable* physical or mental impairment...." § 423(d)(1)(A) (emphasis supplied). In short, a medical assessment of the worker's physical or mental condition is required. This is a more sharply focused and easily documented decision than the typical determination of welfare entitlement....

The decision in *Goldberg* also was based on the Court's conclusion that written submissions were an inadequate substitute for oral presentation because they did not provide an effective means for the recipient to communicate his case to the decisionmaker. Written submissions were viewed as an unrealistic option, for most recipients lacked the "educational attain-

ment necessary to write effectively" and could not afford professional assistance. In addition, such submissions would not provide the "flexibility of oral presentations" or "permit the recipient to mold his argument to the issues the decision maker appears to regard as important." 397 U.S., at 269, 90 S.Ct., at 1021. In the context of the disability-benefits-entitlement assessment the administrative procedures under review here fully answer these objections.

The detailed questionnaire which the state agency periodically sends the recipient identifies with particularity the information relevant to the entitlement decision, and the recipient is invited to obtain assistance from the local SSA office in completing the questionnaire. More important, the information critical to the entitlement decision usually is derived from medical sources, such as the treating physician. Such sources are likely to be able to communicate more effectively through written documents than are welfare recipients or the lay witnesses supporting their cause. The conclusions of physicians often are supported by X-rays and the results of clinical or laboratory tests, information typically more amenable to written than to oral presentation....

E

In striking the appropriate due process balance the final factor to be assessed is the public interest. This includes the administrative burden and other societal costs that would be associated with requiring, as a matter of constitutional right, an evidentiary hearing upon demand in all cases prior to the termination of disability benefits. The most visible burden would be the incremental cost resulting from the increased number of hearings and the expense of providing benefits to ineligible recipients pending decision. No one can predict the extent of the increase, but the fact that full benefits would continue until after such hearings would assure the exhaustion in most cases of this attractive option. . . .

In assessing what process is due in this case, substantial weight must be given to the good-faith judgments of the individuals charged by Congress with the administration of social welfare programs that the procedures they have provided assure fair consideration of the entitlement claims of individuals. This is especially so where, as here, the prescribed procedures not only provide the claimant with an effective process for asserting his claim prior to any administrative action, but also assure a right to an evidentiary hearing, as well as to subsequent judicial review, before the denial of his claim becomes final.

We conclude that an evidentiary hearing is not required prior to the termination of disability benefits and that the present administrative procedures fully comport with due process.

The judgment of the Court of Appeals is

Reversed.

Mr. Justice STEVENS took no part in the consideration or decision of this case.

Mr. Justice BRENNAN, with whom Mr. Justice MARSHALL concurs, dissenting.

For the reasons stated in my dissenting opinion in Richardson v. Wright, 405 U.S. 208, 212, 92 S.Ct. 788, 791, 31 L.Ed.2d 151 (1972), I agree with the District Court and the Court of Appeals that, prior to termination of benefits, Eldridge must be afforded an evidentiary hearing of the type required for welfare beneficiaries. . . .

While the Court was at pains to distinguish *Goldberg* from *Mathews*, the consensus among commentators is that the latter is one in a line of cases that moved away from the broad implications of the former: "Without saying so directly, the Court set *Goldberg*'s rigid model aside and replaced it with an admittedly vague procedural balancing test." [6] This due process balancing is brought out clearly in the excerpts from section E of the *Mathews* opinion quoted above. The major emphasis in *Goldberg* was on two considerations: (1) the right to be heard prior to the deprivation of an interest, and (2) the use of a rather elaborate hearing process to adjudicate the private party's claim. *Mathews* dealt with the first of these, but in rejecting the need for a pretermination hearing it didn't have to reach the second. Both of these matters, the timing of the hearing and the degree of its formality, have been the subjects of important further development.

THE TIMING OF THE HEARING

The majority in *Mathews* concluded that Eldridge was entitled only to the posttermination hearing provided by Social Security Administration regulations, and that such a hearing could be considered to be within the period of "final administrative decision on his claim." Thus, the Court's action was consistent with the following statement found elsewhere in the opinion:

---

[6] Paul R. Verkuil, "The Emerging Concept of Administrative Procedure," 78 *Columbia Law Review* 258, 288 (1978). See also Schwartz, above, note 3, at 301, and Jerry L. Mashaw, "The Supreme Court's Due Process Calculus for Administrative Adjudication in *Mathews v. Eldridge*: Three Factors in Search of a Theory of Value," 44 *University of Chicago Law Review* 28 (1976).

"This Court consistently has held that some form of hearing is required before an individual is finally deprived of a property interest" (424 U.S. 333).[7] That is, due process required a hearing, but not a pretermination hearing.

On the authority of *Mathews*, the Supreme Court has sustained an Illinois statute authorizing the revocation of a driver's license for repeated conviction of traffic offenses without a prior hearing but with a postrevocation hearing. *Dixon* v. *Love*, 431 U.S. 105, 97 S.Ct. 1723, 52 L.Ed.2d 172 (1977). And in a pair of five-to-four decisions handed down on the same day in 1979, the Supreme Court upheld state statutory schemes that allowed license suspensions without a prior hearing but with a posthearing of: (1) a driver who refused to take a breathalyzer test upon arrest for driving while intoxicated, *Mackey* v. *Montrym*, 443 U.S. 1, 99 S.Ct. 2612, 61 L.Ed.2d 321 (1979); and (2) a harness racehorse trainer whose horse was revealed, on the basis of a postrace urinalysis, to have been given a stimulant. *Barry* v. *Barchi*, 443 U.S. 55, 99 S.Ct. 2642, 61 L.Ed.2d 365 (1979).[8] Both of these cases relied strongly on the due process balancing concept articulated in *Mathews* v. *Eldridge*.

One of the justifications for not requiring a prior hearing in the cases discussed above is the assertion that this would forestall necessary administrative action. The point is even made that removing drunken drivers from the highways is within the ambit of the "summary procedures" which the courts "have traditionally accorded the states great leeway in adopting." *Mackey* v. *Montrym*, 443 U.S. 1, 99 S.Ct. 2612, 61 L.Ed.2d 321. This is one of the illustrations of the recent expansion of the concept of summary powers. The use of such authority "had its roots in the common law of nuisance."[9] Its early application was typically premised on the existence of "extraordinary" or "emergency"[10] circumstances, upon a "pressing need for quick action."[11]

If the grounds for employing summary authority have been expanded recently, there are still occasions when summary administrative activity, in the more traditional sense, is necessary. In such cases, the need for swift administrative action will obviate any possible justification for a prior hearing. The following case is an example.

---

[7] This statement is virtually identical to one in *Wolff* v. *McDonnell*: "The Court has consistently held that some kind of hearing is required at some time before a person is finally deprived of his property interests." 418 U.S. 539, 557–8, 94 S.Ct. 2963, 2975, 41 L.Ed.2d 935, 952 (1974). This statement, in turn, was the inspiration for the title of Judge Friendly's article "Some Kind of Hearing," above, note 2.

[8] In *Barry* v. *Barchi* the suspension was found to be contrary to due process because the statutory provision for a post-suspension hearing, as applied in the case, failed to assure a prompt proceeding.

[9] James O. Freedman, *Crisis and Legitimacy: The Administrative Process and American Government* 208 (1978).

[10] Ibid. 209.

[11] Jerry L. Mashaw and Richard A. Merrill, *Introduction to the American Public Law System* 374 (1975).

Hodel v. Virginia Surface Mining and Reclamation Association, Inc.

SUPREME COURT OF THE UNITED STATES, 1981.
452 U.S. 264, 101 S.CT. 2352, 69 L.ED.2D 1.

[An association of coal producers brought suit challenging the constitutionality of parts of the Surface Mining Control and Reclamation Act of 1977, 30 U.S.C. § 1201 et seq., which was designed to combat the adverse effects of surface coal-mining operations. The act is administered by the secretary of the interior in cooperation with the state governments. The Office of Surface Mining Reclamation and Enforcement (OSM), within the Department of Interior, actually carries out the regulatory and enforcement programs, including inspecting surface-mining operations for violations of the act. The complaints alleged that several of the act's provisions were unconstitutional. The district court ruled in favor of some of the plaintiff's constitutional claims and against others. The issue of relevance here is the association's assertion that the act violated procedural due process requirements, a claim which the district court supported. In its review the Supreme Court ruled against the association on all of its constitutional challenges. The excerpt below, from the long majority opinion of Justice Marshall, only involves the part of the decision pertaining to the procedural due process implications of summary action permitted under the act. As the numerous citations included in this excerpt indicate, the Supreme Court has been called upon on numerous occasions to rule on the constitutionality of the exercise of summary powers.]

Justice MARSHALL delivered the opinion of the Court. . . .

The District Court next ruled that the Act contravenes the Fifth Amendment because a number of its enforcement provisions offend the Amendment's Due Process Clause. One such provision is § 521(a)(2), 30 U.S.C. § 1271(a)(2), which instructs the Secretary immediately to order total or partial cessation of a surface mining operation whenever he determines, on the basis of a federal inspection, that the operation is in violation of the Act or a permit condition required by the Act and that the operation

> creates an immediate danger to the health or safety of the public, or is causing, or can reasonably be expected to cause significant, imminent environmental harm to land, air, or water resources. . . .

The District Court held that § 521(a)(2)'s authorization of immediate cessation orders violates the Fifth Amendment because the statute does not provide sufficiently objective criteria for summary administrative action. . . .

Our cases have indicated that due process ordinarily requires an opportunity for "some kind of hearing" prior to the deprivation of a significant property interest. See *Parratt* v. *Taylor*, 451 U.S. 527, 540, 101 S.Ct. 1908, 1915, 68 L.Ed.2d 420 (1981); *Boddie* v. *Connecticut*, 401 U.S. 371, 379, 91 S.Ct. 780, 786, 28 L.Ed.2d 113 (1971). The Court has often acknowledged, however, that summary administrative action may be justified in emergency situations. See, e.g., *Calero-Toledo* v. *Pearson Yacht Leasing Co.*, 416 U.S. 663, 677–680, 94 S.Ct. 2080, 2088–2090, 40 L.Ed.2d 452 (1974); *Boddie* v. *Connecticut*, supra, 401 U.S., at 378–379, 91 S.Ct., at 786; *Ewing* v. *Mytinger & Casselberry, Inc.*, 339 U.S. 594, 599–600, 70 S.Ct. 870, 872–873, 94 L.Ed. 1088 (1950); *Fahey* v. *Mallonee*, 332 U.S. 245, 253–254, 67 S.Ct. 1552, 1555–1556, 91 L.Ed. 2030 (1947); *Yakus* v. *United States*, 321 U.S. 414, 442–443, 64 S.Ct. 660, 675–676, 88 L.Ed. 834 (1944); *Bowles* v. *Willingham*, 321 U.S. 503, 519–520, 64 S.Ct. 641, 649–650, 88 L.Ed. 892 (1944); *Phillips* v. *Commissioner*, 283 U.S. 589, 595–599, 51 S.Ct. 608, 611–612, 75 L.Ed. 1289 (1931); *North American Cold Storage*

Co. v. *Chicago*, 211 U.S. 306, 315–321, 29 S.Ct. 101, 104–106, 53 L.Ed. 195 (1908). The question then, is whether the issuance of immediate cessation orders under § 521(a) falls under this emergency situation exception to the normal rule that due process requires a hearing prior to deprivation of a property right. We believe that it does.

The immediate cessation order provisions reflect Congress' concern about the devastating damage that may result from mining disasters. They represent an attempt to reach an accommodation between the legitimate desire of mining companies to be heard before submitting to administrative regulation and the governmental interest in protecting the public health and safety and the environment from imminent danger. Protection of the health and safety of the public is a paramount governmental interest which justifies summary administrative action. Indeed, deprivation of property to protect the public health and safety is "one of the oldest examples" or permissible summary action. *Ewing* v. *Mytinger & Casselberry, Inc.,* supra, 339 U.S., at 599, 70 S.Ct., at 872. See *Mackey* v. *Montrym*, 443 U.S. 1, 17–18, 99 S.Ct. 2612, 2620–2621, 61 L.Ed.2d 321; id., at 21, n. 1, 25, 99 S.Ct., at 2622, n. 1, 2624 (Stewart, J., dissenting); *North American Cold Storage Co.* v. *Chicago*, supra, 211 U.S., at 315–316, 29 S.Ct., at 104. Moreover, the administrative action provided through immediate cessation orders responds to situations in which swift action is necessary to protect the public health and safety. This is precisely the type of emergency situation in which this Court has found summary administrative action justified. See *Ewing* v. *Mytinger & Casselberry, Inc.,* supra; *North American Cold Storage Co.* v. *Chicago*, supra.

Rather than taking issue with any of these principles, the District Court held that the Act does not establish sufficiently objective criteria governing the issuance of summary cessation orders. We disagree. In our judgment, the criteria established by the Act and the Secretary's implementing regulations are specific enough to control governmental action and reduce the risk of erroneous deprivation. Section 701(8) of the Act, 30 U.S.C. § 1291(8), defines the threat of "imminent danger to the health and safety of the public" as the existence of a condition or practice which could:

> reasonably be expected to cause substantial physical harm to persons outside the permit area before such condition, practice, or violation can be abated. A reasonable expectation of death or serious injury before abatement exists if a rational person, subjected to the same conditions or practices giving rise to the peril, would not expose himself or herself to the danger during the time necessary for abatement.

If anything, these standards are more specific than the criteria in other statutes authorizing summary administrative action that have been upheld against due process challenges. See, e.g., *Ewing* v. *Mytinger & Casselberry, Inc.*, supra, 339 U.S., at 595, 70 S.Ct., at 871 ("dangerous to health . . . or would be in a material respect misleading to the injury or damage of the purchaser or consumer"); *Fahey* v. *Mallonee*, supra, 332 U.S., at 250–251, n. 1, 67 S.Ct., at 1554, n. 1 ("is unsafe or unfit to manage a Federal savings and loan association" or "[i]s in imminent danger of becoming impaired"); *Air East, Inc.* v. *National Transportation Safety Board*, 512 F.2d 1227, 1232 (CA3), cert. denied, 423 U.S. 863, 96 S.Ct. 122, 46 L.Ed.2d 92 (1975) ("emergency requiring immediate action . . . in respect to air safety in commerce").

The fact that OSM inspectors have issued immediate cessation orders that were later overturned on administrative appeal does not undermine the adequacy of the Act's criteria but instead demonstrates the efficacy of the review procedures. The relevant inquiry is not whether a cessation order should have been issued in a particular case, but whether the statutory procedure itself is incapable of affording due process. *Yakus* v. *United States*, supra, 321 U.S., at 434–435, 64 S.Ct., at 671–672. The possibility of administrative error inheres in any regulatory program; statutory programs authorizing emergency administrative action prior to a hearing are no exception. As we explained in *Ewing* v. *Mytinger & Casselberry, Inc.*, supra, 339 U.S., at 599, 70 S.Ct., at 872:

> Discretion of any official action may be abused. Yet it is not a requirement of due process that there be judicial inquiry before discretion can be exercised. It is sufficient, where only property rights are concerned,

that there is at some stage an opportunity for a hearing and a judicial determination.

Here, mine operators are afforded prompt and adequate post-deprivation administrative hearings and an opportunity for judicial review. We are satisfied that the Act's immediate cessation order provisions comport with the requirements of due process. . . .

[The concurring opinions of the Chief Justice and Justice Powell, and the opinion of Justice Rehnquist concurring with judgment, are omitted.]

The authority for the use of summary power in cases of seizure of dangerous or illegal products has been sanctioned by the Supreme Court at least as far back as before the turn of the century. The Court upheld early statutes providing not only for seizure but also for summary destruction of the offending objects. See, for instance, *Lawton* v. *Steele*, 152 U.S. 133, 14 S.Ct. 499, 38 L.Ed. 385 (1894) (illegal fish nets), and *North American Cold Storage Co.* v. *Chicago*, 211 U.S. 306, 29 S.Ct. 101, 53 L.Ed. 195 (1908) (allegedly putrid poultry). Although the *North American Cold Storage* case is still cited approvingly by the Supreme Court,[12] it seems unlikely that the Court would today approve summary administrative action which involved destruction of private property unless that destruction were absolutely necessary. The alternative of a postseizure hearing seems clearly preferable. One commentator has referred to this category of activity as "temporary action pending hearing."[13]

DEGREE OF FORMALITY

Justice Hugo Black complained in a dissenting opinion in *Goldberg* v. *Kelly* (not included in the excerpt printed above) that the procedural complexity ordered in that case would work against the welfare recipient by inducing welfare agencies to carry out more exhaustive investigations before putting claimants on the welfare rolls in the first place. Other commentators have voiced further concerns about highly complex hearings, suggesting that welfare recipients may not be competent to take advantage of the procedures provided: "due process protections would favor not the neediest but only the

---

[12] "States surely have at least as much interest in removing drunken drivers from their highways as in summarily seizing mislabeled drugs or destroying spoiled foodstuffs; e.g., *Ewing* v. *Mytinger & Casselberry, Inc.*, 339 U.S. 594, 70 S.Ct. 870, 94 L.Ed. 1088 (1950); *North American Cold Storage Co.* v. *Chicago*, 211 U.S. 306, 29 S.Ct. 101, 53 L.Ed. 195 (1908)." *Mackey* v. *Montrym*, 443 U.S. 1, 99 S.Ct. 2612, 61 L.Ed.2d 321 (1979).

[13] Kenneth Culp Davis, 2 *Administrative Law Treatise* 462 (2d Edition, 1979).

most aggressive of recipients."[14] Beyond the area of welfare benefits, a more general concern about overjudicialization of administrative processes has been expressed by several analysts, including the former chairman of the Administrative Conference of the United States.[15] Something is to be said, therefore, for protecting due process rights through less formal procedures. The following case represents an example of the Supreme Court's efforts to mandate an approach of that kind.

Goss v. Lopez

SUPREME COURT OF THE UNITED STATES, 1975.
419 U.S. 565, 95 S.CT. 729, 42 L.ED.2D 725.

[Several Columbus, Ohio high school students were temporarily suspended without a hearing, either prior to the suspensions or within a reasonable time thereafter. The students sued for a declaration that the Ohio statute under which they were suspended was unconstitutional. The U.S. district court ruled that the students had been denied due process and ordered school administrators to remove all references to the suspensions from the students' records. The school administrators appealed.]

Mr. Justice WHITE delivered the opinion of the Court. . . .

At the outset, appellants contend that because there is no constitutional right to an education at public expense, the Due Process Clause does not protect against expulsions from the public school system. This position misconceives the nature of the issue and is refuted by prior decisions. The Fourteenth Amendment forbids the State to deprive any person of life, liberty, or property without due process of law. Protected interests in property are normally "not created by the Constitution. Rather, they are created and their dimensions are defined" by an independent source such as

state statutes or rules entitling the citizen to certain benefits. Board of Regents v. Roth, 408 U.S. 564, 577, 92 S.Ct. 2701, 2709, 33 L.Ed.2d 548 (1972).

Accordingly, a state employee who under state law, or rules promulgated by state officials, has a legitimate claim of entitlement to continued employment absent sufficient cause for discharge may demand the procedural protections of due process. So may welfare recipients who have statutory rights to welfare as long as they maintain the specified qualifications. Goldberg v. Kelly, 397 U.S. 254, 90 S.Ct. 1011, 25 L.Ed. 2d 287 (1970). Morrissey v. Brewer, 408 U.S. 471, 92 S.Ct. 2593, 33 L.Ed.2d 484 (1972), applied the limitations of the Due Process Clause to governmental decisions to revoke parole, although a parolee has no constitutional right to that status. In like vein was Wolff v. McDonnell, 418 U.S. 539, 94 S.Ct. 2963, 41 L.Ed.2d 935 (1974), where the procedural protections of the Due Process Clause were triggered by official cancellation of a prisoner's good-time credits accumulated under state law, although those benefits were not mandated by the Constitution.

---

[14] The quotation is from J. S. Fuerst and Roy Petty, "Due Process—How Much is Enough?" 79 *Public Interest* 99 (1985); see also Jerry Mashaw, "The Management Side of Due Process," 59 *Cornell Law Review* 772 (1974).

[15] Loren A. Smith, "Judicialization: The Twilight of Administrative Law," 1985 *Duke Law Journal* 427 (1985); see also John Earl Haynes, "Democracy and Due Process: The Case of Handicapped Education," 1982 *Regulation* 29 (November/December, 1982).

Here, on the basis of state law, appellees plainly had legitimate claims of entitlement to a public education.... Having chosen to extend the right to an education to people of appellees' class generally, Ohio may not withdraw that right on grounds of misconduct absent, fundamentally fair procedures to determine whether the misconduct has occurred....

Appellants proceed to argue that even if there is a right to a public education protected by the Due Process Clause generally, the Clause comes into play only when the State subjects a student to a "severe detriment or grievous loss." The loss of 10 days, it is said, is neither severe nor grievous and the Due Process Clause is therefore of no relevance. Appellants' argument is again refuted by our prior decisions; for in determining "whether due process requirements apply in the first place, we must look not to the 'weight' but to the *nature* of the interest at stake." Board of Regents v. Roth, supra, at 570–571, 92 S.Ct., at 2705–2706. Appellees were excluded from school only temporarily, it is true, but the length and consequent severity of a deprivation, while another factor to weigh in determining the appropriate form of hearing, "is not decisive of the basic right" to a hearing of some kind. Fuentes v. Shevin, 407 U.S. 67, 86, 92 S.Ct. 1983, 1997, 32 L.Ed.2d 556 (1972). The Court's view has been that as long as a property deprivation is not *de minimis*, its gravity is irrelevant to the question whether account must be taken of the Due Process Clause. A 10-day suspension from school is not *de minimis* in our view and may not be imposed in complete disregard of the Due Process Clause.... Disciplinarians, although proceeding in utmost good faith, frequently act on the reports and advice of others; and the controlling facts and the nature of the conduct under challenge are often disputed. The risk of error is not at all trivial, and it should be guarded against if that may be done without prohibitive cost or interference with the educational process.

The difficulty is that our schools are vast and complex. Some modicum of discipline and order is essential if the educational function is to be performed. Events calling for discipline are frequent occurrences and sometimes require immediate, effective action. Suspension is considered not only to be a necessary tool to maintain order but a valuable educational device. The prospect of imposing elaborate hearing requirements in every suspension case is viewed with great concern, and many school authorities may well prefer the untrammeled power to act unilaterally, unhampered by rules about notice and hearing. But it would be a strange disciplinary system in an educational institution if no communication was sought by the disciplinarian with the student in an effort to inform him of his dereliction and to let him tell his side of the story in order to make sure that an injustice is not done. "[F]airness can rarely be obtained by secret, one-sided determination of facts decisive of rights...." "Secrecy is not congenial to truth-seeking and self-righteousness gives too slender an assurance of rightness. No better instrument has been devised for arriving at truth than to give a person in jeopardy of serious loss notice of the case against him and opportunity to meet it." Joint Anti-Fascist Committee v. McGrath, supra, 341 U.S., at 170, 172–173, 71 S.Ct., at 647–649 (Frankfurter, J., concurring).

We do not believe that school authorities must be totally free from notice and hearing requirements if their schools are to operate with acceptable efficiency. Students facing temporary suspension have interests qualifying for protection of the Due Process Clause, and due process requires, in connection with a suspension of 10 days or less, that the student be given oral or written notice of the charges against him and, if he denies them, an explanation of the evidence the authorities have and an opportunity to present his side of the story. The Clause requires at least these rudimentary precautions against unfair or mistaken findings of misconduct and arbitrary exclusion from school.

There need be no delay between the time "notice" is given and the time of the hearing. In the great majority of cases the disciplinarian may informally discuss the alleged misconduct with the student minutes after it has occurred. We hold only that, in being given an opportunity to explain his version of the facts at this discussion, the student first be told what he is accused of doing and what the basis of the accusation is. Lower courts which have addressed the question of the *nature* of the procedures required in short suspension cases have reached the same conclusion. Since the hearing may occur almost immediately following the misconduct, it follows that as a general rule notice and hearing should precede removal of the student from school. We agree with the District Court, however, that there are recurring situations in which prior notice and hearing cannot be insisted upon. Students whose presence poses a continuing danger to persons or property or an ongoing threat of disrupting the academic process may be immediately removed from school. In such cases, the necessary notice and rudimentary hearing should follow as soon as practicable, as the District Court indicated.

In holding as we do, we do not believe that we have imposed procedures on school disciplinarians which are inappropriate in a classroom setting. Instead we have imposed requirements which are, if anything, less than a fair-minded school principal would impose upon himself in order to avoid unfair suspensions. Indeed, according to the testimony of the principal of Marion-Franklin High School, that school had an informal procedure, remarkably similar to that which we now require, applicable to suspensions generally but which was not followed in this case. Similarly, according to the most recent memorandum applicable to the entire CPSS, . . .

school principals in the CPSS are now required by local rule to provide at least as much as the constitutional minimum which we have described.

We stop short of construing the Due Process Clause to require, countrywide, that hearings in connection with short suspensions must afford the student the opportunity to secure counsel, to confront and cross-examine witnesses supporting the charge, or to call his own witnesses to verify his version of the incident. Brief disciplinary suspensions are almost countless. To impose in each such case even truncated trial-type procedures might well overwhelm administrative facilities in many places and, by diverting resources, cost more than it would save in educational effectiveness. Moreover, further formalizing the suspension process and escalating its formality and adversary nature may not only make it too costly as a regular disciplinary tool but also destroy its effectiveness as part of the teaching process.

On the other hand, requiring effective notice and informal hearing permitting the student to give his version of the events will provide a meaningful hedge against erroneous action. At least the disciplinarian will be alerted to the existence of disputes about facts and arguments about cause and effect. He may then determine himself to summon the accuser, permit cross-examination, and allow the student to present his own witnesses. In more difficult cases, he may permit counsel. In any event, his discretion will be more informed and we think the risk of error substantially reduced.

Requiring that there be at least an informal give-and-take between student and disciplinarian, preferably prior to the suspension, will add little to the factfinding function where the disciplinarian himself has witnessed the conduct forming the basis for the charge. But things are not always as they seem to be, and the student will at least have the opportunity to characterize his conduct and put it in what he deems the proper context.

We should also make it clear that we have addressed ourselves solely to the short suspension, not exceeding 10 days. Longer suspensions or expulsions for the remainder of the school term, or permanently, may require more formal procedures. Nor do we put aside the possibility that in unusual situations, although involving only a short suspension, something more than the rudimentary procedures will be required.

IV

The District Court found each of the suspensions involved here to have occurred without a hearing, either before or after the suspension, and that each suspension was therefore invalid and the statute unconstitutional insofar as it permits such suspensions without notice or hearing. Accordingly, the judgment is

Affirmed.

Mr. Justice POWELL, with whom THE CHIEF JUSTICE, Mr. Justice BLACKMUN, and Mr. Justice REHNQUIST join, dissenting.

The Court today invalidates an Ohio statute that permits student suspensions from school without a hearing "for not more than ten days." The decision unnecessarily opens avenues for judicial intervention in the operation of our public schools that may affect adversely the quality of education. The Court holds for the first time that the federal courts, rather than educational officials and state legislatures, have the authority to determine the rules applicable to routine classroom discipline of children and teenagers in the public schools. It justifies this unprecedented intrusion into the process of elementary and secondary education by identifying a new constitutional right: the right of a student not to be suspended for as much as a single day without notice and a due process hearing either before or promptly following the suspension.

The Court's decision rests on the premise that, under Ohio law, education is a property interest protected by the Fourteenth Amendment's Due Process Clause and therefore that any suspension requires notice and a hearing. In my view, a student's interest in education is not infringed by a suspension within the limited period prescribed by Ohio law. Moreover, to the extent that there may be some arguable infringement, it is too speculative, transitory, and insubstantial to justify imposition of a *constitutional* rule. . . .

The *Goss* opinion was a central case in Judge Friendly's frequently cited analysis of the due process explosion. It led him to wonder "whether the government can do anything to a citizen without affording him 'some kind of hearing.' " [16] But events would quickly show that the implications of *Goss* were not so broad. This is perhaps best illustrated by a case decided by the Supreme Court two years after *Goss*. Like *Goss*, the case of *Ingraham* v. *Wright* involved the disciplining of school students.

---

[16] Above, note 2, at 1275.

Ingraham v. Wright

SUPREME COURT OF THE UNITED STATES, 1977.
430 U.S. 651, 97 S.CT. 1401, 51 L.ED.2D 711.

[Two students in a Dade County, Florida junior high school instituted an action under 42 U.S.C.A. §§ 1981–1988 against certain school officials, alleging violation of their Eighth and Fourteenth Amendment rights based on disciplinary paddling incidents. They sought damages and injunctive and declaratory relief, and their evidence indicated that pursuant to Florida law they were subjected to disciplinary paddling without prior notice and hearing, and that the paddlings were so severe as to keep one of the plaintiffs out of school for eleven days and to deprive the other plaintiff of full use of his arm for a week. The plaintiffs charged, in effect, that the paddlings constituted cruel and unusual punishment (Eighth Amendment) and that the procedure was defective in that the paddlings were not preceded by notice and hearing (due process clause of Fourteenth Amendment). Two lower federal courts ruled against the plaintiffs and the case came to the U.S. Supreme Court on certiorari.]

Mr. Justice POWELL delivered the opinion of the Court.... [I]t is not surprising to find that every decision of this Court considering whether a punishment is "cruel and unusual" within the meaning of the Eighth and Fourteenth Amendments has dealt with a criminal punishment....

Petitioners acknowledge that the original design of the Cruel and Unusual Punishments Clause was to limit criminal punishments, but urge nonetheless that the prohibition should be extended to ban the paddling of schoolchildren. Observing that the Framers of the Eighth Amendment could not have envisioned our present system of public and compulsory education, with its opportunities for noncriminal punishments, petitioners contend that extension of the prohibition against cruel punishments is necessary lest we afford greater protection to criminals than to schoolchildren. It would be anomalous, they say, if schoolchildren could be beaten without constitutional redress, while hardened criminals suffering the same beatings at the hands of their jailers might have a valid claim under the Eighth Amendment. Whatever force this logic may have in other settings, we find it an inadequate basis for wrenching the Eighth Amendment from its historical context and extending it to traditional disciplinary practices in the public schools.

The prisoner and the schoolchild stand in wholly different circumstances, separated by the harsh facts of criminal conviction and incarceration. The prisoner's conviction entitles the State to classify him as a "criminal," and his incarceration deprives him of the freedom "to be with family and friends and to form the other enduring attachments of normal life." Morrissey v. Brewer, 408 U.S. 471, 482, 92 S.Ct. 2593, 2600, 33 L.Ed.2d 484 (1972). Prison brutality, as the Court of Appeals observed in this case, is "part of the total punishment to which the individual is being subjected for his crime and, as such, is a proper subject for Eighth Amendment scrutiny." 525 F.2d, at 915. Even so, the protection afforded by the Eighth Amendment is limited. After incarceration, only the " 'unnecessary and wanton infliction of pain,' " Estelle v. Gamble, 429 U.S., at 103, 97 S.Ct., at 291, quoting Gregg v. Georgia, 428 U.S. at 173, 96 S.Ct., at 2925, constitutes cruel and unusual punishment forbidden by the Eighth Amendment.

The schoolchild has little need for the protection of the Eighth Amendment. Though attendance may not always be voluntary, the public school remains an open institution. Except perhaps when very young, the child is not physically restrained from leaving school during school hours; and at the end of the school day, the child is invariably free to return home. Even while at school, the child brings with him the support of family and friends and is rarely apart from teachers and other pupils who may witness and protest any instances of mistreatment.

The openness of the public school and its supervision by the community afford significant safeguards against the kinds of abuses from which the Eighth Amendment protects the prisoner. In virtually every community where corporal punishment is permitted in the schools, these safeguards are reinforced by the legal constraints of the common law. Public school teachers and administrators are privileged at common law to inflict only such corporal punishment as is reasonably necessary for the proper education and discipline of the child: any punishment going beyond the privilege may result in both civil and criminal liability. As long as the schools are open to public scrutiny, there is no reason to believe that the common-law constraints will not effectively remedy and deter excesses such as those alleged in this case.

We conclude that when public school teachers or administrators impose disciplinary corporal punishment, the Eighth Amendment is inapplicable. The pertinent constitutional question is whether the imposition is consonant with the requirements of due process.

IV

The Fourteenth Amendment prohibits any state deprivation of life, liberty, or property without due process of law. Application of this prohibition requires the familiar two-stage analysis: We must first ask whether the asserted individual interests are encompassed within the Fourteenth Amendment's protection of "life, liberty or property"; if protected interests are implicated, we then must decide what proce-

dures constitute "due process of law." Morrissey v. Brewer, 408 U.S. at 481, 22 S.Ct., at 2600; Board of Regents v. Roth, 408 U.S. 564, 569–572, 92 S.Ct. 2701, 2705–2707, 33 L.Ed.2d 548 (1972). See Friendly, Some Kind of Hearing, 123 U.Pa.L.Rev. 1267 (1975). Following that analysis here, we find that corporal punishment in public schools implicates a constitutionally protected liberty interest, but we hold that the traditional common-law remedies are fully adequate to afford due process.

A

"[T]he range of interests protected by procedural due process is not infinite." Board of Regents v. Roth, supra, at 570, 92 S.Ct., at 2705. We have repeatedly rejected "the notion that *any* grievous loss visited upon a person by the State is sufficient to invoke the procedural protections of the Due Process Clause." Meachum v. Fano, 427 U.S. at 224, 96 S.Ct., at 2538. Due process is required only when a decision of the State implicates an interest within the protection of the Fourteenth Amendment. And "to determine whether due process requirements apply in the first place, we must look not to the 'weight' but to the *nature* of the interest at stake." Roth, supra, 408 U.S., at 570–571, 92 S.Ct., at 2705.

The Due Process Clause of the Fifth Amendment, later incorporated into the Fourteenth, was intended to give Americans at least the protection against governmental power that they had enjoyed as Englishmen against the power of the Crown. The liberty preserved from deprivation without due process included the right "generally to enjoy those privileges long recognized at common law as essential to the orderly pursuit of happiness by free men." Meyer v. Nebraska, 262 U.S. 390, 399, 43 S.Ct. 625, 626, 67 L.Ed. 1042 (1923). Among the historic liberties so protected was a right to be free from and to obtain judicial relief, for unjustified intrusions on personal security.

While the contours of this historic liberty interest in the context of our federal system of government have not been defined precisely, they always have been thought to encompass freedom from bodily restraint and punishment. It is fundamental that the state cannot hold and physically punish an individual except in accordance with due process of law.

This constitutionally protected liberty interest is at stake in this case. There is, of course a *de minimis* level of imposition with which the Constitution is not concerned. But at least where school authorities, acting under color of state law, deliberately decide to punish a child for misconduct by restraining the child and inflicting appreciable physical pain, we hold that Fourteenth Amendment liberty interests are implicated.

B

"[T]he question remains what process is due." Morrissey v. Brewer, supra, at 481, 92 S.Ct., at 2600. Were it not for the common-law privilege permitting teachers, to inflict reasonable corporal punishment on children in their care, and the availability of the traditional remedies for abuse, the case for requiring advance procedural safeguards would be strong indeed. But here we deal with a punishment—paddling—within that tradition, and the question is whether the common-law remedies are adequate to afford due process. . . .

Florida has continued to recognize, and indeed has strengthened by statute, the common-law right of a child not to be subjected to excessive corporal punishment in school. Under Florida law the teacher and principal of the school decide in the first instance whether corporal punishment is reasonably necessary under the circumstances in order to discipline a child who has misbehaved. But they must exercise prudence and restraint. For Florida has preserved the traditional judicial proceedings for determining whether the punishment was justified. If the punishment inflicted is later found to have been excessive—not reasonably believed at the time to be necessary for the child's discipline or training—the school authorities inflicting it may be held liable in damages to the child and, if malice is shown, they may be subject to criminal penalties. . . .

It still may be argued, of course, that the child's liberty interest would be better protected if the common-law remedies were supplemented by the administrative safeguards of prior notice and a hearing. We have found frequently that some kind of prior hearing is necessary to guard against arbitrary impositions on interests protected by the Fourteenth Amendment. But where the State has preserved what "has always been the law of the land," the case for administrative safeguards is significantly less compelling. . . .

But even if the need for advance procedural safeguards were clear, the question would remain whether the incremental benefit could justify the cost. Acceptance of petitioners' claims would work a transformation in the law governing corporal punishment in Florida and most other States. Given the impracticability of formulating a rule of procedural due process that varies with the severity of the particular imposition, the prior hearing petitioners seek would have to precede *any* paddling, however moderate or trivial.

Such a universal constitutional requirement would significantly burden the use of corporal punishment as a disciplinary measure. Hearings—even informal hearings—require time, personnel, and a diversion of attention from normal school pursuits. School authorities may well choose to abandon corporal punishment rather than incur the burdens of complying with the procedural requirements. Teachers, properly concerned with maintaining authority in the classroom, may well prefer to rely on other disciplinary measures—which they may view as less effective—rather than confront the possible disruption that prior notice and a hearing may entail.... In view of the low incidence of abuse, the openness of our schools, and the common-law safeguards that already exist, the risk of error that may result in violation of a schoolchild's substantive rights can only be regarded as minimal. Imposing additional administrative safeguards as a constitutional requirement might reduce that risk marginally, but would also entail a significant intrusion into an area of primary educational responsibility. We conclude that the Due Process Clause does not require notice and a hearing prior to the imposition of corporal punishment in the public schools, as that practice is authorized and limited by the common law....

Affirmed.

Mr. Justice WHITE, with whom Mr. Justice BRENNAN, Mr. Justice MARSHALL, and Mr. Justice STEVENS join, dissenting....

The Eighth Amendment places a flat prohibition against the infliction of "cruel and unusual punishments."...

Nevertheless, the majority, holds that the Eighth Amendment "was designed to protect [only] those convicted of crimes," relying on a vague and inconclusive recitation of the history of the Amendment. Yet the constitutional prohibition is against cruel and unusual *punishments*; nowhere is that prohibition limited or modified by the language of the Constitution. Certainly the fact that the Framers did not choose to insert the word "criminal" into the language of the Eighth Amendment is strong evidence that the Amendment was designed to prohibit all inhumane or barbaric punishments, no matter what the nature of the offense for which the punishment is imposed.

No one can deny that spanking of schoolchildren is "punishment" under any reasonable reading of the word, for the similarities between spanking in public schools and other forms of punishment are too obvious to ignore. Like other forms of punishment, spanking of schoolchildren involves an institutionalized response to the violation of some official rule or regulation proscribing certain conduct and is imposed for the purpose of rehabilitating the offender, deterring the offender and others like him from committing the violation in the future, and inflicting some measure of social retribution for the harm that has been done.... The Court would have us believe ... that there is a recognized distinction between criminal and noncriminal punishment for purposes of the Eighth Amendment. This is plainly wrong. "[E]ven a clear legislative classification of a statute as 'non-penal' would not alter the fundamental nature of a plainly penal statute." Trop v. Dulles, 356 U.S. 86, 95, 78 S.Ct. 590, 595, 2 L.Ed.2d 630 (1958) (plurality opinion). The relevant inquiry is not whether the offense for which a punishment is inflicted has been labeled as criminal, but whether the purpose of the deprivation is among those ordinarily associated with punishment, such as retribution, rehabilitation, or deterrence....

If this purposive approach were followed in the present case, it would be clear that spanking in the Florida public schools is punishment within the meaning of the Eighth Amendment....

II

The majority concedes that corporal punishment in the public schools implicates an interest protected by the Due Process Clause—the liberty interest of the student to be free from "bodily restraint and punishment" involving "appreciable physical pain" inflicted by persons acting under color of state law. The question remaining, as the majority recognizes, is what process is due.

The reason that the Constitution requires a State to provide "due process of law" when it punishes an individual for misconduct is to protect the individual from erroneous or mistaken punishment that the State would not have inflicted had it found the facts in a more reliable way. In Goss v. Lopez, 419 U.S. 565, 95 S.Ct. 729, 42 L.Ed.2d 725 (1975), the Court applied this principle to the school disciplinary process, holding that a student must be given an informal opportunity to be heard before he is finally suspended from public school....

The Court now holds that these "rudimentary precautions against unfair or mistaken findings of misconduct," are not required if the student is punished with "appreciable physical pain" rather than with a suspension, even though both punishments deprive the student of a constitutionally protected interest. Although the respondent school authorities provide absolutely *no* process to the student before the punishment is finally inflicted, the majority concludes that the student is nonetheless given due process because he can later sue the teacher and recover damages if the punishment was "excessive."

This tort action is utterly inadequate to protect against erroneous infliction of punishment for two reasons. First, under Florida law, a student punished for an act he did not commit cannot recover damages from a teacher "proceeding in utmost good faith ... on the reports and advice of others," the student has no remedy at all for punishment imposed on the basis of mistaken facts, at least as long as the punishment was reasonable from the point of view of the disciplinarian, uninformed by any prior hearing. The "traditional common-law remedies" on which the majority relies, thus do nothing to protect the student from the danger that concerned the

Court in *Goss*—the risk of reasonable, good-faith mistake in the school disciplinary process.

Second, and more important, even if the student could sue for good-faith error in the infliction of punishment, the lawsuit occurs after the punishment has been finally imposed. The infliction of physical pain is final and irreparable; it cannot be undone in a subsequent proceeding. There is every reason to require, as the Court did in *Goss*, a few minutes of "informal give-and-take between student and disciplinarian" as a "meaningful hedge" against the erroneous infliction of irreparable injury....

The majority emphasizes, as did the dissenters in *Goss*, that even the "rudimentary precautions" required by that decision would impose some burden on the school disciplinary process. But those costs are no greater if the student is paddled rather than suspended; the risk of error in the punishment is no smaller; and the fear of "a significant intrusion" into the disciplinary process is just as exaggerated. The disciplinarian need only take a few minutes to give the student "notice of the charges against him and, if he denies them, an explanation of the evidence the authorities have and an opportunity to present his side of the story." In this context the Constitution requires, "if anything, less than a fair-minded school principal would impose upon himself" in order to avoid injustice.

I would reverse the judgment below.

[The dissenting opinion of Mr. Justice STEVENS is omitted.]

Effects of Recent Court Decisions

Just as *Mathews* v. *Eldridge* represents a moving away from the expansive opportunity to be heard enunciated in *Goldberg*, so *Ingraham* v. *Wright* amounts to a cutting back on the implications of *Goss* regarding informal hearings in the school setting. These cases are important, but as numerous analysts have documented,[17] they are not the only examples of the trend. From the latter 1970s on, the Supreme Court has taken a generally more restrictive stance with regard to hearing rights under the due process clause. For the present, it seems, the "due process revolution" is over.[18]

The complaint of commentators who analyze Supreme Court decisions in this area is not so much that hearing rights have been cut back as that there is so little consistency or pattern to the decisions. Professor Jerry Mashaw expressed the view of a number of analysts when he concluded in 1985 that "the basic methodology of administrative due process adjudication has gone awry."[19]

Further uncertainty exists concerning the present situation with regard to the right-privilege distinction. Professor Van Alstyne wrote in 1968 of the "demise" of the right-privilege distinction,[20] and a series of Supreme Court opinions, culminating in *Roth* ("the Court has fully and finally rejected the wooden distinction between 'rights' and 'privileges' ")[21] seemed to support this conclusion. While the right-privilege distinction has not been discussed by the Supreme Court in recent years, the Court has continued to search for a satisfactory rationale for its decisions and has, as shown, struggled with inconsistency. Some scholars have seen in recent Court decisions a "reemergence" of the right-privilege distinction.[22]

Finding a Middle Ground

Solutions to the present confusion have been suggested by numerous analysts.[23] But it is the Supreme Court itself which will ultimately have to provide the solution. In addition to a more restrictive view in recent years regarding due process protection, the Court has, as Professors Gellhorn and Boyer put it, become "more skeptical about the value of trial-type procedures."[24] This is brought out clearly in a number of Supreme Court opinions, including *Goss*.

---

[17] See in particular Richard J. Pierce, Jr., Sidney A. Shapiro, and Paul R. Verkuil, *Administrative Law and Process* 273–277 (1985). See also the sources cited below in notes 18 and 19.

[18] "Did we really once believe that Goldberg v. Kelly was the opening volley in a due process 'revolution'? We may be forgiven the sense of mild embarrassment that accompanies such memories. Of course, we know better now. There was no revolution—at least not the one expected . . . *Goldberg* itself looks very different now." Colin S. Diver, "The Wrath of *Roth*," (book review), 94 *Yale Law Journal* 1529 (1985). As an indicator of what Diver considers the key cases in this change of direction by the Supreme Court, he asks (at 1529): "Was there some implacable logic that transformed the generous constitutionalism of *Goldberg* into the niggardly positivism of *Roth* and *Eldridge*?"

[19] *Due Process in the Administrative State* 32, 108–115 (1985). See also, e.g., Diver, above, note 18; Pierce, Shapiro and Verkuil, above note 17; and John Hart Ely, *Democracy and Distrust: A Theory of Judicial Review*, 19–20 (1980).

[20] See above, note 1.

[21] See above, pp. 194–195.

[22] See Rodney A. Smolla, "The Reemergence of the Right-Privilege Distinction in Constitutional Law: The Price of Protesting Too Much," 35 *Stanford Law Review* 69 (1982), and sources cited therein. See also Davis, above, note 13, 350.

[23] See, e.g., Smolla, above, note 22, 76; Pierce, Shapiro, and Verkuil, above, note 17, 274.

[24] Ernest Gellhorn and Barry B. Boyer, *Administrative Law and Process in a Nutshell* 177 (2d ed., 1981).

It has been suggested that a reasonable middle ground between a full trial-type hearing and none at all might be the requirement of a reasoned explanation of adverse actions affecting a person's due process rights.[25] At least in some kinds of cases that may be a reasonable solution. A result of that kind is achieved in the following lower court case.

Sherrill v. Knight

UNITED STATES COURT OF APPEALS, DISTRICT OF COLUMBIA CIRCUIT, 1977.
569 F.2D 124.

Before McGOWAN, LEVENTHAL and ROBB, Circuit Judges.

Opinion for the Court filed by McGOWAN, Circuit Judge.

McGOWAN, Circuit Judge: . . .

In 1966, plaintiff-appellee Robert Sherrill, who has been the Washington Correspondent for *The Nation* since 1965 and who has throughout this period had credentials for the House and Senate press galleries, applied for and was denied a White House press pass. The denial resulted solely from the determination of the Secret Service, after investigating Mr. Sherrill, that he not be issued the pass. A memorandum from the Secret Service to then White House Press Secretary Moyers requested that the background information obtained about Mr. Sherrill upon which this determination was based "not be disclosed to Mr. Sherrill or his employer."

Although there exist no written procedures pertaining to the issuance of press passes for the White House, it was established in the District Court that these passes are routinely obtained in the following manner. A journalist submits a request for a pass to the White House Press Office. After determining that the applicant has obtained a pass for the House and Senate press galleries, resides in the Washington, D. C. area, and needs to report from the White House on a regular basis (the latter usually being verified by an editor of the publication for which the applicant is a correspondent), the Press Office forwards the application to the Secret Service for a security check, including a background FBI investigation. Whether a pass is then issued depends solely on the recommendation of the Secret Service. There exist no published or internal regulations stating the criteria upon which a White House press pass security clearance is based.

If the application is denied, the journalist is informed, orally or in writing, that the denial is "for reasons relating to the security of the President and/or the members of his immediate family." When Mr. Sherrill asked why he had been rejected, Secret Service personnel replied that "we can't tell you the reasons." According to affidavits of the Secret Service obtained during discovery below, Mr. Sherrill apparently reapplied for and was denied a press credential in January of 1972, again on the basis of the original Secret Service recommendation. . . .

After a subsequent refusal by Mr. Rossides to change his decision, appellee filed this action in District Court, alleging, *inter alia*, that the denial of a press pass under the foregoing circumstances violated the first and fifth amendments to the Constitution. Although appellee requested the District Court to order appellants to grant him a White House press pass, the District Court determined, correctly we believe,

---

[25] Robert L. Rabin, "Job Security and Due Process: Monitoring Administrative Discretion Through a Reasons Requirement," 44 *University of Chicago Law Review* 60 (1976).

that it had no occasion to pass on the merits of the press pass denial. Rather, on cross-motions for summary judgment, the Court remanded the case to the Secret Service, which was instructed to "devise and publicize narrow and specific standards" for press pass denials, and to institute procedures whereby an applicant is given notice of the evidence upon which the Secret Service proposes to base its denial, the journalist is afforded an opportunity to rebut or explain this evidence, and the Secret Service issues a final written decision specifying the reasons for its refusal to grant a press pass. The Service was instructed to reconsider the appellee's application under these newly instituted standards and procedures. 416 F.Supp. at 1039–40.

The District Court based its requirement of a written decision upon its determination that denial of a White House press pass to a bona fide journalist violates the first amendment unless it furthers a compelling governmental interest identified by narrowly and specifically drawn standards. The Court felt it would be unable to undertake proper judicial review of the denial of the press pass to Sherrill unless the Secret Service first explained why application of such standards to Sherrill necessitated the denial. With respect to its requirement of notice and opportunity to rebut, the Court relied on its determination that a denial of a White House press pass constitutes a deprivation of "liberty" without due process of law within the meaning of the fifth amendment because it interferes with the free exercise of the profession of journalism.

We agree with the District Court that both first and fifth amendment concerns are heavily implicated in this case.[26] We conclude, however, that neither of these concerns requires the articulation of detailed criteria upon which the granting or denial of White House press passes is to be based. We further conclude that notice, opportunity to rebut, and a written decision are required because the denial of a pass potentially infringes upon first amendment guarantees. Such impairment of this interest cannot be permitted to occur in the absence of adequate procedural due process. . . .

[W]e are presented with a situation where the White House has voluntarily decided to establish press facilities for correspondents who need to report therefrom. These press facilities are perceived as being open to all bona fide Washington-based journalists, whereas most of the White House itself, and press facilities in particular, have not been made available to the general public. White House press facilities having been made publicly available as a source of information for newsmen, the

---

[26] We reject at the outset the contention of appellants that this case is nonjusticiable either because protection of the President is vested within the sole discretion of the Executive or because there are no judicially manageable standards for presidential protection. The former argument is wholly without force. Nothing in the Constitution suggests that courts are not to be the final arbiters of the legality of the actions of those protecting the President, cf. In re Neagle, 135 U.S. 1, 10 S.Ct. 658, 34 L.Ed. 55 (1890). The congressional grants of authority to the Secret Service to protect the President, see 18 U.S.C.A. § 3056, and to control access to temporary presidential residences, 3 U.S.C.A. § 202, cannot be said to authorize procedures or actions violative of the Constitution. Cf. Cafeteria Workers v. McElroy, 367 U.S. 886, 894, 81 S.Ct. 1743, 6 L.Ed.2d 1230 (1961).

Appellant's second argument is precisely that made in A Quaker Action Group v. Hickel, 137 U.S.App.D.C. 176, 421 F.2d 1111 (1969). We reassert our conclusion in that case that

we cannot agree with the Government's argument that mere mention of the President's safety must be allowed to trump any First Amendment issue. . . . [A]bsent a compelling showing . . . that courts cannot evaluate the questions of fact in estimating danger to the President, the final judgment must rest with the courts.

Id. at 137 U.S.App.D.C. at 182, 421 F.2d at 1117–18. See also Frank v. Herter, 106 U.S.App.D.C. 54, 269 F.2d 245 (Secretary of State's manner of selecting correspondents allowed to travel to China is subject to judicial review), cert. denied, 361 U.S. 918, 80 S.Ct. 256, 4 L.Ed.2d 187 (1959).

protection afforded newsgathering under the first amendment guarantee of freedom of the press, requires that this access not be denied arbitrarily or for less than compelling reasons. Not only newsmen and the publications for which they write, but also the public at large have an interest protected by the first amendment in assuring that restrictions on newsgathering be no more arduous than necessary, and that individual newsmen not be arbitrarily excluded from sources of information.... Merely informing individual rejected applicants that rejection was for "reasons of security" does not inform the public or other potential applicants of the basis for exclusion of journalists from White House press facilities. Moreover, we think that the phrase "reasons of security" is unnecessarily vague and subject to ambiguous interpretation.

Therefore, we are of the opinion that appellants must publish or otherwise make publicly known the actual standard employed in determining whether an otherwise eligible journalist will obtain a White House press pass. We do agree with appellants that the governmental interest here does not lend itself to detailed articulation of narrow and specific standards or precise identification of all the factors which may be taken into account in applying this standard. It is enough that the Secret Service be guided solely by the principle of whether the applicant presents a potential source of physical danger to the President and/or his immediate family so serious as to justify his exclusion. This standard is sufficiently circumspect so as to allow the Secret Service, exercising expert judgment which frequently must be subjective in nature, considerable leeway in denying press passes for security reasons. At the same time, the standard does specify in a meaningful way the basis upon which persons will be deemed security risks, and therefore will allow meaningful judicial review of decisions to deny press passes. We anticipate that reviewing courts will be appropriately deferential to the Secret Service's determination of what justifies the inference that an individual constitutes a potential risk to the physical security of the President or his family.

IV

In our view, the procedural requirements of notice of the factual bases for denial, an opportunity for the applicant to respond to these, and a final written statement of the reasons for denial are compelled by the foregoing determination that the interest of a bona fide Washington correspondent in obtaining a White House press pass is protected by the first amendment. This first amendment interest undoubtedly qualifies as liberty which may not be denied without due process of law under the fifth amendment. The only further determination which this court must make is "what process is due," Morrissey v. Brewer, 408 U.S. 471, 481, 92 S.Ct. 2593, 33 L.Ed. 2d 484 (1972). We think that notice to the unsuccessful applicant of the factual bases for denial with an opportunity to rebut is a minimum prerequisite for ensuring that the denial is indeed in furtherance of Presidential protection, rather than based on arbitrary or less than compelling reasons. The requirement of a final statement of denial and the reasons therefor is necessary in order to assure that the agency has neither taken additional, undisclosed information into account, nor responded irrationally to matters put forward by way of rebuttal or explanation. This requirement also will avoid situations such as occurred in the case before us, where an applicant does not receive official written notification of his status until more than five years after the status decision is made....

Not all deprivations of interests merit a statement of reasons from governmental agencies. In 1981 the Supreme Court, voting seven to two, reversed two lower courts in ruling that a board of pardons' failure to provide a life inmate with a written statement of reasons for denying commutation of his sentence did not violate due process. *Connecticut Board of Pardons* v. *Dumschat*, 452 U.S. 458, 101 S.Ct. 2460, 69 L.Ed.2d 158.

THE NATURE OF THE HEARING

As cases such as *Goss* v. *Lopez* indicate, in some situations considerably less than a full trial-type hearing is required to satisfy due process. The range of required elements is great, and what is necessary in a given case will depend on a number of factors, including the gravity of the interest at stake and the provisions of the relevant legislation. A large part of a law school course on administrative law is devoted to the examination of particular aspects of the hearing process and its product, the administrative decision. This section of the chapter will provide only a brief discussion of several selected issues that fall into this broad category. These are the right to counsel, the right to confrontation and cross examination, standing to intervene in administrative proceedings, the problem of bias, and the institutional decision.

The Right to Counsel

APA section 555(b) contains a broad entitlement to counsel for persons compelled to appear before an agency or for parties to agency proceedings. But important issues involving the right to counsel occur in informal proceedings or in hearings not governed by the APA. As discussed above, *Goldberg* v. *Kelly* affirmed the right of the welfare recipient to retain counsel if desired, but did not require counsel to be provided for an indigent recipient. In *Morrissey* v. *Brewer* the Court declined to consider the question of the parolee's entitlement to counsel, while in *Goss* v. *Lopez* the Court stopped short of requiring that students be provided the opportunity to secure counsel. In the absence of clear legislative guidance on this matter, it appears that the courts will continue to fashion rules regarding counsel on a case-by-case basis.

Confrontation and Cross-Examination

A good general statement on this subject comes from a portion of *Goldberg* v. *Kelly* not quoted in the excerpt set forth earlier in this chapter: "In almost every setting where important decisions turn on questions of fact, due process requires an opportunity to confront and cross examine adverse witnesses." 397 U.S. 254, 269, 90 S.Ct. 1011, 1021, 25 L.Ed.2d 287, 300. Some exceptions to this general principle are recognized, however. For instance, in *Hannah* v. *Larche*, 363 U.S. 420, 80 S.Ct. 1502, 4 L.Ed.2d 1307 (1960), the Supreme Court ruled that because the U.S. Civil Rights Commission is a purely investigative body that cannot take action which will affect an individual's legal rights, its procedural rules, including those which deny those summoned to testify the right to confront and cross-examine other witnesses called by the commission, do not violate due process. And in *Wolff* v. *McDonnell*, 418 U.S. 539, 94 S.Ct. 2963, 41 L.Ed.2d 935 (1974), the Supreme Court ruled that in a prison disciplinary hearing the right to confrontation and cross-examination may be denied at the discretion of prison officials in the interest of avoiding potential disruption in the prison setting.

Parties and Standing to Intervene

Traditionally, agencies possessed considerable discretion in determining who might participate in agency adjudicatory proceedings. Of primary importance were the parties most directly involved with agency action, such as licensees in license renewal proceedings. The recent period has been one of heightened emphasis on public participation in the administrative process, however, and this trend has been reflected to some extent in the development of the law. The seminal case is *Office of Communication of the United Church of Christ* v. *FCC*, 359 F.2d 994 (D.C.Cir., 1966), in which a U.S. court of appeals overruled the FCC's position denying the status as a "party in interest" to appellants, members of the general listening public, in a television renewal proceeding. Since the *Office of Communication* case, the principle stated therein has to some extent found reflection in other case law.[27]

Bias

In both judicial and administrative proceedings, a party is entitled to expect fair treatment. Rules have been developed over time to prevent bias in adjudicatory decision making. Following the ancient maxim that "no man shall be a judge in his own cause," the Supreme Court in 1927 ruled illegal an arrangement under which a village mayor acting as judge received compensation only from fines levied against convicted violators. *Tumey* v. *Ohio*, 273 U.S. 510, 47 S.Ct. 437, 71 L.Ed. 749 (1927). And in 1972 the Court ruled that where a mayor of an Ohio village who had responsibility for revenue production also served as a judge in traffic offense cases, petitioner who was convicted and fined by the mayor did not receive the impartial adjudication to which he was entitled. *Ward* v. *Village of Monroeville, Ohio*, 409 U.S. 57, 93 S.Ct. 80, 34 L.Ed. 2d 267 (1972). Disqualification for bias is not limited only to cases of personal interest, however. Personal bias or prejudice may also serve as a basis for the disqualification of an adjudicator. *Texaco, Inc.* v. *FTC*, is an example. 336 F.2d 754 (D.C.Cir. 1964), vacated on other grounds, 381 U.S. 739, 85 S.Ct. 1798, 14 L.Ed.2d 714 (1965). While a proceeding against two companies for violation of section 5 of the Federal Trade Commission Act was pending before the FTC, the FTC chairman made a speech in which he discussed the allegedly illegal practices and the companies involved. A court of appeals ruled that the chairman should be disqualified from the case because of the appearance of bias and prejudgment demonstrated in the speech. But if a function is deemed essentially prosecutorial rather than judicial, the bias charge may not be sustained. In 1980 the Supreme Court unanimously upheld a provision of the

---

[27] See Bernard Schwartz, *Administrative Law* 263–268 (1976).

Fair Labor Standards Act that provided that sums collected as civil penalties for unlawful employment of child labor are turned over to the Employment Standards Administration of the Labor Department in reimbursement for the costs of determining violations and assessing penalties. The Court reversed a district court ruling that this provision "created an impermissible risk of bias" on the part of administrators investigating alleged violations and that it therefore violated the Due Process Clause of the Fifth Amendment. *Marshall* v. *Jerrico, Inc.*, 446 U.S. 238, 100 S.Ct. 1610, 64 L.Ed.2d 182 (1980).

The Institutional Decision

Decisions made by administrative agencies are often institutional rather than personal. Dean Acheson, the chairman of the Attorney General's Committee on Administrative Procedure stated the problem well nearly forty years ago:

> [T]he agency is one great obscure organization with which the citizen has to deal. It is absolutely amorphous. He pokes it in one place and it comes out another. No one seems to have specific authority. There is someone called the commission, the authority; a metaphysical omniscient brooding thing which sort of floats around the air and is not a human being. That is what is baffling. . . . There is no [*sic*] idea that Mr. A heard the case and then it goes into this great building and mills around and comes out with a commissioner's name on it but what happens in between is a mystery. That is what bothers people.[28]

Courts have sought to grapple with the problem of the institutional decision in various ways. In the famous *Morgan* cases, which reached the Supreme Court four times between 1936 and 1941, the Court first ruled that it was the responsibility of the official charged by law with making the decision, in this case the secretary of agriculture, to participate meaningfully in the process. This did not preclude "practicable administrative procedure in obtaining the aid of assistants in the department. Assistants may prosecute inquiries. Evidence may be taken by an examiner. Evidence thus taken may be sifted and analyzed by competent subordinates." But "the officer who makes the determinations must consider and appraise the evidence which justifies them. That duty undoubtedly may be an onerous one, but the performance of it in a substantial way is inseparable from the exercise of the important authority conferred." *Morgan* v. *United States*, 298 U.S. 468, 481–2, 56 S.Ct. 906, 912, 80 L.Ed. 1288, 1295–6 (1936).

The Court later made a determination of the role actually played by the Secretary:

> The evidence had been received before he took office. He did not hear the oral argument. The bulky record was placed on his desk and he dipped into it from time to time to get its drift. He decided that probably the essence of the evidence was contained in appellants' briefs. These, together with the transcript of the oral argument, he took home with him and read. He had several conferences with the

---

[28] Administrative Procedure, Hearings on S. 674, S. 675 and S. 918 before a Subcommittee of the Senate Committee on the Judiciary, 77th Cong., 1st sess. 816 (1941), as quoted in Schwartz, above, note 27, at 378.

Solicitor of the Department and with officials in the Bureau of Animal Industry and discussed the proposed findings. He testified that he considered the evidence before signing the order. Morgan v. United States, 304 U.S. 1, 17–18, 58 S.Ct. 773, 776, 82 L.Ed. 1129, 1132 (1938).

Still later the Court concluded that the secretary's "testimony shows that he dealt with the enormous record in a manner not unlike the practice of judges in similar situations," suggesting that his level of participation was adequate. Importantly, however, the Court added that "the Secretary should never have been subject to this proceeding." Because courts and administrative agencies are "collaborative instrumentalities of justice and the appropriate independence of each should be respected by the other," the Supreme Court asserted that "it was not the function of the court to probe the mental processes of the Secretary." *United States* v. *Morgan*, 313 U.S. 409, 422, 61 S.Ct. 999, 1004, 85 L.Ed. 1429, 1435–6 (1941).

As a court of appeals decision of 1974 put it, "what emerges from the *Morgan* quartet is the principle that those legally responsible for a decision must in fact make it, but that their method of doing so . . . is largely beyond judicial scrutiny." *K.F.C. Nat. Management Corp.* v. *NLRB*, 497 F.2d 298, 304 (2d Cir., 1974).

Other ways have also been developed to attempt to bring responsibility to administrative decisions. Among these are the requirements of findings and reasoned opinions to accompany administrative decisions. Clearly these requirements are associated with proceedings involving hearings rather than informal proceedings. Section 557(c) of the APA, which applies only to orders or rules made on the record after opportunity for agency hearing, provides in part:

All decisions, including initial, recommended, and tentative decisions, are a part of the record and shall include a statement of—

(A) findings and conclusions, and the reasons or basis therefor, on all material issues of fact, law, or discretion presented on the record; and
(B) the appropriate rule, order, sanction, relief, or denial thereof.

While the language of the APA is quite explicit on findings and reasons, this requirement is no panacea with regard to the problems of the institutional decision. This is demonstrated in the following passage written by former CAB Chairman Alfred E. Kahn in 1979:

I have been told by people who have been at the C.A.B. a long time . . . that in the past the Board would often choose among competing applicants for the right to operate a particular route in secret sessions, held in a closed room from which all staff were rigidly excluded; that somehow out of that process emerged a name attached to the route in question; that the Chairman—or perhaps his assistant— would then pick up the telephone and call the General Counsel and tell him who the lucky winner was, and nothing more; that then a lawyer on the General Counsel's staff, amply supplied with blank legal tablets and a generous selection of cliches—some, like "beyond-area benefits," "route strengthening" or "subsidy need reduction," tried and true, others the desperate product of a feverish imagination—would construct a work of fiction that would then be published as the Board's opinion. Need I add that any resemblance between it and the Board's actual reasons for its decision would be purely coincidental? And then the courts solemnly reviewed these opinions, accepting the fiction that they truly explained the Board's decision, to determine whether the proffered reasons were supported by substantial evidence of record.

Well, we have come to grips with the institutional decision. The Sunshine law has helped force us to do so, but I would like to take some small credit too. My highly publicized preoccupation with the style of our orders and our opinions is not merely aesthetic, though it is surely that; it also goes to the very heart of what we do. All too often, the use in opinions of such pomposities as "we reject the proposed course of action because we deem it inappropriate"—which means no more than "we're not going to do it because we don't want to"—or such oblique methods of expression as the passive voice—"he was hit by a rock," when what really happened was that you threw a rock at him—all too often the purpose of those pomposities and circumlocutions is to conceal information, and to seem to explain while actually saying absolutely nothing—but very impressively. I was taught as a child that "because" is not an answer to the question "why?" No more is "because it is appropriate" or "inappropriate"—the only difference being that the child does not sound like a pompous ass. So, my campaign for the active voice and for the elimination of pomposities and circumlocutions is fundamentally a campaign for clear explanations—real explanations—of what we are doing and why.[29]

The answer to the problem of the institutional decision, in other words, may lie not so much in legal devices as in the competence and good intentions of the people who administer the law.

ADJUDICATION AND POLICY MAKING

Agencies can develop policies through adjudication as well as through rule making. Commentators and judges often express a strong preference for rule making and, as discussed in the last chapter, the use of rule making has increased significantly in recent years. Among the suggested advantages of rule making are the following: the notice and opportunity-for-comment provisions in rule making offer the chance for wider public participation than in regular adjudicatory hearings; the use of rule making allows an agency to plan a broad administrative program to carry out its legislative mandate rather than proceeding on a piecemeal basis; since rules are basically prospective, they avoid the problem of retroactivity of application that sometimes characterizes administrative decisions; rules guarantee a uniformity of application which a case-by-case approach might not achieve; rules are normally direct statements of agency policy which are published or otherwise available to the public; and they thereby have the qualities of accessibility and clarity of formulation that adjudicatory decisions may not possess.[30]

Some agencies do not possess clear rule-making power, however, and some manifest a definite preference for adjudication, even when rule-making

---

[29] Alfred E. Kahn and Michael Roach, "Commentary: A Paean to Legal Creativity," 31 *Administrative Law Review* 97, 101–102 (1979). Reprinted by permission of the *Administrative Law Review*, a publication of the Administrative Law Section of the American Bar Association.

[30] See David L. Shapiro, "The Choice of Rulemaking or Adjudication in the Development of Administrative Policy," 78 *Harvard Law Review* 921 (1975).

authority exists. Among the suggested reasons why agencies might resort to adjudication rather than rule making are a greater ability of adjudicatory decisions to survive judicial challenge, especially if rule-making authority is unclear, and greater freedom to depart from prior adjudicatory decisions than from regulations.[31] A good discussion of judicial views on rule making versus adjudication is found in the landmark *Chenery* case.

Securities and Exchange Comm'n v. Chenery Corp.

SUPREME COURT OF THE UNITED STATES, 1947.
332 U.S. 194, 67 S.CT. 1575, 1760, 91 L.ED. 1995.

[This is the second time this case came to the Supreme Court. In *SEC* v. *Chenery Corporation*, 318 U.S. 80, 63 S.Ct. 454, 87 L.Ed. 626 (1943), the Court ruled that the SEC's order could not be upheld because it was based on judicial precedents which did not support the order. The case was remanded, the SEC reconsidered the issue, and, on the basis of a new rationale, reached the same result.

Several matters of importance are treated in Justice Murphy's opinion for the majority: whether the SEC's recast reasoning will now support the decision and order; the choice between rule making and adjudication for developing agency policy; and the issue of retroactive application of decisions reached in adjudicatory proceedings.]

Mr. Justice MURPHY delivered the opinion of the Court. . . .

The Commission had been dealing with the reorganization of the Federal Water Service Corporation (Federal), a holding company registered under the Public Utility Holding Company Act of 1935, 49 Stat. 803, 15 U.S.C.A. § 79 et seq. During the period when successive reorganization plans proposed by the management were before the Commission, the officers, directors and controlling stockholders of Federal purchased a substantial amount of Federal's preferred stock on the over-the-counter market. Under the fourth reorganization plan, this preferred stock was to be converted into common stock of a new corporation; on the basis of the purchases of preferred stock, the management would have received more than 10% of this new common stock. It was frankly admitted that the management's purpose in buying the preferred stock was to protect its interest in the new company. It was also plain that there was no fraud or lack of disclosure in making these purchases.

But the Commission would not approve the fourth plan so long as the preferred stock purchased by the management was to be treated on a parity with the other preferred stock. It felt that the officers and directors of a holding company in process of reorganization under the Act were fiduciaries and were under a duty not to trade in the securities of that company during the reorganization period. 8 S.E.C. 893, 915–921. And so the plan was amended to provide that the preferred stock acquired by the management, unlike that held by others, was not to be converted into the new common stock; instead, it was to be surrendered at cost plus dividends accumulated since the purchase dates. As amended, the plan was approved by the Commission over the management's objections. 10 S.E.C. 200. . . .

After the case was remanded to the Commission, Federal Water and Gas Corp.

---

[31] Ibid.

(Federal Water), the surviving corporation under the reorganization plan, made an application for approval of an amendment to the plan to provide for the issuance of new common stock of the reorganized company. This stock was to be distributed to the members of Federal's management on the basis of the shares of the old preferred stock which they had acquired during the period of reorganization, thereby placing them in the same position as the public holders of the old preferred stock. The intervening members of Federal's management joined in this request. The Commission denied the application in an order issued on February 7, 1945. Holding Company Act Release No. 5584. That order was reversed by the Court of Appeals, 154 F.2d 6, which felt that our prior decision precluded such action by the Commission.

The latest order of the Commission definitely avoids the fatal error of relying on judicial precedents which do not sustain it. This time, after a thorough reexamination of the problem in light of the purposes and standards of the Holding Company Act, the Commission has concluded that the proposed transaction is inconsistent with the standards of §§ 7 and 11 of the Act. It has drawn heavily upon its accumulated experience in dealing with utility reorganizations. And it has expressed its reasons with a clarity and thoroughness that admit of no doubt as to the underlying basis of its order.

The argument is pressed upon us, however, that the Commission was foreclosed from taking such a step following our prior decision. It is said that, in the absence of findings of conscious wrongdoing on the part of Federal's management, the Commission could not determine by an order in this particular case that it was inconsistent with the statutory standards to permit Federal's management to realize a profit through the reorganization purchases. All that it could do was to enter an order allowing an amendment to the plan so that the proposed transaction

could be consummated. Under this view, the Commission would be free only to promulgate a general rule outlawing such profits in future utility reorganizations; but such a rule would have to be prospective in nature and have no retroactive effect upon the instant situation.

We reject this contention, for it grows out of a misapprehension of our prior decision and of the Commission's statutory duties. We held no more and no less than that the Commission's first order was unsupportable for the reasons supplied by that agency. But when the case left this Court, the problem whether Federal's management should be treated equally with other preferred stockholders still lacked a final and complete answer. It was clear that the Commission could not give a negative answer by resort to prior judicial declarations. And it was also clear that the Commission was not bound by settled judicial precedents in a situation of this nature. 318 U.S. at page 89, 63 S.Ct. at page 460, 87 L.Ed. 626. Still unsettled, however, was the answer the Commission might give were it to bring to bear on the facts the proper administrative and statutory considerations, a function which belongs exclusively to the Commission in the first instance. The administrative process had taken an erroneous rather than a final turn. Hence we carefully refrained from expressing any views as to the propriety of an order rooted in the proper and relevant considerations.

When the case was directed to be remanded to the Commission for such further proceedings as might be appropriate, it was with the thought that the Commission would give full effect to its duties in harmony with the views we had expressed. This obviously meant something more than the entry of a perfunctory order giving parity treatment to the management holdings of preferred stock. The fact that the Commission had committed a legal error in its first disposition of the case certainly gave Federal's management no vested right to receive the benefits of such an order. After the remand was made, therefore, the Commission was bound to deal with the problem afresh, performing the function delegated to it by Congress. It was again charged with the duty of measuring the proposed treatment of the management's preferred stock holdings by relevant and proper standards. Only in that way could the legislative policies embodied in the Act be effectuated. . . .

It is true that our prior decision explicitly recognized the possibility that the Commission might have promulgated a general rule dealing with this problem under its statutory rule-making powers, in which case the issue for our consideration would have been entirely different from that which did confront us. But we did not mean to imply thereby that he failure of the Commission to anticipate this problem and to promulgate a general rule withdrew all power from that agency to perform its statutory duty in this case. To hold that the Commission had no alternative in this proceeding but to approve the proposed transaction, while formulating any general rules it might desire for use in future cases of this nature, would be to stultify the administrative process. That we refuse to do.

Since the Commission, unlike a court, does have the ability to make new law prospectively through the exercise of its rule-making powers, it has less reason to rely upon ad hoc adjudication to formulate new standards of conduct within the framework of the Holding Company Act. The function of filling in the interstices of the Act should be performed, as much as possible, through this quasi-legislative promulgation of rules to be applied in the future. But any rigid requirement to that effect would make the administrative process inflexible and incapable of dealing with many of the specialized problems which arise. Not every principle essential to the effective administration of a statute can or should be cast immediately into the mold of a general rule. Some principles

must await their own development, while others must be adjusted to meet particular, unforeseeable situations. In performing its important functions in these respects, therefore, an administrative agency must be equipped to act either by general rule or by individual order. To insist upon one form of action to the exclusion of the other is to exalt form over necessity.

In other words, problems may arise in a case which the administrative agency could not reasonably foresee, problems which must be solved despite the absence of a relevant general rule. Or the agency may not have had sufficient experience with a particular problem to warrant rigidifying its tentative judgment into a hard and fast rule. Or the problem may be so specialized and varying in nature as to be impossible of capture within the boundaries of a general rule. In those situations, the agency must retain power to deal with the problems on a case-to-case basis if the administrative process is to be effective. There is thus a very definite place for the case-by-case evolution of statutory standards. And the choice made between proceeding by general rule or by individual, ad hoc litigation is one that lies primarily in the informed discretion of the administrative agency.

Hence we refuse to say that the Commission, which had not previously been confronted with the problem of management trading during reorganization, was forbidden from utilizing this particular proceeding for announcing and applying a new standard of conduct. That such action might have a retroactive effect was not necessarily fatal to its validity. Every case of first impression has a retroactive effect, whether the new principle is announced by a court or by an administrative agency. But such retroactivity must be balanced against the mischief of producing a result which is contrary to a statutory design or to legal and equitable principles. If that mischief is greater than the ill effect of the retroactive application of a new standard, it is not the type of retroactivity which is condemned by law.

And so in this case, the fact that the Commission's order might retroactively prevent Federal's management from securing the profits and control which were the objects of the preferred stock purchases may well be outweighed by the dangers inherent in such purchases from the statutory standpoint. If that is true, the argument of retroactivity becomes nothing more than a claim that the Commission lacks power to enforce the standards of the Act in this proceeding. Such a claim deserves rejection.

The problem in this case thus resolves itself into a determination of whether the Commission's action in denying effectiveness to the proposed amendment to the Federal reorganization plan can be justified on the basis upon which it clearly rests. As we have noted, the Commission avoided placing its sole reliance on inapplicable judicial precedents. Rather it has derived its conclusions from the particular facts in the case, its general experience in reorganization matters and its informed view of statutory requirements. It is those matters which are the guide for our review.

The Commission concluded that it could not find that the reorganization plan, if amended as proposed, would be "fair and equitable to the persons affected [thereby]" within the meaning of § 11(e) of the Act, under which the reorganization was taking place. Its view was that the amended plan would involve the issuance of securities on terms "detrimental to the public interest or the interest of investors" contrary to §§ 7(d)(6) and 7(e), and would result in an "unfair or inequitable distribution of voting power" among the Federal security holders within the meaning of § 7(e). It was led to this result "not by proof that the interveners [Federal's management] committed acts of conscious wrongdoing but by the character of the conflicting interests created by the inter-

veners' program of stock purchases carried out while plans for reorganization were under consideration." . . .

Drawing upon its experience, the Commission indicated that all these normal and special powers of the holding company management during the course of a § 11(e) reorganization placed in the management's command "a formidable battery of devices that would enable it, if it should choose to use them selfishly, to affect in material degree the ultimate allocation of new securities among the various existing classes, to influence the market for its own gain and to manipulate or obstruct the reorganization required by the mandate of the statute." In that setting, the Commission felt that a management program of stock purchase would give rise to the temptation and the opportunity to shape the reorganization proceeding so as to encourage public selling on the market at low prices. No management could engage in such a program without raising serious questions as to whether its personal interests had not opposed its duties "to exercise disinterested judgment in matters pertaining to subsidiaries' accounting, budgetary and dividend policies, to present publicly an unprejudiced financial picture of the enterprise, and to effectuate a fair and feasible plan expeditiously." . . .

The scope of our review of an administrative order wherein a new principle is announced and applied is no different from that which pertains to ordinary administrative action. The wisdom of the principle adopted is none of our concern. Our duty is at an end when it becomes evident that the Commission's action is based upon substantial evidence and is consistent with the authority granted by Congress.

We are unable to say in this case that the Commission erred in reaching the result it did. The facts being undisputed, we are free to disturb the Commission's conclusion only if it lacks any rational and statutory foundation. . . . There is thus a reasonable basis for a value judgment that the benefits and profits accruing to the management from the stock purchases should be prohibited, regardless of the good faith involved. And it is a judgment that can justifiably be reached in terms of fairness and equitableness, to the end that the interests of the public, the investors and the consumers might be protected. But it is a judgment based upon public policy, a judgment which Congress has indicated is of the type for the Commission to make.

The Commission's conclusion here rests squarely in that area where administrative judgments are entitled to the greatest amount of weight by appellate courts. It is the product of administrative experience, appreciation of the complexities of the problem, realization of the statutory policies, and responsible treatment of the uncontested facts. It is the type of judgment which administrative agencies are best equipped to make and which justifies the use of the administrative process. Whether we agree or disagree with the result reached, it is an allowable judgment which we cannot disturb.

Reversed.

Mr. Justice BURTON concurs in the result.

The CHIEF JUSTICE and Mr. Justice DOUGLAS took no part in the consideration or decision of this case.

Mr. Justice JACKSON, dissenting.

The Court by this present decision sustains the identical administrative order which only recently it held invalid. Securities and Exchange Commission v. Chenery Corp., 318 U.S. 80, 63 S.Ct. 454, 87 L.Ed. 626. As the Court correctly notes, the Commission has only "recast its rationale and reached the same result." . . . There being no change in the order, no additional evidence in the record and no amendment of relevant legislation, it is clear that there has been a shift in attitude between that of the controlling membership of the Court when the case was first here and that of those who have the power of decision on this second review.

I feel constrained to disagree with the reasoning offered to rationalize this shift. It makes judicial review of administrative orders a hopeless formality for the litigant, even where granted to him by Congress. It reduces the judicial process in such cases to a mere feint. While the opinion does not have the adherence of a majority of the full Court, if its pronouncements should become governing principles they would, in practice, put most administrative orders over and above the law. . . .

The reversal of the position of this Court is due to a fundamental change in prevailing philosophy. The basic assumption of the earlier opinion as therein stated was, *"But before transactions otherwise legal can be outlawed or denied their usual business consequences, they must fall under the ban of some standards of conduct prescribed by an agency of government authorized to prescribe such standards."* Securities and Exchange Commission v. Chenery Corp., 318 U.S. 80, 92, 93, 63 S.Ct. 454, 461, 87 L.Ed. 626. The basic assumption of the present opinion is stated thus: *"The absence of a general rule or regulation governing management trading during reorganization did not affect the Commission's duties in relation to the particular proposal before it."* (Par. 13.) This puts in juxtaposition the two conflicting philosophies which produce opposite results in the same case and on the same facts. The difference between the first and the latest decision of the Court is thus simply the difference between holding that administrative orders must have a basis in law and a holding that absence of a legal basis is no ground on which courts may annul them.

As there admittedly is no law or regulation to support this order we peruse the Court's opinion diligently to find on what grounds it is now held that the Court of Appeals, on pain of being reversed for error, was required to stamp this order with its approval. We find but one. That is the principle of judicial deference to administrative experience. . . .

What are we to make of this reiterated deference to "administrative experience" when in another context the Court says, "Hence we refuse to say that the Commission, *which had not previously been confronted with the problem of management trading during reorganization*, was forbidden from utilizing this particular proceeding for announcing and applying *a new standard of conduct.*"? (Par. 17.) (Emphasis supplied.)

The Court's reasoning adds up to this: The Commission must be sustained because of its accumulated experience in solving a problem with which it had never before been confronted! . . .

Whether, as matter of policy, corporate managers during reorganization should be prohibited from buying or selling its stock, is not a question for us to decide. But it is for us to decide whether, so long as no law or regulation prohibits them from buying, their purchases may be forfeited, or not, in the discretion of the Commission. If such a power exists in words of the statute or in their implication, it would be possible to point it out and thus end the case. Instead, the Court admits that there was no law prohibiting

these purchases when they were made, or at any time thereafter. And, except for this decision, there is none now.

The truth is that in this decision the Court approves the Commission's assertion of power to govern the matter *without law*, power to force surrender of stock so purchased whenever it will, and power also to overlook such acquisitions if it so chooses. The reasons which will lead it to take one course as against the other remain locked in its own breast, and it has not and apparently does not intend to commit them to any rule or regulation. This administrative authoritarianism, this power to decide without law, is what the Court seems to approve in so many words: "The absence of a general rule or regulation governing management trading during reorganization did not affect the Commission's duties." . . .

I have long urged, and still believe, that the administrative process deserves fostering in our system as an expeditious and nontechnical method *applying law* in specialized fields. I can not agree that it be used, and I think its continued effectiveness is endangered when it is used, as a method of *dispensing with law* in those fields.

Mr. Justice FRANKFURTER joins in this opinion.

The *Chenery* case was complicated by the fact that it involved a retroactive application of the principle developed in the case: the trading in stocks which the SEC disallowed in the case had not been considered illegal or improper prior to the case itself. The fact that the SEC was adopting a *new* policy in an unsettled area of the law appears to be significant to some commentators, who argue that it would be undesirable, and legally questionable, for an administrative agency to change settled policy through adjudication and apply it retroactively to the case at hand.[32] What is somewhat surprising is that the SEC, once it had been upheld in *Chenery*, did not move to articulate the

---

[32] See Davis, above, note 13 at 122 and Schwartz, above note 26 at 186–190. A case which ruled against retroactive application of a change in settled law is *Retail, Wholesale and Dept. Store Union, AFL–CIO v. NLRB*, 466 F.2d 380 (D.C.Cir., 1972). But in *NLRB v. Bell Aerospace Co. Division of Textron, Inc.*, 416 U.S. 267, 94 S.Ct. 1757, 40 L.Ed.2d 134 (1974), the Supreme Court approved the use of adjudication rather than rule making in the NLRB's articulation of what has been described

substantive policy of the order through rule making. But in the opinion of SEC personnel, the issue raised in *Chenery* is one of the areas where "comprehensive rules of general application cannot substitute for the adjudicative process." [33]

As suggested above, some administrative bodies manifest a definite preference for adjudication over rule making. As many commentators have documented,[34] one such agency is the National Labor Relations Board. A particularly interesting case dealing with this NLRB preference is *NLRB* v. *Wyman-Gordon*. The reader should pay special attention to two aspects of the four judicial opinions excerpted below: the holdings with regard to the question at issue, and the expressions of approval or disapproval of the NLRB's choice of a policy-making tool.

National Labor Relations Bd. v. Wyman-Gordon Co.

SUPREME COURT OF THE UNITED STATES, 1969.
394 U.S. 759, 89 S.CT. 1426, 22 L.ED.2D 709.

Mr. Justice FORTAS announced the judgment of the Court and delivered an opinion in which the CHIEF JUSTICE, Mr. Justice STEWART, and Mr. Justice WHITE join.

On the petition of the International Brotherhood of Boilermakers and pursuant to its powers under § 9 of the National Labor Relations Act, 49 Stat. 453, 29 U.S.C.A. § 159, the National Labor Relations Board ordered an election among the production and maintenance employees of the respondent company. At the election, the employees were to select one of two labor unions as their exclusive bargaining representative, or to choose not to be represented by a union at all. In connection with the election, the Board ordered the respondent to furnish a list of the names and addresses of its employees who could vote in the election, so that the unions could use the list for election purposes. The respondent refused to comply with the order, and the election was held without the list. Both unions were defeated in the election.

The Board upheld the unions' objections to the election because the respondent had not furnished the list, and the Board ordered a new election. The respondent again refused to obey a Board order to supply a list of employees, and the Board issued a subpoena ordering the respondent to provide the list or else produce its personnel and payroll records showing the employees' names and addresses. The Board filed an action in the United States District Court for the District of Massachusetts seeking to have its subpoena enforced or to have a mandatory injunction issued to compel the respondent to comply with its order.

---

as "arguably a new principle" replacing one already in effect. See Robert A. Gorman, *Basic Text on Labor Law* 17 (1976).

[33] Letter of March 13, 1979, from Andrew MacDonald, special counsel for the SEC, to one of the authors.

[34] See, e.g., Cornelius J. Peck, "The Atrophied Rule-Making Power of the National Labor Relations Board," 70 *Yale Law Journal* 729 (1961); Peck, "A Critique of the National Labor Relations Board's Performance in Policy Formulation: Adjudication and Rulemaking," 117 *University of Pennsylvania Law Review* 254 (1968); Merton C. Bernstein, "The N.L.R.B.'s Adjudication-Rulemaking Dilemma Under the Administrative Procedure Act," 79 *Yale Law Journal* 571 (1970); Glenn Robinson, "The Making of Administrative Policy: Another Look at Rulemaking and Adjudication and Administrative Procedure Reform," 118 *University of Pennsylvania Law Review* 485 (1970).

The District Court held the Board's order valid and directed the respondent to comply. 270 F.Supp. 280 (1967). The United States Court of Appeals for the First Circuit reversed. 397 F.2d 394 (1968). The Court of Appeals thought that the order in this case was invalid because it was based on a rule laid down in an earlier decision by the Board, Excelsior Underwear Inc., 156 N.L.R.B. 1236 (1966), and the *Excelsior* rule had not been promulgated in accordance with the requirements that the Administrative Procedure Act prescribes for rule making, 5 U.S.C.A. § 553. We granted certiorari to resolve a conflict among the circuits concerning the validity and effect of the *Excelsior* rule. 393 U.S. 932, 89 S.Ct. 301, 21 L.Ed. 2d 268 (1968).

I

The *Excelsior* case involved union objections to the certification of the results of elections that the unions had lost at two companies. The companies had denied the unions a list of the names and addresses of employees eligible to vote. In the course of the proceedings, the Board "invited certain interested parties" to file briefs and to participate in oral argument of the issue whether the Board should require the employer to furnish lists of employees. 156 N.L.R.B., at 1238. Various employer groups and trade unions did so, as *amici curiae*. After these proceedings, the Board issued its decision in *Excelsior*. It purported to establish the general rule that such a list must be provided, but it declined to apply its new rule to the companies involved in the *Excelsior* case. Instead, it held that the rule would apply "only in those elections that are directed, or consented to, subsequent to 30 days from the date of [the] Decision." Id., at 1240, n. 5.

Specifically, the Board purported to establish "a requirement that will be applied in all election cases. That is, within 7 days after the Regional Director has approved a consent-election agreement entered into

by the parties . . ., or after the Regional Director or the Board has directed an election . . ., the employer must file with the Regional Director an election eligibility list, containing the names and addresses of all the eligible voters. The Regional Director, in turn, shall make this information available to all parties in the case. Failure to comply with this requirement shall be grounds for setting aside the election whenever proper objections are filed." Id., at 1239–1240.

Section 6 of the National Labor Relations Act empowers the Board "to make . . ., in the manner prescribed by the Administrative Procedure Act, such rules and regulations as may be necessary to carry out the provisions of this Act." 29 U.S.C.A. § 156. The Administrative Procedure Act contains specific provisions governing agency rule making, which it defines as "an agency statement of general or particular applicability and future effect," 5 U.S.C.A. § 551(4). The Act requires among other things, publication in the Federal Register of notice of proposed rule making and of hearing; opportunity to be heard; a statement in the rule of its basis and purposes; and publication in the Federal Register of the rule as adopted. The Board asks us to hold that it has discretion to promulgate new rules in adjudicatory proceedings, without complying with the requirements of the Administrative Procedure Act.

The rule-making provisions of that Act, which the Board would avoid, were designed to assure fairness and mature consideration of rules of general application. See H.R.Rep. No. 1980, 79th Cong., 2d Sess., 21–26 (1946); S.Rep. No. 752, 79th Cong., 1st Sess., 13–16 (1945). They may not be avoided by the process of making rules in the course of adjudicatory proceedings. There is no warrant in law for the Board to replace the statutory scheme with a rule-making procedure of its own invention. Apart from the fact that the device fashioned by the Board does not comply with statutory command, it obviously falls short of the substance of the requirements of the Administrative Procedure Act. The "rule" created in *Excelsior* was not published in the Federal Register, which is the statutory and accepted means of giving notice of a rule as adopted; only selected organizations were given notice of the "hearing," whereas notice in the Federal Register would have been general in character; under the Administrative Procedure Act, the terms or substance of the rule would have to be stated in the notice of hearing, and all interested parties would have an opportunity to participate in the rule making.

The Solicitor General does not deny that the Board ignored the rule-making provisions of the Administrative Procedure Act. But he appears to argue that *Excelsior's* command is a valid substantive regulation, binding upon this respondent as such, because the Board promulgated it in the *Excelsior* proceeding, in which the requirements for valid adjudication had been met. This argument misses the point. There is no question that, in an adjudicatory hearing, the Board could validly decide the issue whether the employer must furnish a list of employees to the union. But that is not what the Board did in *Excelsior*. The Board did not even apply the rule it made to the parties in the adjudicatory proceeding, the only entities that could properly be subject to the order in that case. Instead, the Board purported to make a rule: i.e., to exercise its quasi-legislative power.

Adjudicated cases may and do, of course, serve as vehicles for the formulation of agency policies, which are applied and announced therein. See H. Friendly, The Federal Administrative Agencies 36–52 (1962). They generally provide a guide to action that the agency may be expected to take in future cases. Subject to the qualified role of *stare decisis* in the administrative process, they may serve as precedents.

But this is far from saying, as the Solicitor General suggests, that commands, decisions, or policies announced in adjudication are "rules" in the sense that they must, without more, be obeyed by the affected public.

In the present case, however, the respondent itself was specifically directed by the Board to submit a list of the names and addresses of its employees for use by the unions in connection with the election. This direction, which was part of the order directing that an election be held, is unquestionably valid. Even though the direction to furnish the list was followed by citation to "Excelsior Underwear Inc., 156 NLRB No. 111," it is an order in the present case that the respondent was required to obey. Absent this direction by the Board, the respondent was under no compulsion to furnish the list because no statute and no validly adopted rule required it to do so.

Because the Board in an adjudicatory proceeding directed the respondent itself to furnish the list, the decision of the Court of Appeals for the First Circuit must be reversed....

Mr. Justice BLACK, with whom Mr. Justice BRENNAN and Mr. Justice MARSHALL join, concurring in the result.

I agree with Parts II and III [a] of the prevailing opinion of Mr. Justice FORTAS, holding that the *Excelsior* requirement that an employer supply the union with the names and addresses of its employees prior to an election is valid on its merits and can be enforced by a subpoena. But I cannot subscribe to the criticism in that opinion of the procedure followed by the Board in adopting that requirement in the *Excelsior* case, 156 N.L.R.B. 1236 (1966). Nor can I accept the novel theory by which the opinion manages to uphold enforcement of the *Excelsior* practice in spite of what it considers to be statutory violations present

---

[a] Parts II and III have been omitted by the editors.

in the procedure by which the requirement was adopted. Although the opinion is apparently intended to rebuke the Board and encourage it to follow the plurality's conception of proper administrative practice, the result instead is to free the Board from all judicial control whatsoever regarding compliance with procedures specifically required by applicable federal statutes such as the National Labor Relations Act, 29 U.S.C.A. § 151 et seq., and the Administrative Procedure Act, 5 U.S.C.A. § 551 et seq. Apparently, under the prevailing opinion, courts must enforce any requirement announced in a purported "adjudication" even if it clearly was not adopted as an incident to the decision of a case before the agency, and must enforce "rules" adopted in a purported "rule making" even if the agency materially violated the specific requirements that Congress has directed for such proceedings in the Administrative Procedure Act. I for one would not give judicial sanction to any such illegal agency action.

In the present case, however, I am convinced that the *Excelsior* practice was adopted by the Board as a legitimate incident to the adjudication of a specific case before it, and for that reason I would hold that the Board properly followed the procedures applicable to "adjudication" rather than "rule making." . . .

The prevailing opinion seems to hold that the *Excelsior* requirement cannot be considered the result of adjudication because the Board did not apply it to the parties in the *Excelsior* case itself, but rather announced that it would be applied only to elections called 30 days after the date of the *Excelsior* decision. But the *Excelsior* order was nonetheless an inseparable part of the adjudicatory process. The principal issue before the Board in the *Excelsior* case was whether the election should be set aside on the ground, urged by the unions, that the employer had refused to make the employee lists available to them. See 156 N.L.R.B., at 1236–1238. The Board decided

that the election involved there should not be set aside and thus rejected the contention of the unions. In doing so, the Board chose to explain the reasons for its rejection of their claim, and it is this explanation, the Board's written opinion, which is the source of the *Excelsior* requirement. The Board's opinion should not be regarded as any less an appropriate part of the adjudicatory process merely because the reason it gave for rejecting the unions' position was not that the Board disagreed with them as to the merits of the disclosure procedure but rather, see 156 N.L.R.B., at 1239, 1240, n. 5, that while fully agreeing that disclosure should be required, the Board did not feel that it should upset the Excelsior Company's justified reliance on previous refusals to compel disclosure by setting aside this particular election.

Apart from the fact that the decisions whether to accept a "new" requirement urged by one party and, if so, whether to apply it retroactively to the other party are inherent parts of the adjudicatory process, I think the opposing theory accepted by the Court of Appeals and by the prevailing opinion today is a highly impractical one. In effect, it would require an agency like the Labor Board to proceed by adjudication only when it could decide, *prior* to adjudicating a particular case, that any new practice to be adopted would be applied retroactively. Obviously, this decision cannot properly be made until all the issues relevant to adoption of the practice are fully considered in connection with the final decision of that case. If the Board were to decide, after careful evaluation of all the arguments presented to it in the adjudicatory proceeding, that it might be fairer to apply the practice only prospectively, it would be faced with the unpleasant choice of either starting all over again to evaluate the merits of the question, this time in a "rule-making" proceeding, or overriding the considerations of fairness and applying its order retroactively anyway, in order to preserve the validity of the new practice and avoid duplication of effort. I see no good reason to impose any such inflexible requirement on the administrative agencies.

For all of the foregoing reasons I would hold that the Board acted well within its discretion in choosing to proceed as it did, and I would reverse the judgment of the Court of Appeals on this basis.

Mr. Justice DOUGLAS, dissenting.

The Administrative Procedure Act, 5 U.S.C.A. § 553(b) provides that general notice "of proposed rule making" shall be published in the Federal Register. Public participation—in essence a hearing—is provided, § 553(c). And "interested" persons are given the right to petition for the issuance, amendment, or repeal of a rule, § 553(c).

In Excelsior Underwear Inc., 156 N.L.R.B. 1236, the Board in 1966 decided (1) that an employer would be required to furnish the Regional Director, prior to the conducting of a representation election, the names and addresses of the eligible voters, which list would then be made available to all contestants in the election, but (2) that this requirement would apply only prospectively, to all elections directed or consented to subsequent to 30 days after the date of its decision there.

The notice and hearing procedure prescribed by § 553(b) was not followed; and in this case, an election was directed seven months after the *Excelsior* decision, the Board applying the *Excelsior* rule.

I am willing to assume that, if the Board decided to treat each case on its special facts and perform its adjudicatory function in the conventional way, we should have no difficulty in affirming its action. The difficulty is that it chose a different course in the *Excelsior* case and, having done so, it should be bound to follow the procedures prescribed in the Act as my Brother HARLAN has outlined them. When we hold otherwise, we let the Board "have its cake and eat it too." . . .

Rule making is no cure-all; but it does force important issues into full public display and in that sense makes for more responsible administrative action.

I would hold the agencies governed by the rule making procedure strictly to its requirements and not allow them to play fast and loose as the National Labor Relations Board apparently likes to do. . . .

Mr. Justice HARLAN, dissenting.

The language of the Administrative Procedure Act does not support the Government's claim that an agency is "adjudicating" when it announces a rule which it refuses to apply in the dispute before it. The Act makes it clear that an agency "adjudicates" only when its procedures result in the "formulation of an *order*." 5 U.S.C.A. § 551(7). (Emphasis supplied.) An "order" is defined to include "the whole or a *part* of a final disposition . . . of an agency *in a matter other than rule making* . . . ." 5 U.S.C.A. § 551(6). (Emphasis supplied.) This definition makes it apparent that an agency is not adjudicating when it is making a rule, which the Act defines as "an agency statement of general or particular applicability and *future effect* . . . ." 5 U.S.C.A. § 551(4). (Emphasis supplied.) Since the Labor Board's *Excelsior* rule was to be effective only 30 days after its promulgation, it clearly falls within the rule-making requirements of the Act. . . .

Given the fact that the Labor Board has promulgated a rule in violation of the governing statute, I believe that there is no alternative but to affirm the judgment of the Court of Appeals in this case. If, as the plurality opinion suggests, the NLRB may properly enforce an invalid rule in subsequent adjudications, the rule-making provisions of the Administrative Procedure Act are completely trivialized. Under today's prevailing approach, the agency may evade the commands of the Act whenever it desires and yet coerce the regulated industry into compliance. . . .

One cannot always have the best of both worlds. Either the rule-making provisions are to be enforced or they are not. Before the Board may be permitted to adopt a rule that so significantly alters pre-existing labor-management understandings, it must be required to conduct a satisfactory rule-making proceeding, so that it will have the benefit of wide-ranging argument before it enacts its proposed solution to an important problem.

In refusing to adopt this position, the prevailing opinion not only undermines the Administrative Procedure Act, but also compromises the most basic principles governing judicial review of agency action established in our past decisions. This Court's landmark opinion in SEC v. Chenery Corp., 318 U.S. 80, 94, 63 S.Ct. 454, 462, 87 L.Ed. 626 (1943), makes it clear that we are obliged to remand a case if the agency has relied upon an improper reason to justify its action. . . .

I would affirm the judgment of the Court of Appeals.

The complicated result in *Wyman-Gordon* involved seven justices upholding the NLRB's order, but six justices disapproving of the means by which it was imposed. The preference for rule making and sense of moderate uneasiness with the use of adjudication on issues where new ground is broken also comes out in *Chenery*. And this is understandable: the prospective character of genuine rules and the broader potential accessibility of interested parties to rule-making proceedings make that process appear fairer than agency action which lays down general (and possibly retroactive) rules through adjudicatory proceedings. While both *Chenery* and *Wyman-Gordon* remain good law, it is not surprising that some commentators [35] and courts [36] continue to object to the choice of adjudication in circumstances of this sort.

---

[35] See, e.g., Arthur Earl Bonfield, "State Law in the Teaching of Administrative Law: A Critical Analysis of the Status Quo," 61 *Texas Law Review* 95, at 100 (1982).

[36] In *Ford Motor Company* v. *Federal Trade Commission*, 673 F.2d 1009 (1981), the U.S. Court of Appeals for the Ninth Circuit ruled than an FTC decision, based on adjudicatory proceedings, which ordered defendants to stop using certain credit practices in repossessing automobiles, "changes existing law, and has widespread application" and therefore "should be addressed by rulemaking." For a thorough analysis of this case, in the context of discussion of like cases, see Kenneth Culp Davis, *1982 Supplement to Administrative Law Treatise* 179–186 (1982).

Chapter 8

Informal Activity and the Exercise of Discretion

The past two chapters are among the longest in the book, a fact which is symptomatic of the state of development of administrative law. For they deal with the most important formal aspects of the administrative process, the part of the subject which has received the greatest attention, and on which the most progress has been made. The present chapter, rather short by contrast, involves an area which, until recently, received scant attention from commentators. This is not to suggest that students of administrative law did not appreciate the importance of the informal aspects of the process. One can go all the way back to the founders of American administrative law and find concern expressed about the dangers of uncontrolled administrative discretion.[1] And more recent analyses of the subject typically recite how the overwhelming proportion of the actual activity of most administrative agencies is accomplished through informal means.[2] But the very fact that informal activity *is* informal makes it hard to analyze systematically, and this explains the lack of attention given to it over the years. It wasn't until the 1960s that the subject began to be examined in a serious way.

What is provided in this chapter is merely a sampling of some of the problems that fall into the category of informal activity and the exercise of discretion. The chapter begins with a selection from an article by Warner W. Gardner, for eight years chairman of the Committee on Informal Action of the

---

[1] Ernst Freund wrote in 1894 that "the greatest drawback of our system . . . lies in the fact that it makes no provision for the review of discretionary action." As quoted in Oscar Kraines, *The World and Ideas of Ernst Freund: The Search for General Principles of Legislation and Administrative Law* 104 (1974). Frank Goodnow, in 1905 stated that "it is the purpose of all administrative legislation to lessen as far as possible the realm of administrative discretion and to fix limits within which the administration must move." *The Principles of the Administrative Law of the United States* 368 (1905).

[2] For example, Warner W. Gardner, in the selection below, says that the commonly cited figure of 90 percent of such activity "is much too low."

Administrative Conference of the United States. In the excerpt Gardner reviews some of the recent scholarly attention given to the informal process and describes what he sees as the problems of bringing informal activity within the framework of administrative law. In 1972 Gardner described the general contours of an "Informal Procedure Act of 1980" which he hoped would be promulgated.[3] In the present article he expresses skepticism that such legislation can or should be undertaken, concluding that informal activity can be well understood and evaluated only in the context of the substantive governmental program to which it applies.

The Informal Actions of the Federal Government

Warner W. Gardner

26 *American University Law Review* 799 (1977).[a]

I

This paper undertakes to bring into focus the intractable and perhaps insoluble dilemmas that are likely to hamper any effort either to structure the informal actions of government or even to study them. From that introduction, which comes close to a confession of futility for all which follows, the paper addresses a few of the major issues that have developed in this newly discovered area of concern. It concludes with a suggestion that the objectives of reform should be modest and that studies of expansive scope should be given confined application.

The government actions that are here considered to be "informal" are those that are taken without an evidentiary hearing and formal record. However defined, informal action is the mode in which government operates. A common and loose figure is that 90 percent of the government's business is accomplished by informal action.[4] The figure is much too low. In terms of quantity, surely much less than 1 percent of the actions of the federal government are based upon evidentiary hearings. And, if one were possessed of a divine calibrator that could measure "importance," it is doubtful that weighing the transactions by their importance would reduce the predominance of informal action in the operations of government.

Yet, until a decade ago, the field of informal action was substantially untouched by legal scholarship. The 1941 studies of the attorney general's

---

[3] "The Procedures By Which Informal Action is Taken," 24 *Administrative Law Review* 155 (1972).

[a] Reprinted with permission of the *American University Law Review*. In the excerpt printed below some of the footnotes have been omitted and others have been renumbered.

[4] The figure derives from Verkuil, *A Study of Informal Adjudicative Procedures*, 43 U.Chi.L.Rev. 739, 741 (1976), which in turn relies upon Gardner, *The Procedures By Which Informal Action Is Taken*, 24 Ad.L.Rev. 155, 156 (1972). We thus have research by bootstrap in a form of classical purity.

Committee on Administrative Procedure,[5] to be sure, recognized that "informal procedures constitute the vast bulk of administrative adjudication and are truly the lifeblood of the administrative process,"[6] and followed with a perceptive discussion of a score or so of representative informal functions.[7] A number of particular recommendations were directed at particular agencies and functions,[8] but the committee wisely avoided any legislative recommendation. The Landis Report[9] in 1960 gave some attention to policy making but otherwise confined itself to formal proceedings. None of the thirty recommendations of the 1961–62 Temporary Administrative Conference dealt with informal action.[10] The professional literature, judging by a casual browsing through the *Index to Legal Periodicals*, dealt with the informal administrative process only as a part of the substantive work of one agency or another, and not as a field lending itself to procedural study.[11]

We are long past that comfortable inattention. Walter Gellhorn's formidable surveys of the ombudsman function have necessarily caused him, a quarter century after the attorney general's report, to revisit the vast territory outside of the Administrative Procedure Act (APA).[12] Kenneth Davis brought his growing concern to a focus in his 1966 lectures that in due course grew into his seminal *Discretionary Justice*.[13] The Administrative Conference of the

---

[5] Attorney General's Comm. on Administrative Procedure, Final Report, S. Doc. No. 8, 77th Cong., 1st Sess. 5, 35 (1941) [hereinafter cited as Final Report].

[6] Id. at 35. But see K. Davis, Administrative Law Treatise § 4.13 at 208 (Supp.1970) [hereinafter cited as Davis Treatise], in which Professor Davis objects that "[t]he [committee's] statement never should have put administrative adjudication at the center; the lifeblood is informal procedures, but informal procedures far transcend administrative adjudication."

[7] Some of the functions that the attorney general's report characterized as informal include: issuance or denial of second-class mailing privileges by the Post Office Department without a hearing; the Securities and Exchange Commission's practice of allowing applicants to remedy and amend deficient registration statements following informal conferences at which the adequacy of such statements is reviewed; and spot-checks of inspectors' work by the Grain and Seed Division of the Agricultural Marketing Service of the Department of Agriculture to ensure continued competency for the purposes of licensing. Final Report, supra note e, at 35–38.

[8] Recommendations pertained to FCC Safety Convention certificates, Final Report, supra, at 133; poultry licensing, id. at 137–38; railroad retirement disability ratings, id. at 139–40; rulings of and licensing by the banking agencies, id. at 141–43; marine casualty investigations, id. at 143–44; licensing of navigable obstructions, id. at 155–56; oil and gas leasing and land classification, id. at 162–63; uncontested workmen's compensation cases, id. at 164; income tax procedures, id. at 167–72; and customs entries, id. at 184–85.

[9] *Staff of Senate Comm. on the Judiciary*, 86th Cong., 2d Sess., *Report to the President-Elect on Regulatory Agencies* (Comm. Print 1960).

[10] See *Selected Reports of the Administrative Conference of the United States*, S. Doc. No. 24, 88th Cong., 1st Sess. 37–64 (1963).

[11] The reason for the inattention was probably that lawyers, accustomed to thinking of legal procedures in terms of trials and hearings, thought that simple government "action" was hardly deserving of professional analysis. As a token that no condemnation is intended, I note that in 1958 I authored a forty-page survey on the administrative process which included only two casual paragraphs on informal government. Gardner, *The Administrative Process*, in M. Paulson, *Legal Institutions Today and Tomorrow* 108 (1959).

[12] W. Gellhorn, *Ombudsman and Others: Citizens' Protectors in Nine Countries* (1966); W. Gellhorn, *When Americans Complain: Governmental Grievance Procedures* (1966).

[13] K. Davis, *Discretionary Justice—A Preliminary Inquiry* (1969) [hereinafter cited as *Discretionary Justice*].

United States (ACUS) [14] has received studies from its consultants and made recommendations on thirty-nine aspects of the administrative process and has considered another two or three studies in this area, which the agencies accepted without the necessity of formal recommendation.[15] About two-thirds of the thirty-nine recommendations adopted by the conference in the past five years have related to the field of informal action.[16] The literature seems to be growing at a rate of nearly a hundred pieces a year.[17] The field, accordingly, no longer offers virgin territory. Yet it is far from being fully cultivated. Indeed, it may fairly be concluded that both the objectives and the methodology of the study of informal action remain both wholly fluid and open to most vigorous debate.

II

No work, whether of reform or of study, can be done in the field of informal action without plunging immediately into its central dilemma. Quite obviously, we want a government of laws, not of men. That is, in approximate conformity to Professor Davis analysis, we should confine discretion, so far as is feasible, by publishing rules and policy statements which will both advise the citizen and limit the room for official caprice; and, so far as is feasible, we should structure its exercise by requiring statements of reasons and adherence to open precedents.[18]

None could quarrel with objectives so plainly desirable. But so, too, it is hard to suppress doubts that the path is really so clear. Do we really want to be ruled by codified rules to the fullest feasible extent? Drafting skills will be uneven, and the inability to anticipate either offsetting factors or future issues will be constant. Do we want perhaps to double the 141 volumes and twelve feet of shelf space now occupied by the *Code of Federal Regulations*, or to

---

[14] The Administrative Conference of the United States is a permanent, independent federal agency established in 1964 by the Administrative Conference Act. 5 U.S.C. §§ 571–576 (1970). Its purposes are to monitor all aspects of the administrative process in all of the executive and independent agencies; to identify and analyze the causes of administrative inefficiency, inadequacy, and unfairness; to recommend to the agencies, the President, the Congress, and the Judicial Conference of the United States specific means of improvement; and to furnish assistance and advice on matters of administrative procedure. Id. § 574.

[15] See R. Hamilton, ACUS Memorandum (March 1975) (unpublished memorandum summarizing the studies and recommendations of the Administrative Conference as of March 1975).

[16]

| | Recommendations | |
Year	Informal Action	Other
1971	5	4
1972	4	4
1973	4	1
1974	2	2
1975	8	2
1976 (Jan.-June)	4	1
	27	14

[17] A most casual count reflected ninety-three articles in the *Index to Legal Periodicals* which appeared to be directed in significant part to the procedures of informal action. Index To Legal Periodicals, September 1974–August 1975, 5–9, 71, 115, 129–35, 174, 190, 244–46.

[18] Discretionary Justice, supra note 13, passim.

double the daily *Federal Register* from its average length of possibly two-hundred pages? Do we want to slow the course of all official action by meticulous adherence to procedural requirements of notice, opportunity to state one's case, and statement of reasons? Do we want by profusion of regulation and precedent to increase very considerably the citizen's need for an attorney to deal with his government? . . .

It is indeed possible that we have strayed into an area where the Washington journalist is more "expert" than the attorney. Against that heretical possibility it is appropriate to consider the conclusions of an experienced and perceptive reporter, Meg Greenfield:

> I think there is a dynamic at work among both Federal government officials and the affected public that puts a premium on framing impossible new rules and preserving impossible old ones. It begins with a desirable goal or public policy, moves on to a bureaucratic decision to transfer the onus of enforcement from individuals to ostensibly fair and immutable pages of written rules and builds up a body of regulation that acquires a political, symbolic and legal life of its own. . . .
> . . . By formulating endless rules, we put the problem on "automatic," and there are very few officials in this town who are willing to take the heat that goes with trying to make common-sense rulings instead of just more rules.
> And why do the rest of us go along? Probably because we have an abiding fear of discretionary government and a misplaced belief in the capacity of written regulations to ensure fairness and to prevent our officeholders from treating us in capricious or tyrannical ways.[19]

Between flexible, informal approaches and codification, there can be no choice that will suit every situation. The United States government carries out many thousands of functions by informal means. Each is different from all others. No generalization can be true, and no proposal can be practicable, if it reflects the circumstances of one informal activity and is applied without reexamination to another. The annual volume of business may vary from three construction-differential subsidy contracts for ship construction [20] to the processing of 125 million tax returns [21] or the issuance of 700 million payments to social security beneficiaries.[22] The dollar amounts involved will range from the few cents in a claim for overdue postage to a good many billions of dollars in the development of a new aircraft. One function will be discharged by a scandalously underemployed staff, another by a staff too desperately overburdened to give thoughtful attention to any part of its business. One function has by long tradition been discharged with meticulous care for the rights of those affected, another by an equally long tradition of substantial indifference to the individual consequences. Delay in decisions may be viewed within one agency as the normal prerogative of government, but by another as unforgivable inefficiency. We have, in short, an almost infinite diversity among the agency functions and practices. Only one general-

---

[19] Greenfield, *Can Ford Break the Rules?*, Newsweek, Aug. 4, 1975, at 76.

[20] [1975] Maritime Ad. Ann. Rep. 5.

[21] [1975] Commissioner of IRS Ann. Rep. 13.

[22] Staff of House Comm. on Ways and Means, 94th Cong., 2d Sess., [1975] Ann. Rep. of Social Security Ad. 10, 15, 19, 22, 33 (Comm. Print 1976) (the report lists a total of 59.8 million beneficiaries of the five social security programs, each of whom presumably receives a monthly check).

ization may be made safely: there can be no sound generalization about informal procedures.

One should be able to reach at least a rough judgment as to the degree of formalization appropriate for a particular function. But that judgment is not entitled to even presumptive weight when applied to other forms of governmental action. It would seem beyond argument that even Ms. Greenfield would, one may suppose, object to paying an income tax assessed by an auditor who cast the code and regulations aside and relied upon his own discretion and perceptions of fairness. Even Professor Davis, one may suppose, would be content if the park ranger undertakes to aid visitors and control vandals on the basis of what seems sensible at the time rather than by thumbing through a codification of policy and instructions.

The provisional conclusion is that the procedural incidents of informal action and the degree of discretionary decision are so closely related to the substantive program that they cannot be sensibly studied, much less "reformed," except from the foundation of a close understanding of the particular substantive program.[23] . . .

ADVICE FROM GOVERNMENTAL OFFICIALS: AN EXAMPLE OF INFORMAL ACTIVITY

As Professor Michael Asimow put it in *Advice to the Public from Federal Administrative Agencies*: "Providing advice to the public on proposed private transactions is a significant government function. It consumes an appreciable quantity of the resources of many agencies; it provides an invaluable benefit to a vast number of citizens each year."[24] It also is an activity, however, from which unfortunate consequences—and legal problems—may ensue for the unwary citizen.

Almost all citizens need to consult a government agency at one time or another for advice or information: is a certain expenditure tax-deductible?; is a building permit needed to build an addition to the house or a zoning variance needed to build in a certain part of the city?; am I entitled to this specific kind of benefit from the government, and if so, what must I do to get it? On such questions as these, and many others that one could imagine, an individual might turn to a government agency before proceeding to take action. But what if the advice that one relied on in such situations turned out to be erroneous, and one stood to suffer a loss as a result? The doctrine of *equitable estoppel* is relevant to this problem. Under the doctrine, a person

---

[23] It seems obligatory that the author record that in the period 1971–1972 he made a most vigorous effort to have the Administrative Conference make a major inquiry to determine if it were possible to develop a general and enforceable set of procedural standards for informal action. Gardner, *The Procedures By Which Informal Action is Taken*, 24 AD.L.REV. 155 (1972). The project foundered because of the prudent reluctance of the consultants who were approached to take on the job and because of the skepticism of the committee that the job should or could be done. As the accompanying text indicates, the prudence and the skepticism now seem to me to be sound.

[24] *Advice to the Public From Federal Administrative Agencies* 2 (1973).

"may be precluded by his act or conduct from asserting a right or defense which he otherwise would have had." [25]

An actual example is the following: a worker was assured by his employer that he could initiate a compensation claim for an industrial accident within a seven-year period. However, under the Federal Employers' Liability Act, the actual period of limitation was three years. The worker, who brought his claim after the three-year period had elapsed, sued to estop his employer from raising the three-year limitation as a defense. The Supreme Court unanimously ruled in his favor, quoting the maxim that "no man may take advantage of his own wrong." [26]

Estopping the Government

One problem with equitable estoppel in administrative law, is that it traditionally has been held not to apply to governmental units. As "an offshoot of sovereign immunity," [27] a doctrine that will be discussed in more detail in chapter 9, it has often been held by courts that the government cannot be estopped. An often-cited decision is the 1947 case of *Federal Crop Ins. Corp.* v. *Merrill*, 332 U.S. 380, 68 S.Ct. 1, 92 L.Ed. 10. Merrill, an Idaho farmer, received advice from the local agent of the F.C.I.C., a wholly government-owned enterprise, that a certain crop was insurable, and the F.C.I.C. accepted the application. The advice was inaccurate, however (the Wheat Crop Insurance Regulations, published in the *Federal Register*, prohibited insuring the type of crop in question), and when the crop was destroyed by drought, the corporation refused to pay the loss. In a five to four decision, the Supreme Court reversed the Idaho Supreme Court and ruled that the government could not be estopped in this case. Although assuming "that recovery could be had against a private insurance company," the Court stated that it "is too late in the day to urge that the Government is just another private litigant" and that "anyone entering into an arrangement with the Government takes the risk of having accurately ascertained that he who purports to act for the government stays within the bounds of his authority." [28]

The rule against estopping the government is not as consistently applied as the *Merrill* case might suggest, however. Some state and lower federal

---

[25] "Annotation: Equitable Estoppel as Precluding Reliance on Statute of Limitations—Federal Cases," 3 L.Ed.2d 1886 (1959). A useful summary and analysis is David K. Thompson, "Equitable Estoppel of the Government", 79 *Columbia Law Review* 551 (1979).

[26] *Glus* v. *Brooklyn Eastern Dist. Terminal*, 359 U.S. 231, 79 S.Ct. 760, 3 L.Ed.2d 770 (1959).

[27] "Modern Status of Applicability of Doctrine of Estoppel Against Federal Government and Its Agencies," 27 A.L.R.Fed. 702, 708 (1976).

[28] But see *Moser* v. *United States*, 341 U.S. 41, 71 S.Ct. 553, 95 L.Ed. 729 (1951), in which the Supreme Court reversed a court of appeals decision and ruled that a Swiss national residing in the U.S. did not waive his right to gain American citizenship even though he signed a form in connection with being relieved from serving in the U.S. Army, which expressly stated that under the applicable statute, a person who in such circumstances did seek to be excused from military service "shall thereafter be debarred from becoming a citizen of the United States." Professor Davis, in juxtaposing the *Merrill* and *Moser* cases, has argued persuasively that it would make more sense if the result in each case were reversed, with estoppel being granted in *Merrill* and denied in *Moser*. Kenneth Culp Davis, *Administrative Law: Cases—Text—Problems* 540 (6th ed., 1977).

courts have permitted the government to be estopped in certain situations. Estoppel, as noted, is identified as *equitable* estoppel, meaning that it developed as a part of the law of equity, a body of law that grew side by side with the common law in order to prevent injustices that a too-rigid application of the common law might entail. Equitable estoppel is thus a doctrine designed to promote basic fairness. As stated in a 1973 estoppel decision by a federal district court, protecting the public treasury "cannot be carried so far as to permit the government to deal capriciously with its citizens." [29]

The first case excerpted below, a state court case, seems to the authors to be a good example of a court considering whether basic fairness requires estopping the government, and acting accordingly. But there is no clear and certain rule on when estoppel will or will not be allowed. On the federal level, the strong inclination is not to invoke estoppel against the government. Some lower federal courts, upon finding that the government or its agent has engaged in "affirmative misconduct," have allowed the government to be estopped.[30] The Supreme Court has not gone that far. In *Schweiker* v. *Hansen*, the second case excerpted below, the Supreme Court addresses the concept of affirmative misconduct, but finds that it does not apply to the case at hand.

Tillman v. City of Pompano Beach

SUPREME COURT OF FLORIDA, 1957.
100 SO.2D 53.

HOBSON, Justice.

This appeal arises from the action of the court in striking certain allegations of a pleading which had been filed by appellant, plaintiff below. The action had been commenced by appellant against the city and its truck driver, to recover damages for injuries sustained by appellant when a city-owned truck collided with the rear of appellant's automobile.

The city contended below that appellant was barred from prosecuting his claim by virtue of provisions of the city charter [Secs. 1 and 2, Art. 7, Part XII, Chap. 24835, Special Acts of 1947] to the effect that no suit of this nature should be maintained against the city "unless it shall be made to appear that written notice of such damage was, within thirty (30) days after the receiving of the injury alleged, given to the

City Commission or the City Manager, with such reasonable specifications as to time, and place and witnesses as would enable the proper City officials to investigate the matter. . . ." (Emphasis supplied.)

In the pleading with which we are concerned, appellant alleged that at the time of the accident the city manager and a member of the city commission were in the immediate vicinity. These officials promptly visited the scene, interrogated the appellant, and made a full and complete investigation of the collision on the spot. Appellant further alleged that on the day following the accident he reported the accident and his injuries and damages to an agent of the city, that such agent assured appellant the city was covered by insurance and that the accident had been or would be promptly and properly re-

---

[29] *Oil Shale Corp.* v. *Morton*, 370 F.Supp. 108, 125 (D.C.Colo., 1973).

[30] "Estopping the Federal Government: Still Waiting for the Right Case," 53 *George Washington Law Review* 191 (1984–1985).

ported to the city and its insurance carrier. Appellant went on to allege in substance that various representatives of the city, including the city manager, discussed the accident and appellant's injuries with him on numerous occasions within thirty days following the accident, conceding the liability of the city and discussing only the amount of the payment due appellant. Relying upon the representations made by the city through its agents, appellant was led to believe, so he alleges, that no further action on his part was necessary, and he therefore remained inactive until the time specified in the city charter had run.

Two unusual features of this case are immediately apparent: first, the very city officials to whom the statutory notice was to be given had immediate actual notice of the accident and conducted an investigation of it; and second, the city, through its agents, actively represented that the city was liable, leaving open only the question of damages, which was to be settled when the amount was finally determined. In other words, the basic representation made to appellant was that the matter would not proceed to the litigation stage, and it was with this assurance that appellant delayed obtaining representation by counsel until after the time for filing written notice had run. Both sections of the city charter here involved contemplate the giving of written notice only as a condition precedent to commencing litigation, as the use of the words "suit" and "cause of action" in the statute indicate. According to the stricken allegations, however, the city officials said in effect that they would render litigation unnecessary by settling appellant's claim, but later, after the time for performing the technical condition precedent to filing suit had run, they refused to fulfill their earlier promises, making it necessary for appellant to seek his remedies at law. Appellant could have not told the city officials in

writing anything he did not tell them verbally or that they did not already know by virtue of their own investigation of the accident. We conclude that under the peculiar facts of this case the appellee was estopped to insist upon the requirement of written notice as a condition precedent to filing suit.

We have held that in a proper case the doctrine of estoppel may be applied against the interest of an entity of government. . . .

We have frequently expressed our views regarding the purpose of municipal charter provisions requiring notice to the city within a time certain. There can be no doubt that the actual notice which was had by the city officials in the instant case fulfilled the purpose of the charter provisions. When the city manager and a member of the city commission, directly after the accident occurred, made an investigation thereof, the city was then on an equal footing with appellant and had an opportunity to investigate the matter in detail in order to determine whether a settlement was indicated and prepare the city's case for a trial if necessary.

We are not unmindful that the result which we have reached is inconsistent with the position taken by the courts of several other states. . . . In this connection we can say only that under the peculiar facts of this case, where it is alleged that city officials, who had actual knowledge of all the facts which a notice required by the charter provision would have disclosed, won the confidence of a bona fide claimant, causing him, by their affirmative acts and assurances, to defer seeking his remedies at law, the requirements of fair play compel us to hold that the city may not now be heard to say that the claimant is barred from adjudication of his rights.

Reversed and remanded.

Schweiker v. Hansen

SUPREME COURT OF THE UNITED STATES, 1981.
450 U.S. 785, 101 S.CT. 1468, 67 L.ED.2D 685.
REH DEN 451 U.S. 1032, 101 S.CT. 3023, 69 L.ED.2D 401.

PER CURIAM.

On June 12, 1974, respondent met for about 15 minutes with Don Connelly, a field representative of the Social Security Administration (SSA), and orally inquired of him whether she was eligible for "mother's insurance benefits" under § 202(g) of the Social Security Act (Act), 64 Stat. 485, as amended, 42 U.S.C. § 402(g). Connelly erroneously told her that she was not, and she left the SSA office without having filed a written application. By the Act's terms, such benefits are available only to one who, among other qualifications, "has filed application." 42 U.S.C. § 402(g)(1)(D). By a regulation promulgated pursuant to the Act, only written applications satisfy the "filed application" requirement. 20 CFR § 404.601 (1974). The SSA's Claims Manual, and internal Administration handbook, instructs field representatives to advise applicants of the advantages of filing written applications and to recommend to applicants who are uncertain about their eligibility that they file written applications. Connelly, however, did not recommend to respondent that she file a written application; nor did he advise her of the advantages of doing so. The question is whether Connelly's erroneous statement and neglect of the Claims Manual estop petitioner, the Secretary of Health and Human Services, from denying retroactive benefits to respondent for a period in which she was eligible for benefits but had not filed a written application.

Respondent eventually filed a written application after learning in May 1975 that in fact she was eligible. She then began receiving benefits. Pursuant to § 202(j)(1) of the Act, she also received retroactive benefits for the preceding 12 months, which was the maximum retroactive benefit allowed by the Act. Respondent contended, however, that she should receive retroactive benefits for the 12 months preceding her June 1974 interview with Connelly. An Administrative Law Judge rejected this claim, concluding that Connelly's erroneous statement and neglect of the Claims Manual did not estop petitioner from determining respondent's eligibility for benefits only as of the date of respondent's written application. The Social Security Appeals Council affirmed.

Respondent then brought this lawsuit in the District Court for the District of Vermont, which held that the written-application requirement was "unreasonably restrictive" as applied to the facts of this case. A divided panel of the Court of Appeals for the Second Circuit affirmed. 619 F.2d 942 (1980). It agreed with petitioner as an initial matter that the regulation requiring a written application is valid and that the Claims Manual has no legally binding effect. But it considered the written-application requirement a mere "procedural requirement" of lesser import than the fact that respondent in June 1974 had been "substantively eligible" for the benefits. Id., at 948. In such circumstances, the majority held, "misinformation provided by a Government official combined with a showing of misconduct (even if it does not rise to the level of a violation of a legally binding rule) should be sufficient to require estoppel." Ibid. In summarizing its holding, the majority stated that the Government may be estopped "where (a) a procedural not a substantive requirement is involved and (b) an internal procedural manual or guide or some other source of objective standards of conduct exists and supports an inference of misconduct by a Government employee." Id., at 949.

Judge Friendly dissented. He argued that the majority's conclusion is irreconcilable with decisions of this Court, e.g., Federal Crop Insurance Corp. v. *Merrill*, 332 U.S. 380, 68 S.Ct. 1, 92 L.Ed. 10 (1947); *Montana* v. *Kennedy*, 366 U.S. 308, 81 S.Ct. 1336, 6 L.Ed.2d 313 (1961); *INS* v. *Hibi*, 414 U.S. 5, 94 S.Ct. 19, 38 L.Ed.2d 7 (1973) (per curiam), and with decisions of other Courts of Appeals, *Leimbach v. Califano*, 596 F.2d 300 (CA8 1979); *Cheers v. Secretary of HEW*, 610 F.2d 463 (CA7 1979).

We agree with the dissent. This Court has never decided what type of conduct by a Government employee will estop the Government from insisting upon compliance with valid regulations governing the distribution of welfare benefits. In two cases involving denial of citizenship, the Court has declined to decide whether even "affirmative misconduct" would estop the Government from denying citizenship, for in neither case was "affirmative misconduct" involved. *INS* v. *Hibi*, supra, at 8–9, 94 S.Ct., at 21–22; *Montana* v. *Kennedy*, supra, at 314–315, 81 S.Ct., at 1340–1341. The Court has recognized, however, "the duty of all courts to observe the conditions defined by Congress for charging the public treasury." *Federal Crop Insurance Corp.* v. *Merrill*, supra, at 385, 68 S.Ct., at 3. Lower federal courts have recognized that duty also, and consistently have relied on *Merrill* in refusing to estop the Government where an eligible applicant has lost Social Security benefits because of possibly erroneous replies to oral inquiries. . . . This is another in that line of cases, for we are convinced that Connelly's conduct—which the majority conceded to be less than "affirmative misconduct," 619 F.2d, at 948— does not justify the abnegation of that duty.

Connelly erred in telling respondent that she was ineligible for the benefit she sought. It may be that Connelly erred because he was unfamiliar with a recent amendment which afforded benefits to respondent. Id., at 947. Or it may be that respondent gave Connelly too little information for him to know that he was in

error. Id., at 955 (Friendly, J., dissenting). But at worst, Connelly's conduct did not cause respondent to take action, cf. *Federal Crop Insurance Corp.* v. *Merrill*, supra, or fail to take action, cf. *Montana* v. *Kennedy*, supra, that respondent could not correct at any time.

Similarly, there is no doubt that Connelly failed to follow the Claims Manual in neglecting to recommend that respondent file a written application and in neglecting to advise her of the advantages of a written applications. But the Claims Manual is not a regulation. It has no legal force, and it does not bind the SSA. . . .

Finally, the majority's distinction between respondent's "substantiv[e] eligib[ility]" and her failure to satisfy a "procedural requirement" does not justify estopping petitioner in this case. Congress expressly provided in the Act that only one who "has filed application" for benefits may receive them, and it delegated to petitioner the task of providing by regulation the requisite manner of application. A court is no more authorized to overlook the valid regulation requiring that applications be in writing than it is to overlook any other valid requirement for the receipt of benefits.

In sum, Connelly's errors "fal[l] far short" of conduct which would raise a serious question whether petitioner is estopped from insisting upon compliance with the valid regulation. *Montana* v. *Kennedy*, supra, at 314, 81 S.Ct., at 1340. Accordingly, we grant the motion of respondent for leave to proceed *in forma pauperis* and the petition for certiorari and reverse the judgment of the Court of Appeals.

It is so ordered.

Justice MARSHALL, with whom Justice BRENNAN, joins, dissenting.

A summary reversal is a rare disposition, usually reserved by this Court for situations in which the law is settled and stable, the facts are not in dispute, and the decision below is clearly in error. Because this is not such a case, I dissent from the majority's summary reversal of the judgment of the Court of Appeals, and would instead grant the petition and set the case for plenary consideration.

The issue here is important, not only in economic terms to respondent Hansen, but in constitutional terms as well. The question of when the Government may be equitably estopped has divided the distinguished panel of the Court of Appeals in this case, has received inconsistent treatment from other Courts of Appeals, and has been the subject of considerable ferment. See, e.g., *Corniel-Rodriquez* v. *INS*, 532 F.2d 301 (CA2 1976); *United States* v. *Lazy FC Ranch*, 481 F.2d 985 (CA9 1973); *United States* v. *Fox Lake State Bank*, 366 F.2d 962 (CA7 1966); *Walsonavich* v. *United States*, 335 F.2d 96 (CA3 1964); *Simmons* v. *United States*, 308 F.2d 938 (CA5 1962); *Semaan* v. *Mumford*, 118 U.S.App.D.C. 282, 335 F.2d 704 (1964); *Eichelberger* v. *Commissioner of Internal Revenue*, 88 F.2d 874 (CA5 1937). See generally K. Davis, Administrative Law of the Seventies § 17.01 (1976); Note, Equitable Estoppel of the Government, 79 Colum.L.Rev. 551 (1979). Indeed, the majority today recognizes that "[t]his Court has never decided what type of conduct by a Government employee will estop the Government from insisting upon compliance with valid regulations governing the distribution of welfare benefits." *Ante*, at 1470. The majority goes on to suggest that estoppel may be justified in some circumstances. Yet rather than address the issue in a comprehensive fashion, the Court simply concludes that this is not such a case. The apparent message of today's decision—that we will know an estoppel when we see one—provides inadequate guidance to the lower courts in an area of the law that, contrary to the majority's view, is far from settled. . . .

Moreover, in summarily reversing the judgment of the Court of Appeals, the majority glosses over the sorts of situations— such as that presented by this case—that

have increasingly led courts to conclude that in some cases hard and fast rules against estoppel of the Government are neither fair nor constitutionally required. The majority characterizes Connelly's conduct in this case a little more than an innocent mistake, based possibly on his unfamiliarity with a "recent amendment" rendering respondent eligible for benefits, or possibly the majority speculates, on respondent's failure to give Connelly sufficient "information . . . to know that he was in error." The majority further concludes that this error was essentially harmless, because, in the majority's view, it "did not cause respondent to . . . fail to take action . . . that respondent could not correct at any time."

While these characterizations certainly facilitate the summary disposition the majority seeks, they do not fit this case. The "recent amendment" had been in effect for a year and a half when respondent was incorrectly informed that she was not eligible. Moreover, it is quite clear that respondent provided Connelly with sufficient information on which to make a correct judgment, had he been so inclined. Finally, to conclude that Connelly's incorrect assessment to respondent's eligibility did not cause her to act to her detriment in a manner that she "could not correct at any time" is to blink in the face of the obvious. Connelly, and not respondent, had the legal duty to meet with Social Security applicants and advise them concerning their eligibility for benefits. While not necessarily free of error, such preliminary advice is inevitably accorded great weight by applicants who—like respondent—are totally uneducated in the intricacies of the Social Security laws. Hence, the majority's effort to cast respondent as the architect of her own predicament is wholly unpersuasive. Instead, the fault for respondent's failure to file a timely application for benefits that she was entitled to must rest squarely with the Government, first, because its agent incorrectly advised her that she was ineligible for benefits, and, second, because the same agent breached his duty to encourage to file a written application regardless of his views on her eligibility.

In my view, when this sort of governmental misconduct directly causes an individual's failure to comply with a purely procedural requirement established by the agency, it may be sufficient to estop the Government from denying that individual benefits that she is substantively entitled to receive. Indeed, in an analogous situation, we concluded that before an agency "may extinguish the entitlement of . . . otherwise eligible beneficiaries, it must comply, at a minimum, with its own internal procedures." *Morton* v. *Ruiz*, 415 U.S. 199, 235, 94 S.Ct. 1055, 1074, 39 L.Ed.2d 270 (1974). At the very least, the question deserves more than the casual treatment it receives from the majority today.

Since *Schweiker* v. *Hansen*, the Supreme Court has refused to estop the government on two further occasions. *I.N.S.* v. *Miranda*, 459 U.S. 14, 103 S.Ct. 281, 74 L.Ed.2d 12 (1982); *Heckler* v. *Community Health Services of Crawford County*, 467 U.S. 51, 104 S.Ct. 2218, 81 L.Ed.2d 42 (1984). But it has not closed the door on estoppel completely. In the *Heckler* case just cited, the government urged the Court to lay down "a flat rule that estoppel may not in any circumstances run against the Government." But the Court refused to go this far:

> We have left the issue open in the past, and do so again today. Though the arguments the Government advances for the rule are substantial, we are hesitant, when it is unnecessary to decide this case, to say that there are *no cases* in which the public interest in ensuring that the Government can enforce the law free from estoppel might be outweighed by the countervailing interest of citizens in some minimum standard of decency, honor and reliability in their dealings with their Government.

DISCRETION AND ITS CONTROL

As suggested at the beginning of the chapter, commentators have long been aware of the significance of discretion in administrative law, and of the desirability of keeping it within reasonable bounds. The problem has been to find ways to limit discretion without unduly restricting the flexibility of the administrator. Kenneth Culp Davis, in his pioneering study, *Discretionary Justice*, recommends the increased use of administrative rule making to curb unreasonable discretion, and the great rise in the use of rule making in recent years has no doubt had some effect in this area. But the range of possible discretionary activity—and with it the potential for abuse of discretion—remains vast.

In some cases discretion is specifically accorded to administrators by law. A section of the immigration laws, for instance, 8 U.S.C.A. § 1254(a)(1), provides that "the Attorney General may, in his discretion, suspend deportation and adjust the status to that of an alien lawfully admitted for permanent residence. . . . " And the government receives an extraordinary degree of protection in connection with the exercise of discretion by officials. The most important exemption to the Federal Tort Claims Act (28 U.S.C.A. § 2680(a)), a statute that will be discussed in chapter 9, denies governmental liability for any act "based upon the exercise or performance or the failure to exercise or perform a discretionary function or duty . . . , whether or not the discretion involved be abused." But discretion may be provided by law whether or not the word itself is used in the statute. As Ernst Freund wrote in 1928, "a statute confers discretion when it refers an official for the use of his power to beliefs, expectations, or tendencies, instead of facts, or to such terms as 'adequate,' 'advisable,' 'appropriate,' 'beneficial,' 'convenient,' 'detrimental,' 'expedient,' 'equitable,' 'fair,' 'fit,' 'necessary,' 'practicable,' 'proper,' 'reasonable,' 'reputable,' 'safe,' 'sufficient,' 'wholesome,' or their opposites." [31]

Although courts are reluctant to substitute their judgment for that of administrative experts, they are sometimes willing to consider whether administrators have overstepped reasonable limits of discretion. The two cases that follow provide examples of recent Supreme Court attempts to limit the discretion exercised by administrative officials.

Dunlop v. Bachowski

SUPREME COURT OF THE UNITED STATES (1975).
421 U.S. 560, 95 S.CT. 1851, 44 L.ED.2D 377.

Mr. Justice BRENNAN delivered the opinion of the Court.

On February 13, 1973, the United Steelworkers of America (USWA) held district officer elections in its several districts. Respondent Bachowski (hereinafter respondent) was defeated by the incumbent in the election for that office in District 20. After exhausting his remedies within USWA, respondent filed a timely complaint with petitioner, the Secretary of Labor, alleging violations of § 401 of the Labor-Management Reporting and Disclosure Act of 1959 (LMRDA), 73 Stat. 532, 29 U.S.C.A. § 481, thus invoking 29 U.S.C.A. §§ 482(a), (b) which require that the Secretary investigate the complaint and decide whether to bring a civil action to set aside the election. Similar complaints were filed respecting five other district elections. After completing his investigations, the Secretary filed civil actions to set aside the elections in only two districts. With respect to the election in District 20, he advised respondent

by letter dated November 7, 1973, that "[b]ased on the investigative findings, it has been determined . . . that civil action to set aside the challenged election is not warranted."

On November 7, 1973, respondent filed this action against the Secretary and USWA in the District Court for the Western District of Pennsylvania. The complaint asked that, among other relief, "the Court declare the actions of the Defendant Secretary to be arbitrary and capricious and order him to file suit to set aside the aforesaid election." The District Court conducted a hearing on November 8, and after argument on the question of reviewability of the Secretary's decision, concluded that the court lacked "authority" to find that the action was capricious and to order him to file suit. The hearing was followed by an order dated November 12, dismissing the suit. The Court of Appeals for the Third Circuit reversed, 502 F.2d 79 (1974). . . .

---

[31] *Administrative Power Over Persons and Property* 71 as quoted in Kraines, above, note 1, at 112.

We agree that 28 U.S.C.A. § 1337 confers jurisdiction upon the District Court to entertain respondent's suit, and that the Secretary's decision not to sue is not excepted from judicial review by 5 U.S.C.A. § 701(a); rather, §§ 702 and 704 subject the Secretary's decision to judicial review under the standard specified in § 706(2)(A). We hold, however, that the Court of Appeals erred insofar as its opinion construes § 706(2)(A) to authorize a trial-type inquiry into the factual bases of the Secretary's conclusion that no violations occurred affecting the outcome of the election. We accordingly reverse the judgment of the Court of Appeals insofar as it directs further proceedings on remand consistent with the opinion of that court, and direct the entry of a new judgment ordering that the proceedings on remand be consistent with this opinion of this Court.

The LMRDA contains no provision that explicitly prohibits judicial review of the decision of the Secretary not to bring a civil action against the union to set aside an allegedly invalid election. There is no such prohibition in 29 U.S.C.A. § 483. That section states that "[t]he remedy provided by this subchapter for challenging an election already conducted shall be exclusive." Certain LMRDA provisions concerning pre-election conduct, 29 U.S.C.A. §§ 411–413 and 481(c), are enforceable in suits brought by individual union members. Provisions concerning the conduct of the election itself, however, may be enforced only according to the post-election procedures specified in 29 U.S.C.A. § 482. Section 483 is thus not a prohibition against judicial review but simply underscores the exclusivity of the § 482 procedures in post-election cases.

In the absence of an express prohibition in the LMRDA, the Secretary, therefore, bears the heavy burden of overcoming the strong presumption that Congress did not mean to prohibit all judicial review of his decision. "The question is phrased in terms of 'prohibition' rather than 'authorization' because a survey of our cases shows that judicial review of a final agency action by an aggrieved person will not be cut off unless there is persuasive reason to believe that such was the purpose of Congress." Abbott Laboratories v. Gardner, 387 U.S. 136, 140, 87 S.Ct. 1507, 1510, 18 L.Ed.2d 681 (1967). . . .

The Secretary urges that the structure of the statutory scheme, its objectives, its legislative history, the nature of the administrative action involved, and the conditions spelled out with respect thereto, combine to evince a congressional meaning to prohibit judicial review of his decision. We have examined the materials the Secretary relies upon. They do not reveal to us any congressional purpose to prohibit judicial review. Indeed, there is not even the slightest intimation that Congress gave thought to the matter of the preclusion of judicial review. "The only reasonable inference is that the possibility did not occur to the Congress." Wirtz v. Bottle Blowers Assn., 389 U.S. 463, 468, 88 S.Ct. 643, 647, 19 L.Ed.2d 705 (1968).

We therefore reject the Secretary's argument as without merit. He has failed to make a showing of "clear and convincing evidence" that Congress meant to prohibit all judicial review of his decision. . . . Our examination of the relevant materials persuades us, however, that although no purpose to prohibit all judicial review is shown, a congressional purpose narrowly to limit the scope of judicial review of the Secretary's decision can, and should, be inferred in order to carry out congressional objectives in enacting the LMRDA. . . .

Two conclusions follow from this survey of our decisions: (1) since the statute relies upon the special knowledge and discretion of the Secretary for the determination of both the probable violation and the probable effect, clearly the reviewing court is not authorized to substitute its judgment for the decision of the Secretary not to bring suit; (2) therefore, to enable the reviewing court intelligently to review the

Secretary's determination, the Secretary must provide the court and the complaining witness with copies of a statement of reasons supporting his determination. "[W]hen action is taken by [the Secretary] it must be such as to enable a reviewing Court to determine with some measure of confidence whether or not the discretion, which still remains in the Secretary, has been exercised in a manner that is neither arbitrary nor capricious. ... [I]t is necessary for [him] to delineate and make explicit the basis upon which discretionary action is taken, particularly in a case such as this where the decision taken consists of a failure to act after the finding of union election irregularities." *DeVito I*, 300 F.Supp., at 383; see also Valenta v. Brennan, No. C 74–11 (ND Ohio 1974).

Moreover, a statement of reasons serves purposes other than judicial review. Since the Secretary's role as lawyer for the complaining upon member does not include the duty to indulge a client's usual prerogative to direct his lawyer to file suit, we may reasonably infer that Congress intended that the Secretary supply the member with a reasoned statement why he determined not to proceed. "[A]s a matter of law ... the Secretary is not required to sue to set aside the election whenever the proofs before him suggest the suit *might* be successful. There remains in him a degree of discretion to select cases and it is his subjective judgment as to the probable outcome of the litigation that must control." DeVito v. Shultz, 72 L.R.R.M. 2682, 2683 (DC 1969) (DeVito II) (emphasis added). But "[s]urely Congress must have intended that courts would intercede sufficiently to determine that the provisions of Title IV have been carried out in harmony with the implementation of other provisions of [the LMRDA]." *DeVito I*, supra, 300 F.Supp. at 383. Finally, a "reasons" requirement promotes thought by the Secretary and compels him to cover the relevant points and eschew irrelevancies, and as noted by the Court of Appeals in this case, the need to

assure careful administrative consideration "would be relevant even if the Secretary's decision were unreviewable." 502 F.2d, at 88–89, n. 14.

The necessity that the reviewing court refrain from substitution of its judgment for that of the Secretary thus helps define the permissible scope of review. Except in what must be the rare case, the court's review should be confined to examination of the "reasons" statement, and the determination whether the statement, without more, evinces that the Secretary's decision is so irrational as to constitute the decision arbitrary and capricious. Thus, review may not extend to cognizance or trial of a complaining member's challenges to the factual bases for the Secretary's conclusion either that no violations occurred or that they did not affect the outcome of the election. The full trappings of adversary trial-type hearings would be defiant of congressional objectives not to permit individuals to block or delay resolution of post-election disputes, but rather "to settle as quickly as practicable the cloud on the incumbents' titles to office"; and "to protect unions from frivolous litigation and unnecessary interference with their elections." "If ... the Court concludes ... there is a rational and defensible basis [stated in the reasons statement] for [the Secretary's] determination, then that should be an end of this matter, for it is not the function of the Court to determine whether or not the case should be brought or what its outcome would be." *DeVito II*, supra, at 2683.

Thus, the Secretary's letter of November 7, 1973, may have sufficed as a "brief statement of the grounds for denial" for the purposes of the Administrative Procedure Act, 5 U.S.C.A. § 555(e), but plainly it did not suffice as a statement of reasons required by the LMRDA. For a statement of reasons must be adequate to enable the court to determine whether the Secretary's decision was reached for an impermissible reason or for no reason at all. For this essential purpose, although detailed findings of fact are not required, the statement of reasons should inform the court and the complaining union member of both the grounds of decision and the essential facts upon which the Secretary's inferences are based. . . .

There remains the question of remedy. When the district court determines that the Secretary's statement of reasons adequately demonstrates that his decision not to sue is not contrary to law, the complaining union member's suit fails and should be dismissed. Howard v. Hodgson, 490 F.2d 1194 (CA8 1974). Where the statement inadequately discloses his reasons, the Secretary may be afforded opportunity to supplement his statement. *DeVito I*, 300 F.Supp., at 384; Valenta v. Brennan, supra. The court must be mindful, however, that endless litigation concerning the sufficiency of the written statement is inconsistent with the statute's goal of expeditious resolution of post-election disputes.

The district court may, however, ultimately come to the conclusion that the Secretary's statement of reasons on its face renders necessary the conclusion that his decision not to sue is so irrational as to constitute the decision arbitrary and capricious. There would then be presented the question whether the district court is empowered to order the Secretary to bring a civil suit against the union to set aside the election. We have no occasion to address that question at this time. It obviously presents some difficulty in light of the strong evidence that Congress deliberately gave exclusive enforcement authority to the Secretary. We prefer therefore at this time to assume that the Secretary would proceed appropriately without the coercion of a court order when finally advised by the courts that his decision was in law arbitrary and capricious.

III

The opinion of the Court of Appeals authorized review beyond the permissible limits defined in this opinion. After first stating that "judicial review of the Secretary's decision not to bring suit should extend at the very least to an inquiry into his reasons for that decision . . . ," 502 F.2d, at 88–89, the court noted: "The relief requested by the complaint . . . however, goes beyond such an inquiry. . . . [P]laintiff seeks an opportunity to challenge the factual basis for [the Secretary's] conclusion either that no violations occurred or that they did not affect the outcome of the election." Id., at 89. The court concluded that in that circumstance "plaintiff is entitled to a sufficiently specific statement of the factors upon which the Secretary relied in reaching his decision not to file suit so that plaintiff may have information concerning the allegations contained in his complaint." Id., at 90.

But the key allegation of plaintiff's verified complaint is paragraph 18 which alleges: "Notwithstanding the fact that the Defendant Secretary's investigation has substantiated the plaintiff's allegations and notwithstanding the fact that the irregularities charged affected the outcome of the election the Defendant Secretary refuses to file suit to set aside the election." Thus the Court of Appeals' opinion impermissibly authorizes the District Court to allow respondent the full trappings of an adversary trial of his challenge to the factual basis for the Secretary's decision.

IV

The District Court, pursuant to the Court of Appeals' order of remand, ordered the Secretary to furnish a statement of reasons. The petitioner did not cross-petition from the order, and petitioner and USWA conceded that the order was proper in this case. The Secretary furnished the statement and it is attached as an Appendix to this opinion. Its adequacy to support a conclusion whether the Secretary's decision was rationally based or was arbitrary and capricious, is a matter of initial determination by the District Court.

The judgment of the Court of Appeals is reversed insofar as it directs further proceedings consistent with the opinion of the Court of Appeals, and that court is directed to enter a new order that the proceedings on remand be consistent with this opinion of this Court.

Reversed and remanded.

[Mr. Chief Justice Burger's concurring opinion and Mr. Justice Rehnquist's opinion, concurring in part and dissenting in part, are omitted.]

S.E.C. v. Sloan

SUPREME COURT OF THE UNITED STATES, 1978.
436 U.S. 103, 98 S.CT. 1702, 56 L.ED.2D 148.

Mr. Justice REHNQUIST delivered the opinion of the Court.

Under the Securities Exchange Act of 1934 the Securities and Exchange Commission has the authority "summarily to suspend trading in any security . . . for a period not exceeding ten days" if "in its opinion the public interest and the protection of investors so require." Acting pursuant to this authority the Commission issued a series of consecutive orders suspending trading in the common stock of Canadian Javelin Ltd. ("CJL") for over a year. The Court of Appeals for the Second Circuit held that such a series of suspensions was beyond the scope of the Commission's statutory authority. 547 F.2d 152, 157–158 (1976). We granted certiorari to consider this important question, 434 U.S. 901, 98 S.Ct. 295, 54 L.Ed.2d 187 (1977), and, finding ourselves in basic agreement with the Court of Appeals, we affirm. We hold that even though there be a periodic redetermination of whether such action is required by "the public interest" and for "the protection of investors," the Commission is not empowered to issue, based upon a single set of circumstances, a series of summary orders which would suspend trading beyond the initial 10-day period. . . .

Turning to the merits, we note that this is not a case where the Commission, discovering the existence of a manipulative scheme affecting CJL stock, suspended trading for 10 days and then, upon the discovery of a second manipulative scheme or other improper activity unrelated to the first scheme, ordered a second 10-day suspension. Instead it is a case in which the Commission issued a series of summary suspension orders lasting over a year on the basis of evidence revealing a single, though likely sizable, manipulative scheme. Thus, the only question confronting us is whether, even upon a periodic redetermination of "necessity," the Commission is statutorily authorized to issue a series of summary suspension orders based upon a single set of events or circumstances which threaten an orderly market. This question must, in our opinion, be answered in the negative.

The first and most salient point leading us to this conclusion is the language of the statute. Section 12(k) authorizes the Commission "summarily to suspend trading in any security . . . *for a period not exceeding ten days* . . . ." 15 U.S.C.A. § 78*l*(k) (emphasis added). The Commission would have us read the underscored phrase as a limitation only upon the duration of a single suspension order. So read, the Commission could indefinitely suspend trading in a security without any hearing or other procedural safeguards as long as it redetermined every 10 days that suspension was required by the public interest and for the protection of investors. While perhaps not an impossible reading of the statute, we are persuaded it is not the most natural or logical one. The duration limitation rather appears on its face to be just that—a maximum time period for which trading can be suspended for any single set of circumstances.

Apart from the language of the statute, which we find persuasive in and of itself, there are other reasons to adopt this construction of the statute. In the first place, the power to summarily suspend trading in a security even for 10 days, without any notice, opportunity to be heard or findings based upon a record, is an awesome power with a potentially devastating impact on the issuer, its shareholders, and other investors. A clear mandate from Congress, such as that found in § 12(k), is necessary to confer this power. No less clear a mandate can be expected from Congress to authorize the Commission to extend, virtually without limit, these periods of suspension. But we find no such unmistakable mandate in § 12(k). Indeed, if anything, that section points in the opposite direction.

Other sections of the statute reinforce the conclusion that in this area Congress considered summary restrictions to be somewhat drastic and properly used only for very brief periods of time. When explicitly longer term, though perhaps temporary, measures are to be taken against some person, company or security, Congress invariably requires the Commission to give some sort of notice and opportunity to be heard. For example, § 12(j) of the Act authorizes the Commission, as it deems necessary for the protection of investors, to suspend the registration of a security for a period not exceeding 12 months if it makes certain findings *"on the record after notice and opportunity for hearing.... "* 15 U.S.C.A. § 78*l*(j) (emphasis added). Another section of the Act empowers the Commission to suspend broker-dealer registration for a period not exceeding 12 months upon certain findings made only *"on the record after notice and opportunity for hearing."* 15 U.S.C.A. § 78*o*(b)(4) (emphasis added). Still another section allows the Commission,

pending final determination whether a broker-dealer's registration should be revoked, to temporarily suspend that registration, but only *"after notice and opportunity for hearing."* 15 U.S.C.A. § 78*o*(b)(5) (emphasis added). Former § 15(b)(6), which dealt with the registration of broker-dealers, also lends support to the notion that as a general matter Congress meant to allow the Commission to take summary action only for the period specified in the statute when that action is based upon any single set of circumstances. That section allowed the Commission to summarily postpone the effective date of registration for 15 days, and then, *after appropriate notice and opportunity for hearing*, to continue that postponement pending final resolution of the matter. The section which replaced § 15(b)(6) even further underscores this general pattern. It requires the Commission to take some action—either granting the registration or instituting proceedings to determine whether registration should be denied—within 45 days. 15 U.S.C.A. § 78*o*(b) (1). In light of the explicit congressional recognition in other sections of the Act, both past and present, that any long term sanctions or any continuation of summary restrictions must be accompanied by notice and an opportunity for a hearing, it is difficult to read the silence in § 12(k) as an authorization for an extension of summary restrictions without such a hearing, as the Commission contends. The more plausible interpretation is that Congress did not intend the Commission to have the power to extend the length of suspensions under § 12(k) at all, much less to repeatedly extend such suspensions without any hearing....

[T]he Commission argues that for a variety of reasons Congress should be considered to have approved the Commission's construction of the statute as correct. Not only has Congress re-enacted the summary suspension power without disapproving the Commission's construction, but the

Commission participated in the drafting of much of this legislation and on at least one occasion made its views known to Congress in committee hearings. Furthermore, at least one committee indicated on one occasion that it understood and approved of the Commission's practice....

We are extremely hesitant to presume general congressional awareness of the Commission's construction based only upon a few isolated statements in the thousands of pages of legislative documents. That language in a committee report, without additional indication of more widespread congressional awareness, is simply not sufficient to invoke the presumption in a case such as this. For here its invocation would result in a construction of the statute which is not only at odds with the language of the section in question and the pattern of the statute taken as a whole, but is extremely far reaching in terms of the virtually untrammeled and unreviewable power it would vest in a regulatory agency....

In sum, had Congress intended the Commission to have the power to summarily suspend trading virtually indefinitely we expect that it could and would have authorized it more clearly than it did in § 12(k). The sweeping nature of that power supports this expectation. The absence of any truly persuasive legislative history to support the Commission's view, and the entire statutory scheme suggesting that in fact the Commission is not so empowered, reinforce our conclusion that the Court of Appeals was correct in concluding no such power exists. Accordingly, its judgment is

Affirmed.

Mr. Justice BRENNAN, with whom Mr. Justice MARSHALL joins, concurring in the judgment.

Although I concur in much of the Court's reasoning and in its holding that "the Commission is not empowered to issue, based upon a single set of circumstances, a series of summary orders which would suspend trading beyond the initial 10-day period," ante, at 1706, I cannot join the Court's opinion because of its omissions and unfortunate dicta.

I

The Court's opinion does not reveal how flagrantly abusive the Security and Exchange Commission's use of its § 12(k) authority has been. That section authorizes the Commission "summarily to suspend trading in any security . . . for a period not exceeding ten days. . . . " 15 U.S.C.A. § 78*l*(k). As the Court says, this language "is persuasive in and of itself" that 10 days is the "maximum time period for which trading can be suspended for any single set of circumstances." Ante, at 1709. But the Commission has used § 12(k), or its predecessor statutes, see ante, at 1705 n. 1, to suspend trading in a security for up to 13 *years*. And, although the 13-year suspension is an extreme example, the record is replete with suspensions lasting the better part of a year. See App. 184–211. I agree that § 12(k) is clear on its face and that it prohibits this administrative practice. But even if § 12(k) were unclear, a 13-year suspension, or even a one-year suspension as here, without notice or hearing so obviously violates fundamentals of due process and fair play that no reasonable individual could suppose that Congress intended to authorize such a thing.

Moreover, the SEC's procedural implementation of its § 12(k) power mocks any conclusion other than that the SEC simply could not care whether its § 12(k) orders are justified. So far as this record shows, the SEC never reveals the reasons for its suspension orders. To be sure, here respondent was able long after the fact to obtain some explanation through a Freedom of Information Act request, but even the information tendered was heavily excised and none of it even purports to state the reasoning of the Commissioners under whose authority § 12(k) orders issue. Nonetheless, when the SEC finally agreed to give respondent a hearing on the suspension of Canadian Javelin stock, it required respondent to state, in a verified petition (that is, *under oath*) why he thought the unrevealed conclusions of the SEC to be wrong. This is obscurantism run riot.

Accordingly while we today leave open the question whether the SEC could tack successive 10-day suspensions if this were necessary to meet first one and then a different emergent situation, I for one would look with great disfavor on any effort to tack suspension periods unless the SEC concurrently adopted a policy of stating its reasons for each suspension. Without such a statement of reasons, I fear our holding today will have no force since the SEC's administration of its suspension power will be reviewable, if at all, only by the circuitous and time-consuming path followed by respondent here....

Mr. Justice BLACKMUN, concurring in the judgment....

Here, the Commission indulged in 37 suspension orders, all but the last issued "quite bare of any emergency findings," to borrow Professor Loss' phrase. Beyond the opaque suggestion in an April 1975 Release, No. 11,383, that the Commission was awaiting the "dissemination of information concerning regulatory action by Canadian authorities," shareholders of CJL were given no hint why their securities were to be made nonnegotiable for over a year. Until April 22, 1976, see Release No. 12,361, the SEC provided no opportunity to shareholders to dispute the factual premises of a suspension, and, in the absence of any explanation by the Commission of the basis for its suspension orders, such a right to comment would be useless. As such, I conclude that the use of suspension orders in this case exceeded the limits of the Commission's discretion....

INFORMAL REMEDIES: OMBUDSMEN AND OTHERS

The heightened awareness of the significance of informal administrative action has given rise to a number of efforts to find new mechanisms to cope with its problems. Clearly the most important of these is the ombudsman, an institution of Swedish origin for handling citizen complaints against administration which has been widely emulated around the world. Since the ombudsman idea began to spread in the 1960s, an enormous amount of attention and study has been devoted to the institution. The American Bar Association has had an Ombudsman Committee for a number of years. A United States Association of Ombudsmen was established in 1978, as was the International Ombudsman Institute at the University of Alberta, Canada.

A 1982 survey indicated that there are hundreds of ombudsman and other complaint-handling systems in operation in dozens of countries around the world, including numerous such offices in U.S. states, territories, and cities.[32]

A kind of citizen complaint not usually handled by ombudsmen involves the activites of local police. The traditional manner of dealing with allegations of "police brutality" and like complaints has been through internal police

---

[32] International Ombudsman Institute, 11 *Ombudsman and Other Complaint-Handling Systems Survey* (July 1, 1981–June 30, 1982).

department disciplinary proceedings. But because "when five policemen hear a complaint against another policeman, the policeman is always right," [33] pressures for some independent form of review grew in the 1950s and 1960s. In a number of cities "police review boards" were created. Made up partly or wholly of private citizens, these bodies were charged with hearing and ruling on allegations of police irregularities. Even though these bodies usually only had the power to recommend sanctions against police rather than to impose penalties themselves, they met with considerable opposition and, for a variety of reasons, declined greatly in importance after the late 1960s.

An attempt to create a court-imposed scheme of independent review of police action, which might have served as a national model, was rejected by the Supreme Court in 1976. After the Philadelphia Police Advisory Board had been abolished by the city's mayor in 1969, a group of citizens brought suit in federal court alleging a pattern of unconstitutional police mistreatment of citizens. The Court ordered the defendants, Philadelphia city officials, to draft "a comprehensive program for dealing adequately with civilian complaints" and laid down "guidelines," a set of basic procedures, with which the program was required to comply. The Court of Appeals affirmed the District Court's order. But the Supreme Court voted five to three to reverse, holding that the District Court had exceeded its authority under the Civil Rights Act of 1871 (42 U.S.C.A. § 1983) and had contravened principles of federalism by granting an injunction in the circumstances involved in the case. *Rizzo* v. *Goode*, 423 U.S. 362, 96 S.Ct. 598, 46 L.Ed.2d 561 (1976).

---

[33] Arnold Trebach, *The Rationing of Justice* 215 (1964).

PART FOUR

Remedies

Chapter 9

Remedies Against Improper Administrative Acts

As chapter 4 made clear, there are a number of avenues available for obtaining judicial review, including both statutory review and the various forms of nonstatutory review. What we are concentrating on in this chapter are the *forms of relief* that a private party might seek with regard to administrative actions taken against him or her. To put the matter in its simplest form, a private party who considers an administrative act illegal or improper would want, depending upon the timing of the act, either (1) to prevent the action, or stop its being completed, or (2) to have it declared illegal and rescinded. If accomplishing these objectives still left the party injured by the governmental act, compensation might be sought from an official or from the government itself. These are the matters that will be discussed in this chapter, with special attention given to compensation to citizens injured by governmental acts. Another "remedy" of sorts, which has grown considerably in importance in recent years, has to do with the individual's right to gain information about governmental operations. This will be the subject of the next chapter.

DECLARATORY JUDGMENT AND INJUNCTIVE RELIEF

Many of the cases we have discussed in earlier chapters have involved either (1) or (2) above. For example, in *Chrysler Corporation* v. *Brown* in chapter 6 the corporation was seeking to prevent the release of the documents in question; that is, it was asking for *injunctive relief* or an *injunction*. *Marshall* v. *Barlow's* in chapter 5 also involved an effort to enjoin government action, in this instance "injunctive relief against the warrantless searches assertedly permitted by O.S.H.A." In *Dunlop* v. *Bachowski* in chapter 8, the appellant sought to have the court "declare the actions of the Defendant Secretary to be arbitrary and capricious and order him to file suit to set aside aforesaid election." Often plaintiffs will ask for both an injunction and a declaratory judgment. Thus, in

Ingraham v. *Wright* in chapter 7, both injunctive and declaratory relief were sought by the students in connection with the paddling incidents. The students also sued for damages, a subject that will be discussed below.

Even in connection with the doctrine of estoppel discussed in chapter 8, the objective is to prevent the government from acting in a way contrary to a private party's interest. Thus, for instance, in the *Merrill* case, Merrill, the Idaho farmer, sued to estop the government from denying the validity of the insurance contract. As pointed out in chapter 8, the law has changed considerably from the traditional rule that governmental units cannot be estopped. That rule apparently had its roots in the doctrine of sovereign immunity: "the king cannot be estopped, for it cannot be presumed the king would wrong any person." [1]

Sovereign immunity also has relevance to other kinds of suits against the government. In the past, for instance, sovereign immunity was often used successfully to bar suits against the federal government seeking a declaratory judgment, an injunction or other specific relief.[2] In 1976, however, Congress abolished this aspect of sovereign immunity by amending section 702 of the APA pursuant to a recommendation of the American Bar Association and the Administrative Conference of the United States, to provide that an action against the United States for relief other than money damages "shall not be dismissed nor relief therein denied on the ground that it is against the United States or that the United States is an indispensible party."

TORT SUITS AGAINST THE GOVERNMENT

Sovereign immunity still applies, however, in the area of damage suits against the government. Sovereign immunity is one of the common-law inheritances of the United States from England. The basis for the doctrine is the ancient notion that "the king can do no wrong." How a doctrine such as this, originally connected purely with the personality of the English king, every came to be applied in the United States is "one of the mysteries of legal evolution." [3] Whatever the explanation, the main principle of the doctrine, that the government cannot be sued without its consent, became a bedrock maxim of American jurisprudence. As Supreme Court Justice Oliver Wendell Holmes expressed the principle in a 1922 opinion: "The United States has not consented to be sued for torts, and therefore it cannot be said that in the legal sense the United States has been guilty of a tort. For a tort is a tort in a legal sense only because the law has made it so." [4]

Until the 1940s, the government had consented to be sued only in a very narrow range of circumstances. In most cases, sovereign immunity prevailed, and many victims who would have otherwise been entitled to compensation

---

[1] 15 *Halsbury's Laws of England* 248 (1956), quoting from Bacon's Abridgements, as quoted in Kenneth Culp Davis, *Administrative Law Text* 343 (3rd ed., 1972).

[2] See ibid., 494–507.

[3] Edwin M. Borchard, "Governmental Liability in Tort," 34 *Yale Law Journal* 4 (1924).

[4] *U.S.* v. *Thompson*, 257 U.S. 419, 433, 42 S.Ct. 159, 161, 66 L.Ed. 299, 303 (1922).

were left empty-handed because the harm visited upon them was inflicted by the government. Their only recourse in such cases was either a suit against the wrongdoing official (such suits will be discussed below) or the congressional enactment of a private bill giving relief to the individual as a matter of legislative grace. The latter course was a time-consuming and unsure method, which depended greatly on one's having a powerful "angel" in Congress who could carry the fight for a private bill through both houses of the legislature.

A long effort by opponents of sovereign immunity culminated in 1946 in the adoption by Congress of the Federal Tort Claims Act, 60 Stat. 842. The key provision of the Act reads as follows:

> The United States shalll be liable, respecting the provisions of this title relating to tort claims, in the same manner and to the same extent as a private individual under like circumstances....

The direct implication of this passage is that the regular rules of tort law, including the basic requirement of negligence or fault on the part of the wrongdoer, apply to the government. Since these rules are part of state law, not federal law, this meant that governmental liability would depend to some extent on the law of the state in which the tortious act took place.

What caused controversy was the strictness with which the courts interpreted this passage. What the courts initially said, in effect, was that there could be governmental liability only in those instances in which private persons traditionally have been found liable. Thus, in the *Feres* case, which involved injuries inflicted upon soldiers on active duty by other members of the armed services, the Supreme Court could find no analogy in the tort relationships between private individuals, and so it rejected the claims of the soldiers: "We find no parallel liability before and we think no new one has been created by this act. Its effect is to waive immunity from recognized causes of action and was not to visit the Government with novel and unprecedented liabilities." *Feres* v. *United States*, 340 U.S. 135, 142, 71 S.Ct. 153, 157, 95 L.Ed. 152, 159 (1950).

Besides the main provision of the Federal Tort Claims Act discussed above, the act contains thirteen specific exceptions—circumstances in which there can be no governmental liability. Of these, two stand out as of greatest importance. The first of these bars tort actions based on certain intentional torts by public officers such as libel, slander, misrepresentation, deceit and others.[5] The second exception, which has the more far-reaching implications, is the so-called "discretionary-function" exception. It states in part that the act does not extend to claims "based upon the exercise or performance or the failure to exercise or perform a discretionary function or duty on the part of a

---

[5] A 1974 amendment to the Federal Tort Claims Act reduced considerably the number of intentional torts in this exception. The legislation provided that the government would be liable for claims based on acts of U.S. investigative or law enforcement officers involving "assault, battery, false imprisonment, false arrest, abuse of process or malicious prosecution." P.L. 93–253, 88 Stat. 50. The adoption of the amendment followed a particularly shocking act of forced entry and unauthorized search—at the wrong address—by federal narcotics agents. For a vivid description of the incident, see J. Boger, M. Gitenstein and P. Verkuil, "The Federal Tort Claims Act Intentional Tort Amendment: An Interpretive Analysis," 54 *North Carolina Law Review* 497, 500–501 (1976).

federal agency or an employee of the Government, whether or not the discretion involved be abused."

The single most important case to be decided under the Federal Tort Claims Act was *Dalehite* v. *United States*. This case is significant not only because of the huge losses involved (560 deaths, 3000 persons injured, personal and property claims totalling two hundred million dollars), but also because of the significant pronouncements concerning the interpretation of the statute made by the Supreme Court.

Dalehite v. United States

SUPREME COURT OF THE UNITED STATES, 1953.
346 U.S. 15, 73 S.CT. 956, 97 L.ED. 1427.

[As a part of the foreign aid program after World War II, the United States government decided to produce fertilizer for shipment to Europe and elsewhere. Production took place at deactivated ordnance plants used during the war. The fertilizer was manufactured under plans developed by responsible governmental officials, but actual operation of the plants was by private companies which had entered into contracts with the government. The basic ingredient of the fertilizer (FGAN—fertilizer grade ammonium nitrate) was ammonium nitrate, long used as a component in explosives. In undertaking to manufacture the fertilizer, government officials drew up detailed specifications regarding its production.

In April, 1947, almost three-thousand tons of FGAN were loaded onto two ships in the harbor at Texas City, Texas. A fire started and, as the Supreme Court put it in summing up the accident, "[b]oth ships exploded and much of the city was leveled and many people were killed."

The suit brought by the relatives of Henry G. Dalehite, who was killed in the explosion, represented some three-hundred personal and property claims against the U.S. government. The U.S. District Court ruled against the government and awarded damages of $75,000 to each of the individual plaintiffs. The Court of Appeals reversed this judgment, and the case came to the Supreme Court on certiorari.]

Mr. Justice REED delivered the opinion of the Court. . . .

Since no individual acts of negligence could be shown, the suits for damages that resulted necessarily predicated government liability on the participation of the United States in the manufacture and the transportation of FGAN. Following the disaster of course, no one could fail to be impressed with the blunt fact that FGAN would explode. In sum petitioners charged that the Federal Government had brought liability on itself for the catastrophe by using a material in fertilizer which had been used as an ingredient of explosives for so long that industry knowledge gave notice that other combinations of ammonium nitrate with other material might explode. The negligence charged was that the United States, without definitive investigation of FGAN properties, shipped or permitted shipment to a congested area without warning of the possibility of explosion under certain conditions. The District Court accepted this theory. His judgment was based on a series of findings of causal negligence which, for our purposes, can be roughly divided into three kinds—those which held that the Government had been careless in drafting and adopting the fertilizer export plan as a whole, those which found specific negligence in various phases of the manufacturing process and those which emphasized official dereliction of duty in failing to police the shipboard loading. The Court of Appeals *en banc* unanimously reversed....

I. The Federal Tort Claims Act was passed by the Seventy-ninth Congress in 1946 as Title IV of the Legislative Reorganization Act, 60 Stat. 842, after nearly thirty years of congressional consideration. It was the offspring of a feeling that the Government should assume the obligation to pay damages for the misfeasance of employees in carrying out its work. And the private bill device was notoriously clumsy. Some simplified recovery procedure for the mass of claims was imperative. This Act was Congress' solution, affording instead easy and simple access to the federal courts for torts within its scope.

The meaning of the governmental regulatory function exception from suits, § 1680(a) shows most clearly in the history of the Tort Claims Bill in the Seventy-seventh Congress. The Seventy-ninth, which passed the Act, held no hearings on the Act. Instead, it integrated the language of the Seventy-seventh Congress, which had first considered the exception, into the Legislative Reorganization Act as Title IV....

The legislative history indicates that while Congress desired to waive the Government's immunity from actions for injuries to person and property occasioned by the tortious conduct of its agents acting within their scope of business, it was not contemplated that the Government should be subject to liability arising from acts of a governmental nature or function. Section 2680(a) draws this distinction. Uppermost in the collective mind of Congress were the ordinary common-law torts. Of these, the example which is reiterated in the course of the repeated proposals for submitting the United States to tort liability, is "negligence in the operation of vehicles." On the other hand the Committee's reports explain the boundaries of the sovereign immunity waived, as defined by this § 2680 exception, with one paragraph which appears time and again after 1942, and in the House Report of the Congress that adopted in § 2680(a) the limitation in the language proposed for the 77th Congress. It was adopted by the Committee in almost the language of the Assistant Attorney General's explanation. This paragraph characterizes the general exemption as "a highly important exception, intended to preclude any possibility that the bill might be construed to authorize suit for damages against the Government growing out of authorized activity, such as a flood control or irrigation project, where no negligence on the part of any government agent is shown, and the only ground for the suit is the contention that the same conduct by a private individual would be tortious.... The bill is not intended to authorize a suit for damages to test the validity of or provide a remedy on account of such discretionary acts even though negligently performed and involving an abuse of discretion."

II. Turning to the interpretation of the Act, our reasoning as to its applicability to this disaster starts from the accepted jurisprudential principle that no action lies against the United States unless the legislature has authorized it. The language of the Act makes the United States liable "respecting the provisions of this title relating to tort claims, in the same manner and to the same extent as a private individual under like circumstances". 28 U.S.C. § 2674, 28 U.S.C.A. § 2674. This statute is another example of the progressive relaxation by legislative enactments of the rigor of the immunity rule. Through such statutes that change the law, organized government expresses the social purposes that motivate its legislation. Of course, these modifications are entitled to a construction that will accomplish their aim, that is, one that will carry out the legislative purpose of allowing suits against the Government for negligence with due regard for the statutory exceptions to that policy. In interpreting the exceptions to the generality of the grant, courts include only those circumstances which are within the words and reason of the exception. They cannot do less since petitioners obtain their "right to sue from Congress [and they] necessarily must take [that right] subject to such restrictions as have been imposed." Federal Housing Administration v. Burr, 309 U.S. 242, 251, 60 S.Ct. 488, 493, 84 L.Ed. 724.

So, our decisions have interpreted the Act to require clear relinquishment of sovereign immunity to give jurisdiction for tort actions. Where jurisdiction was clear, though, we have allowed recovery despite arguable procedural objections.

One only need read § 2680 in its entirety to conclude that Congress exercised care to protect the Government from claims, however negligently caused, that affected the governmental functions. Negligence in administering the Alien Property Act, or establishing a quarantine, assault, libel, fiscal operations, etc., were barred. An analysis of § 2680(a), the exception with which we are concerned, emphasizes the congressional purpose to except the acts here charged as negligence from the authorization to sue. It will be noted from the form of the section, see 346 U.S. 18, 73 S.Ct. 959, supra, that there are two phrases describing the excepted acts of government employees. The first deals with acts or omissions of government employees, exercising due care in carrying out statutes or regulations whether valid or not. It bars tests by tort action of the legality of statutes and regulations. The second is applicable in this case. It excepts acts of discretion in the performance of governmental functions or duty "whether or not the discretion involved be abused." Not only agencies of government are covered but all employees exercising discretion. It is clear that the just-quoted clause as to abuse connotes both negligence and wrongful acts in the exercise of the discretion because the Act itself covers only "negligent or wrongful act or omission of any employee," "within the scope of his office" "where the

United States, if a private person, would be liable." 28 U.S.C. § 1346(b), 28 U.S.C.A. § 1346(b). The exercise of discretion could not be abused without negligence or a wrongful act. The Committee reports, note 19, supra, show this. They say § 2680(a) is to preclude action for "abuse of discretionary authority—whether or not negligence is alleged to have been involved." They speak of excepting a "remedy on account of such discretionary acts even though negligently performed and involving an abuse of discretion."

So we know that the draftsmen did not intend it to relieve the Government from liability for such common-law torts as an automobile collision caused by the negligence of an employee, see 346 U.S. 28, 73 S.Ct. 964, supra, of the administering agency. We know it was intended to cover more than the administration of a statute or regulation because it appears disjunctively in the second phrase of the section. The "discretion" protected by the section is not that of the judge—a power to decide within the limits of positive rules of law subject to judicial review. It is the discretion of the executive or the administrator to act according to one's judgment of the best course, a concept of substantial historical ancestry in American law.

This contention is met by petitioners with these arguments:

> To accept the foregoing close and narrow reasoning [of the Court of Appeals], which is unrealistic, is to say that a program and undertaking and operation, however like it may be to some private corporation or operation such as the manufacture of an explosive, is nevertheless throughout discretionary, if the concept thereof is born in discretion. . . .
>
> The negligence involved here was far removed from any Cabinet decision to provide aid to Germans and Japanese. . . . It is directed only to the mistakes of judgment and the careless oversight of Government employees who were carrying out a program of manufacturing and shipping fertilizer and who

failed to concern themselves as a reasonable man should with the safety of others.... Congress delegated to Ordnance no "discretion" thus to commit wrong.

It is unnecessary to define, apart from this case, precisely where discretion ends. It is enough to hold, as we do, that the "discretionary function or duty" that cannot form a basis for suit under the Tort Claims Act includes more than the initiation of programs for activities. It also includes determinations made by executives or administrators in establishing plans, specifications or schedules of operations. Where there is room for policy judgment and decision there is discretion. It necessarily follows that acts of subordinates in carrying out the operations of government in accordance with official directions cannot be actionable. If it were not so, the protection of § 2680(a) would fail at the time it would be needed, that is, when a subordinate performs or fails to perform a causal step, each action or nonaction being directed by the superior, exercising, perhaps abusing, discretion.

III. That the cabinet-level decision to institute the fertilizer export program was a discretionary act is not seriously disputed. Nor do we think that there is any doubt that the need for further experimentation with FGAN to determine the possibility of its explosion, under conditions likely to be encountered in shipping, and its combustibility was a matter to be determined by the discretion of those in charge of the production. Obviously, having manufactured and shipped the commodity FGAN for more than three years without even minor accidents, the need for further experimentation was a matter of discretion. Reported instances of heating or bag damage were investigated and experiments, to the extent deemed necessary, were carried on. In dealing with ammonium nitrate in any form, the industry, and of course Ordnance, was well aware that care must be taken. The best indication of the care necessary came from experience in FGAN production. The TVA had produced FGAN since 1943, and their experience, as we have indicated, 73 S.Ct. 960, 961, was not only available to Ordnance but was used by them to the most minute detail. It is, we think, just such matters of governmental duties that were excepted from the Act....

[The Court then turns to the specific acts of negligence charged in the manufacture of FGAN, including the general plan of manufacture, the temperature for bagging of the material, the type of bagging, and its labeling. It finds that all of these were carried out in accordance with the detailed specifications drawn up by governmental officials.]

In short, the alleged "negligence" does not subject the Government to liability. The decisions held culpable were all responsibly made at a planning rather than operational level and involved considerations more or less important to the practicability of the Government's fertilizer program.

"There must be knowledge of a danger, not merely possible, but probable," MacPherson v. Buick Motor Co., 217 N.Y. 382, 389, 111 N.E. 1050, 1053, L.R.A. 1919F, 696. Here, nothing so startling was adduced. The entirety of the evidence compels the view that FGAN was a material that former experience showed could be handled safely in the manner it was handled here. Even now no one has suggested that the ignition of FGAN was anything but a complex result of the interacting factors of mass, heat, pressure and composition.

IV. The findings of negligence on the part of the Coast Guard in failing to supervise the storage of the FGAN, and in fighting the fire after it started, were rejected by a majority of the Court of Appeals. 197 F.2d 777, 780, 781. We do not enter into an examination of these factual findings. We prefer, again, to rest our decision on the Act.

The District Court's holding that the Coast Guard and other agencies were negligent in failing to prevent the fire by regulating storage or loading of the fertilizer in some different fashion is like his specific citations of negligence discussed above. They are classically within the exception. "The power to adopt regulations or bylaws . . . for the preservation of the public health, or to pass ordinances prescribing the regulating the duties of policemen and firemen . . . are generally regarded as discretionary, because, in their nature, they are legislative." Weightman v. Corporation of Washington, 1 Black 39, 49, 17 L.Ed. 52. The courts have traditionally refused to question the judgments on which they are based.

As to the alleged failure in fighting the fire, we think this too without the Act. The Act did not create new causes of action where none existed before.

> . . . the liability assumed by the Government here is that created by "all the circumstances," not that which a few of the circumstances might create. We find no parallel liability before, and we think no new one has been created by, this Act. Its effect is to waive immunity from recognized causes of action and was not to visit the Government with novel and unprecedented liabilities. Feres v. United States, 340 U.S. 135, 142, 71 S.Ct. 153, 157, 95 L.Ed. 152.

It did not change the normal rule that an alleged failure or carelessness of public firemen does not create private actionable rights. Our analysis of the question is determined by what was said in the Feres case. See 28 U.S.C. §§ 1346 and 2674, 28 U.S.C.A. §§ 1346, 2674. The Act, as was there stated, limited United States liability to "the same manner and to the same extent as a private individual under like circumstances." 28 U.S.C. § 2674, 28 U.S.C.A. § 2674. Here, as there, there is no analogous liability; in fact, if anything is doctrinally sanctified in the law of torts it is the immunity of communities and other public bodies for injuries due to fighting fire.

This case, then, is much stronger than Feres. We pointed out only one state decision which denied government liability for injuries incident to service to one in the state militia. That cities, by maintaining firefighting organizations, assume no liability for personal injuries resulting from their lapses is much more securely entrenched. The Act, since it relates to claims to which there is no analogy in general tort law, did not adopt a different rule. To impose liability for the alleged nonfeasance of the Coast Guard would be like holding the United States liable in tort for failure to impose a quarantine for, let us say, an outbreak of foot-and-mouth disease.

V. Though the findings of specific and general negligence do not support a judgment of government liability, there is yet to be disposed of some slight residue of theory of absolute liability without fault. This is reflected both in the District Court's finding that the FGAN constituted a nuisance, and in the contention of petitioner here. We agree with the six judges of the Court of Appeals, 197 F.2d 771, 776, 781, 786, that the Act does not extend to such situations, though of course well known in tort law generally. It is to be invoked only on a "negligent or wrongful act or omission" of an employee. Absolute liability, of course, arises irrespective of how the tortfeasor conducts himself; it is imposed automatically when any damages are sustained as a result of the decision to engage in the dangerous activity. The degree of care used in performing the activity is irrelevant to the application of that doctrine. But the statute requires a negligent act. So it is our judgment that liability does not arise by virtue either of United States ownership of an "inherently dangerous commodity" or property, or of engaging in an "extra hazardous" activity. United States v. Hull, 1 Cir., 195 F.2d 64, 67.

Petitioners rely on the word "wrongful" though as showing that something in addition to negligence is covered. This argument, as we have pointed out, does not override the fact that the Act does require some brand of misfeasance or nonfeasance, and so could not extend to liability without fault; in addition, the legislative history of the word indicates clearly that it was not added to the jurisdictional grant with any overtones of the absolute liability theory. Rather, Committee discussion indicates that it had a much narrower inspiration: "trespasses" which might not be considered strictly negligent. Hearings before a Subcommittee of the Senate Committee on the Judiciary on S. 2690, 76th Cong., 3d Sess., 43–44. Had an absolute liability theory been intended to have been injected into the Act, much more suitable models could have been found, e.g., the Suits in Admiralty Act, 41 Stat. 525, 46 U.S.C. §§ 742–743, 46 U.S.C.A. §§ 742, 743, in regard to maintenance and cure.

Affirmed.

Mr. Justice DOUGLAS and Mr. Justice CLARK took no part in the consideration or decision of this case.

Mr. Justice JACKSON, joined by Mr. Justice BLACK and Mr. Justice FRANKFURTER, dissenting. . . .

We think that the statutory language, the reliable legislative history, and the common-sense basis of the rule regarding municipalities, all point to a useful and proper distinction preserved by the statute other than that urged by the Government. When an official exerts governmental authority in a manner which legally binds one or many, he is acting in a way in which no private person could. Such activities do and are designed to affect, often deleteriously, the affairs of individuals, but courts have long recognized the public policy that such official shall be controlled solely by the statutory or administrative mandate and not by the added threat of private damage suits. For example, the Attorney General will not be liable for false arrest in circumstances where a private person performing the same act would be liable, and such cases could be multiplied. The official's act might inflict just as great an injury and might be just as wrong as that of the private person, but the official is not answerable. The exception clause of the Tort Claims Act protects the public treasury where the common law would protect the purse of the acting public official.

But many acts of government officials deal only with the housekeeping side of federal activities. The Government, as landowner, as manufacturer, as shipper, as warehouseman, as shipowner and operator, is carrying on activities indistinguishable from those performed by private persons. In this area, there is no good reason to stretch the legislative text to immunize the Government or its officers from responsibility for their acts, if done without appropriate care for the safety of others. Many official decisions even in this area may involve a nice balancing of various considerations, but this is the same kind of balancing which citizens do at their peril and we think it is not within the exception of the statute.

The Government's negligence here was not in policy decisions of a regulatory or governmental nature, but involved actions akin to those of a private manufacturer, contractor, or shipper. Reading the discretionary exception as we do, in a way both workable and faithful to legislative intent, we would hold that the Government was liable under these circumstances. Surely a statute so long debated was meant to embrace more than traffic accidents. If not, the ancient and discredited doctrine that "The King can do no wrong" has not been uprooted; it has merely been amended to read, "The King can do only little wrongs."

The *Dalehite* decision was eventually "appealed" to Congress, where relief was granted by means of private bills.[6] When the last claim had been processed in 1957, 1394 awards, totaling nearly $17,000,000 had been made.[7]

Effects of the Dalehite Case

Some of the rules laid down in the *Dalehite* case were modified in later cases. In *Indian Towing Co.* v. *United States*, 350 U.S. 61, 76 S.Ct. 122, 100 L.Ed. 48 (1955), the company sued the government for damages to one of its tugboats which ran aground because of the alleged negligence of the Coast Guard in allowing the light in a lighthouse to become extinguished. The government argued in defense that a close analogy to the extinguishing of a lighthouse would be the faulty operation of a traffic light and that since, under the municipal law of Louisiana (in whose waters the accident happened), the operation of traffic lights was a "governmental" function, for which there could be no liability, the same should apply to the present case. But the Supreme Court refused to be pushed into the " 'governmental-non-governmental' quagmire," referring to this distinction as "inherently unsound." The Court also rejected the contentions of the *Feres* and *Dalehite* cases that there can be no liability for negligence in the performance of activities which private persons do not perform. The majority opinion stated:

> [I]f the United States were to permit the operation of private lighthouses—not at all inconceivable—the Government's basis of differentiation would be gone and the negligence charged in this case would be actionable. . . . [A]ll Government activity is inescapably "uniquely governmental" in that it is performed by the Government. . . . On the other hand, it is hard to think of any governmental activity on the "operational level," . . . which is "uniquely governmental," in the sense that its kind has not at one time or another been, or could not conceivably be, privately performed.

The decision in *Indian Towing Co.* did not clear up the meaning of the exception for discretionary functions, but it came to some different conclusions concerning discretion. It was held that once the Coast Guard "exercised its discretion" to maintain the lighthouse light, "and engendered reliances on the guidance afforded by the light, it was obligated to use due care to make certain that the light was kept in working order." [8]

A similar conclusion was reached in the lower court case of *United States* v. *Union Trust Co.*, 221 F.2d 62 (D.C.Cir.1954), affirmed 350 U.S. 907, 76 S.Ct. 192, 100 L.Ed. 799 (1955). This case was brought against the government as a

---

[6] P.L. 378, 69 Stat. 707 (1955).

[7] Milton Mackay, "Death on the Waterfront," *The Saturday Evening Post* 100 (October 26, 1957). The irony of this result is that the Federal Tort Claims Act was adopted, in part, to obviate the need for private legislation. The Act was adopted as Title IV of the broader Congressional Reorganization Act of 1946, "an Act to provide for increased efficiency in the legislative branch of the government." P.L. 601, 60 Stat. 812 (1946).

[8] It is important to note that the Supreme Court did not hold the government liable to pay damages to the Indian Towing Company. It merely stated that the immunity defenses the government sought to assert would not be allowed. When the case was finally tried on the merits, the plaintiffs did not succeed in persuading the lower court that the government was negligent. See *Indian Towing Company* v. *United States*, 276 F.2d 300 (5th Cir.1960).

result of a collision of two airplanes caused when a government control tower operator directed the two planes to land on the same airstrip at the same time. The government contended that the tower operators' duties involved discretion, and that, therefore, the government should be exempted from liability. The court held, however, that "discretion was exercised when it was decided to operate the tower, but the tower personnel had no discretion to operate it negligently." And in 1963 the Supreme Court partially denied another aspect of the *Dalehite* and *Feres* cases by holding that prisoners in federal prisons could recover from the government for injuries sustained while in prison, even though no individual would run a prison and no analogous liability had existed before the adoption of the Federal Tort Claims Act.[9]

An aspect of *Dalehite* that remains of great importance is the planning level-operational level distinction articulated by the majority opinion. To the objection that the chain of events which led to the disaster may have been "born in discretion," but that the tortious acts themselves (the packaging, handling and loading of the fertilizer, the fighting of the fire, and so on) were not discretionary, the Court stated that the decisions upon which these actions were based "were all responsibly made at a planning rather than operational level." This distinction, whether or not it was applied correctly in *Dalehite* (and some commentators argue that it was not), remains to this day a cornerstone of the interpretation of the discretionary function exception.

Interpreting the Federal Tort Claims Act

In addition to *Dalehite* and its direct progeny, thousands [10] of cases involving the Federal Tort Claims Act have been decided by the courts. The following are three recent examples that suggest something of the wide range of activity which exposes the government to potential liability. They represent decisions from all three levels of the federal courts (U.S. Supreme Court, U.S. court of appeals, and U.S. district court). And, while each case involves the assertion of substantial injury or loss, one can distinguish levels of seriousness in the harm suffered. The defects in the house not detected by the government official in the first case, and the homicide attributed to the lack of care of government doctors in the second basically involved injury to single individuals or small numbers of people. The harm allegedly resulting from nuclear testing in the southwestern part of the country affected a large number of persons, and potential money damages could be substantial. Claims of this magnitude are no doubt, in part, behind recent efforts to place limits on governmental liability—a matter discussed later in this chapter. Note that in all three of the cases set forth below the government asserts as a defense that its activity fell within one of the exceptions to the Federal Tort Claims Act.

---

[9] *United States* v. *Muniz*, 374 U.S. 150, 83 S.Ct. 1850, 10 L.Ed.2d 805 (1963).

[10] According to Peter Schuck, civil suits under the Federal Tort Claims Act were recorded separately only until the late 1970s. At that time such actions were running at over two-thousand per year. Schuck, *Suing Government* 201 (1983). Kenneth Culp Davis discusses the liability of governmental entities and their officers more broadly and concludes: "The new reality is unquestionably that suits for damages against governments and their employees have become a major part of the total legal system. Suits filed in district courts under 42 U.S.C. § 1983 grew from 296 in 1961 to 8,443 in 1974, and 38,162 in 1983." Davis, 5 *Administrative Law Treatise* xiv (2nd ed., 1984).

Block v. Neal

SUPREME COURT OF THE UNITED STATES, 1983.
460 U.S. 289, 103 S.CT. 1089, 75 L.ED.2D 67.

[Onilia Neal obtained a loan from the Farmers Home Administration (FmHA), a governmental agency, for the construction of a prefabricated house. She contracted with Home Marketing Associates Inc. to build the House, which was to be constructed in conformance with plans approved by FmHA. The contract granted FmHA the right to inspect the house with regard to materials and workmanship, and to reject anything found to be defective. Three inspections were made by an FmHA official, who issued a final report indicating that construction was in accordance with agency specifications.

Shortly after moving in, Neal complained about problems in the house. Other FmHA officials, after inspection, identified fourteen construction defects, including the heat pump, the plumbing, the floor, and the roof. The builder refused FmHA's request to correct the defects, and Neal turned to FmHA to pay for the repair. When it declined to do so, Neal sued under the Federal Tort Claims Act. The district court dismissed the suit, but the court of appeals reversed. The Supreme Court reviewed the case on certiorari.]

Justice MARSHALL delivered the opinion of the Court. . . .

The question before us is a narrow one. The Government argues only that respondent's claim is a claim of "misrepresentation" within the meaning of § 2680(h). . . . Thus, we need not decide precisely what Neal must prove in order to prevail on her negligence claim, nor even whether such a claim lies. Nor are we called on to consider whether recovery is barred by any other provision of the Tort Claims Act, including the exception for any action "based upon the exercise or performance or the failure to exercise or perform a discretionary function." Id.,

§ 2680(a). Finally, we are not asked to determine whether the administrative remedy created by the Housing Act of 1949, 42 U.S.C. § 1479(c) (1976 ed., Supp. IV), provides the exclusive remedy against the Government for damages attributable to the negligence of FmHA officials.

The scope of the "misrepresentation" exception to the Tort Claims Act was the focus of this Court's decision in *United States* v. *Neustadt*, 366 U.S. 696, 81 S.Ct. 1294, 6 L.Ed.2d 614 (1961). Neustadt purchased a house in reliance on an appraisal undertaken by the Federal Housing Administration (FHA) for mortgage insurance purposes. After he took up residence, cracks appeared in the ceilings and walls of his house. The cracks were caused by structural defects that had not been noticed by the FHA appraiser during the course of his inspection. Neustadt sued the Government under the Tort Claims Act to recover the difference between the fair market value of the property and the purchase price. He alleged that the FHA had negligently inspected and appraised the property, and that he had justifiably relied on the appraisal in paying a higher price for the house than he would otherwise have paid.

This Court held that the claim in *Neustadt* arose out of "misrepresentation" under § 2680(h). We determined initially that § 2680(h) applies to claims arising out of negligent, as well as intentional, misrepresentation. 366 U.S., at 703–706, 81 S.Ct., at 1298–1300. This Court found that Neustadt's claim that the Government had breached its "duty to use due care in obtaining and communicating information upon which [the plaintiff] may reasonably be expected to rely in the conduct of his economic affairs," merely restated the traditional legal definition of "negligent misrepresentation" as would have been understood by Congress when the Tort Claims Act was enacted. Id., at 706–707, 81 S.Ct., at 1300–1301. Finally, we examined the National Housing Act of 1934, as amended, under which the FHA had conducted its appraisal, and found nothing to indicate "that Congress intended, in a case such as this, to limit or suspend the application of the 'misrepresentation' exception of the Tort Claims Act." Id., at 708–710, 81 S.Ct., at 1301–1302.

We cannot agree with the Government that this case is controlled by *Neustadt*. As we recognized in that decision, the essence of an action for misrepresentation, whether negligent or intentional, is the communication of misinformation on which the recipient relies. The gravamen of the action against the Government in *Neustadt* was that the plaintiff was misled by a "Statement of FHA Appraisal" prepared by the Government. Neustadt alleged no injury that he would have suffered independently of his reliance on the erroneous appraisal. Because the alleged conduct that was the basis of his negligence claim was in essence a negligent misrepresentation, Neustadt's action was barred under the "misrepresentation" exception.

Section 2680(h) thus relieves the Government of tort liability for pecuniary injuries which are wholly attributable to reliance of the Government's negligent misstatements. As a result, the statutory exception undoubtedly preserves sovereign immunity with respect to a broad range of government actions. But it does not bar negligence actions which focus not on the Government's failure to use due care in communicating information, but rather on the Government's breach of a different duty.

In this case, unlike *Neustadt*, the Government's misstatements are not essential to plaintiff's negligence claim. The Court of Appeals found that to prevail under the Good Samaritan doctrine, Neal must show that FmHA officials voluntarily undertook to supervise construction of her house;

that the officials failed to use due care in carrying out their supervisory activity; and that she suffered some pecuniary injury proximately caused by FmHA's failure to use due care. FmHA's duty to use due care to ensure that the builder adhere to previously approved plans and cure all defects before completing construction is distinct from any duty to use due care in communicating information to respondent. And it certainly does not "appea[r] beyond doubt" that the only damages alleged in the complaint to be caused by FmHA's conduct were those attributable to Neal's reliance on FmHA inspection reports. *Conley v. Gibson*, 355 U.S. 41, 45–46, 78 S.Ct. 99, 101–102, 2 L.Ed.2d 80 (1957). Neal's factual allegations would be consistent with proof at trial that Home Marketing would never have turned the house over to Neal in its defective condition if FmHA officials had pointed out defects to the builder while construction was still underway, rejected defective materials and workmanship, or withheld final payment until the builder corrected all defects.

Of course, in the absence of the "misrepresentation" exception to the Tort Claims Act, respondent could also have brought a claim for negligent misrepresentation to recover for any injury caused by her misplaced reliance on advice provided by FmHA officials and on the FmHA inspection reports. Common to both the misrepresentation and the negligence claim would be certain factual and legal questions, such as whether FmHA officials used due care in inspecting Neal's home while it was under construction. But the partial overlap between these two tort actions does not support the conclusion that if one is excepted under the Tort Claims Act, the other must be as well. Neither the language nor history of the Act suggest that when one aspect of the Government's conduct is not actionable under the "misrepresentation" exception, a claimant is barred from pursuing a distinct claim arising out of other aspects of the Government's conduct. " 'The exemption of the sovereign from suit involves hardship enough where consent has been withheld. We are not to add to its rigor by refinement of construction where consent has been announced.' " *United States* v. *Aetna Surety Co.*, 338 U.S. 366, 383, 70 S.Ct. 207, 216, 94 L.Ed. 171 (1949), quoting *Anderson* v. *Hayes Constr. Co.*, 243 N.Y. 140, 147, 153 N.E. 28, 29–30 (1926) (Cardozo, J.). Any other interpretation would encourage the Government to shield itself completely from tort liability by adding misrepresentations to whatever otherwise actionable torts it commits.

We therefore hold that respondent's claim against the government for negligence by FmHA officials in supervising construction of her house does not "aris[e] out of . . . misrepresentation" within the meaning of 28 U.S.C. § 2680(h). The Court of Appeals properly concluded that Neal's claim is not barred by this provision of the Tort Claims Act because Neal does not seek to recover on the basis of misstatements made by FmHA officials. Although FmHA in this case may have undertaken both to supervise construction of Neal's house and to provide Neal information regarding the progress of construction, Neal's action is based solely on the former conduct. Accordingly, the judgment of the Court of Appeals is

Affirmed.

THE CHIEF JUSTICE concurs in the judgment.

Liability for Failure to Warn

The next two cases fall into a general category that might be called "failure to warn." This is a developing area of the law in which the principles are not yet well-settled. The first case involves failure to warn concerning a potentially dangerous person. A sense of the complexity of this problem can be gained from examining the growing body of scholarly literature. See, for instance, Jones, "Annotation: Liability of Governmental Officer or Entity for Failure to Warn or Notify of Release of Potentially Dangerous Individual from Custody," 12 *ALR* 4th 722 (1982).

Jablonski by Pahls v. United States

UNITED STATES COURT OF APPEALS, NINTH CIRCUIT, 1983.
712 F.2D 391 (1983).

Before WRIGHT, WALLACE, and KENNEDY, Circuit Judges.

WALLACE, Circuit Judge:

Meghan Jablonski (Meghan), a minor, brought suit under the Federal Tort Claims Act, 28 U.S.C. §§ 1346(b) & 2671–80 (the Act), for the wrongful death of her mother, Melinda Kimball. Kimball was murdered by the man she was living with, Phillip Jablonski. Meghan charged that psychiatrists at the Loma Linda Veterans Administration Hospital (the hospital) committed malpractice proximately resulting in her mother's death. The case was tried before the district judge who decided in favor of Meghan.

On appeal, the government first claims that Meghan's suit is barred by subsection 2680(h) of the Act because the suit arose out of an assault and battery. 28 U.S.C. § 2680(h). Second, it argues that the suit is barred under subsection 2680(a) of the Act because the claims arose out of the performance by federal employees of discretionary functions. Id. § 2680(a). Finally, the government contends that, under California law, no duty was owed to Meghan, that Kimball was not a foreseeable victim of Jablonski's violent tendencies, and that the alleged negligence was not the proximate cause of Kimball's death. We reject all of the government's contentions and affirm the judgment of the district court.

I

On July 7, 1978, Jablonski threatened Isobel Pahls, Kimball's mother, with a sharp object and apparently attempted to rape her. Pahls had also been the object of obscene telephone calls and other malicious acts which the police believed had been committed by Jablonski. Although Pahls did not file formal charges against Jablonski, she discussed with the police the possibility of his receiving psychiatric treatment. Shortly thereafter, Jablonski volunteered to undergo a psychiatric examination at the hospital.

The police immediately called the hospital and were informed that Jablonski would be treated by Dr. Kopiloff. Because Kopiloff was unable to come to the telephone, the policeman spoke instead with Dr. Berman, the head of psychiatric services. The policeman advised Berman of Jablonski's prior criminal record, the recent history of obscene telephone calls and malicious damage, and stated that, in his opinion, Jablonski needed to be treated on an in-patient basis. Although Berman stated that he would transmit this information to Kopiloff, he failed to do so. Kopiloff testified that had he received this information from the police, he would have involuntarily hospitalized Jablonski if possible.

On Monday, July 10, Kimball drove Jablonski to the hospital. In the interview with Jablonski and Kimball, Kopiloff learned that Jablonski had served a five year prison term for raping his wife, and that four days earlier he had attempted to rape Pahls. Jablonski informed Kopiloff

that he had undergone psychiatric treatment previously, but refused to state where he had received the treatment. Kopiloff concluded that the patient was vague, non-communicative and unwilling to share his prior medical history. He diagnosed Jablonski as an "anti-social personality" and "potentially dangerous." He recommended that Jablonski voluntarily hospitalize himself, but Jablonski refused. Kopiloff concluded that there was no emergency and that there was no basis for involuntary hospitalization. Jablonski was to return in two weeks.

In a private conference following the diagnostic interview, Kimball told Kopiloff that she felt insecure around Jablonski and was concerned about his unusual behavior. Kopiloff recommended that she leave Jablonski at least while he was being evaluated. When Kimball responded "I love him," Kopiloff did not warn her further because he believed she would not listen to him.

No attempt was made to locate Jablonski's prior medical records. Meghan's retained expert witness, Dr. Thompson, testified that under professional standards commonly practiced in the community, Kopiloff should have recognized that Jablonski was potentially very dangerous. He further testified that given the potential danger and the patient's reluctance to reveal his past medical treatment, Kopiloff should have obtained Jablonski's prior medical history at the veterans facilities in the Los Angeles and Long Beach area. He stated that these records could have been obtained by telephone without Jablonski's consent.

The hospital records of Jablonski's prior treatment revealed that in 1968 he had received extensive care at an Army hospital in El Paso. The El Paso records reported that Jablonski had a "homicidal ideation toward his wife," that on numerous occasions he had tried to kill her, that he "had probably suffered a psychotic break and the possibility of future violent behavior was a distinct probability," and that he was "demonstrating some masculine identification in beating his wife as his father did frequently to his mother." The final diagnosis concluded in part that Jablonski had a "schizophrenic reaction, undifferentiated type, chronic, moderate; manifested by homicidal behavior toward his wife."

On Tuesday or Wednesday, July 11 or 12, Pahls telephoned Kopiloff and complained because Jablonski was not to return for two weeks. Kopiloff persuaded her not to call the police and agreed to see Jablonski on Friday, July 14. On Wednesday, July 12, Kimball and Meghan moved out of Jablonski's apartment and into Pahl's apartment because of warnings Kimball had received earlier that day from her priest. Kimball continued to see Jablonski, however, and drove him to the hospital for his second appointment.

On July 14, Jablonski met with both Kopiloff and Dr. Hazle, Kopiloff's supervisor. Although Jablonski volunteered that he had had frequent problems all his life with violent reactions, he was again vague as to his prior treatment and again refused a request to admit himself as an in-patient. Kopiloff concluded that Jablonski possessed an "antisocial personality with explosive features." Although Hazle believed that Jablonski was dangerous and that his case was an "emergency," both doctors concluded that there was no basis for involuntary hospitalization. Again, no effort was made to seek the prior medical records. Instead, Jablonski was scheduled for more tests and given a prescription for valium.

During Jablonski's appointment with Hazle and Kopiloff, Kimball stood in the hall-way outside. Noticing that she seemed to be in distress, a third doctor, Dr. Warnell, chief of the Mental Health Clinic, invited her into his office. Kimball expressed fear for her personal safety. Warnell replied that "if she was afraid of her husband and that he didn't fit the criteria to be held in the hospital, that she could con-

sider staying away from him." Although Warnell later relayed this information to Kopiloff and Hazle, they concluded that Jablonski was not homicidal or suicidal, and that he could not be involuntarily hospitalized. Another appointment was made for Jablonski for Monday, July 17.

On Sunday, July 16, Kimball went to Jablonski's apartment, apparently to pick up some baby diapers. Jablonski either was at the apartment at the time or arrived soon after. He then attacked and murdered her.

The district judge found that Meghan had proven several claims of malpractice against the hospital psychiatrists. The district judge's findings of malpractice for failure to record and transmit the information from the police, for failure to obtain the past medical records, and for failure adequately to warn Kimball, each of which the district court found proximately caused Kimball's death, are significant for purposes of our disposition. . . .

A

The government argues first that it is immune from Meghan's suit because the claim "arises out of an assault and battery," and thus is excluded by subsection 2680(h). Subsection 2680(h) states in relevant part that the Act, as well as the jurisdiction based on it, does not apply to "[a]ny claim arising out of assault, battery, false imprisonment, false arrest, malicious prosecution, abuse of process, libel, slander, misrepresentation, deceit, or interference with contract rights." . . .

Under subsection 2680(h) the government retains its immunity from claims arising from assaults and batteries committed by government employees. The question presented here is whether subsection 2680(h) is intended to prohibit a suit for injuries resulting from an attack by a non-governmental employee, when the attack was alleged to have been proximately caused by the negligence of government employees. Although we have never faced this question, all circuits passing on the issue have held that the assault and battery exception does not bar such suits. . . .

The government attempts to distinguish the decisions holding that the assault and battery exception does not bar suits for negligence. It asserts that each of these cases concerned a plaintiff who was committed to the custody of the government, either as a prisoner or a patient. This distinction is not meaningful. It is more significant that these cases, like the one before us, are based on negligence, not on assault and battery. Moreover, it seems likely that the policy underlying subsection 2680(h) was to insulate the government from liability for acts it was powerless to prevent or which would make defense of a lawsuit unusually difficult. . . . Meghan's suit is based on the negligence of government employees that could have been prevented by an exercise of due care. We hold that Meghan's suit is not precluded by subsection 2680(h).

B

The government argues next that Meghan's suit is barred by 28 U.S.C. § 2680(a). That subsection exempts from the waiver of immunity any claim "based upon the exercise or performance or the failure to exercise or perform a discretionary function or duty on the part of a federal agency or an employee of the Government, whether or not the discretion involved be abused." The district judge's relevant findings of malpractice are that the government doctors failed to record and communicate the police warning, to obtain medical records, and to warn Kimball. The question posed is whether these acts or omissions relate to "discretionary functions" within the meaning of subsection 2680(a).

Our determination of whether or not a governmental employee's function is discretionary requires us to determine whether the act or omission occurred at the plan-

ning level or at the operational level. *Lindgren* v. *United States*, 665 F.2d 978, 980 (9th Cir.1982); *Thompson* v. *United States*, 592 F.2d 1104, 1111 (9th Cir.1979); *Driscoll* v. *United States*, 525 F.2d 136, 138 (9th Cir. 1975). The general rule is that discretionary functions are ones which involve policy choices. *Lindgren* v. *United States,* supra, 665 F.2d at 980. As we elaborated in *Thompson* v. *United States,* supra:

> Obviously, attending to many day-to-day details of management involves decisions and thus some element of discretion. The exercise of this kind of discretion does not fall within the discretionary function exemption. The distinction generally made in the application of the discretionary function exemption is between those decisions which are made on a policy or planning level, as opposed to those made on an operational level.

592 F.2d at 1111. . . . The acts and omissions of the doctors in the present case were operational acts, not discretionary acts involving planning. No general policy regarding veteran medical records prevented the doctors in this case from obtaining Jablonski's records. Nothing prevented them from recording and communicating the information relayed by the police. Providing a warning is a day-to-day hospital activity.

Moreover, policy considerations warrant the conclusion that these acts or omissions were not discretionary. In *Driscoll* v. *United States*, supra, 525 F.2d at 138, we cited a list of factors to be considered in distinguishing decisions made at the planning level from those made at the operational level. These include "the character and severity of the plaintiff's injury, the existence of alternative remedies, the capacity of a court to evaluate the propriety of the official's action, and the effect of liability on the effective administration of the function in question." Id., citing Jaffe, *Suits Against Governments and Officers: Damage Actions*, 77 Harv.L.Rev. 209, 219

(1963). The application of these factors to the case before us supports our conclusion. The injury obviously was severe, and there are no meaningful alternative remedies available to plaintiff. Courts should encounter no difficulty in evaluating the official's action, since they are experienced in deciding medical malpractice cases. Finally, there is no evidence that our decision will affect the effective administration of veterans hospitals. Requiring doctors to obtain, communicate, and use relevant information on dangerous patients will not burden the hospitals financially. Furthermore, the doctors will be held only to standards of adequate medical care in their community. Therefore, we find that Meghan's suit is not barred by subsection 2680(a).

III

We now turn to the merits of the case. We apply California tort law because the alleged negligence occurred in California. See 28 U.S.C. § 1346(b).

Only the liability of the hospital is presented to us in this appeal. The district court's primary findings of malpractice concerned a failure to record and communicate the warning by the police, the failure to secure Jablonski's prior records, and the failure to warn Kimball. The district judge found each of these to be separate acts of malpractice, each one of which was a proximate cause of Kimball's death. Thus, any one of the findings, if not clearly erroneous, can support a judgment for Meghan. . . . We conclude that the district judge's findings were not clearly erroneous and his interpretation of the applicable California law was not clearly wrong.

Meghan's failure-to-warn claim is governed by *Tarasoff* v. *Regents of the University of California*, 17 Cal.3d 425, 551 P.2d 334, 131 Cal.Rptr. 14 (1976) (*Tarasoff*). Meghan must show a breach of duty by proving that (1) a psychotherapist-patient relationship existed, (2) that the psycho-

therapist knew, or should have known, that Jablonski was dangerous, (3) that Kimball was a foreseeable victim of Jablonski's violent tendencies, and (4) that the psychotherapist did not take the necessary steps to discharge his duty. 17 Cal.3d at 439. She also must show that the hospital's negligent act proximately caused her injury. See 4 B. Witkin, Summary of California Law, Torts, § 488 (8th ed. 1974).

The government argues first that it did not owe any duty to Kimball because Jablonski was an outpatient and therefore no special relationship existed between the doctors and Jablonski. Such an interpretation is contrary to the express holding of *Tarasoff*, which stated that a special relationship exists between any psychotherapist and his patient. *Tarasoff*, supra, 17 Cal.3d at 435, 436 n. 6, 131 Cal.Rptr. 14, 551 P.2d 334. Indeed, the patient in *Tarasoff* was an outpatient. Id. at 430 n. 2, 432, 131 Cal.Rptr. 14, 551 P.2d 334.

The government argues next that no duty was owed to Kimball because she was not the foreseeable victim of Jablonski's violence; that is, she was not sufficiently targeted as a victim of the mentally sick individual. We need not decide whether our review of a foreseeability issue is a question of fact or law, because we would arrive at the same conclusion under either standard.

Although the case before us falls somewhere between the extremes of *Tarasoff* and *Thompson* v. *Alameda*, 27 Cal.3d 741, 614 P.2d 728, 167 Cal.Rptr. 70 (1980), we find *Tarasoff* to be more clearly on point. Unlike the killer in *Tarasoff*, Jablonski made no specific threats concerning any specific individuals. Nevertheless, Jablonski's previous history indicated that he would likely direct his violence against Kimball. He had raped and committed other acts of violence against his wife. His psychological profile indicated that his violence was likely to be directed against women very close to him. This, in turn, was borne out by his attack on Pahls. Thus,

Kimball was specifically identified or "targeted" to a much greater extent than were the neighborhood children in *Thompson*. Moreover, the difficulties in giving a warning that were present in *Thompson* are not present here. See id. at 755–56, 167 Cal.Rptr. 70, 614 P.2d 728. Warning Kimball would have posed no difficulty for the doctors, especially since she twice expressed her fear of Jablonski directly to them. Neither can it be said, as was the case in *Thompson*, that direct and precise warnings would have had little effect. . . .

The finding that Kimball was a foreseeable victim was dependent on the district judge's finding that the doctors had been negligent in failing to obtain Jablonski's prior medical history. The government claims that this latter finding was incorrect. However, the government must show that the finding was clearly erroneous. *Rooney* v. *United States*, 634 F.2d 1238, 1244 (9th Cir.1980). The district judge chose to believe Thompson, Meghan's expert witness, that the failure to obtain Jablonski's records was negligent in light of accepted community standards. His finding was not clearly erroneous.

The government argues next that even if it owed the decedent a duty of care, that duty was properly discharged by the warnings given by Kopiloff and Warnell to Kimball. The district judge found that the warnings from both doctors, if given, were totally unspecific and inadequate under the circumstances. The district court's finding was not clearly erroneous.

Finally, the government argues that Kimball received sufficient warning from a variety of sources, including a psychological hotline, her attorney, her priest, and her mother. The government does not cite any specific language in *Tarasoff* or otherwise attempt to classify its argument under any specific legal doctrine.

The government's argument may be that Kimball was contributorily negligent in continuing to see Jablonski or that she assumed the risk that she would be harmed by Jablonski. The government did argue in the district court that Meghan's award should be reduced due to Kimball's comparative negligence, but its argument was rejected by the district judge. His finding was not clearly erroneous.

To the extent the government's argument is that the doctors' failure to warn was not the proximate cause of Meghan's loss, we conclude that the government failed to show that a finding of proximate cause was clearly erroneous. *Rudelson* v. *United States*, supra, 602 F.2d at 1330. The district judge referred to the information from Jablonski's prior medical records and found that "this data properly used, would have prevented the murder in question." The judge's finding is not clearly erroneous.

The district judge also found, as separate acts of malpractice, that the doctors failed to secure Jablonski's prior records and failed to record and communicate the warning by the police. These findings were not clearly erroneous. The record adequately supports the finding that preventative action would have been taken but for these failures.

Affirmed.

Allen v. United States

UNITED STATES DISTRICT COURT, UTAH, 1984.
588 F.SUPP. 247.

[The complex and long opinion in this case runs to over two hundred pages and is supplemented by more than two hundred footnotes. It is preceded by ninety-four headnotes provided by the case editors. The opinion, which is replete with tables, formulae, and drawings, contains a great amount of technical information concerning nuclear physics and radiation which the judge felt was necessary to provide support for his conclusions. The same judge had already ruled on some aspects of this case three years earlier, and refers in this decision to "the first *Allen* opinion."

The excerpt included below deals with just three parts of Judge Jenkins' long and thoughtful opinion: basic background information (including the judge's views on the possibility of establishing scientific and legal certainty), conclusions concerning the discretionary function exception, and the issue of damages.]

Memorandum Opinion

JENKINS, District Judge. . . .

This case is concerned with what reasonable men in positions of decision-making in the United States government between 1951 and 1963 knew or should have known about the fundamental nature of matter.

It is concerned with the duty, if any, that the United States government had to tell its people, particularly those in proximity to the experiment site, what it knew or should have known about the dangers to them from the government's experiments with nuclear fission conducted above ground in the brushlands of Nevada during those critical years.

This case is concerned with the perception and the apprehension of its political leaders of international dangers threatening the United States from 1951 to 1963. It is concerned with high level determinations as to what to do about them and whether such determinations legally excuse the United States from being answerable to a comparatively few members of its population for injuries allegedly resulting from open air nuclear experiments conducted in response to such perceived dangers.

It is concerned with the method and quantum of proof of the cause in fact of claimed biological injuries. It is concerned with the passage of time, the attendant diminishment of memory, the availability of contemporary information about open air atomic testing and the application of a statute of repose.

It is concerned with what plaintiffs—laymen, not experts—knew or should have known about the biological consequences that could result from open air nuclear tests and when each plaintiff knew or should have known of such consequences.

It is ultimately concerned with who in fairness should bear the cost in dollars of injury to those persons whose injury is demonstrated to have been caused more likely than not by nation-state conducted open air nuclear events.

The complaint in this action alleges that each plaintiff, or his predecessor, has suffered injury or death as a proximate result of exposure to radioactive fallout that drifted away from the Nevada Test Site and settled upon communities and isolated populations in southern Utah, northern Arizona and southeastern Nevada. Each of the plaintiffs or their decedents resided in that area. Each claims serious loss due to radiation-caused cancer or leukemia. Each asserts that the injury suffered resulted from the negligence of the United States in conducting open-air nuclear testing, in monitoring testing results, in failing to inform persons at hazard of attendant dangers from such testing and in failing to inform such persons how to avoid or minimize or mitigate such dangers....

This action is a consolidation of the individual claims of the 1,192 named plaintiffs in this lawsuit. This is not a class action. Cf. Annot., 48 A.L.R.Fed. 860 (1980). Trial was held in this action beginning September 14, 1982 and concluding with final arguments on December 17, 1982. The trial encompassed 24 of the claims in their entirety. Pursuant to the suggestion of the court these cases were selected by plaintiffs' and defendant's counsel as "bellwether" cases. The effort was to provide a selection of "typical" cases which when decided and reviewed may provide a legal and factual pattern against which the remaining issues in the pending cases may be subsequently matched.

The trial was conducted as well so as to make a full and complete record concerning legal, historic, and scientific matters common to all of the 1,192 plaintiffs with the idea in mind of avoiding future duplication of effort. See *Park Lane Hosiery Company, Inc.* v. *Shore*, 439 U.S. 322, 99 S.Ct. 645, 58 L.Ed.2d 552 (1979). Other than as noted in this opinion, this court has not decided the remaining issues in the claims of the more than 1,100 plaintiffs that are still pending in the consolidated case.

This opinion decides claims of individuals, each with his own history and relationship to the open air nuclear tests. It fully decides 24 separate cases, tied together by common legal, historic and scientific threads of unique importance....

During the course of trial, this court received into evidence the testimony of 98 witnesses as well as more than 1,692 documentary exhibits.[11] The evidence provides testimony of witnesses ranging from those who participated in the testing program and related operations to highly trained and gifted "experts" offering conflicting opinions, to claimants who seek solace for their test-blamed sorrow....

We all seek to simplify and to order. The mind eschews the uncertain. We strain for certainty and perfect knowledge in an infinitely complex and dynamic universe. In doing so, we often fail to distinguish between those things which we directly experience, see, feel, hear, taste, smell—facts we experience—from those facts we infer. Each is a form of knowledge. Each we say we know. But we must be constantly aware of the nature of that which we say we "know." ...

In the law, as in science, one always faces uncertainty. This court, faced with the duty of judgment in this case, does not have the luxury of the zealous absolutists who "know beyond doubt" that each and every cancer in the Great Basin is the result of open air atomic testing, or of their absolutist counterparts who "know beyond doubt" that none resulted. The court is disciplined by the record and the application of rules of law.

The court's findings of fact have a certainty that is relative to the evidence presented to the court by others. They are not fixed in absolute terms. Judicial determination of facts in this case is indistinguishable from fact-finding in other cases no matter how "complex" the facts here might be.

Thus, this opinion speaks in terms of "natural and probable" consequences, "substantial" factors and things "more likely than not."

In the pragmatic world of "fact" the court passes judgment on the probable. Dispute resolution demands rational decision, not perfect knowledge....

---

[11] The trial transcript [hereinafter cited as "Tr."] extends to more than 7,000 pages. The exhibits now in evidence before this court amount to over 54,000 pages of written material contained in 19 cardboard boxes....

V. Discretionary Function

At the end of the trial the United States moved to dismiss this matter on the grounds that the actions of the United States of which plaintiffs complain are insulated from complaint by the discretionary function exception found in the Tort Claims Act....

Let us look beyond the words and see what the United States did or did not do about which plaintiffs complain. Then let us see if such acts were so imbued with considerations of public policy and governance as to be immunized from the reach of the Federal Tort Claims Act.

First, there is no complaint that testing took place. To test or not to test is a policy decision. See e.g., "Review of Establishment of Continental Test Site," AEC Santa Fe Operations Office (Sept. 1953), PX–52/DX–1A. Obviously the United States has not consented to be sued for what Harry Truman or Dwight Eisenhower or the Atomic Energy Commission or the Congress determined as a matter of policy and governance ought to be done. E.g., DX–127, 120–21, 146, 147, 177, 804, 171, 203, 330, 331, 333, 406 (memoranda concerning Presidential approval of the Buster-Jangle, Tumbler-Snapper, Upshot-Knothole, Teapot, and Plumbbob series of tests). This action does not challenge the decision to test.

The United States seems to argue that because a choice has been made, a discretionary choice at the highest levels of government, that *all* subsequent operational choices and actions executing the original policy choice are to be regarded as identical with the original policy choice, and insulated as the original choice is insultated from the *reach* of the Tort Claims Act.

The United States misperceives the intent of the act. For example, we choose the objective: Rome. We choose the road: the Appian Way. Discretionary choices both. We make such choices as a matter of power and as a matter of right.

The manner in which we drive from our location to Rome, carelessly or carefully, is also a matter of choice. But, it is not a matter of discretion as used in the Tort Claims Act. It is not a matter of discretion because such a choice is subject to a standard, a limitation. It is subject to a limitation imposed by a civilized society as to *appropriate conduct*.

It is not a matter of discretion because while we have a power to choose, we have no right to breach the standard and without responsibility choose to drive carelessly. If we do, we are answerable for exercising power without right.

In 1951, in response to international pressures, the United States chose the objective—to try to stabilize the restless balance of world power. It chose the road—open air atomic testing.

Discretionary choices both. Both choices were made as a matter of power and as a matter of right.

The manner in which the tests were conducted, carefully or carelessly, was also a matter of choice but was not a matter of discretion because such operational conduct was subject to a standard, a limitation. That limiting standard of conduct, due care, reasonable care under the circumstances, is called a duty. The person to whom a duty is owed is said to have a right.

At the operational level employees of the United States had a duty to prepare and conduct tests carefully with full regard for public safety. The citizen adjacent to the testing site had a right to have that duty fulfilled....

Much like the driver on the road to Rome, an operational employee had the power to conduct such tests carelessly, but he had a duty to do otherwise. The duty limits choice and thus belies discretion or its exercise.

When a decisionmaker with genuine power and right to make discretionary choices makes such a choice, an operational person down the decision-making and administrative ladder—charged by the decisionmaker with the responsibility for executing but not making such choice—is not in a position to overrule or to nullify the original discretionary choice, either through choices of his own or through negligent operational actions of his own. That original discretionary choice has been made. There are no rightful operational vetoes of appropriate discretionary choices. That kind of discretion does not exist. This is simply another reason why the position of the United States lacks persuasion. . . .

In the first *Allen* opinion, this court observed that "one must understand that the case here is not footed on the fact that high level policy decisions were made—but is footed on the allegedly inappropriate manner in which such policy distinctions were carried out. The distinction cries out," even more loudly now than before.

For the reasons set forth in the first *Allen* opinion as amplified here, the discretionary function exception for the operational activities complained of is simply unavailable.

Jurisdiction is proper. Defendant's Motion to Dismiss based on the discretionary exception is denied. . . .

X. Damages

After careful examination of the factors discussed in detail above in all of the preceding sections, it appears that ten of the twenty-four, bellwether cases merit compensation. . . .

The court finds in the following cases that the claimants indicated have been damaged by the wrongful death of the deceased person indicated in the sums indicated:

Deceased	Claimant	Status	Amount
Arthur F. Bruhn	Lorna C. Bruhn	Spouse	$400,000
	Michael F. Bruhn	Child(M)	150,000
	Eleanor K. McDonald	Child(A)	75,000
John E. Crabtree	Florence M. Crabtree	Spouse	125,000
	Wendy C. Snipe	Child(M)	25,000
	Glenna C. Giddens	Child(M)	25,000
	Joyce C. Messer	Child(A)	15,000
	Phyllis C. Gillins	Child(A)	15,000
	John A. Crabtree	Child(A)	15,000
	Carroll J. Smith	Child(A)	15,000
Karlene Hafen	Leora Hafen	Parent	250,000
Sybil D. Johnson	Blaine Johnson	Parent	125,000
	Loah J. Johnson	Parent	125,000
Lenn McKinney	Vonda McKinney	Spouse	200,000
	Donna McK. Patzke	Child(M)	50,000
	Stephen L. McKinney	Child(A)	25,000
	Arthur Y. McKinney	Child(A)	25,000
Sheldon D. Nisson	Darrell A. Nisson	Parent	250,000
Peggy L. Orton	Rula D. Orton	Parent	250,000
LaVier Tait	VaRene E. Tait	Spouse	240,000
	Nan T. Avent	Child(M)	40,000
	Teresa T. Hollenbeck	Child(M)	40,000
	Lindsey C. Tait	Child(M)	40,000
	Pattie T. Heaton	Child(M)	40,000

The court finds that the claimants indicated below have suffered damage in the sums indicated:

Claimant	Amount
Norma Jean Pollitt (now dead)	* * * (not yet fixed)
Jacqueline M. Sanders	$100,000

XI. Findings of Ultimate Fact

The court finds that defendant failed to adequately warn the plaintiffs or their predecessors of known or foreseeable long-range biological consequences to adults and to children from exposure to fallout radiation from open-air atomic testing and that such failure was negligent.

The court finds that defendant failed to measure adequately and concurrently with open-air atomic testing the actual fallout in communities and population centers near the Nevada Test Site on a *person-specific* basis, or its equivalent, and that such failure was negligent.

The court finds that contemporaneously with atmospheric atomic testing the defendant failed to adequately and continuously inform individuals and communities near the test site of well-known and inexpensive methods to prevent, minimize or mitigate the known or foreseeable long-range biological consequences of exposure to radioactive fallout, and that such failure was negligent.

The court finds that as a direct and proximate result of such negligent failures, individually and in combination, defendant unreasonably placed plaintiffs or their predecessors at risk of injury and as a direct and proximate result of such failures that each prevailing plaintiff designated in Part X, beginning at page 446, suffered injury for which the sums set opposite their respective names should be paid. . . .

As the excerpt from the *Allen* case indicates, only a small number of the suits filed over radiation fallout from the Nevada test site were resolved by that decision.[12] Much more litigation is in process. Moreover, numerous suits have been filed by ex-servicemen who were exposed to nuclear radiation while on active duty and who claim that the government was negligent in not warning them, after their separation from the military, of the dangers of radiation.[13] The general issue of governmental liability for exposure to nuclear radiation appears to be an issue that is ripe for Supreme Court consideration.

The potential magnitude of governmental liability in suits such as these has become a matter of concern for governments at all levels in the United States. As will be discussed at the end of the chapter, a movement is now

---

[12] For a broad analysis of this issue see Howard Ball, *Justice Downwind: America's Atomic Testing Program in the 1950s* (1986).

[13] The standard defense asserted by the government in such cases is the *Feres* doctrine. See above, p. 261. But two 1985 court of appeals cases ruled that *Feres* did not bar a claim against the United States for failure to warn servicemen of the dangers of exposure to nuclear radiation. See *Cole* v. *U.S.*, 755 F.2d 873 (11th Cir., 1985) and *Molsbergen* v. *U.S.*, 757 F.2d 1016 (9th Cir., 1985). And see "Postdischarge Failure to Warn: Judicial Response to Veterans' Attempts to Circumvent *Feres*," 30 *Villanova Law Review* 263 (1985).

under way to make broad legislative changes in tort liability, including governmental tort liability. It might be noted here that both the failure to warn, the theory on which liability was posited in the two cases just covered, and the second of these cases in particular, *Allen* v. *United States*, were specifically criticized in a 1986 U.S. Department of Justice report which recommended numerous changes in tort law.[14]

STATE TORT LIABILITY

States have a dual protection against tort suits: the common-law doctrine of sovereign immunity and the Eleventh Amendment to the U.S. Constitution. That amendment bars federal court suits against states by individuals.[15] Thus, as on the federal level, the extent to which a state can be liable for the torts of its agents depends upon the extent of its waiver of immunity. A traditional basis for deciding questions of liability on the state and local level has been the so-called "governmental-proprietary" distinction. Essentially this holds that if a governmental agency is performing a function that could be performed by a private party (a "proprietary" function) it could be held liable for an injury-causing tort that ensued, but if it were performing a "purely governmental" function, immunity would prevail. But in the course of years of inconsistent and sometimes irrational application, this distinction "became one of the most unsatisfactory known to law." [16]

A 1954 survey showed that only one state, New York, had made itself amenable to suit for substantially all state torts. In a dozen other states liability was allowed in many or most cases, while in all of the others tort claims were satisfied only occasionally, seldom, or not at all.[17] But since the late 1950s, and especially since the middle 1960s, more and more states have permitted at least some level of liability. By the 1980s only a handful of states maintained the traditional common-law position of no waiver of immunity.[18]

Waiver of Immunity

In many jurisdictions the waiver of immunity was accomplished by court decision, on the theory that the doctrine of sovereign immunity was judicially

---

[14] See *Report of the Tort Policy Working Group on the Causes, Extent and Policy Implications of the Current Crisis in Insurance Availability and Affordability*, 32 and 34.

[15] For a thorough analysis of the origins and evolution of the Eleventh Amendment, see Clyde E. Jacobs, *The Eleventh Amendment and Sovereign Immunity* (1972). The Eleventh Amendment may serve as a bar to suits for other than money damages as well as tort suits.

[16] Kenneth Culp Davis, *Administrative Law: Cases—Text—Problems* 189 (6th ed., 1977).

[17] Robert A. Leflar and Benjamin F. Kantrowitz, "Tort Liability of the States," 29 *New York University Law Review* 1407 (1954).

[18] "As of 1984, the generalization seems justified that state courts and state legislatures have produced a nationwide movement away from sovereign immunity of state and local governments from tort liability." Davis, above, note 10, 9. But the degree of waiver of immunity from state to state varies widely. It is difficult to generalize without considering many narrow areas of potential liability. For instance "[m]ore than half of the states have statutes prohibiting suits against the state which claim damages arising out of any type of negligent inspection." "Negligent State Fire Inspection," 13 *Columbia Journal of Law and Social Problems* 305 (1977).

created in the first place.[19] But in some states, the courts have ruled that sovereign immunity must be abolished or modified by the legislature. Pennsylvania has gone through an interesting development in this respect recently. In 1973 the Pennsylvania Supreme Court abolished local governmental immunity,[20] while upholding it on the state level.[21] In 1975 the court extended liability to state-level entities that are not part of the "Commonwealth"—in this case, the Pennsylvania Turnpike Commission.[22] In 1978 the same court stated: "This rule of 'sovereign immunity' has been recently upheld by this Court. We today abrogate this doctrine of 'sovereign immunity.' " [23] Two months later the Pennsylvania Legislature restored sovereign immunity except in cases where immunity had already been waived by statute, such as damages arising from the operation of state vehicles, defects in state-owned real estate or highways, injury caused by state-owned animals, and several other categories of activities.[24]

THE LIABILITY OF INDIVIDUAL OFFICERS

Although the government has traditionally been protected by sovereign immunity, this doctrine did not extend the cloak of protection to individual governmental servants. As the great English jurist Dicey said in an oft-quoted statement, "every official, from the Prime Minister down to a constable or a collector of taxes, is under the same responsibility for every act done without justification as any other citizen." [25] And indeed, some early American cases ruled that public officials could be held liable for improper acts, even if undertaken reasonably and in good faith.[26] But the modern law on the subject is much different. Generally speaking, it is fair to say that if a public official is performing a function requiring judgment or discretion, if that function is within the sphere of his or her duties, and if it is performed in good faith and in a reasonable manner, the official will not be held liable by a court for injuries or property damage that might ensue.[27]

There are varying levels of official protection, depending upon the function being performed. Judges performing judicial functions are usually said to have "absolute immunity," meaning that they are protected from liability

---

[19] See, for instance, *Muskopf* v. *Corning Hospital Dist.*, 55 Cal.2d 211, 11 Cal.Rptr. 89, 359 P.2d 457 (1961).

[20] *Ayala* v. *Philadelphia Bd. of Public Educ.*, 453 Pa. 584, 305 A.2d 877 (1973).

[21] *Brown* v. *Commonwealth*, 453 Pa. 566, 305 A.2d 868 (1973).

[22] *Specter* v. *Commonwealth*, 462 Pa. 474, 341 A.2d 481 (1975).

[23] *Mayle* v. *Pennsylvania Dept. of Highways*, 479 Pa. 384, 388 A.2d 709 (1978).

[24] 1 Purdon's Pennsylvania Statutes Annotated § 2310 (Supplementary Pamphlet, 1964 to 1978), 148.

[25] A. V. Dicey, *Introduction to the Study of the Law of the Constitution* 189 (8th ed., 1915).

[26] A frequently-cited case is *Miller* v. *Horton*, 152 Mass. 540, 26 N.E. 100 (1891). This much-criticized case was overruled in 1973. *Gildea* v. *Ellershaw*, 363 Mass. 800, 298 N.E. 847.

[27] See generally Bernard Schwartz, *Administrative Law* 554–561 (1976).

even if acting maliciously or in bad faith.[28] The same level of immunity was long considered applicable to legislators, although recent cases, to be discussed below, cast some doubt on this generalization. Other public officials were not put in the same category as those performing judicial or legislative functions, and their level of immunity has varied with the circumstances. The best way to examine these matters in detail is to consider several concrete cases, but first the legal bases for suits against governmental officials should be discussed.

Basically, a person may sue an officer on the basis of common-law principles, civil rights legislation, and the Constitution.[29] Common-law tort liability will be discussed in the cases presented below and needs no further examination here. The Civil Rights Act of 1871, 42 U.S.C.A. § 1983, provides in part: "Every person who, under color of any statute, ordinance, regulation, custom, or usage, of any State or Territory, subjects, or causes to be subjected, any citizen of the United States or other person within the jurisdiction thereof to the deprivation of any rights, privileges or immunities secured by the Constitution and laws, shall be liable to the party injured in an action at law, suit in equity, or other proper proceeding for redress." The constitutional basis for suing officials in tort was articulated in *Bivens* v. *Six Unknown Named Agents of the Fed. Bureau of Narcotics*, 403 U.S. 388, 91 S.Ct. 1999, 29 L.Ed.2d 619 (1971). In this case the Supreme Court ruled that the Fourth Amendment could provide the basis for a damage suit where federal agents made a warrantless, early morning raid at the plaintiff's apartment and ransacked the premises in a fruitless and illegal attempt to find evidence.[30]

Liability of Judges

At common law, it has long been clear that judges are absolutely immune from tort suits.[31] Suits against judges based on § 1983 of the 1871 Civil Rights Act date from more recent times, but the Supreme Court ruled in favor of absolute immunity in such a suit in 1967.[32] The following case is a recent affirmation of that principle, but the contrasting views of the majority and the dissenters are interesting to consider.

---

[28] "Qualified immunity" protects an official from liability unless it can be shown that he acted maliciously or in bad faith. The standard of "bad faith" is discussed by Jerry L. Mashaw in "Civil Liability of Government Officers: Property Rights and Official Accountability," 42 *Law and Contemporary Problems* 8, esp. at 20. (1976). This issue is devoted to "Civil Liability of Government Officials."

[29] See Kenneth W. Clarkson and Timothy J. Muris, "Foreword," 42 *Law and Contemporary Problems* 2 (1976). Also Davis, above, note 16, at 209.

[30] The Supreme Court remanded the case to the court of appeals for consideration of the question of official immunity. That court ruled that the officers were entitled to qualified rather than absolute immunity. 456 F.2d 1339 (2nd Cir., 1972).

[31] See the discussion and cases cited in Mashaw, above, note 28, at 15.

[32] *Pierson* v. *Ray*, 386 U.S. 547, 87 S.Ct. 1213, 18 L.Ed.2d 288 (1967). See "Liability of Judicial Officers Under Section 1983," 79 *Yale Law Journal* 322 (1969).

Stump v. Sparkman

Supreme Court of the United States, 1978.
435 U.S. 349, 98 S.Ct. 1099, 55 L.Ed.2d 331,
reh den 436 U.S. 951, 98 S.Ct. 2862, 56 L.Ed.2d 795.

[The mother of the respondent petitioned the Circuit Court of DeKalb County, Indiana to have her "somewhat retarded" daughter sterilized. The petition was approved by Judge Stump on the same day. The operation was performed, the daughter having been told that she was to have her appendix removed. Two years later the daughter was married and, when she discovered that she had been sterilized, she sued the judge and others under § 1983 seeking damages for the alleged violation of her constitutional rights. The district court ruled that Judge Stump was absolutely immune from liability, but the court of appeals reversed, holding that the judge had not "acted within his jurisdiction" and had forfeited his immunity for "failure to comply with elementary principles of procedural due process." The case came to the Supreme Court on certiorari.]

Mr. Justice WHITE delivered the opinion of the Court. . . .

The governing principle of law is well established and is not questioned by the parties. As early as 1872, the Court recognized that it was "a general principle of the highest importance to the proper administration of justice that a judicial officer, in exercising the authority vested in him, [should] be free to act upon his own convictions, without apprehension of personal consequences to himself." Bradley v. Fisher [13 Wall. 335], at 347. For that reason the Court held that "judges of courts of superior or general jurisdiction are not liable to civil actions for their judicial acts, even when such acts are in excess of their jurisdiction, and are alleged to have been done maliciously or corruptly." 13 Wall., at 351. Later we held that this doctrine of judicial immunity was applicable in suits under § 1 of the Civil Rights Act of 1871, 42 U.S.C.A. § 1983, for the legislative record gave no indication that Congress intended to abolish this long-established principle. Pierson v. Ray, 386 U.S. 547, 87 S.Ct. 1213, 18 L.Ed.2d 288 (1967).

The Court of Appeals correctly recognized that the necessary inquiry in determining whether a defendant judge is immune from suit is whether at the time he took the challenged action he had jurisdiction over the subject matter before him. . . .

We cannot agree that there was a "clear absence of all jurisdiction" in the DeKalb County Circuit Court to consider the petition presented by Mrs. McFarlin. As an Indiana circuit court judge, Judge Stump had "original exclusive jurisdiction in all cases at law and in equity whatsoever. . . ." jurisdiction over the settlement of estates and over guardianships, appellate jurisdiction as conferred by law, and jurisdiction over "all other causes, matters and proceedings where exclusive jurisdiction thereof is not conferred by law upon some other court, board or officer." Ind.Code § 33–4–4–3 (1975). This is indeed a broad jurisdictional grant; yet the Court of Appeals concluded that Judge Stump did not have jurisdiction over the petition authorizing Linda Sparkman's sterilization.

In so doing, the Court of Appeals noted that the Indiana statutes provided for the sterilization of institutionalized persons under certain circumstances, see Ind.Code §§ 16–13–13–1 through 16–13–13–4 (1973), but otherwise contained no express authority for judicial approval of tubal ligations. It is true that the statutory grant of general jurisdiction to the Indiana circuit courts does not itemize types of cases those courts may hear and hence does not expressly mention sterilization petitions presented by the parents of a minor. But in our view, it is more significant that there was no Indiana statute and no case law in 1971 prohibiting a circuit court, a court of general jurisdiction, from considering a petition of the type presented to Judge Stump. The statutory authority for the sterilization of institutionalized persons in the custody of the State does not warrant the inference that a court of general jurisdiction has no power to act on a petition for sterilization of a minor in the custody of her parents, particularly where the parents have authority under the Indiana statutes to "consent to and contract for medical or hospital care or treatment of [the minor] including surgery." Ind.Code § 16–8–4–2 (1973). The District Court concluded that Judge Stump had jurisdiction under § 33–4–4–3 to entertain and act upon Mrs. McFarlin's petition. We agree with the District Court, it appearing that neither by statute or case law has the broad jurisdiction granted to the circuit courts of Indiana been circumscribed to foreclose consideration of a petition for authorization of a minor's sterilization. . . .

Perhaps realizing the broad scope of Judge Stump's jurisdiction, the Court of Appeals stated that, even if the action taken by him was not foreclosed under the Indiana statutory scheme, it would still be "an illegitimate exercise of his common law power because of his failure to comply with elementary principles of procedural due process." 552 F.2d, at 176. This misconceives the doctrine of judicial immunity. A judge is absolutely immune from liability for his judicial acts even if his exercise of authority is flawed by the commission of grave procedural errors. . . .

We conclude that the Court of Appeals, employing an unduly restrictive view of the scope of Judge Stump's jurisdiction, erred in holding that he was not entitled to judicial immunity. Because the court over which Judge Stump presides is one of general jurisdiction, neither the procedural errors he may have committed nor the lack of a specific statute authorizing his approval of the petition in question rendered

him liable in damages for the consequences of his actions.

The respondents argue that even if Judge Stump had jurisdiction to consider the petition presented to him by Mrs. McFarlin, he is still not entitled to judicial immunity because his approval of the petition did not constitute a "judicial" act. It is only for acts performed in his "judicial" capacity that a judge is absolutely immune, they say. We do not disagree with this statement of the law, but we cannot characterize the approval of the petition as a nonjudicial act. . . .

The relevant cases demonstrate that the factors determining whether an act by a judge is a "judicial" one relate to the nature of the act itself, i.e., whether it is a function normally performed by a judge, and to the expectations of the parties, i.e., whether they dealt with the judge in his judicial capacity. Here, both factors indicate that Judge Stump's approval of the sterilization petition was a judicial act. State judges with general jurisdiction not infrequently are called upon in their official capacity to approve petitions relating to the affairs of minors, as for example, a petition to settle a minor's claim. Furthermore, as even respondents have admitted, at the time he approved the petition presented to him by Mrs. McFarlin, Judge Stump was "acting as a county circuit court judge." See supra, at 1106. We may infer from the record that it was only because Judge Stump served in that position that Mrs. McFarlin, on the advice of counsel, submitted the petition to him for his approval. Because Judge Stump performed the type of act normally performed only by judges and because he did so in his capacity as a circuit court judge, we find no merit to respondents' argument that the informality with which he proceeded rendered his action nonjudicial and deprived him of his absolute immunity.

Both the Court of Appeals and the respondents seem to suggest that, because of the tragic consequences of Judge Stump's actions, he should not be immune. For example, the Court of Appeals noted that "[t]here are actions of purported judicial character that a judge, even when exercising general jurisdiction, is not empowered to take," 552 F.2d, at 176, and respondents argue that Judge Stump's action was "so unfair" and "so totally devoid of judicial concern for the interests and well-being of the young girl involved" as to disqualify it as a judicial act. Brief for Respondents 18. Disagreement with the action taken by the judge, however, does not justify depriving that judge of his immunity. Despite the unfairness to litigants that sometimes results, the doctrine of judicial immunity is thought to be in the best interests of "the proper administration of justice.... [, for it allows] a judicial officer, in exercising the authority vested in him [to] be free to act upon his own convictions, without apprehension of personal consequences to himself." Bradley v. Fisher, 13 Wall., at 347. The fact that the issue before the judge is a controversial one is all the more reason that he should be able to act without fear of suit....

The Indiana law vested in Judge Stump the power to entertain and act upon the petition for sterilization. He is, therefore, under the controlling cases, immune from damages liability even if his approval of the petition was in error. Accordingly, the judgment of the Court of Appeals is reversed and the case is remanded for further proceedings consistent with this opinion.

It is so ordered.

Mr. Justice BRENNAN took no part in the consideration or decision of this case.

Mr. Justice STEWART, with whom Mr. Justice MARSHALL and Mr. Justice POWELL join, dissenting.

It is established federal law that judges of general jurisdiction are absolutely immune from monetary liability "for judicial acts, even when such acts are in excess of their jurisdiction, and are alleged to have been done maliciously or corruptly." Brad-

ley v. Fisher, 13 Wall. 335, 351, 20 L.Ed. 646. It is also established that this immunity is in no way diminished in a proceeding under 42 U.S.C.A. § 1983. Pierson v. Ray, 386 U.S. 547, 87 S.Ct. 1213, 18 L.Ed.2d 288. But the scope of judicial immunity is limited to liability for "judicial acts," and I think that what Judge Stump did on July 9, 1971, was beyond the pale of anything that could sensibly be called a judicial act.

Neither in Bradley v. Fisher nor in Pierson v. Ray was there any claim that the conduct in question was not a judicial act, and the Court thus had no occasion in either case to discuss the meaning of that term. Yet the proposition that judicial immunity extends only to liability for "judicial acts" was emphasized no less than seven times in Mr. Justice Field's opinion for the Court in the *Bradley* case. Cf. Imbler v. Pachtman, 424 U.S. 409, 430, 96 S.Ct. 984, 995, 47 L.Ed.2d 128. And if the limitations inherent in that concept have any realistic meaning at all, then I cannot believe that the action of Judge Stump in approving Mrs. McFarlin's petition is protected by judicial immunity.

The Court finds two reasons for holding that Judge Stump's approval of the sterilization petition was a judicial act. First, the Court says, it was "a function normally performed by a judge." Second, the Court says, the act was performed in Judge Stump's "judicial capacity." With all respect, I think that the first of these grounds is factually untrue and that the second is legally unsound.

When the Court says that what Judge Stump did was an act "normally performed by a judge," it is not clear to me whether the Court means that a judge "normally" is asked to approve a mother's decision to have her child given surgical treatment generally, or that a judge "normally" is asked to approve a mother's wish to have her daughter sterilized. But whichever way the Court's statement is to be taken, it is factually inaccurate. In Indiana, as elsewhere in our country, a parent is authorized to arrange for and consent to medical and surgical treatment of his minor child. Ind.Code § 16–8–4–2 (1973). And when a parent decides to call a physician to care for his sick child or arranges to have a surgeon remove his child's tonsils, he does not, "normally" or otherwise, need to seek the approval of a judge. On the other hand, Indiana did in 1971 have statutory procedures for the sterilization of certain people who were *institutionalized.* But these statutes provided for *administrative proceedings* before a board established by the superintendent of each public hospital. Only if after notice and an evidentiary hearing, an order of sterilization was entered in these proceedings could there be review in a circuit court. See Ind.Code §§ 16–13–13–1 through 16–13–13–4 (1973).

In sum, what Judge Stump did on July 9, 1971, was in no way an act "normally performed by a judge." Indeed, there is no reason to believe that such an act has ever been performed by *any* other Indiana judge, either before or since.

When the Court says that Judge Stump was acting in "his judicial capacity" in approving Mrs. McFarlin's petition, it is not clear to me whether the Court means that Mrs. McFarlin submitted the petition to him only because he was a judge, or that, in approving it, he *said* that he was acting as a judge. But however the Court's test is to be understood, it is, I think, demonstrably unsound.

It can safely be assumed that the Court is correct in concluding that Mrs. McFarlin came to Judge Stump with her petition because he was a county circuit court judge. But false illusions as to a judge's power can hardly convert a judge's response to those illusions into a judicial act. In short, a judge's approval of a mother's petition to lock her daughter in the attic would hardly be a judicial act simply because the mother had submitted her petition to the judge in his official capacity.

If, on the other hand, the Court's test depends upon the fact that Judge Stump

said he was acting in his judicial capacity, it is equally invalid. It is true that Judge Stump affixed his signature to the approval of the petition as "Judge, DeKalb Circuit Court." But the conduct of a judge surely does not become a judicial act merely on his own say-so. A judge is not free, like a loose cannon, to inflict indiscriminate damage whenever he announces that he is acting in his judicial capacity.

If the standard adopted by the Court is invalid, then what is the proper measure of a judicial act? Contrary to implications in the Court's opinion, my conclusion that what Judge Stump did was not a judicial act is not based upon the fact that he acted with informality, or that he may not have been "in his judge's robes," or "in the courtroom itself." Ante, p. 1107. And I do not reach this conclusion simply "because the petition was not given a docket number, was not placed on file with the clerk's office, and was approved in an *ex parte* proceeding without notice to the minor, without a hearing, and without the appointment of a *guardian ad litem*." Ante, p. 1106.

It seems to me, rather that the concept of what is a judicial act must take its content from a consideration of the factors that support immunity from liability for the performance of such as act. Those factors were accurately summarized by the Court in Pierson v. Ray, 386 U.S. 547, at 554, 87 S.Ct. 1213, at 1218, 18 L.Ed.2d 288:

> [I]t "is ... for the benefit of the public, whose interest it is that the judges should be at liberty to exercise their functions with independence and without fear of consequences." ... It is a judge's duty to decide all cases within his jurisdiction that are brought before him, including controversial cases that arouse the most intense feelings in the litigants. His errors may be corrected on appeal, but he should not have to fear that unsatisfied litigants may hound him with litigation charging malice or corruption. Imposing such a burden on judges would con-

tribute not to principled and fearless decision-making but to intimidation.

Not one of the considerations thus summarized in the *Pierson* opinion was present here. There was no "case," controversial or otherwise. There were no litigants. There was and could be no appeal. And there was not even the pretext of principled decision-making. The total absence of *any* of these normal attributes of a judicial proceeding convinces me that the conduct complained of in this case was not a judicial act.

The petitioners' brief speaks of "an aura of deism which surrounds the bench . . . essential to the maintenance of respect for the judicial institution." Though the rhetoric may be overblown, I do not quarrel with it. But if aura there be, it is hardly protected by exonerating from liability such lawless conduct as took place here. And if intimidation would serve to deter its recurrence, that would surely be in the public interest.

Mr. Justice POWELL, dissenting.

While I join the opinion of Mr. Justice STEWART, I wish to emphasize what I take to be the central feature of this case—petitioner's preclusion of any possibility for the vindication of respondent's rights elsewhere in the judicial system.

Bradley v. Fisher, 13 Wall. 335, 20 L.Ed. 646 (1872), which established the absolute judicial immunity at issue in this case, recognized that the immunity was designed to further the public interest in an independent judiciary, sometimes at the expense of legitimate individual grievances. . . . Underlying the *Bradley* immunity . . . is the notion that private rights can be sacrificed in some degree to the achievement of the greater public good deriving from a completely independent judiciary, because there exist alternative forums and methods for vindicating those rights.

But where a judicial officer acts in a manner that precludes all resort to appellate or other judicial remedies that otherwise would be available, the underlying assumption of the *Bradley* doctrine is inoperative. . . . The complete absence of normal judicial process foreclosed resort to any of the "numerous remedies" that "the law has provided for private parties." *Bradley*, supra, at 354.

In sum, I agree with Mr. Justice STEWART that respondent's actions were not "judicial," and that he is entitled to no judicial immunity from suit under 42 U.S. C.A. § 1983.

An important disagreement between the majority and the dissenters in *Stump* v. *Sparkman* was whether a "judicial act" was involved, i.e., whether the judge was acting within the sphere of his official duties. This is a question that keeps recurring in the cases that follow. Prosecutors, like judges, have been accorded absolute immunity at common law, and in *Imbler* v. *Pachtman*, 424 U.S. 409, 96 S.Ct. 984, 47 L.Ed.2d 128 (1976) the Supreme Court unanimously ruled that absolute immunity for prosecutors applies to § 1983 suits as well. Three of the eight Justices participating, however, felt that the immunity extended by the majority was broader than necessary and that, in general, prosecutors are not entitled to absolute immunity in suits based on claims of unconstitutional suppression of evidence because such an act "is beyond the scope of duties constituting an integral part of the judicial process." 424 U.S. 443, 96 S.Ct. 1001, 47 L.Ed.2d 151.

As further cases challenging judicial-type acts have come to the courts, the immunity doctrine has been extended and refined. Absolute immunity has been accorded to administrative law judges, witnesses and police officers who testify in court, and grand jurors.[33] But a sense of the limits of absolute immunity has also begun to emerge. *Pulliam v. Allen*, decided by the Supreme Court in 1984, is one relevant case.

Gladys Pulliam, a state magistrate in Virginia, imposed bail on Allen and Nicholson for nonjailable offenses, and then jailed them when they couldn't post bail. They brought a § 1983 action against her and the district court both enjoined the practice of committing persons to jail in such circumstances and awarded the respondents more than $7000 in costs and attorney's fees (the money award was made under § 1988, a related part of the statute). Over the vigorous dissent of four justices, the Supreme Court majority ruled that absolute judicial immunity prohibited neither the injunction nor the awarding of attorney's fees. 466 U.S. 522, 104 S.Ct. 1970, 80 L.Ed.2d 565.

Two more recent cases involved the extent of immunity for nonjudges performing what were arguably judicial-type functions. In *Cleavinger v. Saxner*, the Supreme Court considered the immunity of a prison's Institution Discipline Committee, which held a disciplinary hearing involving respondent inmates. The inmates, alleging that their constitutional rights had been violated at the hearing, sued for declaratory and injunctive relief, as well as for compensatory damages. The Supreme Court ruled, six to three, that the members of the Institution Discipline Committee were entitled only to qualified immunity, not absolute immunity. ___ U.S. ___, 106 S.Ct. 496, 88 L.Ed.2d 507 (1985). And a police officer who allegedly caused the unconstitutional arrest of a plaintiff, and who sought absolute immunity because "his function in seeking an arrest warrant was similar to that of a complaining witness," was held by the Supreme Court in 1986 to be protected only by a qualified immunity. *Malley v. Briggs*, ___ U.S. ___, 106 S.Ct. 1092, 89 L.Ed.2d 271.

Liability of Legislators

The "Speech and Debate" Clause of the Constitution provides broad protection from tort suits to members of Congress. This principle has been expressed on numerous occasions by the Supreme Court, although it has also been indicated recently that this blanket protection does not extend to subordinate employees of legislators.[34] But when congressmen "act outside of this 'sphere of legitimate legislative activity,' they enjoy no special immunity from local laws protecting the good name or the reputation of the ordinary citizen." [35]

Thus, members of Congress are wholly immune for speeches made in Congress, which are published in the *Congressional Record*, and for committee reports and associated work. But newsletters and press releases by individual congressmen are outside of this protection. This was the basis for the

---

[33] For references to Supreme Court cases where these rulings are cited, see *Cleavinger v. Saxner*, ___ U.S. ___, 106 S.Ct. 496, 500, 88 L.Ed.2d 507, 513–514.

[34] *Tenney v. Brandhove*, 341 U.S. 367, 71 S.Ct. 783, 95 L.Ed. 1019 (1951); *Dombrowski v. Eastland*, 387 U.S. 82, 87 S.Ct. 1425, 18 L.Ed.2d 577 (1967); *Doe v. McMillan*, 412 U.S. 306, 93 S.Ct. 2018, 36 L.Ed. 2d 912 (1973).

[35] *Doe v. McMillan*, 412 U.S. 306, 324, 93 S.Ct. 2018, 2030, 36 L.Ed.2d 912, 927–8 (1973).

Supreme Court's 1979 ruling that Senator William Proxmire was not immune from a defamation suit by a behavorial scientist based on a "Golden Fleece Award" aimed at allegedly egregious examples of wasteful government spending, which was distributed by the senator in a news release in 1975. *Hutchinson* v. *Proxmire*, 443 U.S. 111, 99 S.Ct. 2675, 61 L.Ed.2d 411 (1979). Of the nine participating justices, only Justice Brennan dissented, arguing that "public criticism by legislators of unnecessary governmental expenditures, whatever its form, is a legislative act shielded by the Speech and Debate Clause." 443 U.S. 111, 136, 99 S.Ct. 2675, 2689, 61 L.Ed.2d 411, 432.[36]

Liability of Other Officials

The following case is important in that it involves the question of the level of immunity accorded to the country's chief executive. For that reason, however, it can't be called a *typical* case involving the liability of public officials. But the excerpt included below provides a discussion of other relevant case law. This will be followed by an examination of some of the significant cases decided since *Nixon* v. *Fitzgerald*.

Nixon v. Fitzgerald

SUPREME COURT OF THE UNITED STATES, 1982.
457 U.S. 731, 102 S.CT. 2690, 73 L.ED.2D 349.

[A. Ernest Fitzgerald was a civilian Air Force employee who testified in 1968 before a congressional subcommittee concerning cost overruns and other difficulties of a particular airplane. In 1970, when Richard Nixon was president, Fitzgerald was dismissed from his job during a departmental reorganization. He complained to the Civil Service Commission that the dismissal was actually in retaliation for his congressional testimony.

While the commission did not agree with this allegation, it found that Fitzgerald lost his job through "reasons purely personal" to him, which was an impermissible basis for dismissal. It ordered his reappointment with backpay, and although Fitzgerald had to go to court to achieve it, he was eventually restored to his former position.

After the Civil Service Commission's decision in 1973, Fitzgerald filed a suit for damages against several officials of the United States. Considerable preliminary legal maneuvering ensued, including several rulings by the district court and the court of appeals. By March 1980, more than ten years after he complained to the Civil Service Commission about his dismissal, three defendants remained: former President Nixon, and presidential aides Bryce Harlow and Alexander Butterfield. The present case involves only former President Nixon. The case against the presidential aides was decided separately by the Supreme Court on the same day, and will be discussed below.

Fitzgerald claimed that the president and his aides had violated his First Amendment rights and certain statutory rights. He

---

[36] Senator Proxmire later settled the case out of court. He issued an apology and paid $10,000 to Dr. Hutchinson. Court costs of $5,123 and Senator Proxmire's legal defense costs of $124,351 were paid from public funds. The *New York Times*, March 25, 1980, B18.

alleged that the defendants had conspired to have him dismissed on improper grounds, namely, his congressional testimony. Among the evidence submitted to support his claim were: a) transcriptions of taped conversations between the president and other officials that were released as a result of the Watergate controversy; and b) an assertion by President Nixon at a news conference in January 1973 that he was aware of the Fitzgerald case and took full responsibility for the discharge; this statement was retracted the next day.

Before the case reached the Supreme Court, Nixon and Fitzgerald made an agreement under which Nixon paid Fitzgerald $142,000 and agreed to pay him $28,000 more if the Supreme Court ruled that Nixon was not entitled to absolute immunity. If the Court upheld the absolute immunity claim, no further payments were to be made. The question was raised as to whether this agreement, characterized by some commentators as a "sidebet," rendered the case moot. The majority ruled that it did not, and then turned to the issue of presidential immunity.]

Justice POWELL delivered the opinion of the Court. . . .

This Court consistently has recognized that government officials are entitled to some form of immunity from suits for civil damages. In *Spalding* v. *Vilas*, 161 U.S. 483, 16 S.Ct. 631, 40 L.Ed. 780 (1896), the Court considered the immunity available to the Postmaster General in a suit for damages based upon his official acts. Drawing upon principles of immunity developed in English cases at common law, the Court concluded that "[t]he interests of the people" required a grant of absolute immunity to public officers. Id., at 498, 16 S.Ct., at 637. In the absence of immunity, the Court reasoned, executive officials would hesitate to exercise their discretion in a way "injuriously affect[ing] the claims of particular individuals," id., at 499, 16 S.Ct., at 637, even when the public interest required bold and unhesitating action. Considera-

tions of "public policy and convenience" therefore compelled a judicial recognition of immunity from suits arising from official acts. . . .

Decisions subsequent to *Spalding* have extended the defense of immunity to actions besides those at common law. In *Tenney* v. *Brandhove*, 341 U.S. 367, 71 S.Ct. 783, 95 L.Ed. 1019 (1951), the Court considered whether the passage of 42 U.S.C. § 1983, which made no express provision for immunity for any official, had abrogated the privilege accorded to state legislators at common law. *Tenney* held that it had not. Examining § 1983 in light of the "presuppositions of our political history" and our heritage of legislative freedom, the Court found it incredible "that Congress . . . would impinge on a tradition so well grounded in history and reason" without some indication of intent more explicit than the general language of the statute. Id., at 376, 71 S.Ct., at 788. . . .

In *Scheuer* v. *Rhodes*, 416 U.S. 232, 94 S.Ct. 1683, 40 L.Ed.2d 90 (1974), the Court considered the immunity available to state executive officials in a § 1983 suit alleging the violation of constitutional rights. In that case we rejected the officials' claim to absolute immunity under the doctrine of *Spalding* v. *Vilas*, finding instead that state executive officials possessed a "good faith" immunity from § 1983 suits alleging constitutional violations. Balancing the purposes of § 1983 against the imperatives of public policy, the Court held that "in varying scope, a qualified immunity is available to officers of the executive branch of government, the variation being dependent upon the scope of discretion and responsibilities of the office and all the circumstances as they reasonably appeared at the time of the action on which liability is sought to be based." 416 U.S., at 247, 94 S.Ct., at 1692.

Here a former President asserts his immunity from civil damages claims of two kinds. He stands named as a defendant in a direct action under the Constitution and in two statutory actions under federal laws of general applicability. In neither case has Congress taken express legislative action to subject the President to civil liability for his official acts.

Applying the principles of our cases to claims of this kind, we hold that petitioner, as a former President of the United States, is entitled to absolute immunity from damages liability predicated on his official acts. We consider this immunity a functionally mandated incident of the President's unique office, rooted in the constitutional tradition of the separation of powers and supported by our history. . . .

In arguing that the President is entitled only to qualified immunity, the respondent relies on cases in which we have recognized immunity of this scope for governors and cabinet officers. E.g., *Butz* v. *Economou*, 438 U.S. 478, 98 S.Ct. 2894, 57 L.Ed.2d 895 (1978); *Scheuer* v. *Rhodes*, 416 U.S. 232, 94 S.Ct. 1683, 40 L.Ed.2d 90 (1974). We find these cases to be inapposite. The President's unique status under the Constitution distinguishes him from other executive officials. . . .

Courts traditionally have recognized the President's constitutional responsibilities and status as factors counseling judicial deference and restraint. For example, while courts generally have looked to the common law to determine the scope of an official's evidentiary privilege, we have recognized that the Presidential privilege is "rooted in the separation of powers under the Constitution." *United States* v. *Nixon*, 418 U.S., at 708, 94 S.Ct., at 3107. It is settled law that the separation-of-powers doctrine does not bar every exercise of jurisdiction over the President of the United States. See, e.g., *United States* v. *Nixon*, supra; *United States* v. *Burr*, 25 F.Cas. 187, 191, 196 (No. 14,694) (CC Va. 1807); cf. *Youngstown Sheet & Tube Co.* v. *Sawyer*, 343 U.S. 579, 72 S.Ct. 863, 96 L.Ed. 1153 (1952). But our cases also have established that a court, before exercising jurisdiction, must balance the constitutional weight of the interest to be

served against the dangers of intrusion on the authority and functions of the Executive Branch. See *Nixon* v. *Administrator of General Services*, 433 U.S. 425, 443, 97 S.Ct. 2777, 2790, 53 L.Ed.2d 867 (1977); *United States* v. *Nixon*, supra, at 703–713, 94 S.Ct., at 3105–3110. When judicial action is needed to serve broad public interests—as when the Court acts, not in derogation of the separation of powers, but to maintain their proper balance, cf. *Youngstown Sheet & Tube Co.* v. *Sawyer*, supra, or to vindicate the public interest in an ongoing criminal prosecution, see *United States* v. *Nixon*, supra—the exercise of jurisdiction has been held warranted. In the case of this merely private suit for damages based on a President's official acts, we hold it is not.

In defining the scope of an official's absolute privilege, this Court has recognized that the sphere of protected action must be related closely to the immunity's justifying purposes. Frequently our decisions have held that an official's absolute immunity should extend only to acts in performance of particular functions of his office. See *Butz* v. *Economou*, 438 U.S., at 508–517, 98 S.Ct., at 2911–2916; cf. *Imbler* v. *Pachtman*, 424 U.S., at 430–431, 96 S.Ct., at 994–995. But the Court also has refused to draw functional lines finer than history and reason would support. See, e.g., *Spalding* v. *Vilas*, 161 U.S., at 498, 16 S.Ct., at 637 (privilege extends to all matters "committed by law to [an official's] control or supervision"); *Barr* v. *Matteo*, 360 U.S. 564, 575, 79 S.Ct. 1335, 1341, 3 L.Ed.2d 1434 (1959) (fact "that the action here taken was within the outer perimeter of petitioner's line of duty is enough to render the privilege applicable . . ."); *Stump* v. *Sparkman*, 435 U.S., at 363 and n. 12, 98 S.Ct., at 1108 and n. 12 (judicial privilege applies even to acts occurring outside "the normal attributes of a judicial proceeding"). In view of the special nature of the President's constitutional office and functions, we think it appropriate to recognize absolute Presidential immunity from damages liability for acts within the "outer perimeter" of his official responsibility. . . .

A rule of absolute immunity for the President will not leave the Nation without sufficient protection against misconduct on the part of the Chief Executive. There remains the constitutional remedy of impeachment. In addition, there are formal and informal checks on Presidential action that do not apply with equal force to other executive officials. The President is subjected to constant scrutiny by the press. Vigilant oversight by Congress also may serve to deter Presidential abuses of office, as well as to make credible the threat of impeachment. Other incentives to avoid misconduct may include a desire to earn re-election, the need to maintain prestige as an element of Presidential influence, and a President's traditional concern for his historical stature.

The existence of alternative remedies and deterrents establishes that absolute immunity will not place the President "above the law." For the President, as for judges and prosecutors, absolute immunity merely precludes a particular private remedy for alleged misconduct in order to advance compelling public ends. . . .

[The concurring opinion of Chief Justice Burger is omitted.]

Justice WHITE, with whom Justice BRENNAN, Justice MARSHALL, and Justice BLACKMUN join, dissenting.

The four dissenting Members of the Court in *Butz* v. *Economou*, 438 U.S. 478, 98 S.Ct. 2894, 57 L.Ed.2d 895 (1978), argued that all federal officials are entitled to absolute immunity from suit for any action they take in connection with their official duties. That immunity would extend even to actions taken with express knowledge that the conduct was clearly contrary to the controlling statute or clearly violative of the Constitution. Fortunately, the major-ity of the Court rejected that approach: We held that although public officials perform certain functions that entitle them to absolute immunity, the immunity attaches to particular functions—not to particular offices. Officials performing functions for which immunity is not absolute enjoy qualified immunity; they are liable in damages only if their conduct violated well-established law and if they should have realized that their conduct was illegal.

The Court now applies the dissenting view in *Butz* to the Office of the President: A President, acting within the outer boundaries of what Presidents normally do, may, without liability, deliberately cause serious injury to any number of citizens even though he knows his conduct violates a statute or tramples on the constitutional rights of those who are injured. Even if the President in this case ordered Fitzgerald fired by means of a trumped-up reduction in force, knowing that such a discharge was contrary to the civil service laws, he would be absolutely immune from suit. By the same token, if a President, without following the statutory procedures which he knows apply to himself as well as to other federal officials, orders his subordinates to wiretap or break into a home for the purpose of installing a listening device, and the officers comply with his request, the President would be absolutely immune from suit. He would be immune regardless of the damage he inflicts, regardless of how violative of the statute and of the Constitution he knew his conduct to be, and regardless of his purpose.[37]

The Court intimates that its decision is grounded in the Constitution. If that is the case, Congress cannot provide a remedy against Presidential misconduct and the criminal laws of the United States are wholly inapplicable to the President. I find this approach completely unacceptable. I

---

[37] This, of course, is not simply a hypothetical example. See *Halperin* v. *Kissinger*, 196 U.S.App. D.C. 285, 606 F.2d 1192 (1979), aff'd by an equally divided Court, 452 U.S. 713, 101 S.Ct. 3132, 69 L.Ed.2d 367 (1981).

do not agree that if the Office of President is to operate effectively, the holder of that Office must be permitted, without fear of liability and regardless of the function he is performing, deliberately to inflict injury on others by conduct that he knows violates the law.

We have not taken such a scatter-gun approach in other cases. *Butz* held that absolute immunity did not attach to the office held by a member of the President's Cabinet but only to those specific functions performed by that officer for which absolute immunity is clearly essential. Members of Congress are absolutely immune under the Speech or Debate Clause of the Constitution, but the immunity extends only to their legislative acts. We have never held that in order for legislative work to be done, it is necessary to immunize all of the tasks that legislators must perform. Constitutional immunity does not extend to those many things that Senators and Representatives regularly and necessarily do that are not legislative acts. Members of Congress, for example, repeatedly importune the executive branch and administrative agencies outside hearing rooms and legislative halls, but they are not immune if in connection with such activity they deliberately violate the law. *United States* v. *Brewster*, 408 U.S. 501, 92 S.Ct. 2531, 33 L.Ed.2d 507 (1972), for example, makes this clear. Neither is a Member of Congress or his aide immune from damages suits if in order to secure information deemed relevant to a legislative investigation, he breaks into a house and carries away records. *Gravel* v. *United States*, 408 U.S. 606, 92 S.Ct. 2614, 33 L.Ed.2d 583 (1972). Judges are absolutely immune from liability for damages, but only when performing a judicial function, and even then they are subject to criminal liability. See *Dennis* v. *Sparks*, 449 U.S. 24, 31, 101 S.Ct. 183, 188, 66 L.Ed.2d 185 (1980); *O'Shea* v. *Littleton*, 414 U.S. 488, 503, 94 S.Ct. 669, 679–80, 38 L.Ed. 2d 674 (1974). The absolute immunity of prosecutors is likewise limited to the prosecutorial function. A prosecutor who directs that an investigation be carried out in a way that is patently illegal is not immune. . . .

Attaching absolute immunity to the Office of the President, rather than to particular activities that the President might perform, places the President above the law. It is a reversion to the old notion that the King can do no wrong. Until now, this concept had survived in this country only in the form of sovereign immunity. That doctrine forecloses suit against the Government itself and against Government officials, but only when the suit against the latter actually seeks relief against the sovereign. *Larson* v. *Domestic & Foreign Commerce Corp.*, 337 U.S. 682, 687, 69 S.Ct. 1457, 1460, 93 L.Ed. 1628 (1949). Suit against an officer, however, may be maintained where it seeks specific relief against him for conduct contrary to his statutory authority or to the Constitution. Id., at 698, 69 S.Ct., at 1465. Now, however, the Court clothes the Office of the President with sovereign immunity, placing it beyond the law. . . .

The functional approach to the separation-of-powers doctrine and the Court's more recent immunity decisions converge on the following principle: The scope of immunity is determined by function, not office. The wholesale claim that the President is entitled to absolute immunity in all of his actions stands on no firmer ground than did the claim that all Presidential communications are entitled to an absolute privilege, which was rejected in favor of a functional analysis, by a unanimous Court in *United States* v. *Nixon*, 418 U.S. 683, 94 S.Ct. 3090, 41 L.Ed.2d 1039 (1974). Therefore, whatever may be true of the necessity of such a broad immunity in certain areas of executive responsibility, the only question that must be answered here is whether the dismissal of employees falls within a constitutionally assigned executive function, the performance of which would be substantially impaired by the possibility of a private action for damages. I believe it does not. . . .

[The dissenting opinion of Justice Blackmun, joined by Justices Brennan and Marshall, is omitted.]

Qualified Immunity

Codefendants with former President Nixon in the same civil damage suit brought by Fitzgerald were former presidential aides Bryce Harlow and Alexander Butterfield. They also sought the protection of absolute immunity. But in a separate decision the Supreme Court ruled eight to one that they were only entitled to qualified immunity. Noting that for "executive officials in general . . . our cases make plain that qualified immunity represents the norm," the Court concluded that public policy did not require that presidential aides be afforded absolute immunity. *Harlow* v. *Fitzgerald*, 457 U.S. 800, 102 S.Ct. 2727, 73 L.Ed.2d 396 (1982).

A notable further point made in *Harlow* v. *Fitzgerald* involves the standard for determining whether qualified immunity will apply. It was suggested above (see note 28) that qualified immunity protects an official unless maliciousness or bad faith can be shown. In *Harlow* the Court asserted that "substantial costs attend the litigation of the subjective good faith of governmental officials," allowing some cases to go to trial which should be dismissed as falling within the protection of qualified immunity. The Court therefore ruled that henceforth "governmental officials performing discretionary functions generally are shielded from liability for civil damages insofar as their conduct does not violate clearly established constitutional rights of which a reasonable person would have known." 457 U.S. 818, 102 S.Ct. 2738, 73 L.Ed.2d 410. It is too early to know whether this new standard will be workable in practice. Some commentators doubt that it will.[38]

Another point made in passing in *Harlow* is that not just presidential aides, but also Cabinet members, would normally be entitled only to qualified immunity. The Court got a chance to assert this view directly in 1985 in *Mitchell* v. *Forsyth*, ___ U.S. ___, 105 S.Ct. 2806, 86 L.Ed.2d 411. A suit was brought against former Attorney General Mitchell for his authorization of a warrantless wiretap for purposes of gathering information about a radical group. Warrantless wiretaps in cases involving domestic threats to national security were later ruled illegal, and the plaintiff sued Mitchell for violation of his constitutional and statutory rights. The Supreme Court held that Mitchell was entitled to only qualified rather than absolute immunity.

As just indicated, *Mitchell* was based on an alleged constitutional tort, and allows a defendant only qualified immunity. This result appears to be at odds with immunity principles where a common-law tort is at issue. The leading recent case is *Barr* v. *Matteo*, 360 U.S. 564, 79 S.Ct. 1335, 3 L.Ed.2d 1434 (1959), which was mentioned in passing in the excerpt from *Nixon* v. *Fitzgerald* printed above. Without going into the details of the case, suffice it to say that

---

[38] See, e.g., Davis, above, note 10, 127–136. Among Davis' conclusions is the following (at 136): "The lower courts pay lip service to the Harlow case but to a great extent continue to use the test of 'reasonable and in good faith'."

it stands for the principle that high governmental officials (in this case the Acting Director of the Office of Rent Stabilization) are absolutely immune from liability for injury-causing acts committed "within the outer perimeter of petitioner's line of duty." This seeming inconsistency is another area where the commentators have called upon the Supreme Court to bring uniformity to the law.[39]

Barr v. *Matteo* has not been overruled, but it appears to be out of line with many recent decisions. If a trend is developing, it is that executive-branch officials other than the president, when performing normal executive functions, will be entitled to no more than the protection of qualified immunity. This generalization applies not just to the federal level, but to state officials sued under § 1983 as well. In *Scheuer* v. *Rhodes*, 416 U.S. 232, 94 S.Ct. 1683, 40 L.Ed. 90 (1974), a case which grew out of the National Guard shootings of students at Kent State University in 1970, the Supreme Court reversed a lower court dismissal of a § 1983 suit against the governor of Ohio and other officials and declared that only a qualified immunity was available to the defendants. The next year this principle was extended to a § 1983 suit against school administrators in a school expulsion case. *Wood* v. *Strickland*, 420 U.S. 308, 95 S.Ct. 992, 43 L.Ed.2d 214 (1975). Since then, other relevant cases have reached a similar conclusion.

THE INTEGRATION OF GOVERNMENT AND OFFICERS' LIABILITY

Developments described in this chapter outline a trend in the direction of greater governmental liability in tort accompanied by a reduction in the liability of governmental officials. Several recent developments suggest that this trend will continue, to the point where liability of officials may be largely absorbed by governmental liability. Among the relevant developments are those discussed in this chapter section.

Legislation Protecting Government Employees from Liability

Legislation making the government the sole defendant in tort suits that might be filed against individuals has been adopted on several occasions. A 1961 amendment to the Federal Tort Claims Act provided that for personal injuries resulting from a government employee's operation of a motor vehicle, only the government and not the employee could be sued, upon certification by the attorney general that the employee was acting within the scope of his office. P.L. 87–258, 75 Stat 539 (1961) as amended by P.L. 89–506 (1966), codified as 28 U.S.C.A. § 2679.[40]

Other such legislation protects certain government contractors from liability. For example, a 1976 statute provided that the exclusive remedy for

---

[39] See, e.g., Davis, above, note 10, 117–122; also Schuck, above, note 10, 40–43.

[40] See the discussion of four other statutes that similarly protect governmental medical personnel in 5 Davis 21 (above, note 10).

claimants seeking damages for liability arising from the swine flu immunization program being administered at that time would be a suit against the United States. P.L. 94–380, 90 Stat. 1115 (1976). And a 1984 statute substituted the United States as a defendant in all suits against private contractors with the government arising out of injuries connected with the atomic weapons testing program. P.L. 98–525, 98 Stat. 2646, codified as 42 U.S.C.A. 2212.

In a more general way, legislation has been introduced in Congress several times over the past few years that would extend the principle of substituting governmental liability for the liability of federal officials for all "constitutional torts." In 1982 the Administrative Conference of the United States endorsed this proposal.[41] Some commentators would transfer liability in general to governmental entities, whether constitutional torts or other torts were involved. Still unanswered under such an arrangement is how governmental employees might be held accountable for clearly irresponsible acts, a problem that is addressed in some legislative proposals through a provision for intraagency disciplinary proceedings.[42]

A related question is whether the government should be entitled, as a defense in tort suits, to the immunity that would have been available to individual employees. No clear answer has yet emerged on this issue. In *Norton* v. *United States*, 581 F.2d 390 (1978), the Court of Appeals for the Fourth Circuit ruled, in a Federal Tort Claims Act suit, that the United States could assert as a defense the good faith and reasonable belief of their officers in the legality of their conduct. But other courts have ruled to the contrary.[43] And the Supreme Court has come to the opposite conclusion when the issue was the liability of a municipality under § 1983. In *Owen* v. *City of Independence, Missouri*, 445 U.S. 622, 100 S.Ct. 1398, 63 L.Ed.2d 673 (1980) the Court ruled five to four that a municipality was not entitled to a qualified immunity based on the good faith of their officials.

Liability under Section 1983

Monroe v. *Pape*, 365 U.S. 167, 81 S.Ct. 473, 5 L.Ed.2d 492 (1961) was an important case that "resurrected Section 1983 from ninety years of obscurity."[44] It allowed police officers to be held liable for illegal acts against individuals even if the acts were done without state authority. But the Supreme Court ruled that the City of Chicago was immune from liability under § 1983, reasoning that a municipality could not be considered a "person" whose acts, which deprived others of their civil rights, the statute was designed to remedy. In 1978 the Supreme Court overruled the latter aspect of *Monroe* v. *Pape*, holding that that case had been based on an erroneous interpretation of legislative

---

[41] Recommendation 82–6: Federal Officials' Liability for Constitutional Violations (Adopted December 16, 1982), *1982 Report of the Administrative Conference of the United States* 58 (1983).

[42] See, for example, S.695, *Congressional Record*, March 15, 1979, S2919–2923. Professor Davis, while endorsing the general transfer of liability to governmental entities, states that "retaining liability of the employee for malicious action might be reasonable." Davis, above, note 10, 246.

[43] See the cases discussed in Davis, above, note 10, 141.

[44] "Developments in the Law: Section 1983 and Federalism," 90 *Harvard Law Review* 1133, 1169 (1977).

history and that local governments, municipal corporations, and school boards were "persons" subject to liability under § 1983. *Monell* v. *Department of Social Services of City of New York*, 436 U.S. 658, 98 S.Ct. 2018, 56 L.Ed.2d 611 (1978).[45]

Paying Judgments Against Officials from Public Funds

On some occasions governmental units protect their officials from tort liability by assuming the obligations themselves, either through the payment of insurance premiums or by settling claims against officials from public funds. An important recent example of a state government assuming financial responsibility for a potentially large damage award against state officials was the State of Ohio's $675,000 out-of-court settlement in 1978 of a suit against Governor Rhodes and a number of National Guardsmen, brought by the victims and families of victims of the Kent State University shootings.[46]

While paying judgments against officials from public funds has been assumed to be a fairly frequent practice on the state and local level,[47] it apparently is not so frequent at the federal level.[48] Davis suggests that the Court "should always inquire of counsel for the employee (a) whether a judgment against the employee will be paid by the employee or by his governmental employer, and (b) what, if any, disciplinary action is likely to be taken against the employee if he is found to be at fault."[49]

WHERE DOES GOVERNMENTAL LIABILITY GO FROM HERE?

The government is a unique kind of entity. A question that is increasingly being raised is not whether the government ought to be less liable than a private party (on the basis of sovereign immunity) but whether it ought to be

---

[45] Another aspect of *Monell* is at odds with the Supreme Court's views on governmental liability at the federal level, however. Under the Federal Tort Claims Act the United States can be considered vicariously liable for the torts of its officials under a legal concept known as *respondeat superior* ("let the master answer"). According to *Monell*, however, a local government "cannot be held liable under § 1983 on a *respondent superior* theory." Instead, governmental liability must be based on the execution of a "policy" of a local governmental unit. 463 U.S. 691, 694. This issue has divided the Supreme Court and has caused confusion as to the circumstances under which a governmental entity may be liable under § 1983. It appears that the Court may be moving away from the view that liability must be based on governmental policy. In a 1986 case, the Court ruled that a single decision to take a particular action may be considered to constitute "policy" for purposes of liability under § 1983. *Pembaur* v. *City of Cincinnati*, ___ U.S. ___, 106 S.Ct. 1299, 89 L.Ed.2d 452 (1986). For a critical analysis of the differences between the Supreme Court's view of liability of the federal government as compared to local governments, see Davis, above, note 10, 216.

[46] The *New York Times*, January 5, 1978, 12.

[47] Writing for the majority in a 1974 case, Justice Rehnquist asserted in a decision reversing a compensation award of the basis of the Eleventh Amendment, that the award "will to a virtual certainty be paid from state funds, and not from the pockets of individual state officials who were defendants in the action." *Edelman* v. *Jordan*, 415 U.S. 651, 668, 94 S.Ct. 1347, 1358, 39 L.Ed.2d 662, 676 (1974). But the practice may not be so frequent as is assumed by the Supreme Court. See Davis, above, note 10, 222–224.

[48] Ibid. 224.

[49] Ibid. 226.

more liable. The bases for this kind of thinking are the rise of the welfare state and the greater ability of the government than of most private parties to pay for damages caused by it. Professor Davis has summarized the relevant reasoning as follows:

> ... After all, a governmental unit differs significantly from a private party: it is supported by taxation, and it is not dependent upon private investment or private profit. A large enough governmental unit is the best of all possible loss spreaders, especially, perhaps if its taxes are geared to ability to pay. This basic fact, which so far has been given too little heed, will in time lead us to see that the basis for government liability should not be fault but should be equitable loss spreading. The ultimate principle may be that the taxpaying public should usually bear the fortuitous and heavy losses that result from governmental activity.... The key idea will be simply that a beneficent governmental unit ought not to allow exceptional losses to be borne by those upon whom the governmental activity has happened to inflict harm.[50]

This line of thinking is quite different from more traditional views. It is not argued today (as it was put in an old English case) that "it is better that an individual should sustain an injury than that the public should suffer an inconvenience."[51] But there are still many who do not favor so-called "collectivization of risk," who hold that "individual well-being is not in itself absolutely assured by any government.... The individual must pay for the privilege of living in an organized society."[52]

Even if one favors the further extension of governmental liability, there remains the question of how far government should be held liable for its acts. Nearly all governmental activity, legislative, executive, judicial, and administrative, hurts someone, but should there be liability for all such acts? This would be neither reasonable nor possible. The government must be given some latitude for performing its functions. As Mr. Justice Jackson has stated, "it is not a tort for the government to govern." *Dalehite* v. *United States*, 346 U.S. 15, 57, 73 S.Ct. 956, 979, 97 L.Ed. 1427, 1452 (1953).

Up to the present, the basis of governmental tort liability, as of tort liability in general in the United States, has been the concept of negligence or fault. Normally it must be shown that the defendant in a case has acted negligently in causing injury to another person before a judgment can be made against him. In private tort law, one of the important trends in modern times has been the replacement of the fault principle in certain circumstances (the use of dangerous substances or the conducting of ultrahazardous activities, for instance) by the principle of "strict liability" or liability regardless of fault. But *Dalehite* v. *United States* ruled that liability under the Federal Tort Claims Act could be based only on negligence. 346 U.S. 15, 45, 73 S.Ct. 956, 972, 97 L.Ed. 1427, 1445 (1953). More recently this principle was reaffirmed in *Laird* v. *Nelms*, 406 U.S. 797, 92 S.Ct. 1899, 32 L.Ed.2d 499 (1972), where the Supreme

---

[50] 3 *Administrative Law Treatise* 503–504 (1958). This view is affirmed in the second edition of Davis' treatise. See above, note 10, 140.

[51] *Russell* v. *Men of Devon*, 100 Eng.Rep. 359, as cited in *Muskopf* v. *Corning Hospital Dist.*, 55 Cal.2d 211, 11 Cal.Rptr. 89, 359 P.2d 457 (1961).

[52] Harry Street, "Governmental Liability for Tort in Britain and the United States," 18 *Public Administration* 48 (1950).

Court ruled that a plaintiff could not recover damages caused by sonic booms by military aircraft because no negligence was shown to have taken place in the flight. Yet it seems clear that this cost of living in a highly technological society should not be borne by an individual.

Most people would probably agree that a person who has been arrested, convicted, and has served time in prison for a crime of which he is innocent should have recourse against the government for the financial damages caused to him. And indeed he does, at least in some jurisdictions. On the federal level the "Unjust Conviction Statute" provides this kind of possibility of compensation.[53]

Compensation for Crime Victims

Imagine this situation: an individual is mugged and robbed by an unknown assailant and feels that he is entitled to better police protection than he received. Should he be able to sue the government for not protecting him? Traditionally the answer has been no, and even with changes in attitudes in recent times with regard to the plight of crime victims, there has been little advocacy of a "right" to sue the government for failing to protect its citizens from crime.[54] In 1963 New Zealand adopted the "Criminal Injuries Compensation Act," which provides a comprehensive plan for compensation to the victims of violent crimes. A tribunal hears claims and makes awards. Compensation is paid "as a matter of social welfare and not because of the State's liability for not successfully protecting a citizen from crime." [55] This principle has become the basis for the adoption of similar laws in Great Britain and other foreign countries, and by the mid-1980s thirty-nine states in the U.S. had adopted such legislation. In addition, in 1982, after several years of efforts, Congress enacted the Victim and Witness Protection Act which, among other things, provides guidelines for the fair treatment of crime victims and witnesses, and spells out the kinds of services that are available to victims. P.L. 97–291, 96 Stat. 1248. Two years later Congress adopted the Victims of Crime Act of 1984. It created a Crime Victims Fund which provides grants to state crime victim programs and retains a small reserve for compensation of victims of federal crimes. P.L. 98–473, Title II, § 1402, 98 Stat. 2170.

In addition to compensation from public funds, a crime victim may be able to bring a civil action for damages against a criminal, and may be awarded restitution by a court in a criminal proceeding against a defendant. And a number of states have enacted statutes (often called Son of Sam statutes) giving victims the right to share in the profits from the criminal's depiction of the crime in commercial presentations.[56]

---

[53] 52 Stat. 438 (1938), 28 U.S.C.A. § 2513.

[54] In some jurisdictions, suits have been successfully brought against the state for failure to protect a citizen from crime, particularly where there was due warning to the authorities of the likelihood of a crime. See, for instance, *Schuster* v. *New York*, 5 N.Y.2d 75, 180 N.Y.S.2d 265, 154 N.E. 534 (1958).

[55] *Correctional Research*, Bulletin No. 16, November 1966, 8.

[56] On these matters see generally James H. Stark and Howard W. Goldstein, *The Rights of Crime Victims* (1985).

Liability for Mob Violence

A somewhat different situation exists with regard to governmental liability for losses resulting from mob violence. Some fifteen states have statutes providing that municipalities will be liable for damages caused by civil disturbances.[57] The motivation for adopting at least some of these statutes was to create an incentive for local officials to prevent such uprisings. Why should a government be liable for not preventing large-scale personal injury and property damage, but not that visited upon single individuals by common criminals? Some people have pointed out the inconsistency here, but the reason for the existence of liability statutes for riot damage is apparently a historical one. A number of such statutes, modeled after the English Riot Act of 1714, were enacted during the nineteenth century, when the problems of municipal disturbances had not approached the proportions that they later reached. Recently some states have cut back their liability in this area[58]

Liability for Malfeasance

So far the discussion has involved new potential areas of governmental liability where the government has failed to take proper action, "nonfeasance" in legal language. Another sphere of possible governmental liability concerns positive acts of governmental authority that are harmful in nature ("malfeasance" or "misfeasance"). For instance, the Food and Drug Administration erroneously declared a harvest of spinach to be contaminated by the pesticide heptachlor; as a result, the crop had to be destroyed. Under the Federal Tort Claims Act there was no liability, because the FDA declaration qualified as "misrepresentation," one of the specific circumstances under the act for which the government will not be liable. In this particular case, the farmers were able to prevail upon Congress to pass a private bill allowing them to get a court hearing on their loss claims.[59]

Private Bills

As indicated earlier, the avenue of private legislation is still resorted to frequently where a suit against the government fails or the government is declared immune. The victims of the Texas City Disaster finally benefited from private legislation, although the test case, *Dalehite* v. *United States*, was lost in the courts. And in 1976 Congress provided $750,000 to the family of Dr. Frank

---

[57] "Municipal Liability for Riot Damage," 81 *Harvard Law Review* 653 (1968): "Aftermath of the Riot: Balancing the Budget," 116 *University of Pennsylvania Law Review* 649 (1968).

[58] For instance, statutes dating back as far as 1841 which provided for county liability for property damage as a result of mob violence or riots in three large Pennsylvania counties were repealed in 1968 and 1970. 16 Purdon's Pennsylvania Statutes Annotated §§ 11821–11826. In place of such liability Pennsylvania created in 1968 the Pennsylvania Civil Disorder Authority, an insurance arrangement against riots and civil disorders. 40 Ibid. § 1600.301 et seq. But the deputy attorney general of Pennsylvania wrote to one of the authors in November, 1979, that "the Pennsylvania, Civil Disorder Authority has not been active in recent years, and may never have been active."

[59] 78 Stat. 1195 (1964). *Mizokami* v. *U.S.*, 414 F.2d 1375 (Ct.Cl.1969). The Court of Claims awarded plaintiffs $301,974.33.

Olson, a civilian biochemist working for the federal government, who died in 1953. Dr. Olson plunged to his death from a Manhattan hotel room after CIA agents, engaged in testing the effects of LSD on humans, placed some of the drug in his after-dinner drink during a conference of government scientists.[60] These are just several examples of hundreds of such pieces of private legislation.

But private bills cannot and should not be the main road to a remedy in cases of this kind. The delays and uncertainties, as well as the inevitability of some deserving cases not making their way through Congress, suggest that another means of handling these problems would be preferable. While saying this, it is worth noting that the number of potential claims against the government, in its ever more pervasive presence in American life, is truely staggering. The FDA error with regard to the spinach crop described above is only a single example of a vast area of governmental activity in inspecting and certifying that certain products, foods, or activities are safe or permissible. With regard to most such inspections and certifications, the government can avoid being held liable, even if negligence could be shown, by the FTCA's "misrepresentation" clause or some other exception in the law. Thus, for example, in 1969 the FDA banned the use of the artificial sweetner cyclamate after earlier having listed it among food substances "generally recognized as safe." Those who claimed to incur losses as a result of the ban lobbied Congress for private legislation for their benefit, since they could not sue the government directly.[61] Whether or not the government should compensate in such cases may be open to question[62] but private legislation does not seem the appropriate way to gain such relief.

Other Avenues for Compensation

There are two other ways on the federal level by which compensation can be awarded in deserving cases. Section 2672 of Title 28 of the U.S. Code is a part of the Federal Tort Claims Act, as amended. It provides an alternative to instituting a tort suit: administrative settlement of claims for personal injury or property damage by the heads of appropriate federal agencies. The amount of such settlement is unlimited, but any award in excess of $25,000 must be approved by the attorney general. And § 2677 of the same title provides that the attorney general or his designee may arbitrate, compromise, or settle any claim against the United States that has already been commenced.

There have been some notable awards under these sections. A $9-million settlement was made in 1975 in a suit against the United States Public Health Service for a forty-year study of the effects of untreated syphilis in which six-

---

[60] The private legislation on behalf of the Olson family is Private Law 94–126, October 12, 1976, 90 Stat. 3006. The facts of the death of Dr. Olson were widely reported in the press, including the *New York Times*, December 19, 1975, 24.

[61] See the *New York Times*, July 25, 1972, 1.

[62] There is a distinct possibility of governmental liability in cases of this kind in French law. See Bernard Schwartz, *French Administrative Law and the Common-Law World* 298–302 (1954).

hundred black males were subjects.[63] Later the same decade, the federal government settled hundreds of claims of persons who were apparently paralyzed as a result of being inoculated in a mass swine flu immunization program established by the federal government in 1976.[64]

Looking Ahead

In the long run, however, administrative settlement or compromise will probably not be a sufficient remedy. For while agency heads or the attorney general may be prepared to settle claims for rather modest amounts, it is less likely that they will be prepared to recommend payment in situations involving scores of millions of dollars. Moreover, the administrative settlement of claims by agency heads carries at least the suggestion of conflict of interest: in settling a claim an administrator is admitting in a sense that his agency did something wrong. It may be unreasonable to expect consistent objectivity from high-level bureaucrats under this arrangement.

Whether the traditional tort suit provides any better answer is also open to question. Critics cite the "explosion of tort liability," the burgeoning number and size of awards against governmental entities, and the difficulties municipalities and other organizations have in getting adequate insurance to protect them from potentially devastating lawsuits as among the problems that tort law has recently created.[65]

One response is to alter the tort-law rules as currently applied, and a movement in that direction seems to be taking hold in the latter part of the 1980s. For instance, the Reagan administration in 1986 sent a proposal to Congress to amend the Federal Tort Claims Act in various ways. Declaring that "tort liability awards against the United States in recent years have become increasingly unreasonable and unfair," the proposal contains several provisions for containing the costs of judgments against the United States, such as limiting noneconomic damage payments to $100,000, making economic loss payments on a periodic basis rather than as a single lump sum, and putting a cap on attorneys' fees.[66]

---

[63] This case was widely reported in the press. See, for instance, the *New York Times*, February 6, 1975, 3 and July 29, 1979, 26.

[64] See the *New York Times*, June 10, 1979, 1 and June 15, 1979, A26. Some plaintiffs have chosen to sue rather than settling out of court in these cases. An analogous earlier situation was the mass polio innoculations begun in the 1960s. Some suits against the government under the Federal Tort Claims Act for injuries allegedly resulting from polio shots have been won. See, e.g., *Griffin* v. *United States*, 500 F.2d 1059 (3d Cir.1974). See Marc A. Franklin and Joseph E. Mais, "Tort Law and Mass Immunization Programs: Lessons from the Polio and Flu Episodes," 65 *California Law Review* 754 (1977).

[65] On these points, including the quoted phrase, see the U.S. Department of Justice's *Report of the Tort Policy Working Group on the Causes, Extent and Policy Implications of the Current Crisis in Insurance Availability and Affordability*, esp. 2–5 (February, 1986). This report covers not only governmental tort liability but also private sector problems of tort law as well.

[66] The proposed legislation is known as the "Federal Tort Claims Reform Act of 1986." See U.S. Department of Justice release, April 30, 1986. This release contains two other proposals also aimed at alleviating current problems in tort law. They are "The Government Contractor Reform Act of 1986" and "The Product Liability Reform Act of 1986." New York State, among other states, also appears to be moving toward changes in these areas. See, e.g., *The New York Times*, March 17, 1986, A1.

This proposal is part of a broader attack on tort law in general,[67] but not one that goes unopposed by some segments of American society.[68] It is a fair guess, however, that these proposals express a general mood or attitude that is growing in strength. It is probable that concrete alterations in tort law and insurance arrangements will follow in the not too distant future.

---

[67] See above, sources cited in notes 65 and 66.

[68] Several groups, including the American Bar Association, the National Insurance Consumer Organization, and Public Citizen, Inc., are said to oppose these proposals. See *The New York Times*, May 1, 1986, B9.

Chapter 10

Opening Up the Government

The late 1960s and 1970s saw a significant shift in the direction of increased public access to government operations. This shift was accomplished largely through legislation, but the contours of the movement were shaped by judicial and administrative action as well. The most important aspects of this development, which will be discussed in this chapter, are the following: the federal Freedom of Information Act, the concept of executive privilege, the Privacy Act, the "government-in-the-sunshine" laws, and the provisions for increased citizen participation in the governmental policy-making and decision-making processes.

THE FREEDOM OF INFORMATION ACT

A key development was the adoption of the federal Freedom of Information Act (FOIA) in 1966. P.L. 89–487, 80 Stat. 250. Some very significant amendments were added in 1974. P.L. 93–502, 88 Stat. 1561. The act is codified as section 552 of Title 5 of the U.S.Code, a part of the Administrative Procedure Act.[1] Prior to the adoption of the act, government records were required to be revealed only to "persons properly and directly concerned" with such records. Any records could be kept secret if such a policy was "in the public interest" or if the records related "solely to the internal management of an agency." [2] The Freedom of Information Act, described by the House Committee on Government Operations as "milestone legislation that reversed long-standing government

---

[1] The Administrative Procedure Act is appendix A of this book. The reader may consult section 552 for the specific provisions of the Freedom of Information Act. Two other important acts discussed in this chapter are also part of the Administrative Procedure Act: The Privacy Act (section 552a of the APA) and the Government in the Sunshine Act (section 552b).

[2] 60 Stat. 237 (1946) (section 3 of the original Administrative Procedure Act).

information practices," [3] provides, by contrast, that "each agency" shall make available records or other information requested by "any person." The burden of proof for withholding information is placed on the agency, which is required to respond to all requests for information within ten working days after receipt of a request, except when "unusual circumstances" permit an extension of ten more working days. A denial of information may be appealed to a higher level in the agency, and if the information request is still denied, the party may go to federal district court to seek an order that the records be produced.

Not all information in the hands of the government need be released, of course. The act lists nine specific matters to which the disclosure section does not apply, including such information as "trade secrets and commercial or financial information obtained from a person" which are deemed "privileged or confidential," and "personnel and medical files and similar files the disclosure of which would constitute a clearly unwarranted invasion of personal privacy." Perhaps the most important exemption is for information "specifically authorized under criteria established by an Executive order to be kept secret in the interest of national defense or foreign policy."

Whether the disclosure of certain files *would* constitute an unwarranted invasion of privacy, or whether information in the government's possession *is* privileged or confidential, are matters about which opinions may differ. These are the kinds of issues that the courts are called upon to decide, and the case of *Chrysler* v. *Brown*, excerpted below, involves the second exemption just mentioned. The exemption involving information pertaining to national defense and foreign policy has also been the subject of some significant litigation. Many Americans are fearful that this provision could be used unreasonably to keep information from the public, and, in the first few years of the operation of the FOIA, courts seemed quite willing to go along with government use of the exemption. A key case was *Environmental Protection Agency* v. *Mink*, 410 U.S. 73, 93 S.Ct. 827, 35 L.Ed.2d 119 (1973). In relation to the documents sought by Congresswoman Patsy Mink and her colleagues, the district court ruled in favor of the government, partly on the basis of the national defense and foreign policy exemption. The court of appeals reversed, concluding that this exemption permits the withholding of only the secret portions of the documents and ordering the district judge to examine the documents *in camera* (behind closed doors) for purposes of separating the secret from the nonsecret components and allowing the latter to be disclosed. The Supreme Court, in turn, reversed the court of appeals, upholding the principle of nondisclosure. The excerpt below provides a description of the matters at issue and the Supreme Court's reasoning in the case.

---

[3] *A Citizen's Guide on How to Use the Freedom of Information Act and the Privacy Act in Requesting Government Documents*, Thirteenth Report by the Committee on Government Operations, 95th Congress, 1st session, House Report No. 95–793, Washington, 1977, 5.

Environmental Protection Agency v. Mink

SUPREME COURT OF THE UNITED STATES, 1973.
410 U.S. 73, 93 S.CT. 827, 35 L.ED.2D 119.

Mr. Justice WHITE delivered the opinion of the Court....

Respondents' lawsuit began with an article that appeared in a Washington, D.C., newspaper in late July 1971. The article indicated that the President had received conflicting recommendations on the advisability of the underground nuclear test scheduled for that coming fall and, in particular, noted that the "latest recommendations" were the product of "a departmental under-secretary committee named to investigate the controversy." Two days later, Congresswoman Patsy Mink, a respondent, sent a telegram to the President urgently requesting the "immediate release of recommendations and report by inter-departmental committee...." When the request was denied, an action under the Freedom of Information Act was commenced by Congresswoman Mink and 32 of her colleagues the House....

Subsection (b)(1) of the Act (hereafter sometimes Exemption) exempts from forced disclosure matters "specifically required by Executive order to be kept secret in the interest of the national defense or foreign policy." According to the Irwin affidavit,[a] the six documents for which Exemption 1 is now claimed were all duly classified Top Secret or Secret, pursuant to Executive Order 10501, 3 CFR 280 (Jan. 1, 1970). That order was promulgated under the authority of the President in 1953, 18 Fed.Reg. 7049, and, since that time, has served as the basis for the classification by the Executive Branch of information "which requires protection in the interests of national defense." We do not believe that Exemption 1 permits compelled disclosure of documents, such as the six here that were classified pursuant to this Executive Order. Nor does the Exemption permit *in camera* inspection of such documents to sift out so-called "nonsecret components." Obviously, this test was not the only alternative available. But Congress chose to follow the Executive's determination in these matters and that choice must be honored....

What has been said thus far makes wholly untenable any claim that the Act intended to subject the soundness of executive security classifications to judicial review at the insistence of any objecting citizen. It also negates the proposition that Exemption 1 authorizes or permits *in camera* inspection of a contested document bearing a single classification so that the court may separate the secret from the supposedly nonsecret and order disclosure of the latter. The Court of Appeals was thus in error. The Irwin affidavit stated that each of the six documents for which Exemption 1 is now claimed "are and have been classified" Top Secret and Secret "pursuant to Executive Order No. 10501" and as involving "highly sensitive matter that is vital to our national defense and foreign policy." The fact of those classifications and the documents' characterizations have never been disputed by respondents. Accordingly, upon such a showing and in such circumstances, petitioners had met their burden of demonstrating that the documents were entitled to protection under Exemption 1, and the duty of the District Court under § 552(a)(3) was therefore at an end....

---

[a] John N. Irwin II, undersecretary of state, headed a committee which annually reviewed the underground nuclear test program and reported to the president. He submitted an affidavit supporting the EPA's view that the materials sought were exempt under the FOIA.

Judgment reversed and case remanded. . . .

Mr. Justice DOUGLAS, dissenting. . . .

The Government is aghast at a federal judge's even looking at the secret files and views with disdain the prospect of responsible judicial action in the area. It suggests that judges have no business declassifying "secrets," that judges are not familiar with the stuff with which these "Top Secret" or "Secret" documents deal.

This is to misconceive and distort the judicial function under § 552(a)(3) of the Act. The Court of Appeals never dreamed that the trial judge would declassify documents. His first task would be to determine whether nonsecret material was a mere appendage to a "Secret" or "Top Secret" file. His second task would be to determine whether under normal discovery procedures contained in Fed.Rule Civ.Proc. 26, factual material in these "Secret" or "Top Secret" materials is detached from the "Secret" and would therefore, be available to litigants confronting the agency in ordinary lawsuits.

Unless the District Court can do those things, the much-advertised Freedom of Information Act is on its way to becoming a shambles. Unless federal courts can be trusted, the Executive will hold complete sway and by *ipse dixit* make even the time of day "Top Secret." Certainly, the decision today will upset the "workable formula," at the heart of the legislative scheme, "which encompasses, balances, and protects all interests, yet places emphasis on the fullest responsible disclosure." S.Rep. No. 813, p. 3. The Executive Branch now has *carte blanche* to insulate information from public scrutiny whether or not that information bears any discernible relation to the interests sought to be protected by subsection (b)(1) of the Act. . . .

1974 Amendments to FOIA

EPA v. *Mink* played a significant role in the further development of the Freedom of Information Act. It would not be too much to say that some of the 1974 amendments to the act were written to overrule *Mink*.[4] The relevant amendments provide that information classified under the exemptions must be "in fact properly classified"; that the court may make the *in camera* examination of documents that the Supreme Court had denied in *Mink* "to determine whether such records or any part thereof shall be withheld" under any of the exemptions; and that "[a]ny reasonably segregable portion of a record shall be provided to any person requesting such record after deletion of the portions which are exempt under this subsection."

Other important 1974 amendments set the ten-day time limits mentioned above for responding to information requests, provided for the disciplining of persons responsible for arbitrary and capricious withholding of information, and allowed court costs and attorney fees to be awarded if the plaintiff has "substantially prevailed" in a case taken to court under the FOIA. Under the latter provision, the Justice Department in 1978 agreed to pay over $195,000 to the two sons of Julius and Ethel Rosenberg, who were executed in 1953 on

---

[4] See "National Security and the Amended Freedom of Information Act," 85 *Yale Law Journal* 401, 402 (1976); "National Security and the Public's Right to Know: A New Role for the Courts Under the Freedom of Information Act," 123 *University of Pennsylvania Law Review* 1438, 1488 (1975); and Bernard Schwartz, *Administrative Law* 130 (1976).

espionage charges, in their suit to obtain information on the government's case against their parents.[5]

An important case involving the FOIA is *Chrysler* v. *Brown*. Another aspect of that case was presented in chapter 6. The excerpt below treats the part of the case having to do with Chrysler's "reverse Freedom of Information Act" suit.

Chrysler Corp. v. Brown

Supreme Court of the United States, 1979.
441 U.S. 281, 99 S.Ct. 1705, 60 L.Ed.2d 208.

Mr. Justice REHNQUIST delivered the opinion of the Court.

The expanding range of federal regulatory activity and growth in the Government sector of the economy have increased federal agencies' demand for information about the activities of private individuals and corporations. These developments have paralleled a related concern about secrecy in Government and abuse of power. The Freedom of Information Act (hereinafter "FOIA") was a response to this concern, but it has also had a largely unforeseen tendency to exacerbate the uneasiness of those who comply with governmental demands for information. For under the FOIA third parties have been able to obtain Government files containing information submitted by corporations and individuals who thought the information would be held in confidence.

This case belongs to a class that has been popularly denominated "reverse-FOIA" suits. The Chrysler Corporation (hereinafter "Chrysler") seeks to enjoin agency disclosure on the grounds that it is inconsistent with the FOIA and 18 U.S.C.A. § 1905, a criminal statute with origins in the 19th century that proscribes disclosure of certain classes of business and personal information.[a] We agree with the Court of Appeals for the Third Circuit that the FOIA is purely a disclosure statute and affords Chrysler no private right of action to enjoin agency disclosure....

I

As a party to numerous Government contracts, Chrysler is required to comply with Executive Orders 11246 and 11375, which charge the Secretary of Labor with ensuring that corporations who benefit from Government contracts provide equal employment opportunity regardless of race or sex. The U.S. Department of Labor's Office of Federal Contract Compliance Programs (OFCCP) has promulgated regulations which require Government contractors to furnish reports and other information about their affirmative action programs and the general composition of their work forces.

The Defense Logistics Agency (DLA) (formerly the Defense Supply Agency) of the Department of Defense is the designated compliance agency responsible for monitoring Chrysler's employment practices. OFCCP regulations require that Chrysler make available to this agency written affirmative action programs (AAPs) and annually submit Employer Information Reports, known as EEC–1 Reports. The agency may also conduct "compliance reviews" and "complaint investigations," which culminate in Compliance Review

---

[5] The *New York Times*, June 27, 1978, 10.

[a] On the Court's disposition of the issue of 18 U.S.C.A. § 1905, see above, p. 160.

Reports (CRRs) and Complaint Investigation Reports (CIRs), respectively.

Regulations promulgated by the Secretary of Labor provide for public disclosure of information from records of the OFCCP and its compliance agencies. Those regulations state that notwithstanding exemption from mandatory disclosure under the Freedom of Information Act, 5 U.S.C.A. § 552,

> records obtained or generated pursuant to Executive Order 11246 (as amended) . . . shall be made available for inspection and copying . . . if it is determined that the requested inspection or copying furthers the public interest and does not impede any of the functions of the OFCC[P] or the Compliance Agencies except in the case of records disclosure of which is prohibited by law.

It is the voluntary disclosure contemplated by this regulation, over and above that mandated by the FOIA, which is the gravamen of Chrysler's complaint in this case.

This controversy began in May of 1975 when the DLA informed Chrysler that third parties had made a FOIA request for disclosure of the 1974 AAP for Chrysler's Newark, Del. assembly plant and an October 1974 CIR for the same facility. Nine days later Chrysler objected to release of the requested information, relying on OFCCP's disclosure regulations and on exemptions to the FOIA. Chrysler also requested a copy of the CIR, since it had never seen it. DLA responded the following week that it had determined that the requested material was subject to disclosure under the FOIA and the OFCCP disclosure rules, and that both documents would be released five days later.

On that day Chrysler filed a complaint in the United States District Court for Delaware seeking to enjoin release of the Newark documents. The District Court granted a temporary restraining order barring disclosure of the Newark documents and requiring that DLA give five days' notice to Chrysler before releasing any similar documents. Pursuant to this order, Chrysler was informed on July 1, 1975, that DLA had received a similar request for information about Chrysler's Hamtramck, Mich. plant. Chrysler amended its complaint and obtained a restraining order with regard to the Hamtramck disclosure as well. . . .

II

We have decided a number of FOIA cases in the last few years. Although we have not had to face squarely the question whether the FOIA *ex proprio vigore* forbids governmental agencies from disclosing certain classes of information to the public, we have in the course of at least one opinion intimated an answer. We have, moreover, consistently recognized that the basic objective of the Act is disclosure.

In contending that the FOIA bars disclosure of the requested equal employment opportunity information, Chrysler relies on the Act's nine exemptions and argues that they require an agency to withhold exempted material. In this case it relies specifically on Exemption 4:

> (b) [FOIA] does not apply to matters that are— . . .
>
> (4) trade secrets and commercial or financial information obtained from a person and privileged or confidential. . . . 5 U.S.C. § 552(b)(4).

Chrysler contends that the nine exemptions in general, and Exemption 4 in particular, reflect a sensitivity to the privacy interests of private individuals and nongovernmental entities. That contention may be conceded without inexorably requiring the conclusion that the exemptions impose affirmative duties on an agency to withhold information sought. In fact, that conclusion is not supported by the language, logic or history of the Act.

The organization of the Act is straightforward. Subsection (a), 5 U.S.C.A. § 552(a), places a general obligation on the agency to make information available to the public and sets out specific modes of disclosure for certain classes of information. Subsection (b), 5 U.S.C.A. § 552(b), which lists the exemptions, simply states that the specified material is not subject to the disclosure obligations set out in subsection (a). By its terms, subsection (b) demarcates the limits of the agency's obligation to disclose; it does not foreclose disclosure.

That the FOIA is exclusively a disclosure statute is, perhaps, demonstrated most convincingly by examining its provision for judicial relief. Subsection (a)(4)(B) gives federal district courts "jurisdiction to enjoin the agency from withholding agency records and to order the production of any agency records improperly withheld from the complainant." 5 U.S.C.A. § 552(a) (4)(B). That provision does not give the authority to bar disclosure, and thus fortifies our belief that Chrysler, and courts which have shared its view, have incorrectly interpreted the exemption provisions to the FOIA. The Act is an attempt to meet the demand for open government while preserving workable confidentiality in governmental decisionmaking. Congress appreciated that with the expanding sphere of governmental regulation and enterprise, much of the information within Government files has been submitted by private entities seeking Government contracts or responding to unconditional reporting obligations imposed by law. There was sentiment that Government agencies should have the latitude, in certain circumstances, to afford the confidentiality desired by these submitters. But the congressional concern was with the *agency's* need or preference for confidentiality; the FOIA by itself protects the submitters' interest in confidentiality only to the extent that this interest is endorsed by the agency collecting the information.

Enlarged access to governmental information undoubtedly cuts against the privacy concerns of nongovernmental entities, and as a matter of policy some balancing and accommodation may well be desirable. We simply hold here that Congress did not design the FOIA exemptions to be mandatory bars to disclosure.

This conclusion is further supported by the legislative history. The FOIA was enacted out of dissatisfaction with § 3 of the Administrative Procedure Act, which had not resulted in as much disclosure by the agencies as Congress later thought desirable. Statements in both the Senate and House Reports on the effect of the exemptions support the interpretation that the exemptions were only meant to permit the agency to withhold certain information, and were not meant to mandate nondisclosure. For example, the House Report states:

> [The FOIA] sets up workable standards for the categories of records which *may* be exempt from disclosure....
>
> ... There may be legitimate reasons for nondisclosure and [the FOIA] is designed to *permit* nondisclosure in such cases.
>
> [The FOIA] lists in a later subsection the specific categories of information which *may* be exempted from disclosure.

We therefore conclude that Congress did not limit an agency's discretion to disclose information when it enacted the FOIA. It necessarily follows that the Act does not afford Chrysler any right to enjoin agency disclosure....

By almost any measure, the Freedom of Information Act can be considered a very significant milestone in American administrative law. Proponents of open government may be disappointed with those court decisions that have rejected access to information sought under the act, but none can deny that the FOIA has made a great difference in the amount and kind of information it has been possible to gain.

Backlash Against FOIA

Recently, the view seems to be gaining ground that restrictions on information released have become too loose, and that too many government employees are being diverted from other tasks to do FOIA work, and a backlash of sorts has set in. It has been asserted that the FOIA has had an adverse effect on law enforcement, particularly with regard to information collection by investigatory agencies and the protection of police informants; that processing information requests has become enormously expensive and has placed a great burden in taxpayers; that a large proportion of FOIA requests come not from private citizens, scholars, journalists, and public interest groups, for whom the act was presumably intended, but from businessmen seeking advantages over competitors, criminals, and representatives of foreign (including Communist) governments.[6]

While the act still has numerous supporters, a consensus may be emerging that favors modifications in the act to achieve a more reasonable balance between the public's right to know and the government's ability to carry out its functions. Small modifications have already been achieved in several areas. For instance, in 1984 Congress put beyond the reach of the FOIA the "operational files" of the CIA. P.L. 98–477, 98 Stat. 2209. Interestingly, this was accomplished not through amendment of the Freedom of Information Act but by amending the National Security Act, the enabling legislation covering the CIA.[7]

More comprehensive legislation is also under consideration. The so-called FOIA Regulatory Reform Act passed the Senate but not the House of Representatives in 1984. This bill, if eventually adopted, would result in numerous changes, the cumulative effect of which would be to restrict disclosure in a number of ways.[8] Even without new legislation, however, greater restrictions on information access have been imposed in recent years. The president by executive order can create classification categories and increase the duration of classifications. The practices adopted under President Reagan in this area have been considerably more restrictive than those of his predecessors,[9] to the

---

[6] See the discussion and sources cited in Richard J. Pierce, Jr., Sidney A. Shapiro, and Paul R. Verkuil, *Administrative Law and Process* 444, 478–82 (1985). A source which acknowledges these problems but still, on balance, favors the FOIA essentially in its present form is U.S. Court of Appeals Judge Patricia M. Wald. See her article, "The Freedom of Information Act: A Short Case Study in the Perils and Paybacks of Legislating Democratic Values," 33 *Emory Law Journal* 648 (1984).

[7] This legislation received support not just from the "security establishment," but also from the American Civil Liberties Union. On this and other aspects of the legislative history of this act, see 4 *U.S.Code Congressional and Administrative News* 3471 (98th Congress, 2d Session, 1984). Also, *The New York Times*, January 16, 1985, A16. In supporting this amendment the ACLU argued that the files in question were likely to be protected from public access in any case, and that a blanket exclusion would allow the agency more time to handle information requests more likely to be honored.

[8] See Pierce, et al., above, note 6, 478–482.

[9] See the analyses of Reagan, Carter, and Nixon executive orders in Pierce, et al., above, note 6, 446. On this matter as well as broader questions of recent government information policies, see Donna A. Demac, *Keeping America Uninformed: Government Secrecy in the 1980s* (1984).

point where even high government officials have wondered whether too much information was being classified.[10]

Another aspect of the trend toward more restricted access has to do with the role of the courts. Particularly in the area of national security, the courts have tended to take a highly deferential attitude in reviewing government secrecy claims.[11] The following case illustrates the problems faced by judges in deciding such cases and, if the concurring view of Justice Marshall is accurate, amounts to a more restrictive stance on public access than Congress intended.

Central Intelligence Agency v. Sims

SUPREME COURT OF THE UNITED STATES, 1985.
471 U.S. 159, 105 S.CT. 1881, 85 L.ED.2D 173.

[A CIA-funded research project on countering Soviet and Chinese brainwashing and interrogation techniques (code-named MKULTRA) was carried out in the 1950s and 1960s. Universities, research foundations, and other institutions conducted the research under contracts with the CIA. In the late 1970s respondents filed a request under the FOIA seeking, among other things, the names of the institutions and individuals who had performed the research.

The CIA declined to release some of the information requested, citing Exemption 3 of the FOIA, which states than an agency may withhold "matters that are . . . specifically exempted from disclosure by statute . . . provided that such statute . . . refers to particular types of matters to be withheld." The exempting statute invoked by the CIA was § 102(d)(3) of the National Security Act of 1947, which provides that "the Director of Central Intelligence shall be responsible for protecting intelligence sources and methods from unauthorized disclosure."

Before reaching the Supreme Court, the case was heard twice by a district court and twice by a court of appeals. The two issues the Supreme Court was called upon to decide were: (1) whether the quoted section of the National Security Act can be considered a withholding statute under Exemption 3 of the FOIA; and (2) whether the researchers are "intelligence sources" within the meaning of the National Security Act.

Justice Marshall's opinion, concurring in the result, expresses the view that the Court goes too far in deferring to the CIA's definition of "intelligence source," and thereby gives that agency more independence and discretion than Congress intended.]

Chief Justice BURGER delivered the opinion of the Court. . . .

Between 1953 and 1966, the Central Intelligence Agency financed a wide-ranging project, code-named MKULTRA, concerned with "the research and development of chemical, biological, and radiological materials capable of employment in clandestine operations to control human behavior." The program consisted of some 149 subprojects which the Agency contracted out to various universities, re-

---

[10] Attorney General Meese was quoted in 1985 as saying: "We have far too much classified information in the Federal Government. A lot of things which shouldn't be classified are." He urged a tightening of the system "so that only material that really has to be kept secret in the interests of national defense or national security is classified." *The New York Times*, April 2, 1985, A18.

[11] On this point see Pierce, et al., above, note 6, 446–7.

search foundations, and similar institutions. At least 80 institutions and 185 private researchers participated. Because the Agency funded MKULTRA indirectly, many of the participating individuals were unaware that they were dealing with the Agency.

MKULTRA was established to counter perceived Soviet and Chinese advances in brainwashing and interrogation techniques. Over the years the program included various medical and psychological experiments, some of which led to untoward results.[12] These aspects of MKULTRA surfaced publicly during the 1970's and became the subject of executive and congressional investigations.

On August 22, 1977, John C. Sims, an attorney, and Sidney M. Wolfe, M.D., the director of the Public Citizen Health Research Group, filed a request with the Central Intelligence Agency seeking certain information about MKULTRA. Respondents invoked the Freedom of Information Act (FOIA), 5 U.S.C. § 552. Specifically respondents sought the grant proposals and contracts awarded under the MKULTRA program and the names of the institutions and individuals that had performed research.

Pursuant to respondents' request, the Agency made available to respondents all of the MKULTRA grant proposals and contracts. Citing Exemption 3 of the FOIA, 5 U.S.C. § 552(b)(3)(B), however, the Agency declined to disclose the names of all individual researchers and 21 institutions. . . .

The mandate of the FOIA calls for broad disclosure of Government records. Congress recognized, however, that public disclosure is not always in the public interest and thus provided that agency records may be withheld from disclosure under any of the nine exemptions defined in 5

U.S.C. § 552(b). Under Exemption 3 disclosure need not be made as to information "specifically exempted from disclosure by statute" if the statute affords the agency no discretion on disclosure, 5 U.S.C. § 552(b)(3)(A), establishes particular criteria for withholding the information, or refers to the particular types of material to be withheld, § 552(b)(3)(B). . . .

Congress has made the Director of Central Intelligence "responsible for protecting intelligence sources and methods from unauthorized disclosure." 50 U.S.C. § 403(d)(3). As part of its postwar reorganization of the national defense system, Congress chartered the Agency with the responsibility of coordinating intelligence activities relating to national security. In order to carry out its mission, the Agency was expressly entrusted with protecting the heart of all intelligence operations—"sources and methods."

Section 102(d)(3) of the National Security Act of 1947, which calls for the Director of Central Intelligence to protect "intelligence sources and methods," clearly "refers to particular types of matters," 5 U.S.C. § 552(b)(3)(B), and thus qualifies as a withholding statute under Exemption 3. The "plain meaning" of the relevant statutory provisions is sufficient to resolve the question. . . . Moreover, the legislative history of the FOIA confirms that Congress intended § 102(d)(3) to be a withholding statute under Exemption 3. Indeed, this is the uniform view among other federal courts. . . .

Congress expressly made the Director of Central Intelligence responsible for "protecting intelligence sources and methods from unauthorized disclosure." This language stemmed from President Truman's Directive of January 22, 1946, 11 Fed. Reg. 1337, in which he established the Na-

---

[12] Several MKULTRA subprojects involved experiments where researchers surreptitiously administered dangerous drugs, such as LSD, to unwitting human subjects. At least two persons died as a result of MKULTRA experiments, and others may have suffered impaired health because of the testing. . . . This type of experimentation is now expressly forbidden by executive order. Exec. Order No. 12333, § 2.10 3 CFR 213 (1982).

tional Intelligence Agency and the Central Intelligence Group, the Agency's predecessors. These institutions were charged with "assur[ing] the most effective accomplishment of the intelligence mission related to the national security," ibid., and accordingly made "responsible for fully protecting intelligence sources and methods," id., at 1339. The fact that the mandate of § 102(d)(3) derives from this Presidential Directive reinforces our reading of the legislative history that Congress gave the Agency broad power to control the disclosure of intelligence sources.

Applying the definition of "intelligence sources" fashioned by the Congress in § 102(d)(3), we hold that the Director of Central Intelligence was well within his statutory authority to withhold the names of the MKULTRA researchers from disclosure under the FOIA....

Consistent with its responsibility to maintain national security, the Agency reasonably determined that major research efforts were necessary in order to keep informed of our potential adversaries' perceived threat. We thus conclude that MKULTRA researchers are "intelligence sources" within the broad meaning of § 102(d)(3) because these persons provided, or were engaged to provide, information the Agency needs to fulfill its statutory obligations with respect to foreign intelligence....

We hold that the Director of Central Intelligence properly invoked § 102(d)(3) of the National Security Act of 1947 to withhold disclosure of the identities of the individual MKULTRA researchers as protected "intelligence sources." We also hold that the FOIA does not require the Director to disclose the institutional affiliations of the exempt researchers in light of the record which supports the Agency's determination that such disclosure would lead to an unacceptable risk of disclosing the sources' identities.

Accordingly, we reverse that part of the judgment of the Court of Appeals re-

garding the disclosure of the individual researchers and affirm that part of the judgment pertaining to disclosure of the researchers' institutional affiliations.

It is so ordered.

Justice MARSHALL, with whom Justice BRENNAN joins, concurring in the result.

To give meaning to the term "intelligence source" as it is used in § 102(d)(3) of the National Security Act of 1947, the Court today correctly concludes that the very narrow definition offered by the Court of Appeals is incorrect. That the Court of Appeals erred does not, however, compel the conclusion that the Agency's sweeping alternative definition is in fact the correct one. The Court nonetheless simply adopts wholesale the Agency's definition of "intelligence source." That definition is mandated neither by the language or legislative history of any congressional act, nor by legitimate policy considerations, and it in fact thwarts congressional efforts to balance the public's interest in information and the Government's need for secrecy. I therefore decline to join the opinion of the Court....

[Justice Marshall, turning to the exemptions available under the FOIA, raises the question of the applicability of Exemption 1 to this case.]

A second exemption, known as Exemption 1, covers matters that are "(A) specifically authorized under criteria established by an Executive order to be kept secret in the interest of national defense or foreign policy and (B) are in fact properly classified pursuant to such Executive order." 5 U.S.C. § 552(b)(1). This latter exemption gives to the Executive Branch the authority to define material that will not be disclosed, subject of course to congressional amendment of the exemption. Agency decisions to withhold are subject to *de novo* review in the courts, which must ascertain whether documents are correctly classified, both substantively and procedurally.

Exemption 1 is the keystone of a congressional scheme that balances deference to the Executive's interest in maintaining secrecy with continued judicial and congressional oversight. In the past, Congress has taken affirmative steps to make clear the importance of this oversight.... Exemption 1 allows the Government to protect from the scrutiny of this Nation's enemies classes of information that warrant protection, as long as the Government proceeds through a publicly issued, congressionally scrutinized, and judicially enforced executive order. See Hearing on Executive Order on Security Classification before the Subcommittee of the Committee on Government Operations of the House of Representatives, 97th Cong., 2d Sess. (1982) (Hearing).

Exemption 1 thus plays a crucial role in the protection of Central Intelligence Agency information. That the Court does not mention this exemption even once, in the course of its lengthy analysis on the *policy* reasons for broadly interpreting the "intelligence source" provision, is extraordinary. By focusing myopically on the single statutory provision on which the Agency has chosen to rely in asserting its secrecy right, the Court rewards the agency's decision not to invoke Exemption 1 in this case.[13] Of course, the Agency may fairly assert any possible ground for decision, and it has no duty to select that which is narrowest. But the Court, intent to assure that important information is protected, today plays into the Agency's hands by stretching the "intelligence source" exception beyond its natural limit; it does so while simply ignoring the fact that the in-

formation sought could properly have been withheld on other grounds—on which the Agency chose not to rely. The cost of acceding to the Agency's litigation strategy, rather than undertaking a thorough analysis of the entire statutory scheme, is to mangle, seriously, a carefully crafted statutory scheme....

The scope of Exemption 1 is defined by the Executive, and its breadth therefore quite naturally fluctuates over time. For example, at the time this FOIA action was begun, Executive Order 12065, promulgated by President Carter, was in effect. That order established three levels of secrecy—top secret, secret, and confidential—the lowest of which, "confidential," was "applied to information, the unauthorized disclosure of which reasonably could be expected to cause identifiable damage to the national security." 43 Fed.Reg. 28949, 28950 (1978).

The order also listed categories of information that could be considered for classification, including "military plans, weapons, or operations," "foreign government information," and "intelligence activities and sources." Id., at 28951. As it is now, nondisclosure premised on Exemption 1 was subject to judicial review. A court reviewing an Agency claim to withholding under Exemption 1 was required to determine *de novo* whether the document was properly classified and whether it substantively met the criteria in the Executive Order. If the claim was that the document or information in it contained military plans, for example, a court was required to determine whether the document was classified, whether it in fact con-

---

[13] Indeed, this case presents a curious example of the Government's litigation strategy. Despite the repeated urging of the District Court, the Agency steadfastly refused to invoke Exemption 1 to withhold the information at issue. The lists of names of MKULTRA researchers were in fact once classified under an Executive Order and were therefore within the potential scope of Exemption 1, but the Agency elected to declassify them. See 479 F.Supp. 84, 88 (DC 1979). The District Court went so far as to postpone the effective date of its disclosure order, so the Agency could "act on the possibility of classifying the names of institutions and researchers which would otherwise be disclosable," ibid., and thereby withhold the information under Exemption 1. The Agency refused to do so, however.

tained such information *and* whether disclosure of the document reasonably could be expected to cause at least identifiable damage to national security. The burden was on the Agency to make this showing. At one time, this Court believed that the judiciary was not qualified to undertake this task. See *EPA v. Mink*, 410 U.S. 73, 93 S.Ct. 827, 35 L.Ed.2d 119 (1973). . . . Congress, however, disagreed, overruling both a decision of this Court and a Presidential veto to make clear that precisely this sort of judicial role is essential if the balance that Congress believed ought to be struck between disclosure and national security is to be struck in practice.

Today's decision enables the Agency to avoid making the showing required under the carefully crafted balance embodied in Exemption 1 and thereby thwarts Congress' effort to limit the Agency's discretion. The Court identifies two categories of information—the identity of individuals or entities, whether or not confidential, that contribute material related to Agency information-gathering, and material that might enable an observer to discover the identity of such a "source"—and rules that all such information is *per se* subject to withholding as long as it is related to the Agency's "intelligence function." The Agency need not even assert that disclosure will conceivably affect national security, much less that it reasonably could be expected to cause at least identifiable damage. It need not classify the information,

much less demonstrate that it has properly been classified. Similarly, no court may review whether the source had, or would have been to have had any interest in confidentiality, or whether disclosure of the information would have any effect on national security. No court may consider whether the information is properly classified, or whether it fits the categories of the executive order. By choosing to litigate under Exemption 3, and by receiving this Court's blessing, the Agency has cleverly evaded all these carefully imposed congressional requirements.[14] . . .

Congress gave to the Agency considerable discretion to decide for itself whether the topics of its interest should remain secret, and through Exemption 1 it provided the Executive with the means to protect such information. If the Agency decides to classify the identities of non-confidential contributors of information so as not to reveal the subject matter or kinds of interests it is pursuing, it may seek an Exemption 1 right to withhold. Under Congress' scheme, that is properly a decision for the Executive. It is not a decision for this Court. Congress has elsewhere identified particular types of information that it believes may be withheld regardless of the existence of an Executive order, such as the identities of Agency employees, or, recently, the contents of Agency operational files. See 50 U.S.C. § 403g (exempting from disclosure requirements the organization, functions, names, official titles, salaries, or

---

[14] The current Executive Order moves Exemption 1 a step closer to Exemption 3, given the manner in which the Court interprets the National Security Act exemption. Like its predecessor, the Order establishes three classification levels, but unlike the prior Order, the "confidential" classification no longer requires a reasonable possibility of *identifiable* damage. Instead, the label "confidential" now shall be applied to "information the unauthorized disclosure of which reasonably could be expected to cause damage to the national security." Executive Order 12356, 3 CFR 166 (1983). In addition, the new Order not only lists "intelligence sources" as a category subject to classification, but it also creates a presumption that such information is confidential. This presumption shifts from the Agency the burden of proving the possible consequence to national security of disclosure. As a result, if the Agency defines "intelligence source" under the Executive Order as broadly as the Court defines the term in § 102(d)(3), the Agency need make but a limited showing to a court to invoke Exemption 1 for that material. In light of this new Order, the Court's avid concern for the national security consequences of a narrower definition of the term is quite puzzling.

numbers of personnel employed by the Agency); Central Intelligence Agency Information Act, Pub.L. 98–477, § 701(a), 98 Stat. 2209 (exempting the Agency's operational files from disclosure under FOIA). Each of these categorical exemptions reflects a congressional judgment that as to certain information, the public interest will always tip in favor of nondisclosure. In this case, we have absolutely no indication that Congress has ever determined that the broad range of information that will hereinafter be enshrouded in secrecy should be inherently and necessarily confidential. Nevertheless, today the Court reaches out to substitute its own policy judgments for those of Congress.

To my mind, the language and legislative history of § 102(d)(3), along with the policy concerns expressed by the Agency, support only an exemption for sources who provide information based on an implicit or explicit promise of confidentiality and information leading to disclosure of such sources. That reading of the "intelligence source" exemption poses no threat that sources will "clam up" for fear of exposure, while at the same time it avoids an injection into the statutory scheme of the additional concerns of the Members of this Court. The Court of Appeals, however, ordered the release of even more material than I believe should be disclosed. Accordingly, I would reverse and remand this case for reconsideration in light of what I deem to be the proper definition of the term "intelligence source."

EXECUTIVE PRIVILEGE

In the previous chapter the reader met the word *privilege* in connection with libel suits against governmental officials. Privilege, as used there, involved the issue of whether an official was entitled to some level of protection or immunity—either "qualified privilege" or "absolute privilege"—regarding utterances made in the course of official duties. Another use of the term privilege has to do with the protection of information or communications from access by the legal process. Examples of privileged communications which are recognized in some jurisdictions are those between physician and patient, and those between husband and wife.

"Executive privilege" is a doctrine that has some relevance to administrative law. It is not mentioned in the FOIA, although the exemption for national defense and foreign policy information has to do with analogous matters. But there is a doctrine of executive privilege outside of the FOIA. A key case is *United States* v. *Reynolds*, 345 U.S. 1, 73 S.Ct. 528, 97 L.Ed. 727 (1953). The Supreme Court overruled a district court decision ordering that the government produce, for examination by the court, the Air Force's official accident investigation report sought by the widows of three deceased civilian observers who were killed in the crash of a military aircraft carrying secret electronic equipment. The plaintiffs were suing the government under the Federal Tort Claims Act, and the Supreme Court ruled that "the Court should not jeopardize the security which the privilege is meant to protect by insisting upon an examination of the evidence, even by the judge alone, in chambers."

In *United States* v. *Nixon*, 418 U.S. 683, 94 S.Ct. 3090, 41 L.Ed.2d 1039 (1974), the Watergate tapes case, the Supreme Court reaffirmed the doctrine of executive privilege, but ruled that it did not apply in the case at hand: "The generalized assertion of privilege must yield to the demonstrated, specific need for evidence in a pending criminal trial." [15]

THE PRIVACY ACT

Like the FOIA, the Privacy Act of 1974 (P.L. 93–579, 88 Stat. 1897) is codified as part of the Administrative Procedure Act (5 U.S.C.A. § 552a; the FOIA is 5 U.S. C.A. § 552).[16] The act is designed

> to give citizens more control over what information is collected about them and how that information is used." As stated in House Report No. 95–93, the Privacy Act accomplishes this in five basic ways: "It requires agencies to publicly report the existence of all systems of records maintained on individuals. It requires that the information contained in these record systems be accurate, complete, relevant, and up-to-date. It provides procedures whereby individuals can inspect and correct inaccuracies in almost all Federal files about themselves. It specifies that information about an individual gathered for one purpose not be used for another without the individual's consent. And, finally, it requires agencies to keep an accurate accounting of the disclosure of records and, with certain exceptions, to make these disclosures available to the subject of the record.[17]

General exemptions to the Privacy Act apply to files maintained by the CIA and criminal law enforcement agencies, and there are seven specific exemptions which apply to all agencies and cover such matters as classified documents concerning national defense and foreign policy, Secret Service intelligence files, and certain materials pertaining to government employment.

The act establishes agency appeal procedures, and a person dissatisfied with agency action may take his case to the federal court. There has been some potential for conflict between the FOIA and the Privacy Act. While the Privacy Act contains a statement (§ 552a(b)(2)) mandating disclosure if it is "required under Section 552 of this title [i.e., the Freedom of Information Act]," the issue was raised in several cases as to whether the Privacy Act itself might be considered a "withholding statute" under Exemption 3 of the FOIA (the matter of "withholding statutes" was discussed above in *CIA* v. *Sims*). The lower courts had given inconsistent views on this question,[18] and in 1984 Congress amended the Privacy Act to make clear that "[n]o agency shall rely on any exemption contained in section 552 of this title [i.e., the Freedom of

---

[15] A thorough and highly critical analysis of executive privilege may be found in Arthur S. Miller, "Executive Privilege: A Political Theory Masquerading as Law," in Harold C. Relyea, ed., *The Presidency and Information Policy* 48 (1981).

[16] Actually, only the main section of the Privacy Act, Section 3, is published as § 552a of the APA. There are several other sections to the Privacy Act, including one that gives the Office of Management and Budget the responsibility for developing guidelines for implementing the act and monitoring compliance with it. See Kenneth Culp Davis, *1982 Supplement to Administrative Law Treatise* 94 (1982).

[17] *A Citizen's Guide on How to Use the Freedom of Information Act and the Privacy Act in Requesting Government Documents*, Thirteenth Report by the Committee on Government Operations, 95th Congress, 1st session, House Report No. 95–793, Washington, 1977, 16.

[18] See Pierce, et al., above, note 6, 471–474.

Information Act] to withhold from an individual any record which is otherwise accessible to such individual under the provisions of this section." P.L. 98–477, 98 Stat. 2209, 2211.

"GOVERNMENT–IN–THE–SUNSHINE" ACTS

Since 1950, "Government-in-the-Sunshine" or open-meeting statutes have been adopted in all fifty states and on the federal level.[19] The latest jurisdiction to do so was the federal government, in 1976. P.L. 94–409, 90 Stat. 1241. Like the FOIA and the Privacy Act, the Federal Sunshine Act has been codified as part of the Administrative Procedure Act, 5 U.S.C.A. § 552b.[20] While the Sunshine Act applies only to multi-headed federal agencies, other legislation covers parts of the rest of the federal government: the Federal Advisory Committee Act, P.L. 92–463, 86 Stat. 770 (1972) provides for public access to meetings of advisory committees, study panels, and ad hoc committees within the executive branch; and resolutions by the House of Representatives and the Senate, in 1973 and 1975, respectively, apply the principle of openness to congressional committee meetings and "markup sessions." [21]

Obviously, the purpose of the sunshine laws is to enhance citizen access to government operations. The degree of openness provided varies considerably from statute to statute, however. On the federal level, and in some states, a body can go into executive session and close a meeting to the public simply by a majority vote. In other states even informal meetings are required to be open. Most statutes allow for some exceptions to the principle of openness, as in the case of labor negotiations or other personnel matters. As mentioned, the federal statute applies only to multi-headed agencies, even though some of the single-headed agencies perform similar functions. The implications of this point are well put in an analysis of the federal statute written shortly after its adoption: "The Securities and Exchange Commission, for instance, has enforcement powers comparable to those of the Attorney General and regulatory powers comparable to those of the Comptroller of the Currency: yet, of the three, only the Securities and Exchange Commission is covered by the Act." [22]

As indicated above, the Freedom of Information Act has been the focus of considerable litigation over the years. This has been much less the case with regard to the Privacy Act and the federal Sunshine Act. The Supreme Court has ruled on the latter only once, in *Federal Communications Commission* v. *ITT World Communications*, 466 U.S. 463, 104 S.Ct. 1936, 80 L.Ed.2d 480 (1984). Members of the FCC met with Canadian and European counterparts in confer-

---

[19] Howard I. Fox, "Government in the Sunshine," *1978 Annual Survey of American Law* 305–306, (1979). The State of New York adopted a sunshine act in 1976, and became the fiftieth state to do so, after the publication of the source cited by Fox in note 15, 306. For further background information see "Open Meeting Statutes," 75 *Harvard Law Review* 1199 (1962).

[20] See Richard K. Berg and Stephen H. Klitzman, *An Interpretive Guide to the Government in the Sunshine Act*, a publication of the Administrative Conference of the United States, Washington, 1978.

[21] Fox, above, note 19, at 306.

[22] Ibid., 307.

ences to discuss joint planning of telecommunications facilities. ITT brought suit, complaining, among other things, that these "Consultative Process" sessions were "meetings" within the meaning of the Sunshine Act and should be held in public. A unanimous Supreme Court ruled against ITT on two grounds: the sessions in question were not "meetings" since they could not, as the Sunshine Act provided, "determine or result in the joint conduct or disposition of official agency business"; and the sessions were not meetings "of an agency" within the meaning of the act, since they were not subject to the FCC's unilateral control.[23]

CITIZEN PARTICIPATION

Some of the matters discussed above, such as sunshine laws, are relevant to citizen participation. Basically, however, the discussion up to now has been of "access" rather than "activity." Citizen participation suggests an active role in government operations, rather than merely being able to ascertain what has been done.

As Stuart Langton has pointed out, two kinds of citizen participation may be delineated: citizen-initiated activities (the "citizen action movement") and government-initiated activities (the "citizen involvement movement").[24] The second of these has a close relationship to administrative law and will be discussed here.

Some degree of citizen involvement in the administrative process has long existed. The APA, for instance, has provided since its inception for general notice and the opportunity for interested persons to participate in proposed rule making (section 553), as well as for oral participation, including certain basic procedural rights, in adjudications requiring an agency hearing (sections 554–556). As pointed out in chapter 6, a number of statutes go well beyond the requirements of section 553 and require "on the record" hearings for rule making. In addition, several recent statutes provide funding for interested parties to participate in agency proceedings. The FTC Improvement Act of 1975 allows the commission to compensate a necessary party for attorney's fees and the costs of participation in rule making if that party could not otherwise be represented. Bills have been introduced in Congress to make such aid available for participation in agency proceedings generally.

As mentioned in chapter 7, agencies traditionally possessed considerable discretion in controlling participation in adjudicatory proceedings. Since the important case of *Office of Communication of United Church of Christ* v. *FCC*, 359 F.2d 994 (D.C.Cir.1966), however, in which the Court allowed members of the general listening public to be considered a "party in interest" in a televi-

---

[23] On the basis of this case, Larry W. Thomas, concluded that the Supreme Court "left no doubt that in the future lower federal courts should interpret the Sunshine Act quite narrowly." "The Courts and the Implementation of the Government in the Sunshine Act," 37 *Administrative Law Review* 259, 279 (1985).

[24] Stuart Langton, ed., *Citizen Participation in America* 1–3 (1978). See also the bimonthly journal *Citizen Participation*. The journal was started in 1979 and is published by the Lincoln Filene Center for Citizenship and Public Affairs, Tufts University.

sion license renewal proceeding, the opportunities for such citizen participation have been increased.

In large part on the basis of congressional mandates, it is fair to say that there are now literally hundreds of provisions requiring or permitting some form of citizen participation in administrative policy making or decision making.[25] These range from the kinds of participation described above to provisions for the creation of citizen advisory committees, requirements that public hearings be held before a policy is promulgated, and rather vague statutory mandates such as the following: "Public participation in the development, revision and enforcement of any regulation, standard, effluent limitations, plan or program established by the Administrator, or any State under this Act shall be provided for, encouraged and assisted by the Administrator and the States . . . ."[26]

This heightened level of citizen participation is not without its detractors. Some doubt has been expressed that citizen involvement helps in improving the governmental process. It has also been suggested that citizen participation is often actually "elite participation" and therefore not very significant in terms of democratic goals. In addition, greater costs, in time, money, and efforts of government officials, are inevitable in any significant public participation program. On the latter point in particular, the citizen participation movement is seen as being in conflict with another important development— the recent emphasis on the use of economic impact analysis in judging whether programs being considered by administrative agencies ought to be implemented.[27] The extent to which the growth of concern about economic impact affects the level of citizen participation remains to be seen.

---

[25] See Community Services Administration, *Citizen Participation*, Washington, 1978; see also Langton, above, note 20, 3. There has also been a notable, though less fully examined, increase in citizen participation programs at the state level. See ibid., 5–6.

[26] Section 101(e) of the Federal Water Pollution Control Act Amendments of 1972, P.L. 92–500, 86 Stat. 816, as quoted in ibid., 83. See the classification of 226 federal public participation programs by type and date of creation, ibid., 84.

[27] Robert B. Reich, "Warring Critiques of Regulation," *Regulation* 37 (January/February, 1979).

Appendixes

Appendix A

Administrative Procedure Act

P.L. 404, 60 Stat. 237 (1946), as amended through 98th Congress, Second Session (1984). 5 U.S.C.A. §§ 551–559, 701–706, 1305, 3105, 3344, 5372, 7521.

TITLE 5—GOVERNMENT ORGANIZATION AND EMPLOYEES

PART I
The Agencies Generally

CHAPTER 5
Administrative Procedure

SUBCHAPTER II
Administrative Procedure

Table of Sections

§ 551.   Definitions

For the purpose of this subchapter—

(1) "agency" means each authority of the Government of the United States, whether or not it is within or subject to review by another agency, but does not include—

(A) the Congress;

(B) the courts of the United States;

(C) the governments of the territories or possessions of the United States;

(D) the government of the District of Columbia; or except as to the requirements of section 552 of this title—

(E) agencies composed of representatives of the parties or of representatives of organizations of the parties to the disputes determined by them;

(F) courts martial and military commissions;

(G) military authority exercised in the field in time of war or in occupied territory; or

(H) functions conferred by sections 1738, 1739, 1743, and 1744 of title 12; chapter 2 of title 41; or sections 1622, 1884, 1891–1902, and former section 1641(b)(2), of title 50, appendix;

(2) "person" includes an individual, partnership, corporation, association, or public or private organization other than an agency;

(3) "party" includes a person or agency named or admitted as a party, or properly seeking and entitled as of right to be admitted as a party, in an agency proceeding, and a person or agency admitted by an agency as a party for limited purposes;

(4) "rule" means the whole or a part of an agency statement of general or particular applicability and future effect designed to implement, interpret, or prescribe law or policy or describing the organization, procedure, or practice requirements of an agency and includes the approval or prescription for the future of rates, wages, corporate or financial structures or reorganizations thereof, prices, facilities, appliances, services or allowances therefor or of valuations, costs, or accounting, or practices bearing on any of the foregoing;

(5) "rule making" means agency process for formulating, amending, or repealing a rule;

(6) "order" means the whole or a part of a final disposition, whether affirmative, negative, injunctive, or declaratory in form, of an agency in a matter other than rule making but including licensing;

(7) "adjudication" means agency process for the formulation of an order;

(8) "license" includes the whole or a part of an agency permit, certificate, approval, registration, charter, membership, statutory exemption or other form of permission;

(9) "licensing" includes agency process respecting the grant, renewal, denial, revocation, suspension, annulment, withdrawal, limitation, amendment, modification, or conditioning of a license;

(10) "sanction" includes the whole or a part of an agency—

(A) prohibition, requirement, limitation, or other condition affecting the freedom of a person;

(B) withholding of relief;

(C) imposition of penalty or fine;

(D) destruction, taking, seizure, or withholding of property;

(E) assessment of damages, reimbursement, restitution, compensation, costs, charges, or fees;

(F) requirement, revocation, or suspension of a license; or

(G) taking other compulsory or restrictive action;

(11) "relief" includes the whole or a part of an agency—

(A) grant of money, assistance, license, authority, exemption, exception, privilege, or remedy;

(B) recognition of a claim, right, immunity, privilege, exemption, or exception; or

(C) taking of other action on the application or petition of, and beneficial to, a person;

(12) "agency proceeding" means an agency process as defined by paragraphs (5), (7), and (9) of this section;

(13) "agency action" includes the whole or a part of an agency rule, order, license, sanction, relief, or the equivalent or denial thereof, or failure to act; and

(14) "ex parte communication" means an oral or written communication not on the public record with respect to which reasonable prior notice to all parties is not given, but it shall not include requests for status reports on any matter or proceeding covered by this subchapter.

§ 552. Public Information; Agency Rules, Opinions, Orders, Records, and Proceedings

(a) Each agency shall make available to the public information as follows:

(1) Each agency shall separately state and currently publish in the Federal Register for the guidance of the public—

(A) descriptions of its central and field organization and the established places at which, the employees (and in the case of a uniformed service, the members) from whom, and the methods whereby, the public may obtain information, make submittals or requests, or obtain decisions;

(B) statements of the general course and method by which its functions are channeled and determined, including the nature and requirements of all formal and informal procedures available;

(C) rules of procedure, descriptions of forms available or the places at which forms may be obtained, and instructions as to the scope and contents of all papers, reports, or examinations;

(D) substantive rules of general applicability adopted as authorized by law, and statements of general policy or interpretations of general applicability formulated and adopted by the agency; and

(E) each amendment, revision, or repeal of the foregoing.

Except to the extent that a person has actual and timely notice of the terms thereof, a person may not in any manner be required to resort to, or be adversely affected by, a matter required to be published in the Federal Register and not so published. For the purpose of this paragraph, matter reasonably available to the class of persons affected thereby is deemed published in the Federal Register when incorporated by reference therein with the approval of the Director of the Federal Register.

(2) Each agency, in accordance with published rules, shall make available for public inspection and copying—

(A) final opinions, including concurring and dissenting opinions, as well as orders, made in the adjudication of cases;

(B) those statements of policy and interpretations which have been adopted by the agency and are not published in the Federal Register; and

(C) administrative staff manuals and instructions to staff that affect a member of the public;

unless the materials are promptly published and copies offered for sale. To the extent required to prevent a clearly unwarranted invasion of personal privacy, an agency may delete identifying details when it makes available or publishes an opinion, statement of policy, interpretation, or staff manual or instruction. However, in each case the justification for the deletion shall be explained fully in writing. Each agency shall also maintain and make available for public inspection and copying current indexes providing identifying information for the public as to any matter issued, adopted, or promulgated after July 4, 1967, and required by this paragraph to be made available or published. Each agency shall promptly publish, quarterly or more frequently, and distribute (by sale or otherwise) copies of each index or supplements thereto unless it determines by order published in the Federal Register that the publication would be unnecessary and impracticable, in which case the agency shall nonetheless provide copies of such index on request at a cost not to exceed the direct cost of duplication. A final order, opinion, statement of policy, interpretation, or staff manual or instruction that affects a member of the public may be relied on, used, or cited as precedent by an agency against a party other than an agency only if—

(i) it has been indexed and either made available or published as provided by this paragraph; or

(ii) the party has actual and timely notice of the terms thereof.

(3) Except with respect to the records made available under paragraphs (1) and (2) of this subsection, each agency, upon any request for records which (A) reasonably describes such records and (B) is made in accordance with published rules stating the time, place, fees (if any), and procedures to be followed, shall make the records promptly available to any person.

(4)(A) In order to carry out the provisions of this section, each agency shall promulgate regulations, pursuant to notice and receipt of public comment, specifying a uniform schedule of fees applicable to all constituent units of such agency. Such fees shall be limited to reasonable standard charges for document search and duplication and provide for recovery of only the direct costs of such search and duplication. Documents shall be furnished without charge or at a reduced charge where the agency determines that waiver or reduction of the fee is in the public interest because furnishing the information can be considered as primarily benefiting the general public.

(B) On complaint, the district court of the United States in the district in which the complainant resides, or has his principal place of business, or in which the agency records are situated, or in the District of Columbia, has jurisdiction to enjoin the agency from withholding agency records and to order the production of any agency records improperly withheld from the complainant. In such a case the court shall determine the matter de novo, and may examine the contents of such agency records in camera to determine whether such records or any part thereof shall be withheld under any of the exemptions set forth in subsection (b) of this section, and the burden is on the agency to sustain its action.

(C) Notwithstanding any other provision of law, the defendant shall serve an answer or otherwise plead to any complaint made under this subsection within thirty days after service upon the defendant of the pleading in which such complaint is made, unless the court otherwise directs for good cause shown.

[(D) Repealed. Pub.L. 98–620, Title IV, § 402(2), Nov. 8, 1984, 98 Stat. 3357]

(E) The court may assess against the United States reasonable attorney fees and other litigation costs reasonably incurred in any case under this section in which the complainant has substantially prevailed.

(F) Whenever the court orders the production of any agency records improperly withheld from the complainant and assesses against the United States reasonable attorney fees and other litigation costs, and the court additionally issues a written finding that the circumstances surrounding the withholding raise questions whether agency personnel acted arbitrarily or capriciously with respect to the withholding, the Special Counsel shall promptly initiate a proceeding to determine whether disciplinary action is warranted against the officer or employee who was primarily responsible for the withholding. The Special Counsel, after investigation and consideration of the evidence submitted, shall submit his findings and recommendations to the administrative authority of the agency concerned and shall send copies of the findings and recommendations to the officer or employee or his representative. The administrative authority shall take the corrective action that the Special Counsel recommends.

(G) In the event of noncompliance with the order of the court, the district court may punish for contempt the responsible employee, and in the case of a uniformed service, the responsible member.

(5) Each agency having more than one member shall maintain and make available for public inspection a record of the final votes of each member in every agency proceeding.

(6)(A) Each agency, upon any request for records made under paragraph (1), (2), or (3) of this subsection, shall—

(i) determine within ten days (excepting Saturdays, Sundays, and legal public holidays) after the receipt of any such request whether to comply with such request and shall immediately notify the person making such request of such determination and the reasons therefor, and of the right of such person to appeal to the head of the agency any adverse determination; and

(ii) make a determination with respect to any appeal within twenty days (excepting Saturdays, Sundays, and legal public holidays) after the receipt of such appeal. If on appeal the denial of the request for records is in whole or in part upheld, the agency shall notify the person making such request of the provisions for judicial review of that determination under paragraph (4) of this subsection.

(B) In unusual circumstances as specified in this subparagraph, the time limits prescribed in either clause (i) or clause (ii) of subparagraph (A) may be extended by written notice to the person making such request setting forth the reasons for such extension and the date on which a determination is expected to be dispatched. No such notice shall specify a date that would result in an extension for more than ten working days. As used in this subparagraph, "unusual circumstances" means, but only to the extent reasonably necessary to the proper processing of the particular request—

(i) the need to search for and collect the requested records from field facilities or other establishments that are separate from the office processing the request;

(ii) the need to search for, collect, and appropriately examine a voluminous amount of separate and distinct records which are demanded in a single request; or

(iii) the need for consultation, which shall be conducted with all practicable speed, with another agency having a substantial interest in the determination of the request or among two or more components of the agency having substantial subject-matter interest therein.

(C) Any person making a request to any agency for records under paragraph (1), (2), or (3) of this subsection shall be deemed to have exhausted his administrative remedies with respect to such request if the agency fails to comply with the applicable time limit provisions of this paragraph. If the Government can show exceptional circumstances exist and that the agency is exercising due diligence in responding to the request, the court may retain jurisdiction and allow the agency additional time to complete its review of the records. Upon any determination by an agency to comply with a request for records, the records shall be made promptly available to such person making such request. Any notification of denial of any request for records under this subsection shall set forth the names and titles or positions of each person responsible for the denial of such request.

(b) This section does not apply to matters that are—

(1)(A) specifically authorized under criteria established by an Executive order to be kept secret in the interest of national defense or foreign policy and (B) are in fact properly classified pursuant to such Executive order;

(2) related solely to the internal personnel rules and practices of an agency;

(3) specifically exempted from disclosure by statute (other than section 552b of this title), provided that such statute (A) requires that the matters be withheld from the public in such a manner as to leave no discretion on the issue, or (B) establishes particular criteria for withholding or refers to particular types of matters to be withheld;

(4) trade secrets and commercial or financial information obtained from a person and privileged or confidential;

(5) inter-agency or intra-agency memorandums or letters which would not be available by law to a party other than an agency in litigation with the agency;

(6) personnel and medical files and similar files the disclosure of which would constitute a clearly unwarranted invasion of personal privacy;

(7) investigatory records compiled for law enforcement purposes, but only to the extent that the production of such records would (A) interfere with enforcement proceedings, (B) deprive a person of a right to a fair trial or an impartial adjudication, (C) constitute an unwarranted invasion of personal privacy, (D) disclose the identity of a confidential source and, in the case of a record compiled by a criminal law enforcement authority in the course of a criminal investigation, or by an agency conducting a lawful

national security intelligence investigation, confidential information furnished only by the confidential source, (E) disclose investigative techniques and procedures, or (F) endanger the life or physical safety of law enforcement personnel;

(8) contained in or related to examination, operating, or condition reports prepared by, on behalf of, or for the use of an agency responsible for the regulation or supervision of financial institutions; or

(9) geological and geophysical information and data, including maps, concerning wells.

Any reasonably segregable portion of a record shall be provided to any person requesting such record after deletion of the portions which are exempt under this subsection.

(c) This section does not authorize withholding of information or limit the availability of records to the public, except as specifically stated in this section. This section is not authority to withhold information from Congress.

(d) On or before March 1 of each calendar year, each agency shall submit a report covering the preceding calendar year to the Speaker of the House Representatives and President of the Senate for referral to the appropriate committees of the Congress. The report shall include—

(1) the number of determinations made by such agency not to comply with requests for records made to such agency under subsection (a) and the reasons for each such determination;

(2) the number of appeals made by persons under subsection (a)(6), the result of such appeals, and the reason for the action upon each appeal that results in a denial of information;

(3) the names and titles or positions of each person responsible for the denial of records requested under this section, and the number of instances of participation for each;

(4) the results of each proceeding conducted pursuant to subsection (a)(4)(F), including a report of the disciplinary action taken against the officer or employee who was primarily responsible for improperly withholding records or an explanation of why disciplinary action was not taken;

(5) a copy of every rule made by such agency regarding this section;

(6) a copy cf the fee schedule and the total amount of fees collected by the agency for making records available under this section; and

(7) such other information as indicates efforts to administer fully this section.

The Attorney General shall submit an annual report on or before March 1 of each calendar year which shall include for the prior calendar year a listing of the number of cases arising under this section, the exemption involved in each case, the disposition of such case, and the cost, fees, and penalties assessed under subsections (a)(4)(E), (F), and (G). Such report shall also include a description of the efforts undertaken by the Department of Justice to encourage agency compliance with this section.

(e) For purposes of this section, the term "agency" as defined in section 551(1) of this title includes any executive department, military department, Government corporation, Government controlled corporation, or other establishment in the executive branch of the Government (including the Executive Office of the President), or any independent regulatory agency.

§ 552a. Records Maintained on Individual

(a) **Definitions.** For purposes of this section—

(1) the term "agency" means agency as defined in section 552(e) of this title;

(2) the term "individual" means a citizen of the United States or an alien lawfully admitted for permanent residence;

(3) the term "maintain" includes maintain, collect, use, or disseminate;

(4) the term "record" means any item, collection, or grouping of information about an individual that is maintained by an agency, including, but not limited to, his education, financial transactions, medical history, and criminal or employment history and that contains his name, or the identifying number, symbol, or other identifying particular assigned to the individual, such as a finger or voice print or a photograph;

(5) the term "system of records" means a group of any records under the control of any agency from which information is retrieved by the name of the individual or by some identifying number, symbol, or other identifying particular assigned to the individual;

(6) the term "statistical record" means a record in a system of records maintained for statistical research or reporting purposes only and not used in whole or in part in making any determination about an identifiable individual, except as provided by section 8 of title 13; and

(7) the term "routine use" means, with respect to the disclosure of a record, the use of such record for a purpose which is compatible with the purpose for which it was collected.

(b) **Conditions of disclosure.** No agency shall disclose any record which is contained in a system of records by any means of communication to any person, or to another agency, except pursuant to a written request by, or with the prior written consent of, the individual to whom the record pertains, unless disclosure of the record would be—

(1) to those officers and employees of the agency which maintains the record who have a need for the record in the performance of their duties;

(2) required under section 552 of this title;

(3) for a routine use as defined in subsection (a)(7) of this section and described under subsection (e)(4)(D) of this section;

(4) to the Bureau of the Census for purposes of planning or carrying out a census or survey or related activity pursuant to the provisions of title 13;

(5) to a recipient who has provided the agency with advance adequate written assurance that the record will be used solely as a statistical research or reporting record, and the record is to be transferred in a form that is not individually identifiable;

(6) to the National Archives and Records Administration as a record which has sufficient historical or other value to warrant its continued preservation by the United States Government, or for evaluation by the Archivist of the United States or the designee of the Archivist to determine whether the record has such value;

(7) to another agency or to an instrumentality of any governmental jurisdiction within or under the control of the United States for a civil or criminal law enforcement activity if the activity is authorized by law, and if the head of the agency or instrumentality has made a written request to the agency which maintains the record specifying the particular portion desired and the law enforcement activity for which the record is sought;

(8) to a person pursuant to a showing of compelling circumstances affecting the health or safety of an individual if upon such disclosure notification is transmitted to the last known address of such individual;

(9) to either House of Congress, or, to the extent of matter within its jurisdiction, any committee or subcommittee thereof, any joint committee of Congress or subcommittee of any such joint committee;

(10) to the Comptroller General, or any of his authorized representatives, in the course of the performance of the duties of the General Accounting Office;

(11) pursuant to the order of a court of competent jurisdiction; or

(12) to a consumer reporting agency in accordance with section 3711(f) of title 31.

(c) **Accounting of certain disclosures.** Each agency, with respect to each system of records under its control, shall—

(1) except for disclosures made under subsections (b)(1) or (b)(2) of this section, keep an accurate accounting of—

(A) the date, nature, and purpose of each disclosure of a record to any person or to another agency made under subsection (b) of this section; and

(B) the name and address of the person or agency to whom the disclosure is made;

(2) retain the accounting made under paragraph (1) of this subsection for at least five years or the life of the record, whichever is longer, after the disclosure for which the accounting is made;

(3) except for disclosures made under subsection (b)(7) of this section, make the accounting made under paragraph (1) of this subsection available to the individual named in the record at his request; and

(4) inform any person or other agency about any correction or notation of dispute made by the agency in accordance with subsection (d) of this

section of any record that has been disclosed to the person or agency if an accounting of the disclosure was made.

(d) **Access to records.** Each agency that maintains a system of records shall—

(1) upon request by any individual to gain access to his record or to any information pertaining to him which is contained in the system, permit him and upon his request, a person of his own choosing to accompany him, to review the record and have a copy made of all or any portion thereof in a form comprehensible to him, except that the agency may require the individual to furnish a written statement authorizing discussion of that individual's record in the accompanying person's presence;

(2) permit the individual to request amendment of a record pertaining to him and—

(A) not later than 10 days (excluding Saturdays, Sundays, and legal public holidays) after the date of receipt of such request, acknowledge in writing such receipt; and

(B) promptly, either—

(i) make any correction of any portion thereof which the individual believes is not accurate, relevant, timely, or complete; or

(ii) inform the individual of its refusal to amend the record in accordance with his request, the reason for the refusal, the procedures established by the agency for the individual to request a review of that refusal by the head of the agency or an officer designated by the head of the agency, and the name and business address of that official;

(3) permit the individual who disagrees with the refusal of the agency to amend his record to request a review of such refusal, and not later than 30 days (excluding Saturdays, Sundays, and legal public holidays) from the date on which the individual requests such review, complete such review and make a final determination unless, for good cause shown, the head of the agency extends such 30-day period; and if, after his review, the reviewing official also refuses to amend the record in accordance with the request, permit the individual to file with the agency a concise statement setting forth the reasons for his disagreement with the refusal of the agency, and notify the individual of the provisions for judicial review of the reviewing official's determination under subsection (g)(1)(A) of this section;

(4) in any disclosure, containing information about which the individual has filed a statement of disagreement, occurring after the filing of the statement under paragraph (3) of this subsection, clearly note any portion of the record which is disputed and provide copies of the statement and, if the agency deems it appropriate, copies of a concise statement of the reasons of the agency for not making the amendments requested, to persons or other agencies to whom the disputed record has been disclosed; and

(5) nothing in this section shall allow an individual access to any information compiled in reasonable anticipation of a civil action or proceeding.

(e) **Agency requirements.** Each agency that maintains a system of records shall—

(1) maintain in its records only such information about an individual as is relevant and necessary to accomplish a purpose of the agency required to be accomplished by statute or by executive order of the President;

(2) collect information to the greatest extent practicable directly from the subject individual when the information may result in adverse determinations about an individual's rights, benefits, and privileges under Federal programs;

(3) inform each individual whom it asks to supply information, on the form which it uses to collect the information or on a separate form that can be retained by the individual—

(A) the authority (whether granted by statute, or by executive order of the President) which authorizes the solicitation of the information and whether disclosure of such information is mandatory or voluntary;

(B) the principal purpose or purposes for which the information is intended to be used;

(C) the routine uses which may be made of the information, as published pursuant to paragraph (4)(D) of this subsection; and

(D) the effects on him, if any, of not providing all or any part of the requested information;

(4) subject to the provisions of paragraph (11) of this subsection, publish in the Federal Register upon establishment or revision a notice of the existence and character of the system of records, which notice shall include—

(A) the name and location of the system;

(B) the categories of individuals on whom records are maintained in the system;

(C) the categories of records maintained in the system;

(D) each routine use of the records contained in the system, including the categories of users and the purpose of such use;

(E) the policies and practices of the agency regarding storage, retrievability, access controls, retention, and disposal of the records;

(F) the title and business address of the agency official who is responsible for the system of records;

(G) the agency procedures whereby an individual can be notified at his request if the system of records contains a record pertaining to him;

(H) the agency procedures whereby an individual can be notified at his request how he can gain access to any record pertaining to him contained in the system of records, and how he can contest its content; and

(I) the categories of sources of records in the system;

(5) maintain all records which are used by the agency in making any determination about any individual with such accuracy, relevance, timeliness, and completeness as is reasonably necessary to assure fairness to the individual in the determination;

(6) prior to disseminating any record about an individual to any person other than an agency, unless the dissemination is made pursuant to subsection (b)(2) of this section, make reasonable efforts to assure that such records are accurate, complete, timely, and relevant for agency purposes;

(7) maintain no record describing how any individual exercises rights guaranteed by the First Amendment unless expressly authorized by statute or by the individual about whom the record is maintained or unless pertinent to and within the scope of an authorized law enforcement activity;

(8) make reasonable efforts to serve notice on an individual when any record on such individual is made available to any person under compulsory legal process when such process becomes a matter of public record;

(9) establish rules of conduct for persons involved in the design, development, operation, or maintenance of any system of records, or in maintaining any record, and instruct each such person with respect to such rules and the requirements of this section, including any other rules and procedures adopted pursuant to this section and the penalties for noncompliance;

(10) establish appropriate administrative, technical, and physical safeguards to insure the security and confidentiality of records and to protect against any anticipated threats or hazards to their security or integrity which could result in substantial harm, embarrassment, inconvenience, or unfairness to any individual on whom information is maintained; and

(11) at least 30 days prior to publication of information under paragraph (4)(D) of this subsection, publish in the Federal Register notice of any new use or intended use of the information in the system, and provide an opportunity for interested persons to submit written data, views, or arguments to the agency.

(f) **Agency rules.** In order to carry out the provisions of this section, each agency that maintains a system of records shall promulgate rules, in accordance with the requirements (including general notice) of section 553 of this title, which shall—

(1) establish procedures whereby an individual can be notified in response to his request if any system of records named by the individual contains a record pertaining to him;

(2) define reasonable times, places, and requirements for identifying an individual who requests his record or information pertaining to him be-

fore the agency shall make the record or information available to the individual;

(3) establish procedures for the disclosure to an individual upon his request of his record or information pertaining to him, including special procedure, if deemed necessary, for the disclosure to an individual of medical records, including psychological records, pertaining to him;

(4) establish procedures for reviewing a request from an individual concerning the amendment of any record or information pertaining to the individual, for making a determination on the request, for an appeal within the agency of an initial adverse agency determination, and for whatever additional means may be necessary for each individual to be able to exercise fully his rights under this section; and

(5) establish fees to be charged, if any, to any individual for making copies of his record, excluding the cost of any search for and review of the record.

The Office of the Federal Register shall annually compile and publish the rules promulgated under this subsection and agency notices published under subsection (e)(4) of this section in a form available to the public at low cost.

(g)(1) **Civil remedies.** Whenever any agency

(A) makes a determination under subsection (d)(3) of this section not to amend an individual's record in accordance with his request, or fails to make such review in conformity with that subsection;

(B) refuses to comply with an individual request under subsection (d)(1) of this section;

(C) fails to maintain any record concerning any individual with such accuracy, relevance, timeliness, and completeness as is necessary to assure fairness in any determination relating to the qualifications, character, rights, or opportunities of, or benefits to the individual that may be made on the basis of such record, and consequently a determination is made which is adverse to the individual; or

(D) fails to comply with any other provision of this section, or any rule promulgated thereunder, in such a way as to have an adverse effect on an individual, the individual may bring a civil action against the agency, and the district courts of the United States shall have jurisdiction in the matters under the provisions of this subsection.

(2)(A) In any suit brought under the provisions of subsection (g)(1)(A) of this section, the court may order the agency to amend the individual's record in accordance with his request or in such other way as the court may direct. In such a case the court shall determine the matter de novo.

(B) The court may assess against the United States reasonable attorney fees and other litigation costs reasonably incurred in any case under this paragraph in which the complainant has substantially prevailed.

(3)(A) In any suit brought under the provisions of subsection (g)(1)(B) of this section, the court may enjoin the agency from withholding the records and order the production to the complainant of any agency records improperly withheld from him. In such a case the court shall determine the matter de novo, and may examine the contents of any agency records in camera to determine whether the records or any portion thereof may be withheld under any of the exemptions set forth in subsection (k) of this section, and the burden is on the agency to sustain its action.

(B) The court may assess against the United States reasonable attorney fees and other litigation costs reasonably incurred in any case under this paragraph in which the complainant has substantially prevailed.

(4) In any suit brought under the provisions of subsection (g)(1)(C) or (D) of this section in which the court determines that the agency acted in a manner which was intentional or willful, the United States shall be liable to the individual in an amount equal to the sum of—

(A) actual damages sustained by the individual as a result of the refusal or failure, but in no case shall a person entitled to recovery receive less than the sum of $1,000; and

(B) the costs of the action together with reasonable attorney fees as determined by the court.

(5) An action to enforce any liability created under this section may be brought in the district court of the United States in the district in which the complainant resides, or has his principal place of business, or in which the agency records are situated, or in the District of Columbia, without regard to the amount in controversy, within two years from the date on which the cause of action arises, except that where an agency has materially and willfully misrepresented any information required under this section to be disclosed to an individual and the information so misrepresented is material to establishment of the liability of the agency to the individual under this section, the action may be brought at any time within two years after discovery by the individual of the misrepresentation. Nothing in this section shall be construed to authorize any civil action by reason of any injury sustained as the result of a disclosure of a record prior to September 27, 1975.

(h) **Rights of legal guardians.** For the purposes of this section, the parent of any minor, or the legal guardian of any individual who has been declared to be incompetent due to physical or mental incapacity or age by a court of competent jurisdiction, may act on behalf of the individual.

(i)(1) **Criminal penalties.** Any officer of employee of an agency, who by virtue of his employment or official position, has possession of, or access to, agency records which contain individually identifiable information the disclosure of which is prohibited by this section or by rules or regulations established thereunder, and who knowing that disclosure of the specific material is so prohibited, willfully discloses the material in any manner to any person or agency not entitled to receive it, shall be guilty of a misdemeanor and fined not more than $5,000.

(2) Any officer or employee of any agency who willfully maintains a system of records without meeting the notice requirements of subsection (e)(4) of this section shall be guilty of a misdemeanor and fined not more than $5,000.

(3) Any person who knowingly and willfully requests or obtains any record concerning an individual from an agency under false pretenses shall be guilty of a misdemeanor and fined not more than $5,000.

(j) **General exemptions.** The head of any agency may promulgate rules, in accordance with the requirements (including general notice) of sections 553(b) (1), (2), and (3), (c), and (e) of this title, to exempt any system of records within the agency from any part of this section except subsections (b), (c)(1) and (2), (e) (4)(A) through (F), (e)(6), (7), (9), (10), and (11), and (i) if the system of records is—

(1) maintained by the Central Intelligence Agency; or

(2) maintained by an agency or component thereof which performs as its principal function any activity pertaining to the enforcement of criminal laws, including police efforts to prevent, control, or reduce crime or to apprehend criminals, and the activities of prosecutors, courts, correctional, probation, pardon, or parole authorities, and which consists of (A) information compiled for the purpose of identifying individual criminal offenders and alleged offenders and consisting only of identifying data and notations of arrests, the nature and disposition of criminal charges, sentencing, confinement, release, and parole and probation status; (B) information compiled for the purpose of a criminal investigation, including reports of informants and investigators, and associated with an identifiable individual; or (C) reports identifiable to an individual compiled at any stage of the process of enforcement of the criminal laws from arrest or indictment through release from supervision.

At the time rules are adopted under this subsection, the agency shall include in the statement required under section 553(c) of this title, the reasons why the system of records is to be exempted from a provision of this section.

(k) **Specific exemptions.** The head of any agency may promulgate rules, in accordance with the requirements (including general notice) of sections 553(b)(1), (2), and (3), (c), and (e) of this title, to exempt any system of records within the agency from subsections (c)(3), (d), (e)(1), (e)(4)(G), (H), and (I) and (f) of this section if the system of records is—

(1) subject to the provisions of section 552(b)(1) of this title;

(2) investigatory material compiled for law enforcement purposes, other than material within the scope of subsection (j)(2) of this section: *Provided, however*, That if any individual is denied any right, privilege, or benefit that he would otherwise be entitled by Federal law, or for which he would otherwise be eligible, as a result of the maintenance of such material, such material shall be provided to such individual, except to the extent that the disclosure of such material would reveal the identity of a source who furnished information to the Government under an express promise that the identity of the source would be held in confidence, or, prior to the effective date of this section, under an implied promise that the identity of the source would be held in confidence;

(3) maintained in connection with providing protective services to the President of the United States or other individuals pursuant to section 3056 of title 18;

(4) required by statute to be maintained and used solely as statistical records;

(5) investigatory material compiled solely for the purpose of determining suitability, eligibility, or qualifications for Federal civilian employment, military service, Federal contracts, or access to classified information, but only to the extent that the disclosure of such material would reveal the identity of a source who furnished information to the Government under an express promise that the identity of the source would be held in confidence, or, prior to the effective date of this section, under an implied promise that the identity of the source would be held in confidence;

(6) testing or examination material used solely to determine individual qualifications for appointment or promotion in the Federal service the disclosure of which would compromise the objectivity or fairness of the testing or examination process; or

(7) evaluation material used to determine potential for promotion in the armed services, but only to the extent that the disclosure of such material would reveal the identity of a source who furnished information to the Government under an express promise that the identity of the source would be held in confidence, or, prior to the effective date of this section, under an implied promise that the identity of the source would be held in confidence.

At the time rules are adopted under this subsection, the agency shall include in the statement required under section 553(c) of this title, the reasons why the system of records is to be exempted from a provision of this section.

(*l*)(1) **Archival records.** Each agency record which is accepted by the Archivist of the United States for storage, processing, and servicing in accordance with section 3103 of title 44 shall, for the purposes of this section, be considered to be maintained by the agency which deposited the record and shall be subject to the provisions of this section. The Archivist of the United States shall not disclose the record except to the agency which maintains the record, or under rules established by that agency which are not inconsistent with the provisions of this section.

(2) Each agency record pertaining to an identifiable individual which was transferred to the National Archives of the United States as a record which has sufficient historical or other value to warrant its continued preservation by the United States Government, prior to the effective date of this section, shall, for the purposes of this section, be considered to be maintained by the National Archives and shall not be subject to the provisions of this section, except that a statement generally describing such records (modeled after the requirements relating to records subject to subsections (e)(4)(A) through (G) of this section) shall be published in the Federal Register.

(3) Each agency record pertaining to an identifiable individual which is transferred to the National Archives of the United States as a record which has sufficient historical or other value to warrant its continued preservation by the United States Government, on or after the effective date of this

section, shall, for the purposes of this section, be considered to be maintained by the National Archives and shall be exempt from the requirements of this section except subsections (e)(4)(A) through (G) and (e)(9) of this section.

(m)(1) **Government contractors.** When an agency provides by a contract for the operation by or on behalf of the agency of a system of records to accomplish an agency function, the agency shall, consistent with its authority, cause the requirements of this section to be applied to such system. For purposes of subsection (i) of this section any such contractor and any employee of such contractor, if such contract is agreed to on or after the effective date of this section, shall be considered to be an employee of an agency.

(2) A consumer reporting agency to which a record is disclosed under section 3711(f) of title 31 shall not be considered a contractor for the purposes of this section.

(n) **Mailing lists.** An individual's name and address may not be sold or rented by an agency unless such action is specifically authorized by law. This provision shall not be construed to require the withholding of names and addresses otherwise permitted to be made public.

(*o*) **Report on new systems.** Each agency shall provide adequate advance notice to Congress and the Office of Management and Budget of any proposal to establish or alter any system of records in order to permit an evaluation of the probable or potential effect of such proposal on the privacy and other personal or property rights of individuals or the disclosure of information relating to such individuals, and its effect on the preservation of the constitutional principles of federalism and separation of powers.

(p) **Annual report.** The President shall annually submit to the Speaker of the House of Representatives and the President pro tempore of the Senate a report—

(1) describing the actions of the Director of the Office of Management and Budget pursuant to section 6 of the Privacy Act of 1974 during the preceding year;

(2) describing the exercise of individual rights of access and amendment under this section such year;

(3) identifying changes in or additions to systems of records;

(4) containing such other information concerning administration of this section as may be necessary or useful to the Congress in reviewing the effectiveness of this section in carrying out the purposes of the Privacy Act of 1974.

(q)(1) **Effect of other laws.** No agency shall rely on any exemption contained in section 552 of this title to withhold from an individual any record which is otherwise accessible to such individual under the provisions of this section.

(2) No agency shall rely on any exemption in this section to withhold from an individual any record which is otherwise accessible to such individual under the provisions of section 552 of this title.

§ 552b. Open Meetings

(a) For purposes of this section—

(1) the term "agency" means any agency, as defined in section 552(e) of this title, headed by a collegial body composed of two or more individual members, a majority of whom are appointed to such position by the President with the advice and consent of the Senate, and any subdivision thereof authorized to act on behalf of the agency;

(2) the term "meeting" means the deliberations of at least the number of individual agency members required to take action on behalf of the agency where such deliberations determine or result in the joint conduct or disposition of official agency business, but does not include deliberations required or permitted by subsection (d) or (e); and

(3) the term "member" means an individual who belongs to a collegial body heading an agency.

(b) Members shall not jointly conduct or dispose of agency business other than in accordance with this section. Except as provided in subsection (c), every portion of every meeting of an agency shall be open to public observation.

(c) Except in a case where the agency finds that the public interest requires otherwise, the second sentence of subsection (b) shall not apply to any portion of an agency meeting, and the requirements of subsections (d) and (e) shall not apply to any information pertaining to such meeting otherwise required by this section to be disclosed to the public, where the agency properly determines that such portion or portions of its meeting or the disclosure of such information is likely to—

(1) disclose matters that are (A) specifically authorized under criteria established by an Executive order to be kept secret in the interests of national defense or foreign policy and (B) in fact properly classified pursuant to such Executive order;

(2) relate solely to the internal personnel rules and practices of an agency;

(3) disclose matters specifically exempted from disclosure by statute (other than section 552 of this title), provided that such statute (A) requires that the matters be withheld from the public in such a manner as to leave no discretion on the issue, or (B) establishes particular criteria for withholding or refers to particular types of matters to be withheld;

(4) disclose trade secrets and commercial or financial information obtained from a person and privileged or confidential;

(5) involve accusing any person of a crime, or formally censuring any person;

(6) disclose information of a personal nature where disclosure would constitute a clearly unwarranted invasion of personal privacy;

(7) disclose investigatory records compiled for law enforcement purposes, or information which if written would be contained in such

records, but only to the extent that the production of such records or information would (A) interfere with enforcement proceedings, (B) deprive a person of a right to a fair trial or an impartial adjudication, (C) constitute an unwarranted invasion of personal privacy, (D) disclose the identity of a confidential source and, in the case of a record compiled by a criminal law enforcement authority in the course of a criminal investigation, or by an agency conducting a lawful national security intelligence investigation, confidential information furnished only by the confidential source, (E) disclose investigative techniques and procedures, or (F) endanger the life or physical safety of law enforcement personnel;

(8) disclose information contained in or related to examination, operating, or condition reports prepared by, on behalf of, or for the use of an agency responsible for the regulation or supervision of financial institutions;

(9) disclose information the premature disclosure of which would—

(A) in the case of an agency which regulates currencies, securities, commodities, or financial institutions, be likely to (i) lead to significant financial speculation in currencies, securities, or commodities, or (ii) significantly endanger the stability of any financial institution; or

(B) in the case of any agency, be likely to significantly frustrate implementation of a proposed agency action, except that subparagraph (B) shall not apply in any instance where the agency has already disclosed to the public the content or nature of its proposed action, or where the agency is required by law to make such disclosure on its own initiative prior to taking final agency action on such proposal; or

(10) specifically concern the agency's issuance of a subpena, or the agency's participation in a civil action or proceeding, an action in a foreign court or international tribunal, or an arbitration, or the initiation, conduct, or disposition by the agency of a particular case of formal agency adjudication pursuant to the procedures in section 554 of this title or otherwise involving a determination on the record after opportunity for a hearing.

(d)(1) Action under subsection (c) shall be taken only when a majority of the entirc membership of the agency (as defined in subsection (a)(1)) votes to take such action. A separate vote of the agency members shall be taken with respect to each agency meeting a portion or portions of which are proposed to be closed to the public pursuant to subsection (c), or with respect to any information which is proposed to be withheld under subsection (c). A single vote may be taken with respect to a series of meetings, a portion or portions of which are proposed to be closed to the public, or with respect to any information concerning such series of meetings, so long as each meeting in such series involves the same particular matters and is scheduled to be held no more than thirty days after the initial meeting in such series. The vote of each agency member participating in such vote shall be recorded and no proxies shall be allowed.

(2) Whenever any person whose interests may be directly affected by a portion of a meeting requests that the agency close such portion to the

public for any of the reasons referred to in paragraph (5), (6), or (7) of subsection (c), the agency, upon request of any one of its members, shall vote by recorded vote whether to close such meeting.

(3) Within one day of any vote taken pursuant to paragraph (1) or (2), the agency shall make publicly available a written copy of such vote reflecting the vote of each member on the question. If a portion of a meeting is to be closed to the public, the agency shall, within one day of the vote taken pursuant to paragraph (1) or (2) of this subsection, make publicly available a full written explanation of its action closing the portion together with a list of all persons expected to attend the meeting and their affiliation.

(4) Any agency, a majority of whose meetings may properly be closed to the public pursuant to paragraph (4), (8), (9)(A), or (10) of subsection (c), or any combination thereof, may provide by regulation for the closing of such meetings or portions thereof in the event that a majority of the members of the agency votes by recorded vote at the beginning of such meeting, or portion thereof, to close the exempt portion or portions of the meeting, and a copy of such vote, reflecting the vote of each member on the question, is made available to the public. The provisions of paragraphs (1), (2), and (3) of this subsection and subsection (e) shall not apply to any portion of a meeting to which such regulations apply: *Provided*, That the agency shall, except to the extent that such information is exempt from disclosure under the provisions of subsection (c), provide the public with public announcement of the time, place, and subject matter of the meeting and of each portion thereof at the earliest practicable time.

(e)(1) In the case of each meeting, the agency shall make public announcement, at least one week before the meeting, of the time, place, and subject matter of the meeting, whether it is to be open or closed to the public, and the name and phone number of the official designated by the agency to respond to requests for information about the meeting. Such announcement shall be made unless a majority of the members of the agency determines by a recorded vote that agency business requires that such meeting be called at an earlier date, in which case the agency shall make public announcement of the time, place, and subject matter of such meeting, and whether open or closed to the public, at the earliest practicable time.

(2) The time or place of a meeting may be changed following the public announcement required by paragraph (1) only if the agency publicly announces such change at the earliest practicable time. The subject matter of a meeting, or the determination of the agency to open or close a meeting, or portion of a meeting, to the public, may be changed following the public announcement required by this subsection only if (A) a majority of the entire membership of the agency determines by a recorded vote that agency business so requires and that no earlier announcement of the change was possible, and (B) the agency publicly announces such change and the vote of each member upon such change at the earliest practicable time.

(3) Immediately following each public announcement required by this subsection, notice of the time, place, and subject matter of a meeting, whether the meeting is open or closed, any change in one of the preceding, and the name and phone number of the official designated by the agency to respond to requests for information about the meeting, shall also be submitted for publication in the Federal Register.

(f)(1) For every meeting closed pursuant to paragraphs (1) through (10) of subsection (c), the General Counsel or chief legal officer of the agency shall publicly certify that, in his or her opinion, the meeting may be closed to the public and shall state each relevant exemptive provision. A copy of such certification, together with a statement from the presiding officer of the meeting setting forth the time and place of the meeting, and the persons present, shall be retained by the agency. The agency shall maintain a complete transcript or electronic recording adequate to record fully the proceedings of each meeting, or portion of a meeting, closed to the public, except that in the case of a meeting, or portion of a meeting, closed to the public pursuant to paragraph (8), (9)(A), or (10) of subsection (c), the agency shall maintain either such a transcript or recording, or a set of minutes. Such minutes shall fully and clearly describe all matters discussed and shall provide a full and accurate summary of any actions taken, and the reasons therefor, including a description of each of the views expressed on any item and the record of any rollcall vote (reflecting the vote of each member on the question). All documents considered in connection with any action shall be identified in such minutes.

(2) The agency shall make promptly available to the public, in a place easily accessible to the public, the transcript, electronic recording, or minutes (as required by paragraph (1)) of the discussion of any item on the agenda, or of any item of the testimony of any witness received at the meeting, except for such item or items of such discussion or testimony as the agency determines to contain information which may be withheld under subsection (c). Copies of such transcript, or minutes, or a transcription of such recording disclosing the identity of each speaker, shall be furnished to any person at the actual cost of duplication or transcription. The agency shall maintain a complete verbatim copy of the transcript, a complete copy of the minutes, or a complete electronic recording of each meeting, or portion of a meeting, closed to the public, for a period of at least two years after such meeting, or until one year after the conclusion of any agency proceeding with respect to which the meeting or portion was held, whichever occurs later.

(g) Each agency subject to the requirements of this section shall, within 180 days after the date of enactment of this section, following consultation with the Office of the Chairman of the Administrative Conference of the United States and published notice in the Federal Register of at least thirty days and opportunity for written comment by any person, promulgate regulations to implement the requirements of subsections (b) through (f) of this section. Any person may bring a proceeding in the United States District Court for the District of Columbia to require an agency to promulgate such regulations if such agency has not promulgated such regulations within the time period specified herein. Subject to any limitations of time provided by law, any person may bring a proceeding in the United States Court of Appeals for the District of Columbia to set aside agency regulations issued pursuant to this subsection that are not in accord with the requirements of subsections (b) through (f) of this section and to require the promulgation of regulations that are in accord with such subsections.

(h)(1) The district courts of the United States shall have jurisdiction to enforce the requirements of subsections (b) through (f) of this section by declaratory judgment, injunctive relief, or other relief as may be appropriate. Such actions may be brought by any person against an agency prior to, or within sixty days after, the meeting out of which the violation of this section arises, except that if public announcement of such meeting is not initially provided by the agency in accordance with the requirements of this section, such action may be instituted pursuant to this section at any time prior to sixty days after any public announcement of such meeting. Such actions may be brought in the district court of the United States for the district in which the agency meeting is held or in which the agency in question has its headquarters, or in the District Court for the District of Columbia. In such actions a defendant shall serve his answer within thirty days after the service of the complaint. The burden is on the defendant to sustain his action. In deciding such cases the court may examine in camera any portion of the transcript, electronic recording, or minutes of a meeting closed to the public, and may take such additional evidence as it deems necessary. The court, having due regard for orderly administration and the public interest, as well as the interests of the parties, may grant such equitable relief as it deems appropriate, including granting an injunction against future violations of this section or ordering the agency to make available to the public such portion of the transcript, recording, or minutes of a meeting as is not authorized to be withheld under subsection (c) of this section.

(2) Any Federal court otherwise authorized by law to review agency action may, at the application of any person properly participating in the proceeding pursuant to other applicable law, inquire into violations by the agency of the requirements of this section and afford such relief as it deems appropriate. Nothing in this section authorizes any Federal court having jurisdiction solely on the basis of paragraph (1) to set aside, enjoin, or invalidate any agency action (other than an action to close a meeting or to withhold information under this section) taken or discussed at any agency meeting out of which the violation of this section arose.

(i) The court may assess against any party reasonable attorney fees and other litigation costs reasonably incurred by any other party who substantially prevails in any action brought in accordance with the provisions of subsection (g) or (h) of this section, except that costs may be assessed against the plaintiff only where the court finds that the suit was initiated by the plaintiff primarily for frivolous or dilatory purposes. In the case of assessment of costs against an agency, the costs may be assessed by the court against the United States.

(j) Each agency subject to the requirements of this section shall annually report to Congress regarding its compliance with such requirements, including a tabulation of the total number of agency meetings open to the public, the total number of meetings closed to the public, the reasons for closing such meetings, and a description of any litigation brought against the agency under this section, including any costs assessed against the agency in such litigation (whether or not paid by the agency).

(k) Nothing herein expands or limits the present rights of any person under section 552 of this title, except that the exemptions set forth in subsection (c) of this section shall govern in the case of any request made pursuant to section 552 to copy or inspect the transcripts, recordings, or minutes described in subsection (f) of this section. The requirements of chapter 33 of title 44, United States Code, shall not apply to the transcripts, recordings, and minutes described in subsection (f) of this section.

(*l*) This section does not constitute authority to withhold any information from Congress, and does not authorize the closing of any agency meeting or portion thereof required by any other provision of law to be open.

(m) Nothing in this section authorizes any agency to withhold from any individual any record, including transcripts, recordings, or minutes required by this section, which is otherwise accessible to such individual under section 552a of this title.

§ 553. Rule Making

(a) This section applies, according to the provisions thereof, except to the extent that there is involved—

(1) a military or foreign affairs function of the United States; or

(2) a matter relating to agency management or personnel or to public property, loans, grants, benefits, or contracts.

(b) General notice of proposed rule making shall be published in the Federal Register, unless persons subject thereto are named and either personally served or otherwise have actual notice thereof in accordance with law. The notice shall include—

(1) a statement of the time, place, and nature of public rule making proceedings;

(2) reference to the legal authority under which the rule is proposed; and

(3) either the terms or substance of the proposed rule or a description of the subjects and issues involved.

Except when notice or hearing is required by statute, this subsection does not apply—

(A) to interpretative rules, general statements of policy, or rules of agency organization, procedure, or practice; or

(B) when the agency for good cause finds (and incorporates the finding and a brief statement of reasons therefor in the rules issued) that notice and public procedure thereon are impracticable, unnecessary, or contrary to the public interest.

(c) After notice required by this section, the agency shall give interested persons an opportunity to participate in the rule making through submission of written data, views, or arguments with or without opportunity for oral presentation. After consideration of the relevant matter presented, the agency shall incorporate in the rules adopted a concise general statement of their basis and purpose. When rules are required by statute to be made on the record after opportunity for an agency hearing, sections 556 and 557 of this title apply instead of this subsection.

(d) The required publication or service of a substantive rule shall be made not less than 30 days before its effective date, except—

(1) a substantive rule which grants or recognizes an exemption or relieves a restriction;

(2) interpretative rules and statements of policy; or

(3) as otherwise provided by the agency for good cause found and published with the rule.

(e) Each agency shall give an interested person the right to petition for the issuance, amendment, or repeal of a rule.

§ 554. Adjudications

(a) This section applies, according to the provisions thereof, in every case of adjudication required by statute to be determined on the record after opportunity for an agency hearing, except to the extent that there is involved—

(1) a matter subject to a subsequent trial of the law and the facts de novo in a court:

(2) the selection or tenure of an employee, except an administrative law judge appointed under section 3105 of this title;

(3) proceedings in which decisions rest solely on inspections, tests, or elections;

(4) the conduct of military or foreign affairs functions;

(5) cases in which an agency is acting as an agent for a court; or

(6) the certification of worker representatives.

(b) Persons entitled to notice of an agency hearing shall be timely informed of—

(1) the time, place, and nature of the hearing;

(2) the legal authority and jurisdiction under which the hearing is to be held; and

(3) the matters of fact and law asserted.

When private persons are the moving parties, other parties to the proceeding shall give prompt notice of issues controverted in fact or law; and in other instances agencies may by rule require responsive pleading. In fixing the time and place for hearings, due regard shall be had for the convenience and necessity of the parties or their representatives.

(c) The agency shall give all interested parties opportunity for—

(1) the submission and consideration of facts, arguments, offers of settlement, or proposals of adjustment when time, the nature of the proceeding, and the public interest permit; and

(2) to the extent that the parties are unable so to determine a controversy by consent, hearing and decision on notice and in accordance with sections 556 and 557 of this title.

(d) The employee who presides at the reception of evidence pursuant to section 556 of this title shall make the recommended decision or initial decision required by section 557 of this title, unless he becomes unavailable to the agency. Except to the extent required for the disposition of ex parte matters as authorized by law, such an employee may not—

(1) consult a person or party on a fact in issue, unless on notice and opportunity for all parties to participate; or

(2) be responsible to or subject to the supervision or direction of an employee or agent engaged in the performance of investigative or prosecuting functions for an agency.

An employee or agent engaged in the performance of investigative or prosecuting functions for an agency in a case may not, in that or a factually related case, participate or advise in the decision, recommended decision, or agency review pursuant to section 557 of this title, except as witness or counsel in public proceedings. This subsection does not apply—

(A) in determining applications for initial licenses;

(B) to proceedings involving the validity or application of rates, facilities, or practices of public utilities or carriers; or

(C) to the agency or a member or members of the body comprising the agency.

(e) The agency, with like effect as in the case of other orders, and in its sound discretion, may issue a declaratory order to terminate a controversy or remove uncertainty.

§ 555. Ancillary Matters

(a) This section applies, according to the provisions thereof, except as otherwise provided by this subchapter.

(b) A person compelled to appear in person before an agency or representative thereof is entitled to be accompanied, represented, and advised by counsel or, if permitted by the agency, by other qualified representative. A party is entitled to appear in person or by or with counsel or other duly qualified representative in an agency proceeding. So far as the orderly conduct of public business permits, an interested person may appear before an agency or its responsible employees for the presentation, adjustment, or determination of an issue, request, or controversy in a proceeding, whether interlocutory, summary, or otherwise, or in connection with an agency function. With due regard for the convenience and necessity of the parties or their representatives and within a reasonable time, each agency shall proceed to

conclude a matter presented to it. This subsection does not grant or deny a person who is not a lawyer the right to appear for or represent others before an agency or in an agency proceeding.

(c) Process, requirement of a report, inspection, or other investigative act or demand may not be issued, made, or enforced except as authorized by law. A person compelled to submit data or evidence is entitled to retain or, on payment of lawfully prescribed costs, procure a copy or transcript thereof, except that in a nonpublic investigatory proceeding the witness may for good cause be limited to inspection of the official transcript of his testimony.

(d) Agency subpenas authorized by law shall be issued to a party on request and, when required by rules of procedure, on a statement or showing of general relevance and reasonable scope of the evidence sought. On contest, the court shall sustain the subpena or similar process or demand to the extent that it is found to be in accordance with law. In a proceeding for enforcement, the court shall issue an order requiring the appearance of the witness or the production of the evidence or data within a reasonable time under penalty of punishment for contempt in case of contumacious failure to comply.

(e) Prompt notice shall be given of the denial in whole or in part of a written application, petition, or other request of an interested person made in connection with any agency proceeding. Except in affirming a prior denial or when the denial is self-explanatory, the notice shall be accompanied by a brief statement of the grounds for denial.

§ 556. Hearings; Presiding Employees; Powers and Duties; Burden of Proof; Evidence; Record as Basis of Decision

(a) This section applies, according the provisions thereof, to hearings required by section 553 or 554 of this title to be conducted in accordance with this section.

(b) There shall preside at the taking of evidence—

(1) the agency;

(2) one or more members of the body which comprises the agency; or

(3) one or more administrative law judges appointed under section 3105 of this title.

This subchapter does not supersede the conduct of specified classes of proceedings, in whole or in part, by or before boards or other employees specially provided for by or designated under statute. The functions of presiding employees and of employees participating in decisions in accordance with section 557 of this title shall be conducted in an impartial manner. A presiding or participating employee may at any time disqualify himself. On the filing in good faith of a timely and sufficient affidavit of personal bias or other disqualification of a presiding or participating employee, the agency shall determine the matter as a part of the record and decision in the case.

(c) Subject to published rules of the agency and within its powers, employees presiding at hearings may—

(1) administer oaths and affirmations;

(2) issue subpenas authorized by law;

(3) rule on offers of proof and receive relevant evidence;

(4) take depositions or have depositions taken when the ends of justice would be served;

(5) regulate the course of the hearing;

(6) hold conferences for the settlement or simplification of the issues by consent of the parties;

(7) dispose of procedural requests or similar matters;

(8) make or recommend decisions in accordance with section 557 of this title; and

(9) take other action authorized by agency rule consistent with this subchapter.

(d) Except as otherwise provided by statute, the proponent of a rule or order has the burden of proof. Any oral or documentary evidence may be received, but the agency as a matter of policy shall provide for the exclusion of irrelevant, immaterial, or unduly repetitious evidence. A sanction may not be imposed or rule or order issued except on consideration of the whole record or those parts thereof cited by a party and supported by and in accordance with the reliable, probative, and substantial evidence. The agency may, to the extent consistent with the interests of justice and the policy of the underlying statutes administered by the agency, consider a violation of section 557(d) of this title sufficient grounds for a decision adverse to a party who has knowingly committed such violation or knowingly caused such violation to occur. A party is entitled to present his case or defense by oral or documentary evidence, to submit rebuttal evidence, and to conduct such cross-examination as may be required for a full and true disclosure of the facts. In rule making or determining claims for money or benefits or applications for initial licenses an agency may, when a party will not be prejudiced thereby, adopt procedures for the submission of all or part of the evidence in written form.

(e) The transcript of testimony and exhibits, together with all papers and requests filed in the proceeding, constitutes the exclusive record for decision in accordance with section 557 of this title and, on payment of lawfully prescribed costs, shall be made available to the parties. When an agency decision rests on official notice of a material fact not appearing in the evidence in the record, a party is entitled, on timely request, to an opportunity to show the contrary.

§ 557. Initial Decisions; Conclusiveness; Review by Agency; Submissions by Parties; Contents of Decisions; Record

(a) This section applies, according to the provisions thereof, when a hearing is required to be conducted in accordance with section 556 of this title.

(b) When the agency did not preside at the reception of the evidence, the presiding employee or, in cases not subject to section 554(d) of this title, an employee qualified to preside at hearings pursuant to section 556 of this title, shall initially decide the case unless the agency requires, either in specific cases or by general rule, the entire record to be certified to it for decision. When the presiding employee makes an initial decision, that decision then becomes the decision of the agency without further proceedings unless there is an appeal to, or review on motion of, the agency within time provided by rule. On appeal from or review of the initial decision, the agency has all the powers which it would have in making the initial decision except as it may limit the issues on notice or by rule. When the agency makes the decision without having presided at the reception of the evidence, the presiding employee or an employee qualified to preside at hearings pursuant to section 556 of this title shall first recommend a decision, except that in rule making or determining applications for initial licenses—

(1) instead thereof the agency may issue a tentative decision or one of its responsible employees may recommend a decision; or

(2) this procedure may be omitted in a case in which the agency finds on the record that due and timely execution of its functions imperatively and unavoidably so requires.

(c) Before a recommended, initial, or tentative decision, or a decision on agency review of the decision of subordinate employees, the parties are entitled to a reasonable opportunity to submit for the consideration of the employees participating in the decisions—

(1) proposed findings and conclusions; or

(2) exceptions to the decisions or recommended decisions of subordinate employees or to tentative agency decisions; and

(3) supporting reasons for the exceptions or proposed findings or conclusions.

The record shall show the ruling on each finding, conclusion, or exception presented. All decisions, including initial, recommended, and tentative decisions, are a part of the record and shall include a statement of—

(A) findings and conclusions, and the reasons or basis therefor, on all the material issues of fact, law, or discretion presented on the record; and

(B) the appropriate rule, order, sanction, relief, or denial thereof.

(d)(1) In any agency proceeding which is subject to subsection (a) of this section, except to the extent required for the disposition of ex parte matters as authorized by law—

(A) no interested person outside the agency shall make or knowingly cause to be made to any member of the body comprising the agency, administrative law judge, or other employee who is or may reasonably be expected to be involved in the decisional process of the proceeding, an ex parte communication relevant to the merits of the proceeding;

(B) no member of the body comprising the agency, administrative law judge, or other employee who is or may reasonably be expected to be involved in the decisional process of the proceeding, shall make or knowingly cause to be made to any interested person outside the agency an ex parte communication relevant to the merits of the proceeding;

(C) a member of the body comprising the agency, administrative law judge, or other employee who is or may reasonably be expected to be involved in the decisional process of such proceeding who receives, or who makes or knowingly causes to be made, a communication prohibited by this subsection shall place on the public record of the proceeding:

(i) all such written communications;

(ii) memoranda stating the substance of all such oral communications; and

(iii) all written responses, and memoranda stating the substance of all oral responses, to the materials described in clauses (i) and (ii) of this subparagraph;

(D) upon receipt of a communication knowingly made or knowingly caused to be made by a party in violation of this subsection, the agency, administrative law judge, or other employee presiding at the hearing may, to the extent consistent with the interests of justice and the policy of the underlying statutes, require the party to show cause why his claim or interest in the proceeding should not be dismissed, denied, disregarded, or otherwise adversely affected on account of such violation; and

(E) the prohibitions of this subsection shall apply beginning at such time as the agency may designate, but in no case shall they begin to apply later than the time at which a proceeding is noticed for hearing unless the person responsible for the communication has knowledge that it will be noticed, in which case the prohibitions shall apply beginning at the time of his acquisition of such knowledge.

(2) This subsection does not constitute authority to withhold information from Congress.

§ 558. Imposition of Sanctions; Determination of Applications for Licenses; Suspension, Revocation, and Expiration of Licenses

(a) This section applies, according to the provisions thereof, to the exercise of a power or authority.

(b) A sanction may not be imposed or a substantive rule or order issued except within jurisdiction delegated to the agency and as authorized by law.

(c) When application is made for a license required by law, the agency, with due regard for the rights and privileges of all the interested parties or adversely affected persons and within a reasonable time, shall set and complete proceedings required to be conducted in accordance with sections 556 and 557 of this title or other proceedings required by law and shall make its decision. Except in cases of willfulness or those in which public health, interest, or safety requires otherwise, the withdrawal, suspension, revocation, or annulment of a license is lawful only if, before the institution of agency proceedings therefor, the licensee has been given—

> (1) notice by the agency in writing of the facts or conduct which may warrant the action; and

> (2) opportunity to demonstrate or achieve compliance with all lawful requirements.

When the licensee has made timely and sufficient application for a renewal or a new license in accordance with agency rules, a license with reference to an activity of a continuing nature does not expire until the application has been finally determined by the agency.

§ 559. Effect on Other Laws; Effect of Subsequent Statute

This subchapter, chapter 7, and sections 1305, 3105, 3344, 4301(2)(E), 5372, and 7521 of this title, and the provisions of section 5335(a)(B) of this title that relate to administrative law judges, do not limit or repeal additional requirements imposed by statute or otherwise recognized by law. Except as otherwise required by law, requirements or privileges relating to evidence or procedure apply equally to agencies and persons. Each agency is granted the authority necessary to comply with the requirements of this subchapter through the issuance of rules or otherwise. Subsequent statute may not be held to supersede or modify this subchapter, chapter 7, sections 1305, 3105, 3344, 4301(2)(E), 5372, or 7521 of this title, or the provisions of section 5335(a)(B) of this title that relate to administrative law judges, except to the extent that it does so expressly.

CHAPTER 7
Judicial Review

Table of Sections

§ 701. Application; Definitions

(a) This chapter applies, according to the provisions thereof, except to the extent that—

> (1) statutes preclude judicial review; or

> (2) agency action is committed to agency discretion by law.

(b) For the purpose of this chapter—

(1) "agency" means each authority of the Government of the United States, whether or not it is within or subject to review by another agency, but does not include—

(A) the Congress;

(B) the courts of the United States;

(C) the governments of the territories or possessions of the United States;

(D) the government of the District of Columbia;

(E) agencies composed of representatives of the parties or of representatives of organizations of the parties to the disputes determined by them;

(F) courts martial and military commissions;

(G) military authority exercised in the field in time of war or in occupied territory; or

(H) functions conferred by sections 1738, 1739, 1743, and 1744 of title 12; chapter 2 of title 41; or sections 1622, 1884, 1891–1902, and former section 1641(b)(2), of title 50, appendix; and

(2) "person", "rule", "order", "license", "sanction", "relief", and "agency action" have the meanings given them by section 551 of this title.

§ 702.   Right of Review

A person suffering legal wrong because of agency action, or adversely affected or aggrieved by agency action within the meaning of a relevant statute, is entitled to judicial review thereof. An action in a court of the United States seeking relief other than money damages and stating a claim that an agency or an officer or employee thereof acted or failed to act in an official capacity or under color of legal authority shall not be dismissed nor relief therein be denied on the ground that it is against the United States or that the United States is an indispensable party. The United States may be named as a defendant in any such action, and a judgment or decree may be entered against the United States: *Provided*, That any mandatory or injunctive decree shall specify the Federal officer or officers (by name or by title), and their successors in office, personally responsible for compliance. Nothing herein (1) affects other limitations on judicial review or the power or duty of the court to dismiss any action or deny relief on any other appropriate legal or equitable ground; or (2) confers authority to grant relief if any other statute that grants consent to suit expressly or impliedly forbids the relief which is sought.

§ 703.   Form and Venue of Proceeding

The form of proceeding for judicial review is the special statutory review proceeding relevant to the subject matter in a court specified by statute or, in the absence or inadequacy thereof, any applicable form of legal action, including actions for declaratory judgments or writs of prohibitory or mandatory injunction or habeas corpus, in a court of competent jurisdiction. If no special statutory review proceeding is applicable, the action for judicial review may be brought against the United States, the agency by its official title, or the appropriate officer. Except to the extent that prior, adequate, and exclusive opportunity for judicial review is provided by law, agency action is subject to judicial review in civil or criminal proceedings for judicial enforcement.

§ 704. Actions Reviewable

Agency action made reviewable by statute and final agency action for which there is no other adequate remedy in a court are subject to judicial review. A preliminary, procedural, or intermediate agency action or ruling not directly reviewable is subject to review on the review of the final agency action. Except as otherwise expressly required by statute, agency action otherwise final is final for the purposes of this section whether or not there has been presented or determined an application for a declaratory order, for any form of reconsideration, or, unless the agency otherwise requires by rule and provides that the action meanwhile is inoperative, for an appeal to superior agency authority.

§ 705. Relief Pending Review

When an agency finds that justice so requires, it may postpone the effective date of action taken by it, pending judicial review. On such conditions as may be required and to the extent necessary to prevent irreparable injury, the reviewing court, including the court to which a case may be taken on appeal from or on application for certiorari or other writ to a reviewing court, may issue all necessary and appropriate process to postpone the effective date of an agency action or to preserve status or rights pending conclusion of the review proceedings.

§ 706. Scope of Review

To the extent necessary to decision and when presented, the reviewing court shall decide all relevant questions of law, interpret constitutional and statutory provisions, and determine the meaning or applicability of the terms of an agency action. The reviewing court shall—

(1) compel agency action unlawfully withheld or unreasonably delayed; and

(2) hold unlawful and set aside agency action, findings, and conclusions found to be—

(A) arbitrary, capricious, an abuse of discretion, or otherwise not in accordance with law;

(B) contrary to constitutional right, power, privilege, or immunity;

(C) in excess of statutory jurisdiction, authority, or limitations, or short of statutory right;

(D) without observance of procedure required by law;

(E) unsupported by substantial evidence in a case subject to sections 556 and 557 of this title or otherwise reviewed on the record of an agency hearing provided by statute; or

(F) unwarranted by the facts to the extent that the facts are subject to trial de novo by the reviewing court.

In making the foregoing determinations, the court shall review the whole record or those parts of it cited by a party, and due account shall be taken of the rule of prejudicial error.

PART II
The United States Civil Service Commission

CHAPTER 13
Special Authority

§ 1305. Administrative Law Judges

For the purpose of sections 3105, 3344, 4301(2)(D), and 5372 of this title and the provisions of section 5335(a)(B) of this title that relate to administrative law judges, the Office of Personnel Management may, and for the purpose of section 7521 of this title, the Merit Systems Protection Board may investigate, require reports by agencies, issue reports, including an annual report to Congress, prescribe regulations, appoint advisory committees as necessary, recommend legislation, subpena witnesses and records, and pay witness fees as established for the courts of the United States.

PART III
Employees

SUBPART B
Employment and Retention

CHAPTER 31
Authority for Employment

§ 3105. Appointment of Administrative Law Judges

Each agency shall appoint as many administrative law judges as are necessary for proceedings required to be conducted in accordance with sections 556 and 557 of this title. Administrative law judges shall be assigned to cases in rotation so far as practicable, and may not perform duties inconsistent with their duties and responsibilities as administrative law judges.

CHAPTER 33
Examination, Selection, and Placement

§ 3344.   Details; Administrative Law Judges

An agency as defined by section 551 of this title which occasionally or temporarily is insufficiently staffed with administrative law judges appointed under section 3105 of this title may use administrative law judges selected by the Office of Personnel Management from and with the consent of other agencies.

SUBPART D
Pay and Allowances

CHAPTER 53
Pay Rates and Systems

§ 5372.   Administrative Law Judges

Administrative law judges appointed under section 3105 of this title are entitled to pay prescribed by the Office of Personnel Management independently of agency recommendations or ratings and in accordance with subchapter III of this chapter and chapter 51 of this title.

SUBPART F
Employee Relations

CHAPTER 75
Adverse Actions

§ 7521.   Actions Against Administrative Law Judges

(a) An action may be taken against an administrative law judge appointed under section 3105 of this title by the agency in which the administrative law judge is employed only for good cause established and determined by the Merit Systems Protection Board on the record after opportunity for hearing before the Board.

(b) The actions covered by this section are—

    (1) a removal;

    (2) a suspension;

    (3) a reduction in grade;

    (4) a reduction in pay; and

    (5) a furlough of 30 days or less;

but do not include—

(A) a suspension or removal under section 7532 of this title;

(B) a reduction-in-force action under section 3502 of this title; or

(C) any action initiated under section 1206 of this title [i.e., by the Special Counsel of the Board].

Appendix B

The Constitution of the United States of America [a]

We the People of the United States, in Order to form a more perfect Union, establish Justice, insure domestic Tranquility, provide for the common defence, promote the general Welfare, and secure the Blessings of Liberty to ourselves and our Posterity, do ordain and establish this Constitution for the United States of America.

Article I

Section. 1.   All legislative Powers herein granted shall be vested in a Congress of the United States, which shall consist of a Senate and House of Representatives.

Section. 2.   The House of Representatives shall be composed of Members chosen every second Year by the People of the several States, and the Electors in each State shall have the Qualifications requisite for Electors of the most numerous Branch of the State Legislature.

No Person shall be a Representative who shall not have attained to the age of twenty-five Years, and been seven Years a Citizen of the United States, and who shall not, when elected, be an Inhabitant of that State in which he shall be chosen.

Representatives and direct Taxes shall be apportioned among the several States which may be included within this Union, according to their respective Numbers, *which shall be determined by adding to the whole Number of free Persons, including those bound to Service for a Term of Years*, and excluding Indians not taxed, *three fifths of all other persons.*[1] The actual Enumeration shall be made within three Years after the first Meeting of the Congress of the

---

[a] Italics are used to indicate provisions that have been modified by subsequent amendments.

[1] See Amendment XIV.

United States, and within every subsequent Term of ten Years, in such Manner as they shall by Law direct. The Number of Representatives shall not exceed one for every thirty Thousand, but each State shall have at Least one Representative; and until such enumeration shall be made, the State of New Hampshire shall be entitled to chuse three, Massachusetts eight, Rhode-Island and Providence Plantations one, Connecticut five, New-York six, New Jersey four, Pennsylvania eight, Delaware one, Maryland six, Virginia ten, North Carolina five, South Carolina five, and Georgia three.

When vacancies happen in the Representation from any State, the Executive Authority thereof shall issue Writs of Election to fill such Vacancies.

The House of Representatives shall chuse their Speaker and other Officers; and shall have the sole Power of Impeachment.

Section. 3.   The Senate of the United States shall be composed of two Senators from each State, *chosen by the Legislature thereof,*[2] for six Years; and each Senator shall have one Vote.

Immediately after they shall be assembled in Consequence of the first Election, they shall be divided as equally as may be into three Classes. The Seats of the Senators of the first Class shall be vacated at the Expiration of the second Year, of the second Class at the Expiration of the fourth Year, and of the third Class at the Expiration of the sixth Year, so that one third may be chosen every second Year; *and if Vacancies happen by Resignation, or otherwise, during the Recess of the Legislature of any State, the Executive thereof may make temporary Appointments until the next Meeting of the Legislature, which shall then fill such Vacancies.*[3]

No Person shall be a Senator who shall not have attained to the Age of thirty Years, and been nine Years a Citizen of the United States, and who shall not, when elected, be an Inhabitant of that State for which he shall be chosen.

The Vice President of the United States shall be President of the Senate, but shall have no Vote, unless they be equally divided.

The Senate shall choose their other Officers, and also a President pro tempore, in the Absence of the Vice President, or when he shall exercise the Office of President of the United States.

The Senate shall have the sole Power to try all Impeachments. When sitting for that Purpose, they shall be on Oath or Affirmation. When the President of the United States is tried, the Chief Justice shall preside: And no Person shall be convicted without the Concurrence of two thirds of the Members present.

Judgment in Cases of Impeachment shall not extend further than to removal from Office, and disqualification to hold and enjoy any Office of honor, Trust or Profit under the United States: but the Party convicted shall nevertheless be liable and subject to Indictment, Trial, Judgment and Punishment, according to Law.

---

[2] See Amendment XVII.

[3] Ibid.

Section. 4. The Times, Places and Manner of holding Elections for Senators, and Representatives, shall be prescribed in each State by the Legislature thereof; but the Congress may at any time by Law make or alter such Regulations, except as to the Places of chusing Senators.

The Congress shall assemble at least once in a Year, and such Meeting shall be on the first Monday in December, unless they shall by Law appoint a different Day.[4]

Section. 5. Each House shall be the Judge of the Elections, Returns and Qualifications of its own Members, and a Majority of each shall constitute a Quorum to do Business; but a smaller Number may adjourn from day to day, and may be authorized to compel the Attendance of absent Members, in such Manner, and under such Penalties as each House may provide.

Each House may determine the Rules of its Proceedings, punish its Members for disorderly Behavior, and, with the Concurrence of two thirds, expel a Member.

Each House shall keep a Journal of its Proceedings, and from time to time publish the same, excepting such Parts as may in their Judgment require Secrecy; and the Yeas and Nays of the Members of either House on any question shall, at the Desire of one fifth of those Present, be entered on the Journal.

Neither House, during the Session of Congress, shall, without the Consent of the other, adjourn for more than three days, nor to any other Place than that in which the two Houses shall be sitting.

Section. 6. The Senators and Representatives shall receive a Compensation for their Services, to be ascertained by Law, and paid out of the Treasury of the United States. They shall in all Cases, except Treason, Felony and Breach of the Peace, be privileged from Arrest during their Attendance at the Session of their respective Houses, and in going to and returning from the same; and for any Speech or Debate in either House, they shall not be questioned in any other Place.

No Senator or Representative shall, during the Time for which he was elected, be appointed to any civil Office under the Authority of the United States, which shall have been created, or the Emoluments whereof shall have been encreased during such time; and no Person holding any Office under the United States, shall be a Member of either House during his Continuance in Office.

Section. 7. All Bills for raising Revenue shall originate in the House of Representatives; but the Senate may propose or concur with Amendments as on other Bills.

Every Bill which shall have passed the House of Representatives and the Senate, shall, before it become a Law, be presented to the President of the United States; if he approve he shall sign it, but if not he shall return it, with his Objections to that House in which it shall have originated, who shall enter

---

[4] See Amendment XX.

the Objections at large on their Journal, and proceed to reconsider it. If after such Reconsideration two thirds of that House shall agree to pass the Bill, it shall be sent, together with the Objections, to the other House, by which it shall likewise be reconsidered, and if approved by two thirds of that House, it shall become a Law. But in all such Cases the Votes of both Houses shall be determined by Yeas and Nays, and the Names of the Persons voting for and against the Bill shall be entered on the Journal of each House respectively. If any Bill shall not be returned by the President within ten Days (Sundays excepted) after it shall have been presented to him, the Same shall be a Law, in like Manner as if he had signed it, unless Congress by their Adjournment prevent its Return, in which Case it shall not be a Law.

Every Order, Resolution, or Vote to which the Concurrence of the Senate and House of Representatives may be necessary (except on a question of Adjournment) shall be presented to the President of the United States; and before the Same shall take Effect, shall be approved by him, or being disapproved by him, shall be repassed by two thirds of the Senate and House of Representatives, according to the Rules and Limitations prescribed in the Case of a Bill.

Section. 8.   The Congress shall have Power to lay and collect Taxes, Duties, Imposts, and Excises, to pay the Debts and provide for the common Defence and general Welfare of the United States; but all Duties, Imposts and Excises shall be uniform throughout the United States;

To borrow Money on the credit of the United States;

To regulate Commerce with foreign Nations, and among the several States, and with the Indian Tribes;

To establish an uniform Rule of Naturalization, and uniform Laws on the subject of Bankruptcies throughout the United States;

To coin Money, regulate the Value thereof, and of foreign Coin, and fix the Standard of Weights and Measures;

To provide for the Punishment of counterfeiting the Securities and Current Coin of the United States;

To establish Post Offices and post Roads;

To promote the Progress of Science and useful Arts, by securing for limited Times to Authors and Inventors the exclusive Right to their respective Writings and Discoveries:

To constitute Tribunals inferior to the Supreme Court;

To define and punish Piracies and Felonies committed on the high Seas and Offences against the Law of Nations;

To declare War, grant letters of Marque, and Reprisal, and make Rules concerning Captures on Land and Water;

To raise and support Armies, but no Appropriation of Money to that Use shall be for a longer Term than two Years;

To provide and maintain a Navy;

To make Rules for the Government and Regulation of the land and naval Forces;

To provide for calling forth the Militia to execute the Laws of the Union, suppress Insurrections and repel Invasions;

To provide for organizing, arming, and disciplining, the Militia, and for governing such Part of them as may be employed in the Service of the United States, reserving to the States respectively, the Appointment of the Officers, and the Authority of training the Militia according to the discipline prescribed by Congress;

To exercise exclusive Legislation in all Cases whatsoever, over such District (not exceeding ten Miles square) as may, by Cession of particular States, and the Acceptance of Congress, become the Seat of the Government of the United States, and to exercise like Authority over all Places purchased by the Consent of the Legislature of the State in which the Same shall be, for the Erection of Forts, Magazines, Arsenals, dock-Yards, and other needful Buildings;—And

To make all Laws which shall be necessary and proper for carrying into Execution the foregoing Powers, and all other Powers vested by this Constitution in the Government of the United States, or in any Department or Officer thereof.

Section. 9.   The Migration or Importation of such Persons as any of the States now existing shall think proper to admit, shall not be prohibited by the Congress prior to the Year one thousand eight hundred and eight, but a Tax or duty may be imposed on such Importation, not exceeding ten dollars for each Person.

The Privilege of the Writ of Habeas Corpus shall not be suspended, unless when in Cases of Rebellion or Invasion the public Safety may require it.

No Bill of Attainder or ex post facto Law shall be passed.

No Capitation, or other direct, Tax shall be laid, unless in Proportion to the Census or Enumeration herein before directed to be taken.

No Tax or Duty shall be laid on Articles exported from any State.

No Preference shall be given by any Regulation of Commerce or Revenue to the Ports of one State over those of another: nor shall Vessels bound to, or from, one State, be obliged to enter, clear, or pay Duties in another.

No Money shall be drawn from the Treasury, but in Consequence of Appropriations made by Law; and a regular Statement and Account of the Receipts and Expenditures of all public Money shall be published from time to time.

No title of Nobility shall be granted by the United States: And no Person holding any Office of Profit or Trust under them, shall, without the Consent of the Congress, accept of any present, Emolument, Office, or Title, of any kind whatever, from any King, Prince, or foreign State.

Section. 10.   No State shall enter into any Treaty, Alliance, or Confederation; grant Letters of Marque and Reprisal; coin Money; emit Bills of Credit; make any Thing but gold and silver Coin a Tender in Payment of Debts; pass any Bill of Attainder, ex post facto Law, or Law impairing the Obligation of Contracts, or Grant any Title of Nobility.

No State shall, without the Consent of the Congress, lay any Imposts or Duties on Imports or Exports, except what may be absolutely necessary for executing its inspection Laws: and the net Produce of all Duties and Imposts, laid by any State on Imports or Exports, shall be for the Use of the Treasury of the United States; and all such Laws be subject to the Revision and Control of the Congress.

No State shall, without the Consent of Congress, lay any Duty of Tonnage, keep Troops, or Ships of War in time of Peace, enter into any Agreement or Compact with another State, or with a foreign Power, or engage in War, unless actually invaded, or in such imminent Danger as will not admit of delay.

Article II

Section. 1.   The executive Power shall be vested in a President of the United States of America. He shall hold his Office during the Term of four Years, and, together with the Vice President, chosen for the same Term be elected as follows:

Each State shall appoint, in such Manner as the Legislature thereof may direct, a Number of Electors, equal to the whole Number of Senators and Representatives to which the State may be entitled in the Congress; but no Senator or Representative, or Person holding an Office of Trust or Profit under the United States, shall be appointed an Elector.

The Electors shall meet in their respective States, and vote by Ballot for two Persons, of whom one at least shall not be an Inhabitant of the same State with themselves. And they shall make a List of all the Persons voted for, and of the Number of Votes for each; which List they shall sign and certify, and transmit sealed to the Seat of the Government of the United States, directed to the President of the Senate. The President of the Senate shall, in the Presence of the Senate and House of Representatives, open all the Certificates, and the Votes shall then be counted. The Person having the greatest Number of Votes shall be the President, if such Number be a Majority of the whole Number of Electors appointed; and if there be more than one who have such Majority, and have an equal Number of Votes, then the House of Representatives shall immediately chuse by Ballot one of them for President; and if no Person have a Majority, then from the five highest on the List the said House shall in like Manner chuse the President. But in chusing the President, the votes shall be taken by States, the Representation from each State having one Vote; A quorum for this purpose shall consist of a Member or Members from two thirds of the States, and a majority of all the States shall be necessary to a Choice. In every Case, after the Choice of the President, the Person having the Greatest Number of Votes of the Electors shall be the Vice President. But if there should remain two or more who have equal Votes, the Senate shall chuse from them by Ballot the Vice President.[5]

---

[5] See Amendment XII.

The Congress may determine the Time of chusing the Electors, and the Day on which they shall give their Votes; which Day shall be the same throughout the United States.

No Person except a natural born Citizen, or a Citizen of the United States, at the time of the Adoption of this Constitution, shall be eligible to the Office of President; neither shall any Person be eligible to that Office who shall not have attained to the Age of thirty-five Years, and been fourteen Years a Resident within the United States.

The Case of the Removal of the President from Office, or of his Death, Resignation, or Inability to discharge the Powers and Duties of the said Office, the Same shall devolve on the Vice President, and the Congress may by Law provide for the Case of Removal, Death, Resignation, or Inability, both of the President and Vice President, declaring what Officer shall then act as President, and such Officer shall act accordingly, until the Disability be removed, or a President shall be elected.

The President shall, at stated Times, receive for his Services, a Compensation which shall neither be encreased nor diminished during the Period for which he shall have been elected, and he shall not receive within that Period any other Emolument from the United States, or any of them.

Before he enter on the Execution of his Office, he shall take the following Oath or Affirmation:—"I do solemnly swear (or affirm) that I will faithfully execute the Office of President of the United States, and will to the best of my Ability, preserve, protect, and defend the Constitution of the United States."

Section. 2.   The President shall be Commander in Chief of the Army and Navy of the United States; and of the Militia of the several States, when called into the actual service of the United States; he may require the Opinion, in writing, of the principal Officer in each of the executive Departments, upon any Subject relating to the Duties of their respective Offices, and he shall have Power to grant Reprieves and Pardons for Offences against the United States, except in Case of Impeachment.

He shall have Power, by and with the Advice and Consent of the Senate, to make Treaties, provided two thirds of the Senators present concur; and he shall nominate, and by and with the Advice and Consent of the Senate, shall appoint Ambassadors, and other public Ministers and Consuls, Judges of the supreme Court, and all other Officers of the United States, whose Appointments are not herein otherwise provided for, and which shall be established by Law; but the Congress may by Law vest the Appointment of such inferior Officers, as they think proper, in the President alone, in the Courts of Law, or in the Heads of Departments.

The President shall have Power to fill up all Vacancies that may happen during the Recess of the Senate, by granting Commissions which shall expire at the End of their next Session.

Section. 3.   He shall from time to time give to the Congress Information of the State of the Union, and recommend to their Consideration such Measures as he shall judge necessary and expedient; he may, on extraordinary Occasions, convene both Houses, or either of them, and in Case of Disagreement between them, with Respect to the Time of Adjournment, he may adjourn them to such Time as he shall think proper; he shall receive Ambassadors and other public Ministers, he shall take Care that the Laws be faithfully executed, and shall Commission all the Officers of the United States.

Section. 4. The President, Vice President, and all civil Officers of the United States, shall be removed from Office on Impeachment for, and Conviction of, Treason, Bribery, or other High Crimes and Misdemeanors.

Article III

Section. 1. The judicial Power of the United States, shall be vested in one supreme Court and in such inferior Courts as the Congress may from time to time ordain and establish. The Judges, both of the supreme and inferior Courts, shall hold their Offices during good Behavior, and shall, at stated Times, receive for their Services, a Compensation, which shall not be diminished during their Continuance in Office.

Section. 2. The Judicial Power shall extend to all Cases, in Law and Equity, arising under this Constitution, the Laws of the United States, and Treaties made, or which shall be made, under their Authority;—to all Cases affecting Ambassadors, other public Ministers and Consults;—to all Cases of admiralty and maritime Jurisdiction;—to Controversies to which the United States shall be a Party;—to Controversies between two or more States;—*between a State and Citizens of another State*; [6]—between Citizens of different States;—between Citizens of the same State claiming Lands under Grants of different states, *and between a State, or the Citizens thereof, and foreign States, Citizens, or Subjects*.[7]

In all cases affecting Ambassadors, other public Ministers and Consuls, and those in which a State shall be Party, the supreme Court shall have original Jurisdiction. In all the other Cases before mentioned, the supreme Court shall have appellate Jurisdiction, both as to Law and Fact, with such Exceptions, and under such Regulations as the Congress shall make.

The Trial of all Crimes, except in Cases of Impeachment, shall be by Jury; and such Trial shall be held in the State where the said Crimes shall have been committed; but when not committed within any State, the Trial shall be at such Place or Places as the Congress may by Law have directed.

Section. 3. Treason against the United States, shall consist only in levying War against them, or in adhering to their Enemies, giving them Aid and Comfort. No person shall be convicted of Treason unless on the Testimony of two Witnesses to the same overt Act, or in Confession in open Court.

The Congress shall have Power to declare the Punishment of Treason, but no Attainder of Treason shall work Corruption of Blood, or Forfeiture except during the Life of the Person attainted.

---

[6] See Amendment XI.

[7] *Ibid.*

Article IV

Section. 1.   Full Faith and Credit shall be given in each State to the public Acts, Records, and judicial Proceedings of every other State. And the Congress may by general Laws prescribe the Manner in which such Acts, Records, and Proceedings shall be proved, and the Effect thereof.

Section. 2.   The Citizens of each State shall be entitled to all Privileges and Immunities of Citizens in the several States.

A Person charged in any State with Treason, Felony, or other Crime, who shall flee from Justice, and be found in another State, shall on Demand of the executive Authority of the State from which he fled, be delivered up, to be removed to the State having Jurisdiction of the Crime.

No Person held to Service or Labour in one State, under the Laws thereof, escaping into another, shall, in Consequence of any Law or Regulation therein, be discharged from such Service or Labour, but shall be delivered up on Claim of the Party to whom such Service or Labour may be due.[8]

Section 3.   New States may be admitted by the Congress into this Union; but no new State shall be formed or erected within the Jurisdiction of any other State; nor any State be formed by the Junction of two or more States, or Parts of States, without the Consent of the Legislatures of the States concerned as well as of the Congress.

The Congress shall have Power to dispose of and make all needful Rules and Regulations respecting the Territory or other Property belonging to the United States; and nothing in this Constitution shall be so construed as to Prejudice any claims of the United States, or of any particular State.

Section. 4.   The United States shall guarantee to every State in this Union a Republican Form of Government, and shall protect each of them against Invasion; and on Application of the Legislature, or of the Executive (when the Legislature cannot be convened) against domestic Violence.

Article V

The Congress, whenever two thirds of both Houses shall deem it necessary, shall propose Amendments to this Constitution, or, on the Application of the Legislatures of two thirds of the several States, shall call a Convention for proposing Amendments, which, in either Case, shall be valid to all Intents and Purposes, as Part of this Constitution, when ratified by the Legislatures of three fourths of the several States, or by Conventions in three fourths thereof, as the one or the other Mode of Ratification may be proposed by the Congress; Provided that no Amendment which may be made prior to the Year One thousand eight hundred and eight shall in any Manner affect the first and fourth Clauses in the Ninth Section of the first Article; and that no State, without its Consent, shall be deprived of its equal Suffrage in the Senate.

---

[8] See Amendment XIII.

Article VI

All Debts contracted and Engagements entered into, before the Adoption of this Constitution, shall be as valid against the United States under this Constitution, as under the Confederation.

This Constitution, and the Laws of the United States which shall be made in Pursuance thereof; and all Treaties made, or which shall be made, under the Authority of the United States, shall be the supreme Law of the Land; and the Judges in every State shall be bound thereby, any Thing in the Constitution or Laws of any State to the Contrary notwithstanding.

The Senators and Representatives before mentioned, and the Members of the several State Legislatures, and all executive and judicial Officers, both of the United States and of the several States, shall be bound by Oath or Affirmation, to support this Constitution; but no religious Test shall ever be required as a Qualification to any Office or public Trust under the United States.

Article VII

The Ratification of the Conventions of nine States, shall be sufficient for the Establishment of this Constitution between the States so ratifying the Same.

Done in Convention by the Unanimous Consent of the States present the Seventeenth Day of September in the Year of our Lord one thousand seven hundred and eighty seven and of the Independence of the United States of America the twelfth. In witness whereof We have hereunto subscribed our Names.

* * *

Articles in addition to, and amendment of, the Constitution of the United States of America, proposed by Congress, and ratified by the several States, pursuant to the Fifth Article of the original Constitution.

Amendment I [9]

Congress shall make no law respecting an establishment of religion, or prohibiting the free exercise thereof; or abridging the freedom of speech, or of the press; or the right of the people peaceably to assemble, and to petition the Government for a redress of grievances.

Amendment II

A well regulated Militia, being necessary to the security of a free State, the right of the people to keep and bear Arms, shall not be infringed.

Amendment III

No Soldier shall, in time of peace be quartered in any house, without the consent of the Owner, nor in time of war, but in a manner to be prescribed by law.

---

[9] Ratification of the first ten amendments was completed December 15, 1791.

Amendment IV

The right of the people to be secure in their persons, houses, papers, and effects, against unreasonable searches and seizures, shall not be violated, and no Warrants shall issue, but upon probable cause, supported by Oath or affirmation, and particularly describing the place to be searched, and the persons or things to be seized.

Amendment V

No person shall be held to answer for a capital, or otherwise infamous crime, unless on a presentment or indictment of a Grand Jury, except in cases arising in the land or naval forces, or in the Militia, when an actual service in time of War or public danger; nor shall any person be subject for the same offence to be twice put in jeopardy of life or limb; nor shall be compelled in any criminal case to be a witness against himself, nor be deprived of life, liberty, or property, without due process of law; nor shall private property be taken for public use, without just compensation.

Amendment VI

In all criminal prosecutions, the accused shall enjoy the right to a speedy and public trial, by an impartial jury of the State and district wherein the crime shall have been committed, which district shall have been previously ascertained by law, and to be informed of the nature and cause of the accusation; to be confronted with the witness against him; to have compulsory process for obtaining witness in his favor, and to have the Assistance of Counsel for his defence.

Amendment VII

In Suits at common law, where the value in controversy shall exceed twenty dollars, the right of trial by jury shall be preserved, and no fact tried by a jury, shall be otherwise re-examined in any Court of the United States, than according to the rules of the common law.

Amendment VIII

Excessive bail shall not be required, nor excessive fines imposed, nor cruel and unusual punishments inflicted.

Amendment IX

The enumeration in the Constitution, of certain rights, shall not be construed to deny or disparage others retained by the people.

Amendment X

The powers not delegated to the United States by the Constitution, nor prohibited by it to the States, are reserved to the States respectively, or to the people.

Amendment XI   [January 8, 1798]

The Judicial power of the United States shall not be construed to extend to any suit in law or equity, commenced or prosecuted against one of the United States by Citizens of another State, or by Citizens or Subjects of any Foreign State.

Amendment XII   [September 25, 1804]

The Electors shall meet in their respective states and vote by ballot for President and Vice President, one of whom, at least, shall not be an inhabitant of the same state with themselves; they shall name in their ballots the person voted for as President, and in distinct ballots the person voted for as Vice President, and they shall make distinct lists of all persons voted for as President, and of all persons voted for as Vice President, and of the number of votes for each, which lists they shall sign and certify, and transmit sealed to the seat of the government of the United States, directed to the President of the Senate:—The President of the Senate shall, in the presence of the Senate and House of Representatives, open all the certificates and the votes shall then be counted;—The person having the greatest number of votes for President, shall be the President, if such number be a majority of the whole number of Electors appointed; and if no person have such majority, then from the persons having the highest numbers not exceeding three on the list of those voted for as President, the House of Representatives shall choose immediately, by ballot, the President. But in choosing the President, the votes shall be taken by states, the representation from each state having one vote; a quorum for this purpose shall consist of a member or members from two thirds of the states, and a majority of all the states shall be necessary to a choice. And if the House of Representatives shall not choose a President whenever the right of choice shall devolve upon them, *before the fourth day of March next following*,[10] then the Vice President shall act as President as in the case of the death or other constitutional disability of the President.—The person having the greatest number of votes as Vice President, shall be the Vice President, if such number be a majority of the whole number of Electors appointed, and if no person have a majority, then from the two highest numbers on the list, the Senate shall choose the Vice President; a quorum for the purpose shall consist of two-thirds of the whole number of Senators, and a majority of the whole number shall be necessary to a choice. But no person constitutionally ineligible to the office of President shall be eligible to that of Vice President of the United States.

Amendment XIII   [December 18, 1865]

Section 1.   Neither slavery nor involuntary servitude, except as a punishment for crime whereof the party shall have been duly convicted, shall exist within the United States, or any place subject to their jurisdiction.

Section 2.   Congress shall have power to enforce this article by appropriate legislation.

---

[10] See Amendment XX.

Amendment XIV   [July 28, 1868]

Section 1.   All persons born or naturalized in the United States, and subject to the jurisdiction thereof, are citizens of the United States and of the State wherein they reside. No state shall make or enforce any law which shall abridge the privileges or immunities of citizens of the United States; nor shall any state deprive any person of life, liberty, or property, without due process of law; nor deny to any person within its jurisdiction the equal protection of the laws.

Section 2.   Representatives shall be apportioned among the several States according to their respective numbers, counting the whole number of persons in each State, excluding Indians not taxed. But when the right to vote at any election for the choice of electors for President and Vice President of the United States, Representatives in Congress, the Executive and Judicial officers of a State, or the members of the Legislature thereof, is denied to any of the male inhabitants of such State, being twenty one years of age, and citizens of the United States, or in any way abridged, except for participation in rebellion, or other crime, the basis of representation therein shall be reduced in the proportion which the number of such male citizens shall bear to the whole number of male citizens twenty one years of age in such State.

Section 3.   No person shall be a Senator or Representative in Congress, or elector of President and Vice President, or hold any office, civil or military, under the United States, or under any State who having previously taken an oath, as a member of Congress, or as an officer of the United States, or as a member of any State legislature, or as an executive or judicial officer of any State, to support the Constitution of the United States, shall have engaged in insurrection or rebellion against the same, or given aid or comfort to the enemies thereof. But Congress may by a vote of two thirds of each House remove such disability.

Section 4.   The validity of the public debt of the United States authorized by law, including debts incurred for payment of pensions and bounties for services in suppressing insurrection or rebellion shall not be questioned. But neither the United States nor any State shall assume or pay any debt or obligation incurred in aid of insurrection or rebellion against the United States, or any claim for the loss or emancipation of any slave; but all such debts, obligations, and claims shall be held illegal and void.

Section 5.   The Congress shall have power to enforce, by appropriate legislation, the provisions of this article.

Amendment XV   [March 30, 1870]

Section 1.   The right of citizens of the United States to vote shall not be denied or abridged by the United States or by any State on account of race, color, or previous condition of servitude.

Section 2.   The Congress shall have power to enforce this article by appropriate legislation.

Amendment XVI   [February 25, 1913]

The Congress shall have power to lay and collect taxes on incomes, from whatever source derived, without apportionment among the several States, and without regard to any census or enumeration.

Amendment XVII   [May 31, 1913]

The Senate of the United States shall be composed of two Senators from each State, elected by the people thereof, for six years; and each Senator shall have one vote. The electors in each State shall have the qualifications requisite for electors of the most numerous branch of the State legislatures.

When vacancies happen in the representation of any State in the Senate, the executive authority of such State shall issue writs of election to fill such vacancies: *Provided*, That the legislature of any State may empower the executive thereof to make temporary appointments until the people fill the vacancies by election as the legislature may direct.

This amendment shall not be so construed as to affect the election or term of any Senator chosen before it becomes valid as part of the Constitution.

Amendment XVIII   [January 29, 1919]

Section 1.   *After one year from the ratification of this article the manufacture, sale, or transportation of intoxicating liquors within, the importation thereof into, or the exportation thereof from the United States and all territory subject to the jurisdiction thereof for beverage purposes is hereby prohibited.*

Section 2.   *The Congress and the several States shall have concurrent power to enforce this article by appropriate legislation.*

Section 3.   *This article shall be inoperative unless it shall have been ratified as an amendment to the Constitution by the legislatures of the several States, as provided in the Constitution, within seven years from the date of submission hereof to the States by the Congress.*[11]

Amendment XIX   [August 26, 1920]

The right of citizens of the United States to vote shall not be denied or abridged by the United States or by any State on account of sex.

Congress shall have power to enforce this article by appropriate legislation.

Amendment XX   [February 6, 1933]

Section 1.   The terms of the President and Vice President shall end at noon on the 20th day of January, and the terms of Senators and Representatives at noon on the 3rd day of January, of the years in which such terms would have ended if this article had not been ratified; and the terms of their successors shall then begin.

---

[11] Repealed by Amendment XXI.

Section 2. The Congress shall assemble at least once in every year, and such meeting shall begin at noon on the 3rd day of January unless they shall by law appoint a different day.

Section 3. If, at the time fixed for the beginning of the term of the President, the President elect shall have died, the Vice President elect shall become President. If a President shall not have been chosen before the time fixed for the beginning of his term, or if the President elect shall have failed to qualify, then the Vice President elect shall act as President until a President shall have qualified; and the Congress may by law provide for the case where-in neither a President elect nor a Vice President elect shall have qualified, declaring who shall then act as President, or the manner in which one who is to act shall be selected, and such person shall act accordingly until a President or Vice President shall have qualified.

Section 4. The Congress may by law provide for the case of the death of any of the persons from whom the House of Representatives may choose a President whenever the right of choice shall have devolved upon them, and for the case of the death of any of the persons from whom the Senate may choose a Vice President whenever the right of choice shall have devolved upon them.

Section 5. Sections 1 and 2 shall take effect on the 15th day of October following the ratification of this article.

Section 6. This article shall be inoperative unless it shall have been ratified as an amendment to the Constitution by the legislatures of three fourths of the several States within seven years from the date of its submission.

Amendment XXI   [December 5, 1933]

Section 1. The eighteenth article of amendment to the Constitution of the United States is hereby repealed.

Section 2. The transportation or importation into any State, Territory, or possession of the United States for delivery or use therein of intoxicating liquors, in violation of the laws thereof, is hereby prohibited.

Section 3. This article shall be inoperative unless it shall have been ratified as an amendment to the Constitution by conventions in the several States, as provided in the Constitution, within seven years from the date of the submission hereof to the States by the Congress.

Amendment XXII   [February 26, 1951]

Section 1. No person shall be elected to the office of the President more than twice, and no person who has held the office of President, or acted as President, for more than two years of a term to which some other person was elected President shall be elected to the office of President more than once. But this Article shall not apply to any person holding the office of President when this Article was proposed by the Congress, and shall not prevent any person who may be holding the office of President, or acting as President, during the term within which this Article becomes operative from holding the office of President or acting as President during the remainder of such term.

Section 2.   This article shall be inoperative unless it shall have been ratified as an amendment to the Constitution by the legislatures of three fourths of the several States within seven years from the date of its submission to the States by the Congress.

Amendment XXIII   [March 29, 1961]

Section 1.   The District constituting the seat of Government of the United States shall appoint in such manner as the Congress may direct:

A number of electors of President and Vice President equal to the whole number of Senators and Representatives in Congress to which the District would be entitled if it were a State, but in no event more than the least populous State; they shall be in addition to those appointed by the States, but they shall be considered, for the purposes of the election of President and Vice President, to be electors appointed by a State; and they shall meet in the District and perform such duties as provided by the twelfth article of amendment.

Section 2.   The Congress shall have power to enforce this article by appropriate legislation.

Amendment XXIV   [January 23, 1964]

Section 1.   The rights of citizens of the United States to vote in any primary or other election for President or Vice President, for electors for President or Vice President, or for Senator or Representative in Congress, shall not be denied or abridged by the United States or any state by reason of failure to pay any poll tax or other tax.

Section 2.   The Congress shall have power to enforce this article by appropriate legislation.

Amendment XXV   [February 10, 1967]

Section 1.   In case of the removal of the President from office or of his death or resignation, the Vice President shall become President.

Section 2.   Whenever there is a vacancy in the office of the Vice President, the President shall nominate a Vice President who shall take office upon confirmation by a majority vote of both Houses of Congress.

Section 3.   Whenever the President transmits to the President pro tempore of the Senate and the Speaker of the House of Representatives his written declaration that he is unable to discharge the powers and duties of his office, and until he transmits to them a written declaration to the contrary, such powers and duties shall be discharged by the Vice President as Acting President.

Section 4.   Whenever the Vice President and a majority of either the principal officers of the executive departments or of such other body as Congress may by law provide, transmit to the President pro tempore of the Senate and the Speaker of the House of Representatives their written declaration that the President is unable to discharge the powers and duties of his office, the Vice President shall immediately assume the powers and duties of the office as Acting President.

Thereafter, when the President transmits to the President pro tempore of the Senate and the Speaker of the House of Representatives his written declaration that no inability exists, he shall resume the powers and duties of his office unless the Vice President and a majority of either the principal officers of the executive department[s] or of such other body as Congress may by law provide, transmit within four days to the President pro tempore of the Senate and the Speaker of the House of Representatives their written declaration that the President is unable to discharge the powers and duties of his office. Thereupon Congress shall decide the issue, assembling within forty-eight hours for that purpose if not in session. If the Congress, within twenty-one days after receipt of the latter written declaration, or, if Congress is not in session, within twenty-one days after Congress is required to assemble, determines by two-thirds vote of both Houses that the President is unable to discharge the powers and duties of his office, the Vice President shall continue to discharge the same as Acting President; otherwise, the President shall resume the powers and duties of his office.

Amendment XXVI   [June 30, 1971]

Section 1.   The right of citizens of the United States, who are 18 years of age or older, to vote shall not be denied or abridged by the United States or by any state on account of age.

Section 2.   The Congress shall have power to enforce this article by appropriate legislation.

INDEX

References are to Pages